COGNITION AND INSTRUCTION
Twenty-Five Years of Progress

Carnegie Mellon Symposia on Cognition
David Klahr, Series Editor

COGNITION AND INSTRUCTION
Twenty-Five Years of Progress

Edited by

Sharon M. Carver
David Klahr
Carnegie Mellon University

LEA LAWRENCE ERLBAUM ASSOCIATES, PUBLISHERS
2001   Mahwah, New Jersey   London

Lawrence Erlbaum Associates, Inc., Publishers
10 Industrial Avenue
Mahwah, NJ 07430

Cover design by Kathryn Houghtaling Lacey

Library of Congress Cataloging-in-Publication Data

Cognition and instruction: Twenty-five years of progress / edited by Sharon M. Carver and David Klahr.
p. cm.
Includes bibliographical references and indexes.
ISBN 0-8058-3823-6 (cloth : alk. paper) — ISBN 0-8058-3824-4 (pbk. : alk. paper)
1. Learning, psychology of. 2. Cognition. 3. I. Carver, Sharon M. II. Klahr, David.

LB1060. C615 2001
370.15'23—dc21   2001023195
                                                    CIP

Printed in the United States of America
10 9 8 7 6 5 4 3 2 1

*In memory of Ann Brown
for her insight, example, and inspiration
in our personal and professional spheres*

Contents

TRIBUTE TO ANN BROWN
January 26, 1943–June 4, 1999

It is hard to imagine that anyone familiar with Ann Brown and her work did not feel an enormous sense of loss on hearing of her death June 4, 1999. Her contributions to educational and psychological research and to scholarship were extraordinary, whether measured by their number, their generativity, or their impact. Perhaps more than most scholars, Ann's work can be characterized as a journey—a journey toward a theoretical model of learning and instruction—a journey in which she integrated and applied her vast knowledge of teaching, learning, curriculum, assessment, and the social contexts of classrooms and schools—a journey always focused on the goal of expanding learners' capabilities.

Ann's life journey began January 26, 1943 in Portsmouth, England. She was the middle child and only daughter of Kathryn and John Lesley Taylor. Her own history as a learner is noteworthy as she experienced considerable difficulty learning to read and did not attain fluency until the age of 13, an accomplishment that she attributed to a teacher who recognized Ann's potential and worked to unleash it. Ann's higher education was completed at the University of London, where, drawn to the study of animal learning, she pursued her degrees in psychology, completing a dissertation study in 1967 entitled, *Anxiety and Complex Learning Performance in Children.*

Attracted by research in developmental psychology that was taking place in the United States, Ann took a leave from her first academic position at the University of Sussex and accepted a position as a visiting assistant professor in the Department of Psychology and an appointment as a research scientist at the Children's Research Center at the University of

Illinois at Champaign-Urbana. In a rare turn in academia, but in a move that signaled Ann's talent, she was awarded tenure at the University of Sussex while in absentia!

As a postdoctoral fellow with Zeaman and House at the University of Connecticut, Ann began a long and productive program of research on human memory. It was in this early work that an attribute strongly identified with Ann's research emerged; that is, her interest in enhancing cognitive performance. In her foundational scholarship in metacognition, she asked about the value of strategies to support knowledge about and control of learning activity. Initially, she raised these questions while studying the learning and achievement of students with mental retardation while engaged in simple recall and recognition tasks; over time, she asked these questions in the context of more challenging tasks, such as the comprehension and use of complex text.

In 1969, Ann met Joseph C. Campione, who became her dearest companion, husband, and closest collaborator. Together, Ann and Joe, leading various teams of researchers, conducted research that reverberated throughout the worlds of educational research and practice in a number of ways. For example, their work in metacognition spurred the development of a new strand of curriculum and instruction that focused on strategy instruction for the purpose of enhancing learners' abilities and the inclination to engage in self-regulation. Their research in strategy instruction led to an examination of fundamental issues regarding the difference between "blind training" and "informed instruction"; and their work on dynamic assessment demonstrated how dormant skills could be awakened with the assistance of others.

Had Ann's career contributions ended here, she would have left an indelible mark on educational research and practice; but they did not end here. In the last decade of her research with Joe, while at the University of California, Berkeley, she launched a new program of inquiry, *Fostering Communities of Learners*, that had an amazing synthetic quality both in substance and form. The substance included the use of a diverse array of participant structures in which students—engaged as collaborative researchers—pursued deep understanding of content knowledge and domain-specific reasoning in the biological sciences. Working closely with educators in urban schools, Ann and Joe reconceptualized classrooms as contexts in which diversity was not only tolerated but was, in fact, integral to success. This research has taken the form of design experiments in which first principles guide the engineering and investigation of educational innovation. Although these contributions were of significant value to advancing educational practice, they were all the more valuable for the ways in which they advanced learning theory, for these are the kinds of studies that put flesh on abstract notions such as "constructivist pedagogy" and "socially mediated learning."

Ann's gifts were many and she gave of them generously. She served on the most prestigious boards and panels in our profession. The youngest scholar ever elected to the *National Academy of Education*, she was its president from 1997 until her death. She served as president of *AERA* and president of Division 7 of the *American Psychological Association*. She contributed tirelessly to the writing and dissemination of reports that would spur reform efforts and garner additional attention to and support for educational research; the most recent example being the report of the *National Research Council, How people learn: Brain, mind, experience, and school* (coedited with Bransford and Cocking in 1999).

Chief among Ann's gifts was her ability to write. The clarity of Ann's writing reflected the fact that she wrote as much from her heart as from her intellect. For example, the children about whom Ann wrote were not just the subjects of her research; thoughts of these children flooded her mind at night; fears of what they would confront as they matriculated to middle school—questions about the possible futures of these children who lived in poverty. When Ann wrote, "what most recent developmental theories ask of teachers is so hard," it was because she came to a deep respect and appreciation for the work of teachers and the challenging sociopolitical contexts in which they do this work. Ann derived enormous satisfaction from her conversations with the children in her research and glowed as she recounted tales of their accomplishments, filing stories away to enliven future presentations and writing.

Ann was a generous teacher and mentor. To this I can attest personally. As I completed my dissertation study on reciprocal teaching, many was the morning that she met me at her door as the sun was rising, with thoughtful feedback and an encouraging smile that would carry me through the next revision. What I came to understand later is that she had probably retired only several hours before my tentative knocks at her door. Her support did not stop with the awarding of a degree; she was a very dear and steadfast friend.

In recognition of her seminal work in metacognition, her outstanding theoretical and practical contributions to the design of interactive learning environments, her contributions to the development of reasoning in young children, and for her leadership and inspiration to other researchers and students, Ann received the AERA's Award for Distinguished Contributions to Educational Research in 1991. This award was followed by the Distinguished Scientific Contribution Award for the Application of Psychology by the American Psychological Association in 1996. Then, in recognition of her "... distinguished achievements in psychological science. For brilliantly combining the fields of developmental psychology, learning theory, and the design of learning environments in a career of theoretical and experimental work and their applications to education" she was honored, in 1997, by the American Psychological Society with the James McKeen Catell Award for Distinguished Achievements.

Ann was a fellow of the American Psychological Society, Society for Experimental Psychologists, Spencer Foundation, Society for Research in Child Development, and the American Psychological Association. In addition, she was twice a fellow at the Center for Advanced Study in the Behavioral Sciences. She provided leadership on a number of editorial boards in education and psychology, using her position to build a stronger community of scholars, as well as to translate research into practice by communicating the interests and achievements of that community of scholars to others.

The many responsibilities she shouldered in her professional life were made lighter by the pleasure she found in her friendships and in the care of her family. She loved her son, Richard, and took great joy in his accomplishments and in the fact that he married a young woman of Ann's Irish heritage, named Mary. She loved her granddaughter, Sophie, and gathered observations that vied with Piaget's for their specificity and perspicacity; furthermore, she expressed unabashed pride at Sophie's precocious nature. The love, mutual respect, and support that she and Joe provided one another has few parallels in academia.

Ann's death at the age of 56 clearly brought her journey to a premature end. There is no question, however, that her legacy will endure in the work of so many of us who have inherited the powerful tools that are represented in her ideas, in her methods, and in the challenges she posed to reveal and extend the capabilities of learners. Were Ann in attendance at this symposium, she would have encouraged, as every fine teacher does—further, deeper, keep going ...

—*Annemarie Sullivan Palincsar*
University of Michigan

Preface

This volume is based on papers presented in June 1999 at the 30th Carnegie Symposium on Cognition. This particular symposium was unusual in that it was conceived in reference to the 1974 symposium entitled *Cognition and Instruction* (Klahr, 1976). The central question for that symposium was not so different from the basic question that we all still face: "What contributions can current research in cognitive psychology make to the solution of problems in instructional design?" Speakers discussed a variety of topics, including innovative strategies for instructional research, process and structure in learning, processes for comprehending instructions, and the development of what Robert Glaser dubbed "a linking science—a science of instructional design."

A lot has happened since then, as the cognition and instruction components of the developing field have forged a reciprocal relation in which researchers and teachers have (a) applied cognitive science theories and methods to the complex world of the classroom, (b) built on advances in cognitive science to improve education, and (c) enriched cognitive science by studying effective instruction experimentally (Larkin, 1994).

Institutional developments have further strengthened the field. We have seen the establishment of interdisciplinary journals, teacher education courses, research funding initiatives, and research institutes with graduate training programs. In 1984, the journal *Cognition and Instruction* was founded as a vehicle for sharing cognitive investigations of instruction and learning, specifically cognitive analyses of instructionally relevant tasks and performance, theories of skill and knowledge acquisition, and theoretical analyses of instructional interventions. In 1991, the new *Journal of the Learning Sciences* initiated a multidisciplinary forum for presenting cognitively oriented research and discussion related to changing our understanding of learning and the practice of education. During this same period, many teacher–educators began to offer preservice courses that emphasized the links between theory, research, and practice.

The cognition–instruction link was substantially strengthened in 1987 when Jill Larkin of Carnegie Mellon and John Bruer of the James S. McDonnell Foundation initiated their innovative program in Cognitive Studies in Educational Practice (CSEP). CSEP offered large multiyear grants to encourage the development of collaborations between "bench psychologists" and educational researchers and teachers. CSEP further fostered such collaborations by holding annual miniconferences during which teams of grantees could interact with each other, to share both research advances and ideas for accomplishing the difficult task of close interdisciplinary collaboration. The two volumes resulting from the CSEP program (Bruer, 1993; McGilly, 1994) represent the type of synergy that promises to sustain the emergent field of Cognition and Instruction. After nearly 15 years of supporting this kind of research—both financially and intellectually—the McDonnell Foundation decided to terminate the CSEP program, suggesting that researchers in this now well-established field seek funding from the better endowed government agencies—such as the National Science Foundation and the Office of Naval Research. Indeed, the interest of these agencies in the new field is evidenced by the fact that they both enthusiastically supported the symposium on which this volume is based.

Although Robert Glaser's Learning Research and Development Center (LRDC) provided an institutional venue for this kind of work long ago, several more recent institutional innovations have produced university research institutes and centers aimed at both encouraging exchange and collaboration among researchers, and training graduate students in this emerging interdisciplinary field. Such centers can be found at Berkeley, Carnegie Mellon, Northwestern, Vanderbilt, and Wisconsin—to name just a few.

So, with all of this activity ... where is the field of Cognition and Instruction? How much progress have we made in 25 years? What remains to be done? The goal of this volume is to propose and illustrate some exciting and challenging answers to these questions. In choosing contributors, we sought a balance between senior researchers who participated in the original 1974 symposium, other established researchers who joined the field after that time, and new investigators with innovative and promising research programs. Finally, we decided to emphasize the challenges that we must face in the next 25 years and the inclusion of perspectives beyond what is commonly called Cognition and Instruction work. Chapters 6, 7, and 13 through 17 are based on the comments of discussants (Robert Siegler and Earl Hunt) and other invited speakers (Herbert Simon, Timothy Koschmann, Paul Cobb, Sam Wineburg, and Robert Glaser) that highlight research questions, methods, and contexts that will most productively expand and advance the field in the years to come.

This book is organized into five sections according to the primary focus of the chapter. Discussant comments and other invited addresses are included in the order they occurred to preserve the references between contributions that occurred at the symposium.

PART I:
DEVELOPMENT AND INSTRUCTION

This section of the anniversary volume includes the topics most similar to the original symposium. In the past 25 years, detailed analyses of tasks, subjects' knowledge and processes, and the changes in performance over time have led to new understanding of learners' representations, their use of multiple strategies, and the important role of metacognitive processes. New methods for assessing and tracking the development and elaboration of knowledge structures and processing strategies have yielded new conceptualizations of the process of change. Kalchman, Moss, and Case (chap. 1) and Klahr, Chen, and Toth (chap. 3) extend their theoretical stances on cognitive development and their empirical findings in laboratory studies to the creation of effective instructional approaches. Kalchman, Moss, and Case focus mainly on preschool and elementary mathematics instruction, and Klahr, Chen, and Toth address problems of basic scientific reasoning among elementary school children. Lehrer, Schauble, Strom, and Pligge (chap. 2) have also moved from laboratory studies of isolated aspects of thinking to complex, embedded instructional procedures with an emphasis on model-based reasoning in mathematics instruction in elementary school.

PART II:
TEACHERS AND INSTRUCTIONAL
STRATEGIES

Detailed cognitive analysis of expert teachers, as well as a direct focus on enhancing teachers' cognitive models of learners and use of effective instructional strategies, is another area that has seen tremendous growth and refinement in the past 25 years. Minstrell (chap. 4) is uniquely able to address the role of the teacher from the dual perspective of a teacher–researcher. Insights from his own learning process as a teacher studying cognitive science complement his research on diagnosing students' understanding and application of physics principles, and both highlight the key role of the teacher in the learning process. Palincsar and Magnusson (chap. 5) build on a long history of collaboration with teachers in the process of moving laboratory research relating cognition and instruction into the classroom, while maintaining both experimental control and ecological validity. They worked closely with educators to design and evaluate novel instructional materials and strategies to both model and support the development of scientific knowledge and reasoning.

Siegler (chap. 6) provides a sophisticated synthesis of the chapters in Parts I and II by focusing on their common "quest for meaning." He suggests a research agenda that would provide evidence to support what he sees as important issues raised by the work described in those chapters: (a) how to assess "meaningful understanding of a domain," (b) how to determine what levels of meaning are attainable by children at different ages, (c) how to inculcate a search for meaning in all children. Perhaps the answers to these questions will emerge in the next 25 years.

Herbert Simon in chapter 7, which is based on his keynote address at the symposium, articulates what is often an implicit—albeit fundamental—assumption in this area; "learning is one of the most important activities in which human beings engage, occupying a very large fraction of their lives and absorbing a substantial fraction of the national income" (p. 205). Then, having established the importance of the learning process, he reminds us of its location; "learning takes place inside the learner and only inside the learner" (p. 210). He then provides a concise history of methodological developments over the past 25 years or more that have enabled us to better understand the learning process— or, as he puts it, to "banish mysteries." Some of the best of these tools are described in Part III.

PART III:
TOOLS FOR LEARNING
FROM INSTRUCTION

The impact of intelligent tutors, complex computer based instructional interfaces, internet and distance learning, and so forth, are an important feature of cognition and instruction research that did not exist in 1974. Anderson and Gluck (chap. 8), and Reiser, Tabak, Sandoval, Smith, Steinmuller, and Leone (chap. 9) demonstrate ways in which computer-based intelligent tutors have moved from being a laboratory research tool to a pragmatic instructional medium in several urban schools, with dramatic effects on learning. Lesgold and Nahemow (chap. 10), faced with the challenge of real-world training contexts, use computer technology to amplify and instantiate the venerable concept of learning by doing.

PART IV:
SOCIAL CONTEXTS
OF INSTRUCTION AND LEARNING

Both the shift to conducting a significant portion of the cognition and instruction research in real classrooms and the increased collaboration between academics and educators have brought the role of the social context to center stage. Lovett (chap. 11) emphasizes the importance of communication for successful multidisciplinary collaboration among her team of cognitive psychologists, statistics instructors, educational researchers, and instructional technologists whose goal it is to understand and improve undergraduates' statistical reasoning. Carver (chap. 12) discusses the large-scale integration of cognition and instruction at Carnegie Mellon's early childhood laboratory school. She suggests five cognitive "metaprinciples" that can be used to develop learning goals, program designs, and assessments for the preschool and kindergarten children, as well as ways in which the same principles can be applied to staff development, parent education, and undergraduate learning experiences.

Earl Hunt's comments (chap. 13) on Parts III and IV provide a cautionary note about the extent to which the science of cognition provides a basis for engineering instructional innovations. In addition, he suggests that we carefully examine many of the assumptions that underlie the "social engineering" that accompanies many instructional innovations in order to better understand the nature of collaborative work.

PART V:
COGNITION AND INSTRUCTION:
THE NEXT 25 YEARS

Koschmann (chap. 14) notes that, in the past 25 years, the community of psychologists interested in cognition and instruction has expanded substantially, such that the previously dominant "information processing" view is now challenged by quite a different perspective; that of "situated cognition," and he utilizes a Deweyan framework to propose a resolution of the sometimes acrimonious debate among those who hold these different perspectives. Cobb (chap. 15) highlights and exemplifies the benefits of using design experiments, as opposed to traditional controlled experiments, within the social context of the classroom for developing theories of learning that account for the effects of broader factors, such as cultural diversity and institutional systems. Wineburg and Grossman (chap. 16) provide a case study of the significant ways that such factors affected their attempt to apply cognitive science principles to the development of a community among history and literature teachers who were planning to collaborate on developing curriculum materials for their urban high school students. Together, these chapters emphasize the challenges raised by the increasing integration of research and practice in the field of Cognition and Instruction. We look forward to the creative ways in which we and our colleagues will address these issues and advance the field in the next 25 years.

The final task, that of pulling it all together, would be overwhelming for most people. But, perhaps because he started it all over 40 years ago (Glaser, 1962/1965), Robert Glaser rises to the occasion in his concluding comments (chap. 17). He provides an interesting contrast between the first *Cognition and Instruction* volume (Klahr, 1976) and the present one, and he reiterates—with a more optimistic stance—Hunt's (chap. 13) theme of science-based engineering as the path to a future in which he anticipates a teaching profession empowered by modern knowledge of mature cognition and child development, and the related design of curriculum content and teaching methods.

Acknowledgments

The symposium that is the basis for the chapters in this volume was generously funded by the Office of Naval Research and the Directorate for Education & Human Resources at the National Science Foundation. The Psychology Department and the Children's School at Carnegie Mellon University also supported the conference in diverse ways. We thank Mary Anne Cowden, Anna Marie Joyce, Queenie Kravitz, Donna Perovich, and Jolene Watson for their valuable assistance in organization prior to the conference and for their gracious hostessing during it.

We extend our deep appreciation to each of the symposium participants. The contributors of chapters for this volume made our jobs easier by preparing their materials in a timely fashion and improved the quality of the work by reviewing each others' chapters and revising their own according to their peers' feedback. Bennett Bertenthal, Susan Chipman, Shari Ellis, and Michele Gregoire contributed significantly to the symposium via presentations that are, unfortunately, not represented in this volume. Thanks also to the Junior Scientists—supported by the Directorate for Education & Human Resources at NSF—who enriched the intellectual dialogue at the symposium by their active participation: Alla Keselman (Columbia), Eugene Matusov (University of Delaware), Anandi Nagarajan (Rutgers University), Mitchell Nathan (University of Colorado), Michael Nussbaum (California State University), Michelle Simmons (University of Florida), Judith Sinclair (Catholic College of America), Gregg Solomon (MIT), John St. Julien (University of Delaware), Michelle Stephan (IPFW), Joyce Tang Boyland (Alverno

College), Aaron Yarlas (Ohio State / UCLA), and Corinne Zimmerman (University of Alberta).

Sadly, the excitement and optimism with which this project was conceived and executed has been associated with two tragic losses. Just a week prior to the symposium, Ann Brown, who had been scheduled to be one of the discussants, died after a very brief illness. We are grateful to Buz Hunt for selflessly agreeing to serve as a discussant on very short notice and to Annemarie Palincsar, who graciously honored Ann with a moving tribute—included in this volume (p. xi)—at the opening session of the symposium. The second blow came a little over a year later, as the chapters were being copy edited, when Robbie Case—another major contributor to the field, and a participant in the symposium (chap. 1) suddenly died. Although the field has lost two of its most prolific and influential contributors, perhaps there is some comfort in knowing that their work has inspired others to continue to advance our knowledge about the intersection of cognition and instruction.

Each of the editors, Sharon Carver and David Klahr, would like to publicly express to the other a note of appreciation for being such an excellent colleague and collaborator, from the very beginning of this project to this final stage (introductions are always written last, placed first, and remembered not at all!). We both consider ourselves fortunate to have had the opportunity to work on a project in which both the product and the process were of such high quality.

In addition, Sharon Carver would like to express her gratitude to each of the Children's School staff members, children, families, and undergraduates, all of whom are part of her continuing opportunities for integrating cognition and instruction. More importantly, she wants her husband, Dave, and daughter, Ariel, to know how much she values them for calmly supporting her efforts on multiple simultaneous projects and for encouraging her to balance her work with family activities. David Klahr expresses deep appreciation to his wife, Pam, and his children, Anna, Joshua, Sophia, and Benjamin, for their continual support and encouragement on this and many other endeavors.

—*Sharon M. Carver*
—*David Klahr*
   Carnegie Mellon University
   Pittsburgh, Pennsylvania

REFERENCES

Bruer, J.T. (1993). *Schools for thought: A Science of learning in the classroom.* Cambridge, MA: MIT Press.

Glaser, R. (Ed.). (1965). *Training research and education.* New York: Science Editions, Wiley. (Original work published in 1962.)

Glaser, R. (1976). Cognitive psychology and instructional design. In D. Klahr (Ed.), *Cognition and instruction.* Hillsdale, NJ: Lawrence Erlbaum Associates.

Klahr, D. (Ed.). (1976). *Cognition and instruction.* Hillsdale, NJ: Lawrence Erlbaum Associates.

Larkin, J.H. (1994). Foreword. In K. McGilly (Ed.), *Classroom lessons: Integrating cognitive theory and classroom practice.* Cambridge, MA: MIT Press.

McGilly, K. (Ed.). (1994). *Classroom lessons: Integrating cognitive theory and classroom practice.* Cambridge, MA: MIT Press.

Part I

Development and Instruction

1

Psychological Models for the Development of Mathematical Understanding: Rational Numbers and Functions

Mindy Kalchman
Joan Moss
Robbie Case
University of Toronto

The domains of rational number and functions are foundational to many topics in advanced mathematics, and underpin the understanding necessary for participation in the pure and applied sciences (Lamon, 1999). Both domains are also known to be extremely difficult to master. Although many students do eventually learn to perform the basic operations and algorithms that the domains require, their conceptual knowledge remains remarkably weak, as does their ability to tackle novel problems (Carpenter, Fennema, & Romberg, 1993; Harel & Dubinsky, 1992). In this chapter, we discuss a program of research in which we have been trying to model the conceptual understanding that underpins novel performance in these two domains on the one hand, and to design improved curricular approaches for developing this sort of conceptual competence on the other.

The particular form of conceptual competence that we have been interested in has been characterized as *number sense*. As a number of authors have pointed out, the characteristics of good number sense include (a) fluency in estimating and judging magnitude, (b) ability to recognize unreasonable results, (c) flexibility when mentally computing, (d) ability to move among different representations and to use the most appropriate representation for a given situation, and (e) ability to represent the same number or function in multiple ways, depending on the context and purpose of this representation (Bereiter & Scardamalia, 1996; Case, 1998; Greeno, 1991; Sowder, 1992).

Our primary psychological assumption about number sense is that it depends on the presence of powerful organizing schemata that we refer to as *central conceptual structures*. We believe that these structures, which we model as complex networks of semantic nodes, relations, and operators, represent the core content in a domain of knowledge, help children to think about the problems that the domain presents, and serve as a tool for the acquisition of higher order insights into the domain in question. In an earlier series of articles, we proposed that central conceptual structures are normally assembled by the integration of two intuitive or "primitive" schemata. The first of these is primarily digital, verbal, and sequential; the second is primarily spatial, analogic, and nonsequential (Case & Okamoto, 1996; Griffin & Case, 1997; Kalchman & Case 1998; Moss & Case, 1999). In the first phase of children's learning (which we shall refer to as Level 1), these two core schemata are consolidated in isolation. In the second phase (Level 2), both of these two early schemata become more complex, while at the same time they are mapped onto each other. The result is that the students' understanding of the domain is transformed and a new psychological unit is constructed. During the next phase (Level 3), students slowly begin to discriminate among the different contexts in which the new unit can be applied, and to create slightly different representations of it—each with its own distinctive properties. In the final phase (Level 4), students build explicit representations of how these different variants of the core structure are related to each other, and learn to move among them freely and fluently depending on their purpose. More than anything else, it is this flexible movement that demonstrates that children have acquired true number sense, and not just a set of isolated conceptual understandings and algorithms.

In order to understand the way in which this general progression takes place in mathematics, it is useful to consider a concrete example. Consider, therefore, the domain of the whole number and the central conceptual structure on which children's number sense depends. According to the model proposed by Case and his colleagues (Griffin & Case, 1997; Okamoto & Case, 1996), the two primitive schemata on which the development of whole number depends are the schema for verbal counting (digital, sequential; Gelman, 1978), and the schema for global quantity comparison (spatial, analogic; Starkey, 1992). Although young children have strong intuitions for both counting and global quantity comparisons, these two schemata initially develop separately. Evidence in support of this assertion comes from several sources. In a recent factor analysis, Okamoto and her colleagues (personal communication, February 14, 2000) found two factors at this age level that corresponded with counting and quantity evaluation. Other evidence includes the fact that children have difficulty answering a question posed in one mode (e.g., verbal/sequential) that depends on the other mode for its answer. For example, they have a hard time answering the question "Which is more, 5 or 4?" although they can count to 5 without error, and can pick out an array of 5 objects as the larger, when it is contrasted with an array of 4 objects (Griffin, Case, & Siegler, 1994; Okamoto & Case, 1996; Siegler & Robinson, 1982).

As children make the transition to a higher level of cognitive development (Level 2) at about the age of 6, and as their thinking is stimulated by the numerical problems that they encounter at home and in school, they gradually elaborate on these two schemata and map them onto each other. Factor analytic studies now reveal a single factor, and children can answer a variety of questions requiring the coordination of the two initial schemata. Their new structure also permits them to solve a wide variety of cross-modal questions, including symbolically or verbally posed addition and subtraction problems, which they solve by counting forward and backward along the verbal counting sequence (Fuson, 1992; Siegler, 1996). In Okamoto's study, a single factor also emerged at this age level among the more advanced students.

As children begin to understand how mental counting works, as they continue to encounter problems that require mental counting, and as they continue to develop more generally, they move on to the next phase (Level 3), typically at about the age of 7 years. During this phase of their learning, they gradually form representations of multiple number lines, such as those for counting by 2, 5, 10, and 100. The construction of these representations gives new meaning to problems such as double digit addition and subtraction, which can now be understood as involving separate number lines, one for 10s and one for 1s.

In the final phase of their learning about whole number (Level 4), which typically begins around 9 or 10 years of age, children gradually develop both a generalized and an explicit understanding of the entire whole number system and the way in which different forms of counting are related to each other. Addition or subtraction with regrouping, estimation problems using large numbers, and mental math problems involving compensation are all understood at a higher level as this understanding gradually takes shape. The progression through the various phases is summarized in the second column of Table 1.1. The central numerical structure (the "mental number line") that emerges in the second phase is illustrated in greater detail in Fig. 1.1. The

TABLE 1.1

Modelling the Development of Conceptual Understanding
In Three Different Mathematical Domains

Level of Understanding	Mathematical Domain		
	Whole Numbers	Rational Numbers	Functions
Level 1: Consolidation of primitive schemata A: digital B: analog	A: Counting schema B: Qualitative quantity schema (more/ less; addition & subtraction).	A: Formal halving and doubling schema, for numbers from 1 to 100 B: Qualitative proportionality schema, including visual halving and doubling.	A: Recursive computation schema B: Bar graph schema
Level 2: Construction of new element A–B	Mental number line, with counting as an operation that is equivalent to addition and subtraction	Rational number line, with each number half or double previous one (e.g., whole, $1/2$, $1/4$, $1/8$, or we believe more appropriately; 100%, 50%, 25%, 12.5%)	Function schema, with line on Cartesian graph understood to represent results of iterative computation for different values of x
Level 3: Differentiation of new elements $A_1 - B_1; A_2 - B_2$	1s, 10s, 100s, and their relationship, understood and generalized to full whole number system	Decimals, fractions, percents, and their relationship understood	Confusable functions differentiated from each other, (e.g., $y = 2x; y = x^2; y = 2^x$. Function as object differentiated from function as sequence of operations
Level 4: Understanding of full system $A_1 - B_1 \times A_2 - B_2 \times A_3 - B_3$	1s, 10s, 100s, and their relationship, understood and generalized to full whole number system	Decimals, fractions, percents, and their relationship understood	Elements of polynomial (x, x^2, x^3) and the way they can relate, understood.

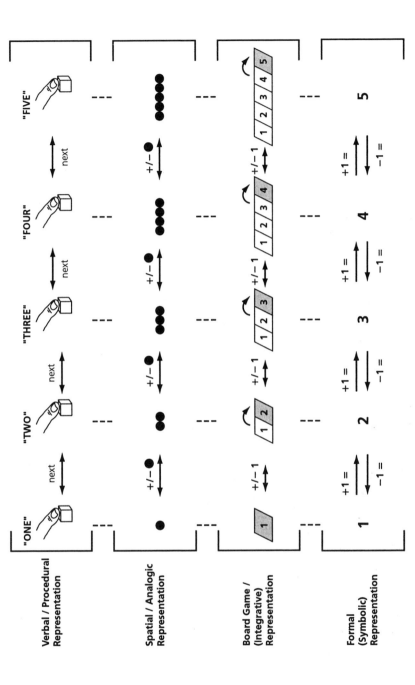

FIG. 1.1. Central conceptual structure for whole number. The four rows indicate different representations. The horizontal arrows indicate an understanding of the relation between adjacent items within each different type of representations. The vertical lines indicate that subjects understand the equivalence of these different representations, and the relations between them.

integrative representation in the middle of the figure is one that we have found useful in helping children to differentiate, elaborate, and integrate their earlier analogic and digital representations of numbers in our instructional studies (Griffin & Case, 1997).

How general is the psychological progression that is illustrated in Figure 1.1? How general is the sort of reciprocal mapping that the structure illustrates? How general is the finding that an integrative external representation, appropriately used, can facilitate the internal process of integration, thus deepening children's conceptual understanding and improving their number sense? (Case, 1985; Case & Griffin, 1990). In the present study, we investigated all three of these questions, and came to the conclusion that all three processes are quite general indeed.

UNDERSTANDING IN THE DOMAINS OF RATIONAL NUMBER AND FUNCTIONS

Rational Number

Our model of the developmental sequence on which a deep and flexible understanding of rational numbers depends is formally identical to that for whole number. In the first phase (Level 1), we proposed that children develop two separate schemata; (1) a global, qualitative structure for proportional evaluation that is spatial and analogic, and that encodes one quantity in relation to another (Moss & Case, 1999; Resnick & Singer, 1993; Spinillo & Bryant, 1991); and (2) a numerical structure for *splitting* or *doubling* that is digital and sequential, and that includes the results of a number of familiar splitting operations (e.g., $2 \times 50 = 100$; $^{100}/_2 = 50$; Case, 1985; Confrey, 1994; Kieren, 1992). Both of these schemata appear to be in place by about 9 to 10 years, and the latter depends on the availability of the central conceptual structure for whole number described earlier.

The new unit that is formed as these schemata are elaborated and integrated is the rational number line, a structure that permits children to solve a number of problems that involve ratio, rates, and/or equal sharing, provided that they involve simple halves or doubles. Once children understand a system for representing rational numbers (e.g., fractions or percents), they can gradually expand their understanding to include other forms of representation. Finally, after another period that is quite extended, they can come to understand the relationship among the various forms of representation, and can learn to move fluidly among them. This

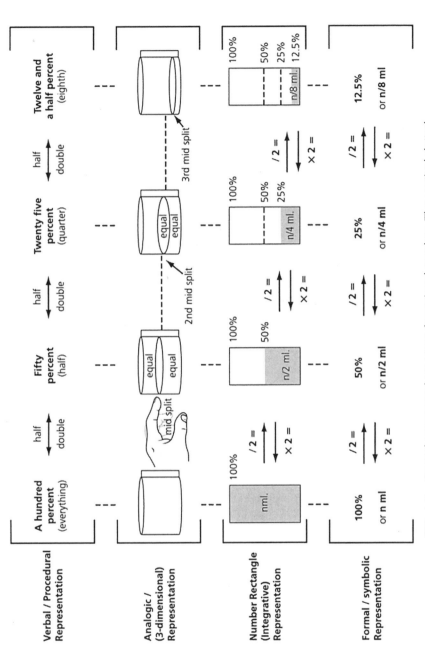

FIG. 1.2. Central conceptual structure for rational number. The vertical dotted lines in the figure indicate the knowledge that each row maps conceptually onto the next; the horizontal arrows indicate an understanding of the relation between adjacent items.

7

structural progression is summarized in the third column of Table 1.1. The core structure for rational number is illustrated in Fig. 1.2.

The top line of the figure represents the fractional and percent language that students use to describe a sequence of halved and doubled quantities. The (left to right) arrows connecting the expressions in this row indicate the operations by which we presume children move from one element to the next in the sequence. The second line illustrates the perceptually based sequence of ratios that children learn to recognize and to order. This operation, which might best be termed visual–motor halving, is most easily executed by putting one's forefinger beside an object—then moving it up and down until one finds the point at which the top and bottom halves of the object are symmetrical. In the third row, we depict the number rectangle—the integrative representation that we use in our instruction, and that helps the digital and spatial schemata to merge. This integrative representation also facilitates children's learning of benchmark percent values and the numerical operations that connect them. Thus, they are able to compose and decompose percents that were calculated in this fashion (e.g., to determine the size of 75% by finding the sizes of 50% and 25% and then combining them). Finally, the bottom row of the figure is meant to represent the corresponding set of measurement techniques and formal arithmetic procedures that children learn to use when the goal is to express a ratio in some standard set of units such as milliliters. For example, if one knows that the total volume a beaker can hold is 120 ml, one can determine what 75% of that volume must be by first computing half of 120 (60), then computing half of the resulting total (30), then adding these two values.

In our instructional work, we have shown that once children possess a ratio measurement structure such as that diagrammed in Fig. 1.2, they are able to use this structure as a starting point for learning about decimals and fractions (Moss & Case, 1999).

MATHEMATICAL FUNCTIONS

We hypothesize that a formally similar progression takes place in the domain of functions, as summarized in the third column of Table 1.1. For this domain, the primitive schemata are; (1) a digital, sequential schema in which a series of iterative numerical calculations is made, resulting in a string of numbers with a clear pattern (e.g., 0, 4, 8, 12, 16, etc. that occurs from adding 4 to each successive number); and (2) a spatial or analogic schema in which quantities are represented as bars on a graph in such a fashion that a pattern is perceived by a left to right visual scan (e.g., each bar is longer than the previous bar). The bars on the graph are read off the vertical axis (y-axis) as discrete quantities, and the categories along the horizontal axis (x-axis) are qualitative ones (e.g., a graph of individual people represented along the x-axis, where each person has more money than the previous one). These schemata are hypothesized to be in place by the time children are 9 or 10 years of age, with the latter one dependent on the development of children's central conceptual structure for representing space (Case, Marra, Bleiker, & Okamoto, 1996; Okamoto & Case, 1996).

In the second phase (Level 2), these two schemata are elaborated and mapped onto each other. The elaboration of the digital/sequential schema is one in which the numerical operation is applied iteratively to a string of positive, ascending whole numbers in order to generate pairs of quantitative values (e.g., multiplying each number by 4 to generate the following pairs of numbers: 0–0, 1–4, 2–8, 3–12, 4–16, etc.). A parallel elaboration is presumed to take place in the analogic schema during the same phase. In this elaboration, the categories along the horizontal axis become continuous rather than discrete, and thus can be used to represent quantitative rather than qualitative data. Any pair of numbers with two values is now understood to be representable in this (Cartesian) space, and the pattern that these pairs yield is representable by joining up the points, and looking at the sort of line that results.

These two initial schemata, as they are elaborated, are also mapped onto each other in such a fashion that the base set of whole numbers on which a computation is executed becomes points that can be represented from left to right along the x-axis. The results of this computation (e.g., multiply by 4) become points that can be represented along the y-axis. The overall pattern can be seen in the size of the step that is taken from one point to the next when the points are joined up (e.g., "up by 4" in a table representing pairs of numeric values, and "up by 4" on the graph). The result of this elaboration and coordination is a new element, which corresponds to children's first bimodal representation of a functional relationship. When this new element has been formed, an algebraic representation such $y = 4x$ can be constructed and can begin to have real meaning for children.

Figure 1.3 illustrates the structure of the central conceptual structure for function using the function $y = 4x$. The top row of the figure represents a string of positive, ascending whole numbers on which children operate to generate a second series of numbers. For this particular function, a constant multiplier of 4 is shown in the second row of the figure. The "+ 4" indicates that the values generated by this iterative operation consistently

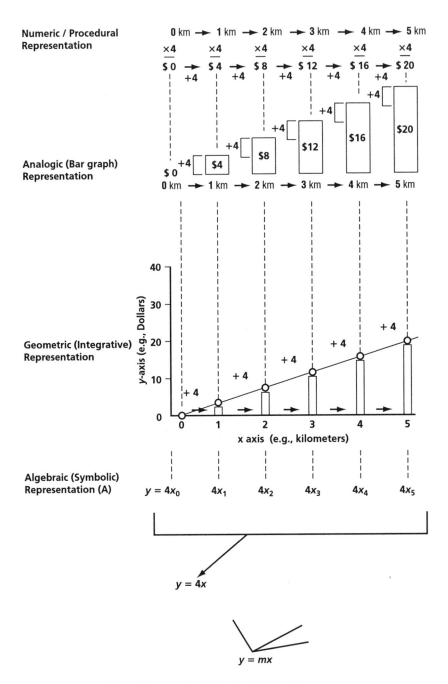

Numeric / Procedural Representation

Analogic (Bar graph) Representation

Geometric (Integrative) Representation

Algebraic (Symbolic) Representation (A)

FIG. 1.3. Central conceptual structure for function.

increase by 4. The bars found along the next row are also seen to increase successively by 4. The integrative representation, on which we place a heavy emphasis in our instructional work (Kalchman & Case, 1999), shows how the digital and analogic schemata are mapped onto one another and that the constant increase of 4 is a numeric measure of the steepness of the line, that is, the slope. Finally, the last two lines of this figure show an increasing ability for students to algebraically abstract the newly differentiated representations, and to categorize types of functions accordingly. Our hypothesis is that the general structure of the model is maintained for all other types of functions, including nonlinear. All that differs is the notation and operations that must be employed. For example, for the nonlinear function $y = x^2$, each kilometer in the first row of Fig. 1.3 is multiplied by itself, and the result is a set of values that grows exponentially and that is represented as a curved line in the integrative representation.

As children progress to the third phase in their learning (Level 3), they can begin to differentiate among families of functions, for example, linear and nonlinear functions. For a full differentiation to occur, however, it is necessary for children to understand integers, and to elaborate their Cartesian schema to the point where they can differentiate the four quadrants of the Cartesian plane, and can understand the relationship of these quadrants to each other.

Finally, at Level 4, children learn how linear and nonlinear terms can themselves be related and how to understand the properties of the resulting entities (polynomials) by analyzing these relations.

Our hypothesis is that the development of understanding in each of these individual domains (rational number and functions) progresses in a similar fashion to the way it progresses in the domain of whole number. In each case, we expect a recursive series of differentiations, integrations, and elaborations of increasingly complex cognitive structures.

INSTRUCTIONAL PROGRAMS

The question to which we now turn is how to design instruction that will facilitate children's movement through such a developmental sequence. At a general level, what we try to accomplish in our instruction is to help children move through the structural sequence that our developmental analyses have suggested underpin deep conceptual understanding and the achievement of "number sense." Working within the framework of central conceptual structures, we must first consider the prerequisite sequential and analogic structures that children already possess for a domain, and determine what differentiation and elaboration of these structures is necessary.

Our next task is to create a core context—often one involving an analogy or a metaphor—that serves as a conceptual bridge between the initial, separate schemata and the integrated conceptual structure that is the ultimate target. To enable children to move from their existing structures to the desired structure as expeditiously as possible, we often attempt to create external, pencil and paper representations that contain both analogic and digital information and that foster their interlinkage. The board game plays an integrative role of this sort in our programs for teaching whole number. Other similar devices, described later, appear in our programs for teaching rational numbers and functions.

Often, in order to maximize the gains from these multimodal representations, we create situations in which quantities are represented as objects having locations that are fixed in physical space, and through which children can literally move. We also create a semantic context that makes this movement familiar to children, and relates it to their everyday lives. Under these circumstances, we believe that children often come to appreciate properties of the numbers that their spatial cognition naturally predisposes them to notice (adjacency, closeness, etc.), and that they might otherwise miss.

As our figures indicate, central conceptual structures contain a great deal of verbal as well as symbolic and spatial information. Thus, another important component of our instructional design is the way in which we encourage children to create and integrate their purely verbal representations with their symbolic and analogic representations. We do so by having them talk about the integrative representations that we use, and the other representations that they themselves create, using natural language. We then try to form a bridge between the natural language that children use spontaneously and the more formal linguistic and symbolic mathematical terms of each domain, in a fashion that maps the two as directly and simply as possible.

Finally, we try to design situations in which children themselves can choose how to move back and forth among the different representations to which they are exposed, thus getting practice from the start in the sorts of problems that are often considered criterial for demonstrating number sense.

Consider now how these general procedures have been applied in each of the two domains in question.

Teaching Rational Numbers

The standard approach to teaching rational numbers is to introduce children to pie chart representations of fractions in the third or fourth grade, and then to proceed to exercises involving the addition or subtraction of fractions. By the fifth or sixth grade, students are expected to be able to add and subtract fractions with different denominators, using a standard algorithm for conversion to a common denominator. As fractions are mastered, decimals are introduced. Finally, between sixth and eighth grade, percents are introduced.

In our own curriculum, the thrust is on building the underlying psychological structure whose development was previously described. Accordingly, our goal is to begin with the two isolated schemata on which we believe rational number understanding depends and then to foster children's movement through the general sequence that is summarized in Table 1.1.

Overview of the Curricular Sequence

Level 1. The two basic schemata whose presence must be established, in our view, and that must be elaborated in order to move from the first to second phase of rational number learning, are the intuitive proportionality schema and the formal halving and doubling schema for the whole numbers from 1 to 100. The context in which we introduce the first of these two schemata is one in which children are filling large tubes with water, and estimating and comparing how much different tubes contain in proportional terms. Young children have difficulty perceiving narrow, upright containers in proportional terms. Although they can see which of two such containers has more liquid in absolute terms, they can also see which has more in proportional terms. That is to say, they can see which one is fuller. The comparison of beakers thus provides a context in which children can naturally apply and elaborate this qualitative schema.

Further, by the time children are 10 or 11, they have also had 4 or 5 years of instruction in arithmetic with whole numbers and are familiar with the numbers from 1 to 100 and the operations of addition and subtraction. As well, students have by now acquired basic knowledge of multiplication and division, including the knowledge of certain halving/doubling pairs by heart. Thus, for example, they know that 50 is half 100, and that 25 is half of 50. Using their well-automated computation skills, they can figure out that $12^1/_2$ is half of 25. They can also partition 100 a variety of ways, such as 25/75 or 90/10.

Level 2.   As previously mentioned, most programs begin children's instruction in rational numbers by teaching fractions. Moreover, they do so by introducing pizza pies, which must be divided equally for the purpose of sharing. The disadvantage of this is that children tend to encode each piece in absolute rather than in relative terms. They see a number like one fourth as being a thing, and three fourths as being three of these things, taken away from a whole pizza (Kerslake, 1986; Silver, 1997).

In our program, we create a context where children's proportional understanding of liquids and containers can be mapped onto their understanding of the whole number system from 1 to 100. We do so by beginning with the special case of percents. We begin the lessons with activities in which students estimate fullness of beakers using percent terminology. We then go on to computational problems such as figuring out what 50% or 75% of 120 ml would be, and so forth. The two strategies that we stress are *numerical halving* (100, 50, 25, etc.), which corresponds to the sequence of visual motor splits that children use naturally with their fingers, and *composition* (e.g., 100 = 75+25), which corresponds to visual motor addition of the results. Once children understand how percent values can be computed numerically, in a fashion that corresponds directly to intuitively based visual motor operations, we consider that they have moved into the second phase of their learning (Level 2) and have constructed the core rational number line that was indicated in Fig.1.2.

Level 3.   Our next step is to move them to the third phase—where they begin to understand other ways of representing rational numbers. The next form of rational number we introduce is the two-place decimal. We do so in a measurement context by explaining that a two-place decimal number indicates the percent of the way between two adjacent whole number distances that an intermediate point lies (e.g., 5.25 is a distance that is 25% of the way between 5 and 6). We then gradually expand this original idea to include multiplace decimals, using a transitional double decimal notation that the children spontaneously invent (e.g., 5.25.25 is a number that lies 25% of the way between 5.25 and 5.26), and using both spatial and temporal measurement situations.

Level 4.   Finally, as children become comfortable in understanding decimals and percents, we move on to the fourth phase, where children develop explicit representations of all possible rational numbers, including fractions, and begin to move among them freely and in a fashion that suits their particular purpose in the problems that they are confronting. At this point, a number of exercises are presented in which fractions, decimals, and percents are used interchangeably.

DETAILS OF INSTRUCTIONAL SEQUENCE
FOR FOURTH GRADE

Each time the curriculum is implemented, we follow the general procedures described earlier. The following is a sequence of activities that took place in a mixed-ability fourth-grade classroom in one of our trials. The lessons that are summarized were presented over a 3-month period at a rate of 1 or 2 classes per week. Each class lasted for approximately 1 hour.

Estimating Percents (Lessons 1–3)

The first lesson started with an introduction to percents. Students were challenged to think about instances where percents occur in their daily lives and to report these instances to the class as a whole. Not only were they able to volunteer a number of different contexts in which percents appeared (their siblings' school marks, price reductions in stores having sales, and tax on restaurant bills were the ones most frequently mentioned), the students were able to indicate a good qualitative understanding of what different numerical values "meant," for example, that 100% meant "everything," 99% meant "almost everything," 50% meant "exactly half," and 1% meant "almost nothing." Following these discussions, we presented the students with large drainage pipes of varying lengths covered with specially fitted sleeves made of flexible venting tube that fit around the pipes and could be pulled up and down and set to various levels. The children spontaneously estimated the various percentages of the pipes that were covered using the perceptual halving strategy. The students also continued percent estimations using beakers and vials filled with sand or water. These estimation exercises were designed to allow the students to integrate their natural halving strategies with percent terminology. The students were then introduced to a standard numerical form of notation for labeling percents.

Computing Percents (Lessons 4–6)

The visual estimation exercises using vials and beakers were continued with a new focus on computation and measurement. Children were instructed to compare visual estimates with estimates based on measurement and computation. For example, if a vial were 20 mm tall, 50% of that should be 10 mm. The children then began to estimate and mentally compute percentage of volume; for example, this vial holds 60 ml of water, 50% full should be 30 ml, and 25% full should be 15 ml. Other challenges included measuring objects in the classroom and then estimating and calculating different benchmark points such as 50%, 25%, 12^1/$_2$%, and 75%.

The children were not given any standard rules to perform these calculations and thus they employed a series of strategies of their own invention. For example, to calculate 75% of the length of an 80cm desktop, the students typically considered this task in a series of steps. Step 1—find half, and then build up as necessary (50% of 80 is 40). Step 2—find the difference between 75% and 50% (75% − 50% = 25%). Step 3—find 25% of 80, (25% × 80 = 20). Step 4—sum parts (40 + 20 = 60). Other exercises included comparing heights of children to teacher, for example, and then assigning an estimated numerical value using the language of percents. For example, "Peter's height is what percent of Joan's?" or "What percent of your father's height is your height?" A series of specially made laminated cutout dolls ranging in height from 5 cm to 25 cm provide additional practice at comparing heights. Percent lessons were concluded with the students planning and teaching a percent lesson to a child from a lower grade.

Introduction to Decimals
Using Stopwatches (Lessons 7–8)

In these two lessons, children were introduced to decimals as an extension of their work on percents. The lessons started with discussions of decimals and how they permit more precise measurement than do whole numbers. Two-place decimals were introduced as a way of indicating what "percent" of the distance between two whole numbers a particular quantity occupies. LCD stopwatches with screens that display seconds and hundredths of seconds (hundredths of seconds are indicated by two small digits to the right of the numbers) were used as the introduction to decimals. After lengthy discussions of what these small numbers represent quantitatively, the students came to refer to these hundredths of seconds as "centiseconds." The stopwatch activities served to build up children's intuitive sense of small time intervals, and to give students the experience of the magnitude of "centiseconds."

More importantly, use of these stopwatches provided the students with the opportunity to represent these intervals as decimal numbers. In the stopwatch activities, centiseconds indicated the percentage of time that had passed between any two whole seconds; they came to represent the temporal analogs of distance. Many activities and games were devised for the purpose of helping the students to actively manipulate the decimal numbers in order to illuminate the conceptually difficult concepts of magnitude and order. The first challenge that was presented to the students was "The Stop/Start Challenge." In this exercise, students attempted to start and stop the watch as quickly as possible, several times in succession. They then compared their personal quickest reaction time with that of their classmates. In this exercise, they had the opportunity to experience the ordering of decimal numbers as well as to have an informal look at computing differences in decimal numbers (scores).

Another difficult initial aspect of using decimal symbols is the ordering of decimals when the numbers move from 0.09 to 0.10, for example. Some students are able to respond quickly enough to the challenge to achieve a score of .09 seconds. Therefore, such traditionally difficult rational number tasks such as, what is bigger, .09 or .40? can be naturally introduced. Another stopwatch game that offered active participation in the understanding of magnitude was "Stop the Watch Between." The object of this game was for the student to decide which decimal numbers come in between two given decimal numbers and then to stop the watch somewhere in that span of decimal numbers. In the game "Crack the Code," the students moved between representations as they were challenged to stop the watch at the decimal equivalent of, for example, $\frac{1}{2}$ (.50). As an extension to these exercises, the students were encouraged to invent variations of these games to use as challenges for their classmates.

Learning About Decimals on Number Lines (Lesson 9)

A second approach to decimals was through the use of meter-long, laminated number lines that are calibrated in centimeters. This approach was based on students' work with percents using number lines. The first activities served as a review. Each child was given a small number line and was asked to find designated percents of the whole line by placing a unit block on the appropriate spot. ("Please place a unit block on the line that indicates 44% of your number line.") The students were then told that these percent quantities could also be expressed as a decimal number; thus, for example, 44% could also be shown as 0.44. Other activities included "Percent/Decimal Walks" where several number lines (which are referred to as "sidewalks" by the students) were lined up end-to-end on the class-room floor with small gaps between each. Students walked a given indicated distance on the number lines, for example, "Can you please walk 3.67 sidewalks."

Playing and Inventing
Decimal Board Games (Lessons 10–13)

A board game called the "The Dragon game" was devised with the intention of giving the students the opportunity to learn about the magnitude of decimal numbers, as well as to add and subtract decimal numbers. The game board was approximately 60 cm x 90 cm and was composed of 20 individual laminated 10-cm number lines that were arranged as a winding path. Each number line was marked as a ruler; 10 thick black lines indicated cm measures, 10 slightly shorter blue lines highlighted the .5 cm measures, and 100 red lines provided the mm measures. This game directly followed from the "sidewalk" exercises mentioned earlier. The object of the game was to get from the beginning (the first sidewalk) to the end (the 20th sidewalk) before the other players. At each turn, a child picked two cards, an "add" or "subtract" card and a "number" card. Each number card had two digits written on it. The rule was that before making a move on the board, the player had to expand the two digits on the card by adding both a zero and a decimal point strategically so as to optimize the distance that the player would travel. For example, if a child picked a card with the digits 1 and 2, she had the options of calling that card .120, 1.20, 12.0, or 120. Three lessons followed where the students invented and planned their own rational number board game and then played each other's games.

Fractions (Lessons 14–17)

In keeping with the curriculum focus of translating among representations, fraction lessons were taught in relationship to decimals and percents. In these lessons, the children were challenged, for example, to represent the fraction $1/4$ in as many ways as they could, using a variety of shaded geometric shapes as well as using formal fraction, decimal, and percent representations. They also worked on problems and invented their own challenges for solving mixed-representation equations involving decimals, percents, and fractions. For example, a student might compose the following challenge: "Is this true or false; $1/8 + 10\% + 0.75 = 1$?"

Review (Lessons 18–20)

Games were played where students had to add and subtract decimals, fractions, and percents by creating their own hands-on concrete materials. For example, students invented card games with mixed-representations and challenged their classmates to solve a variety of problems that were posed. As a final culminating project, students were invited to either invent their own rational number teaching strategies and lessons that could be taught to another group, or design a game or video presentation that incorporated specific rational number teaching objectives.

RESULTS
FROM THE RATIONAL NUMBER STUDIES

In order to assess the effectiveness of the curriculum, we designed a series of measures that we administered both as pre- and posttests to students in the experimental programs as well as to students who served as control and comparative groups. To analyze results, items were assigned to subcategories that are generally taken to be indicators of rational number sense, and that are specific to the indicators of general number sense that were mentioned at the beginning of the chapter. These subcategories included comparing and ordering rational numbers; translating among decimals, fractions, and percents; solving problems that include misleading visual features; and inventing procedures for calculating with rational numbers. We also included items that were of a standard nature and that reflected traditional tasks. In the following section, we present items from each of these subcategories along with representative responses that students gave to these items at posttest. These examples are taken from three different empirical studies that we conducted where the experimental rational number curriculum was implemented and assessed. In the first, we presented the curriculum to a group of high-achieving fourth-grade students ($n = 16$) and compared their pre- and posttest performance to a well-matched treatment-control group (Moss & Case, 1999). In the second and third studies, the students who participated in the experimental program were from intact mixed-ability classrooms, one, a class of fourth graders ($n = 21$), and the other, a group of sixth graders ($n = 16$). For these latter studies, we compared the posttest performance of the experimental students to the performance of several traditionally instructed normative groups of students from fourth grade ($n = 30$), sixth grade ($n = 36$), and eighth grade

($n = 26$). The comparison group also included 32 preservice teachers in a postgraduate teacher training program, (Moss, 2000).

Quantitative analyses of the results revealed that all of the students in the experimental groups made significant gains from pre- to posttest, achieving effect sizes in the range of 2.3 to 3.5 standard deviations. The results also revealed that the posttest scores of the fourth and sixth-grade experimental students were higher than those obtained on the same measure by the eighth-grade comparison students and were equal to the scores that the preservice teachers achieved. Moreover, as we show in the examples that follow, the experimental students showed less reliance on whole number strategies when solving novel problems, and made more frequent reference to proportional concepts in justifying their answers than did the students in the normative groups.

The first item that we present was from the subcategory *Interchangeability*, which was comprised of items that required students to translate among the representations of rational number system—an important factor in rational number sense (Sowder, 1992). Although none of the students in the experimental groups was able to answer the following question at pretest, more than 80% of these students achieved a correct answer at posttest.

Interviewer: Do you know what one eighth is as a decimal?

Student: Well one eighth is half of one fourth. And one quarter is 25%, so half of that is $12^{1}/2\%$. So as a decimal, that would have to be point 12 and a half. So that is point 12 point 5, so that means that it is .125.

The reasoning of this student is representative of the kind of strategies that most of the students used to arrive at a solution to this problem. Furthermore, this solution strategy illustrates several features that became central to students' reasoning: First is the use of percents as a guide even when the problem does not contain the percent representation. Second, the student used the familiar 25% benchmark to convert from a fraction to a decimal. Third, this same protocol reveals that when working on problems with decimals, students often employ a mixed decimal and fraction representation. And fourth, the usefulness of the halving and doubling operation is clear. By contrast, over 50% of all the students in the comparison groups asserted that 0.8 must be the answer as $^{1}/8$ was the fraction to be translated.

Closely associated with interchangeability is the ability to compare and order rational numbers. Not only must students assign a quantitative referent to the rational numbers that are represented, but as is illustrated in the following example, they must also have an understanding of the density property of the rational number system.

Interviewer: Can any fractions fit between one fourth and two fourths? And if so, can you name one?

Student A: Well, I know that one quarter is 25% and so two quarters is 50%. So, 40% fits between them. So that would be 40 hundredths.

Student B: One quarter is the same as two eighths and two quarters is the same as four eighths so the answer is three eighths.

This item that was answered correctly by 80% of the high-achieving students as posttest, (0% at pretest), was very difficult for the students from the comparison group, most of whom either did not know the answer or asserted that no such fraction existed. These students achieved a passing rate of 46%.

A third item that we present was designed to assess students' ability to overcome misleading features. The item that we now present that appeared on the measures used in both of the fourth-grade studies, challenged the students to ignore an irrelevant partitioning of a geometric region in order to correctly answer the question. At posttest, 90% of the students in the experimental groups were able to provide a correct answer. The following three examples of student reasoning are representative of the strategies that were used by these young students.

Interviewer: Can you shade three quarters of this pizza. (The pizza was partitioned into 8 sections).

Student A: Well let me see .... This is a half (student shaded 4 sections), ... so you would need 2 more to make three quarters. (Shades 2 more sections).

Student B: There are 2 slices in a quarter so you need 6 [slices] to make three quarters (shades them).

Student C: (Shades 6 sections) I just keep the quarters and forget about the eighths.

By contrast, the students in the control group only achieved a passing rate of 50% and made the kind of error that is reported in the literature and is considered to be indicative of whole number interference. They asserted that "since it says $^3/_4$, you need to shade in three parts."

Finally, the ability to invent procedures to solve standard and nonstandard computation problems is generally seen as an important feature of number sense. The types of errors that are consistently shown in the rational number literature demonstrate that students are overly dependent on the use of procedures. Even when uncertain of the rules, they misuse a procedure, preferring to accept an improbable answer rather than to invent an alternate strategy (Mack, 1995). The results of the previously mentioned studies reveal that the students acquired the ability to invent procedures for calculating with rational numbers. The next item that we present appeared on all of the measures in the three studies. Overall, 68% of the students were able to correctly answer this question. By contrast, virtually none of the school-age children and only 60% of the preservice teachers were able to answer this question.

The following two examples of students' reasoning is typical of the reasoning that the students used on this item.

Interviewer: What is 65% of 160?

Student A: Okay, 50% of 160 is 80. Half of 80 is 40 so that is 25%. So if you add 80 and 40 you get 120 but that is too much because that's 75%. So you need to minus 10% and that's 16. So, 120 take away 16 is 104.

Student B: The answer is 104. First I did 50% which was 80. Then I did 10% of 160, which is 16. Then I did 5% of it, which was 8. I added them (16 + 8) to get 24, and added that to 80 to get 104.

The reasoning in these examples clearly indicates that using benchmark quantities when working with percents and translating among representations is an effective strategy for solving unfamiliar problems.

DISCUSSION
OF RATIONAL NUMBER STUDIES

The foregoing examples of students' reasoning, while limited in number, are representative of the kinds of understandings that have emerged with each iteration of the curriculum (Moss, 2000). The scope of students' acquired understandings includes an overall understanding of the number system, which is illustrated in their ability to use the representations of decimals, fractions, and percents interchangeably; an appreciation of the magnitude of the rational numbers as seen in their ability to compare and order numbers within this system; an understanding of the proportional- and ratio-based constructs of this domain, which underpins their facility with equivalencies; an understanding of percent as an operator, which is evident in their ability to invent a variety of solution strategies for calcu- lating with these numbers; and a general confidence and fluency in their ability to think about the domain, using the benchmark values that they have learned, which is a hallmark of number sense.

Recently, several other investigators have reported success in produc- ing a deeper, more proportionally based understanding of fractions or dec- imals in the middle school years (e.g., Confrey, 1994; Kieren, 1995; Mack, 1995; Streefland, 1993). Not coincidentally, we believe, our pro- gram shares several important features with the programs designed by these other investigators, including a greater emphasis on the meaning or semantics of the rational numbers, a greater emphasis on the proportional nature of rational numbers, a greater emphasis on children's natural way of viewing problems, and their spontaneous solution strategies, and the use of an alternative form of visual representation (i.e., an alternative to the standard "pie chart"). In addition, our program shares several particu- lar features with Confrey's program that, like ours, attempted to move children beyond the understanding of any single form of rational number representation toward a deeper understanding of the rational number sys- tem as a whole. These common features include a strong emphasis on con- tinuous quantity and measurement, as opposed to discrete quantity and counting, on splitting as a natural form of computation that can be used in a measurement context, and on the equivalence between different forms of rational number representation.

We do, however, see our program as unique in several ways and it is our conjecture that the following three features are particularly crucial. (1) Our program begins with percents, thus permitting children to take advan- tage of and to combine their qualitative understanding of proportions and their knowledge of the numbers from 1 to 100 while avoiding (or at least postponing) the problems that fractions present, either on their own or as a basis for understanding decimals. (2) Our program uses a unidimen- sional form of number representation (the rational number line) in a con- text that emphasizes the global, proportional nature of any quantity, rather than the multiple units or "shares" into which it may be divided. (3) Our program emphasizes benchmark values for moving among equivalencies among percents, decimals, and fractions, an emphasis that permits stu- dents to think about problems in a much more flexible fashion and to use procedures of their own invention for approaching them.

CURRICULUM
FOR MATHEMATICAL FUNCTIONS

The topic of functions is generally introduced in the ninth grade, where the graphic, numeric (tabular), and algebraic representations are typically taught in isolation. In this standard approach, algebraic equations are presented as the primary representation of functions, whereas graphs and numeric patterns found in tables of values are secondary and are loosely connected to the meaning of the algebra. The primary goal is for students to achieve competence in identifying and manipulating a few standard types of functions, such as linear functions, quadratic functions, and so forth. By contrast, in our experimental curriculum, we introduce students to the domain as early as sixth grade, with an emphasis that is considerably different. As is the case with curricula designed to foster number sense with whole numbers (Griffin & Case, 1997) or rational numbers (Moss & Case, 1999) our primary goal is to bring children through the developmental sequence that is summarized in Table 1.1.

Overview of Curricular Sequence

Levels 1 and 2. We begin by helping students elaborate their digital and analogic schemata, and map them onto each other so that they can begin to create a new psychological (and mathematical) object. To do so, the "bridging context" used is one in which both the digital or computational aspect of a function, and the graphic aspect, can be represented and understood simultaneously. The particular context we use for this purpose is a walkathon, in which the sponsorship rule varies from one participant to the next, and the results can be represented as tables of numbers or as a series of bar graphs. This context was chosen over other possible contexts because children have experience with and understand the variables in question (distance and money) as mathematical variables, and understand the functional (dependent) relationship between them; children are interested in the impact of different rules on the rate at which money accumulates; and children naturally think of distance as a continuous variable and are interested in what happens if they complete only part of the last kilometer.

The following is an example of how this walkathon context is used in the classroom. Children understand that when earning $1.00 per kilometer walked, their total earnings depend on the ultimate distance traveled, and are calculated by multiplying one times the number of kilometers walked. A table of values and a Cartesian grid—both of which are mathematical constructs with which sixth-grade children are familiar from previous schooling—are basic representations that children can use to keep track of kilometer by kilometer earnings. A symbolic representation is also easily and intuitively constructed by introducing the symbol of $ as the money earned and km as the distance walked. So, the sponsorship agreement of earning $1.00 per kilometer can be represented as $1.00 \times km = \$$. Thus, from the onset, the graphic, tabular, and algebraic/symbolic representations of a function are seen as equivalent forms of the same mathematical relationship.

Level 3. Students move from the walkathon context to a computer lab where they are introduced to a spreadsheet technology for graphing. Here, they consolidate and apply the ideas from the first part of the program, and begin differentiating different functions by empirically varying the parameters of different formulae (e.g., the slope, the y-intercept, an exponent, etc.). We chose spreadsheet technology because it simultaneously displays the tabular, graphic, and algebraic representations with any change in one representation being instantly reflected in the others. The general idea is for students to understand the properties and behaviors of individual functions; to generalize these features to entire families of functions (e.g., $y = mx + b$ and $y = ax^2 + b$); to differentiate these families of function from each other (e.g., $y = mx + b$ from $y = ax^2 + b$); and to understand the relationship between changes in the basic function, and changes in its various representations (e.g., tabular, graphic, algebraic).

Level 4. In the final component of the program, groups of students investigate further one particular type of function (e.g., linear, quadratic, or cubic) using the computer. They explore that function, and then use computer generated output of exemplary graphs, equations, and tables to illustrate the function's general properties and behaviors. Students then develop a presentation and share their new expertise with classmates. In sixth grade, we do not expect students to be able to understand quadratic equations, or to break them into components. Thus, these final exercises primarily serve to consolidate the understanding that they have already achieved. In higher grades, students go on to more complex functions including quadratic, cubic, and reciprocal functions.

Typical Instructional Sequence for Grade 8

The following sequence of instruction is set out lesson by lesson. However, because this curriculum is implemented differently in different schools and with different classes, the amount of time available to cover a single lesson varies, and one lesson does not necessarily correspond to one day's instruction. Still, we consider one lesson to involve approximately a one-hour period of time. Generally, we try to implement the lessons in 10 to 15 successive school days.

Lesson 1: Introduction to Functions and Slope. The walkathon context is introduced and children are given the example of being sponsored $1.00 for every kilometer walked for a 10 km walkathon. Using that rule, the first task is to record in a table of values the money earned at each kilometer walked. As one student completes the table for walking 0, 1, 2, 3, and so forth km, a second student marks on a large graph the coordinates identified in the table. For example, at 0 km, 0 times 1 equals 0, so $0 has been earned and a marker is put at the point where 0 km along the horizontal axis and 0 dollars along the vertical axis meet; the next marker is put at 1–1, and so on.

Here, we emphasize the physical action of walking *along* the horizontal axis from kilometer to kilometer and then going *up* to the number of dollars earned. This motion serves to enforce the dynamic aspect of a function—that is, change in one quantity brings about change in the other, and the left to right "movement" of a function, which is important for determining the direction of the slope of a linear function. Once the table of values and the graph are constructed, we consider ways of representing the function symbolically using km to represent the distance walked and $ to represent the money earned. Before settling on a representation, however, we first look at what operation we performed at each kilometer to get the money earned. In this first case, we multiplied each kilometer by 1 to get the money earned. This translates into the expression km $\times$ 1 = $. The significance of the "1" in the above symbolic expression is highlighted and its meaning considered in the corresponding graph and the table of values. In the table, we notice that the difference between consecutive $ values is always 1; and the line on the graph always goes *up by* one value as we go across by one value. Thus, students develop a feel for the spatial and numeric properties intrinsic to the $y = 1 \times x$ ($y = x$) line, and determine that it has an up by amount of 1. This up by amount corresponds to the mathematical term of slope, although this term is not introduced at this time.

The same procedures are then carried out for sponsorship agreements such as $2.00 per kilometer, $5.00 per kilometer, $10.00 per kilometer, 50¢ per kilometer, 25¢ per kilometer, and for rules created by the students. Before each rule is graphed, students predict the steepness of the line relative to the $y = x$ line, thus establishing a sort of "benchmark." Then, common characteristics of these functions are discussed. Characteristics typically noted by the students include: "They're all straight lines because the $'s all go up by the same amount each time [in the graphs and in the tables]"; "they all go through zero because zero times anything is zero"; and "the bigger the number you multiply by, the steeper the line is." The term *slope* is introduced at this point, and students are asked to determine a value for the slope of each of the functions we explore. At no time is an algorithm for determining slope introduced.

Lesson 2: The Y-Intercept. The idea of a starting bonus is introduced and is explained as an initial amount of money that may be contributed before the walkathon even begins. This starting amount is called the "starter offer"—a phrase coined by students in pilot studies. We begin these lessons also with a sponsorship arrangement of $1.00 for every kilometer walked. Students graph this function, make a table of values, and write a symbolic representation for it. Students are then told that they will be given a $5.00 starter offer just for participating in the walkathon. As one student constructs the table, a second student places markers on the graph at each coordinate, and the markers are joined. Each student is then asked to construct a symbolic representation of the function (km × 1 + 5 = $).

Other rules in which students earn $1.00 per kilometer but have different starter offer amounts such as $2.00, $10.00, and $3.50 are given. For each new rule, the table and graph are created, and an equation written. Then, all of the starter offer rules are compared. The following common features typically emerge; (a) all are still straight lines, (b) all lines with the same per kilometer sponsorship rule are parallel, (c) all of the functions go up by one, and (d) changing the starter offer only changes the starting position of the line on the graph and not the slope of it. The term *y-intercept* is introduced as the mathematical name for the starter offer.

Next, a group discussion is initiated in which we talk about the effects of changing the starter offer on the graph versus the effects of changing the amount we multiply the kilometers by (the slope, or up by amount). We then review all of the functions with which we have worked and determine how the slope and y-intercept may be found in each of the representations used (tables, graphs, and equations).

Students, either individually or in pairs, then work on an activity where they invent two functions that will allow them to earn $153.00 at the completion of a 10 km walkathon. Both strategies must produce straight line functions. Tables, graphs, and equations are constructed to show their work. Students are also asked to identify the slope and y-intercept of each function they use. Individual or pairs of students then show their functions to the whole group. Students are also challenged to work "backwards," that is, to find what the starter offer would have to be if the slope were 10, or what the slope would have to be if the starter offer were 20.

Lesson 3: Curved Lines.   It is explained to students that there are some functions that generate curved-line rather than straight-line graphs. Students are asked to recall the numeric properties of those that produce straight line graphs. The notion of a constant up by amount in both a table of values and a graph is discussed, as well as the corresponding coefficient in a $y = mx + b$ equation. Students are then shown a table of values for the function $y = x^2$ and are asked to try and find the function. Students first notice that the sequence of values generated do not "go up by the same amount each time," and thus, they cannot use their strategy of multiplying the first set of numbers by a constant value. The rule of multiplying each number by itself invariably is discovered and represented as $\$ = km \times km$. Because younger students are not familiar with exponents as a mode of mathematical operation, it is explained that km^2 is the same as km times km; likewise, km^3 is the same as km times km times km, and so on. Thus, the equation for this function may be written as $\$ = km^2$. It is then explained that the coordinates of these functions are connected on a graph using a smooth curve rather than the series of line segments that students tend to spontaneously draw.

Next, we explore the idea of including a starter offer with these types of functions and students come to recognize that the inclusion of a starter offer has the same effect on this type of function as on the straight line functions. That is, the steepness of the line (or curve) is not altered, merely the place at which the function meets the vertical axis. A rule where one is being sponsored the number of kilometers by itself plus a starter offer of $10.00 is easily symbolized by students as $\$ = km^2 + 10$. Students are then challenged to come up with a function that would produce a curved line, and that they could use for earning $153.00 over 10 km.

Lesson 4: Negative Slopes and Y-intercept.   Negative values along the y-axis are introduced by asking students to think about how the negative values along the vertical axis could be used. Students generally recognize that lines would contain a *down by* amount if a certain amount of money was given away for each kilometer walked. For example, if $2.00 were given away for each kilometer walked, a table of values would show that the $ or y values would go down by 2 each time, and in the equation it would be necessary to multiply the km by –2. Graphing the function would give a decreasing straight line with a slope of –2, and a starter offer of 0.

A context is then introduced for negative y-intercepts. The idea of debt is suggested whereby students have to pay off a starter offer. For example, students are asked to make a table, graph, and equation for paying off a $10.00 debt at $1.00 per kilometer walked. The equation for this type of function is written as $ = 1 \times$ km $+ -10$. Students are then challenged to invent several of their own functions in which they have to pay off a chosen amount of money over a certain number of kilometers. They are asked to make tables and graphs for these functions, and to write equations that represent their ideas.

Lessons 5–8 Computer Activities.   Students spend the next several lessons working in pairs on computers using spreadsheet charting tools (see Fig. 1.4 for a sample computer screen). The activities for the computer were designed for children to consolidate and move beyond the tasks they have been doing in the classroom. In these activities, students are asked to change single parameters of functions, that is, just the slope, intercept, or exponent, of the $y = x$ or the $y = x^2$ function, in order to manipulate the graphic representation through preplotted colored points. They are then asked to change more than one parameter at a time in order to manipulate the given line or curve through the points.

Throughout, students are required to record the equations of the new functions, the numeric sequence found in the generated tables, and the graphic implications. In addition, students are asked to create their own functions that have certain visual and numeric characteristics (e.g., slopes steeper than 4, or inverted curves), program the equations for those functions into the computer, and record the results.

Lessons 9–10: In–Class Presentations.   The final component of the curriculum requires students to prepare and then give a presentation on a specified type of function, which was featured in the computer activities. Students are asked to capture the general characteristics and behaviors of "their" function with exemplary graphs, equations, and tables, and to share their expertise with their classmates. When participating as a member of the audience, children are required to provide

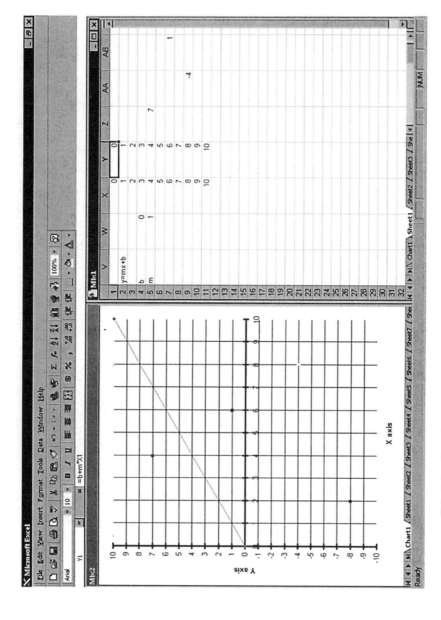

FIG. 1.4. Sample computer screen. With this configuration, students work on activities having to do with altering the slope and *y*-intercept of the function (m and b, respectively).

feedback, ask clarifying questions, and challenge the presenters on any information that is inconsistent with their own understandings.

RESULTS FROM FUNCTION STUDIES

The test designed to measure students' understanding of function presents items in an order that is intended to reflect the levels of understanding hypothesized in the developmental model. Because the curriculum for functions is implemented with classes of children in the sixth, eighth, and 11th grades, expectations for posttest success are relative to the grade level of the students. Thus, examples of items that increase in difficulty are presented, along with corresponding responses from students who have participated in our experimental curriculum and who were in the sixth, eighth, and 11th grades, respectively. Control conditions have been used at the eighth- and 11th-grade levels only. This is because there is no local, standard sixth-grade curriculum that introduces comparable concepts. In the present work, sixth-grade responses were drawn from studies carried out with two different sixth-grade classes ($n = 34$). The eighth-grade students' responses are from a study in which there were both experimental and control conditions (Kalchman & Case, 1998, 1999 $n = 24$ and $n = 21$, respectively). Full results for a study conducted at the 11th-grade level where both control and experimental conditions were employed ($n = 16$ for both group) are in preparation (Kalchman, 2000). Some earlier analyses of 11th graders' reasoning about functions were done with students who had experienced a text-based program (Kalchman & Katz, 1999).

In the first example, students are responding to the item seen in Fig. 1.5. For this question, students must provide an equation for a function that, when graphed, will cross the given line within the Cartesian territory seen on the page. There are an unlimited number of possible linear and curvilinear functions that could cross this line. Linear solutions include functions that have a slope of approximately 3.5 or greater and a y-intercept of 0 (e.g., $y = 6x$; $y = 10x$); those that have a y-intercept less than 7 and a slope greater than 1 (e.g., $y = 2x + 5$; $y = 4x + 1$); those that have a negative slope and have a y-intercept greater than 7 and less than or equal to 10 (e.g., $y = -3x + 8$, $y = -2x + 9$).

Increasing and decreasing curvilinear graphs are also possible. For example, an increasing curvilinear function must either rise fast enough to

Can you think of a function that would cross the function seen in the graph below? What is the equation of the function you thought of?

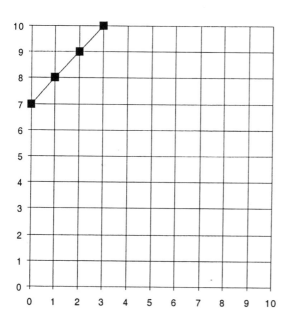

Explain why the equation you chose is a good one.

FIG. 1.5.   Sample level 2 item for the functions measure.

cross the given function if it has a y-intercept of 0 (e.g., $y = x^3$), or must have a y-intercept great enough to pass the curve through the line (e.g., $y = x^2 + 5$). Responses from students who have participated in our programs vary considerably and include all of the above types of functions. The following are samples of students' reasoning. In one case (Student B), the supporting context of the walkathon is evident in his thinking.

Student A: $y = -2x + 10$ is one because the $+10$ is where it starts and when you multiply [x] by -2 [the function] goes down by that [amount] each time.

Student B: If it's $y = 2x + 6$ then [the function's] starting at 6 and going up by 2 every kilometer and that will cross.

Student C: $y = 100x$. It could really be anything. You could just make it times 100 and it'll go straight up. (By drawing on the graph with his finger, he showed how multiplying x by a large number such as 100 would produce a line on the graph that would shoot almost straight up and cross the given one by the time the function reached $x = 1$.)

Student D: This student began by drawing in the function $y = x^2$ and continually redrawing the same function with a greater and greater y-intercept until she was satisfied that the function $y = x^2 + 6$ would cross the given line.

The previous responses from sixth-grade students must be considered against a backdrop of only 9% of students in an advanced level 11th-grade mathematics class ($n = 33$) giving correct responses to this item following their unit on functions (Kalchman & Katz, 1999). Seventy percent of the sixth-grade students who experienced our program gave a correct solution to this item following instruction (0% prior to instruction). Most of the older students tried unsuccessfully to apply the general equation for a straight line (i.e., $y = mx + b$) to the problem by simply inserting negative signs into the equation (e.g., $y = -mx - b$). Few of these older students even attempted to use numeric values for m and b.

In the next question, students were asked to look at the following sequence of numbers; 2, 5, 8, 11, 14, 17, ...; and to write an equation for a function that would generate this pattern of values.

For success with this item, students must have clearly distinguished the domain (x values) of a function from its range (y values), and must also understand that a generated set of numbers provides key information about certain parameters of a function (i.e., what x is multiplied by and where the function will be when x is equal to 0). The most common response to this item from both younger students and a control group was $y = x + 3$ "... since the pattern goes up by 3." Eighty percent of the eighth-grade students who participated in the experimental group were successful on this item following instruction, versus 4% in the control group (with 0% correct for both groups on the pretest). Responses from our eighth-grade students included the following reasoning:

Student E: "Well, it can't be $y = x + 3$, because the first number in the sequence would be 3 when x equals 0.... This sequence is increasing by 3 each time, which means there is a slope of 3 and when x equals 0, then you have to add 2 so the equation is $y = 3x + 2$."

Write an equation for a function that would have the following shape:

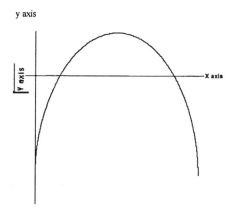

FIG. 1.6.   Sample level 4 item for the functions measure.

Student F: "If I make a table of values I can see that the y-intercept is
                at 2 and that the y values go up by 3 each time. So, that
                means it's 3 times x and then plus 2. The equation would be
                $y = 3x + 2$."[1]

In the final example, students were asked to give an equation for the
graph of a function seen in Fig.1.6. For competence with this sort of item,
students must be able to differentiate functions within families of functions (i.e., a particular representation of the general quadratic function) as
well as to understand the meaning of the algebraic, graphic, and numeric
parameters that comprise the function. Students who had experienced a
text-based curriculum and younger students generally provided incorrect
equations that included a negative exponent with the reasoning that it
would "... make the curve come back down."

The following response indicates the sort of reasoning we have found
older students to use following our program:

---

[1]The function y = 3x − 1 was also a correct response that was given by students.

Student G: To make this shape I need to start with $y = x^2$. Then because it's upside-down, it needs to have a maximum value so I have to multiply it by a negative. Then I still have to move it up and over. To move it up I have to add something like 10, and to move it over I have to subtract something [from the x]. So an equation would be $y = -2 \times (x - 5)^2 + 10$.

DISCUSSION OF FUNCTION STUDIES

Results of studies carried out with the functions curriculum have shown that, first, even young students are able to use relatively sophisticated strategies when reasoning about functions. Second, there are some problems specific to the domain that are beyond the ability of some younger students, possibly because of their earlier stage of intellectual development and their limited experience with more advanced ideas in mathematics. Third, most of our students, regardless of age, emerge from the program with flexibility with respect to moving among representations and operating in the domain, an understanding of the mathematical meaning inherent to the individual representations of a function, and an ability to interconnect these isolated representations. We believe that introducing a powerful context (i.e., the walkathon) fosters these aforementioned abilities. In this context, students have the opportunity to merge their core digital and analogic schemata. They also have the opportunity to interconnect the numeric, graphic, and algebraic representations of a function early in the curriculum. This foundation for understanding function is expanded when students engage in computer activities, which allow them to make the more elaborate connections necessary for moving toward a complete conceptual structure for the domain.

GENERAL DISCUSSION

The results from the rational number and functions programs now join those that we reported earlier for whole number programs (Griffin & Case, 1997). We believe that they show how students develop a deeper understanding for the domain as a whole when they are brought through a natural developmental sequence, and are provided with a context in which the digital and analog representations on which the sequence is founded can be mapped onto each other—in a meaningful and familiar context—and where they themselves can choose to explore the conjoint space so created in a variety of fashions. An additional feature that the curricula embody is the use of natural language and the creation of unique products that children can display and talk about to others. Not only is there an improved curricular sequence, then, but an improved sense of ownership, and the ability to assume a metaposition in regard to their own and others' learning. Given the known challenges that these domains have presented historically for students of all ages, the accomplishments of the curricula that we have described seem noteworthy, as does the diversity, the fluency, and the sense of individual ownership that the protocols reveal.

A point with which we would like to conclude is one that has not been stressed in the foregoing account of the psychological structures on which the curricula are based. The relationship between structural modeling and curricular design is actually a circular one. Given a rich description of the central conceptual structures whose development is thought to underpin a domain, one can begin the task of designing a curricular sequence, and piloting various bridging devices immediately. But it may also happen that, as the curriculum is actually implemented, students' errors sensitize one to the fact that information that one thought students had automatic access to from other sources, must actually be included in the central conceptual structure itself. All of the structural sequences that have been presented in this chapter had their original origins in the developmental tradition, where underlying processes, rules, and structures were inferred from tests and test protocols. However, in each case, as we attempted to implement the original (relatively sparse) model via the designated curriculum, we discovered ways in which the model had to be expanded or modified in light of children's performance in a learning context. The models we ended up with thus became richer and richer, and included more numerical, linguistic, and iconic detail.

It is our hope that as the developmental models are refined further and the techniques of instruction are refined and generalized in parallel with them, we will be on our way to a deeper understanding of the psychological processes that are involved in successful learning and teaching in these subject areas, across the full range of ages that the elementary school and high school comprise.

ACKNOWLEDGMENTS

Joan Moss and Mindy Kalchman contributed equally to this chapter; order of authorship reflects alphabetical convention. This work was supported in part by the James S. McDonnell Foundation and by the Social Sciences and Humanities Research Council of Canada. We thank the teachers, children, and administrators of the schools in which this research was conducted. We also thank Cheryl Zimmerman for her technical and administrative support.

REFERENCES

Bereiter, C., & Scardamalia, M. (1996). Rethinking learning. In D. Olson & N. Torrance (Eds.)., *The handbook of education and human development* (pp.485–513). Malden, MA: Blackwell.

Carpenter, T. P., Fennema, E., & Romberg, T. A. (1993). Toward a unified discipline of scientific inquiry. In T. Carpenter, E. Fennema, & T. A. Romberg (Eds.), *Rational numbers: An integration of research* (pp. 1–12). Hillsdale, NJ: Lawrence Erlbaum Associates.

Case, R. (1985). *Intellectual development: Birth to adulthood*. New York: Academic Press.

Case, R. (1998, April). *A psychological model of number sense and its development*. Paper presented at the annual meeting of the American Educational Research Association, San Diego, CA.

Case, R., & Griffin, S. (1990) Child cognitive development: The role of central conceptual structures in the development of scientific and social thought. In C. A. Hauert (Ed.), *Developmental Psychology: Cognitive perceptuo-motor and neuropsychological perspectives* (pp. 193–230). Amsterdam: Elsevier.

Case, R., Marra, K., Bleiker, C., & Okamoto, Y. (1996). Central spatial structures and their development. In R. Case & Y. Okamoto (Eds.), *The role of central conceptual structures in the development of children's thought. Monographs of the Society for Research in Child Development, 61* (1–2, Serial No. 246, pp. 103–130). Chicago: University of Chicago Press.

Case, R., & Okamoto, Y. (1996). The role of central conceptual structures in the development of children's thought. *Monographs of the Society for Research in Child Development*, 61 (1–2, Serial No. 246).

Confrey, J. (1994). Splitting, similarity, and the rate of change: A new approach to multiplication and exponential functions. In G. Harel & J. Confrey (Eds.), *The development of multiplicative reasoning in the learning of mathematics* (pp. 293–332). Albany, NY: State University of New York Press.

Fuson, K. (1992). Research on learning and teaching addition and subtraction of whole numbers. In G. Leinhardt, R. Putnam, & R. Hattrup (Eds.), *Analysis of arithmetic for mathematics teaching* (pp. 53–187). Hillsdale, NJ: Lawrence Erlbaum Associates.

Gelman, R. (1978). Counting in the preschooler: What does and what does not develop? In R. Siegler (Ed.), *Children's thinking: What develops?* Hillsdale, NJ: Lawrence Erlbaum Associates.

Greeno, J. G. (1991). Number sense as situated knowing in a conceptual domain. *Journal for Research in Mathematics Education, 22* (3), 170–218.

Griffin, S., & Case, R. (1997). Rethinking the primary school math curriculum: An approach based on cognitive science. *Issues in Education, 3*, 1–65.

Griffin, S., Case, R., & Siegler, R. S. (1994). Rightstart: Providing the central conceptual structures for children at risk of school failure. In K. McGilly (Ed.), *Classroom lessons: Integrating cognitive theory and classroom practice* (pp. 25–49). Cambridge, MA: MIT Press.

Harel, G., & Dubinsky, E. (Eds.). (1992). *The concept of function: Aspects of epistemology and pedagogy*. West LaFayette, IN: Mathematical Association of America.

Kalchman, M. (2000) *Learning and Teaching Mathematical Functions: A Neo-Piagetian Framework for Instruction and Analysis*. Manuscript in preparation.

Kalchman, M., & Case, R. (1998). Teaching mathematical functions in primary and middle school: An approach based on Neo-Piagetian theory. *Scientia Pedagogica Experimentalis, 35* (1), 7–53.

Kalchman, M. & Case, R. (1999). Diversifying the Curriculum in a Mathematics Class Streamed for High-Ability Learners: A Necessity Unassumed. *School Science and Mathematics 99* (6), 320–329.

Kalchman, M., & Katz, S. (1999). Symbol or experience: A mathematics education quandary illustrated in the context of functions. *Curriculum, 20* (2), 131–144.

Kerslake, D. (1986). *Fractions: Children's strategies and errors.* Windsor, England: NFER Nelson.

Kieren, T.E. (1992). Rational and fractional numbers as mathematical and personal knowledge. In G. Leinhardt, R. Putnam, & R. A. Hattrup (Eds.), *Analysis of arithmetic for mathematics teaching* (pp. 323–372). Hillsdale, NJ: Lawrence Erlbaum Associates.

Kieren, T. E. (1995). Creating spaces for learning fractions. In J. T. Sowder & B. P. Schappelle (Eds.), *Providing a foundation for teaching mathematics in the middle grades* (pp. 31–65). New York: State University of New York Press.

Lamon, S. J. (1999). *Teaching fractions and ratios for understanding: Essential content knowledge and instructional strategies for teachers.* Mahwah, NJ: Lawrence Erlbaum Associates.

Mack, N. K. (1995). Confounding whole-number and fraction concepts when building on informal knowledge. *Journal for Research in Mathematics Education, 26* (5), 422–441.

Moss, J. (2000). *Deepening children's understanding of rational number: A developmental model and two experimental studies.* Unpublished doctoral dissertation, University of Toronto.

Moss, J., & Case, R. (1999). Developing children's understanding of rational numbers: A new model and experimental curriculum. *Journal for Research in Mathematics Education, 30* (2), 122–147.

Okamoto, Y., & Case, R. (1996). Exploring the microstructure of children's central conceptual structures in the domain of number. *Monographs of the Society for Research in Child Development, 61* (1–2, Serial No. 246, pp. 27–58).

Resnick, L. B., & Singer, J. (1993). Protoquantitative origins of ratio reasoning. In T. P. Carpenter, E. Fennema, & T. A. Romberg (Eds.), *Rational numbers: An integration of research* (pp. 107–130). Hillsdale, NJ: Lawrence Erlbaum Associates.

Siegler, R. S. (1996). A grand theory of development. *Monographs of the Society for Research in Child Development, 61* (1–2, Serial No. 246, pp. 266–275).

Siegler, R. S., & Robinson, M. (1982). The development of numerical understanding. In H.W. Reese & L. P. Lipsitt (Eds.), *Advances in child development and behavior (Vol. 16).* New York: Academic Press.

Silver, E. A. (1997). Learning from NAEP: Looking back and looking ahead. In P. A. Kenney (Ed.), *Research from the sixth mathematics assessment of the National Association of Educational Progress* (pp. 279–287). Reston, VA: NCTM.

Sowder, J. T. (1992). Making sense of numbers in school mathematics. In G. Leinhardt, R. Putnam, & R. Hattrup (Eds.), *Analysis of arithmetic for mathematics* (pp. 1–51). Hillsdale, NJ: Lawrence Erlbaum Associates.

Spinillo, A. G., & Bryant, P. (1991). Children's proportional judgements: The importance of "half." *Child Development, 62,* 427–440.

Starkey, P. (1992). The early development of numerical reasoning. *Cognition, 43,* 93–126.

Streefland, L. (1993). Fractions: A realistic approach. In T. Carpenter, E. Fennema, & T. A. Romberg (Eds.), *Rational numbers: An integration of research* (pp. 289–327). Hillsdale, NJ: Lawrence Erlbaum Associates.

2

Similarity of Form and Substance: Modeling Material Kind

Richard Lehrer
Leona Schauble
Dolores Strom
Margie Pligge
University of Wisconsin, Madison

This chapter describes one study within a multiyear investigation of the emergence and development of model-based reasoning. Our emphasis on models follows from the widespread observation that, regardless of their domain or specialization, scientists' work involves building and refining models (Giere, 1993; Stewart & Golubitsky, 1992). Although models are central to the everyday work of scientists, they are nearly invisible in school science, especially in the elementary grades. Moreover, modeling is a form of thinking that is difficult to study, because it coalesces only over years of instruction in contexts where it is consistently valued and supported.

Accordingly, to conduct our research program, we have been collaborating for the last several years with elementary school teachers in a local district to reorient mathematics and science instruction around the construction, evaluation, and revision of models. We work closely with participating teachers to plan instruction and then study together the forms of student thinking that emerge. The emphasis is on cross-grade collaboration with an eye toward understanding the development of student thinking across the 5 years of elementary schooling. Because we seek to study the *development* of model-based reasoning, we focus especially on promising precursors to this form of reasoning in young school students, including physical models, maps, diagrams, and other forms of inscription (Lehrer, Jacobson, Kemeny, & Strom, 1999; Lehrer & Schauble, 2000). We are particularly interested in how young students come to mathematize the world, an activity that modern science has been pursuing since the time of Newton (Kline, 1980; Olson, 1994).

For example, in the first and second grades, students were provided with baskets of hardware and invited to construct models that showed how their elbows work (Penner, Giles, Lehrer, & Schauble, 1997). Children's first models reflected a preoccupation with resemblance. That is, these models primarily captured features that children found perceptually salient, like styrofoam balls to represent the "bump where your elbow goes" and pop-sicle sticks to represent fingers. As they reviewed these first models in their classrooms, children decided that resemblance was not a sufficient crite-rion for an acceptable model because, by and large, these models did *not* "work like"—for example, bend like—elbows. The children next gener-ated a variety of new design solutions; springs, bending straws, and rubber balloons were used to construct "elbows" that could bend. During this sec-ond round of model construction, concern for perceptual salience faded and children focused instead on function. All the groups of students suc-ceeded in getting their elbow models to bend, but initially, no one seemed concerned with the fact that they all bent a full 360°! However, as the class evaluated these models, one child objected, "Your real elbow doesn't bend that way...it gets stuck!" In the final round of model revision, student atten-tion turned to modifying the models so that they reflected both potential sources of motion and constraints on motion.

In the third grade, other students carried these explorations further, and as they did so, their models showed an increasing concern for mathemat-ical description (Penner, Lehrer, & Schauble, 1998). First, the third-graders conducted a series of investigations with a device constructed of two dowels connected with a hinge. The dowels could be connected at varying positions so that students could investigate the function of "elbows" with different points of tendon attachment. Students developed graphical and functional descriptions of the relationships between the position of a load and the point of attachment of the tendon—in effect, modeling the elbow as a third-class lever. They eventually concluded that the elbow trades off lift for reach, that is, although it takes more effort to lift a load at a distance from one's body, there are, nevertheless, advantages in mobility to this kind of "design."

This brief example reflects some of the principles of the overall program of research. These principles include (1) collaborative design of instruction with teachers to focus on "big ideas" in mathematics and science that are amenable to modeling approaches; (2) intensive professional development to help teachers understand both content and student thinking about content; (3) emphasis on classroom tasks that make student thinking visible via inscriptions, maps, diagrams, models, and related mathematical descriptions; (4) expansion of mathematics beyond arithmetic, for example, to data, space, and geometry, measure, and uncertainty; and (5) recruitment of these mathematical resources for reasoning about science. We are interested in the development of student knowledge about mathematics and science and, equally important, as we explain later, about students coming to understand the epistemologies of mathematics and science. In this chapter, space precludes discussion of our work on professional development; this topic and the design of the overarching research program are explained in Lehrer and Schauble (2000).

Over the years our research, we have studied student thinking both within and across concentrated units of modeling instruction. Here, we report results of a study of one fifth grade classroom where students recruited a variety of mathematical resources to construct and evaluate models of material kind—that is, density. Before describing the instruction, however, we first discuss a particular commitment in this research that contrasts sharply with prevailing approaches to model-based reasoning—that is, its reliance on mathematical resources.

"QUALITATIVE" VERSUS "QUANTITATIVE" MODELS

The pioneering work on expertise performed in the 1980s by researchers like Larkin, McDermott, Simon, & Simon (1980) and Chi, Feltovich, and Glaser (1981) focused educators and psychologists on the important role that qualitative analysis plays in the reasoning of practicing scientists. Today, researchers in education (e.g., White & Frederiksen, 1998; Wiser, Grosslight, & Unger, 1989), psychology (e.g., Clement, 1989), and philosophy (e.g., Nercessian, 1993) continue research in this tradition, uncovering new knowledge about the contribution of conceptual, causal, or "mental" models, analogies, and images to thinking and problem solution. This research has been both influential and instructionally fruitful. However, the work has also spawned a by-product that, in our view, has been less salutary. Specifically, the dichotomy between quantitative and qualitative reasoning (sometimes referred to as formal and informal reasoning) has been overgeneralized and reified. Many now believe that qualitative reasoning, which builds on students' existing conceptual structures, is a better starting point for instruction than is quantitative reasoning, which is widely assumed to be mere calculation—the proceduralized manipulation of algorithms. For example, it is taken for granted within the field of science education that students should learn to engage in qualitative forms of reasoning before they reason mathematically or quantitatively about problems.

This position can result in two kinds of distortions. First, it trivializes mathematics itself. Although school instruction places undue focus on the manipulation of arithmetic algorithms, we later argue that mathematics is not equivalent to computation (National Council of Teachers of Mathematics, 2000). Second, a commitment to the priority of qualitative reasoning cuts students off from one of the fundamental trends in modern science, particularly modeling activity in modern science—the progressive mathematization of nature (Kline, 1980; Olson, 1994).

Although mathematics is often viewed as the discovery of preexisting structure, an alternative perspective is that it develops within a history of collective argument and inscription (Davis & Hersch, 1981; Kline, 1980; Lakatos, 1976). An implication for mathematics education is that students, even at an early age, should have opportunities to develop their understanding of the nature of mathematical argument and the relationship between mathematical procedures and concepts (Strom, Kemeny, Lehrer, & Forman, 2000). More broadly, learning mathematics includes developing an epistemology in which mathematics is experienced as purposeful and meaningful. School instruction often caricatures mathematics by reducing it to procedures, framed within an epistemology of "answer." Yet, studies of mathematical learning in reform classrooms paint a strikingly different picture, one in which mathematical cognition is a joint product of individuals' attempts to achieve meaning and collective "norms" (standards for evidence and ways of thinking) about the nature of mathematics (Cobb, Gravemeijer, Yackel, McClain, & Whitenack, 1997).

Accordingly, as we considered ways to develop mathematics that could conceivably be employed to make sense of material kind (i.e., density), we were careful to ensure that students would first have the opportunity to develop an understanding of the "big ideas" in mathematics that could serve as effective resources for this purpose. Practically, this meant that students learned mathematics *before* attempting to employ mathematical reasoning as a tool for understanding nature. Our rationale for separating rather than "integrating" strands of instruction for mathematics and science was that these two disciplines have contrasting epistemic roots. Mathematics often relies on a logic of certainty, illustrated canonically by proof as a form of explanation. In contrast, science relies on a logic of reasoning about uncertainty, moderated through models (and the related idea of residual between the model and the modeled world) or other means of inscribing the world.

Too early integration of mathematics and science runs the risk of short-changing one at the expense of the other. For example, students could learn about the mathematics of ratio by employing ratio to calculate the density of a material, but this emphasis would foreshorten other mathematical senses of ratio that might profitably be developed (we later discuss some of these). Similarly, density could be used merely as a "context" for teaching students about ratio, but only with a corresponding foreshortening of related ideas about material kind. Given these shortcomings of traditional forms of integration, we decided to separate mathematics and science instruction. Specifically, we decided to lead with mathematics instruction and to follow with instruction about density in which students were encouraged to use mathematical ideas to model material kind. As we later describe, we did not adhere rigidly to distinguishing mathematics from science when it made more sense to consider them jointly. For instance, precision of measure arises whenever attributes of the world are considered, so students grappled with this aspect of measure during instruction about density and material kind.

THE TEACHING STUDY

Participants in this study were 20 students and their teacher in a fifth-grade classroom in a suburban public school in south central Wisconsin. Many, but not all, of the students had been instructed in previous grades by teachers participating in our research program. Students were otherwise representative of children in the community. They were White and of mixed socioeconomic status. A few were classified as having special needs, such as cognitive or learning disabilities. One was autistic and is not represented in this study, but participated in class activities.

The study was conducted in the spring semester, so most of the students were 11 years old. Our general approach was to work intensively with the teacher to plan instruction and then to study the forms of student thinking that emerged, both by tracking discussion, small group activity, and student work in the classroom, and by administering one-on-one interviews with the participating students. Data sources included daily video of classroom instruction supplemented by our field notes, collection of student work, and tape recordings of student interviews.

Over the spring semester, researchers worked closely with the teacher, Mark Rohlfing, to plan a series of lessons organized around two topics. During February and March, Mr. Rohlfing worked toward developing in his students a firm understanding of measure and ratio. As described later, the emphasis was on understanding, not on the calculation of rote procedures. To that end, the researchers and Mr. Rohlfing emphasized the accessible idea of *similarity* as the foundation from which to build an increasingly mathematical understanding of ratio and proportion (Lehrer, Strom, & Confrey, 2000). Students explored ratios of lengths of two-dimensional and three-dimensional geometric figures and expressed these ratios in various mathematical forms. They also explored volume measure with an eye toward developing mathematical descriptions of the structure of the space occupied by an object. This unit took approximately 8 weeks and included a total of 29 classes, usually of about 1 1/2 hours in duration.

During the late spring (April and May), Mr. Rohlfing's students began to explore the properties of various kinds of materials. As we later explain, modeling approaches were emphasized throughout this unit. Of interest to the researchers were whether and how students would use the mathematics of measure and similarity as a means for modeling ideas about material kind—that is, density. Approximately 20 classes were devoted to investigation of material kind. Most of these classes lasted about 1 1/2 hours.

We first describe the mathematical ideas that Mr. Rohlfing's students investigated and provide some highlights of the varieties of student thinking that these classroom activities elicited. We then follow by outlining the classroom instruction on material kind, again providing examples of student thinking. Finally, we report the results of final interviews in which students were asked to reason about complex problems in both of these two domains.

DEVELOPING
MATHEMATICAL RESOURCES

We developed and posed a series of tasks in volume measure and similarity, many of which were drawn from work the previous year in a third-grade classroom. In each strand of mathematics, we began with a careful description of everyday perception and then helped students develop mathematical explanations for their perceptions.

Volume

We first focused on helping students develop a theory of measure, rather than merely achieving simple procedural competence. Because many of these students had had extensive prior experience in earlier grades with core ideas about length and area measure (such as the need for standard units and zero point; see Lehrer, Jacobson et al., 1998; Lehrer et al., 1999), we extended consideration of these fundamental ideas to volume measure, using activities and ideas derived from previous research (Lehrer, et al., 2000). To forestall students considering volume as a product of a simple algorithm, we first emphasized qualities of volume as space occupied. Students began by exploring different ways to partition three rectangular prisms ("fish tanks") composed of cubes to decide which tank could hold the most water. Despite differences in appearance, all three rectangular prisms had equal volume measure, and students arrived at this conclusion by considering various ways of structuring the space (i.e., by counting individual cubes or by partitioning the prisms into arrays and then counting groups of cubes). These counting strategies for given units helped students recognize that measure of volume often requires consideration of "hidden" units (some of the units in the prisms were not visible from the surface).

From these initial investigations, we posed a series of increasingly complex tasks that involved structuring three dimensions into units and arrays of units. For example, students designed different rectangular prisms given a constraint of constant volume, or estimated the cubic volume of different boxes (also rectangular prisms) given only the lengths (as edges of cubes). Most students in the class solved problems like these by forming rectangular arrays of cubes organized into layers. Some multiplied the number of cubes in each layer by the number of layers, whereas others relied on skip counting the number of cubes in each layer by the total number of layers (see Battista & Clements, 1996). In short, students' counting strategies became progressively more efficient, and their structuring of the space occupied nearly always accounted for hidden units.

To develop ideas about volume when a simple counting strategy is apt to be inefficient or impossible, students also attempted to find the volume of forms that were not rectangular prisms. One student's solution to a problem of this kind is displayed in Fig. 2.1. Here, the area of the base of the cylinder was approximated; then the student multiplied the area by the height to arrive at the volume. Note the use of color-coding (simulated in gray tone in our figure) to delineate fractions of units that could be combined to yield a whole.

Solution strategies like these afforded students an opportunity to think of volume as the iteration of the area of "slices" (which were conceptualized by some students as vanishingly small). Although volume formulae typically assume this understanding, we found it necessary to provide students with experiences of structuring and restructuring three-dimensional space in a variety of ways. Not all of the student inventions proved useful, but exploration of the strengths and weaknesses of students' proposed strategies elaborated the class' understanding of the structure of "the space occupied." For example, when comparing the volumes of an open one-liter cylinder and an open one-liter rectangular prism (students did not know either volume, or that the two containers were equivalent, but did establish that they were the same height), students proposed seven different strategies within the span of the lesson. Several of these proposed strategies partitioned and rearranged parts of each base to compare the areas. The argument was that equal heights implied that comparative volumes could be established by comparative areas of the bases, taking a view of volume as a product of area and height. Another student suggested that these area-based strategies could be circumvented by using string to measure the perimeter of each base. He claimed (incorrectly) that the larger perimeter would imply the greater volume. Although this conjecture proved untenable, counterclaims made by students to examine it helped them further differentiate among perimeter, area, and volume. For example, students compared the volumes and circumferences of two 8.5 × 11 inch sheets of paper, one folded in half and the other rolled to create a cylinder. (Use of extreme cases like these is a good mathematical heuristic or "habit of mind.") In summary, class invention and investigation of measurement strategies related conceptions of the structure of space occupied to ways of finding its measure. These served as an important preamble to considering other aspects of measure, like precision, that arose during the unit on material kind that we describe later.

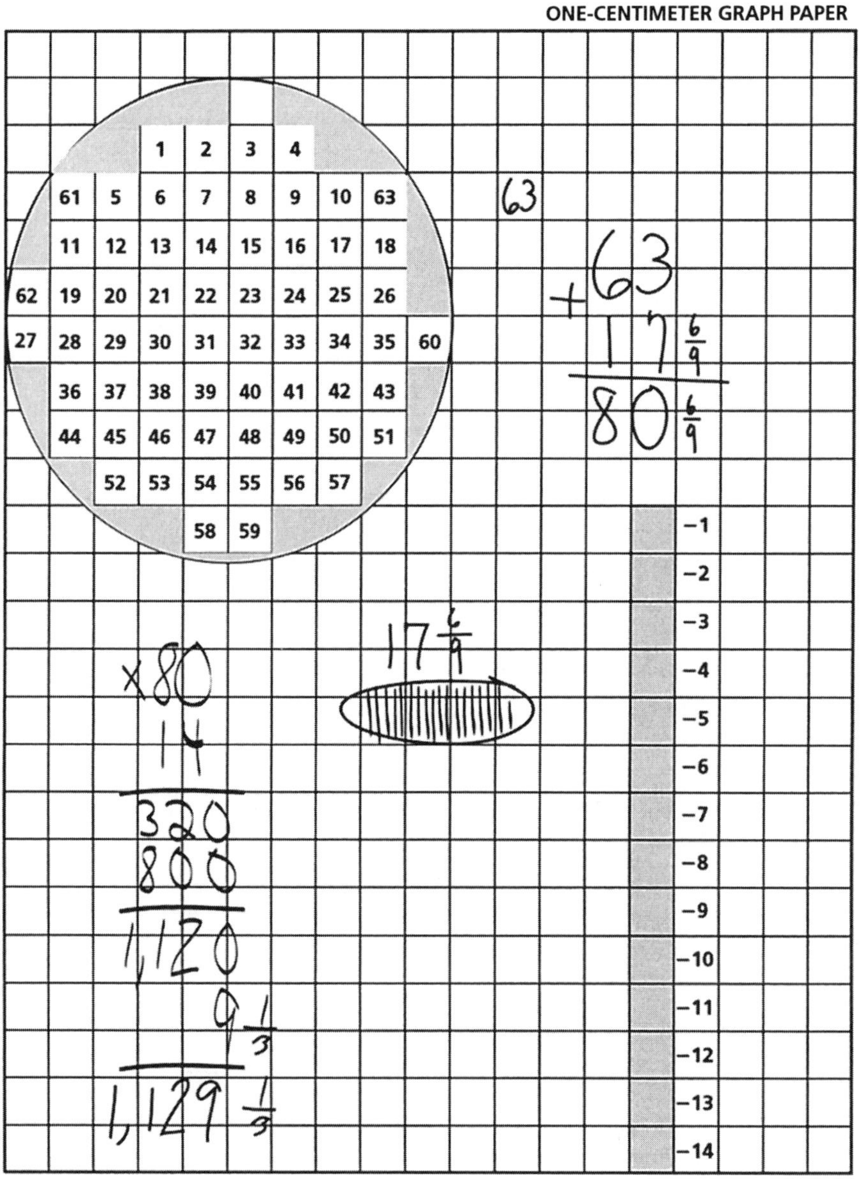

FIG. 2.1. Finding the volume of a cylinder by estimating the area of the base and multiplying it by height.

Similarity

We anchored similarity to students' experiences with magnification. Our aim was to help students develop a mathematical explanation for their perception of "same, but bigger." In our view, this perceptual grounding served as a resource for making sense in ways that typical word problems about recipes or relative sweetness of solutions do not. That is, in the scale of geometric figures, students can readily perceive both constant ratio and violations of constant ratio.

Students first picked out "families" of magnified rectangles from collections of rectangles with different dimensions. Then they described what was the same about the rectangles in each family. We told students that similar rectangles (those within a common family) are described as those with the same relationship between the sides. Students next sorted another dozen rectangles into three different groups of similar rectangles. For each group, students found a "rule" relating the long side of each rectangle in that group to the short side, for example, "2 × short side = long side." Follow-up tasks included finding other rules that described different groups of rectangles and using these simple algebraic expressions to generate new instances of similar rectangles. Although ratios of sides were expressed as simple algebraic relationships, not all relationships were integers. For example, a 2:3 ratio was expressed as "ss = $^2/_3$ ls" and "ls = ss + $^1/_2$ ss." After students generated these algebraic expressions of ratio, they plotted bivariate graphs of short versus long sides of their families of rectangles, as displayed in Fig. 2.2.

All similar rectangles on these graphs were described by lines through the origin, and different families were characterized by different lines. Constructing these graphs afforded students the opportunity of thinking about the meaning of lines of different steepness when the long side of the rectangle was represented on the ordinate and the short side on the abscissa. Students expressed an interest in characterizing the extent of steepness, so we introduced notions of "stairs" (right triangles) and slopes. Students "tried on" ratios of both legs of the triangles that characterized the slope of each line, finding that changes in x per unit y resulted in quantities that decreased with steepness. Consequently, they represented steepness numbers as changes in y per unit x, so that higher quantities were associated with greater steepness (although some students suggested simply switching the axes). Students also constructed and compared lines with and without "shift numbers" (their terminology for expressing the distance of a line from the origin at the x-intercept). These comparisons distinguished between multiplicative (e.g., ls = 2 × ss) and additive

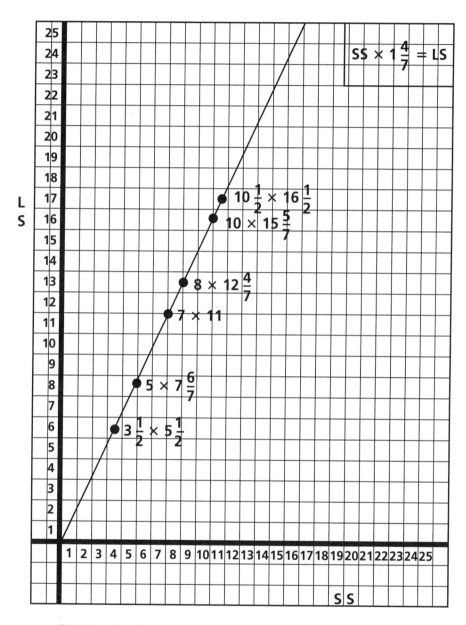

FIG. 2.2. Graph representing a "family" of rectangles.

relationships (e.g., ls = 2 × ss + 3), and also, between similar and non-similar figures.

Following these experiences with similarity in two dimensions, we moved to a comparatively simple case in three dimensions. Students worked with similar cylinders and developed graphical displays of similar solids by jointly considering the circumference of the base and height of the cylinder. Steepness numbers and shift numbers again figured prominently in representing families of similar forms. In addition, students rea-

Date: 4/22/97

Rules for families of cylinders

Here are three rules for relating the circumference of a cylinder (C) to its height (H).

$C \times \frac{1}{4} = H$	$C \div \frac{1}{4} = H$	$C \times 4 = H$
● C|H	● C|H	● C|H
$1\|1\frac{1}{4}$	1|4	1|4
$2\|2\frac{2}{4}$ or $\frac{1}{2}$	2|8	2|8
$3\|3\frac{3}{4}$	3|12	3|12
4|1	4|16	4|16
$5\|1\frac{1}{4}$	5|20	5|20
$6\|1\frac{2}{4}$ or $1\frac{1}{2}$	6|24	6|24
$7\|1\frac{3}{4}$	7|28	7|28
8|2	8|32	8|32
$9\|2\frac{1}{4}$	9|36	9|36
$10\|2\frac{2}{4}$ or $2\frac{1}{2}$	10|40	10|40

Use the table and make a graph to find out which rules make the same line. How do the stairs of the lines compare? Write a paragraph about how the numbers in these rules relate to each other and to the graph.

The numbers in these rules relate to each other by the #s and answers they have. What I mean by this is that the purple one is using the # $\frac{1}{4}$ and so is the pink one. The only difference in those 2 rules is that one is multiplying the C and the other is dividing it. The way the pink and green relate to each other is, that even though they have different rules, when you do the equation you get the same # for an answer. There really isn't much relationship.

FIG. 2.3. Katie's report about three formulae relating the circumference of a cylinder to its height.

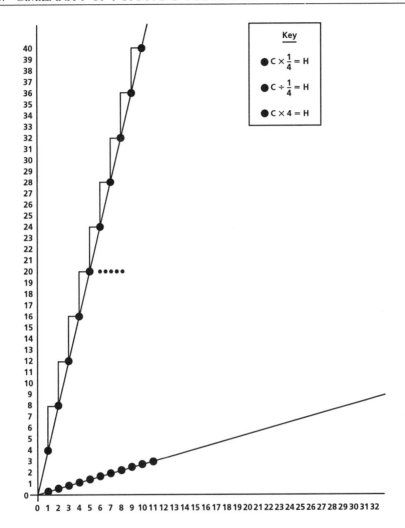

FIG. 2.4.   The graph that goes with Katie's report.

soned about the equivalence of different algebraic expressions of similarity, as depicted in Fig. 2.3 and Fig. 2.4.

In summary, similarity lent itself to initial perceptual grounding, followed by development of multiple ways of representing ratio. One form of expression used by the students was the quantitative relationship, $^a/_b$, interpreted as "a units per unit of b." For example, students noted: "For every one of the short side, there's two of the long," or, "The long side is $3^1/_2$ times the short side." Another form of expression that we cultivated was graphical. This graphical description of similar forms extended the sense of ratio by making its generality explicit. A line described any similar figure of a particular ratio, even figures that had not been plotted, or often even conceived. The quantitative expression of the ratio was readily recovered as the slope of the line, a concept that itself relied on similarity (i.e., similar right triangles).

In addition to these mathematical considerations of the sensibility and extension of ratio, similarity also provided a ready analogy for understanding the densities of materials. Just as different similar forms are characterized by different ratios of lengths or angles, material kinds (e.g., brass, aluminum, wood, water) are characterized by unique ratios of mass and volume. Working from the assumption that models are basically analogies (Hesse, 1965), we intended to work with students on the mathematics of similar form and then use these concepts to serve as a base domain for helping students understand the target domain of density.

The analogical mappings between base and target domains were, in principle, sustained by mathematical descriptions of the two cases that were nearly identical. For example, substituting mass and volume for short and long sides in Fig. 2.2 makes the analogy evident. However, central to the differing epistemologies in mathematics and science is the kind of relationship that the line expresses in each of these cases. In the case of mathematical similarity, the line describes a relation of necessity. The two-dimensional figures are ideal cases, and by definition, every similar figure will fall exactly on the same line. In contrast, in the case of material kind, the points plotted represent the measured mass and volume of actual three-dimensional figures. Here, cases may or may not fall exactly on the line, so the line serves as a potential model. The difference between mathematical similarity and material kind highlights a central aspect in the epistemology of modeling that we wanted students to consider explicitly—that is, the idea of mismatch, or residual between the model and the world.

MODELING MATERIAL KIND

Fundamental properties of material are foundational concepts in science, but many of these properties—volume, mass, and especially density—are notoriously difficult for students to grasp. Many science curricula and texts present volume and mass as mere definitions (one gets the impression that these are regarded as the formal definitions for ideas that students should already find self-evident) and then define density as a mathematical formula expressing the ratio of mass per unit volume. Smith, Snir, and Grosslight (1992) and Smith, Maclin, Grosslight, and Davis (1997) suggest that the problem with these approaches is that they fail to connect with students' intuitive theories about material and substance. According to the research conducted by Smith and her colleagues, children do not necessarily regard matter as continuous, as occupying volume, and as having the property of mass. Instead, they define matter by its readily perceptual qualities; for example, one can see it, one can feel it, it has "felt weight." The implication is that what one cannot see or feel (e.g., very small particles) is not counted as substance. Moreover, preadolescent children typically fail to differentiate weight and density, and instead, conflate both of these concepts into a general sense of "heaviness." Smith and her colleagues provide compelling evidence of these aspects of students' theories concerning weight and density, and we begin from the premise that their insights are largely on target. One means for addressing these alternative conceptions is through analogy (e.g., to sweetness) and qualitative modeling, a route that Smith and her colleagues extensively explored.

Here, we suggest an alternative, largely unexplored route—through deep understanding of the relevant mathematics. We are not advocating the application of what Smith et al. (1997) referred to as "quantitative reasoning" (e.g., "formal knowledge of a density calculation procedure," p. 350). This type of procedural approach to mathematical pedagogy has not proven a fruitful foundation for understanding density. For example, in earlier research, when high school students were taught procedures to plot coordinate graphs representing mass–volume relationships as lines, they failed to understand that the line signaled an invariant ratio and thus, did not understand the line as a representation of density (Rowell & Dawson, 1977a). Moreover, despite accurate calculations, many students cannot flexibly partition volumes or understand the equivalencies among various algebraic expressions of mass, volume, and density (Hewson, 1986; Hewson & Hewson, 1983; Leoni & Mullet, 1993; Rowell & Dawson, 1977b; Smith et al., 1997). Mathematical understanding, as opposed to cranking out computations prescribed by a mathematical formula, has its own intuitive bases and typical trajectories (Fennema & Romberg, 1999). We conjecture that when these ideas are cultivated and supported, they can serve as invaluable resources for reasoning about science. Moreover, these resources are essential for helping students capitalize on modeling approaches that fully acknowledge the epistemological foundations of modeling.

Design of classroom pedagogy about material kind was guided by consideration of the mathematical resources students had developed. We designed instruction to capitalize on students' general understandings of the mathematics of measure, as well as their specific experiences with volume measure. We also counted on students' ability to draw on similarity as a model for substance. Yet, the instruction did not ignore the physical grounding afforded by material kinds. Consequently, students hefted, submerged, and compared objects and generally acted on them in ways consistent with building physical intuitions. Classroom instruction was oriented toward using mathematics as explanations and extensions of these emerging intuitions. Our hypothesized developmental trajectory for material kind began with comparisons and orderings of weight, volume, and kind, and then proceeded to quantification of differences (e.g., how much heavier?) and invariants like density.

Weight

In the classroom, we opened the discussion of material kind by asking students to rank by weight 24 small, three-dimensional figures composed of wood, Teflon, aluminum, and brass (six of each kind). Discussions about the relative weight of these objects, which began with the simple idea of rank-order comparison, eventually expanded into consideration of how much heavier and related issues about precision.

Mr. Rohlfing presented the collection of 24 objects. In order of increasing volume, each of the four sets of materials included six identical figures; a small sphere, a small cube, a short cylinder, a short rectangular prism, a tall cylinder (same circumference as the short cylinder but twice the height), and a tall rectangular prism (same perimeter as the short prism, but twice the height). Mr. Rohlfing arrayed the objects on a table at the front of the class and challenged students to find an efficient way to rank-order the 24 objects by weight: "How can we order them by weight without comparing every object to every other one?"

As previous research would predict, this challenge motivated some debate about what it means for objects to be "heavy." However, compared with middle school participants in previous studies, these students readily differentiated volume from material kind as independent variables that determined the weight of any object in the set. For example, Craig asserted that the "gold" objects were the heaviest materials, but then was uncertain about whether the tall rectangular prism or the tall cylinder had the greater volume. He went on to note that whichever had the greater volume would be the heaviest object of all. We conjecture that students' strong foundational understanding of volume was important in helping them achieve this differentiation. In fact, after these initial discussions, students generated an algorithm for identifying the minimum number of pairwise comparisons that could still ensure a correct rank order of objects; the form of this algorithm was essentially a bubble sort. In subsequent classes, students used a pan balance to execute the algorithm (e.g., comparing pairs of objects on the balance to conclude which was heavier). Within short order, the objects (labeled by letter) were listed on a master chart by rank order of weight, heaviest to lightest.

Mr. Rohlfing next "upped the ante" by posing the question, "Can we tell how much heavier one object is than another?" This is a question that was deliberately sidestepped by Smith et al. (1997), who decided to rely on qualitative forms of modeling partly because, "Students find it extremely difficult to measure the mass and volume of different samples of the same kind of material with enough accuracy to determine that different sample sizes have the same density" (p. 368). As one might expect, given our commitment to mathematical understanding, we took the opposite tact. That is, we regarded the issue of precision as an opportunity for making a fundamental point about modeling—that modeling entails not only mapping, but also making decisions about how to interpret mismapping or residual.

Groups of students worked to weigh and then double-check the weight of the objects (in fact, they found the mass of objects, but in this instruction, we deliberately did not differentiate between weight and mass). The tools that they used were chosen to foreground the same concepts about measure that they had earlier encountered while measuring volume (and, moreover, in their earlier years of instruction while measuring length and area). First, students needed to come to regard the very idea of measure as *comparison* (as opposed, for example, to simply reading numbers off a scale). Ideas about standard units, appropriate units, and zero point (i.e., origin of the scale) emerged once again in the context of weight. For example, only a few sets of standard masses were available for use on the balance. Even using all the available masses was insufficient to balance the large, brass rectangular prism (the heaviest object in the set). To surmount this difficulty, students spontaneously invented the strategy of finding the weight of one of the lighter objects (for example, the Teflon prism), and then using that object (now of known weight) as one of the standards of comparison for finding the weight of heavier objects. Discussions in the classroom turned to the problem of propagation of error, as students noted that weight measurements conducted with fewer standard weights tended to result in less variable measures across groups of students than measurements made with many weights.

As groups of three students weighed and then reweighed the objects, it became progressively clear, to the consternation of all, that in spite of meticulous care, different groups were recording somewhat different measures. Students identified contributions to variability (e.g., calibration of the scales, placement of objects in the pans, eye level when the scale was read, propagation of error), and were eventually able to reduce, but not to obliterate, the variability of measures.

For several days, students discussed ways of interpreting the distributions of measures that they recorded. These discussions centered around identifying a procedure that the class as a whole could accept for deciding on the true value of the measures. Several students argued for the mode, claiming that if two or more students "got the same answer," that solution must be "right." However, once students observed a case in which the mode was nowhere near the center of the distribution of measures, this reasoning was called into question. As one student argued, "The mode is good, but what if there's like, three 25s and then a 24, 23, 19, and 17? You could take all the 25s because they're the same, but what if they're wrong?" Other students initially preferred averages, but reconsidered when they discovered a case in which a clear outlier pulled the average toward one tail of the distribution. Some students advocated for the median, but others were dissatisfied with a median that did not fall on an observed case (e.g., when there were an even number of measures, and the median fell between two of the observed measures). After several class periods devoted to these discussions of central tendency (students referred to these as "typical numbers"), the class achieved an agreement to use trim means of the observed measures as the true value of weight for each of the objects. The use of the trimmed mean represented a consensus not only about a measure of center, but also about the role that distribution of measurements should play in the selection of a useful indicator of typicality.

Revisiting Volume

As students reviewed their completed table of measures, Mr. Rohlfing asked if they had any conclusions about what affects "how heavy something turns out to be." One of the students summarized, "The gold [that is, the brass] is the heaviest. Silver [aluminum] is next, then white [Teflon], and last is wood."

"That's not always right," another student objected. "Not all the gold ones are heavier than all the silver. It also depends on how big it is."

"What do you mean by how big?" asked Mr. Rohlfing. Students recalled their earlier work at estimating volume of figures and put these tools to work to find the volume of the 24 objects. The tools included centimeter rulers, centicubes (small plastic cubes that are 1 cm on each dimension), graph paper (e.g., for tracing and estimating the base of cylinders), and displacement buckets with graduated cylinders. Students noted that the precision of these forms of measure varied, and moreover, that it varied with the form of the objects. For example, with centicubes, different groups concurred on the volume of the rectangular prisms, but water displacement yielded measures that were far more variable. However, water displacement was the only means children could identify for estimating the volume of the spheres.

Once again, multiple means of measure resulted in varying measures, and the students again debated and came to final decisions about the value that they would provisionally accept as the true value for volume of each of the objects. When the values for both volume and weight were arrayed in a table for all the 24 objects, Mr. Rohlfing brought the students back to a question that had come up in an earlier class about water displacement:

Mr. R: We had two ideas that surfaced with that. One was that the heavier something is, the more water is moved out of the way. The other theory was that it's the amount of space that the object takes up. Were those questions answered? How many people think those questions were answered last time?

Craig: It's the amount of space that's taken up.

Mr. R: What convinced you?

Craig: It was something Katie said. If you stand up in the bathtub, you still weigh the same, but the water doesn't go up as much [as if you lay down].

Luke: My group had a big, light object and someone else had a small, heavy object. And the big, light object displaced more water.

Note that Mr. Rohlfing scaffolded discussion by juxtaposing competing claims about the contributions of volume and weight to water displacement. Moreover, the students' reasoning about volume was tightly connected to experiences, both those generated in the classroom and those from home (tubs). These forms of dialogue contrast sharply with the initiate-respond-evaluate cycle so often observed in studies of classroom discourse.

At this point, Mr. Rohlfing asked another group to measure the weight of different volumes of water with an electronic balance. When the group returned from this task, they recorded their measurements on the board for the class to review:

ML	Weight [of water] in Gm
5	4.9, 4.8
10	9.8, 9.7
20	19.8, 19.7, 19.8
50	49.2, 48.7
100	98.7, 99.8

Katie, one of the students in the group, remarked, "It was always pretty close, within a couple of grams or less. We measured the same amount of water twice and got a range of values, so we know that even the electronic scale isn't very accurate. We also measured out 50 ml in one container and then poured it into another container, and found it was a little over 50 ml in the second container. So we figured out that the water measuring tools [e.g., graduated cylinders] aren't that accurate either."

Mr. Rohlfing asked, "So what conclusions do you make about the measurement of water?"

Katie replied, "Somewhere around one" [e.g., water weighs 1 gm per ml].

The volumes and respective weights of these amounts of water were then added to the chart. As students proceeded next to consider the possibility that there might be "families of materials," as they put it, they had at their fingertips a relatively firm and flexible understanding of (including differentiation of) weight and volume. Understanding these ideas involved many discussions about students' intuitive qualitative conceptions of weight, volume, and material. Equally importantly, mathematizing these ideas provided a firm foundation to which students' intuitive conceptions could be anchored.

Families of Material

After establishing best estimates for the mass and volume of each object, students investigated their families of material hypothesis by taking turns representing each object as a point on a large graph displayed on the wall of the classroom. Mr. Rohlfing labeled the ordinate as G, scaled in units of 20, and the abscissa as ML (cm^3), scaled in units of 10. After brief discussion of the scale and meaning of the labels, students worked in pairs to locate and label each object on the graph.

Reconsidering Error. As students plotted the gold (brass) objects, students noticed that one of the points seemed out of place. Ashley suggested that one of them "... wouldn't work. It wouldn't fit if you were trying to draw a line through it" [gestured sweeping motion with hands]. Mr. Rohlfing agreed with Ashley's identification of the out of place point and then asked how else they might determine that the point in question was out of place. Another student, Craig, noticed that the object being plotted was the "same shape" as some of the other objects plotted, but it was represented on the graph as having a different volume. Craig declared that all objects of the same shape should fall on the same "milliliter line," and he demonstrated what he meant by tracing a vertical line. As they replotted the point, Mr. Rohlfing referred to the brass objects, asking: "Are they all going to be on the same line?"

Most students shook their heads, "No." Adam suggested that the graph itself was a source of imprecision because "It's going up by 20s on the side and so we're not going to be able to graph 28.5 very accurately." He suggested that the graph could be made much more accurate by changing the scale: "If you made each line be one." Other classmates agreed, but pointed out that the graph would then be far too large; they would need a stepladder to plot the points representing some of the objects.

At this point, Rachel raised the possibility that "the numbers might not be accurate." Katie agreed, and then various members of the class recalled particular episodes of imprecision of measure of weight or volume. Adam summarized the discussion up to this point: "... [M]aybe because of propagation of error. Those are probably not all the right numbers there, and then even the graph isn't very accurate. So, putting both of those together make it even worse." As students continued to plot points, Drew proposed an alternative meaning for each point (i.e., in addition to a location):

Drew: I was taking the weight in grams and dividing it by the volumes, and then I look at my answers in the *different families*. And I think gold, it was about volume times 8.5 equals the weight. In the silver, about volume times 2.7 equals the weight. In the white family, it was volume times about 1.4 equals the weight. In wood, it was volume times $^6/_{10}$ was the weight.

Brad: Would you say that again?

Drew: I was trying to find the relationship of the volume to the
                 weight to see what family it was in.

Mr. Rohlfing: Can I stop you for a minute? Remember a long time ago we
                 did families of shapes? What would happen if the shape
                 was in the same family? How did we know that they were
                 in the same family?

Clearly, Drew was building here on the earlier work the class had done
in constructing rules to describe families of two-dimensional figures.
Other students also now proposed that shapes in the same families fall on
the same line and share the same rule, as Mr. Rohlfing wrote each algebraic expression on an easel for consideration by the class (e.g.,
$v \times 8.5 = w$). The class began to predict where other to-be-plotted points
might lie by noting both their measurements and the rules. This discussion
raised the collective awareness of a difference between line in this context
and in the previous context of similarity. Mr. Rohlfing asked the students
why all the points did not fall exactly on the line, and several immediately
volunteered, "Error!"

Which Line?   Having identified a key difference in the two experiences of line, the class was confronted with the problem of exactly where
to draw the line. Using a pair of points on the graph as anchors, two students held up a yardstick to locate a line to describe the family of brass
objects. The proposed result was a line with a nonzero intercept. One student, Cathy, objected, stating that the line needed to start at zero.

Mr. R: We need a line up there to represent gold. Katie was concerned
          that your line didn't go through zero.

Luke: But these two dots do [meaning that the line intercepted the
          dots].

Mr. R: How do you get a line that doesn't start at zero?

Rachel: If it's an added number. [This is a reference to the class' earlier
          work with similar rectangles, in which children discovered that
          expressions like "$w + 4 = l$" yielded lines that did not go
          through the origin and did not define similar figures.]

David: When we used addition, it didn't start at zero, but when it was
          multiplication it did. [e.g., the reference to "multiplication"
          means expressions like "$4w = l$."]

At this point, Mr. Rohlfing asked students to consider what "zero really means." Tara suggested that it meant that the volume was zero. David then added that zero volume implied that the object "wouldn't even be there." A third student proposed that it would weigh "nothing." The class explored the consequences of this implication for a symbolic expression; $v \times 8.75 + 1 = w$. They judged that the application of this expression was impossible ("You can't have nothing that weighs something!"), so that a line representing a family of material would have to go through the origin. Several students proposed trying to induce a rule from the table of measurements and then using the rule to manufacture points for a line, but most suggested that Drew's rule might not be more reliable than fitting a line on the graph. Because of the additional constraint that lines must go through the origin, the strategy of simply intercepting two or more cases receded. Instead, students began to draw lines that appeared to come "close" to the majority of the cases displayed, with a clear bias, however, to ensuring that the line intersected at least one case. One student, Luke, proposed that the class could evaluate the resulting line by considering the rule, "Check the step number."

Lines and Rules: Checking the Steps

In the lessons that followed the initial conjectures about families of materials, students considered the relationships among graphical and algebraic expressions of relationships among mass and volume. Mr. Rohlfing asked about the meaning of steepness in this context. David proposed that they "make steps" (i.e., find the slope), and Melanie suggested that the steps (for the different lines) be compared. Students recalled their experiences with steepness numbers in the context of geometric similarity. They found that if they began at the origin for the line describing the brass objects, one set of stairs could be "up 40 gm" and "over 5 (ml)," resulting in a steepness number of 8.

Several students then responded to a question posed by their teacher about the meaning of this number by rewriting the algebraic expression for brass as $v \times 8 = 40$. Mr. Rohlfing asked if there were another way to express this rule, and Jordan suggested, "Weight divided by volume = 8." Drew compared the steepness number to its counterpart in similarity: "It's like the scale factor between them." Much of the remainder of this lesson was devoted to interpreting each line's slope as a mass to volume ratio, with an emphasis on the slope as a ready means for thinking about grams per milliliter of volume. At the conclusion of the class, students noted that steepness had a material implication. For example, Katie suggested: "This is pretty obvious, but anything below the water line would have less grams than volume." Luke agreed, adding: "Because for the water line, the volume and the weight are the same. So anything above that would have a higher slope. You go over less" (gestures).

Reasoning About Novel Cases

On the final day of instruction, the researchers provoked a discussion to explore how the class might use these ideas to reason about unfamiliar kinds of materials, in particular, novel liquids. One of the authors displayed a bottle of unidentified liquid colored with green food coloring.

RL: I have something in here (shakes bottle). It's greenish.

Natalie: Oh, yuck!

Jordan: It's oil!

Brittany: Colored water!

Tara: Cooking oil!

RL: What I'd like to know is if it belongs with any of the families you've already created, or if it needs its own family.

Brittany: It goes with water.

Luke: I don't think it would. I think it has more molecules per square milliliter than water does.

RL: You can tell this by looking at it?

Luke: It's thicker.

RL: Things that are thicker will have more molecules?

Luke: (Hesitates) ... Not necessarily.

Melanie: Oil is thick, but it's less dense than water.

Danny: If it's water, and you put food coloring in it, it could be just a little bit different.

RL: How could you find out the rule?

Rachel: We should take one ml of that stuff and then weigh it.

Another student objected that if just one measurement were made, it wouldn't be very accurate. Eventually the class agreed to divide into teams, each receiving a different volume of the "mystery liquid" to weigh.

On the basis of their measurements, students concluded that the green mystery liquid (glycerin) weighed 1.3 g/ml, and a mystery gold liquid that RL presented next (cooking oil) weighed .96 g/ml. Eventually, a family line was plotted on the graph for the each of the two mystery liquids.

Students next turned their attention to the graph and discussed which of the represented materials would float in water and which would sink. Students were confident that of the 24 solid objects investigated earlier, only those made of wood would float. David pointed out that wood floats because "it's underneath the water line." In other words, he noted that the line representing the "family" of wooden objects was less steep (hence below) the line representing water. On this basis, students predicted that the mystery gold liquid would float in water and the mystery green liquid would sink.

Natalie: If you pour the gold stuff in the water, the water would stay on the bottom.

RL: What would happen if I poured the green stuff into here (gold liquid)?

Angela: The gold stuff will float on the water, because it's less dense than water. It doesn't float. So the gold would be on top of the green.

Luke: I agree with Angela, because you can look at the graph to see that the gold line is above the green line. So the gold liquid will float on top of the green liquid. The gold is under the water line, and take the green, which is over the water ine.

When RL poured water, green liquid, and gold liquid into a common container, these predictions were confirmed. As the layers separated, Isaac tried to explain: "Let's say you took the green stuff and you've got molecules per milliliter or something like that, and you did the same, like let's say, with the water. The green stuff would have more. It's more compact together. It pushes that stuff [water] away from it, it has more per cubic centimeter."

In sum, over the second part of the semester, students developed a history of common experience and assumptions in measuring the weight and volume of both regularly and irregularly shaped three-dimensional objects made of different materials. These shared experiences provided opportunities to understand principles of measure, reason about precision, and consider sensible ways of resolving its opposite, variability in measure.

Students discovered and reconfirmed in a variety of contexts that water is pushed out of the way when solid objects are immersed in it, and that the amount of water pushed aside is equivalent to (and an alternative measure of) volume.

Relying on their earlier experiences with similar forms, students investigated the possibility that kinds of materials might form families defined by a constant ratio of weight to volume. Their investigations capitalized on the algebraic and graphical notations that they had developed previously in the context of similarity. However, they now debated whether and how a line on a graph could be regarded as an appropriate model for a relationship between weight and volume of a particular kind of material. This debate highlighted an important component of scientific epistemology (the inherent uncertainty of fit between model and world) even as it contrasted with the mathematical generalization (and its certainty) of the line describing similar forms. Finally, students used these ideas—and, in our view, equally importantly, these now-familiar notations—to reason about novel kinds of materials, that is, unfamiliar liquids.

POSTINSTRUCTION INTERVIEW

At the end of the semester, all but three of the students ($n = 17$) participated individually in a clinical interview about material kind (the complete interview is included in the Appendix). The interview lasted approximately 45 minutes. We conducted the interviews not to establish claims that students in this classroom were learning more than those taught in other ways (an objective that would require an experimental design using classrooms as the units of analysis). Rather, the purpose was to learn whether our impressions of student understanding formed during classroom instruction would be confirmed by the performance of individuals, and to develop a finer grained picture of the range of student conceptions. It is one thing be impressed by the performance of a class of students. It is another to be convinced that a majority of the students are benefiting.

Conceptual Differentiation

One pair of interview items (Questions 1 and 6 in the Appendix) assessed whether students thought about density as the coordination of mass and volume (as one student put it, "the amount of stuff packed into the space") or whether, as suggested by other researchers, (Carey, 1991; Smith, Carey,

& Wiser, 1985; Smith et al., 1997), they confounded weight and density into a global, undifferentiated concept of "felt weight," that is, how heavy an item feels when you heft it, as opposed to an idea of "heavy for its size." The fifth-graders did reasonably well with the items in this category.

Weight–Volume. Students were shown two objects of identical size and shape, one made of bronze and one of aluminum. The interviewer pointed out that the objects were of equal volume, and students readily agreed, because these same two objects were among the 24 used in the classroom investigations. Two large graduated cylinders half filled with water were also presented, and the students were asked, "Now, if I put each of these objects into the water, the gold one into this cylinder and the silver into this cylinder, would the water rise higher in one of the cylinders? Or would it rise to the same level in both?"

Approximately 82% of the students explained that because the objects had the same volume, they would displace the same amount of water. Most explicitly rejected the idea that the differing weights of these objects would push out different amounts of water, for example, "Some people think that bronze would go heavier, but both are the same size, so they push out the same amount of water. Weight doesn't matter." The remaining 18% of students were apparently still struggling to unconfound the roles of weight and volume. However, these students, too, provided justifications that seemed to suggest that they were trying to reconcile their convictions (e.g., that the heavier object would displace more water) with the classroom discussions of density, for example: "The gold has more molecules and it's denser, so it will push out more water."

Weight–Density. The interviewer first dropped a dime into a bucket of water and then added a much larger wooden block, asking, "Can you explain why the wood floats and the dime sinks?" If a student simply answered, "Density," the interviewer added, "What does density have to do with it?" On this item, too, students performed well, with 65% of their explanations appealing specifically to conceptions about density. One characteristic reply was, "If you had one milliliter, the dime has more stuff packed into it than one milliliter of water." An additional one fourth of the students told us that wood is a "lighter kind of material" than water. Previous research (e.g., Smith, et al., 1997) suggests that such appeals to kind of material usually mark a transition between undifferentiated conceptions of felt weight and conceptions that fully differentiate weight and volume. The remaining 10% of students talked about either weight or volume, without coordinating the two ideas.

Relative Densities

All but one of the remaining items of the interview concerned relative densities of materials. Some items required interpretation of graphical representations, others, explanation of the observable behavior of physical materials.

Predicting Floating and Sinking by Interpreting a Graph.
The first set of questions (Item 2 in Appendix) posed to students employed the graph displayed in Fig. 2.5, which shows lines representing five novel families of materials.

The interviewer explained, "Jeff made a graph with lines that show families of materials. Each line shows the weights for different volumes of one kind of material. Imagine I had 20 cubic centimeters of these five kinds of material, A, B, C, D, and E. And then, suppose that D is a liquid. Which of these materials will float in D? How do you know?"

About 82% of the students correctly distinguished the lines representing floating materials from those representing sinking materials and pro-

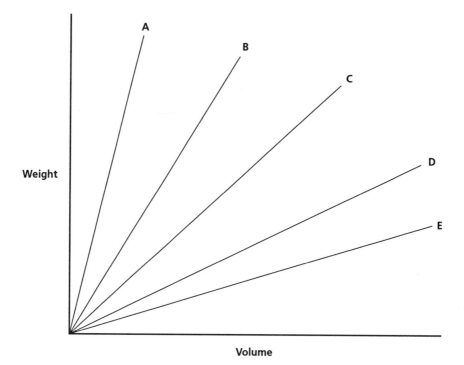

FIG. 2.5.   Graph representing five "families" of material.

vided justifications based on density; for example, "E is less dense. Density is like molecules per cubic centimeter. The lower the weight and the higher the volume, the less dense." An additional 12% of the students ($n = 2$) appropriately identified the floating and sinking materials, but did so by referring only to the position of the lines representing those materials on the graph. That is, their justifications referred to whether the line in question was "above" or "below" the line for material D, but did not include conceptual interpretations of density. One student was unable to interpret the graph.

Finding Densities and Reasoning About the Physical Intelligibility of the Origin. Two additional items also asked students to reason about relative density from graphical representations. From the graph in Fig. 2.6 described as showing "two families of materials, X

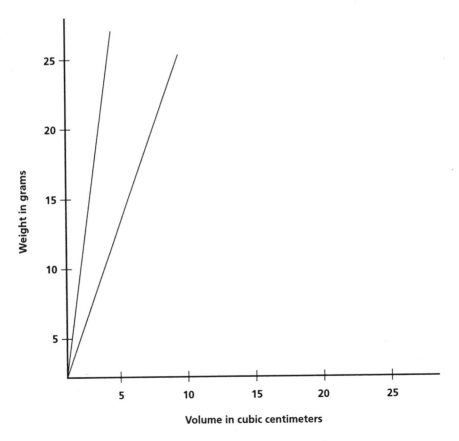

FIG. 2.6.   Graph for calculating densities of materials.

and Y," students were asked to find the density (e.g., a value) of both materials. Seventy one percent of the students were able to find both densities. A final graph, displayed in Fig. 2.7, probed students' understandings of the physical intelligibility of the intercept. The first of these (Item 4 in Appendix, the last of the graph interpretation items) is displayed in Fig. 2.7. The instructions were, "Matt was making a graph to show two families of materials. But Susan told him there was a mistake in his graph. Can you find the mistake and explain why it's a problem?"

Although all the students identified the nonzero intercept as "the mistake," only 47% spontaneously appealed to physical intelligibility to explain why lines representing families of materials must go through the origin. As one student explained, "It can't be nothing and weigh something. Not even air can do that." The remaining students recalled that the

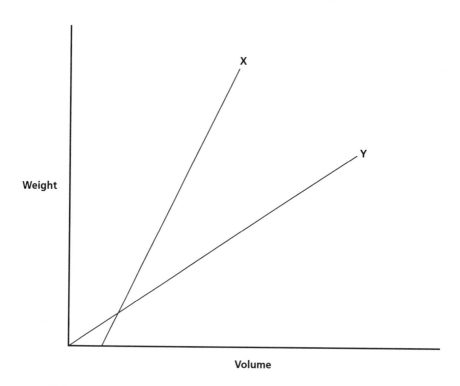

FIG. 2.7. Graph showing an "error" in representing families of materials.

lines must go through the origin, often citing this condition as necessary for comparing densities, but they did not offer physical interpretations to justify this claim. No student cited other features of the graph as problematic.

Reasoning About Composite Materials

The last interview item (Item 5 in the Appendix) required students to reason about the relative density of composite materials. We expected this item to be difficult because our instruction did not include transformations of materials that changed density (e.g., thermal expansion or popping corn). The interviewer adjusted two balls of clay until the participant agreed that they were of equal size and weight. Then, one ball of clay was reshaped into a bowl and both pieces were put into a bucket of water. The interviewer said, "When I put this ball of clay into a bucket of water, it sinks. But when I shape the same amount of clay into a bowl shape like this, it floats on top of the water. How would you explain that?"

Slightly fewer than half the students (47%) referred to the relative densities of the clay versus the clay-plus-air composite, or alternatively, offered appropriate arguments about the amount of water displaced by the two samples of clay. As one student explained, "Ball: Water displaced wasn't more than its weight. Bowl: Water displaced was more than its weight." Another 29% of the students suggested that the differences in volume were important (e.g., "The bowl has greater volume, so it pushes out more water") but failed to integrate these differences with relative densities. The remaining 24% offered vague appeals to "air" to explain why the bowl-shaped piece of clay floats. When asked what air had to do with it, these students either claimed that air is a substance that makes things float by means of some unspecified property or suggested that air floats because it has little weight, giving no evidence that they were regarding the clay-plus-air as a composite substance.

Table 2.1 summarizes student performance across the items in the interview. The table suggests that students did a credible job of displaying differentiated concepts about weight, volume, and density, especially in light of the well-established finding that much older students typically fail to do so (e.g., Hewson & Hewson, 1983; Smith et al., 1992). Most of the fifth-graders were able to reason about density situations from graphical representations of the kind developed in their classroom. Even when physical interpretation of the representations was designed to challenge common misconceptions, half or more of the students performed well.

TABLE 2.1
Summary of Levels of Understanding by Concept

	Level of UnderStanding		
	Full	Transitional	Little
Differentiation			
Weight–Volume	82[a]	18	0
Weight–Density	65	25	10
Graphs of Relative Densities			
Floating/Sinking	82	12	6
Finding Densities	71	---	29
Origin/Intercepts	47	53	0
Composite Densities	47	29	24

[a]Denotes percent of students demonstrating a particular level of understanding.

CONCLUSION

This class of fifth-graders made considerable progress in reasoning about the density of solid objects and liquids, as well as about the relative density of materials and composites. Instead of jumping directly into these difficult ideas through definitions and formulae, the classroom teacher first worked systematically to build student understanding of foundational mathematical ideas about volume, similarity, and distribution. It may seem surprising how much is involved in helping students develop a robust understanding of these concepts. Mr. Rohlfing spent several lessons eliciting different forms of student thinking about apparently simple concepts like volume and encouraged students to discover the contradictions and connections among their ideas. As mentioned, during one lesson that we observed, students proposed seven different ways of ascertaining whether or not two different three-dimensional solids had the identical volume, and spent 2 hours debating which methods were valid and would therefore lead to the same solution. In mathematics, as in science, it is vital to acknowledge the complexity of student thinking about these fundamental ideas. Only when students are urged to cut off their sense making and resort to procedure does the variability of student thinking disappear. When students are routinely encouraged to propose, justify, and evaluate their own algorithms and conjectures, they have reason to reconsider their own prior conceptions and embrace consensual means, via evolving classroom standards of argumentation, to decide which ways of thinking make sense.

In this case, we found that students' conceptual differentiation of weight and volume can be both facilitated and anchored by helping students achieve a firm grasp on mathematics of measure. In Mr. Rohlfing's class, the mathematics helped to anchor definitions and arguments so they did not endlessly drift in a sea of opinions that sounded equally valid to students. Students' well-grounded experience with volume of regular and irregular solids—including inventing various ways to measure volume—served to help students really understand what volume is, and made it correspondingly less likely that they would ignore the idea of per volume when considering the differing weights of kinds of material. Similarly, the class' evolving understanding of concepts about distribution, including typicality and variation, was fundamental to helping them decide what do about the different groups' measurements for weight and volume of the 24 objects. A common challenge for teachers in orchestrating productive classroom argumentation is that students tend to talk past each other when they use terms like heavy and big (e.g., what does one mean by big?) with no clear way to call anyone's claims into account. In contrast, when ideas are mathematized, they can be called into account in very precise ways. Agreeing on what big means is partly a matter of reaching consensus on how to operationalize it in measure. Smith et al. (1997) also found that middle school students' firm understanding of volume as "the total amount of space an object takes up" was related to their differentiation of weight from density, a finding consistent with the interpretation that you can't differentiate what you can't conceive.

A final point is that it makes little sense to regard conceptual and mathematical understanding as opposing and competing ways of approaching science. In our view, it would be preferable to learn more about how these forms of understanding can mutually bootstrap each other. As Smith and Unger (1997) suggested, such bootstrapping involves a dialectical interplay that leads to restructuring knowledge, not simply "abstracting" knowledge from one domain in service of another. Here we have argued that mathematical ideas (e.g., about similarity and measure) can serve as rich resources for reasoning about science (e.g., material kind). It is equally the case that conceptual questions about the world (e.g., How can we decide which objects are heavier than which?) also provoke and lend meaning to mathematical questions (e.g., what is the best typical number for representing a distribution of measures?). When this interplay occurs, mathematics can be recruited as a powerful resource for reasoning about science—a means for modeling nature. Models so constituted are a crucible for grounding and testing arguments and ideas about the material world.

ACKNOWLEDGMENTS

Richard Lehrer and Leona Schauble contributed equally to this research; their order of authorship reflects alphabetical convention.

This research was supported in part by a grant from the U.S. Department of Education, Office of Educational Research and Improvement, to the National Center for Improving Student Learning and Achievement in Mathematics and Science (R305A60007–98). The opinions expressed do not necessarily reflect the position, policy, or endorsement of the supporting agency.

We thank Mark Rohlfing and his students for their participation.

REFERENCES

Battista, M., & Clements, D. (1996). Students' understanding of three-dimensional rectangular arrays of cubes. *Journal for Research in Mathematics Education, 27,* 258–292.

Carey, S. (1991). Knowledge acquisition: Enrichment or conceptual change? In S. Carey & R. Gelman (Eds.), *The epigenesis of mind: Essays on biology and cognition* (pp. 257–291). Hillsdale, NJ: Lawrence Erlbaum Associates.

Chi, M. T. H., Feltovich, P. J., & Glaser, R. (1981). Categorization and representation of physics problems by experts and novices. *Cognitive Science, 5,* 121–152.

Clement, J. (1989). Learning via model construction and criticism: Protocol evidence on sources of creativity in science. In J. Glover, R. Ronning, & C. Reynolds (Eds.), *Handbook of creativity: Assessment, theory, and research* (pp. 341–381). New York: Plenum.

Cobb, P., Gravemeijer, K., Yackel, E., McClain, K., & Whitenack, J. (1997). Mathematizing and symbolizing: The emergence of chains of signification in one first–grade classroom. In D. Kirshner & J. A. Whitson (Eds.), *Situated cognition theory: Social, semiotic, and neurological perspectives* (pp. 151–233). Mahwah, NJ: Lawrence Erlbaum Associates.

Davis, P. J., & Hersch, R. (1981). *The mathematical experience.* Boston: Houghton Mifflin.

Fennema, E., & Romberg, T. A. (Eds.). (1999). *Mathematics classrooms that promote understanding.* Mahwah, NJ: Lawrence Erlbaum Associates.

Giere, R. N. (1993). *Minnesota studies in the philosophy of science: Vol. 15. Cognitive models of science.* Minneapolis, MN: University of Minnesota Press.

Hesse, M. B. (1965). *Forces and fields: A study of action at a distance in the history of physics.* Totowa, NJ: Littlefield, Adams, & Co.

Hewson, M. G. (1986). The acquisition of scientific knowledge: Analysis and representation of student conceptions concerning density. *Science Education, 70,* 159–170.

Hewson, M., & Hewson, P. (1983). Effect of instruction using students' prior knowledge and conceptual change strategies on science learning. *Journal of Research in Science Teaching, 20,* 731–743.

Kline, M. (1980). *The loss of certainty.* Oxford, England: Oxford University Press.

Lakatos, I. (1976). *Proofs and refutations.* Cambridge, England: Cambridge University Press.

Larkin, J. H., McDermott, J., Simon, D. P., & Simon, H. A. (1980). Models of competence in solving physics problems. *Cognitive Science, 4,* 317–345.

Lehrer, R., Jacobson, K., Kemeny, V., & Strom, D. (1999). Building on children's intuitions to develop mathematical understanding of space. In E. Fennema & T. A. Romberg (Eds.), *Mathematics classrooms that promote understanding* (pp. 63–87). Mahwah, NJ: Lawrence Erlbaum Associates.

Lehrer, R., Jacobson, K., Thoyre, G., Kemeny, V., Strom, D., Horvath, J., Gance, S., & Koehler, M. (1998). Developing understanding of geometry and space in the primary grades. In R. Lehrer & D. Chazan (Eds.), *Designing learning environments for developing understanding of geometry and space* (pp. 169–200). Mahwah, NJ: Lawrence Erlbaum Associates.

Lehrer, R., & Schauble, L. (2000). Modeling in mathematics and science. In R. Glaser (Ed.), *Advances in instructional psychology,* (Vol. 5, pp. 101–159). Mahwah, NJ: Lawrence Erlbaum Associates.

Lehrer, R., Strom, D., & Confrey, J. (2000). *Grounding metaphors and inscriptional resonance: Children's emerging understanding of mathematical similarity.* Manuscript submitted for publication.

Leoni, V., & Mullet, E. (1993). Evolution in the intuitive mastery of the relationship between mass, volume, and density. *Genetic, Social, and General Psychology Monographs, 119,* 391–413.

National Council of Teachers of Mathematics, (2000). *Curriculum evaluation standards for school mathematics.* Reston, VA: Author.

Nercessian, N. (1993). How do scientists think? Capturing the dynamic of conceptual change in science. In R. N. Giere (Ed.), *Minnesota studies in the philosophy of science: Vol. 15. Cognitive models of science* (pp. 3–44). Minneapolis, MN: University of Minnesota Press.

Olson, D. R. (1994). *The world on paper: The conceptual and cognitive implications of reading and writing.* Cambridge, England: Cambridge University Press.

Penner, D. E., Giles, N. D., Lehrer, R., & Schauble, L. (1997). Building functional models: Designing an elbow. *Journal of Research in Science Teaching, 34,* 125–143.

Penner, D. E., Lehrer, R., & Schauble, L. (1998). From physical models to biomechanical systems: A design-based modeling approach. *Journal of the Learning Sciences, 7,* 429–449.

Rowell, J. A., & Dawson, C. J. (1977a). Teaching about floating and sinking: An attempt to link cognitive psychology with classroom practice. *Science Education, 61,* 243–251.

Rowell, J. A., & Dawson, C. J. (1977b). Teaching about floating and sinking: Further studies toward closing the gap between cognitive psychology and classroom practice. *Science Education, 61,* 527–540.

Smith, C., Carey, S., & Wiser, M. (1985). On differentiation: A case study of the development of the concepts of size, weight, and density. *Cognition, 21,* 177–237.

Smith, C., Maclin, D., Grosslight, L., & Davis, H. (1997). Teaching for understanding: A study of students' preinstruction theories of matter and a comparison of the effectiveness of two approaches to teaching about matter and density. *Cognition and Instruction, 15,* 317–394.

Smith, C., Snir, Y., & Grosslight, L. (1992). Using conceptual models to facilitate conceptual change: The case of weight-density differentiation. *Cognition and Instruction, 9,* 221–283.

Smith, C., & Unger, C. (1997). What's in dots-per-box? Conceptual bootstrapping with stripped-down visual analogs. *The Journal of the Learning Sciences, 6,* 143–182.

Stewart, I., & Golubitsky, M. (1992). *Fearful symmetry: Is God a geometer?* London, England: Penguin Books.

Strom, D., Kemeny, V., Lehrer, R., & Forman, E. (2000). *Visualizing the emergent structure of children's mathematical argument.* Manuscript submitted for publication.

White, B. Y., & Frederiksen, J. R. (1998). Inquiry, modeling, and metacognition: Making science accessible to all students. *Cognition and Instruction, 16,* 3–118.

Wiser, M., Grosslight, L., & Unger, C. (1989). *Can conceptual models aid ninth graders' differentiation of heat and temperature?* (Tech. Dep 89–6). Cambridge, MA: Harvard Graduate School of Education, Educational Technology center.

APPENDIX:

Density Interview Questions

1. *Differentiation of weight/density*

   This item requires use of the short, bronze cylinder (#28) and the short aluminum cylinder (#20). Place each of the cylinders in front of a graduated cylinder. (Switch left-to-right positions of the cylinder from child to child).

   If I put this solid (pick up bronze cylinder) into the water, what will happen to the level of the water? (Point to water line. If you need to, prompt until child notes that the water level should rise. Record whether child produces this idea spontaneously). Now if I put each of these two cylinders into the water, the gold one into this cylinder and the silver one into this cylinder (pick both up and hold them over their respective cylinders), would this water line rise higher (gesture to one cylinder)? Would this water line rise higher (gesture to the other)? Or would they both rise to the same level? Why? (Justification is important).

2. *Relative density*

   Jeff made a graph with lines that show "families" of materials. Each line shows the weights for different volumes of one kind of material. (Note: These items refer to Fig. 2.5 in the text.)

   2a. Imagine I had 20 cm³ of these five materials, A, B, C, D, and E. And then suppose that D is a liquid. Which of these materials will float in D? How do you know?

   2b. Imagine now that B is a liquid. Which of these materials will float in B? How do you know?

3. *Finding Densities*

   This graph shows two families of materials, X and Y. (Note: This item refers to Fig. 2.6 in the text).

   3a. What does the steepness of the lines tell you about the density of the materials?

   3b. What is the density of X?

   3c. What is the density of Y?

4. *Interpreting Origin* (Note: This item refers to Fig. 2.7 in the text.)

   Matt was making a graph to show two families of materials, X and Y. But Susan told him that there was a mistake in his graph. Can you find the mistake and explain why it's a problem?

5. *Composite Densities*

   This item requires use of two equal-sized pieces of clay, one rolled into a spherical ball and the other shaped into a bowl; also a small bucket of water.

   When I put this lump of clay into a bucket of water, it sinks (gesture with lump of clay over bucket, but do not drop it inside). But when I take the same amount of clay and shape it into a bowlshape like this, it floats on top of the water. How would you explain that?

6. *Differentiation of weight and density*

   For this item you need one bucket with water, one dime, and the wooden cube with the hook removed.

   Drop the dime into the bucket and add the wooden block. The block is much heavier than the dime. So can you explain why the piece of wood floats and the dime sinks? (If the child says "density," ask: What does that have to do with it?)

3

Cognitive Development and Science Education: Ships that Pass in the Night or Beacons of Mutual Illumination?

David Klahr
Zhe Chen
Eva E. Toth
Carnegie Mellon University

Two beliefs widely shared among the contributors to this volume are that (a) theoretical and empirical advances in cognitive and developmental psychology can provide a solid basis for improved instructional practice; and (b) the challenge of instructional innovation can raise new questions for basic cognitive research. Evidence supporting the first belief—implicit in the large dose of cognitive and developmental psychology contained in most degree programs in education—comes from the type of chapters in this and related volumes (e.g., Bruer, 1993, McGilly, 1994), as well as the articles appearing in two influential interdisciplinary journals—*Journal of the Learning Sciences* and *Cognition and Instruction*—that have appeared since the first Carnegie Symposium on this topic (Klahr, 1976). The second belief is a particularization of the commonly held view that applied work always raises novel questions to be addressed by further basic research. In this case, the applications involve the development and implementation of effective instructional methods and the basic research is carried out in the psychologist's laboratory. Taken together, these two beliefs support the "mutual illumination" metaphor in the title of this chapter.

However, there is another view—one that supports instead the second metaphor in our title, in which the two enterprises of cognitive research and instructional practice have no more in common than "ships passing in the night." Consider, for example, the somewhat pessimistic assessment by Strauss (1998) that appeared recently in a prestigious handbook on applied topics in developmental psychology (Sigel & Renninger, 1998). Although Strauss acknowledged that one can find, at the margins of both fields, several atypical examples of such mutual influence, he argued that an honest look at the bulk of the work published in each field reveals that "cognitive developmental psychologists rarely involve themselves in topics that are of interest to science educators" (Strauss, 1998, p. 358). In other words, perhaps the education ship and the research ship traverse the same seas and visit the same ports, but they pass in darkness, with neither one illuminating the other.

Strauss offered several explanations for the relatively small proportion of published work that is of interest to both cognitive psychologists and science educators. One problem is lack of common interest in content: Developmentalists often study topics that, while providing useful indices for cognitive development, may have little relevance for science education. Another problem is that developmentalists focus on universal and invariant sequences that may be largely irrelevant to educators who are more interested in what can, rather than what can't, be changed. A third problem is the tendency for researchers in cognitive development to study the child in isolation, whereas educators have to work in complex social and institutional settings in which cognitive processes may account for only a small part of the variance in outcomes. Finally, Strauss argued that there is scant shared knowledge between developmentalists and science educators: The former know a lot about children, but little about topics in the nonpsychological sciences, whereas the latter know a lot about their science, but little about the psychology of thinking, learning, and development.

Unfortunately, there is much that is correct about Strauss's gloomy assessment. Except for a few notable exceptions (e.g., Brown, 1992, 1997; Fennema, Carpenter, Franke, Levi, Jacobs, & Empson, 1996; White & Frederiksen, 1998), most of the research in the intersection between cognition and instruction is carried out by researchers whose predilection is to conduct their work in either the psychology laboratory or the classroom, but not both. Consequently, reports of laboratory-based research having clear instructional implications typically conclude with a suggested instructional innovation, but one rarely finds a subsequent report on an associated specific action resulting in instructional change. Similarly, many instructional interventions are based on theoretical positions that have been shaped by laboratory findings, but the lab procedures have been adapted to the pragmatics of the classroom by a different set of researchers (e.g., Christensen & Cooper, 1991; Das-Smaal, Klapwijk, & van det Leij, 1996). This division of labor between laboratory-based cognitive research and classroom research is understandable, but, in our view, unnecessary and inefficient because much can be lost in the translation from the psychology laboratory to the classroom.

In this chapter, we propose a two-part remedy to this situation. The first part provides a conceptual framework for classifying research on children's scientific thinking along lines that are relevant to science education. We hope that by providing a kind of "reader's guide" to some of the basic research on the development of scientific reasoning, we may clarify its relevance to science education while at the same time providing some insight into why such work is not always immediately embraced by those facing the challenge of improving instruction. The second part of our chapter provides a counterexample to Strauss's claim: We offer a concrete instance of a productive two-way flow between the psychology lab and the science classroom. The example is based on a project in which, over the past several years, we have been developing, implementing, and assessing a set of instructional materials for teaching children in grades two to four the concepts and skills associated with the design of unconfounded experiments and the derivation of valid inferences.

A TAXONOMY OF APPROACHES TO STUDYING AND TEACHING SCIENTIFIC THINKING

Scientific reasoning—both as it is studied by developmental psychologists and as it is taught by elementary school science teachers—can be classified along two dimensions: one representing the degree of domain specificity or domain generality, and the other representing the type of discovery processes involved, such as generating hypotheses, designing experiments, and evaluating evidence (see Table 3.1). During the course of normal scientific discovery, the various cells in Table 3.1 are traversed repeatedly. However, it is very difficult to study thinking processes that involve all of them simultaneously. Consequently, much of the research on scientific thinking has been intentionally designed to focus on only one or two of the cells in Table 3.1, although some studies have used complex contexts involving several cells. The entries in Table 3.2 illustrate some of the ways that psychologists have attempted to study different aspects of scientific thinking in isolation. (For a more complete description, see Klahr & Carver, 1995, and Klahr, 2000.)

Integrative Investigations of Scientific Reasoning

The types of investigations spanning the bottom row in Table 3.1 and summarized as the final entry in Table 3.2 reveal the large grain of truth in Strauss's complaint about the perceived irrelevance of psychological research to science instruction. On the one hand, the Bruner concept formation task and the Wason "2–4–6" task are among the most widely cited and replicated studies in the cognitive psychology literature. On the other hand, few science teachers would deem it worthwhile to teach children these kinds of skills or to use these puzzlelike materials in their classrooms, even though, from a psychologist's perspective, they elegantly illustrate some of the fundamental cognitive processes involved in scientific thinking.

The classroom teacher does not have the laboratory psychologist's luxury of isolating different components of scientific thinking in order to better understand them. Instead, the teacher must attempt to orchestrate all of these aspects in various combinations. For example, consider the complexity faced by a teacher attempting to teach her students the classic

TABLE 3.1
Types of Foci in Investigations of Scientific Reasoning Processes

	Generating Hypotheses	Designing & Executing Experiments	Evaluating Evidence
Domain-specific knowledge	A	B	C
Domain-general knowledge	D	E	F

TABLE 3.2

Examples of Investigations Located in Various Cells of Table 3.1

Cell(s) from Table 3.1	Focus of Study	Reference
A	Domain-specific hypothesis generation. Participants are asked to make predictions or give explanations in a specific domain in order to reveal their intuitive theories of mechanical or biological phenomena. They are not allowed to run experiments, and they are not presented with any evidence to evaluate.	Carey, 1985; McCloskey, 1983.
B	Domain-specific experimental design. Participants are asked to decide which of a set of prespecified experiments will provide the most informative test of a prespecified hypothesis. There is no search of the hypothesis space and the experiment space search is limited to choosing from among the given experiments, rather than generating them.	Tschirgi, 1980.
E	Domain-general experimental design. People are asked to design factorial experiments in relatively sparse contexts. The use of domain-specific knowledge is minimized as is search in the hypothesis space and the evidence evaluation process.	Case, 1974; Kuhn & Angelev, 1976; Siegler & Liebert, 1975.
C & F	Domain-specific and domain-general evidence evaluation. Studies in this category focus on people's ability to decide which of several hypotheses is supported by evidence. Typically, participants are presented tables of covariation data, and asked to decide which of several hypotheses is supported or refuted by the data. In some cases, the factors are abstract and arbitrary—in which case we would classify the studies in Cell F—and in others, they refer to real world factors, such as studies that present data on plant growth in the context of different amounts of sunlight and water.	Amsel & Brock, 1996; Bullock, Ziegler, & Martin, 1993; Ruffman, Perner, Olson, & Doherty, 1993; Shaklee & Paszek, 1985.
A & C	Domain-specific hypothesis generation and evidence evaluation. Children are asked to integrate a variety of forms of existing evidence in order to produce a theory that is consistent with that evidence. They do not have the opportunity to generate new evidence via experimentation, and the context of their search in the hypothesis space is highly domain specific.	Vosniadou & Brewer, 1992.
A, C, & F	Domain-specific hypothesis generation and domain-specific and domain-general evidence evaluation. In these studies, participants are presented with a complex mixture of covariation data, possible causal mechanisms, analogous effects, sampling procedures, and alternative hypotheses from which they are asked to make a decision about a potentially causal factor. People are given the opportunity to go beyond just the covariation data—that is, to use both their domain-specific knowledge as well as other domain-general features, such as sample size, in making their decisions.	Koslowski, 1996; Koslowski & Okagaki, 1986; Koslowski, Okagki, Lorenz, & Umbach, 1989.

(Continued)

TABLE 3.2

(continued)

Cell(s) from Table 3.1	Focus of Study	Reference
D, E, & F	Domain-general hypothesis generation, experimental design, and evidence evaluation. Participants are asked to discover an arbitrary rule or concept based on formal properties of the stimulus. No domain-specific knowledge of any kind is required, but participants have to use domain-general reasoning processes such as hypothesis formation, instance selection, and rule induction.	Bruner, Goodnow, & Austin, 1956; Wason, 1960.

problem in mechanics of discovering the period of a pendulum. As illustrated in Table 3.3, her students would traverse all of the cells as they worked with this problem. Even though the instruction would tend to focus on the domain-specific aspects of force and acceleration that underlie the phenomenon being investigated, the teacher would also attempt to convey some important domain-general processes and knowledge about scientific methodology. Thus, if they are to be of relevance to educators, psychological studies must somehow be more representative of the complexity faced by the teacher.

First, they must cross the row boundaries in Table 3.1 in order to study the interaction between domain-specific and domain-general knowledge. Second, they must integrate the processes of hypothesis search, experimentation, and evidence evaluation in order to examine their mutual influence. In recent years, several investigators have begun to address these questions by integrating the six different aspects of the scientific discovery process represented in Table 3.1 while still posing the research questions at a sufficiently fine grain so as not to lose relevant detail about the discovery process (cf. Dunbar, 1993; Klahr, 2000; Klahr & Dunbar, 1988; Klahr, Fay, & Dunbar, 1993; Kuhn, 1989; Kuhn, Amsel, & O'Loughlin, 1988; Kuhn, Schauble, & Garcia-Mila, 1992; Kuhn, Garcia-Mila, Zohar, & Andersen, 1995; Schauble, 1990; Schauble, Glaser, Raghavan, & Reiner, 1991).

The study that we describe later in this chapter also focused primarily on a domain-general skill—or what is usually called a "process skill" (in contrast to "content knowledge"). The particular skill had to do with how to design unconfounded experiments, and our study can therefore be classified as belonging primarily in Cell E. However, as will become evident, our experiments also involved evaluation of real experiments with real devices in the physical world, and thus were experiments "about" something. So we would also implicate Cells B, C, and F.

TABLE 3.3
Cells Traversed During Typical Elementary School Science Lab Sessions
on Finding the Period of a Pendulum

	Generating Hypotheses	*Designing & Executing Experiments*	*Evaluating Evidence*
Domain-specific knowledge	• Length? • Initial Force? • Mass?	• Selecting and isolating some aspect (length, mass, force, etc.) • Counting cycles of pendulum • Establishing a timing basis	• Averaging and comparing several trials of same setup • Cross-setup comparisons to look for differences in period length • Eliminate noncasual factors (mass, initial height, initial force, etc.)
Domain-general knowledge	• Asking "good" questions • Proposing plausible causal mechanisms • Inducing "rules" from regularities	• Varying one thing at a time • Choosing tractable values for variables • Minimizing error • Observing relevant outcomes	• Recording data • Making tables • Distinguishing determinate from indeterminant data patterns • Finding most representative measures

To summarize, we have briefly described a taxonomy in which scientific reasoning is classified along two dimensions—domain specificity and type of processes—and we have attempted to illustrate how this classification can be useful for understanding and characterizing both basic lab investigations and classroom teaching. One problem that this taxonomic exercise has revealed is that although science education aims to impart domain-general scientific reasoning skills, it is almost always couched in—perhaps even overwhelmed by—specific context, whereas lab research, although unambiguously identifying general reasoning components, often fails to indicate its relevance to classroom practice.

In the next section, we offer an example of how lab research can generate a solid basis for classroom research, which in turn can generate new theoretical issues for further study in the lab. We describe the process whereby we translated a theoretically motivated, carefully crafted, and laboratory-based instructional procedure of proven effectiveness into a classroom intervention, making minimal modifications to the instructional components while adapting to the constraints of a real classroom. The research-to-practice interface described here further supports both of the widely held beliefs cited in the opening paragraphs of this chapter. First, instruction based on prior laboratory research was educationally effective. Children learned and transferred what they had been taught. Second, once the instruction was situated in a real classroom, a new set of basic research issues arose, and they are currently under investigation. Because we view the move from the laboratory-based research environment to the classroom as fraught with potential pitfalls, we took a very small step—a "baby step" perhaps—in making this move. Nevertheless, or perhaps consequently, we were able to devise an effective curriculum unit that maintained what we believe to be the fundamental features of the laboratory instruction, while still being consistent with everyday classroom practice.

The rest of this chapter is organized as follows. First, we describe the topic of the instruction—the design of controlled experiments—and its place in the elementary school science curriculum. Then, we briefly introduce a contentious issue in instructional methodology, the use of direct instruction versus discovery learning. Next, we summarize the laboratory training study that led us to use direct instruction as the basis for our classroom intervention. With this as background, we describe the design and implementation of the classroom study that aimed to verify the laboratory findings in classroom situations, followed by the basic findings of this study. Finally, we revisit the issue of the mutual influence and relevance of the fields of cognition and instruction.

Before we embark, some terminological clarification might be helpful. Throughout this chapter we use "lab study" when referring to the type of one-on-one study that is typical of the research psychologist—exemplified by the first study described in this chapter. By "classroom study" we mean the kind of study described in the second part of the chapter, where a teacher introduces an experimental curriculum unit and we do several assessments of its effectiveness. The terminology can get confusing because our lab study, although carried out one-on-one with an experimenter and a child, was actually conducted (in a quiet room) in the school and our classroom study took place in the normal science lab in the school. The one additional complexity is that immediately before and after the classroom study, we assessed some children in a one-on-one lab fashion in order to compare their performance to the earlier (true) lab study and to calibrate the lab assessments with the classroom assessments.

DESIGNING UNCONFOUNDED
EXPERIMENTS: THE CONTROL
OF VARIABLES STRATEGY

There is widespread agreement among science educators that "Even at the earliest grade levels, students should learn what constitutes evidence and judge the merits or strength of the data and information that will be used to make explanations" (NSES, 1995). But evidence does not spring forth unbidden. Instead, it must be actively sought or generated. Thus, the ability to create informative experiments and to derive valid inferences from the evidence they yield is one of the fundamental design skills underlying scientific thinking (Klahr, 2000).

A central component of this skill is the control of variables strategy (CVS). Procedurally, CVS is a method for creating experiments in which a single contrast is made between experimental conditions. The full strategy involves not only creating such contrasts, but also being able to distinguish between confounded and unconfounded experiments. Conceptually, CVS involves making appropriate inferences from the outcomes of unconfounded experiments as well as understanding the inherent indeterminacy of confounded experiments.

Both the educational and the psychological literature suggest that elementary school children find these concepts and procedures extremely difficult to acquire. Ross's (1988) meta-analysis of over 60 CVS training studies from the 1970s and 1980s indicated that a variety of training methods can generate improvement in CVS performance, but only a handful of the studies in his sample included young elementary school children (i.e., below grade five). The results of those few studies, as well as more recent ones in that age range, present a decidedly mixed picture of the extent to which young elementary school children can understand and execute CVS (Bullock & Ziegler, 1999; Case, 1974; Kuhn, et al., 1995; Kuhn & Angelev, 1976 ; Schauble, 1996). Moreover, for those studies showing statistically significant differences between trained and untrained groups,[1] the absolute levels of posttest performance are well below educationally desirable levels. Indeed, to get ahead of our story a bit, our first study (Chen & Klahr, 1999) showed that even in schools with strong elementary science programs in which components of CVS were taught repeatedly during the early science curriculum, fourth graders could correctly construct unconfounded experiments on fewer than 50% of their attempts.

---

[1]Ross found a mean effect size of .73 across all of the studies in his sample.

THEORIES
OF INSTRUCTION, LEARNING,
AND TRANSFER

Given that CVS is a fundamental scientific reasoning skill and given that few elementary school children master it even after several years of good science instruction, it is important to know whether there are effective ways to teach it and whether age and instructional method interact with respect to learning and transfer. One controversial issue in instruction is whether or not discovery learning is more effective than the traditional didactic method (called here simply "direct instruction"). Part of the controversy derives from a lack of definitional consensus, so we need to clarify our use of the terms. Although the details will become apparent when we describe our studies, it is important to note at the outset that we do not associate one with "active" and the other with "passive" learning. In all of the learning situations described in this chapter, students were actively engaged in the design and manipulation of experimental apparatus. The main distinction between the situations is that in direct instruction, the instructor told the students how and why CVS worked, whereas in other situations there was no such direct telling.

Even with these distinctions, the relative efficacy of discovery learning versus direct instruction depends on many factors, one of which is the content of the learning tasks. Discovery learning has been considered an effective approach for the acquisition of domain-specific knowledge. Its advocates argue that children who are actively engaged in acquiring new knowledge are more likely to be successful in retaining and applying it than children who passively receive direct instruction (e.g., Jacoby, 1978; McDaniel & Schlager, 1990). Although discovery learning might be effective when problem outcomes provide informative feedback (e.g., Siegler, 1976), direct instruction may be appropriate in those cases where it is unlikely that a multistep strategy would be discovered spontaneously. For example, Klahr and Carver (1988) found that a brief period of direct instruction in how to debug computer programs was more effective than hundreds of hours of discovery learning. Here, too, both groups of children were active, that is, they were writing and running computer programs. But one group was told how to debug, and the other was not. With respect to CVS, unguided experimental designs typically do not provide informative feedback concerning their quality. This lack of feedback might render the discovery of procedures such as CVS particularly difficult for early elementary school children.

BACKGROUND:
A LABORATORY TRAINING STUDY

It is clear that the issue of the relative effectiveness of direct instruction versus discovery learning is extremely complex (and, unfortunately, somewhat politicized). Rather than examine the issue in the "messy" context of an ongoing classroom, we decided to begin by studying it in the relatively controlled confines of a laboratory study. Thus, we compared the effectiveness of different instructional methods for teaching CVS in a situation where children had extensive and repeated opportunities to use CVS while designing, running, and evaluating their own experiments.

Materials

We used three different domains in which children had to design unconfounded experiments: (a) springs, in which the goal was to determine the factors that affected spring elongation; (b) sinking, in which children had to assess the factors that determined how fast various objects sank in water; and (c) ramps, in which children needed to figure out which factors determined how far a ball rolled down the slope. The underlying CVS logic in all three domains was identical. In each, there were four variables that could assume either of two values. In each domain, children were asked to focus on a single outcome that could be affected by any or all of the four variables.

For example, in the springs domain,[2] children had to make comparisons to determine the effects of different variables on how far springs stretch. Materials consisted of eight springs varying in length (long and short), coil width (wide and narrow), and wire diameter (thick and thin). The springs were arranged on a tray such that no pair of adjacent springs made an unconfounded comparison. A pair of heavy and a pair of light weights were also used. Heavy and light weights differed in shape as well as in weight, so that they could be easily distinguished. To set up a comparison, children selected two springs to compare and hung them on hooks on a frame and then selected weight to hang on each spring. To execute a comparison, participants hung the weights on the springs and observed as the springs stretched. The outcome measured was how far the springs stretched down toward the base of the frame. Figure 3.1 depicts the materials and an experiment from the spring domain.

---

[2]In this chapter, we describe only the springs in detail. See Chen and Klahr (1999) for a detailed description of all three domains.

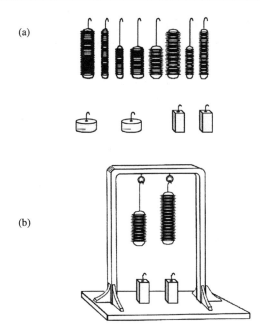

FIG. 3.1. The springs domain. (a) Set of eight springs varying in wire thickness, spring width, and spring length, and set of two heavy weights (cylinders) and light weights (cubes); (b) An unconfounded experiment in which length is varied, and all other factors are held constant.

Training Conditions

1. Explicit Training. Explicit training was provided in the *training/probe* condition. It included an explanation of the rationale behind controlling variables as well as examples of how to make unconfounded comparisons. Children in this condition also received probe questions before and after each comparison that they made. Before the experiment was executed, children were asked to explain and justify the design. After the experiment was executed, children were asked if they could "tell for sure" whether the variable they were testing made a difference and also why they were sure or not sure. The explicit instruction was provided following the exploration phase (see Procedure section below) in which children had designed a few experiments and pondered probe questions about those experiments.

2. Implicit Training. Implicit training was provided in the *no training/probe* condition. Here, children did not receive direct instruction, but—as in the explicit training condition—they did actively construct experiments and receive probe questions before and after each of them.

3. Discovery Learning. Discovery learning opportunities were provided to children in the *no training/no probe* condition. They received neither training nor probes but they did receive the same number of opportunities as children in the other conditions to actively construct experiments.

PARTICIPANTS, PROCEDURE, AND MEASURES USED IN THE LABORATORY STUDY

Eighty-seven second, third, and fourth graders from two private schools[3] in an urban area were randomly assigned to one of the three different instructional methods. Each child worked with one of the three domains on their first day in the study (exploration and assessment phases) and then with two other domains on their second day (transfer-1 and transfer-2). Domain order was counterbalanced, as was the order of focal variables within each domain.

Procedure

Part I consisted of four phases: exploration, assessment, transfer-1, and transfer-2 (see Table 3.4). In each phase, children were asked to construct four different experimental contrasts from which they could make a valid inference about the causal status of some dimension of the domain. The exploration phase established an initial baseline of children's ability to design unconfounded experiments in the first domain (e.g., springs). For the training/probe condition, the instructional session immediately followed the exploration phase. Then followed the assessment phase in which children were asked to design experiments on a different dimension but in the same domain. (Thus, if, in the exploration phase, the experiments focused on spring *length*, then the assessment phase would focus on

---

[3]In School A, we used only third and fourth graders.

TABLE 3.4
Time Line for Laboratory Study

Time	First day			A few days later			7 months later
	Part I						Part II
Phase	Exploration	Training or additional exposure	Assessment	Transfer-1	Transfer-2	Late training	Far transfer
Purpose	Establish baseline of children's ability to design unconfounded experiments in Domain A (e.g., springs)	Explicit training (for training group only) or Additional experiments (for no-training groups) (Factor a; e.g., spring length)	Determine whether children can design an unconfounded test of Factor b (e.g., spring width)	Determine whether children can design an unconfounded test in Domain B (e.g., sinking objects)	Determine whether children can design an unconfounded test in Domain C (e.g., ramps)	Train the two "no training" groups in preparation for far transfer test	Determine whether children can identify good and bad experimental designs on paper and pencil test
Domain	A (springs)	A (springs)	A (springs)	B (sinking)	C (ramps)	C (ramps)	Nonphysical: cooking, plant growth, foot race, etc.

spring *width*.) Transfer-1 and transfer-2 took place a few days after exploration and assessment. Children returned to the lab and were asked to design unconfounded experiments in the other two domains (e.g., in the current example, they would do experiments with ramps and with sinking objects).[4]

Part II was a paper and pencil, experiment evaluation posttest, given 7 months after the individual interviews. This consisted of a set of 15 pairwise experimental comparisons in a variety of domains. The child's task was to examine the experimental setup and decide whether it was a good or a bad experiment. (This type of assessment was also used in the classroom study, and it is described in more detail later.)

RESULTS FROM
THE LABORATORY TRAINING STUDY

Measures

Three measures used in the lab study that were also used in the classroom study[5] were (a) *CVS score*—a simple performance measure based on children's use of CVS in designing experimental contrasts; (b) *robust use of CVS*—a more stringent measure based on both performance and verbal justifications (in responses to probes) about why children designed their experiments as they did; (c) *domain knowledge*—based on children's responses to questions about the effects of different causal variables in the domain.

CVS Score. Children's use of CVS was indexed by their use of valid experimental designs. For example, a valid design to test the effect of the length of a spring is that the pair differs only in the focal variable (i.e., length) while all other variables (coil width, wire size, and weight) are kept constant. Invalid designs included (a) noncontrastive comparisons in which the focal variable was not varied and one or more other variables were varied, and (b) confounded comparisons in which the focal variable as well as one or more other variables were varied. Each valid design was given a score of 1. All other types of design were given a score of 0.

---

[4]Following the transfer-1 and transfer-2 phases, children in the two no-training groups in School A were trained, in preparation for the far transfer test in Part II.

[5]A fourth measure—strategy similarity awareness—was based on children's responses to questions about the similarity across tasks. This is described in Chen and Klahr (1999).

Because children made four comparisons in each phase, the CVS scores for each phase could range from 0 to 4.

Robust Use of CVS. Children's responses to the probe questions "Why did you set up the comparison this way?" and "Can you tell for sure from this comparison?" were classified into four categories: (1) Explanations that included mentions of CVS (e.g., "You just need to make the surface different, but put the gates in the same places, set the ramps the same height, and use the same kind of balls"); (2) Explanations that included controlling some but not all of the other relevant variables (e.g., "Because they're both metal but one was round and one was square"); (3) Explanations that mentioned a comparison within the focal variable (e.g., "Because I had to make the surfaces different"); and (4) Explanations that were irrelevant to CVS.

Children received a robust CVS score of 1 only for those trials for which they produced an unconfounded design *and* provided an explanation or interpretation that mentioned the control of all other variables (i.e., a response fitting category 1, above). Other trials received a score of 0. Again, because children made four designs in each phase, the range of robust use scores was 0 to 4.

Domain Knowledge. Domain knowledge was assessed by asking children, both before and after they designed and implemented their tests, how they thought each variable would affect the outcome. Children's correct prediction/judgment of each variable was given a score of 1, and for incorrect prediction/judgment, a score of 0 was assigned.

Initial Performance in Using CVS

Children's initial performance was measured by the proportion of unconfounded comparisons they produced during the exploration phase. We found significant[6] grade differences in this initial performance with 26%, 34%, and 48% in second, third, and fourth grade, respectively. Note that, even for second graders, these scores are significantly above chance.[7]

---

[6]Statistical detail has been suppressed throughout this chapter. Most of the effects reported as "significant" have *p* values less than .01, although a few are only .05, whereas "marginally significant" values are between .05 and .10. For more detail, see Chen and Klahr (1999) and Toth, Klahr, and Chen (2000).

[7]The chance probability of producing an unconfounded comparison is .083. See Chen and Klahr (1999) for a detailed explanation.

Thus, although continued exposure to science classes in each grade does lead to improvement in children's ability to design unconfounded experiments, their overall performance is far below ceiling.

Acquisition and Transfer of CVS

The three training conditions differed substantially in their effects. As indicated in Fig. 3.2, the frequency of CVS use in the training/probe condition increased immediately following training, and remained at a relatively high level. In contrast, for the no training conditions, the increase was slow (for no training/probe) and unsustained (for no training/no probe). Statistical analysis revealed that, when averaged over all three grade levels, the only significant gains occurred in the training/probe condition.

A more detailed analysis, in which we looked at each grade level separately, revealed that only the third and fourth graders in the training/probe condition showed significant gains after training that were

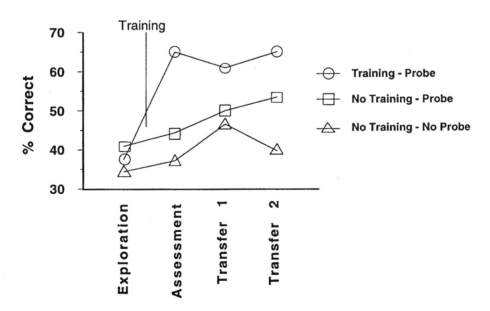

FIG. 3.2.   Percentage of trials with correct use of CVS by phase and condition (lab study).

maintained into the transfer phases (see Fig. 3.3). For second graders in the training/probe condition, transfer performance was not significantly higher than the initial exploration performance.

In order to assess transfer in *individual* students, we defined a "good experimenter" as a child who produced at least 7 out of 8 unconfounded comparisons during transfer-1 and transfer-2, and then we computed the proportion of children who became good experimenters between exploration and transfer. There were substantial effects of condition: 44% of the children in the training/probe condition, 22% in the no training/probe

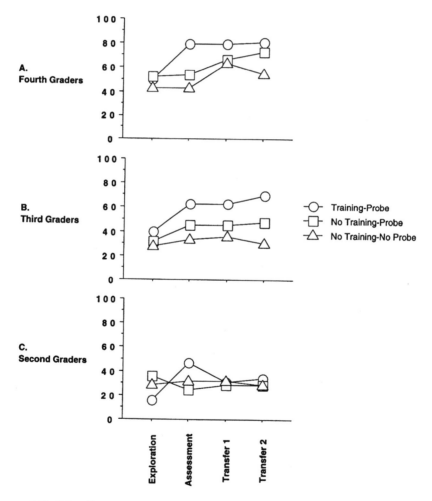

FIG. 3.3. Percentage of correct CVS usage by phase, grade, and condition (lab study).

condition, and 13% in the no training/no probe condition became good experimenters.

Relations Between the Use of CVS and Domain Knowledge

An important issue concerning the function of training in CVS is whether children's domain-specific knowledge—that is, their understanding of the effects of the variables associated with springs, ramps, and sinking— improved as a result of training. Because our primary goal was to examine elementary school children's ability to learn and transfer CVS, neither the training nor the probe questions were directed toward, or contingent on, the children's understanding of the *content* of the domains. However, any change in children's beliefs about the causal mechanisms in the three domains is of obvious interest, because the ultimate goal of good experimental design is to learn about the world. We found that only those children who were directly trained to design informative (i.e., unconfounded) comparisons showed an increase in their domain knowledge (see Fig. 3.4).

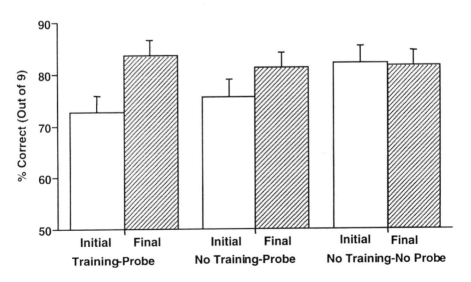

FIG. 3.4.   Initial and final domain knowledge for each condition (lab study).

Posttest Performance

The posttest was designed to see whether children were able to transfer the learned strategy to remote problems after a long (7 months) delay. In School A, all children who participated in the hands-on interviews were trained in CVS, either early in the procedure or at the end of the hands-on study. Because they were all trained at some point, all of these School A children are now, for the purposes of the posttest analysis, considered the experimental group, whereas their classmates who did not participate make up the control group. Posttest data were collected only in School A and therefore only third and fourth graders were included.

Far transfer was indexed by the number of correct responses to the 15 posttest problems. A correct response was given a score of 1, an incorrect one, a score of 0. We found that fourth graders—but not third graders—in the experimental group outperformed those in the control group (see Fig. 3.5).

Another measure of remote transfer involved the percentage of "good reasoners" in the experimental and control groups. Children who made 13

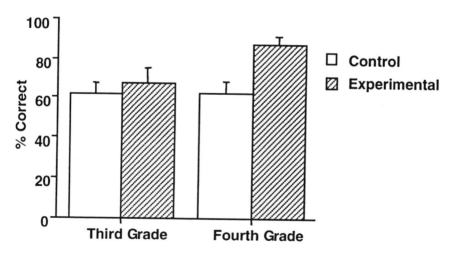

FIG. 3.5.   Percentage of correct posttest answers by grade and condition (lab study).

or more correct judgments out of a total of 15 problems were considered good reasoners. Forty percent of the third and 79% of the fourth graders in the experimental group were categorized as good reasoners, compared to 22% of the third and 15% of the fourth graders in the control group. This difference was significant only for the fourth graders.

MAIN FINDINGS
FROM THE LABORATORY STUDY

To summarize, the key results from our laboratory study are that absent direct instruction, children did not discover CVS on their own, even when they had repeated opportunities to work with hands-on materials; that brief direct instruction on CVS, combined with active participation in experimental setups and execution, was sufficient to promote substantial gains in CVS performance; and that these gains transferred to both near and (for fourth graders) far domains. These results gave us confidence that we were ready to move to the classroom and we began planning to recruit a few elementary school science teachers to let us implement the instructional method that had worked so well in our lab in their classrooms. Thus began the second phase of our project.

MOVING FROM THE LAB
TO THE CLASSROOM

Although our lab study demonstrated that participation in a brief session of direct instruction about CVS produced substantial and long-lasting learning in fourth graders, it was clear to us that the type of one-on-one instruction and assessment used in a typical psychology experiment requiring strict adherence to a carefully crafted script would be impractical for everyday classroom use. Furthermore, we became increasingly aware that our lab study had a relatively narrow focus when compared to the multiple goals and pragmatic constraints that classroom teachers usually have when teaching about experimental design. Thus, we formulated the goal of translating, adapting, and enriching this procedure so that it could be used as a lesson plan for a classroom unit, that is, engineering a classroom learning environment (Brown, 1992; Collins, 1992). In addition, because we wanted to study the effectiveness of this translation process, we recognized the need to include a variety of assessment procedures—assessments that would serve the dual purpose of enhancing students' learning while informing us about the relative effectiveness of our instruction.

With this as background, we began to craft a lesson plan based on our initial laboratory script. In designing the lesson plan and its associated assessments, we addressed the following questions: (a) Can fourth graders learn and transfer CVS when exposed to direct classroom instruction combined with hands-on experimentation? (b) Does the classroom introduce any new issues or difficulties in learning CVS? (c) Will instruction that is focused on the design and justification of students' own experiments increase their ability to evaluate experiments designed by others? (d) What is the relation between students' experimentation skills and the acquisition of domain knowledge?[8]

Throughout this process, we conceptualized our task in terms of differences and similarities between lab and classroom with respect to instructional objectives and pragmatic constraints, and types of assessments. These are summarized in Table 3.5. For a minimalist but still effective intervention, we maintained both the instructional objective (teaching CVS) and the proven instructional strategy (direct instruction interspersed with hands-on experimentation) from the earlier laboratory study. In addition, we attempted, insofar as possible, to make all necessary modifications in terms of our theoretical orientation that the mechanism of transfer from one domain to another was analogical processing. Within these constraints, there were several important differences between the laboratory script and the classroom lesson.

Pragmatic differences were extensive. Because the teacher could not keep track of the experimental setups of all of the groups, we transferred this responsibility to the students. They were instructed in how to record, for each of their experiments, the way that they had set up their pair of ramps. We provided students with worksheets that they completed after each experiment. The worksheets included a preformatted table representation to record ramp setups (see Appendix). The methods for filling out this table and the rest of the questions on the worksheet were discussed before experimentation. Thus, although students had to record the way in which they set up each pair of ramps, they did not have the additional responsibility of devising an external representation for the physical setup.

---

[8]This transition from the lab to the classroom also involved a variety of practical, conceptual, organizational, and interpersonal processes that are described elsewhere (Toth, Klahr, & Chen, 2000).

TABLE 3.5

Comparison of Pragmatics and Instructional Methods in Laboratory and Classroom Study

	Laboratory Study	*Classroom Study*
Instruction		
Instructional objective	Mastery of CVS	Mastery of CVS
Instructional strategy	Didactic instruction of one student	Didactic instruction — group of students
	Active construction, execution, and evaluation of experiments by solo student	Active construction, execution, and evaluation of experiments by group (unequal participation possible)
Materials	Ramps of springs or sinking	Only ramps during classroom work. (Springs and sinking during individual pre and posttest interviews)
Cognitive mechanism targeted	Analogical transfer	Analogical transfer
		Representational transfer with interpretive use of experimenter-provided representation
Pragmatic Constraints		
Timing	Two 45-minute sessions, during or after school	Four 45-minute science classes
Teacher	Outside experimenter	Regular science teacher
Student grouping	Individual students	Entire classroom, organized into five groups of 3–4 students
Teacher–student ratio	1 to 1	1 to 20
Record keeping	By experimenter, not available for students	By students in experimenter-designed data sheets
Assessment		
	Domain knowledge test	Domain knowledge test
	Experimenter's written record of comparisons made by students during individual interviews	Experimenter's written record of comparisons made by students during individual interviews
	Videotaped record of students' answers to questions about comparisons during individual interviews with subset of subjects	Videotaped record of students' answers to questions about comparisons during individual interviews with subset of subjects
		Students' written records of comparisons made and responses given during classroom work
		Paper and pencil pre and posttests for all students in participating classes

However, they did have to negotiate the mapping between physical and tabular representations, and they received detailed instruction on how to do this. During the classroom work, only the ramps domain was used so that the other two domains (sinking and springs) could be used for the individual assessment interviews preceding and following the classroom work. Instead of a single student working with an experimenter, students in the classroom worked in groups of three to five people per pair of ramps. They made joint decisions about how to set up the pair of ramps, but then proceeded to individually record both their setup and the experimental outcome in their laboratory worksheets. (This is explained in more detail later.)

Assessment methods in the classroom were derived from assessments developed for the laboratory study. In both environments, students were tested for their domain knowledge prior to and after instruction. In the laboratory work, this happened in a dialog format between the experimenter and the individual student, whereas in the classroom, each student completed a paper and pencil forced-choice test. Students' ability to compose correct experiments was measured in both situations from the experimental comparisons they made with the set of two ramps. In the classroom study, a paper and pencil experiment evaluation test—similar to the far transfer test used in the lab study—was given before and after instruction.

METHOD

Research Design for Classroom Study

The research design for the classroom study included a set of nested preinstruction and postinstruction measures (see Fig. 3.6). The "inner" set of evaluations—depicted inside the solid box in Fig. 3.6—used several assessment methods, including an in-class paper and pencil test for evaluating experiments that was identical in form to the remote posttest used in the lab study. The full set of assessments was designed to measure students' hands-on experimentation performance as well as their ability to evaluate experiments designed by others. These evaluations were administered by the teacher to all students, in class, immediately before and after the instructional sessions. The "outer" set of individual one-on-one interviews used the same scoring procedures used in Part I of the lab study. For half of the individual interviews, the pretest domain was springs and the posttest domain was sinking objects, and for the other half, the order was reversed.

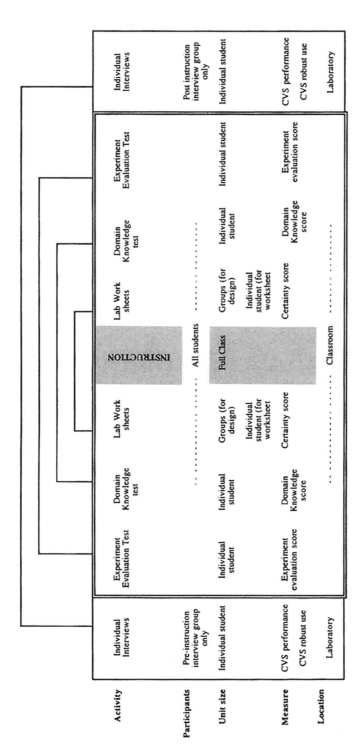

FIG. 3.6. Schedule of various assessments before and after classroom instruction. All activities inside the double-bordered box took place in the classroom.

99

Participants

Seventy-seven students from 4 fourth-grade classrooms in two demographically similar private elementary schools in southwestern Pennsylvania participated. Neither school had participated in the earlier lab study. Schools were selected from among the set of schools represented in our small teacher network on the basis of several pragmatic factors, including permission of school authorities, teacher interest and available time, and the fit between the CVS topic and the normal progression of topics through the fourth-grade science curriculum. From these four classrooms, we recruited volunteers for pre and postinstruction interviews. Of the 77 students participating in the study, 43 students volunteered to be individually interviewed.

Procedure

Individual Interviews

The initial and final assessments were based on individual interviews that were essentially identical to those used throughout the lab study. The pragmatics of conducting research in schools shaped the design of this outer evaluation, because we could only conduct the individual interviews with "volunteers" for whom we had received parental permission.[9] Because we wanted to avoid any potential reactivity between the individual assessments and students' response to the classroom instruction, we included only half of the "permission" students on the individual lab pretest and the other half on the individual lab posttest. Twenty-one of the 43 volunteer students were randomly assigned to the preinstructional interview group and were individually interviewed before the classroom activities began. The rest were assigned to the postinstructional interview group and were individually interviewed after the classroom activities had been completed. The assumption was that in each case, these students were representative of the full classroom and that there would be no reactivity. Subsequent analyses supported both assumptions.

These individual pre and postinstructional interviews—conducted out of the classroom in a separate room—included students' hands-on design of valid experiments as well as verbal justifications for their experiments and the conclusions they drew from them. The interviewer followed the

---

[9]This permission is required by our Institutional Review Board for all experimental work, but not for classroom interventions that do not depart substantially from normal classroom instruction. (This constraint is just one more example of the complexity of applied work.)

same script used in the lab study, except that now students were asked to design and conduct nine experiments: three with each of three variables. After designing each of their experiments, students were asked to justify them. They were also asked to indicate how certain they were about the role of the focal variable, based on the outcome of the experiment. They were asked: "Can you tell for sure from this comparison whether ___ makes a difference? Why are you sure/not sure?" The entire session was recorded on videotape.

Classroom Activities and Assessments

Experiment Evaluation Assessment.   At the start of the first day of the classroom work, all students individually completed a paper and pencil, experiment evaluation test on which they judged precon-structed experiments to be good or bad. Students were presented with 10-page test booklets on which each page displayed a pair of airplanes representing an experimental comparison to test a given variable. For each airplane, there were three variables considered: length of wings, shape of body and size of tailfin. Figure 3.7 depicts one of the types of comparison that were used. Four different types of experiments were presented:

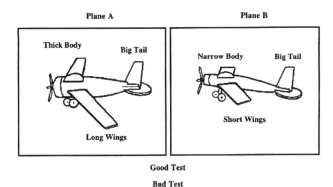

The engineers wanted to compare two planes to figure out whether the length of the wings makes a difference in how fast a model plane flies. Picture A shows one plane they built, and picture B shows the other plane they built.

- They built plane A with a thick body, and they built plane B with a narrow body.
- They built plane A with long wings, and they built plane B with short wings.
- They built plane A with a big tail, and they built plane B with a big tail.

Look at these two pictures carefully. If you think these two pictures show a good way to test if the length of the wings makes a difference, circle the words "Good Test" below. If you think it is a bad way, circle "Bad Test."

Plane A   **Plane B**

Thick Body   Big Tail   Narrow Body   Big Tail

Long Wings   Short Wings

Good Test
Bad Test

FIG. 3.7. Sample page from experiment evaluation assessment booklet used in classroom study (airplanes test). This example has a single confound because the body type is confounded with the focal variable (wing length).

(1) unconfounded comparisons, (2) singly confounded comparisons, (3) multiply confounded comparisons, and (4) noncontrastive comparisons. Students were asked to evaluate these comparisons—that is, to judge whether each picture pair showed a valid experiment to test the focal variable—by circling the word "bad" or "good." (Only unconfounded comparisons are good tests; all others are bad.) This assessment was repeated, using a different set of materials, after classroom instruction (see Fig. 3.6).

Classroom Instruction. Classroom instruction began with a short demonstration of the different ways the ramps can be set up and an explanation of how to map these ramp setups into preformatted tables on the students' individual laboratory worksheets. Following the demonstration, there was a short domain knowledge test, to assess students' prior beliefs about the role of different variables on the ramps. The next phase of classroom work was comprised of three parts: (1) exploratory experiments conducted in small groups,[10] (2) direct instruction for the whole classroom, and (3) application experiments conducted in small groups.

Exploratory Experiments. Students were asked to conduct four different experiments—two to test each of two different variables. Students were required to individually record their experimental setups and data into preformatted worksheets. These worksheets had two sections (see Appendix). The first section asked students to map their ramp setup into a table representation and the second section included questions about the outcome of each experiment and about whether the students were sure or unsure from this experiment about the focal variable's influence on the experimental outcome.

For example, they were asked: "Does the X (the focal variable) of the ramp make a difference? Circle your answer: Yes / No. Think about this carefully, can you tell for sure from this comparison whether X (the current, focal variable) of the ramp makes a difference? Circle your answer: Yes / No." The students were not asked to provide a rationale for their answer. These four experiments conducted in the first stage of classroom work were later analyzed for students' preinstruction knowledge of CVS.

The process whereby these worksheets were designed illustrates some of the complexities of the lab-to-classroom transition. Our initial concep-

---

[10]Assignment of students to groups was determined by the teacher's judgment of the ability of the different students to work together.

tion was very simple: Because we could not simultaneously observe what each group was doing, we needed some way to keep track of their experimental setups. Having each student record them seemed like the most obvious way to do this. In our collaboration with teachers prior to the classroom study, we considered several forms for this worksheet, and finally converged on the one illustrated in the Appendix. Although it seems fairly straightforward, we have no rigorous basis for claiming that it is optimal, or ideally suited for all students or for all CVS instruction. At present, this form simply represents an educated guess of the kind that permeates many transitions between basic research and applied contexts. We return to this issue at the end of the chapter.

Another important difference that emerged in the design of this form—and the classroom process in general—has to do with experimental error. In the course of rolling real balls down real ramps, a variety of errors can occur (even in unconfounded experimental designs). For example, the ball might bump into the side of the ramp, the experimenter (or student) might unintentionally accelerate or impede one of the balls, and so forth. In the lab study, any such anomalous experiments were simply corrected by the experimenter, with a minor comment (e.g., "oops, let's run that one again"). In this way, the experimenter could maintain control over the good and bad executions of each experiment and dismiss any effects of random error. However, in the classroom context, this rigid and artificial control over error is neither possible nor desirable. It is not possible, because—as indicated by the extensive discussions of potential error sources by the children in Lehrer, Schauble, Strom, and Pligge's chapter (chap. 2)—the issue of variation in outcomes becomes a topic of inherent interest when groups of students are running experiments. It is not desirable because students' conceptions of error and their understanding of the distinction between a design error (i.e., a confounded experiment) and other types of error (random error and measurement error) are typically among the instructional objectives of science teachers who—like the teachers in our study—insist that children always do multiple trials for the same experimental setup. Thus, the issue of how students understand error, absent from our lab study, arose for the first time as we moved to the classroom. (As we explain later, it became one of the issues on our list of questions that flowed from the classroom study back to a future lab study.) But this discussion of error is based on hindsight. At the time we designed the worksheet, we encapsulated the entire issue into a simple question about students' certainty about the conclusion they could draw from their experiments.

Direct Instruction. The second stage included about 20 minutes of direct instruction to the entire class on how to create valid experiments. The students' regular science teacher followed these six steps (see Toth, Klahr, & Chen, 2000, for details):

1. *Initiate reflective discussion* based on a "bad comparison"—a multiply confounded comparison between two ramps. After setting up this bad test the teacher asked students whether it was a good or bad test and then provided time and opportunity for students' different views and—often conflicting—explanations. The teacher asked the students to point out what variables were different between the two ramps and asked whether they would be able to tell for sure from this comparison whether the focal variable made a difference in the outcome.

2. *Resolve students' opposing points of view by modeling correct thinking.* After a number of conflicting opinions were heard, the teacher proceeded to reveal that the example was not a good comparison. She explained that other variables, in addition to the focal variable, were different in this comparison, and thus if there was a difference in the outcome, one could *not* tell for sure which variable had caused it. The teacher proceeded to make a good comparison to contrast with the bad one and continued a classroom discussion to determine why the comparison was good.

3. *Test understanding* with another bad comparison. Next, the teacher tested the students' understanding with another bad comparison and asked a similar set of questions.

4. *Reinforce learning* by pointing out the error in the bad comparison.

5. *Summarize the rationale* for CVS. The teacher reinforced her teaching by providing a detailed account of the confounds in the bad test. Next, the teacher created another good comparison and used the same method of classroom discussion as before to review why this test allowed one to tell for sure whether the studied variable makes a difference.

6. Finally, the teacher provided an overall *conceptual justification* for CVS with the following words:

   Now you know that if you are going to see whether something about the ramps makes a difference in how far the balls roll you need to make two ramps that are different only in the one thing that you are testing. Only when you make those kinds of comparisons can you really tell for sure if that thing makes a difference.

Application Experiments. The third phase of the classroom work was created to allow students to apply their newly learned strategy during experimentation. The students' activity in this phase was very similar to what they did in Phase 1, with the exception that during the first application experiment, they tested the effect of a variable they had not tested previously. In the second application, they tested the same variable they had tested in Phase 1.

Measures

We used five measures, similar to those used in the lab study, designed to capture both the procedural and logical components of the control of variables strategy (CVS). They included: (1) *CVS performance score.* We measured students' CVS performance by scoring the experiments students conducted. Each valid (unconfounded) comparison was scored 1, and all other, invalid comparisons were scored 0. (2) *Robust CVS use score.* During individual interviews, a score of 1 was assigned to a valid experiment accompanied by a correct rationale. (3) *Certainty measure.* Probe questions asked students whether they were certain about their conclusion about the role of the focal variable. This question was stated in both the individual interviews and in the classroom worksheets. The certainty measure—not used in the lab study—was intended to capture some of the additional complexity of the type of knowledge students extract from classroom experiences. (4) *Experiment evaluation score.* Correctly indicating whether a given experimental comparison was good or bad gained students a score of 1 and incorrect evaluations were scored 0. (5) *Domain knowledge score.* Correct prediction of the effect for each variable was scored as 1 and incorrect prediction as 0.

RESULTS
FROM THE CLASSROOM STUDY

First, we present the results on procedural knowledge, that is, knowledge about CVS based on all instruments: individual interviews, classroom worksheets, and pre/post experiment evaluation tests. Next, we describe students' domain knowledge, that is, knowledge about which values of the variables make a ball roll farther—before and after classroom instruction. Finally, we report on changes in students' ability to discriminate between good and bad experiments created by others. For each measure, we provide pre and postinstructional comparisons (corresponding to the pairs of connected columns in Fig. 3.6).

Analysis of CVS Performance and Certainty Based on Individual Interviews

CVS performance scores on the individual interviews increased dramatically following instruction, from a mean score of 30% prior to instruction to a mean score of 96% after instruction. With respect to individual students, we defined a CVS "expert" as a student who correctly used CVS on at least eight of the nine trials in the individual interviews. Only one of the 21 children taking the individual pretest interviews was an expert, whereas 20 of the 22 children in the posttest individual interviews exhibited such near-perfect performance.

A similar analysis on robust use (designing an unconfounded experiment *and* providing a CVS rationale) revealed an increase in the mean score from 6% on the pretest to 78% on the posttest. Prior to instruction, none of the 21 students in the preinstructional interview group was a robust expert (i.e., robust use on more than eight of nine trials), whereas after instruction, 12 of the 22 (55%) in the postinstructional interview group were experts. Interestingly, of the 20 CVS use experts, only 12 were robust CVS use experts. That is, a substantial proportion of children who could do CVS failed to explain it adequately.

The analysis of certainty scores also revealed a large improvement in children's confidence about the conclusions they could draw from well-designed experiments. Prior to instruction, children exhibited little differentiation in the confidence with which they drew conclusions from confounded versus unconfounded experiments (see Fig. 3.8). When they designed good experiments, they said they were certain about the effects for 70% of the trials, and when they designed bad experiments, they said they were certain for 60% of the trials. That is, they were only 17% more likely (.70/.60 = 1.17) to be certain about a conclusion drawn from an unconfounded experiment as from a confounded one. In contrast, after instruction, children showed a high degree of differentiation between these two classes of experiments. When they designed good tests, they were certain for 84% of the trials, and when they designed bad tests, they were certain only for 46% of the trials. That is, they were nearly twice as

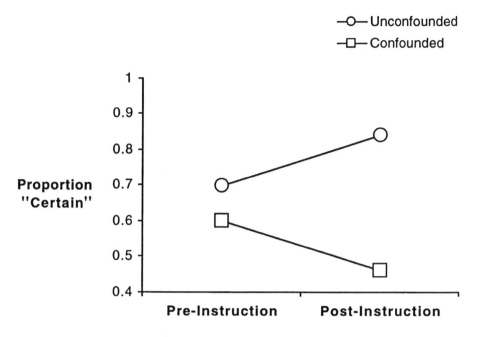

FIG. 3.8.   Proportion of student responses before and after class-room instruction indicating certainty about the conclusions that could be drawn from unconfounded and confounded experiments (based on individual lab interviews).

likely to be confident about the conclusions they could draw from an unconfounded experiment as from a confounded one.

Despite this improvement, we were puzzled by why the proportion of certain conclusions from unconfounded experiments was only 84%, rather than much closer to 100%. We conjecture that there are at least two quite different reasons for this lack of certainty about how to interpret the outcome of what is formally an unconfounded (and therefore unambiguous) experiment. First, the experiment might have been fortuitously unconfounded, even though the student didn't fully understand the logic of CVS. Such uncertainty about the design of an experiment would be likely to be reflected in a low certainty score for the outcome of the experiment. Second, it is possible that some aspect of the execution of an experiment whose design was unconfounded would lead to uncertainty about the outcome. (We return to the different types of error later in the chapter.)

Analysis of CVS Performance and Certainty From Classroom Worksheets

The nested design used in this study allowed us to measure several of the same constructs in both the lab and the classroom (see Fig. 3.6). In this section, we describe the results of the "inner" pairs of pre and postmeasures. As noted earlier, during classroom activities, students worked in small groups. Although the students made their ramp setup decisions and built experimental comparisons together, they each individually filled out a laboratory worksheet. Mean CVS performance scores derived from these worksheets increased from 61% before instruction to 97% after instruction. However, here too, students remained uncertain about the effect of the focal variable on approximately 20% of these experiments.

Analysis of Domain Knowledge Test

Recall that at no point was there any direct instruction regarding the role of the causal variables in the ramps domain. Nevertheless, there was a significant pre to postinstructional increase in domain knowledge. Whereas 79% of the students provided correct answers to all three questions on the domain knowledge test prior to CVS instruction, all students correctly answered all three domain knowledge questions after instruction. Unfortunately, we cannot attribute this gain entirely to the CVS training, because the classroom study had no control group of students who had an equivalent amount of experience in setting up and running experiments without the direct classroom instruction.

Analysis of Experiment Evaluation Scores

We found a similar increase in students' ability to evaluate experiments designed by others. The mean experiment evaluation (airplanes comparison) scores increased from 61% correct on the initial test to 97% correct on the final test. The percentage of students who were evaluation experts—that is, who could correctly evaluate at least 9 of the 10 comparisons—increased from 28% prior to instruction to 75% after instruction. Thus, a brief period of direct instruction interspersed with hands-on experimentation significantly increased students' ability to evaluate the validity of experiments designed by others.

DISCUSSION (CLASSROOM STUDY)

The main goal of the classroom study was to determine whether an instructional procedure that produced substantial and long-lasting learning in the psychology lab could be transformed to an effective instructional unit for everyday classroom use. The laboratory instruction involved one-on-one direct instruction coupled with hands-on experimentation. The classroom teaching also used direct instruction, but now it was instruction directed at several teams of students conducting hands-on experimentation. As indicated by a series of independent but converging measures, the classroom instruction was overwhelmingly successful, not only in terms of statistical significance, but more importantly, with respect to absolute levels of performance. Overall, students' ability to design and assess unconfounded experiments, which ranged from 30% to 60% on various pretests, now was close to perfect.[11] Students learned to do CVS, to explain CVS, and to distinguish between CVS and non-CVS experiments designed by others. Contrary to previous suggestions that early elementary school students are developmentally unable to conduct controlled experiments because it requires formal operational thinking, our results indicate that students' procedural and conceptual knowledge significantly increased after a short, succinct direct instruction session combined with hands-on experimentation.[12]

SHIPS AND BEACONS REVISITED

Our goal in this chapter has been to describe a case in which the intersection between psychological research and classroom practice is not the empty set. In this concluding section, we discuss some of the possible reasons for the success of our lab-to-classroom transition, and then we discuss some of the issues related to the classroom-to-lab aspect of the "mutual illumination" notion.

---

[11]See Toth, Klahr, and Chen (2000) for a more detailed analysis of the classroom study.

[12]One reviewer of this chapter pointed out the fact that we had very "clean" classrooms: private schools, cooperative teachers, well-behaved students. However, these factors still produced average CVS scores of around 50% prior to our intervention.

Why Did Our Instruction Work?

To what can we attribute the success of our classroom instruction? Why was our simple procedure so effective, when, as indicated earlier, even fourth graders who had been exposed to high-quality science curricula for several years could design unconfounded experiments on fewer than one third of their initial attempts, and could correctly explain their designs on fewer than 10% of their attempts (based on the individual interviews)? In order to give a complete answer to this question, we would have to carefully examine these children's prior exposure to CVS instruction and activities. However, in lieu of such information, we can look at a few examples of "model" practice, and contrast our procedures with what we find there.

Our examination of dozens of texts and monographs about science teaching and learning suggests that, at best, CVS receives only a few paragraphs in a handful of books. And in the rare instances when it is taught, instruction is both brief and confusing, as illustrated by the following two examples.

Example 1. A Middle-School Science Text.   Consider the excerpt shown in Table 3.6, taken from the opening chapter of a widely used middle-school science text. (Although students do not use texts extensively in K-4 science instruction, teachers get advice and suggestions from a variety of such books and other teacher-oriented materials; for example, the journal *Science and Children.* The content of such articles tends to be similar to the illustrative example used here.)

At first glance, the excerpt seems like a reasonable treatment of many of the issues involved in CVS. However, a careful examination reveals several potential difficulties. Consider, for example, the presumption that the student would believe that amount of light is a growth factor for mold (sent. 2). To a student lacking any domain knowledge about the growth of mold, this might seem as plausible (or implausible) a factor as type of container, or food source, or day of the week. Indeed, as the student discovers later (sent. 12), the light variable is irrelevant.

Next, while intending to provide a control for another possible causal variable (water), the passage introduces an unnecessary quantification of that variable (i.e., Why 10 drops each? Why not 12 drops each? Is it the "10" that's important here, or the "each"?) and it adds a procedure whose impact is not explicit (Is "cap tightly" important?).

TABLE 3.6

Example of a Description of a Control of Variables Strategy
(from HBJ Science - Nova Edition, 1989)

1. A simple question occurs to you.

2. Will mold grow better in the light or the dark? This, you decide, calls for an investigation.

3. So you divide a slice of bread in half and place each in a jar.

4. You add ten drops of water to each jar and cap tightly.

5. You put one in a dark closet.

6. You keep the other one in the light.

7. In a few days, you make an observation.

8. You observe that the mold in the light is growing better than the mold in the dark.

9. From this observation, you infer that mold grows better in the light.

10. You are sure of your answer.

11. After all, the evidence seems clear.

12. Yet, in truth, scientists know that light has no effect on the growth of mold.

13. Why, then, did the investigation make it seem as though mold grows better in the light?

14. Think a moment.

15. Because the amount of light varied, we say that light was a **variable**.

16. Since light was the only variable considered, you assumed that it was the light that affected the growth of the mold.

17. Was light the only variable you changed? Or could you have changed another variable without realizing it?

18. What about temperature? Suppose that the temperature of the mold in the light was higher.

19. Then it is possible that the higher temperature, not the light itself, caused the growth.

20. Whenever you do an investigation, there may be several possible variables.

21. If you wish to see the effects of changing one variable, such as the amount of light, then you must make sure all the other possible variables remain the same.

22. That is, you must **control** the other variables.

23. In this investigation, to control the variable temperature, you must keep the temperature the same for the mold in the light and the mold in the dark.

24. If you had done so, you would have discovered that the mold grew just as well in the dark closet.

25. However, even then you could not be sure of your conclusion.

26. The investigation must be repeated many times.

27. After all, what happens once can be an accident.

28. Scientists don't base their conclusions on one trial.

29. They repeat the investigation again and again and again.

30. The rest of this year you will be an apprentice.

31. You will be an investigator.

32. You may even decide one day to become a scientist.

Note: Emphasis in original. Sentence numbers added.

Following the quantitative variable, the passage introduces categorical variables (sent. 5–6), but without any explicit statement that the experiment will be run in terms of categorical variables, rather than continuous variables. (And this is in contrast to the unnecessarily specific quantification of the amount of water.)

The goal of the next section (sent. 9–18) appears to be to demonstrate that it is easy to forget potentially important variables. More specifically, the intent is to show the student that it is important to consider causal variables other than light, and that temperature is one such possibility. But this example is problematic because it confounds the domain-general notion of CVS with the domain-specific knowledge that temperature might be a causal variable in this domain. Thus, as stated here, the example might convey the mistaken notion that the logic of the control of variables strategy is flawed in some way. Moreover, the example takes the student down a garden path to a pattern of evidence that is particularly difficult to interpret. Young children are easily misled when they are faced with a single piece of positive evidence, and several remaining sources of unknown evidence (Fay & Klahr, 1996; Piéraut-Le Bonniec, 1980). They tend to believe that the single instance renders the situation determinate, even though they will acknowledge that additional evidence might change that decision.

In closing, the passage abruptly introduces the notion of error variance (sent. 25), but it does so in a way that suggests that just when you think you are sure, you are really not sure. It is not surprising that students come away from such examples believing that their subjective opinions are as valid as the results of scientific investigations.

Finally, as brief as it is, the example represents the *only* explicit attempt in the entire book to teach the principles of good experimental design, the logic of rival hypothesis testing, and the distinctions between valid and invalid inferences or determinate and indeterminate situations.

In summary, the example attempts to cover too many things at once, and it confounds issues pertaining to the abstract logic of unconfounded experimentation and valid inference with other issues having to do with domain-specific knowledge and plausible hypotheses about causal variables.

Example 2. Model Inquiry Unit From NSES.   As noted earlier, the middle-school science text example is used only to illustrate the complexity and subtlety of the topic. More relevant to our point about the inadequacy of the material available to K through 4 teachers who would like to teach CVS is the model inquiry unit entitled "Earthworms" provided in the NSES. The full unit carefully and sensitively elaborates a process whereby third graders interested in creating a habitat for earthworms could learn about the earthworm life cycle, needs, structure, and function. However, its treatment of CVS is extremely sparse:

> Two groups were investigating what kind of environment the earthworms liked best. Both were struggling with several variables at once—moisture, light, and temperature. Ms. F. planned to let groups struggle before suggesting that students focus on one variable at a time. She hoped they might come to this idea on their own. (NSES, 1995, pp. 34–35)

This brief treatment of CVS—consisting of only about 50 of the 1,000 words in the Earthworms inquiry unit—provides virtually no guidance to the teacher on how to present the rationale of CVS, how to provide positive and negative instances, how to draw children's attention to the variables and the design of tests, or how to guide students in interpreting results from controlled or uncontrolled experiments.

Contrasts Between Examples and Our Procedure

These examples suggest several potentially important contrasts between our approach and what children had experienced earlier. First, it is clear that, in typical classroom situations, the detailed components of CVS are not adequately isolated and emphasized either directly, as decontextualized domain-general principles or indirectly, as contextualized skill in a specific domain. In contrast, our instruction avoided, insofar as possible, potential confusion between CVS logic errors and inadequate domain knowledge by making it very clear exactly what dimensions were under consideration at all times. It also used positive and negative examples of CVS designs, and it presented students with both a mechanistic procedure and a conceptual justification for why the procedure worked. We presented several examples of each, so that students could construct an internal representation of CVS that could be transferred, via analogical mapping, to new, but structurally similar situations.

Second, in contrast to the second example's suggestion that children "might come to this idea on their own," we made instruction highly explicit and direct. Prior to the results of our lab study, this focus on explicit instruction was based partly on our own intuitions and partly on the results of other studies of the power of detailed and direct instruction about complex procedures (e.g., Klahr & Carver, 1988). The results of our lab study further demonstrated, in the specific context of CVS, that children find it very difficult to discover CVS on their own. As we have argued several times, we believe that there is too much here for students to acquire on their own, via discovery, so we opted instead for explicit and direct instruction about each of these aspects of CVS.

NEW ISSUES IN BASIC RESEARCH ON SCIENTIFIC THINKING

Although we have argued for a bidirectional flow between lab and classroom, thus far, we have mainly emphasized only one side of that flow: the lab to classroom transition. In this concluding section, we illustrate the other side of that flow by elaborating on some of the new issues that the classroom study has raised—issues that we will continue to investigate in the laboratory.

Representation

Recall that the classroom study used a worksheet on which students recorded the way that they set up their ramps. At the time we prepared these worksheets, we were working under the usual kinds of scheduling deadlines that surround any attempt to intervene in an ongoing "live" classroom during the school year, and so we did not have the luxury of carefully considering just what was involved in asking students to carry out this "trivial" task. However, as psychologists, we are well aware that such mappings entail a complex set of procedures for establishing correspondence between the physical setup of the ramps and a set of marks on paper that represent that setup. Indeed, the ability to move between various equivalent representations for both apparatus and data is one of the commonly stated goals of science educators, and represents the main focus of the chapter by Lehrer, Schauble, Strom, and Pligge (chap. 2). Only with systematic study in a laboratory context on just this issue could we claim that the particular form that we used is the best way to capture students' representations of their experiments. Thus, the issue of the most effective type of representation for this and similar types of classroom exercises has become a topic not only on our research agenda for further laboratory studies, but it has also become a potential instructional objective for subsequent classroom work by the teachers in our schools.

Although the lab studies of representation remain in the planning stages, we have already begun to explore the representation issue in the classroom by introducing a very simple change in our procedure. Rather than providing each group with a pair of ramps, we provide only one ramp. This requires students to set up, execute, and record the effect of one combination of variables, and then follow with another setup, execution, and recording. We believe that this will challenge students to consider the important role of "inscriptions" (Lehrer, Schauble, Strom, & Pligge, chap. 2) as permanent, inspectable representations of transient events, and that it will motivate them to more accurately record and better interpret such external representations and their role in science.

Certainty and Error

Although our classroom instruction produced substantial increases both in students' ability to design unconfounded experiments and in their certainty about the conclusions they could draw from them, there remained a nontrivial proportion of valid experiments from which students were unwilling to draw unambiguous conclusions. Recall that, even after instruction, students indicated uncertainty about the conclusions they could draw from approximately 15% of their valid experiments (see Fig. 3.8). This occurred for both the interview and laboratory assessments. Because *all* the variables in the ramps domain influenced the outcome measure—that is, the distance a ball rolled down a ramp—this finding was, at first, puzzling to us.

Further consideration led to the following conjecture. We believe that children found it difficult to distinguish between a logical error (such as a confounded experiment) and other types of error (such as random error in the execution of the experiment or measurement error), and that they were unsure about which of several replications of the same setup was the "true" result. Although these are important aspects of a rich understanding of experimentation, we did not include them in our highly focused instructional goals. Thus, two additional topics for both detailed lab research and further classroom instruction arose: the distinction among various types of errors involved in scientific experimentation, and a better understanding of how children extract a general conclusion from several replications of the same experiment.

These two particular issues—representational competence and understanding of error—certainly do not exhaust the list of questions arising during our classroom study that could be further investigated in the psychology lab. But they serve to illustrate how complex issues that arise in the authentic and complex setting of the science classroom can be returned to the psychology lab for further controlled investigation. More generally, they provide concrete examples of the two-way influence of relevance and importance between the lab and the classroom. To return to our opening metaphor, we believe that the work described in this chapter, as well as in many of the other chapters in this volume, support the position that the two ships of science education and cognitive development need not pass in darkness, but can, instead, be mutually illuminating.

ACKNOWLEDGMENTS

Portions of the work described in this chapter were supported in part by grants from NICHHD (HD25211) and from the James S. McDonnell Foundation (96–37). We thank Jen Schnakenberg, Sharon Roque, Anne Siegel, and Rose Russo for their assistance with data collection and preliminary analysis, and John Anderson, Milena Koziol Nigam, Amy Masnick, and especially Sharon Carver for their comments and suggestions on earlier drafts of this paper. This project could not have proceeded without the generous cooperation of the parents and administrators at The Ellis School, Winchester-Thurston School, Shady Side Academy, and The Carlow College Campus School, as well as the active involvement of the master teachers who allowed us into their classrooms and their teaching practice, Linn Cline, Patricia Cooper, Cheryl Little, and Dr. Mary Wactlar. Finally, our thanks to the children at all of these schools who participated with enthusiasm and excitement.

REFERENCES

Amsel, E., & Brock, S. (1996). The development of evidence evaluation skills. *Cognitive Development, 11*(4), 523–550.

Brown, A. (1992). Design experiments: Theoretical and methodological challenges in creating complex interventions in classroom settings. *The Journal of the Learning Sciences, 2,* 141–178.

Brown, A. (1997). Transforming schools into communities of thinking and learning about serious matters. *American Psychologist, 52,* 399–413.

Bruer, J. T. (1993). *Schools for thought: A science of learning in the classroom.* Cambridge, MA: MIT Press.

Bruner, J. S., Goodnow, J. J., & Austin, G. A. (1956). A study of thinking. New York: Science Editions.

Bullock, M., Ziegler, A., & Martin, S. (1993). Scientific thinking. In F. E. Weinert & W. Schneider (Eds.), *LOGIC Report 9: Assessment Procedures and Results of Wave 6* (pp. 66–110). New York: Wiley.

Bullock, M., & Ziegler, A. (1999). Scientific reasoning: developmental and individual differences. In F. E. Weinert & W. Schneider (Eds.), *Individual development from 3 to 12: Findings from the Munich Longitudinal Study* (pp. 309–336). Munich: Max Plank Institute for Psychological Research.

Carey, S. (1985). Conceptual change in childhood. Cambridge, MA: MIT Press.

Case, R. (1974). Structures and strictures: Some functional limitations on the course of cognitive growth. *Cognitive Psychology, 6,* 544–573.

Chen, Z., & Klahr, D. (1999). All other things being equal: Children's acquisition of the Control of Variables Strategy. *Child Development, 70* (5), 1098–1120.

Christensen, C. A., & Cooper, T. J. (1991). The effectiveness of instruction in cognitive strategies in developing proficiency in single-digit addition. *Cognition and Instruction, 8,* 363–371.

Collins, A. (1992). Toward a design science of education. In E. Scanlon & T. O'Shea (Eds.), *New directions in educational technology* (pp. 15–22). New York: Springer-Verlag.

Das-Small, E. A., Klapwijk, M. J., & van det Leij, A. (1996). Training of perceptual unit processing in children with a reading disability. *Cognition and Instruction, 14* (2), 221–250.

Dunbar, K. (1993). Concept discovery in a scientific domain. *Cognitive Science, 17,* 397–434.

Fay, A. L., & Klahr, D. (1996). Knowing about guessing and guessing about knowing: Preschoolers' understanding of indeterminacy. *Child Development, 67,* 689–716.

Fennema, E., Carpenter, T. P., Franke, M. L., Levi, L., Jacobs, V. R., & Empson, S. B. (1996). A longitudinal study of learning to use children's thinking in mathematics instruction. *Journal for Research in Mathematics Education, 27,* 403–434.

HBJ Science—Nova Edition. (1989). Orlando, FL: Harcourt Brace.

Jacoby, J. (1978). On interpreting the effects of repetition: Solving a problem versus remembering a solution. *Journal of Verbal Learning and Verbal Behavior, 17,* 649–667.

Klahr, D. (Ed.). (1976). *Cognition and instruction.* Hillsdale, NJ: Lawrence Erlbaum Associates.

Klahr, D. (2000). *Exploring science: The cognition and development of discovery processes* Cambridge, MA: MIT Press.

Klahr, D., & Carver, S. M. (1988). Cognitive objectives in a LOGO debugging curriculum: Instruction, learning, and transfer. *Cognitive Psychology, 20,* 362–404.

Klahr, D., & Carver, S. M. (1995). Scientific thinking about scientific thinking. *Monographs of the Society for Research in Child Development, 245* (60, serial no. 4), 137–151.

Klahr, D., & Dunbar, K. (1988). Dual space search during scientific reasoning. *Cognitive Science, 12,* 1–55.

Klahr, D., Fay, A. L., & Dunbar, K. (1993). Heuristics for scientific experimentation: A developmental study. *Cognitive Psychology, 24* (1), 111–146.

Koslowski, B. (1996). *Theory and evidence: The development of scientific reasoning.* Cambridge, MA: MIT Press.

Koslowski, B., & Okagaki, L. (1986). Non-Humean indices of causation in problem-solving situations: Causal mechanisms, analogous effects, and the status of rival alternative accounts. *Child Development, 57,* 1100–1108.

Koslowski, B., Okagaki, L., Lorenz, C., & Umbach, D. (1989). When covariation is not enough: The role of causal mechanism, sampling method, and sample size in causal reasoning. *Child Development, 60,* 1316–1327.

Kuhn, D. (1989). Children and adults as intuitive scientists. *Psychological Review, 96,* 674–689.

Kuhn, D., & Angelev, J. (1976). An experimental study of the development of formal operational thought. *Child Development, 47,* 697–706.

Kuhn, D., Amsel, E., & O'Loughlin, M. (1988). *The development of scientific reasoning skills.* Orlando, FL: Academic Press.

Kuhn, D., Schauble, L., & Garcia-Mila, M. (1992). Cross-domain development of scientific reasoning. *Cognition and Instruction, 9* (4), 285–327.

Kuhn, D., Garcia-Mila, M., Zohar, A., & Andersen, C. (1995). Strategies of knowledge acquisition. *Monographs of the Society for Research in Child Development. 60* (4, Serial No. 245, pp. 1–128).

McCloskey, M. (1983). Naïve theories of motion. In D. Gentner & A. L. Stevems (Eds.), *Mental Models* (pp. 299–324). Hillsdale, NJ: Lawrence Erlbaum Associates.

McDaniel, M. A., & Schlager, M. S. (1990). Discovery learning and transfer of problem-solving skills. *Cognition and Instruction, 7,* 129–159.

McGilly, K. (Ed.). (1994). *Classroom lessons: Integrating cognitive theory and classroom practice.* Cambridge, MA: MIT Press.

National Science Education Standards (NSES). (1995). Washington, DC: National Academy Press.

Piéraut-Le Bonniec, G. (1980). *The development of modal reasoning: The genesis of necessity and possibility notions.* New York: Academic Press.

Ross, A. J. (1988). Controlling variables: A meta-analysis of training studies. *Review of Educational Research, 58* (4), 405–437.

Ruffman, T., Perner, J., Olsen, D. R., & Doherty, M. (1993). Reflecting on scientific thinking: Children's understanding of the hypothesis-evidence relation. *Child Development, 64,* 1617–1636.

Schauble, L. (1990). Belief revision in children: The role of prior knowledge and strategies for generating evidence. *Journal of Experimental Child Psychology, 49,* 31–57.

Schauble, L. (1996). The development of scientific reasoning in knowledge-rich contexts. *Developmental Psychology, 32,* 102–109.

Schauble, L., Glaser, R., Raghavan, K., & Reiner, M. (1991). Causal models and experimentation strategies in scientific reasoning. *The Journal of the Learning Sciences, 1,* 201–238.

Shaklee, H., & Paszek, D. (1985). Covariation judgment: Systematic rule use in middle childhood. *Childhood Development, 56,* 1229–1240.

Siegler, R. S. (1976). Three aspects of cognitive development. *Cognitive Psychology, 8,* 481–520.

Siegler, R. S., & Liebert, R. M. (1975). Acquisition of formal scientific reasoning by 10- and 13-year-olds: Designing a factorial experiment. *Developmental Psychology, 10,* 401–402.

Sigel, I. E., & Renninger, K. A. (Eds.). (1998). *Handbook of child psychology, Vol 4. Child psychology in practice.* New York: Wiley.

Strauss, S. (1998). Cognitive development and science education: Toward a middle level model. In I. Sigel & K. A. Renninger (Eds.), *Handbook of child psychology, Vol. 4. Child psychology in practice* (pp. 357–400). New York: Wiley.

Toth, E. E., Klahr, D., & Chen, Z. (2000). Bridging research and practice: A research-based classroom intervention for teaching experimentation skills to elementary school children. *Cognition and Instruction, 18* (4), 423–459.

Tschirgi, J. E. (1980). Sensible reasoning: A hypothesis about hypotheses. *Child Development, 51,* 1–10.

Vosniadou, S., & Brewer, W. F. (1992). Mental models of the earth: A study of conceptual change in childhood. *Cognitive Psychology, 24,* 535–585.

Wason, P. C. (1960). On the failure to eliminate hypotheses in a conceptual task. *Quarterly Journal of Experimental Psychology, 12,* 129–140.

White, B. Y., & Frederiksen, J. R. (1998). Inquiry, modeling, and metacognition: Making science accessible to all students. *Cognition and Instruction, 16,* 3–118.

Does the surface make a difference?

I. FIRST COMPARISON FOR SURFACE:

How your ramp was set up:

Teacher reads the table aloud to students and instructs them on how to fill it out: circle answer corresponding to team's ramp setup.

VARIABLES	RAMP A	RAMP B
Surface	Smooth or Rough	Smooth or Rough
Steepness	High or Low	High or Low
Length of run	Long or Short	Long or Short
Type of ball	Golf ball or Rubber ball	Golf ball or Rubber ball

What happened after you rolled the balls down:

1. On which ramp did the ball roll farther most of the time? Circle your answer.

RAMP A   or   RAMP B

Teacher tells students : "Think about why you set up the ramps the way you did."

2. Does the surface of the ramp make a difference? Circle your answer.

YES   or   NO

3. Think about this carefully, can you tell for sure from this comparison whether tl surface of the ramp makes a difference? Circle your answer.

VERY SURE   or   NOT SO SURE

119

Part II

Teachers and Instructional Strategies

4

The Role of the Teacher in Making Sense of Classroom Experiences and Effecting Better Learning

Jim Minstrell
Talaria Inc.

A CHANGE IN PERSPECTIVE

In this chapter, I describe a personal and professional odyssey as I developed from being a teacher alone in my own classroom, to a researcher on students' thinking, to a professional developer of a practical framework for making sense of classroom experiences and designing environments for effecting better learning. No longer alone, I am now a participant in collaborations among teachers, researchers, developers, and policymakers. But, the story starts nearly 40 years ago.

During my first few years of teaching, I focused mostly on what I was doing as a teacher. I carefully crafted my presentations and revised them to make my presentations clearer. I was told by my administrators and by my students that I was "one of the best teachers" they had had, but I wondered precisely what learning effects I had had on my students. The students did well on my tests as long as I kept the questions close to the procedures that I had "trained" them to do. But, when I slipped in questions that required a deep understanding of the concepts and reasoning I supposedly had been teaching, I was disappointed. I became more curious about the nature of learning in my classroom.

After only 4 years of teaching, I had the opportunity to participate in research and curriculum development on the national level with Project Physics (1970). Although the methods used by the researchers in that project were very sophisticated and served the needs of a large curriculum development project, they were not useful for my interest in improving my effectiveness as a teacher in my own classroom. Although the results seemed too far from my issues of learning in my classroom, the experience initiated my interest in research.

Six years into my teaching career, I began working part-time at the University of Washington with Professor Arnold Arons, a colleague and mentor through whom (not from whom) I learned a lot about science and about the capabilities and difficulties of developing conceptual understanding. In working with our university students (mostly teachers and prospective teachers), Arons coached me to keep my hands in my pockets and make the students show me what they did, or what they would do, about the problem. Prior to that, my inclination was not unlike many well-meaning teachers whose approach is: "Here, let me show you how to do it," from which the students learned little more than how "smart" I was.

Arons also coached me to listen to what the students were saying, reminding me that I had two ears but only one mouth and to use them in that proportion. In addition to my learning much about physics, I changed my perspective from a focus on me as a deliverer of knowledge to a focus on my students and what they were learning. My critical questions as a teacher became: "What is the understanding of my students?" and "What experiences can I put before the students to cause them to have to rethink their present understanding and reconstruct their understanding in order to make it more consistent with a broader set of phenomena?"

This has evolved into my line of classroom research and has affected my teaching greatly. When I finished my doctoral dissertation, I applied for a grant to support released time for me to conduct research on the teaching and learning of my students. That has become the natural, and practical, setting within which I conduct a line of research. At the same time, my primary responsibility has been to teach, or, more correctly, to be responsible for my students' learning. Now, in the classroom, I always wear both the hat of a researcher and the hat of a teacher. Each perspective helps me to direct, and to make sense of, the results of the other.

Classroom-based research questions focused my attention on what students were learning. How better could I understand my students' thinking, their conceptual understanding, and their reasoning in the natural setting of the classroom? What effects, if any, did my teaching have on their learning? How could I effect better learning? Will my results be of use beyond my classroom?

In the early stages of my action research, my activities as a researcher were informal. They amounted mostly to anecdotes that, to me, represented evidence of either the learning I intended or the learning that did not occur. I looked for correlation between gross measures like grades in my class (e.g., high school physics) and possibly predicting variables like grades in other courses (e.g., geometry) and more "standardized" measures (e.g., "the Classroom Test of Formal Operations," (A. Lawson, personal communication, 1977).

Sometimes, I was testing an intervention as short as a particular lesson and, at other times, the effects of aspects of an entire year's program. Occasionally, I conducted a controlled experiment. Sometimes, I simply gathered descriptive data and attempted to interpret the results.

Gradually, there evolved a line of investigation in my classroom that focused on describing my students' initial and developing understanding and reasoning about the content of the courses I was teaching. Later, that line of investigation evolved into designing and testing instructional interventions explicitly adapted to address students' difficulties in understanding and reasoning.

This chapter has two parts. First, I describe my attempts as a teacher–researcher to create a coherent view within which I can make sense of my experiences in the classroom. In the second part, I describe how, from this view, I redesign classroom experiences to effect better learning on the part of my students.

MAKING SENSE
OF CLASSROOM EXPERIENCES

Data Gathering in My Classroom

After I began to listen to my students more carefully and to solicit their ideas, I needed to gather data systematically. I enlisted the help of my students and their parents who, at the beginning of the school year, were asked to consider and sign consent forms for participation in my studies. I warned my students that I might be doing some atypical teaching and assessment during my efforts to better understand and address their thinking. I bought a small, battery-run audiorecorder that I kept on my desk in the classroom. Later, I bought a video camera and recorder that I set up when I anticipated discussions that might be informative to other teachers. While students interacted in small groups, I carried the audiorecorder with me and turned it on when I came to an interesting discussion or when students came to me with questions or ideas they had about the phenomena under investigation. During large group discussions, when it appeared that an informative discussion was likely to develop, I started the recorder and let it run throughout the class period.

On one such occasion, early in my experience as a classroom researcher, the audiorecorder was running when we were beginning the study of force and motion. I had asked the students about the forces on a book "at rest" on the front table. The students drew and wrote their answers on paper quietly. While I was walking around the room, I noticed two dominant answers, involving whether the table exerted a force. One suggested that the table exerted an upward force (consistent with the scientists' view), and the other suggested no such upward force. When our discussion began, I drew those two diagrams on the board and took a poll. There was an observer in the class that day, so I asked him to record the number of students who raised their hands during these brief surveys. The answers were divided approximately evenly between those who thought that the table exerted an upward force and those who thought that it did not.

I asked for volunteers to support one or the other of these positions and discovered that the difference revolved around whether one believed that passive objects like tables could exert forces. I decided to test my conjecture by putting the book on the outstretched hand of a student. We took a poll on the students' beliefs about this situation. Nearly everyone thought that the hand exerted an upward force. I inquired about the difference between the two situations, and the students argued that the hand was alive and that the person made muscular adjustments to support the book, especially when I stacked several additional books on top of the first one. The observer recorded the number of students who raised their hands. The teacher side of me wanted the students to be able to see the similarities between the table and the hand situations, but it was clear that the students were seeing the differences. Again thinking about how I would address their concern, I pulled a spring out of a drawer, hung it from hardware, and attached the book to the spring. The spring stretched until the book was supported. I asked again for diagrams and took another poll, recorded by the observer. Nearly all of the students believed that the spring must be exerting an upward force. I countered by asking whether the spring was alive or how this situation was like the book on the hand. The students did not believe that the spring was alive with muscular activity, but that it could stretch or deform and adjust in a way to support the book. And, how was this different from the table? They suggested that the table was rigid; it did not stretch or deform like the spring. "Ability to deform or adjust" now seemed to be the difference between these believable situations and my target situation of the book on the table. I put on my teacher hat, darkened the room, pulled out a light projector, and set it up so that the light reflected off the table top onto the far wall. Using this "light lever," I alternately put heavy objects on and off the table, and we noticed the movement of the light on the far wall. The students concluded that the table must be bending also. With my teacher hat still in place, I summarized by suggesting that force is a concept invented by humankind. As such, we are free to define force in any way we want, but the scientist notes the similarity of "at rest" in several situations. Then, wanting to be consistent, he thinks of one explanation that works for all of the situations; the explanation involving balanced forces. This means that the scientist's definition of force will include "passive" support by tables as well as "active" support by more active things like hands or springs.

The description of this action research became the material in my first published research article (Minstrell, 1982a). The situation has been analyzed since by other researchers and incorporated into curricular materials (Camp et al., 1994). It is important to note that, in this discovery mode, the "hats" of researcher and teacher are being interchanged quickly in an effort to both understand the students' thinking and affect their learning.

It was a memorable lesson for me and for my students. It made them think differently about whether actions are active or passive and about the idea of force. These lessons that students keep referring back to later in the year, or in subsequent years, I have come to call "benchmark lessons," a metaphor from the geographical survey reference to benchmarks that one finds cemented into rocks (diSessa & Minstrell, 1998).

To find out what students were thinking, I designed and set problematic situations before them at the beginning of most units of study. These tasks were typically in the form of preinstruction quizzes, but only the students' honest effort, not the "correctness" of the answer, counted for credit (Minstrell, 1982b). Students were asked for an answer and reasoning for how the answer made sense. From the sorts of tasks I set and from the answers and the rationale students gave, I inferred their conceptual understanding. In this research approach, I was using methods similar to the clinical interviews conducted by cognitive scientists except that I was interviewing my whole class (Bruer, 1993). As a teacher, the activities I set in class tended to be driven by the class as a whole, rather than by an individual learner. Still, the method allowed me to "know" the tentative thinking of most of the individuals in my class as well as the thinking of the class in general.

This procedure allowed me to "discover" aspects of my students' thinking. For example, before I started a dynamics unit, I used the University of Massachusetts Mechanics Diagnostic (J. Clement, personal communication, 1982) to identify ideas my students seemed to have about the forces that objects exerted on each other during interaction. Even though most high school students were able to repeat the phrase "for every action, there is an equal and opposite reaction," they did not apply the idea to objects interacting. I found that most students initially attended to surface features and argued that the heavier, or the stronger, or the most active object, or the one that inflicted the greater change in the other object, exerted the greater force. Often, that was as far as I could go in terms of learning about students' thinking, creating the hypothesis about their thinking, and then instructing with that thinking in mind.

However, as time and opportunity allowed, I also attempted to "verify" my hypotheses about students' thinking. I designed problematic situations that contained those features specifically, and based on my assumptions about the students' thinking, I predicted their answers and rationale. If they responded according to my prediction, I had some degree of confirmation that my assumptions about their thinking were correct.

Notice that the procedure is consistent with science as a method. As a researcher, I was generating and testing hypotheses about students' thinking. As a teacher, I wanted to know generally what the thinking was so that I could choose or design more relevant activities. But, my efforts also had aspects of engineering, that is, designing more effective learning environments. I wanted to design benchmark lessons that might have a better chance of initiating change in students' conceptions, for example, by incorporating a broader set of phenomena, constructing new conceptions or new models that likely would be more consistent with formal scientific thinking. The results of these more systematic approaches to identifying students' ideas have appeared in a working document accumulating facets of students' thinking in physics (Minstrell, 1992; also see www.talariainc.com/facet).

Describing Facets of Students' Thinking About Events and Ideas

Between the research I was doing and the accumulation of research others had done relative to my interests in the teaching of introductory physics, my list of students' misperceptions, misconceptions, procedural errors, and so forth was getting quite long, too long. As a classroom teacher, I needed a practical way of organizing students' thinking so that I could address it in the classroom. I grouped the problematic ideas and approaches around students' understanding or application of significant "big ideas" in the discipline of physics, for example, the meaning of average velocity. Other ideas were organized around explanations or interpretations of some classic event in the physical world, for example, explaining falling bodies.

The usual term applied to these problematic ideas was "misconception," and that bothered me. Many of the ideas seemed valid in certain contexts. For example, "heavier falls faster" is a conclusion that applies pretty well to situations like dropping a marble and a sheet of paper. Part of the complexity of understanding science is to know the conditions under which such a conclusion holds and when it doesn't and to understand why that can happen in some situations and not in others. Also, some of the schema applied were more procedural errors than misconceptions, for example, finding the average velocity by simply adding the initial and final velocities and dividing by 2 in a context in which an object is accelerating in a nonuniform way. In discussions, my colleagues and I talked about these various sorts of problematic aspects of students' thinking as different facets of students' thinking about physics. The reference term "facets" has stuck with us.

Facets, then, are individual pieces, or constructions of a few pieces of knowledge or strategies of reasoning. "Facet clusters" are the small collections of facets about some big idea or explanations of some big event. Most important of all is that facets represent a practical way of talking about students' thinking in the classroom. Teachers should be able to recognize particular facets in what students say or do in the classroom when discussing ideas or events related to the discipline (Minstrell, in press).

I make no claim about what is actually going on inside the learner's head. But, the facets perspective is useful in describing the products of students' thinking and in guiding the subsequent instruction in the classroom. I have attempted to order the facets within a cluster from those that are the most problematic to some that are less troublesome and so on up the ladder to the learning target. This rough ranking is not for scoring but to help teachers monitor progress up the ladder of facets of thinking by individual students or by the class as a whole. The ranking is typically decided based on two criteria: How problematic will future learning be for a student who displays this facet, and/or, based on an effective teaching experience, which facet seems to arise first in the development of the unit. A critical test of the importance of the idea is that if the student leaves my class with this idea, their subsequent learning in this domain could be very deeply curtailed. Those ideas get addressed first. Less problematic ideas likely get treated later in the unit of instruction. Of course, in instruction, while I am challenging each problematic facet, I am attempting to build a case for the goal facet, the learning target, the standard for learning the big ideas of the unit. An example cluster of facets is discussed in the next section along with instructional implications associated with the facets.

INSTRUCTIONAL DESIGN BASED ON STUDENTS' THINKING

Using Facets to Create a Facet-Based Learning Environment

In this section of the chapter, I describe how the facet organization of students' thinking is used to create a facet-based learning environment. The purpose of the environment is to guide students as they construct a more scientific understanding of the related ideas. Facets can be and are being used to diagnose students' ideas, to choose or design instructional activities, and to design assessment activities and interpret results (Bruer, 1993; Hunt and Minstrell, 1994; Minstrell, 1989, 1992, in press; Minstrell & Stimpson, 1996.) I use a particular facet cluster to demonstrate the creation and implementation of such a facet-based learning environment. I consider one part of one unit in our physics program and use this context to discuss the practical implications of my assumptions about students' understanding and learning.

One of the goals in our introductory physics course includes understanding the nature of gravity and its effects and differentiating gravitational effects from the effects of ambient fluid (e.g., air or water) mediums on objects in them, whether the objects are at rest or moving through the fluid. For many introductory physics students, an initial difficulty involves a confusion between which are effects of gravity and which are effects of the surrounding fluid medium. When one attempts to weigh something, does it weigh what it does because the air pushes down on it? Or, is the scale reading that would give the true weight of the object distorted somehow because of the air? Or, is there absolutely no effect by air? Because these have been issues for beginning students, the students are usually highly motivated to engage in thoughtful discussion of the issues. This is the content for my description of a facet-based instructional design.

Eliciting Students' Ideas Prior to Instruction in Order to Build an Awareness of the Initial Understanding

At the beginning of several units or subunits, my teacher colleagues and I administer a preinstruction survey containing one or more questions. One purpose is to provide the teacher with knowledge of what are going to be the learning issues in this content with this group of students and to provide specific knowledge of which students exhibit what sorts of initial ideas. A second purpose is to help students become more aware of the content and issues involved in the upcoming unit.

When I first began doing research on students' conceptions, I apologized to the students for asking these questions at the beginning of units. The students convinced me to stop apologizing, saying "I hate these preinstruction questions, but they help me know what I am going to need to learn and know by the end of the unit." At the end of the year, students reported that these questions were one of the worst things about my course but that they were also one of the best things about the course. They didn't like answering the questions, but the questions were an important tool for promoting the students' learning.

To get students involved in separating effects of gravity from effects of the ambient medium, we use the following question associated with Fig. 4.1.

First, suppose we weigh some object on a large spring scale, not unlike the ones we have at the market. The object apparently weighs 10 lbs, according to the scale. Now we put the same apparatus, scale, object and all, under a very large glass dome, seal the system around the edges, and pump out all the air. That is, we use a vacuum pump to allow all the air to escape out from under the glass dome. What will the scale reading be now? Answer as precisely as you can at this point in time. [pause] And, in the space provided, briefly explain how you decided.

Name _____ School _____ Teacher _____
Period _____   Physics I.D. # _____

Nature and Effects of Gravity Diagnostic Question # 1

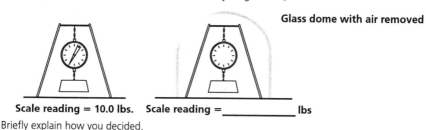

Glass dome with air removed

Scale reading = 10.0 lbs.   Scale reading =_____ lbs
Briefly explain how you decided.

FIG. 4.1.   Pre-instruction question.

Thus, we elicit the students' ideas, their best answer (guess if it need be), and their rationale for how that answer seems to make sense to them at this time. (I encourage the reader to answer this question now as best and as precisely as you can. Or, to let you off the hook a bit, what are the various answers and rationale you believe students would give?)

Students write their answers and their rationale. From their words, a facet diagnosis can be made relatively easily. The facets associated with this cluster, "Separating medium effects from gravitational effects," can be seen in Table 4.1. Students who give an answer of zero pounds for the scale reading in a vacuum usually are thinking that air only presses down, and "without air there would be no weight, like in space" (coded as Facet 319). Other students suggest a number "a little less than 10," because "air is very light, so it doesn't press down very hard, but it does press down some," thus, taking the air away will only decrease the scale reading slightly (Facet 318). Other students suggest there will be no change at all. "Air has absolutely no effect on the scale reading." This answer could result either from a belief that surrounding fluids don't exert any forces or pressures on objects in them (Facet 314), or that fluid pressures on the top and bottom of an object are equal (Facet 315). Typically a few students suggest "the scale reading will be greater because air, like water, pushes upward with a buoyant force on things." A very few students answer that that will yield a large increase in the scale reading, "because of the [buoyant] support by the air." These students seem to be thinking that air or water only exerts upward forces (Facet 317.) Note that many textbooks stop at this point, and readers go away believing that the surrounding fluid only pushes upward on submerged objects. A few students suggest that

TABLE 4.1

Facet Cluster for Separating Fluid Effects From Gravitational Effects

*310	**Pushes from above and below by a surrounding fluid medium lend a slight support (net upward pressure due to differences in depth pressure gradient).**
*310-1	The difference between the upward and downward pushes by the surrounding air results in a slight upward support or buoyancy.
*310-2	Pushes above and below an object in a liquid medium yield a buoyant upward force due to the larger pressure from below.
*311	**Archimedes Principle is correctly applied**
312	**Push up is greater than push down but no difference for difference in depth for a compressible object.**
313	**Knows that things weigh less in water and knows that there is a push up and a push down by the fluid, but not sufficiently relating the "weighing less" to difference in pushes.**
314	**Surrounding fluids don't exert any forces or pushes on objects in them**
315	**Surrounding fluids exert equal pressures all around an object in the medium**
315-1	Air pressure has no up or down influence (neutral).
315-2	Liquid presses equally from all sides regardless of depth.
316	**Which ever surface has greater amount of fluid above or below the object has the greater push by the fluid on that surface. (e.g. an object near the bottom of lake or container will experience a greater force downward because there is more water above than below the object.)**
317	**Fluids exert an upward push only.**
317-1	Air pressure is a big up influence (only direction).
317-2	Liquid presses up only.
317-3	Fluids exert bigger up forces on lighter objects.
318	**Surrounding fluid mediums exert a net downward push.**
318-1	Air pressure is a down influence (only direction).
318-2	Liquid presses (net press) down.
319	**Weight of an object is directly proportional to fluid medium pressure on it.**
319-1	Weight is proportional to air pressure.
319-2	Weight is proportional to liquid pressure.

although there are pressures from above and below, there is a net upward pressure by the fluid. "There is a resultant slight buoyant force" (Facet 310, an acceptable workable idea at this point).

The numbering scheme for the facets allows for more than simply marking the answers "right" or "wrong." The codes ending with a high digit (9, 8, and sometimes 7) represent common facets used by our students at the beginning of the instruction. In the example facet cluster, 319,

318, and 317 each represent an approach that has the fluid pushing in one direction only. Codes ending in 0 or 1 are used to represent goals of learning. In the example cluster 310 is an appropriate conceptual modeling of the situation and 311 represents an appropriate mathematical modeling of the situation. The latter abstractions represent the sort of reasoning or understanding that would be productive at this level of learning and instruction. Middle number codes often represent some formal learning.

The scale is only roughly ordinal in the sense that a facet ending in 5 is less likely to be problematic than a facet ending in 9. But, adjacent numbered facets are not necessarily very distinguishable, for example, Facet 314 is not likely to be distinctly better than 315. More important than the scale is that each facet represents a different sort of understanding, one that likely requires particular lessons to address it. Even so, if and when data are coded, the teacher/researcher can visually scan the class results to identify dominant targets for the focus of instruction.

Benchmark Instruction to Initiate Change in Understanding and Reasoning

By committing their answers and rationale to paper, students demonstrate some ownership of the tentative ideas expressed. They become more engaged and interested in finding out what does happen. Students are now motivated to participate in activities that can lead to resolution. In the classroom, this benchmark lesson usually begins with a discussion of students' answers and rationale. We call this stage "benchmark instruction" because the lesson tends to be a reference point for subsequent lessons (diSessa & Minstrell, 1998). It unpacks the issues in the unit and provides clues to potential resolution of those issues. In this stage, students are encouraged to share their answers and the associated rationale. As the teacher encourages students to express their ideas, teachers attempt to maintain neutrality in leading the discussion. That is, we express sincere interest in hearing what the students are thinking, and we try to help them clarify these initial thoughts. But, we refrain from expressing judgment of the correctness of their answers and rationale. This helps keep the focus on students doing the thinking and it honors the potential (but testable) validity of students' facets of knowledge and reasoning. We accept the students' experiences as valid and we accept, as tentative hypotheses, the sense they make of those experiences (van Zee & Minstrell, 1997.)

Note that many of the ideas and their corresponding facets have valid aspects.

Facet 319: Some students have suggested a correlation with no air in space and no apparent weight in space. What they haven't realized is in an earth orbiting shuttle, one would likely get a zero spring scale reading, whether in the breathable air inside the shuttle or in the airless environment outside. Also, they are thinking that gravity is the result of an interaction between the object and something else. Only they hypothesize an interaction with the surrounding air and the scientist believes the interaction is with the earth. To address Facet 319, students will need to see there is little if any change to the scale reading when the surrounding air has been removed.

Facet 318: It is true that air is light, that is, its density is low relative to most objects we put in it. Air does push downward, but it also pushes in other directions. Students will need to experience this.

Facet 317: Air does help buoy things up, but the buoyant force involves a resolution of the upward and downward forces by the fluid, and that effect is relatively small on most objects in air. (Not so for a helium balloon.) To address Facet 317, students need to see that surrounding fluids like air and water push in all directions, not only upward.

Facet 316: Squishable objects that barely float (such as a scuba diver with a weight belt) near the upper surface of the water may not float when they go deeper than say 30 feet. Thus, it seems like the fluid pushes mostly up when a lot of water is below and pushes mostly down when the object has a lot of water above it. Later in the unit, these students will see that there is no measurable change in the scale reading on a string that supports a solid cylinder whether the cylinder is totally submerged just below the upper surface or submerged to a point slightly above the bottom. (Note this first puts more water below the object and then more water above the object.)

Facet 315: Knowing that the fluid pushes all around but that typical scale readings are not affected, it seems reasonable that the pushes are the same. (This generally happens because the limits of precision of the measurement instruments are too coarse to detect the small difference.) These students will see that there is a difference in scale reading on a string supporting an object submerged in water compared to an object supported out of the water and they will have an opportunity to see that the difference in the support depends on the density of the fluid in which the object is immersed.

Facet 314:   For many situations, the difference between the up and down
forces by air is so little, even the physicist chooses to ignore it.
Thus, there is validity to most of the facets of understanding
and reasoning used by students as they attempt to understand
and reason about this problem situation. The previous information provides guidance for the teacher as she reads students'
answers and explanations and makes plans for instruction.

After the initial sharing of answers and rationale, many threads of students' present understanding of the situation are unraveled and lay on the
table for consideration. The next phase of the discussion moves toward
allowing fellow students to identify strengths and limitations of the various suggested individual threads. "Is this idea ever true? When, in what
contexts? Is this idea valid in this context? Why or why not?"

Seeing the various threads unraveled, students are motivated to know
"what is the right answer?" Because young learners' knowledge (and perhaps that of most anyone for whom a content domain is new) resides more
in features of specific contexts and not in general theoretical principles,
their motivation centers on what will happen in this specific situation. At
this point, they are ready for the question, "How can we find out what happens?" They readily suggest "Try it. Do the experiment and see what happens." In this case, the teacher can "just happen to be prepared" with a
vacuum pump, bell jar, spring scale, and an object to hang on the scale.
After first demonstrating some effects of a vacuum environment, perhaps
using a partially filled balloon, the class is ready to determine the result of
the original problem relating to scale readings in a vacuum.

The experiment is run, air is evacuated, and the result is "no detectable
difference in the scale reading in the vacuum versus in air." Note that this
is not the final understanding I want by the end of the unit, but it does
summarize the results based on the measurements we have taken with the
instruments available so far. This is an opportunity for the class to revisit
their earlier investigations in measurement. "What can we conclude from
the experiment? Given the uncertainty of the scale reading, can we say for
sure that the value is exactly the same? What original suggested answers
can we definitely eliminate? What answers can we not eliminate, knowing
the results of this experiment? What ideas can we conclude do not apply?"
We can eliminate the answer "it would weigh nothing," and we can eliminate the idea that "downward push of air is what causes weight." We can
eliminate the answers reflecting a "great weight increase," and we can
eliminate the idea that "air has a major buoyant effect on this object." We

cannot eliminate "the scale reading would be a tiny bit more" or "a tiny bit less," but also, we don't know that "exactly the same" is the right answer either. Thus, our major conclusion is that the effects of gravity and the effects of a surrounding fluid medium (e.g., air) are different sets of effects. This idea will be important again later when we investigate and try to explain the motions of falling bodies.

Meanwhile, we have addressed the thinking of those students who thought that air pressure was what caused weight, the 319 facet. We still have many other students believing that air only presses down (318). In fact, about 50% of my students typically believe that air only pushes down (318 and 319.) Plus, there is another 10% to 15% who believe that air only pushes up (317). Many of these other issues are left unraveled for now. We don't yet have the definitive answer. We are mirroring an aspect of the nature of science. Rarely do experiments give results indicating exactly the "right" answer (unless the experiments are highly constrained, as in the Klahr, Chen, & Toth chapter in this volume, regarding training on the control of variables). But, experiments usually do eliminate many of the potential answers and ideas. Additional concerns about the direction and magnitude of pushes by air and water are taken up in subsequent investigations.

Elaboration Instruction to Explore Contexts of Application of Other Threads Related to New Understanding and Reasoning

Additional discussion and laboratory investigations allow students to test the contexts of validity for other threads of understanding and reasoning related to the effects of the surrounding fluid medium. Ordinary daily experiences are brought out for investigation; a glass of water with a plastic card over the opening, then inverted (done carefully, the water does not come out); a vertical straw dipped in water and a finger placed over the upper end (the water does not come out of the lower end until the finger is removed from the top); an inverted cylinder is lowered into a larger cylinder of water (it "floats" and as you push the inverted cylinder down, you can see the water rise relative to the inside of the inverted cylinder); and a plastic 2L water filled soda bottle with three holes at different levels down the side (uncapped, water from the lowest hole comes out fastest; capped, air goes in the top hole and water comes out the bottom hole).

It typically takes about two or three class periods for students to work through each of these situations and to present to the rest of the class their results of investigating one of the situations. Although each experiment is a new, specific context, the teacher encourages the students to come to general conclusions about the effects of the surrounding fluid. "In what directions can air and water push?" "What can each experiment tell us that might relate to all of the other situations, including the original benchmark, preinstruction problem?"

Possible related conclusions include "air and water can push upward, and from the side as well as down," and "the push from water is greater the deeper one goes in the container." The latter is probably true of air as well, given reported differences in air pressure between sea level and greater altitudes such as those at the tops of mountains or the levels where planes fly. That can also get brought out through text material and by sharing first-hand experiences, such as siphoning water from a higher level to a lower level or boiling water at high elevation versus at low elevation. Of course, new issues get opened up too, including "stickiness" of water, and "sucking" by vacuums. The former gets us into cohesion and adhesion. Sucking is an hypothesized mechanism that works but is not needed. Addressing it requires raising the issue of parsimony in scientific explanation. Each of these elaboration experiences gives students additional evidence that Facets 319, 318, and 317 are not appropriate. The experiences also provide evidence that water and air can push in all directions and that the push is greater the deeper one goes in the fluid. These are the sorts of big ideas that emerge out of the experiences and consensus discussions.

In addition to encouraging investigation of issues, the teacher can help students note the similarity between what happens to an object submerged in a container of water and what happens to an object submerged in the "ocean of air" around the earth. What are the similarities and differences between air and water as surrounding fluids? To the extent that students learn that the fluid properties of air and water are similar, they can transfer what they learn about water to the less observable properties of water.

A final experiment for this subunit affords students the opportunity to try their new understanding and reasoning in yet one more specific context. A solid, metal slug is weighed successively in air, then partially submerged in water (scale reading is slightly less), then totally submerged just below the surface of the water (scale reading is even less), and finally, totally submerged deep in the container of water (scale reading is the same as in any other position, as long as it is totally submerged). From the scale reading in air, students are asked to predict (qualitatively compare) each of the other results, then do the experiment, record their results, and finally, interpret those results. One last task asks the students to relate these results and the results of the previous experiments to the original benchmark experience. This activity specifically addresses the facets that water does not push on things (314) and that water pushes equally from above and below (315). So, the order of the instructional activities moves gradually up the facet ladder.

By seeing that air and water have similar fluid properties, students are prepared to build an analogy. "Weighing in water is to weighing out of water (in air) as weighing in the ocean of air is to weighing out of the ocean of air (in a vacuum)." Thus, students are now better prepared to answer the original question about weighing in a surround of air, and they have developed a more principled view of the situation.

Some teachers have also had students make the same observations for the metal slug being weighed in other fluids less dense than water (but more dense than air.) The differences in the scale reading turn out to be less dramatic than for water. Thus, they have additional evidence that the same sorts of effects exist, but the magnitude of the effects is less, helping students bridge between more dense fluids (e.g., water), to progressively less dense fluids (e.g., alcohol), to very low density fluid (e.g., air.)

Because students' cognition is often associated with the specific features of each situation, a paramount task for instruction is to help students recognize the common features that cross the various situations. Students argue consistently within a given context. That is, to the extent that different situations have similar surface features, they will employ similar facets. If the surface features in two situations differ, they may alter the facet applied. Thus, we need to guide them in seeing common features across the variety of situations. Only the features we want them to recognize as similar are more like the principles incorporated in the goal facets, for example, 310 and 311. Then, the facets of their understanding and reasoning can be generalized to apply across the situations with different surface features. Air and water push upward and sideways in addition to downward. The push (in all directions) is greater, deeper in the container. Rather than starting with the common, theoretical principles and pointing out the specific applications of the general principles, we start with specific situations, identify ideas that apply in each, attempt to recognize common principles features, and derive ideas (facets) that are more productive across situations.

Some of the students' original ideas may combine to help interpret another situation. In the last experiment, the water pushes upward on the bottom of the metal cylinder and downward on the top of the metal cylinder. The upward push is apparently greater accounting for the drop in the scale reading when the slug is weighed in water. The water in the straw is pushed up by the air beneath the "slug" of water and pushed downward by the air in the straw. The upward push is apparently greater than the downward push, accounting for the need to support the weight of the slug of water in the straw. The surface features of the two experiments are very different. Students need encouragement to see that, in both situations, the slug is apparently partially supported by the difference in pushes by the fluid above and the fluid below the slug. Part of coming to understand physics is coming to see the world differently. The general, principled view can be constructed inductively from experiences and from the ideas that apply across a variety of specific situations. The facets are our representation of the students' ideas. They originate and are used by the students, although they may be elicited from the students by the skilled instructor with curricular tools based on the facets research. Thus, the generalized understandings and explanations are constructed by students from their own earlier ideas. In this way, I am attempting to bridge from students' ideas to the formal ideas of physics.

Assessment Embedded Within Instruction

Sometime after the benchmark instruction and the more focused elaboration lessons, after the class begins to come to tentative resolution on some of the issues, it is useful to give students the opportunity to individually check their understanding and reasoning. Although I sometimes administer these questions on paper in large group format, I prefer to allow the students to quiz themselves at the point they feel they are ready. They think they understand, but they need opportunities to check and fine tune the understanding. To address this need for ongoing formative assessment, Earl Hunt, other colleagues at the University of Washington, and I developed a computerized tool to assist the teacher in individualizing the assessment and keeping records on student progress. When students feel they are ready, they are encouraged to work through computer-presented questions and problems, appropriate to the unit being studied, using a program called DIAGNOSER. I discuss the program in some detail here, because it represents instructional innovation in the form of technological assistance with learning consistent with designing facet-based learning environments.

Technically, the present version of DIAGNOSER is a HyperCard program, carefully engineered to run on a Macintosh Classic or newer. In

1987, we wanted to keep within these design requirements to ensure that we had a program that could be run in the schools. A more complete technical description is presented elsewhere (Levidow, Hunt, & McKee, 1991). Here, I discuss what the DIAGNOSER looks like from the students' view and how it is consistent with my pedagogical framework (Hunt & Minstrell, 1994.)

The DIAGNOSER is organized into units that parallel units of instruction in our physics course. Within our example unit, there is a cluster of questions that focus on the effects of a surrounding medium on scale readings when attempting to weigh an object. Within each cluster, the DIAGNOSER contains several question sets made up of pairs of questions. Each set may address specific situations dealt with in the recent instruction, to emphasize to students that I want them to understand and be able to explain these situations. Sets, also, may depict a novel problem context related to this cluster. I want continually to encourage students to extend the contexts of their understanding and reasoning.

The delivery of each question set consists of four HyperCard screens. The first screen contains a phenomenological question, typically asking the student "what would happen if ... ?" For example, the phenomenological question in Fig. 4.2 asks the student to predict what would happen to an original scale reading of 60 lbs, if air pressure was increased from the normal approximately 15 lbs/sq in to about 20 lbs/sq in.

The appropriate observations or predictions are presented in a multiple choice format with each alternative representing an answer derivable from understanding or reasoning associated with a facet in this cluster. From the student's choice, the system makes a preliminary facet diagnosis. For example, if, in Fig. 4.2, the student had chosen either answer B or E, each

---

Normal air pressure is about 15 lbs/sq. in. When a certain concrete block is weighed in normal air the scale reading is 60 lbs. If the same block was weighed in a special room in which the air pressure has increased to 20 lbs/sq. in., what would the new scale reading be?

A. exactly the same, it still reads 60 lbs, even if we could measure very precisely.

B. very slightly more than 60 lbs. (may not even show up on the scale).

C. about 80 lbs.

D. very slightly less than 60 lbs. (may not even show up on the scale).

E. much more than 60 but not 80 lbs.

F. substantially less than 60 lbs.

FIG. 4.2. DIAGNOSER Phenomenological question screen 3100.

of those answers would be consistent with the thinking that air pushes down and therefore contributes to scale readings (Facet 318.1).

The second screen asks the student "What reasoning best justifies the answer you chose?" Again, the format is multiple choice with each choice briefly paraphrasing a facet as applied to this problem context. From the student's choice, the system makes a second diagnosis. For example, from the screen presented in Fig. 4.3, the student may have picked answer B, suggesting that although air is light, it still does contribute to an increased scale reading (again, Facet 318.1).

On the computer, each of the two screens has an alternative "write a note to the instructor" button. Clicking on this option allows the student to leave a note about their interpretation of the question or about their difficulties with the content. These notes can be scrutinized by the teacher/researcher to assist the individual student. The notes are also helpful in improving DIAGNOSER questions, and in modifying activities to improve learning.

Students are also allowed to move back and forth between the question and the reasoning screens. This is done to encourage students' reflection on experiences, to think about why they have answered the question the way they have, to encourage them to seek more general reasons for answering questions in specific contexts.

The reasoning screen is followed by a diagnosis feedback screen. What this screen says depends on precisely what the student did on the question and reasoning screens. Logically, there are five generic possibilities. First, the student could have chosen the "right" answer for both the phenomenological question and for productive, "physic like" reasoning, in which case the student is given an encouraging message, acknowledging the fact

---

What reasoning would best justify the answer you chose?

A. The weight of an object will change directly proportional to air pressure.

B. Air is light, but greater air pressure will cause an additional downward push. Thus, a greater air pressure will result in an increased scale reading.

C. Air has absolutely nothing to do with the scale reading.

D. Air supports from below. More pressure implies much more support, and so a substantially reduced scale reading.

Air pressure is from all around an object, but it is slightly greater on the bottom of the object. That results in a very slight upward support.

FIG. 4.3.   DIAGNOSER Reasoning question screen 3100.

that she was being consistent. Second, the student could have chosen an incorrect prediction and an associated problematic reasoning, both coded with the same problematic facet, as in our previous example. In this case, the student is encouraged for being consistent but urged to follow a prediction for help (on the next screen; see Fig. 4.4). Third, the student could have chosen a correct prediction but problematic reasons. Fourth, the student could have chosen an incorrect prediction for what seem to be productive reasons. In either of these last two cases, the apparent inconsistency between prediction and reasoning is pointed out, and students are encouraged to follow the prescription for help (see Fig. 4.5). Finally, they may have chosen an incorrect prediction and inconsistent, questionable reasoning. In this case, the double trouble is noted and they are told that the system will attempt to address their phenomenological trouble first, and then address the reasoning, if that is still necessary.

The fourth screen in each sequence is the prescription screen. If the student's answers were diagnosed as associated with productive understanding and reasoning, then the student is very mildly commended and is encouraged to try more questions to be surer. The rationale here is that it should be recognized that although the student's ideas seem ok in this context, overcongratulating the student may allow him to get by with a problematic facet that just didn't happen to show up in this problem situation.

If the student's answers were diagnosed as potentially troublesome, they are issued a prescription lesson associated with the problematic facet. For example, if the student chose one or more answers consistent with "air pushes downward," he would get a prescription suggesting experiences or

---

Both your answer to the question and your reasoning are consistent with each other, but it appears you are using a conception or strategy that will cause you some trouble.

Move ahead for a prescription for help.

FIG. 4.4. DIAGNOSER Feedback screen for consistent answer and reasoning but indicating a conceptual difficulty.

Your answer to the question seems okay, but you need to take a closer look at your reasoning.

Move ahead to get help with the reasoning so that you might be able to generalize what you seem to understand in this one problem to related problems.

FIG. 4.5. DIAGNOSER Feedback screen for inconsistent answer and reasoning and indicating problematic reasoning.

information inconsistent with that facet (318.1; see Fig. 4.6). Typically, the student is encouraged to think about how his ideas would apply to some common, everyday experience or they may be encouraged to do an experiment they may not yet have done. In either case, the experience was chosen because the results would likely challenge the problematic facet apparently invoked by the student. Effectiveness of the prescriptive lessons have been suggested and tested by classroom teachers.

Note the emphasis on consistency. From the students' view, they are generally trying to be consistent. We want to reward students for having thoughtful reasons for the answers they give, thus, the two-part feedback; first for consistency and second for potential productivity of their ideas.

If students generally are seeking consistency, we can challenge situations wherein they have not been consistent. On the DIAGNOSER, one challenge comes if there is an apparent inconsistency between the facet associated with their answer to the question and the facet associated with their reasoning. Even if students are consistent between question and reasoning in the DIAGNOSER, if their facet diagnosis is not consistent with class experiments or with common daily experience, we attempt to point out that inconsistency to them. Thus, we capitalize on the students' nature to be consistent (within a given situation) and then challenge them to extend that consistency within a situation to be applied across situations as well. Note that consistency here means consistency in apparent facet diagnosis. Students are usually more consistent within a particular problem situation than they are between problem situations. Features of different problems tend to cue up different facets.

The DIAGNOSER is typically run in parallel with other instructional activities going on in the classroom. Some students are working on DIAG-

---

If air pressure was down only, then the mountain climber would claim his pack was getting lighter (even without adding anything to or taking anything out). They don't tend to do that.

Suppose we do a thought experiment that goes beyond our lab experiences. What happens when you attempt to "weigh" a cylinder in water versus "weighing" it out of the water? This is the same as when you pick up a big rock under water vs. picking it up out of the water.

We can think of the air around the earth as an ocean of air.

Consider the following analogy: Weighing in the ocean of air is to weighing it out of air as weighing in the ocean of water is to weighing it out of the water. What implication does that have for the direction of air pressure? Does air only push down?

FIG. 4.6.   DIAGNOSER Prescription lesson screen for facet 318.1, "air pressure is downward only."

NOSER while others are working in groups on paper and pencil problem solving or are conducting additional laboratory investigations. In the case of our example subunit, the class may even be moving ahead into the next subunit, more directly investigating gravitational effects. Although students may work on the program individually or in small groups of two or three, they are not graded on their performance on it. It is a formative assessment tool to help them assess their own thinking, and it is a tool to help the teacher assess additional instructional needs for the class as a whole or for students individually. The teacher gets the facet diagnosis for each students' responses or from the small group and can use that information to identify which students or groups still need help addressing what facet of their understanding. It is a device to assist the students and teacher in keeping a focus on understanding and reasoning, on students' learning relative to goal facets.

Application of Ideas and Further Assessment of Knowledge

A unit of instruction may consist of several benchmark experiences and many more elaboration experiences together with the associated DIAGNOSER sessions. Sometime after a unit is completed, students' understanding and reasoning is tested to assess the extent to which instruction has yielded more productive understanding and reasoning. When designing questions for paper and pencil assessment, we attempt to create at least some questions that test for the extent of application of understanding and reasoning beyond the specific contexts dealt with in class. Has learning been a genuine reweave into a new fabric of understanding that generalizes across specific contexts, or has instruction resulted in more brittle situation-bound knowledge?

In designing tests, the cluster of facets becomes the focus for a particular test question. In our example cluster, test questions probe students' thinking about situations in which the local air pressure is substantially changed, questions similar to the elicitation question or the DIAGNOSER question used as examples. Have students moved from believing that air pressure is the cause of gravitational force? Other questions focus on interpreting the effects of a surrounding fluid medium, as they help us infer the forces on an object in that fluid medium. Do students now believe that the fluid pushes in all directions? Can they cite evidence for the idea that greater pushes by the fluid are applied at greater depths? Can they integrate all these ideas together to correctly predict, qualitatively, what effects the fluid medium will have on an object in the fluid? In subsequent units, dynamics for example, do students integrate this qualitative understanding of relative pushes to identify and diagram relative magnitudes of forces acting on submerged objects?

Whether the question is in multiple choice or open response format, I attempt to develop a list of expected answers and associated rationale based on the individual facets in that cluster. After inventing a situation context relevant to the cluster, we read each facet in the cluster and predict the answer and characterize the sort of rationale students would use, if they were operating under this facet. Assuming we have designed clear question situations, and that our lists and characterizations of facets have been sufficiently descriptive of students' understanding and reasoning, we can trace the development of their thinking by recording the trail of facets from preinstruction, through DIAGNOSER, to postunit quizzes, and to final tests in the course.

FACET-BASED LEARNING ENVIRONMENTS PROMOTE LEARNING

For the sample of results described in this section, I continue to focus on separating gravitational effects from effects of the surrounding fluid. The answers for each question associated with diagnosis or assessment were coded using the facets from the cluster for "Separating medium effects from gravitational effects"(see Table 4.1, "310 Cluster of Facets").

The preinstruction question called for free response answers. For that question, 3% of our students wrote answers coded at the most productive level of understanding (see Table 4.2). On the embedded assessment (DIAGNOSER), after students completed the elaboration experiences for a similar multiple choice question and reasoning combination, 81% of the answers to the phenomenological question and 59% of the answers to the reasoning were coded 310.

Revisiting the "object in fluid" context in subsequent instruction helped maintain the most productive level of understanding and reasoning about buoyancy at nearly the 60% level. By the end of the first semester, the class had integrated force related ideas (dynamics) into the context of fluid effects on objects submerged in the fluid medium. On a question in this area, 60% of the students chose, and then briefly defended in writing, an answer coded 310. On the end-of-year final, for the three related questions, answers coded 310 were chosen by students 55%, 56%, and 63% of the time, respectively. Given the difficulty in conceptually understanding the mechanisms of buoyancy and given that the instructional activities took less than 5 hours of class, I consider these numbers a considerable accomplishment.

When we look at the other end of the understanding and reasoning spectrum of facets, we see a substantial development away from believing that "downward pressure causes gravitational effects" (Facet 319) and "fluid mediums push mainly in the downward direction" (Facet 318). On the free response pre-instruction quiz, these two facets accounted for 49% of the data (see Table 4.2). In the DIAGNOSER, those facets accounted for about 5% to 20% of the data, depending on the question. Similar results were achieved on both the first semester final and on the second semester final, some 7 months after the few days of focused instruction. Much of this movement away from the problematic pressure down facets did not make it all the way to the most productive facet. Much student thinking moved to intermediate facets that involve thinking that there are no pushes by the surrounding fluid of air (Facet 314) or that the pushes up and down by the surrounding air are equal (Facet 315). Many of these same students were not stuck on these intermediate facets in the water context, only in the air context. This makes sense because they have direct evidence that when the cylinder is submerged, water pressure causes a difference in the scale reading. In the air case, the preponderance of the evidence is that if there is any difference due to depth, it doesn't matter. For example, force diagrams on a metal slug hung in the air in the classroom don't usually include forces by the surrounding air, because those effects are negligible, except for very lightweight objects, such as balloons.

TABLE 4.2
Student Pre-Instruction Predictions for Scale reading

Scale Reading*	Percent	Facet Code
s≥20 lbs.	2%	317
20>s>11	11	317
11≥s>10	3	310
s = 10	35	314/315
10>s≥9	12	318
9>s>1	17	318
1≥s≥0	20	319

* "s" represents the predicted scale reading

Similar facet-based instruction is now being used by networks of physics teachers across Washington State (Hunt & Minstrell, 1994.) These teachers are getting improved learning effects. After adopting and using a facet-based learning environment in their classes, on the average, these teachers were able to increase the performance of the next cohort of students by 15% over the previous cohort.

The teachers see their role as changed. Formerly, they focused on what they were doing as teachers. They were presenting activities. Now they focus on student learning, on guiding students across the gap from initial facets of thinking toward the learning target facet. The teachers attempt to make sense of what their students are saying and doing, and they design and adjust their instruction to challenge problematic facets and effect improved learning. They have a practical, theoretical view of teaching and learning that they can implement in their classrooms.

The idea of facet-based learning environments is generalizable to other teaching and learning contexts. David Madigan and colleagues have done preliminary research to identify facets of thinking in introductory statistics at the university level. Complete with a web-served version of DIAG-NOSER, they have effected better learning in their courses (Schaffner, 1997.) At Talaria Inc. in Seattle, researchers and developers are building facet-based learning environments to effect better learning within many topics in elder care. Yoshi Nakamura and David Madigan (1997) have identified facets of understanding in pain management for eldercare. By diagnosing learners' understanding of pain management and implementing instruction specific to the diagnosis, they effected significantly better understanding among caregivers. Minstrell at Talaria, in concert with Earl Hunt at the University of Washington and the Office of Superintendent of Public Instruction for Washington State are creating facet-based assessment systems to serve teachers and to effect better learning in science and mathematics for students in the state of Washington. It appears that facets and facet clusters can help teachers in many content areas to better focus on their students' thinking and to effect better learning.

FINAL REMARKS

Teaching is an ill-defined problem where "... every teacher–student interaction can change the teacher's goals and choice of operators" (Bruer, 1993). There are multiple solutions that depend on the prior experiences, knowledge, interests, and motivation of the students and teachers who are present. The teaching–learning process is too complex to completely specify in advance, but I have found that there are specific actions we can take and tools we can use to effect better learning in complex, content-rich learning environments.

Teachers need to be able to make sense of experiences in the classroom and to organize their instructional actions within a coherent framework of learning and teaching, such as that suggested by Donovan, Bransford, and Pellegrino (1997). Facet-based learning environments have provided that coherent framework for me and my fellow teachers. Facets are used to describe students' initial ideas and can be used to track the development of ideas during instruction. The facet clusters provide us with a guide for bridging the gap from students' ideas to the learning standards and from research to practice (Minstrell, in press).

When we know the problematic ideas students use, we can design our curriculum, our assessment items, and our teaching strategies to elicit these ideas and challenge them. Our instructional design to foster development of learner understanding involves eliciting students' ideas with preinstruction questions. Then, we carefully design benchmark lessons that challenge some initial ideas and elaboration lessons that allow students to propose and test initial hypotheses. The classroom becomes a community generating understanding together through respectfully encouraging expression of tentative ideas while at the same time promoting critical reflection and analysis of evidence for and against the shared ideas. Elaboration activities offer an opportunity to test the reliability and validity of new ideas and to explore contexts of application of the new ideas. Through discussions of experiences, we encourage students to summarize principles, the big ideas, that apply across a range of contexts. Assessment embedded within instruction allows students to check on their understanding and allows teachers to monitor progress and identify instructional needs of individuals or of the whole class. Revisiting the ideas and issues by applying them in subsequent units helps students see the value of the new ideas. In subsequent assessments, we go back to the facets of problematic thinking to see the extent to which students have moved away from thinking based on superficial features and have moved toward more principled thinking. The organization and instruction based on facets is effective in promoting development of even the weaker students. Tuning our instruction to address the specific thinking of learners can improve learning across the sciences.

Teachers need to better understand their student's thinking. They need to design or choose instruction to effect better learning. The facets perspective supports teachers' attempts to make sense of classroom experiences and to facilitate more effective learning.

ACKNOWLEDGMENTS

I would like to thank my former students and my teacher colleagues for sharing their classrooms with me and with each other, and for contributing substantially to the data leading to facets descriptions of students' thinking and to benchmark and elaboration lessons. I would also like to thank my colleagues at Talaria Inc. and at the University of Washington, most notably Earl Hunt, for their critical review of theoretical ideas and for their assistance in the transfer of the facets framework into technological tools. Together, I know we have constructed a practical, research-based framework that can assist students and teachers in effecting better learning. Finally, I want to thank the editors of this book and their reviewers for their thoughtful, constructive comments.

Research and development of the facets perspective was supported by grants from the James S. McDonnell Foundation Program in Cognitive Studies for Educational Practice (CSEP) and the National Science Foundation Program for Research in Teaching and Learning (RTL). The writing of this chapter was partially supported by grants #REC–9906098 and REC–9972999 from the National Science Foundation Program for Research in Educational Policy and Practice (REPP). The ideas expressed are those of the author and do not necessarily represent the beliefs of the foundations.

REFERENCES

Bruer, J. (1993). *Schools for thought: A science for learning in the classroom.* Cambridge, MA: MIT Press.

Camp, C., and Clement, J. (1994*). Preconceptions in mechanics: Lessons dealing with students' conceptual difficulties.* Dubuque, IA: Kendall Hunt.

diSessa, A., & Minstrell, J. (1998). Cultivating conceptual change with benchmark lessons. In J. Greeno and S. Goldman (Eds.), *Thinking practices in mathematics and science learning* (pp. 155–187). Mahwah, NJ: Lawrence Erlbaum Associates.

Donovan, M., Bransford, J., & Pellegrino, J. (Eds.). (1999). *How people learn: bridging research and practice.* Washington, DC: National Research Council.

Hunt, E., & Minstrell, J. (1994). A collaborative classroom for teaching conceptual physics. In K. McGilly (Ed.), *Classorrom lessons: Integrating cognitive theory and classroom practice* (pp. 51–74). Cambridge, MA: MIT Press.

Levidow, B., Hunt, E., & McKee, C. (1991). The DIAGNOSER: A HyperCard tool for building theoretically based tutorials. *Behavioral research, method, instruments, and computers, 23* (2), 249–252.

Minstrell, J. (1982a, January). Explaining the "at rest" condition of an object. *The Physics Teacher*, pp. 10–14.

Minstrell, J. (1982b). Conceptual development research in the natural setting of the classroom. In M. B. Rowe (Ed.), *Education for the 80's: Science*, (pp. 129–143). Washington, DC: National Education Association.

Minstrell, J. (1989). Teaching science for understanding. In L. Resnick and L. Klopfer (Eds.), *ASCD 1989 Yearbook: Toward the thinking curriculum: Current cognitive research*, Washington, DC, Association for Supervision and Curriculum Development.

Minstrell, J. (1992). Facets of students' knowledge and relevant instruction. In R. Duit, F. Goldberg, & H. Niedderer (Eds.), *Proceedings of the international workshop: Research in physics learning—theoretical issues and empirical studies* (pp. 110–128). Kiel, Germany: The Institute for Science Education at the University of Kiel (IPN).

Minstrell, J. (in press). Facets of students' thinking: Designing to cross the gap from research to standards-based practice. In K. Crowley, C. Schunn, & T. Okada (Eds.) *Designing for science: Implications from professional, instructional, and everyday science.* Mahwah, NJ: Lawrence Erlbaum Associates.

Minstrell, J., & Stimpson, V. (1996). A classroom environment for learning: Guiding students' reconstruction of understanding and reasoning. In R. Glaser & L. Schauble (Eds), *Innovations in learning: New environments for education* (pp. 175–202). Mahwah, NJ: Lawrence Erlbaum Associates.

Nakamura, Y., & Madigan, D. (1997). *A facet-based learning approach for elder care (FABLE): A computer-based tool for teaching geriatric pain management skills.* Unpublished manuscript.

Project Physics. (1970). New York: Holt, Rinehart & Winston.

Schaffner, A. (1997). *Tools for the advancement of undergraduate statistics education.* Unpublished doctoral dissertation, University of Washington, Seattle.

van Zee, E., & Minstrell, J. (1997). Developing shared understanding in a physics classroom. *The International Journal of Science Education, 19* ,2 (pp. 209–228).

5

The Interplay of First-Hand and Second-Hand Investigations to Model and Support the Development of Scientific Knowledge and Reasoning

Annemarie Sullivan Palincsar
Shirley J. Magnusson
University of Michigan

> *It's pretty cool because we get to share our thinking with the class and we get to also share Lesley's thinking with the class.*
>
> —*(Kenji, May, 1998)*

> *I like to listen to what other scientists do, like Lesley Park. Especially when she started getting more exact.*
>
> —*(Emily, May, 1998)*

These quotes are taken from the remarks of two fourth graders who have been engaged in investigations of light and are commenting on their experiences using notebook entries authored by a fictitious scientist, named Lesley Park, who is documenting her own investigations of light. In this chapter, we consider the nature and role of text designed to advance young children's thinking as they engage in scientific inquiry.

Inquiry is a complex form of thinking that has been developed over thousands of years. It is a cultural legacy that previous generations have imparted to us to employ and revise. From a sociocultural perspective, it is a "cultural tool" (Wertsch, 1998) of a psychological nature, an approach to reasoning that others have found useful. This is not, however, the perspective from which inquiry is generally approached in the worlds of teachers and students. Inquiry is often equated with discovery, or inquiry is framed in a manner that suggests that it is synonymous with activity based, hands-on engagement in investigative activity. The notion that inquiry is discovery is problematic when one considers the impossibility that children will come to meaningful understandings of the nature of scientific thinking simply through the process of interacting with materials and phenomena (see also Brown & Campione, 1994). Furthermore, the notion that inquiry must be exclusively activity based is problematic because, in fact, much of what we know about scientific reasoning has been acquired through the thinking and experiences of others; that is, through learning in a second-hand way. Frequently, although not exclusively, this second-hand learning can be facilitated with the use of text.

Text has generally suffered neglect on the part of the science education community while receiving more attention from the reading and literacy community. Although reading researchers have undertaken vigorous programs of research regarding certain issues related to science text (e.g., students' learning from refutational text), this research has not typically been situated in the context of science curriculum and pedagogy. Hence, the text used is seldom studied in the context of everyday classroom use; the dependent measures seldom reflect the goals that are represented in the science standards documents; and, there is little attention to the integration of text with other modes of experiencing and learning science.

In addition to the argument framed earlier regarding the significant role that second-hand investigations with text can play in advancing science learning, there are at least three other compelling reasons to argue for research related to the study of text in elementary science instruction. First, national standards documents include the recommendation that students "learn how to access scientific information from books, periodicals, videos ... and evaluate and interpret the information they have acquired from these resources" (National Research Council, 1996, p. 45). Furthermore, these reform documents urge that teachers assume an inquiry approach as they guide students in "acquiring and interpreting information" from text (p. 31). These recommendations place challenging demands on classroom teachers, particularly elementary teachers who are unaccustomed to using informational text (Hiebert & Fisher, 1990), much less to using text to promote inquiry. Although the reform documents hint at the use of text as a default experience when students are unable to experience phenomena in a first-hand fashion, we are, in fact, interested in ways that second-hand experiences with text can; (a) prepare students for first-hand experiences in very powerful ways, (b) effectively extend first-hand experiences, and (c) provide a common inquiry that advances students' conceptual understanding in significant ways.

Second, the reform documents suggest that one mark of scientific literacy is the ability to critically read informational text. As the research of Norris and Phillips (1994) demonstrates, even students who experienced advanced level science courses (i.e., high school seniors who had taken four science courses), struggled to be critical of popular science reports and failed to be discriminating regarding truth statements, ascribing higher truth values to statements than were warranted by the information provided. Clearly the competence to understand and critically analyze text will not be developed without careful and systematic attention to cultivating the skills and dispositions to approach science text in a critical fashion throughout the grades.

An additional motivation for the study of text in science instruction is particular to the elementary grades. In this information age, it is well recognized that the attainment of informational literacy is central to achievement, or even to survival, in securing a place in advanced schooling, in one's job, and in one's community. Despite this fact, American schools have failed to develop effective and enduring informational reading and writing skills for many students, particularly those from traditionally disenfranchised social groups (Applebee, Langer, Mullis, Latham, & Gentile, 1994). Chall, Jacobs, and Baldwin (1990) argued that the well-documented "fourth-grade slump" can be explained in terms of the difficulties that students experience with informational text. One likely explanation for this difficulty is the paucity of opportunities students have had to learn from and about informational text (Hiebert & Fisher, 1990; Pappas, 1991).

In this chapter, we describe the design, conduct, and outcomes of a program of research that is focused on students' and teachers' use of text in the context of guided inquiry science instruction. We begin with a discussion of related research and continue with a brief description of the professional development context in which our research has been conducted. This is followed by a description of an observational study in which we examined the practices of an expert elementary classroom teacher who incorporated text in her inquiry instruction. This research contributed to the foundation of the next phase of our research program, which entailed the development and study of the use of an innovative genre of text—text that was written as a scientist's notebook and was specifically designed to support children and teachers to approach text as an inquiry. We then proceed to describe an experimental study comparing student learning from two forms of text. One form was the innovative genre, and the second was a considerate nonrefutational expository text. The experimental study is followed by the description of a naturalistic, observational study of classroom use of the innovative text by fourth graders and their teachers. We conclude with a discussion of issues that have emerged in the course of this program of research.

WHAT IS KNOWN
ABOUT TEXT IN SCIENCE?

If we conceive of the knowledge base regarding science text in terms of three intersecting circles, with one circle representing text features, a second representing student use of text, and a third representing text in context, there are two circles that have been fairly well developed (text features, student use of text), one that is sparse (text in context), and the intersection of these three circles is virtually empty. Studies of naturally occurring science text offer a dismal picture of material that is characterized as incomplete in the provision of explanations (Lloyd & Mitchell, 1989), and sparse with regard to transitions and other devices useful to attaining cohesion (Farris, Kissinger, & Thompson, 1988; Woodward & Noell, 1991). The poor state of affairs regarding naturally occurring text could, in part, be addressed by the research that has been conducted to examine the relative benefits of designing science text with specific features.

For example, there have been numerous studies (reported in a meta-analysis by Guzetti, Snyder, & Glass, 1992) that suggest that refutational expository text, that is, text that explicitly identifies and refutes misconceptions, is more effective (particularly when it is written in a considerate fashion) than is nonrefutational text. However, it is seldom the case that widely available science text has been written in this style; researchers typically generate very short and focused segments of text for the purpose of investigating the effectiveness of refutational text.

One manipulation of text that has captured the interest of researchers is the insertion of embedded questions within the text. For example, Leonard (1987) studied the efficacy of placing questions at the beginning of paragraphs in a college biology text, and calling attention to these questions through the use of an array of devices (use of upper case vs. underlining), when compared with a no-question text. Leonard observed that students who studied from the text with the embedded questions performed significantly better on tests of immediate recall than students in the no-question condition; however, there were no differences on the assessments that were administered 4 weeks later to determine maintenance of the information read. Balluerka (1995) studied the differential effects of providing an advance organizer, engaging students in the generation of an advance organizer, and the provision of illustrations highlighting main ideas in the text. The outcomes were assessed using two types of tasks; the recall of information and the application of information. The findings suggested that illustrations of key ideas facilitated the recall of information, whereas the deeper processing in which students engaged to generate outlines, enhanced comprehension.

Another line of research examines what students do as they read and study from science text. Generally, this research suggests that students, left to their own devices, do not know how to study and learn from scientific expository text (Craig & Yore, 1996; Dee-Lucas & Larkin, 1988; Otero & Companario, 1990). For example, even fairly sophisticated high school physics students in the study by Boyle and Maloney (1991) did not effectively use explicit information regarding Newton's third law, provided them via text, even though it would have facilitated their problem solving regarding the application of forces on an object.

Attempts to teach students to engage more effectively with text through the use of strategies has produced mixed findings. For example, Pearson (1991), working with college students, found that while self-questioning enhanced performance on assessments that measure the short-term recall of information, it did not reliably enhance long-term retention of scientific concepts. In contrast, Woloshyn, Paivio, & Pressley (1994) observed that upper elementary students who engaged in elaborative interrogation in which they made supportive inferences in the course of elaborating on new information, performed better on assessments of conceptual understanding, whether or not their prior conceptions matched scientifically accurate conceptions, when compared with student selected strategies.

Generally, the majority of research regarding text in science has been conducted at the secondary and postsecondary levels. Much of this research has been conducted with the use of contrived text, and little of it has been conducted in the context of naturally occurring science instruction. One line of research that is more closely aligned with the research reported in this chapter is the work of Guthrie and Gaskins and their colleagues (Gaskins, et. al., 1994; Guthrie, McGough, Bennett, & Rice, 1996). In a program of research entitled, *Concept-Oriented Reading Instruction*, they investigated the enactment of year-long curricula in which elementary-aged students and their teachers pursued the study of conceptual issues of the students' choosing. In the course of their inquiry regarding these topics, students are supported to find relevant resources, learn how to use these resources, and learn how to communicate their learning to others. The evaluation of this approach has been conducted using broad ranging assessments that include breadth and amount of reading activity, student motivation for reading, cognitive strategies for reading, as well as the attainment of conceptual knowledge (defined very generally). This is a very ambitious program of research that clearly will inform a large set of significant issues regarding the role of text in inquiry instruction; however, the grain size of the analyses are such that they contribute little to our understanding of the specific nature of the texts students are using, how teachers are mediating students' use of these texts, and what understandings children are achieving that can inform our thinking about the role of text in advancing both conceptual understanding and scientific reasoning.

In the next section of this chapter, we describe a program of research that is at the intersection of text features, student and teacher use of text, and text in the context of inquiry instruction in elementary science teaching. The program began with naturalistic observations of the ways in which elementary teachers, engaged in guided inquiry teaching, used second-hand investigations via text in the course of their teaching. This was followed by a descriptive study of one-third grade teacher for whom we designed a text to complement the first-hand investigation in which her class was engaged. When we began this program of research, we had a fairly clear idea of the nature and role of second-hand investigations; however, our work with teachers was designed to refine our thinking and to inform our understanding of how we could best support teachers to conjoin first- and second-hand investigations. Indeed, this initial phase of the research led us to the design of an innovative text genre to scaffold children's and teachers' use of text in an inquiry fashion. The second phase of the research was a quasi- experimental study designed to compare the outcomes of using the innovative text with the outcomes of a more traditional text. Finally, we engaged in an instructional study in which two fourth-grade teachers used the innovative texts in the course of a program of study on *How Light Interacts With Objects*. We begin by describing the professional development context in which this research occurred.

THE PROFESSIONAL DEVELOPMENT CONTEXT SUPPORTING THIS PROGRAM OF RESEARCH

Before we proceed with the description of our research program, a word is in order regarding the professional development context in which this work is taking place. This context is important because it afforded us the opportunity to conduct this research informed by teachers' experiences. For the past 3 years, we worked with a group of K through 5 teachers[1] who joined this professional development project for the purpose of learning how to effectively teach science from a guided inquiry perspective. Our work together involved biweekly meetings during the school year, week-long institutes during summers, and many hours working alongside these teachers in their classrooms. We refer to the context in which we conducted our research as *The Guided Inquiry supporting Multiple Literacies (GIsML) Community of Practice*. Informed by sociocultural theory regarding the interdependence of social and individual processes in the coconstruction of knowledge (John-Steiner & Mann, 1996; Rogoff, 1994), this professional development project was designed to provide occasions for interaction, joint deliberation, and the collective pursuit of shared goals, particularly with regard to the teaching of science in the elementary grades.[2] (For a complete description of this professional development effort, see Palincsar, Magnusson, Marano, Ford, & Brown, 1998.) The teachers represented 14 schools in six districts, one of which serves a rural community, two of which serve an urban community, and three of which serve primarily suburban communities.

---

[1]There were 18 teacher participants the first 2 years of this work (1996–1998) and there were 14 active participants the third year of this work (1998–1999).

[2]The participants in this Community of Practice met biweekly (for 4 hours each meeting) during the two academic years from 1996 through 1998, and once monthly during 1999. In addition, they committed two weeks of full days during the summers of 1996 and 1997 and one week during 1998.

Our focus was on identifying practices that were consistent with a particular orientation to the teaching of science in the elementary grades. Informed by the research of Grossman (1990), we used the notion of orientation to refer to an overarching conception of how to teach a particular subject. An orientation can be thought of as a conceptual map that guides decision making regarding curriculum, instruction, student understanding, and assessment. The orientation to which we refer is reflected in the heuristic presented in Fig. 5.1. (For a more complete description of this heuristic and the instructional implications, see Magnusson & Palincsar, 1995). The heuristic is organized according to phases of instruction set within a particular problem space, that is, a guiding question that is broad and identifies a general conceptual terrain (e.g., How does light interact with matter? Why do things sink and float?). Inquiry proceeds through cycles of investigation guided by specific questions (e.g., How does light interact with mirrors) or by a particular phenomenon (e.g., shaping a ball of clay to hold the most weight). Integral to this orientation is the conception of the classroom as a community of inquiry (cf. The Cognition and Technology Group at Vanderbilt, 1994; Wells, 1995). Hence, the investigations and documentation of data gathered in the course of the investigation are conducted in pairs or small groups. Furthermore, a critical feature in the instruction is the reporting phase, during which the investigative teams share their data, speak to the evidence they have gathered to support or refute extant claims, and contribute new claims for the class's consideration.

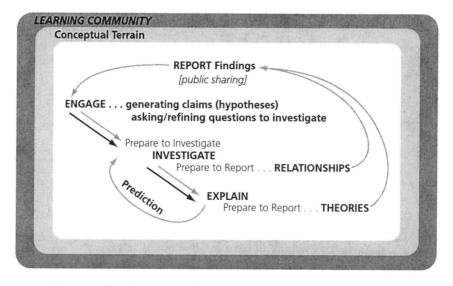

FIG. 5.1. The GIsML heuristic.

The curved lines represent a cycling phenomenon in which students experience the same phase repeatedly in the same or different contexts. This recursive aspect of instruction is required to promote meaningful learning, particularly with respect to scientific inquiry. For example, one needs sufficient experiences examining natural relationships among phenomena before one can meaningfully test explanations for these phenomena.

In the course of GIsML instruction, students and teachers participate in two forms of investigation. Through *first-hand investigations*, children have experiences related to the phenomenon(a) they are investigating. In the course of *second-hand investigations*, children consult text for the purpose of learning about others' interpretations.

The ultimate goal of GIsML instruction is to support children's learning of scientific understandings, and to enable students to experience, understand, and appreciate the ways in which these understandings have evolved by using the tools, language, and ways of reasoning that are characteristic of scientific literacy (Driver, Osoko, Leach, Mortimer, & Scott, 1994; Lemke, 1990; White & Frederiksen, 1998).

During the 1996–1997 school year, the focus of the GIsML Community was on the design, enactment, and evaluation of first-hand investigations. In the spring of 1997, we piloted second-hand investigations in the classroom of a third-grade teacher who is a member of the Community, and in the summer of 1997, we formally introduced the idea of second-hand investigations to the Community. In the next section, we describe the outcomes of this exploratory phase of our research.

DESCRIPTIVE RESEARCH ON SECOND-HAND INVESTIGATIONS

Prior research (e.g., Shymanski, Yore, & Good, 1991) has suggested that when teachers embrace activity-based, project-driven, or guided inquiry practices, text falls into a lacuna; however, this research has been conducted via survey and has not entailed direct observations of teachers who have been supported in the planning and enactment of guided inquiry teaching. As the teachers engaged in the GIsML Community of Practice enacted first-hand investigations with their students, we were interested in how teachers' thinking about the use of text would be influenced by their inquiry experiences. We observed that although these teachers did not systematically introduce the use of text in these investigations, several teachers did in fact acquire topically related books from the library. One teacher used a folk tale to introduce her first graders to the study of shadows, and there were many ways in which the teachers used print literacy, other than prepared text. For example, children's "wonderings" and class claims were posted throughout the room, and students were frequently asked to make and subsequently refer to notebook entries.

Conversations with the teachers about the role that second-hand investigations might play in inquiry provided helpful insights into why other researchers have reported the absence of text in inquiry teaching. Consensus quickly emerged among the teachers that there was a risk inherent in using text to the extent that children might defer to the authority of the text, seeking answers from the text when, in fact, the children themselves had a key role to play in working toward explanations and were indeed quite capable of generating their own "answers" in the course of investigating phenomena. The teachers cautioned against introducing text early in the investigation and urged that text be used following a significant amount of first-hand inquiry. Hence, the preponderance of teachers' ideas suggested that text be used not to supplant children's inquiry and discourse, but rather to extend it (for the full report of focus group conversations with teachers, see Palincsar & Magnusson, 1997).

In preparation for the professional development work that we did at the conclusion of the 1997–1998 school year, we asked Fran S, a third-grade teacher in the GIsML Community, who was well recognized for her expertise as a language arts teacher, if she would be willing to pilot the use of second-hand investigations in GIsML instruction. As a research group, we had now observed 17 iterations of GIsML teaching on the topic of light, which gave us a fairly informed understanding about the role that text might play in this program of study. Ms. S' class first engaged in a week of first-hand investigations of light, which proceeded in the following manner. As the engagement activity, Ms. S asked her students to generate a list regarding what they knew about light. Based on their observations, the class next developed a set of claims regarding light that they would investigate with the use of light boxes and an array of materials, such as mirrors, translucent objects, objects of various colors, and prisms. Working in pairs, students then selected a claim from the list and investigated it with the materials. As they investigated, the students collected data in their notebooks to be presented to the remainder of the class during reporting. There were two iterations of the cycle of inquiry during this week-long investigation.

In this next portion, we describe, in some detail, how Ms. S led her students in this second-hand investigation. We do this because, although we already had a number of ideas regarding second-hand investigations, the experiences of this class were influential in our thinking about the features of text and the features of a second-hand investigation that would be most consonant with the GIsML orientation. The text Ms. S used was specifically designed to reflect the experiences the students had garnered in their first-hand investigations; making reference to familiar concepts and using established vocabulary (e.g., absorption).[3] The question guiding this descriptive study was: What does the interplay of first- and second-hand investigations look like when a class is using nonrefutational expository text?

To prepare the students for the second-hand investigation, which occurred a week and a half after the conclusion of a related first-hand investigation, Ms. S engaged them in recalling the claims for which they had not gathered sufficient evidence in their first-hand investigation. She also elicited those claims that the students indicated could not be investigated first-hand. As the students volunteered, Ms. S recorded their responses on the board. Having reviewed the students' first-hand investigations before class (with the use of student notebooks and posters of class claims), she was able to prompt questions/claims that the students did not initially remember.

Day 1 of Second-hand Investigation

Ms. S: Now, a week and a half ago, when we were doing our investigation of light, during that whole week a lot of questions came up that we found we couldn't answer with the materials we had in the classroom. Frequently people would say, "I guess we need to do that in a second-hand investigation." Do you remember hearing that?

Students: Yeah.

Ms. S: Ok, what were some of those things that were unanswered or that we felt we needed to do different kinds of investigations with? I thought I'd list a few on the board, just to keep a record of it. What were some of the things? Kyla?

Kyla: Um, the speed of light.

Ms. S: Ok. *[writes statement on the board]* I'll just make some quick notes on the board. So, speed of light was one. What else? Evan?

Evan: If light is the fastest thing in the solar system.

...

---

[3]The authors are grateful to Danielle Ford, who prepared the text used in Ms. S's second-hand investigation.

Sarah: Um, light splitting

Katie: *[whispering to* Sarah, *then growing louder]* Water splitting light as well as a prism.

male student off camera: Well, that's not a second-hand investigation.

Katie: I know but we didn't—

Ms. S: But we didn't answer that question. Ok *[writing on board]*, water splitting light into colors. Ok, what else? David.

David: Well, we said this one, the person who said this one said it sorta messed up but we said light absorbs black. They tried to do that one but they said it sorta messed up a bit.

Ms. S: OK, is our claim about black absorbs or soaks up light?

David: Yeah. Some people tried it and they couldn't get it to work.

...

Ms. S: Ok. *[writing on board]* White reflects light. Ok, so we weren't sure about that. Someone tried to, to prove that but we weren't sure about that one. Nick?

Nick: I bet black holes are called black holes because they suck in light. Black.

Ms. S: OK, so that was another thing we couldn't really do a first-hand investigation of. Thank goodness.

Students *[off camera]*:   Yeah ... Yeah 'cause you can't like...

Ms. S: Ok, anything else? I want you to think a little longer. I have a few things I jotted down too when I was trying to recall. Actually, David Brown, you mentioned a couple of things that you couldn't investigate first hand. *[David B. has no response]* Let's see if I have them written down. Oh, how about light as a source of energy?

Katie: Oh, yeah. We kinda did that one.

Ms. S: How did we do that, Katie?

Katie: We put like a thermometer [and we found]...

Student *[off camera]*:   That's heat.

Katie: that it was a source of heat.

Nick: But heat isn't energy.

Ms. S: And you thought that heat might prove that it was a source of energy. But we had some disagreement about whether—Nick—we had some disagreement about that. So can we put that down, that we're not sure about that yet? And we might need more. Ok. *[writing on board]* Light is a source of energy. Ok. Anything else? Ooo, Kevin and Ilya, I remember some controversy in your presentation. Do you remember what that was about?....

Kevin: *[reading from journal]* Light can be reflected by a mirror but not by any object other than a mirror.

Ms. S: So, light isn't reflected by any object but a mirror. Does that say kind of what you're saying there? *[students are talking, "No," some general rumbling]* And we had a controversy about that. People had different opinions. *[writing on board]* Light isn't reflected by objects other than mirrors. All right, let's see if I have anything else here. *[checking notes]* I remember another one. We actually had a long discussion about whether things that, I think you were talking about this, Julian, and you were, Nick—about things that are, excuse me, are all things that glow hot?

Julian: Oh, yeah.

Ms. S: Remember that discussion?

Julian: Everyone was talking about that.

Ms. S: Hmmm. *[writing on board] [Aside: Nick, whatever you're eating, you need to stop, ok? Unless you have enough to share.]* Ok, and the shadow business. Ayaka had some evidence that we couldn't find at the last minute. Why do some objects make darker shadows than other objects? Do you think we needed some, some more information about that? *[no response from Ayaka]*

Student *[off camera]*: Ayaka didn't have hers so we couldn't really discuss it.

Ms. S: Right. *[writing on board]* Some objects make darker shadows than others. Ok, let's take a look at the article.

After this conversation, Ms. S read the first part of the following, text, to the class.

Light and Objects

Everything that we see fits into one of two groups. In one group are objects that give off light. They are called **luminous** objects. Light bulbs, the sun, flashlights are examples of luminous objects. The other group of objects do not give off light. We can see them only because light from luminous objects bounces off them and travels to our eyes. These objects are called **non-luminous** objects.

After reading this portion of the text to the class, Ms. S paused and asked the students to name some luminous objects in their immediate environment. The students offered several other examples, including objects and animals that were not in the classroom environment, and also discussed whether mirrors are luminous or nonluminous They decided that mirrors are nonluminous and Ms. S summarized the discussion, focusing on the luminous objects in their immediate environment, and then asked them to name nonluminous objects. The students had no trouble naming nonluminous objects, and were enthusiastic about this. As Ms. S attempted to continue on to the next paragraph, David made an observation regarding what they had just read about luminous and nonluminous objects and how it related to their claims, still posted on the board.

David: Before we said that light isn't reflected by objects other than mirrors but the article says that light reflects off others so we can see them so we know that claim's wrong.

Ms. S: And I think we'll get maybe some more information about this too as we move along. All right, next paragraph.

> When light travels from a luminous object to your eyes it has to travel through air. It may travel through other materials, too. Light travels through some materials differently than others.

At this point Ms. S stopped and asked the children what they already knew in relation to that segment of text. The students remembered that one of their classmates, Ayaka, had attempted to shine light through various different types of material, including wood, glass, metal, and a paper milk carton, and that her claim was that some objects make darker shadows than others. Ms. S encouraged them to look for more information regarding this claim as they read the next paragraph.

> Light travels straight through objects that are **transparent**, or clear, such as glass windows or pop bottles. Because the light is traveling straight through the transparent object, we can see objects on the other side of the transparent object very clearly. Sometimes, only some light passes through objects. These objects, like plastic milk jugs, are called **translucent**. If you look through a plastic milk jug, you won't see anything clearly on the other side, but you might notice that some light is shining through. Objects that don't allow any light to pass through are called **opaque**. Books and walls are opaque. We can't see anything on the other sides of these objects.

Ms. S stopped at the end of this paragraph and directed the students' attention back to the list of claims on the board:

Ms. S: So, David, you said that there was one up here that this kind of proves as correct.

David: Oh, Ayaka's. Because it said that some lets light come in differently, more light and less light. Less light would probably be a lighter shadow and more light would be a darker shadow.

After this, Ms. S asked the students to name examples of transparent, translucent, and opaque objects in their immediate environment. The students did not have a problem naming transparent objects but the identification of translucent objects proved more elusive. The difference between transparent and translucent objects sparked a lot of discussion as students pointed out the different characteristics of objects on the room, especially the computer screens.

Ms. S: Translucent seems a bit harder. Evan?

Evan: Um, the computer screen.

Student [off camera]: That's what I was gonna say.

Jung Ho: That's more transparent than translucent.

Nick: Yeah, or else you'd see the light.

Ms. S: Guys. Jung Ho, why do you think that?

Jung Ho: Well, 'cause then you wouldn't be able to see through the screen that easily. You can see yourself.

Ms. S: That's kind of a puzzle, but I think the screen itself must at least be transparent.

David: Well, it can be, well, maybe some screen savers are, like that one for instance [points across room] is translucent and it has a picture that lets out some of the light not all of it. But when you move the mouse it gets really transparent.

The discussion about translucent objects continued for a few additional minutes, including more debate regarding the computer screen and whether it should be considered translucent or transparent. Then Ms. S introduced the next section of the text. After reading the subtitle and before reading the next section, she again asked the students for predictions. The class then continued with this section.

Light Bounces

Did you use mirrors when investigating your claims about light? What happens when you hold a mirror facing a light box? You can see the path of the light bouncing off the mirror. The light from the box is hitting the mirror. Then it is bouncing off the mirror and hitting other things—other mirrors, targets, the desk or wall. Why does light bounce this way off mirrors? The surface of a mirror is very smooth. Light bounces off this smooth surface in an even, regular way. Most mirrors are made of glass with a thin coat of shiny silver on the back. What happens when light bouncing off you hits the mirrors? The light bounces off the mirror in the same pattern as it hit the mirror. You see yourself.

At this point Ms. S paused and asked for a volunteer to summarize the paragraph. When the class continued reading, she explicitly drew the students' attention to the claim that two students, Kevin and Ilya, had made following their first-hand investigation, and its relevance to the text:

Ms. S: Did you try to get the light to travel using anything other than mirrors? Kevin, did you try that? *[walks over and places hand on Kevin's shoulder]*

Kevin: *Yeah.*

Ms. S: What do you think would happen if you tried to use white paper instead of a mirror? What happened with white paper, according to Kevin and Ilya? Ilya, what happened?

Ilya: Well, it would just go a little and then it stops.

Ms. S: It just seemed to stop? David?

David: Well, it works sort of like a mirror but it's not quite as smooth I don't think because paper can be folded easily so it won't be as smooth as a mirror so it won't reflect as well. But mirrors, you can't bend a mirror or mess it up. It's very smooth. There's no way to do it. It's like rock.

Ms. S: All right, so we have two thoughts, Kyla and Ayaka. One thought is that light does not bounce off of anything but mirrors. And the other thought is that it does bounce off other things but because they're not smooth, as David said ...

David: They don't bounce as well.

Ms. S: They don't bounce as well. I want you to think about that, which one you kind of agree on at this point.

Compared to a mirror, even the smoothest paper is very rough. Because the surface of the paper is rough, light that strikes it bounces in many directions. We say the light is scattered. It might be hard to see, but a faint light could be seen if you put your hand or a book in front of the paper. Some of the light bounces from the white paper to your hand or the book.

With this, Ms. S stopped and asked the class, "Why don't we see the light as clearly bouncing off the white paper?" When students found this difficult to answer, she asked them what the article said about the surface of the paper. The answer to this question still eluded the class, so Ms. S reread the portion of the text related to this. After rereading, the class voted on whether they thought light was reflected off of objects other than mirrors. Student opinion on this topic was split, and Ms. S continued with the next paragraph.

When light bounces it is said to be **reflected**. Light is reflected from one mirror to another mirror, or to a desk or a chair. Light is reflected from white paper or shiny things to your hand or a book. A page in the book may become bright enough for you to read by the reflected light. However, when light hits black paper, almost no light bounces from it. Instead of reflecting the light, most of the light energy is **absorbed** by the paper.

After this section, Ms. S asked the class to remember Tim's claim from his first-hand investigation. The students recalled that Tim had predicted that black absorbed more light than white, and was therefore hotter, based on his experience playing soccer, while wearing dark and light colored jerseys. They also returned to their discussion of computer screens. Finally, Ms. S concluded the lesson by reviewing each of the claims on the board and having the students discuss, based on what they had learned from the article, whether they agreed or disagreed with each claim.

Day 2 of Second-hand Investigations

Ms. S began this lesson by reviewing the student's claims, recorded on the board. This discussion was similar to the one held at the end of the first day of the second-hand investigation which was 3 days earlier.

Ms. S: I want to review a little bit. Take a look up here. Turn your chairs so you can see if you're like Sarah and you're facing the front. I wrote the questions, the remaining questions we said we had from our second-hand and from our first-hand investigations, I wrote them pretty much how we said them last time. And I want to go through them real quickly. We're just going to read the last section of the article that we didn't get to before. Ok, we said before, was there any information about black holes in the article?

Students: No.

Ms. S: Was there any information on the speed of light?

Students: No.

Ms. S: Hi, Katie. Yes, Nick?

Nick: I have something that shows that it's very, very, very fast. Whenever we turned the light box on, the light immediately shot out. There was no gap.

Ms. S: Right. In any case, it's very fast. We just don't know exactly how fast from that, do we? Yeah, that's good. But the article really didn't say anything about it, or that it was the fastest thing in the solar system. *[points to claim on board]* So we still have no, no evidence about that. How about water splitting light into colors? *[points to next claim on board]* What did we say about that last time? Do we have any evidence in the article to show that that would happen? That water could do that? Nick?

Nick: No, but, um, I did when I put the plastic cup there, there was a little bit of, there was one blue strip of color.

Ms. S: Yeah, we said we needed a little bit more information about that. Zoe?

Zoe: Well, I just, about light is the fastest thing in the solar system?

Ms. S: Hm–mm?

Zoe: Well, we know it's faster than sound because with lightning and thunder.

Ms. S: What happens?

Zoe: Lightning gets here before the thunder.

Ms. S: Interesting. Ok. Good observation. Do you know what she means by that?

Students: Yeah.

Ms. S: Have you heard about that? Ok, good.

Jung Ho: I know why. Because light goes faster than sound.

Ms. S: That's what Zoe was saying. That's kind of a natural proof, isn't it? *[points to next claim on board]* Um, black absorbs, I put most here, we didn't have most on our claim but I think the article said most. Black absorbs most of the light and white reflects most of the light. And last time we proved that that was, or we found out from the article, that that was ...

Students: True.

Ms. S: Um, anyone have anything more to say about that? About what we found out? *[no response from students]* Ok, *[points to next claim]* Light is a source of energy.

Students: no ... yeah ... no

Ms. S: The article said just a teeny bit about that, and I think it was in association, it was associated with this. *[points to previous claim, then to next claim]* How about light is reflected, oh, I changed this one, actually. We had up here last time light is not reflected by objects other than mirrors, and I changed it because we said no, that wasn't true. So I changed it to say, light is reflected by objects other than mirrors. And what did it say in the article about that? How do we know that that is true? That light is reflected by objects other than mirrors? Katie, what do you think?

Katie: Well, because of, it said in here that *[looking at the article]* did you try light to travel with anything other than mirrors? And it bounces off. It's like ...

Ms. S: Ok, how does light bounce off of a mirror? *[no response from students]* Ok, why don't you look at the second page, under light bounces. Right there in the middle. Can you turn to the second page? Kind of skim that paragraph. You see where it says how light bounces off a mirror? About two thirds of the way down?

Students: uh-huh ... yeah

Ms. S: Do you see that? Sarah, do you see that? About two thirds of the way down, that paragraph in the middle of the page? What does it say? What does it say, Katie?

Katie: *[reading]* most mirrors are made of glass, even, re—*[starts again]* Most mirrors are made of glass with a thin coat of shiny silver on the back. What happens when light bouncing off you hits the mirrors? The light bounces off the mirror in the same pattern as it hit the mirror. You see yourself.

Ms. S: Actually even the sentence before that, or the two sentences before that, it says *[reading]* The surface of a mirror is very smooth. Light bounces off this smooth surface in an even, regular way. Ok, how about other objects, then? If we said that light bounces off of all things, all objects, then how is it different than bouncing off a mirror? They used white paper as an example. How is it different? Zoe, did you have an idea about that? *[Zoe shakes head no]* Ok, David.

David: Um, it said in the article that even the smoothest paper is rough so it wouldn't bounce off as well because, um, paper is just not very, um, smooth.

Ms. S: So the light would bounce off in all different

David: directions and scatter.

Ms. S: Scatter.

At this point, Ms. S asked the class to vote again on whether they agreed that light bounces off everything. There were still several students who did not agree. One student, Julian, volunteered that he knew, "... one thing that light does not bounce off of—air." Ms. S added this statement to the class list of claims. The introduction of this topic sparked a debate among the students.

Nick: *Ms. S? [Ms. S is writing Julian's claim on the board]*

Ms. S: Yeah?

Nick: I know, I know, I think no for that one but I know why no. Because we can't see air. [We can't see air.]

Katie: [We can't prove it because we cannot see air.]

Nick: That's because light doesn't reflect onto the air and then go to our eyes. Because it can't reflect off air.

Student *[off camera]*:   Why not?

Katie: We can't, we can't

Ms. S: Just a second. One at a time. Katie?

Katie: Well, we can't see air so it's like impossible to tell if that's true or not.

Nick: Well, it said, it said in the article the way you see things, or something like this, the way we see things is it reflects off that thing and goes to your eyes. But it can't reflect off air so it doesn't go to your eyes.

Ms. S: Interesting. So that's sort of Nick's theory.

Katie: But we can't prove that.

At this point, the discussion began to focus on whether we could test this claim, and whether we can in fact see air or not. Katie offered her dad's help in investigating this, and David B. made comments regarding smoke and steam, which he decided weren't pure air but air with water and "particles" in it. The class' discussion eventually sent them back to the article for information regarding whether light bounces off of or travels through air.

Ms. S: Ok, one more comment about that. Jung Ho?

Jung Ho: Well, it's just that I think light travels through air. It doesn't bounce off.

Ms. S: Do you have any evidence in the article? Did it say anything about that in here?

Jung Ho: Well, not really but about Nick's claim.

Ms. S: Did anyone see anything about that in here? About light traveling through air in the article?

Student [off camera]: No, but I've got something to prove.

Ms. S: Take a look at the first page. Just (?) with me. Look at the second paragraph. Do you see anything in there that talks about light traveling through air?

Students: Yeah...yes...yeah

Ms. S: You see that? What is it? Ilya, can you read that sentence about that?

Ilya: [reading] Luminous objects are objects that give off light.

Ms. S: Look at the top of that paragraph, the second paragraph.

Ilya: Where?

Ms. S: The second paragraph. It says when.

Ilya: Oh, Ok. [reading] When light travels from a luminous object to your eyes it has to travel through air.

David B: So it travels through air.

Ms. S: Air is transparent so light travels right through air.

In discussing the discourse that unfolded in Ms. S's class during the second-hand investigation, these are the features we address; (a) the extension of first-hand investigations, (b) the seamless quality emerging between first- and second-hand investigations in this context, (c) the metacognitive dimension to the discourse, and (d) the role the second hand investigation played in providing a common inquiry that advanced conceptual understanding.

Consistently throughout the discourse, there was attention paid to using the text for the purpose of extending the students' first-hand inquiry. For example, Ms. S focused the students' attentions on those claims for which there was still a lack of consensus. She began the second-hand investigation with the students' claims and models and engaged in a continuous process of tacking back and forth between the text and the student-generated claims; for example, when the text signaled that "light travels through some materials differently than others," Ms. S stopped to inquire what the students already knew about this characteristic of light, given their first-hand experiences. Similarly, when the text raised what is essentially a claim (when light hits black paper, almost no light bounces from it; instead the light energy is absorbed), Ms. S directed the students' attention to the evidence they had mustered for this claim from their own inquiry. Hynd and Alvermann and their colleagues (e.g., Alvermann & Hynd, 1989; Hynd, Qian, Ridgeway, & Pickle, 1992) documented the important role that student dissatisfaction with existing knowledge plays in conceptual change. By engaging in the second-hand investigation so that it was essentially in the service of the first-hand investigation, the students' thinking remained at the forefront; the students' ideas were the touchstones, not to be usurped by the text.

There was a seamless quality relative to tacking between the students' experiences and the ideas presented in the text to determine knowledge claims. For example, when reading about luminous and nonluminous objects, and also when reading about the properties of transparent, translucent, and opaque objects, the class was directed to explore their immediate environment for the purpose of identifying these phenomena. Further evidence of the seamlessness is presented in that portion of the discussion when Ms. S incorporated the investigation and evidence generated by two students (Kevin and Ilya) and encouraged the class to respond to this evidence essentially as "text." The intertextuality is made more salient by the fact that Kevin read from his personal notebook at this point in the discussion. There is evidence that the students had already begun to appropriate this orientation to second-hand investigations; for example, even though Ms. S was drawing the students' attention to whether the text had provided additional information regarding the speed of light, Nick offered additional evidence, drawing from the class' first-hand investigation ("whenever we turned the light box on, the light immediately shot out"). Furthermore, the students used the text as an occasion for generating additional claims (e.g., the role that particles in the air play in reflection).

In addition, there was a metacognitive dimension to the discourse that merits attention. For example, Ms. S was careful to make distinctions between first-and second-hand investigations. She made finer distinctions between those issues (represented as claims) that were unanswered (e.g., the nature of light as energy) and those issues that cannot be investigated first-hand (black holes). She labeled those claims for which there was no consensus [does water "split" (refract) light in the same way that a prism splits light?] as opposed to those on which there was consensus but for which there was insufficient evidence (dark objects absorb more light than lighter colored objects). She called the students' attention to what they already knew relative to the information in the text, and she signaled how the text might advance their emergent understandings of claims they had generated.

Finally, this second-hand investigation revealed the role that text can play when students have had disparate experiences in their first-hand experiences and yet the class is trying to advance class claims. Recall that the students in this class were free to investigate whatever claims regarding light about which they were curious and for which they had the necessary materials and equipment. The value of this approach is that, across the class, students had experienced a broad range of phenomena related to light (e.g., color derived from white light, the relationship between color and the absorption of light, the relationship between the texture of an object and the manner in which light reflects off that object); however, this range of experiences made it more difficult for students to achieve consensus on a particular set of claims regarding the behavior of light. The text, in hand with the diverse experiences of the students, provided a shared context in which the class could advance their consideration and judgment regarding a common set of claims. This finding is reflected on the measure of conceptual understanding that was conducted with these students before their first-hand experiences, following their first-hand experiences, and following their second-hand experiences. On the pretest concept measure, only 2 of the 27 students in this classroom correctly indicated (via drawing) that light (from the sun) is reflected off a target (in this case, a tree) and to the eyes of the viewer. Following their first-hand investigation, 16 students correctly identified how the viewer is able to see the tree. However, following the second-hand investigation, all but one student correctly responded to this question.

The descriptive research in Ms. S' class advanced our understanding of the role that the text, the teacher, the classroom community, and inquiry activity play in advancing students' scientific inquiry and conceptual understanding. The close study of one teacher's implementation of second-hand investigations was invaluable to informing our thinking about the challenges and opportunities inherent in achieving a productive intersection between text and first-hand investigations in the context of guided inquiry science teaching in the elementary grades. Although there were many positive and worthwhile experiences created in the conduct of this second-hand investigation, we were also struck by those features that were missing and yet seemed integral to fully productive second-hand investigations; for example, children were not engaged in assuming a critical stance relative to the text and the text seemed to do little to advance the children's opportunities to learn to think and reason scientifically. These observations influenced our thinking about the design features we would include in the innovative genre we developed to support second-hand investigations in GIsML instruction. Our goal was to design text that would assume some of the burden traditionally on the teacher to engage in the use of text for the broad range of purposes we had in mind.

DESIGNING TEXT TO SUPPORT
GUIDED INQUIRY TEACHING

Our decision to model the text on a scientist's notebook was influenced by our interest in the role that second-hand investigations could play in advancing students' understandings related to both the topic under study (e.g., light), and the use of scientific reasoning through learning about the experiences and thinking of others. Toward this end, there are many ways in which the notebook represents a think-aloud on the part of Lesley who documents the purpose of her investigation, the question(s) guiding her inquiry, the investigative procedures in which she is engaged, the ways in which she is gathering and choosing to represent her data, the claims emerging from her work, the relationships among these claims and her evidence, the conclusions she is deriving, and the new questions that are emerging from her inquiry.

The innovative texts that we designed and investigated are a hybrid of exposition, narration, description, and argumentation. They were designed in conjunction with the inquiry programs of study in use in our GIsML classrooms *(How Light Interacts With Objects, The Study of Floating and Sinking, The Study of Soils)*. One of the features that students have fre-quently commented on with regard to these texts is the presence of "voice" in these notebooks. As the quotes with which we opened this manuscript suggest, students equate the reading of these texts to learning from a "real person," and have suggested that this feature personalizes their reading and renders the text more interesting to them.

There are a number of features that are present in these texts that are consistent with promoting scientific literacy. (See Appendix for a sample text.) The texts include multiple ways of representing data, including tables, figures, and diagrams. For example, diagrams are used to illustrate the setup of the investigation materials. Figures are used to depict data that students can interpret, along with the scientist. Tables model the various ways in which data can be arrayed, and the narrative accompanying the table models the activity of interpreting these data.

There are opportunities for the scientist to revise her thinking based on the collection of additional or more specific data. Students are supported in tracing the source and nature of these revisions. There are reference materials included in these texts that serve to advance the inquiry. For example, in a notebook entry regarding light, the scientist includes what she has learned from studying Newton's investigations of light and color. This provides the opportunity for the scientist to model the use of a second-hand investigation as she critically reads and interprets the reference information and indicates how she will formulate claims from this information to advance her own inquiry. These reference materials are also useful for enriching the conceptual information with which children can work.

Yet another feature of these notebooks is the extent to which they portray the ways in which scientists interact with one another and observe particular conventions to facilitate these interactions. For example, in one entry, Lesley notes that fellow scientists were not persuaded by her data because they were inexact, leading her to use an instrument that would provide more exact data and a process that could be more readily replicated. In the next section of this chapter, we describe a quasi-experimental study in which we compared the outcomes of using this innovative text with the outcomes of using considerate-expository text.

EXPERIMENTAL RESEARCH COMPARING THE INNOVATIVE TEXT WITH TRADITIONAL TEXT

The purpose of this quasi-experimental research was to compare the process and outcomes of using the innovative text, when compared with considerate-expository text (herein referred to as traditional text) to support a second-hand investigation, in the absence of any first-hand experiences. The innovative text was modeled after the scientist's notebook and contained the features described earlier. The traditional text was designed as a considerate, nonrefutational, expository text. We elected to design this study as a within-subject, across-group, study in which each child served as his or her own control and read both the notebook and traditional version of a text. Recognizing the role that background knowledge plays in comprehension, both versions of the text addressed the general topic of light. Both a notebook and traditional text were constructed for the subtopic—reflection, and both a notebook and traditional text were constructed for the subtopic—refraction. Children who read the notebook version of reflection read the considerate-expository version of refraction, and vice versa.

This study took place in two waves. The first wave began in late October 1998 in Granite City. The classroom teachers in three fourth-grade classrooms, all of which were located in different schools in this district, agreed to participate. Our inability to identify a fourth classroom for this wave meant that the design was incomplete; there was no condition in which the students first read the traditional refraction text followed by the notebook reflection text. The second wave began in February 1999. This wave took place in one school in Maple Grove, in which four fourth-grade teachers agreed to participate; hence, for this wave, we had a complete design.

The demographics for each of the two districts suggested important differences in their characteristics. Granite City is an urban district that serves a significant number of families that qualify for free, or reduced-cost, lunch, whereas Maple Grove is a rural district with many fewer families in financial distress. The racial/ethnic profile of Maple Grove is fairly homogenous, whereas Granite City is somewhat heterogeneous, with a significant population (30.3%) of self-identified African Americans. Furthermore, there were potentially important differences in the characteristics of the participating classrooms within the two districts. The Gates MacGinitie Reading Achievement scores (across both vocabulary and comprehension) were consistently lower in the Granite City schools than in the Maple Grove Schools. Because of these sets of differences, we report the results for each district separately.

Table 5.1 presents the characteristics of the two text types across the two topics. We attempted to hold similar all features of the text (e.g., overall length, number of propositional units, readability) that might interfere with our ability to study the differential effects of the features in which we were most interested (those modeling scientific reasoning and the use of inquiry to advance scientific understanding). These features are best represented in the propositional units that are characterized as syntactic ver-

TABLE 5.1
Characteristics of the Two Text Types

| Text | # Sentences | # Prop. Units | | Readability | Figures | Tables |
		Sub.	Synt.	(Fry)		
Refl. N. B.	25	18	14	mid. gr. 5	2	1
Refr. N. B.	23	18	15	beg. gr. 5	3	1
Refl. Trad	25	30		high gr. 5	2	
Refr. Trad	28	31		beg. gr. 5	3	

sus substantive. Substantive units refer to those statements that were written to inform the children's understanding about the reflection or refraction of light (e.g., "the texture of an object will affect the direction that the light is reflected...," "light is energy"). Syntactic units are those that communicate the process and nature of scientific reasoning (e.g., "I need to think about how this information helps me to understand my own data and to answer my questions").

Excerpts from the two text types are provided in Tables 5.2 and 5.3 below.

For each of the two subtopics we designed a paper and pencil assessment to be administered before and after the students read each text. There were seven items on each assessment (some with multiple parts—totaling 14 points). Of these items, three items were designed to measure the recall of factual information. The remaining items were designed to assess students' ability to engage in inferencing from the text. With respect to the items requiring inference, two dealt solely with substantive knowledge and two with a combination of substantive and syntactic knowledge (the ability to engage in scientific reasoning). For example, on the refraction

TABLE 5.2
Sample Text: Traditional Version

When scientists have measured the light reflecting from objects they have found that some light is always reflected. That is, for all objects, some but not all of the light reaching them is reflected. The light that is not reflected can be absorbed by the object. Scientists have wondered what determines the amount of light reflected. They have found that light or white objects reflect most of the light and absorb only a little. Dark or black objects, on the other hand, mostly absorb the light energy and little is reflected from them. You may have experienced this fact about light in your own life as you have touched objects that have had some light shining on them.

TABLE 5.3
Sample Text: Notebook Version

Scientist Lesley Park	Date 10/28/97	Page 2

What I concluded from these data
1. The light reflected from each solid object was always less than the amount of incoming light on the object.
2. The type of material seems to make a difference in how the light is reflected
   - Why are there different amounts of reflected light?
   - Does the amount have to do with the color or the texture of the object?
   - What happens to the light that is NOT reflected? I wondered what other scientists have learned from their investigations of light, so I read about some of their claims.

assessment, students were provided a table with the optical densities of five materials (glass and four other materials). They were asked to indicate which material would bend light the most when the light was moving into this material from glass. The concept of optical density was described in the text; however, to be successful on this item, students needed to know how to read the data represented in the table, they needed to be able to compare the materials as relevant to the issue of optical density, and they had to complete the comparisons required to determine which material would bend light to the greatest extent.

Given the different affordances of the two text types, it was important to consider the relationship between the text and the instruction. We did not expect students to read and respond to these texts independently; rather, the students' reading of the text was mediated by the teacher (Palincsar). This was decided based on the following: It would be uncommon for fourth-grade teachers to assign such text to be read independently, and we did not want students' ability to decode the text to limit what we could determine about their learning from the text. Hence, we were interested in determining how the characteristics of these two text types would interact with the students' use of these texts.

With the traditional text, the teacher employed domain-general strategies, that is, with each paragraph, the teacher elicited a summary in which the students were encouraged to identify the main ideas. The students were also asked to identify the questions that were addressed in the paragraph, and they were asked if any information presented in the paragraph required clarification. When using the notebook text, the teacher mirrored the activities suggested in the GIsML heuristic. At the beginning of the text, the teacher asked the students to identify the purpose of the inquiry. As the text continued, the teacher engaged the students in identifying the investigative procedures, interpreting the data, examining the relationships among the data, and identifying the implications of these relationships with regard to claims one might make.

Using nonparametric statistical analyses, we determined the following outcomes. In Maple Grove, for both topics (reflection and refraction), there were statistically significant differences in learning in favor of the scientist's notebook text with respect to mean posttest scores, mean scores on the *substantive knowledge* items, and mean scores on the *substantive knowledge + reasoning* items. In Granite City, only when considering the refraction topic were there statistically significant differences in favor of the scientist's notebook. There were no learning differences (by text type) for the topic of reflection; however, posttest scores for the items requiring *substantive knowledge* + *reasoning* approached significance (level) in favor of the scientist's notebook text.

In summary, both versions of the text were supportive of students' learning across the two topics concerning light; however, in three of the four conditions in which we could compare the relative benefits of the text genre, the results favored the notebook genre. In one sample (Granite City) for one topic (reflection), there was no significant difference between the outcomes for students who learned about reflection using the notebook versus the traditional text.

To fully understand these differences in outcomes is to examine the nature of the instructional interactions supported by these two text types. Generally, across the seven classrooms, when the notebook text was in use, the instructional conversation reflected the inquiry process. Students were prompted to reflect on the text in terms of the inquiry reported in Lesley's notebook, and across the classes, the students were able to draw on the substantive information in the text to not only follow but to also anticipate the inquiry that was subsequently described. For example, in the refraction notebook version, the text provided opportunities for the students to draw on their relevant background knowledge to generate explanations for an observation quite familiar to them—the appearance that a straw in water is "broken" at the point it enters the water. Because the text was written as an ongoing inquiry, students responded to their reading by bringing to bear their own experiences with this type of phenomenon, making suggestions about how Lesley could proceed to further investigate the phenomenon in other contexts. This type of conversation was far less likely to occur during the reading of the traditional text in which the phenomenon and its explanation were presented explicitly for the students and then illustrated in additional contexts.[4]

Finally, there were substantially more opportunities for students to engage in coconstruction relative to understanding light when responding to the notebook version. For example, the notebook text about reflection provided information in a table about the characteristics of given materials (i.e., color, texture) and the interaction of light with each. Students had to hypothesize about the relationship between the characteristics of objects and the behavior of light. In contrast, in the traditional version, students were provided with a description of the relationship, which they

---

[4]It is, of course, possible for the instructional conversation to override the constraints of the text. For example, in one class, which was using the traditional version of the refraction text, a child promptly placed a pencil in a bottle of water on his desk and proudly displayed his demonstration to his classmates, prompting conversation about this and related phenomena.

then paraphrased; however, this did not engage them in the same constructive process relative to building conceptual understanding about light.

In the final portion of this chapter, we report a subset of findings from
an observational study that was conducted in two fourth-grade classrooms
where teachers used several notebook texts to engage their students in
second-hand investigations that complemented their first-hand inquiries.

Observational Research
With the Innovative Text

In her dissertation study, Danielle Ford examined the experiences of two
fourth-grade teachers and their students as they engaged in first-hand
investigations in a program of study entitled, *How Light Interacts With
Objects,* and in second-hand investigations using two notebook texts
designed for this program of study.

In this section, we highlight a few of the findings from her research,
drawing on the experiences of Ms. Dunbar and her class. (The reader is
referred to Ford, 1999 for complete information regarding this work). As
we engaged in this research, we were especially interested in ascertaining
the instructional opportunities afforded by the text, those features of the
text that were most challenging, and the relationship between the first- and
second-hand investigations. For the purpose of this chapter, we are interested in reporting those observations that influence our current thinking
about the design of these texts.

Ford made a number of observations regarding the ways in which these
teachers made use of the structural features of the text. For example, these
texts contained several tables and figures to which the teachers devoted
considerable time, guiding student thinking about why these features were
included and how they might be used. This is an interesting finding to the
extent that the ability to interpret data that are presented in tables and figures is integral to the comprehension of scientific texts (Roth & McGinn,
1998).

Ms. D: Why do you think she [Lesley] gave us this picture?

Ann: I think she wanted us to understand her thinking, so she put pictures
and labeled it. So we would understand what she was thinking. Not just
the words. It's kinda like what we were doing for our investigations,
because we said that we wanted them [peers] to put pictures on their

[posters] and words and to label them so we would understand. And that's what she's doing.

One of the most obvious ways in which the text influenced the children's thinking was when they returned to conduct another cycle of their own first-hand investigations following their initial second-hand investigation. The students were very attentive to the organization and representation of their data, drawing heavily on the formatting ideas presented in the scientist's notebook. In addition, they quickly appropriated the idea of quantifying the amount of light, adopting the same scale introduced by Lesley.

The second-hand investigation also appeared to be an effective means of introducing the students to a more precise lexicon with which to describe their own observations regarding light. For example, following the reading, the students revised the list of class claims appropriating the terms "absorbed" and "transmitted" to substitute for "goes through" and "stays in."

We purposefully designed the text to report findings that would be revised on further investigation. This feature led to one of the most interesting exchanges to occur in the course of the second-hand investigation, when there was a conflict between a class claim that had received widespread support following the students' first-hand investigations ("Light reflects off all objects") and data that were presented by Lesley in her notebook; i.e., "these data suggested that light did not reflect off a piece of black felt." In the beginning of this exchange, Nat, who is leading the discussion, summarizes and then follows with a question that is focused on the conflicting finding:

Nat: I think on this table what they're trying to tell us is how the objects went with light, and how the shadow was and how it behaved. And my question is, why did the black felt have no light? Byron?

Byron: Cause it was really hard for it to reflect and go into the light catcher.

Mitch, another student in the class, is disturbed with this finding:

Mitch: That's not true! Cause it says light can reflect off anything [*pointing to the class claim that has been posted on the wall*]

Ms. D: Hold on! What does it say there [on the table]?

Mitch: On reflected, it says "no light."

Ms. D: What does that mean?...

Mitch: That she don't believe that light reflects off everything.

Ms. D: Okay, so she wouldn't believe one of our claims.

This incongruity led the children to speculate why it might be that Lesley's observation differed from their own. Among their speculations were the possibility that the black felt with which she was investigating was different than their own and (pointing to the figure that Lesley provided of her experimental setup) noticing that her light catcher was not placed as closely to the object as were their light catchers. As Lesley proceeds with her investigation, she is advised by other scientists to use a light meter for the purposes of obtaining more accurate data.

Ms. D: So, this is a pretty important thing. If you've got a group of scientists, and you're sharing, and they want something else from you. Do they just say, well, Lesley, we're not convinced?

Becca: One of the scientists said for her to use a light meter. They were trying to help her to get more data by one of the scientists saying she could use a light meter... The scientists weren't saying she was wrong or not right.

Ms. D: They actually did a couple of things. They were very specific about what they wanted more from her. They told her they wanted to know more about the amount of light reflected from an object compared to the amount of light transmitted from an object. That's what they wanted her to focus on. And they said, you know, it's not exact, and here's an idea of what you might want to use to go back and make it more exact.

The students were immensely pleased when, with the use of this instrument, Lesley also measured reflected light from the black felt.

Similar to the findings of Dunbar and Klahr (1989), Ford (1999) also found that students were challenged in distinguishing among evidence, claims, and data. In the presentations regarding their own first-hand investigations, as well as in their interpretations and discussions of Lesley's inquiry, these constructs were not used with rigor. Furthermore, consistent with the findings of Kuhn (1989) and Schauble and Glaser (1990), although students were fairly adept at identifying those data that supported their claims, there was little attention to the role of disconfirming evidence. In addition, claims for which there was no evidence were dropped from the class conversation.

As we reflect on findings such as these, we are intrigued with additional possibilities that might be featured in the text. For example, we are interested in the modeling of scientific argumentation in more explicit ways, especially if the text exploits the first-hand experiences that students have engaged in so that they are in a position to coconstruct the argument with the scientist, or to deconstruct another's argument. We will continue to pursue the use of these texts to present the norms and conventions of scientific problem solving and to demonstrate the social ways in which the cannon is generated and refined over time.

THE CHALLENGES AND OPPORTUNITIES ASSOCIATED WITH USING TEXT IN GUIDED INQUIRY SCIENCE

This multifaceted program of research has both shaped and supported our thinking about the role and nature of second-hand investigations in advancing elementary children's learning of science and the processes of scientific reasoning. The early observational work in Ms. S's room, which led to the development of the notebook genre, changed our thinking about the possibilities with text in inquiry instruction in unexpected ways. This research revealed a number of the challenges inherent in conducting second-hand investigations, particularly at the elementary level, where children may have had relatively few experiences using informational text. These challenges included the need to teach students to use text generatively, to assume a critical stance relative to text, to monitor their understanding of text, and to build connections between the information presented in the text and the understandings they developed from their first-hand investigations. Teachers face the additional challenge posed by the paucity of commercially prepared text material that can productively support this kind of second-hand inquiry. This paucity, in hand with thinking about the challenges of second-hand investigations, led us to consider designing our own text, which resulted in the scientist's notebook genre. The quasi-experimental work provided sufficient support for the benefit of the notebook genre over more traditional text to lead us to continue investigating both the instructional possibilities and learning outcomes with this new genre.

Furthermore, the quasi-experimental research and the later observational work represent an initial response to concerns expressed by teachers, experienced with guided inquiry science teaching, about the added value of second-hand investigations. They expressed concerns that text not supplant the important learning that students could experience in the course of first-hand inquiry, for example, examining data for patterns, determining how data constitute evidence and counterevidence for extant claims, thinking through the process of representing one's data and interpreting others' data, and designing further inquiry experiences. In addition, these studies shaped our thinking about additional features to explore to further enhance the ways in which the text could support students in developing knowledge of and facility with scientific reasoning.

The observational research also informed our thinking about the demands that teaching from the notebook texts places on teachers. Engaging children in interacting with the notebook texts in an inquiry fashion requires careful mediation on the part of the teacher. In turn, teachers need to be supported in developing teaching practices that promote the use of text as an inquiry. Similar to the notion advanced by White and Frederiksen (1998), who suggested that their software, *ThinkerTools*, is a valuable way of scaffolding the initial implementation of a guided inquiry curriculum, our hypothesis is that the innovative text genre that assumes the form of a scientists' notebook can be an effective way of scaffolding both students' and teachers' use of text in an inquiry fashion. We are planning future research to investigate this very issue: Does the use of the notebook genre influence the ways teachers and students use commercially prepared text? We are also interested in how we might exploit the design of notebook texts for the purpose of supporting children's learning of some of the more challenging aspects of scientific reasoning, for example, coordinating data, evidence, and claims in the service of constructing a sound scientific argument. These texts might also be used to engage students in the process of evaluating multiple explanations for both accuracy and parsimony. In addition, we are interested in exploring further the interplay of first- and second-hand investigations. For example, our preliminary data suggest that strategically experienced second-hand investigations can have a productive influence on the ways children enact and learn from first-hand investigations. We have seen that second-hand investigations suggest strategies to children regarding how they might most effectively represent their data during first-hand investigations. Similarly, in the course of second-hand investigations, we have observed that children begin to develop a shared lexicon for discussing their inquiries, either first- or second-hand.

In closing, our research program is at an intersection that we believe holds promise for advancing inquiry based teaching and learning of science in the elementary grades by; (a) conceptualizing instruction as guided inquiry teaching consisting of first- and second-hand experiences,

(b) the presence of text features that support both the conduct of first- and second-hand investigations, and (c) the nature of classroom contexts necessary for effective inquiry based teaching and meaningful learning via inquiry.

ACKNOWLEDGMENTS

The comparative text research reported in this paper was supported with a grant from the McDonnell Foundation's Cognitive Studies in Educational Practice Program. The classroom observational research was supported with funding from CIERA. The professional development context reported in this paper was supported with grants from the Spencer/ MacArthur Foundations' Program on Professional Development and the Eisenhower Higher Education Program. The authors gratefully acknowledge reviews of an earlier draft of this chapter by Sharon Carver and Leona Schauble.

REFERENCES

Alvermann, D. R., & Hynd, C. R. (1989). Effects of prior knowledge activation modes and text structure on nonscience majors' comprehension of physics. *Journal of Educational Research, 83* (2), 97–102.

Applebee, A. N., Langer, J. A., Mullis, I. V. S., Latham, A. S., & Gentile, C. A. (1994). *NAEP 1992 writing report card* (Report No. 23–W01). Washington, DC: U.S. Government printing Office.

Balluerka, N. (1995). The influence of instructions, outlines, and illustrations on the comprehension and recall of scientific facts. *Contemporary Educational Psychology, 20*, 369–375.

Boyle, R. K., & Maloney, D. P. (1991). Effect of written text on usage of Newton's third law. *Journal of Research in Science Teaching, 28* (2), 129–139.

Brown, A. L., & Campione, J. C. (1994). Guided discovery in a community of learners. In K. McGilly (Ed.), *Classroom lessons: Integrating cognitive theory and classroom practice* (pp. 229–272). Cambridge, MA: MIT Press.

Chall, J. S., Jacobs, V. A., & Baldwin, L. E. (1990). *The reading crisis: Why poor children fall behind.* Cambridge, MA: Harvard University Press.

Craig, M. T., & Yore, L. D. (1996). Middle school students' awareness of strategies for resolving comprehension difficulties in science reading. *Journal of Research and Development in Education, 29* (4), 226–228.

Dee-Lucas, D., & Larkin, J. H. (1988). Attentional strategies for studying scientific texts. *Memory & Cognition, 16* (5), 469–479.

Driver, R., Osoko, H., Leach, J., Mortimer, E., & Scott, P. (1994). Constructing scientific knowledge in the classroom. *Educational Researcher, 23* (7), 5–12.

Dunbar, K., & Klahr, D. (1989). Developmental differences in scientific discovery processes. In D. Klahr & K. Kotovsky (Eds.), *Complex information processing: The impact of Herbert A. Simon* (pp. 109–143). Hillsdale, NJ: Lawrence Erlbaum Associates.

Farris, P. J., Kissinger, R. W., & Thompson, T. (1988). Text organization and structure in science text-books. *Reading Horizons*, vol. 10, 123–130.

Ford, D. J. (1999). *The role of text in supporting and extending first-hand investigations in guided inquiry science*. Unpublished doctoral dissertation. Ann Arbor, MI: University of Michigan.

Gaskins, I. W., Guthrie, J. T., Satlow, E., Ostertag, J., Six, L., Byrne, J., & Connor, B. (1994). Integrating instruction of science, reading, and writing: Goals, teacher development, and assessment. *Journal of Research in Science Teaching, 31* (9), 1039–1056.

Grossman, P. (1990). *The making of a teacher: Teacher knowledge and teacher education.* New York: Teachers College Press.

Guthrie, J. T., McGough, K., Bennett, L., & Rice, M. E. (1996). Concept-oriented reading instruction: An integrated curriculum to develop motivations and strategies for reading. In L. Baker, P. Afflerbach, & D. Reinking (Eds.), *Developing engaged readers in school and home communities* (pp. 165–190). Mahwah, NJ: Lawrence Erlbaum Associates.

Guzetti, B. J., Snyder, T. E., & Glass, G. V. (1992). Promoting conceptual change in science: Can texts be used effectively? *Journal of Reading, 35* (8), 642–649.

Hiebert, E. H., & Fisher, C. W. (1990). Whole language: Three themes for the future. *Educational Leadership, 47* (6), 62–64.

Hynd, C. R., Qian, G., Ridgeway, V.G., & Pickle, M. (1992). Promoting conceptual change with science texts and discussion. *Journal of Reading, 34* (8), 596–601.

John-Steiner, V., & Mann, H. (1996). Sociocultural approaches to learning and development. *Educational Psychologist, 31*, 191–206.

Kuhn, D. (1989). Children and adults as intuitive scientists. *Psychological Review, 96* (4), 674–689.

Lemke, J. L. (1990). *Talking science: Language, learning, and values.* Norwood, NJ: Ablex.

Leonard, W. H. (1987). Does the presentation style of questions inserted into the text influence understanding and retention of science concepts? *Journal of Research in Science Teaching, 24* (1), 27–37.

Lloyd, C. V., & Mitchell, J. N. (1989). Coping with too many concepts in science texts. *Journal of Reading*, vol. 15, 542–545.

Magnusson, S. J., & Palincsar, A. S. (1995). The learning environment as a site of science education reform. *Theory Into Practice, 34* (1), 43–50.

National Research Council. (1996). *National science education standards.* Washington, DC: National Academy Press.

Norris, S. P., & Phillips, L. M. (1994). Interpreting pragmatic meaning when reading popular reports of science. *Journal of Research in Science Teaching, 31* (9), 947–967.

Otero, J. C., & Companario, J. M. (1990). Comprehension evaluation and regulation in learning from science tests. *Journal of Research in Science Teaching, 27* (5), 447–460.

Palincsar, A. S., & Brown, A.L. (1989). Classroom dialogues to promote self-regulated comprehension. In J. Brophy (Ed.), *Teaching for meaningful understanding and self-regulated learning,* vol. 1. Greenwich, CT: JAI Press.

Palincsar, A. S., & Magnusson, S. J. (1997, Nov.). *The interaction of first and second hand investigations in guided inquiry science teaching.* Paper presented at the annual conference of the National Reading Conference, Austin, TX.

Palincsar, A. S., Magnusson, S. J., Marano, N., Ford, D., & Brown, N. (1998). Designing a community of practice: Principles and practices of the GIsML Community. *Teaching and Teacher Education, 14*, 5–19.

Pappas, C. C. (1991). Fostering full access to literacy by including information books. *Language Arts, 68*, 449–462.

Pearson, J. A. (1991). Testing the ecological validity of teacher-provided vs. student-generated postquestions in reading college science texts. *Journal of Research in Science Teaching, 28*, 485–504.

Rogoff, B. (1994). Developing understanding of the idea of communities of learners. *Mind, Culture, and Activity, 1*, 209–229.

Roth, W. M., & McGinn, M. K. (1998). Inscriptions: Toward a theory of representing as social practice. *Review of Educational Research, 68,* 35–59.

Schauble, L., & Glaser, R. (1990). Scientific thinking in children and adults. In D. Kuhn (Ed.), *Developmental perspectives on teaching and learning thinking skills* (pp. 9–27). Basal, Switzerland: Karger.

Shymanski, J. A., Yore, L. D., & Good, R. (1991). Elementary school teachers' beliefs about and perceptions of elementary school science, science reading, science textbook, and supportive instructional factors. *Journal of Research in Science Teaching, 28* (5), 437–454.

The Cognition and Technology Group at Vanderbilt. (1994). From visual word problems to learning communities: Changing conceptions of cognitive research. In K. McGilly (Ed.), *Classroom lessons: Integrating cognitive theory and classroom practice* (pp. 157–200). Cambridge, MA: MIT Press.

Wells, G. (1995). Language and the inquiry oriented curriculum. *Curriculum Inquiry, 25,* 233–269.

Wertsch, J, (1998). *Mind as action.* New York: Oxford University Press.

White, B.Y., & Frederiksen, J. R. (1998). Inquiry, modeling, and metacognition: Making science accessible to all students. *Cognition and Instruction, 16* (1), 3–118.

Woloshyn, V. E., Paivio, A., & Pressley, M. (1994). Use of elaborative interrogation to help students acquire information consistent with prior knowledge and information inconsistent with prior knowledge. *Journal of Educational Psychology, 86* (1), 79–89.

Woodward, J., & Noell, J. (1991). Science instruction at the secondary level: Implications for students with learning disabilities. *Journal of Learning Disabilities, 24* (5), 251–277.

APPENDIX

Today I investigated how light interacts with different materials. I shined a flashlight on different solid objects and looked at what happened to the light. I used a light catcher to see if light reflected off the object, I looked behind the object to see if light was transmitted by it (traveled through) or if there was a shadow. A shadow would tell me that the object was blocking the light. Figure 1 shows how I used my equipment.

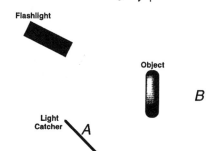

Figure 1. Materials in investigation.
Positions where I described the Light:
   A - on the light catcher
   B - area behind the object

From the data I collected, I made Table 1 to list the ways light interacted with solid objects.

Table 1. How different places looked when I shined light on solid objects.

OBJECT	ON LIGHT CATCHER *[light reflected]*	ON BACK of Object *[light transmitted]*	AREA BEHIND Object *[light blocked]*
Clear Glass	dim light	bright light	light shadow
Purple Glass	dim purple light	bright purple light	dark purple shadow
Silver Wrap	bright light	no light	dark shadow
White Plastic Sheet	dim light	medium light	medium shadow
White Typing Paper	bright light	dim light	medium shadow
Black Felt	no light	no light	very dark shadow
Orange Cardboard	dim orange light	dim reddish light	dark shadow

What I concluded from my data:
- Light reflects off all solid objects, except if they are black.
- Light does not go through all solid objects.
- All objects block the light some amount.
- If a lot of light is reflected off a solid object, not much light is transmitted through it. If a lot of light is transmitted through a solid object, not much light is reflected.

When I showed my claims and evidence to other scientists, they were not convinced of my conclusions because my data were not exact. The other scientists were not confident in my judgments about how the amount of light reflected from an object compared to the amount of light that was transmitted through it.

One scientist suggested that I use a **light meter** to collect more data. She told me a light meter is an instrument that measures the brightness of light. With this tool, I can actually measure the amount of light at any place. Figure 2 shows a picture of a light meter. It measures light in units of candles. I plan to repeat my experiments with the same materials but using a light meter.

Figure 2. Picture of a light meter.

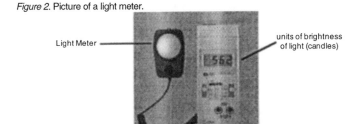

When I repeated the light experiments, I used the same materials in the same way. Figure 3 shows the setup when I measured the light reaching each object. The light meter told me that the light from the flashlight was 10 candles bright.

Figure 3.
Using the light meter.

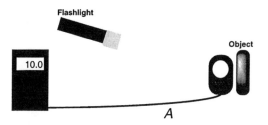

I also used the light meter to measure at two other points (shown in Figure 3). The light at Point A tells me how much light reflected from each object, and the light at Point B tells me how much light was transmitted through each object. I recorded these measurements in Table 2.

Table 2. Measurements of how light interacted with objects.

OBJECT	Light REFLECTED from object (A)	Light TRANSMITTED through object (B)	TOTAL Light measured
Clear Glass	2 candles	7 candles	9 candles
Purple Glass	2 candles	6 candles	8 candles
Silver Wrap	7 candles	0 candles	7 candles
White Plastic Sheet	5 candles	2 candles	7 candles
White Typing Paper	4 candles	3 candle	7 candles
Black Felt	1 candle	0 candles	1 candle
Orange Cardboard	3 candles	2 candles	5 candles

What I concluded from these data:
- The light reflected from each solid object was always less than the amount of light on the object.
- The light transmitted through each solid object was always less than the amount of light on the object.
- The total amount of light transmitted <u>and</u> reflected from a solid object does <u>not</u> add up to the light reaching the object.
  A + B ≠ 10 candles.

Question for me to think about: If they don't add up, where is the other light? Can I assume it is absorbed in the material?

When I thought about whether the light was being absorbed, I thought about how all the objects made a shadow (see Table 1). I know that a shadow means light is blocked, so maybe this means that when light is blocked, some light is absorbed and stays in the object.

I wonder whether other scientists are thinking in this way? To find out, I will go to the library to read what other researchers have claimed about light.

I read several articles in the <u>Journal of Research on Optics</u> to learn about what other scientists have found out about light. Here is what one researcher said:

Our results tell us that light is a form of energy that can interact in several ways with a material. From our measurements of the temperature of solid objects after shining light on them, we determined these relationships:
- all objects reflect <u>and</u> absorb light
- the amount of energy that is absorbed or reflected depends on the material
- white objects mostly reflect light and black objects mostly absorb light; red and yellow objects absorb less light than green and blue objects
- thin objects transmit some light through them, and the thicker an object the more light is absorbed and the less light is transmitted

What I learned from the writings of this scientist:
- Light is energy.
- Light can be reflected, absorbed, and transmitted by the same object.
- All solid objects reflect <u>AND</u> absorb light.
- The color of an object tells us something about how light interacts with it.
- How light interacts with an object is also determined by the thickness of the object.

I need to think about how this information helps me think about my own data and conclusions.

The second claim that I recorded from the work other scientists did helped me the most in my thinking. If light can reflect, transmit, <u>and</u> be absorbed by the same object, I think that helps explain why the light meter readings didn't add up to 10 candles in my investigation. I only measured the light that was reflected or transmitted. I think the "missing" light was light that was absorbed by each object.

I used my measurements from Table 2 and my thinking about absorption to describe how light interacted with each of my objects. Here's how I described the light meter readings:

  1 - 3 = "a little"   4 - 6 = "some"   7 - 9 = "a lot."

I recorded these results in Table 3.

Table 3. Describing my objects by how much light they absorb, transmit, and reflect.

OBJECT	REFLECTS Light	TRANSMITS Light	ABSORBS Light
Clear Glass	Yes, a little	Yes, a lot	Yes, a little
Purple Glass	Yes, a little	Yes, some	Yes, a little
Silver Wrap	Yes, a lot	None	Yes, a little
Whitish Plastic	Yes, some	Yes, a little	Yes, a little
White Typing Paper	Yes, some	Yes, a little	Yes, a little
Black Felt	Yes, a little	None	Yes, a lot
Orange Cardboard	Yes, a little	Yes, a little	Yes, some

What I concluded:
  • Light always interacts with a solid object in at least two ways.

These results tell me that light does not interact in the same way for each object. That made me wonder: why does light behave differently for different objects? I am also wondering how light can interact in <u>different</u> ways with the <u>same</u> object. What does that mean about what light is like? I will have to figure out how to investigate to answer these questions.

6

Cognition, Instruction, and the Quest for Meaning

Robert S. Siegler
Carnegie Mellon University

When the first Carnegie Cognition Symposium on cognition and instruction was held (Klahr, 1976), the field was in its infancy, and many of the presentations were only tangentially related to instruction. Now, as the chapters in Parts I and II of this volume reveal, researchers are producing substantial quantities of rigorous research directly relevant to instruction. As the subtitle of this volume indicates, it has been "25 years of progress" for the field of cognition and instruction.

We should keep in mind, however, that the term "progress" has two different senses. One indicates improvement (i.e., technological progress); the other indicates change but not necessarily improvement (i.e., progress toward the inevitable). As we consider the accomplishments of this field, we should ask ourselves which changes represent improvement and which represent change but not necessarily improvement.

COGNITION AND INSTRUCTION: A TETRAHEDRAL FRAMEWORK

The central message that I derive from these chapters is that the way to produce optimal learning is to lead learners to interact with the target domain in meaningful ways. This perspective suggests a tetrahedral framework for thinking about cognition and instruction (Fig. 6.1). At the apex of the tetrahedron is learning; at the other vertices are learner characteristics, the target domain, and instruction. This framework has three

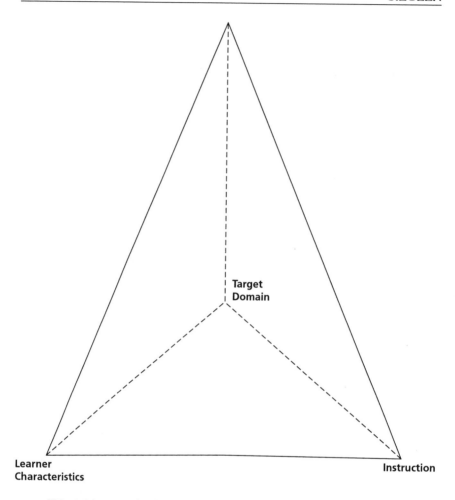

FIG. 6.1.   A tetrahedral framework for thinking about cognition and instruction.

advantages. First, it identifies variables that are central to understanding cognition and instruction, with each face defining a key intersection of three variables. Second, it reminds us that in analyses of cognition of instruction, learning is at the apex; instruction, the target domain, and learner characteristics matter only as they influence learning. Third, the faces of the tetrahedron provide a framework for organizing issues in the field in general and in the present set of chapters in particular. The remainder of this discussion examines issues concerning each of the three faces with learning at the apex.

Target Domain, Instruction, and Learning

What aspects of the target domain should be emphasized in instruction (i.e., "What should be learned?"). At one level, the answers suggested by the present chapters, all of which focus on math and science, are quite traditional; students should learn about ratios and proportions, forces and motion, density and weight, integers, rational numbers, functions, and so on. At another level, however, the chapters in the present volume reflect a more abstract, higher level characterization of target domains and instructional goals than was prevalent in the volume on this topic 25 years ago. Minstrell focuses on promoting scientific discourse skills (chap. 4). Palincsar and Magnusson encourage students to critically evaluate science texts and to understand the thought processes of other scientists (chap. 5). Lehrer, Schauble, Strom, and Pligge's program promotes understanding of the nature of mathematical argument, as well as of the epistemology of science (chap. 2). The goals of Kalchman, Moss, and Case's (chap. 1) and Klahr, Chen, and Toth's (chap. 3) research are somewhat less lofty, but they still are very high-level relative to typical classroom activities as well as to past research on cognition and instruction. Promoting number sense and scientific experimentation skills hardly qualifies as part of the back to basics movement.

To some extent, the views that very high-level goals are central to each target domain and that they should be emphasized in instruction reflect choices of the symposium organizers. They selected the participants and thus, indirectly, the approaches that would be included. However, their choices seem representative of current emphases in the field of cognition and instruction. This emphasis may be a reaction to practices in typical classrooms, where activities aimed at inculcating low-level skills dominate day-to-day activities. Alternatively, it may reflect a more absolute belief that the high-level skills are the most important ones and should be emphasized even if it means that lower level skills receive less practice.

This change from lower level goals certainly represents progress, but it is unclear whether it is progress in the sense of improvement or only in the sense of change. Before we will know, researchers interested in cognition and instruction will need to answer two questions. First, what kinds of evidence do we have that learning would be improved if high-level thinking skills were emphasized to a greater extent than they are? Given time pressures, educators need to choose among competing priorities. What evidence is there that would convince teachers who are skeptical but not cynical about pursuing high-level goals that changing their current approaches would be worthwhile? Comprehensive comparisons of the degree to which children receiving high-level instruction or traditional instruction attain both low-level and high-level objectives are needed to answer this question. Longitudinal comparisons of learning over time would be especially useful, because they would help distinguish between two plausible hypotheses. By one hypothesis, children whose instruction emphasizes high-level skills should be especially motivated to learn more about the domain in the future, and therefore should improve over time relative to those in traditional classrooms. By the other hypothesis, children whose instruction emphasizes high-level skills will be increasingly handicapped by insufficient mastery of the basics and therefore will fall behind over time. The present group of authors clearly hold the first hypothesis; I suspect that they are right, but I would like to see the data.

A second, related question is: What kinds of supports, if any, will be sufficient to allow classroom teachers to inculcate high-level thinking skills if the broader society decides to assign them high priority? Teachers may emphasize low-level skills not because they believe that those skills are the most important but because they understand them and are comfortable teaching them. The fact that professors, graduate students, and trained research assistants can effectively teach high-level content does not imply that most teachers could do the same. What type of help will poor, unmotivated teachers, as well as excellent, highly motivated ones, need to help students understand the thinking of other scientists, to critically evaluate science texts, and to develop scientific discourse skills? I suspect that in many cases, a great deal of help would be needed.

Another major issue within the target domain/instruction/learning area concerns how particular target domains can best be taught. The presenters in this group share the assumption that hands-on activity, guided by instructors' questions, notebooks, and text materials, is the best method for constructing deep knowledge of mathematics and science. Again, the present set of chapters include numerous appealing examples of how such hands-on learning can occur: The whole number and rational number board games used by Kalchman, Moss, and Case (chap. 1), the elbow construction project used by Lehrer, Schauble, Strom, and Pligge (chap. 2), the ramps and springs used to demonstrate experimental design principles by Klahr, Chen, and Toth (chap. 3), and so on. As with the emphasis on high-level instructional/learning goals, the emphasis on hands-on learning is appealing and the results are promising. Again, however, we need evidence that hands-on learning is worth the extra time and effort that would be required for teachers in the classroom to adopt the approach. We also need to ask what types of supports teachers would need to do so.

LEARNER CHARACTERISTICS, INSTRUCTION, AND LEARNING

In the subtitle of their chapter, Klahr, Chen, and Toth (chap. 3) ask if the relation between cognitive development and cognition and instruction is like that of two ships proceeding from different directions toward a single destination, with both ships' beacons illuminating that destination, or like that of ships passing in the night, with beacons trained on different destinations. Their chapter, and that of others in this group, suggests that there is a fair amount of overlapping illumination. This makes sense, given the centrality in both areas of the relation between learner characteristics and learning and the interest of some cognitive developmental researchers in instruction.

A number of themes in current research on cognitive development are evident in these chapters. One is that young children have greater learning capabilities than is usually realized. Palincsar and Magnusson demonstrate that third graders can gain a sophisticated understanding of reflection and refraction of light (chap. 5). Klahr, Chen, and Toth show that fourth graders can learn and transfer scientific experimentation skills (chap. 3). Lehrer, Schauble, Strom, and Pligge find that fifth graders can generate mathematical models of scientific data (chap. 2). Kalchman, Moss, and Case report that sixth graders can gain an understanding of mathematical functions that in some ways is superior to that of eleventh-grade honors students taught with more conventional methods (chap. 1).

A second area of overlap between research on cognitive development and research on cognition and instruction is a shared emphasis on the ways that systematic misconceptions interfere with children's learning. This theme is illustrated especially impressively in Minstrell's system for classifying and addressing errors that reflect different misconceptions about falling objects (chap. 4). It also is aptly illustrated by the probes regarding reflection of light offered by the teacher in Palincsar and Magnusson's chapter (chap. 5). A third theme is the importance of learner characteristics, such as age and conceptual knowledge, on the effectiveness of instruction. Such influences are particularly emphasized by Klahr, Chen, and Toth (chap. 3) and by Kalchman, Moss, and Case (chap. 1). A final shared theme of all of the chapters in this group, as well as of most contemporary research on cognitive development, is that learning is a constructive process, with learners continually striving to understand their experiences. As Palincsar and Magnusson point out, this is true regardless of whether children are learning from text or from physical experience (chap. 5). As Klahr, Chen, and Toth point out, it is true regardless of whether the instructional approach is classified as discovery learning or conceptually oriented didactic instruction (chap. 3).

Instruction always requires going beyond both theory and empirical findings; in many cases, intuitions and past experience are the only bases for making crucial decisions. Although knowledge of cognitive developmental theories and empirical findings may account for part of the instructional success enjoyed by the present group of investigators, the validity of their intuitions and their creative application of their past experience probably play a larger role. Their intuitions raise several questions that need to be addressed by cognitive developmental research:

1. At the outset of their instructional program, Klahr, Chen, and Toth present children flawed experiments as a way of motivating them to learn how to perform valid ones (chap. 3). Do children learn more effectively when the negative consequences of flawed existing procedures are shown to them before they receive instruction in superior ones?

2. Kalchman, Moss, and Case hypothesize that there is a central conceptual structure for rational numbers and another for functions, and that learning these is essential for understanding mathematics beyond arithmetic (chap. 1). What is the evidence that children who acquire these central conceptual structures immediately understand, or are quicker to learn, aspects of mathematics other than rational numbers and functions?

3. Palincsar and Magnusson require children to commit to claims about how light works before instruction begins (chap. 5). They believe that such commitment enhances learning. Does it?

4. Palincsar and Magnusson also hypothesize that greater learning will occur if children do not examine text-based descriptions of phenomena until they have substantial first-hand experience with the phenomena (chap. 5). Are they right?

Thus, just as theories and findings from cognitive development can help guide instructional efforts, so ideas and findings from cognition and instruction can help guide cognitive developmental research.

LEARNER CHARACTERISTICS,
TARGET DOMAIN, AND LEARNING

A common theme in all of these chapters is that regardless of the age and knowledge of the learner, learning of mathematics and science should be organized around the pursuit of meaning. For example, in chap. 2, Lehrer, Schauble, Strom, and Pligge comment, "In reform classrooms ... mathematical cognition is a joint product of individuals' attempts to achieve meaning...about the nature of mathematics," (p. 42) and Minstrell notes that teachers need to make sense of experiences in the classroom (chap. 4).

This theme would not be surprising if we were talking about learning of literature or history. In those areas, the pursuit of meaning has always been viewed as central. The view also would not be surprising if we were talking about students at elite universities learning the deep structure of mathematics or physics. Most researchers who study both psychology and education agree that regardless of the content area or the population of students, the pursuit of meaning should be emphasized. However, the popularity of back to basics movements indicates that many people are skeptical and will need to be convinced of the importance and feasibility of the goal before it will be given high priority in classrooms. Again, researchers who study cognition and instruction need to provide evidence indicating that focusing on meaning represents progress in the sense of improvement, not just in the sense of change.

Emphasizing the pursuit of meaning in mathematics and science raises the issue of what meaning means in these contexts. My understanding of it is a generalized version of the kind of number sense that Kalchman, Moss, and Case try to inculcate in students (chap. 1). Meaningful understanding implies fluent translation among alternative representations and ability to integrate facts, concepts, and procedures in a way that consistent conclusions can be derived via different routes. One of the most hopeful results of the programs described in Parts I and II is the frequency with which they seem to lead students to acquire such meaningful understanding. Thus, Lehrer, Schauble, Strom, and Pligge note that most students who participate in the program demonstrated multiple understandings of similarity: As a ratio, a line, and an algebraic expression (chap. 2). Similarly, Kalchman, Moss, and Case cite the example of a student who, when asked to express one eighth as a decimal, moved fluently between fractional, percentage, and decimal representations, "Well one eighth is half of one fourth. And one quarter is 25%, so half of that is $12^{1}/_{2}\%$. So as a decimal, that would have to be point 12 and a half. So that is point 12 point 5, so that means that it is .125" (chap. 1, p. 20).

Research from cognitive development also suggests that encouraging children to pursue meaning enhances learning of mathematics and science. For example, asking children to explain why the correct answer is correct leads to more learning than simply telling them that the correct answer is correct (Bielaczyc, Pirolli, & Brown, 1995; Chi, Bassok, Lewis, Reimann, & Glasser, 1989; Siegler, 1995). Moreover, asking them to explain both why correct answers are correct and why incorrect answers are incorrect leads to more learning than only asking why correct answers are correct (Siegler, in press). Requests to explain phenomena enhance learning with populations varying from preschoolers to adults and with domains ranging from number conservation to ecosystems to computer programming. Better learners spontaneously generate such explanations more often than less good learners (Bielaczyc et al., 1995; Chi, de Leeuw, Chi, & LaVancher, 1989), and requesting such explanations from randomly selected children or adults causes them to learn more (Chi, de Leeuw, Chi, & LaVancher, 1994; Siegler, in press).

The findings from the present group of chapters raise several questions. First, how can we assess the degree to which children possess meaningful understanding of a domain? More precise specification of the knowledge needed to understand a given area in a meaningful way, and objective measures of that knowledge, are a logical next step in this area. Second, are young children capable of grasping all kinds of meaning in mathematics and science, or are some kinds of meaning best pursued at older ages? Referring to sixth graders learning about mathematical functions, Kalchman, Moss, and Case suggest that "there are some problems specific to the domain that are beyond the ability of some younger students, possibly because of their earlier stage of intellectual development and their limited experience with more advanced ideas in mathematics" (chap. 1, p. 35). What ideas are children unable to understand at given ages, and how exactly does their general intellectual stage limit their learning? Third, can we inculcate in children a "habit of mind" to pursue meaning in all domains? We know that on particular tasks, some children seek explanations far more than do other children. We do not know whether explanation seeking is a general characteristic of some children but not of others; whether explanation seeking is general for a given child within a given domain, but not across different domains; or whether individual children's explanation seeking varies greatly on different tasks within the same domain. We also do not know whether it is possible to instruct children in ways that increase their likelihood of seeking meaning on a broader range of tasks and domains. The answers to this last question will have a lot to do with the long-term success of encouraging children to pursue meaning.

REFERENCES

Bielaczyc, K., Pirolli, P. L., & Brown, A. L. (1995). Training in self-explanation and self-regulation strategies: Investigating the effects of knowledge acquisition activities on problem solving. *Cognition and Instruction, 13*, 221–252.

Chi, M. T. H., Bassok, M., Lewis, M., Reimann, P., & Glasser, R. (1989). Self-explanations: How students study and use examples in learning to solve problems. *Cognitive Science, 13*, 145–182.

Chi, M. T. H., de Leeuw, N., Chiu, M.-H., & LaVancher, C. (1994). Eliciting self-explanations improves understanding. *Cognitive Science, 18*, 439–477.

Klahr, D. (1976). *Cognition and instruction*. Hillsdale, NJ: Lawrence Erlbaum Associates.

Siegler, R. S. (1995). How does change occur: A microgenetic study of number conservation. *Cognitive Psychology, 28*, 225–273.

Siegler, R. S. (in press). Microgenetic studies of self-explanations. In N. Granott & J. Parziale (Eds.), *Microdevelopment: Transition processes in development and learning*. New York: Cambridge University Press.

7

Learning to Research about Learning

Herbert A. Simon
Carnegie Mellon University

The purpose of this chapter is not to introduce wholly new themes into the discussion that is pursued throughout this volume, but to highlight some general implications from the work discussed in the other chapters about directions for learning research, and how our understanding of cognition can define these directions.

LEARNING AS THE LINK

The connection between cognition and instruction lies, of course, in learning; and for at least two very good reasons, learning has been a central topic in psychology for the whole century of that discipline's history.

First, learning is one of the most important activities in which human beings engage, occupying a very large fraction of their lives and absorbing a substantial fraction of the national income (including, of course, the child labor that is invested in education instead of immediately productive occupations). But learning is also important, and perhaps most important, because it is central to the whole psychological enterprise. The survival of living creatures is tied tightly to their adaptability, and one of the two most powerful mechanisms for adapting to an environment is learning; genetic change is the other.

As a consequence of the success of the human species in evolving its learning capabilities, almost all human behavior, from an early age, is learned behavior, and it changes whenever what is learned and stored in memory changes. I am not ignoring or denying the role that nature plays as the foundation for nurture, but simply observing that if the task of science is to find invariant characteristics in its objects of study, many, if not most, of the human invariants do not lie in what is learned, which can exhibit the greatest diversity, for we can learn almost anything, sense or nonsense. The invariants lie mainly in the learning mechanisms themselves, along with the basic mechanisms for sensing, perceiving, and manipulating symbols in the nervous system (which we call thinking) and emoting.

This is why learning theory has played such a central role, perhaps the most important, in psychological research and theory. Of course, learning is also not a strict invariant in an adaptive organism, for we can move up to the first metalevel and learn to learn. I do not think that anyone doubts today that there are more efficient and less efficient ways of learning—for example, learning with understanding versus rote learning. Nor is there any doubt that better ways of learning can be learned, like any other forms of behavior, and become habitual.

That brings us to the second metalevel; learning how to teach people how to learn, that is to say, learning to research about learning, which is the title of my talk and the theme of this conference. Research on learning, as we are all aware, is a complicated affair because learning is a complicated process, or, more accurately a congeries of complex processes. The task of research on learning is to understand all of these processes, and to understand how we can facilitate them.

THE PROCESSES OF LEARNING

The structure of this volume reflects these complexities.

1. Much learning takes place in childhood, a period, and in many respects the most crucial one, during which the child is not only learning but also developing and maturing in an amalgam of biological and psychological changes that continue into adolescence. However much Piaget may have been right or wrong about the specific facts of developmental stages, he taught us that we must study the biological maturation of the infant and child as an essential part of our study of learning. So the relation between development and learning becomes our first theme.

2. Learning is often carried out in a structured environment of facili-
    tators (at least, intended facilitators) called teachers and tutors, and
    nowadays, computer tutors and a whole host of other communica-
    tion devices that have progressed well beyond the blackboard. So
    the role of teachers and their strategies must be another of our
    themes, but never in isolation from our study of the learner.

3. Learning is social. Learning takes place not only in schools or
    other formal settings, but also in every encounter the learner has
    with the natural and social environments. It begins at birth, so that
    the child has already acquired substantial skills of locomotion,
    recognition and manipulation of objects, and oral language long
    before beginning formal education. This early learning most likely
    has a greater aggregate importance, even in a school-saturated
    society like our own, than the subsequent formal learning, for it
    shapes the learning processes themselves, and the frameworks
    within which new knowledge is organized.

    If we observe any peasant society, we see an enormous amount
    of learning taking place without the intercession of schools at all,
    written language being perhaps the most nearly schoolbound of the
    basic human skills. We should not make the mistake of identifying
    learning exclusively with schools. In the future, the association of
    the two may become closer, or as many computer enthusiasts think,
    much more distant. We should also not make the mistake, as is
    sometimes made in the more extreme constructivist circles, of sup-
    posing that learning cannot occur, and even occur efficiently, in
    schools.

    What do we mean by the social context of learning? In speaking
    of learning as a social process, "social" means more than "having
    people around." In a modern society, perhaps the most important
    social influences on learning are the book and other forms of writ-
    ten communication that do not involve having people around at
    all—at least at the moment of learning. Putting learning in books
    does not desocialize it.

    Whether from books or people, at least 90% of what we have in
    our heads (I haven't measured it, that's just a guess) is acquired by
    social processes, including watching others, listening to them, and
    reading their writings. Hence, there is no such thing as individual
    psychology. If we except the rare feral person, all psychology is
    social. Among the most social people are the bookworms, who go

off to hobnob with the scribblers, and who know the world, not through direct contact but mainly by way of its interpretation in books. Others know it by listening to and watching other people. They learn about different worlds, I'm sure, and it's not clear which is more like the real world, but all are learning, and learning socially.

Nor do the scribblers whom the bookworms read or the storytellers we all listen to get most of their information from the external world. The storyteller is a transmitter of tales told by previous storytellers, the preserver of the collective memory. And the traveler is the transmitter of information largely obtained by listening to the inhabitants of other lands. Of course the traveler also looks about (mostly at other people and their artifacts), but is deeply dependent on the local informants to interpret what she or he sees.

4. Learning uses tools. Human tool-building propensities are applicable to learning just as they are applicable to the other aspects of human activity. I have already mentioned three of the most important tools of traditional formal learning systems; written language (including books), teachers, and the blackboard. Today, there are many more, as I have mentioned.

This volume includes many examples of the use of overhead projectors and videotape as learning tools for ourselves, and could have included a productive discussion of the use and misuse of such tools; for example, on the conditions for their compatibility with the limits of human serial, one-at-a-time attention, for the division of labor and coordination between eye and ear, and for the use of the learner's Mind's Eye as a powerful visual display (Tabachneck-Schijf, Leonardo, & Simon, 1997). In learning to research on learning, we must both research the characteristics of these tools, and use these tools in our research, as we are already beginning to do.

With the tools we have today, especially those that can themselves participate in communication, we can aspire to the same kinds of enhancement of learning efficiency that we have achieved historically with tools and machines in a wide host of other productive activities. Notice that I said "aspire." Today, we are not even close to approaching the potential.

We need also to be alert, using foresight as well as hindsight, to the many side effects, desirable and undesirable that new tools invariably bring with them, some of them of societywide and worldwide impact. Today, we are on the brink of the "industrial-ization" (is that the right word? or "mechanization," or "automa-tion"?) of education. Whatever we call it, the "information revolution" is going to have effects over the course of the next century or two—some good, some bad—as sweeping as those of the industrial revolution. These potential effects need to be part of our research agenda, as they were not in the agendas of those who introduced the automobile or the airplane—or the World Wide Web.

5. These are the four main topics around which this volume is organized. However, at least one important topic is absent; the natural environment, which, although I have just been downplaying its importance relative to the social environment, gives very many welcome and unwelcome lessons to all of us (touchings, you might say, of many pleasantly warm and many unpleasantly hot stoves). One of the striking differences between a rural and an urban society is that the former provides all sorts of ways of learning from the natural environment of the farm that are not easily available to city dwellers. Most city kids have very little experience with tools of any kind, unless you consider computers and TV knobs to be tools. Perhaps, but I am not sure of it, this is compensated by broader and more varied social experience.

We especially need to attend to what it is we must learn about the interactions between the natural and the social environment in a world where we humans are so numerous and so powerful that we can produce, quite rapidly, enormous changes for better, and more frequently for worse, in our natural environment. The consequent problems surely require social learning, which calls on the resources of all of our sciences, both natural and behavioral and social, for the required knowledge. In any case, the natural environment also provides important resources and needs for learning, but it is not represented here, and we will need another volume to deal with it.

THE FIRST LAW OF LEARNING

Now we come to the substance of the matter; how we can learn to research on learning, and—not to put the matter wholly into the future—how we have already been learning to do such research. In reading the chapters of my colleagues, I am struck by the fact that most of the cognitive ideas they are using in their educational research and practice are quite general principles that have been around for a long time and that are not couched in any very precise theoretical terms. They might even be mistaken for common sense.

In the chapters on learning tools, we see examples of much more specific and precise use of cognitive theory in education. However, we should not dismiss our heritage of learning about learning just because much of it sounds like common sense. That is the fate of all good theory as it becomes thoroughly understood (like the law of falling bodies, which was transformed in about a century from utter nonsense to obvious common sense).

Therefore, before offering a glimpse of some of the more contemporary trends in cognitive research, I'd like to make explicit the theoretical core of the common sense that I believe my colleagues have been using as the basis for the education procedures they describe.

The long-established first principle, the foundation stone of the entire enterprise, is that *learning takes place inside the learner and only inside the learner.* Learning requires changes in the brain of the learner. We may not understand fully or even approximately what these changes are, especially at the neural level, but we must have some accurate and principled way of characterizing them at least at the symbolic level. If not, we know almost nothing about learning, and can do little to enhance it. The contents of textbooks, the lectures or tutorial activities of teachers, the humming of computer tutors, the murmurings of classroom student discussion and study groups—all of these are wholly irrelevant except insofar as they affect what knowledge and skills are stored inside learners' heads (and sometimes in their fingers and toes).

I must, as a passing remark, observe that during the 1930s, Carnegie Tech (as CMU was then called) was a national leader in introducing into engineering education the so-called "Carnegie Plan," which was squarely based on this principle—that learning depends on what the learner does, and only on what the learner does—and on a focus on problem-solving skills. Neither of the pioneers who accomplished this, Provost Elliott Dunlap Smith nor President Robert Doherty, was by professional training a psychologist, but, wherever they learned this lesson, they were superb learners.

The implication of a learner-centered learning theory (it sounds obvious when you put it that way) is that research on learning must aim at understanding the intracranial learning processes and mechanisms. That is where the action is. In the past 100 years, and especially the past 50 years, psychology has come a very long way along this path. It has identified and characterized some major components of the human cognitive system shown in Fig. 7.1; long-term (LTM) and short-term memory (STM), and subdivisions of these, for example, the iconic memory and the "Mind's Eye" as principal components of visual short-term memory; the echo box and auditory STM (that of the "magic number seven"); long-term semantic memory, both episodic and topical; knowledge in the form of associative list structures, and processes in the form of productions and discrimination nets, together with learned domain-specific retrieval structures in LTM that in effect enlarge STM memory capacity in those domains (Richman, Staszewski, & Simon, 1995).

I am sure you can add to this list, and not everyone's list would be identical with this one (which already defines an important goal for learning research), but a fact-based argument can be made for every box and arrow in the diagram, and there is considerable consensus about the general shape of this picture of memory. Its components are not simply the names of conjectural entities. For each of them, we have substantial data that permits us to estimate its parameters, often within a factor of two or less; capacity, access time, storage time, forgetting rates and so on. Very important: Once estimated, these are no longer free parameters when we fit the models to data.

Each memory component accounts for a range of learning and memory phenomena that do not make sense without them. The general brain locations of more and more of them are being identified with the aid of data from brain-damaged patients and from EEG, PET and MRI scans. fMRI, especially, is beginning to provide us with data about the sequence in which the memories function in the performance of particular tasks (Postle & D'Esposito, in press).

Only to the degree that we understand these processes and mechanisms can we expect to influence them in ways that will enhance learning. This does not mean that we need to understand them all at the neural level—that may still be a long way off. For purposes of applying psychology to learning, what is critical is to understand how the system functions at the level of symbols and their processes. The chapter of John Anderson in this volume makes that very specific and clear (chap. 8).

In addition to the progress that has been made in identifying and characterizing the functional components of the mind, our research has begun to tell us a great deal about the learning processes themselves and how to improve them. Carrying out an educational program consistently with the

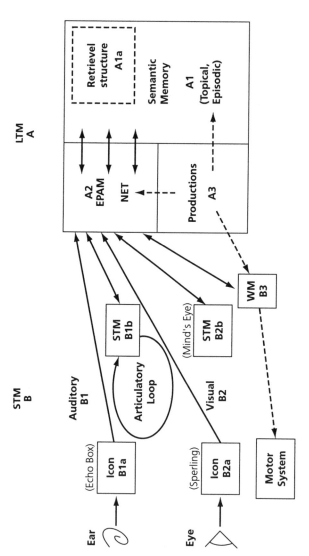

FIG. 7.1. Hypothesized memory structures. The left side of the figure represents the principal short-term memories—auditory, visual and motor—connecting with sensory and motor organs. The right side represents the principal species of long-term memory; (upper left), the network of tests that discriminates stimuli; (lower left), the actions that are triggered by the presence of (internal or external) stimuli; (right) a variety of semantic memory structures, including memory for episodes, for topics (or concepts), and specialized retrieval structures acquired by experts permitting rapid storage of information in their area of expertise. The arrows indicate some of the principal direct connections between components.

basic law of learning requires an understanding of (a) what the learner does during an active learning period, and (b) how the environment can enhance ability and willingness to do it.

As for (a), we shall see that good learners mainly store new information and new processes in memory, organized in such a way as to be *evocable and evoked* when appropriate for the performance of some task. As for (b), the environment, including teachers, can facilitate the storage process, first, by attracting the learners' *attention* to relevant information and processes, organized in ways that make them easy to assimilate in the most useful form, and, second, by *motivating* them to acquire it in a way that will make it readily available for use.

Often, an effective environment will induce learners to spend much time performing tasks that give them *practice in accessing* the information and processes that they are acquiring, and *applying* them to specific situations. If you call this "drill and practice," I will not protest.

A corollary to the basic law of learning is that designing an effective learning environment requires a deep understanding of what knowledge and processes (skills) are needed for performing each class of tasks and how they have to be stored and organized in memory in order to be effective. Thorough *task analysis* is one prerequisite for the environmental design.

A second prerequisite to designing an effective learning environment is understanding the conditions under which learners are likely to respond positively to it and to carry out the activities that have been planned for them. Without appropriate motivation, learners will allot insufficient time to the task. And even with appropriate motivation, but without some understanding of their own learning processes, they are likely to use ineffectively the time they do spend in learning (Simon, 1994).

Motivation is not well represented in the models that have been constructed of learning processes; rather, it has been assumed (as it is in the design of many laboratory experiments on learning). However, where motivation fits in has become relatively clear. Specifically, the attention-focusing mechanisms determine what motives and drives will, from time to time, gain control of the cognitive processes and set their current goals. Attention, then, is the key mechanism linking cognition with motives and drives. These latter include stimuli that attract or threaten, internal drives (e.g., hunger), and memories that have become tinged with affect and that, when evoked by appropriate stimuli, will direct attention to their concerns.

All of these statements are obvious, I think, and will be accepted without debate. The only thing not obvious is why practice so often deviates from them—why, for example, little effort is spent in formal education helping students to understand what learning processes are effective and to practice these processes, whatever content they may be learning. How much attention do we devote, for example, to examining the impact that our testing procedures have on our students' learning practices? Do the structure and frequency of our tests bias them, for example, toward rote learning or toward learning with understanding?

Rote Learning and Understanding

We would all agree that whatever is learned should be learned with understanding and not by rote. Understanding is sometimes regarded as a rather mysterious state of mind. But we cannot learn about learning without understanding "understanding," which is one of the favorite mystery words of both pop and academic psychology. Understanding understanding, and using it meaningfully, turns out not to be a hard problem after all. We define understanding in the same way as we define intelligence or skill, by specifying the observable conditions under which we would say that a person exhibits understanding (Simon, 1975).

In broad terms, a person understands some information to the extent that he or she can use it in performing the tasks for which it is relevant. There is no great difficulty in measuring understanding, thus defined. As we can measure it, we can also carry out careful research to discover when our students are learning by rote and when they are acquiring understanding.

Obviously, understanding is a matter of degree. Do I understand the number "3"? Given the task of adding 3 and 4, I may be able to answer, "7"; but given the task of multiplying 3 by 19, I may fail miserably. That means that I understand how to add 3 to another number, but not (at least not in all cases) to multiply it by another number. Nor does it mean that I understand the sentence, "Three is a cardinal number." There is no mystery in that, or in any situation where we understand something in some respects but not in others. In sum, *rote learning* is learning that allows us only to repeat back what we have learned, and learning brings *understanding* to the extent that it allows us to use what we have learned in order to perform tasks. When other mystery terms like "intuition," "insight," creativity," are treated in this same operational way, their mystery, fortunately for psychology, goes away too.

Tools for Banishing Mysteries

One of the great advances that cognitive psychology has made in the past 50 years has been to find powerful new ways to banish mysteries of the kinds I have just described. One half of the task of removing the mystery from a psychological concept is accomplished in the way I have just described; by specifying the behaviors to which the concept applies. Our ability to do this is enhanced whenever we find a new technique for observing behaviors. The humble tape recorder, and the verbal protocol that it records, the eye movement camera, the videotape are among the tools that have been brought to a practical level of application since World War II. Techniques for moving the observation further inside, like EEG, PET scans and fMRI are now just beginning to deliver important new information. These will be improved further, and there will continue to be others, operating from the information processing level down to the level of neurons.

The other half of the task of removing the mystery is developing languages that allow us to describe clearly and precisely the complexities of the cognitive system and the processes whereby it accomplishes its learning and problem solving. Newton demonstrated that the invention of the calculus was the necessary (and very nearly sufficient) condition for developing a viable theory of motion and applying it to explain the thousands of years old phenomena of the heavens. When physicists could describe what they saw in systems of differential equations—Newton's equations of classical mechanics, Maxwell's equations of electromagnetics, Einstein's equations of special and general relativity, Schrödinger's wave equations of quantum mechanics—they possessed the language necessary for reasoning about physical phenomena.

In exactly the same way, computer programming systems have now provided us with the languages that are necessary for reasoning accurately about physical symbol systems, including the human brain and mind. There are only two differences between the two formalisms. First, there is the unimportant difference that computer programs are systems of difference equations (with a finite time cycle), whereas the calculus employs differential equations (with the cycle going to an infinitesimal limit).

The second difference, an important one, is that the calculus requires that the phenomena it represents be expressed in terms of numbers, real or complex; whereas computer programs can admit and encode any kinds of symbolic patterns; numerical, verbal, graphical, pictorial, auditory—just as the brain can. The Physical Symbol System hypothesis (Newell &

Simon, 1976) asserts that this is exactly the capability a system needs in order to exhibit intelligence. The empirical evidence for that hypothesis is overwhelming today (Anderson, Corbett, Koedinger, & Pelletier, 1995; Feigenbaum & Feldman, 1963; Langley, Simon, Bradshaw, & Zytkow, 1987; Newell & Simon, 1972; Newell, 1990; Simon, 1996).

The remainder of this chapter illustrates how computer models of learning can help us to think clearly about learning processes and what we can do to facilitate learning. I first use the venerable *EPAM* program (Feigenbaum, 1960) to illustrate how we can describe what the expert has learned, and how that learning is organized in memory. Then I use a program, *ZBIE*, (Siklóssy, 1972), to explain the processes that children use to learn natural language, and that can be used in natural language instruction. Finally, I show how a production system language, OPS5, can be used as the first step in constructing effective materials (textbooks and problem books or computer tutors) for school learning tasks (Zhu, Lee, Simon, & Zhu, 1996; Zhu & Simon, 1987). In his chapter, John Anderson uses the Act-R program in a similar way to construct a powerful computer tutor (chap. 8).

My claim is not that these programs, in their present form, are complete or wholly correct theories of the phenomena they address, but that they are powerful tools for interpreting the data we have about these matters, for suggesting what new data we need, for testing our explanatory hypotheses sharply, and for designing tasks for learners. They, and a number of others like them, have clearly demonstrated their efficacy, and they need to be added to the armatorium of tools that we use in improving instruction and learning.

EPAM.   EPAM is a theory expressed as a computer program of human perception and memory, which has been used extensively to explain a wide range of experimental results in human verbal learning (paired associate and serial anticipation learning; Feigenbaum & Simon, 1984), in the structure and content of expert memories (Richman, et al., 1995), and in categorization (Gobet, Richman, Staszewski, & Simon, 1997). Figure 7.1 depicts the general structure of the EPAM, memory, except that in EPAM, the motor component has never been implemented, and the early stages of perception (prior to encoding the stimulus as a vector of features) are implemented very incompletely.

EPAM models the memory structures and processes at a symbolic, not a neural level. It is important to note that "symbolic" means "in terms of patterns." The patterns can represent not only linguistic structures (visual or auditory), but also diagrams, pictures, percepts derived from the tactile and olfactory senses, and so on. The theory is neither language–bound nor rule–bound.

EPAM has two main capabilities. First, when presented with stimuli, and feedback of correctness of responses, it can learn to discriminate among stimuli, dividing them into classes to an arbitrary degree of refinement, and can then associate with each class a body of semantic information about the things that belong to that class. It does this by "growing" a discrimination net, with a test at each node to sort stimuli on the basis of some feature, and by storing the semantic information about discriminated stimuli at the leaf nodes. Second, when the net has been learned, EPAM can use it to recognize familiar stimuli and retrieve the information stored about them.

EPAM, without alternation of its processes or parameters, has been shown to give an excellent account of the memory capabilities of experts in a number of fields, notably mnemonic experts and chess players, but generalizing to the innumerable other kinds of human expertise. For example, in the case of chess, it has been shown, by means of an EPAM-like model, that world-class expertise requires the acquisition of a discrimination net with 300,000 or more branches, each of which provides information about a different class of chess positions ("templates") or features of chess positions ("chunks"; Gobet & Simon, 1998). This number is not surprising, in that it is of the same order of magnitude as the natural language vocabulary of a college graduate, who has certainly put in his or her 10 years and more in acquiring language.

The chess information is usually acquired by humans by studying over a long period of years tens of thousands of positions from chess games, and the merits of various moves in these positions. In terms of our definitions, this material is learned with understanding, and not by rote, because recognizing a familiar template or chunk enables the expert to access information about the goodness or badness of the position and the kinds of moves that are most favorable for continuing the game.

There is every reason to suppose, and a considerable body of evidence, that the expertise, for example, of a physician is organized in a very similar way; the discrimination net distinguishing different symptoms, with which are associated, at the leaf nodes, information about diagnosis, prognosis, and treatment (Pople, 1982). Thus, EPAM provides a quite general model of expertise and of what it takes to become an expert.

The expert, according to this model, operates on a "recognize, then act" cycle. Features in the observed situation are recognized to provide access to the associated knowledge relevant for choosing a response. Of course, there is more to it than that. The associated knowledge does not always, or even usually, provide a complete course of action for the next step in the task at hand, but may be input into a search procedure that uses means-ends analysis to find a likely action. So, a unified model of expert performance would have to include a general problem solver capable of heuristic search (a GPS, Newell & Simon, 1972, or a Soar, Newell, 1990) as well as EPAM. There are strong and fundamental similarities between that architecture and the architecture of Act-R, and, I believe, only modest differences.

The interest of EPAM for this conference is in telling us something about the kinds of knowledge that are needed for high-level performance of a task, and how that knowledge needs to be organized in memory. From that, we can draw conclusions about the content and method of presentation of a curriculum of study. For example, we draw from EPAM the conclusion that if we want students to be competent in arithmetic, we ought to provide them with learning materials and activities that will enable them to master the sums table and the times table, but also materials and activities that will enable them to understand *when* sums and products are appropriate things to compute, and to evoke the tables at those times.

Minstrell's description (chap. 4) of the Diagnoser system for high school physics instructions illustrates how to help students learn about both what the appropriate physics concepts are and when to use them in a particular situation, relating the student's knowledge to the response required in that situation.

From models like EPAM and Diagnoser, we obtain an understanding of the relation between drill and practice and skill in application. We can express the relation in the programming languages called "production systems"; that is, languages each of whose instructions is an "if, then" statement. The if consists of a set of conditions, and the then, of a set of actions. Whenever all the conditions of a production are satisfied, the action is taken. We can see that the actions only tell the student what can be done; he or she needs to understand the conditions in order to know when to do it.

ZBIE.   The program ZBIE (Siklóssy, 1972; its author never disclosed the meaning of the acronym), was constructed by Laurent Siklóssy, inspired by a series of "language by pictures" books developed by the philosopher I. A. Richards as a preferred method of teaching languages. Richards' idea was that second languages should be learned in the same way as first languages are learned; not by translating the words and sentences from and to one's native language, but by learning how to translate visual, auditory, and other sensory experiences directly to and from the new language.

To implement this idea, ZBIE is presented with pairs of stimuli, the first member of the pair being a simple scene (represented internally by a diagram in the form of list structures), the second member, a sentence in the language to be learned. If the sequence begins with very simple scenes and sentences that describe them, ZBIE can begin to match the words in the sentences with objects and relations among objects in the scene. It could, for example, match "dog" with one object in a scene, "cat" with another, and "chases" with the relation in the scene of the dog chasing the cat. Increasingly, after a succession of such pairs, ZBIE can name the objects and relations in scenes correctly, and form sentences that describe the scene.

ZBIE gradually builds up in memory both a lexicon and relational structures that have very much the properties of a grammar. (For example, examination of its memory structures reveals nounlike and verblike classes, and so on.) In fact, it can be said that ZBIE constitutes a realistic model of what, from a psychological standpoint, a grammar really is; not a body of complete and consistent rules, but a set of structures and procedures in memory that govern language understanding and usage.

Notice that ZBIE gets to the very heart of the idea of understanding, for it relates language to the "real world," by creating tight links between syntax and semantics. Its semantics are not limited to dictionary meanings (based on other words) of the vocabulary it learns. It learns to understand the intensions of the sentences it reads; the external situations that the sentences denote.

Moreover, ZBIE acquires these connections between words and situations in a way that closely resembles the way in which a child learns its native language—by hearing the language in the presence of the objects and events being mentioned. ZBIE thereby casts a great deal of light on what is involved in language learning, especially at its earliest stages.

At later stages, things become more complicated because, for example, the meanings of new words can be acquired not only from scenes whose features they denote but also from linguistic expressions that relate them to words already known. Thus, you don't need to see unicorns or pictures of them to learn what a unicorn is, or even how you would recognize one if you did see one: "Horse with a single horn on its forehead" would give the idea.

Only very recently has the linguistic community begun to build further on the achievements of ZBIE. Currently, a new effort is under way to extend the ZBIE program with the means afforded by the much larger computer memories and faster computer processes that are now available. Today, such a program can aspire to attain an adult vocabulary and grammatical skills.

Again, I am less interested in praising the virtues of ZBIE, which was a first effort to address a very complex (and important) problem, than I am in showing how computer models, whether they turn out to be wholly correct or to need major extension, can guide research toward understanding thinking and learning phenomena, and in the interim, can provide an approach to designing learning experiences for students. Operative computer models give clear specifications of what Greeno (1976) called "cognitive objects." In such running programs as the algebra tutor described by Anderson and Gluck (chap. 8) or in Lovett's (chap. 11) analysis of the cognitive objectives of a statistics course, they provide powerful guidelines for the instructional process.

Learning From Examples: Production Systems.   For my last example, I describe a procedure for task analysis that has proved very effective for building curricula in high school algebra and geometry. In this work, a computer model was important in demonstrating the effectiveness of the learning process embodied in the curricula, but a running model of the entire program was not actually needed to develop the curricular materials.

In the late 1970s, David Neves (Neves, 1978) wrote a program, in the production system language, OPS5, that was capable of learning to solve linear equations of the sort one encounters in elementary algebra. I earlier defined a production system as a computer language each of whose instructions take the form: "If condition C is satisfied, then take action A." It also contains priority rules so that if, at any given time, the conditions of more than one of its instructions (productions) are satisfied, it will execute a particular one of them. When Neves' program was presented with a worked-out example of solving an equation, it would examine the example to discover what condition motivated each step in the solution, and what action was taken in response to that condition. The following example will make the process clear.

$$7x - 12 = 4x + 6$$
$$7x = 4x + 18$$
$$3x = + 18$$
$$x = + 6$$

We notice that the second line was obtained by adding 12 to both sides of the first line, thereby getting rid of the numerical term on the left side. Similarly, the third line was obtained from the second by subtracting 4x from both sides, getting rid of the term in x on the right side. Finally, the fourth line was obtained from the third by dividing both sides by 3, putting the expression in the desired form "x equals a number." At each step, a difference was noted between the form of the current expression and the form of the desired expression; a number on the left, or a term in x on the right, or an x with a coefficient different from unity. An action was then taken that removed that difference. The solution path can be summed up in three productions:

If there is a number on the left,
    then subtract the number from both sides.
If there is a term in x on the right,
    then subtract the term in x from both sides.
If there is a term in ax on the left, and a≠1,
    then divide both sides by a.

The information for the if clauses of these productions is obtained by noticing which difference between given expression and desired expression is removed at that step. The information for the then clauses is obtained by noticing what action removed the difference. The actions (operating on both sides of the equation) are those that the students have previously learned to be legitimate (preserving the value of the variable) operations on equations.

Those of you who have been concerned with algebra instruction will observe that textbooks and lesson plans explicitly give time and attention to teaching the legitimate manipulations (actions) of equations; they largely ignore the clues (conditions) that determine what actions would be effective if applied in any particular circumstances. That is, they teach what is permissible, but not what is appropriate—law but not strategy. The same is true of other instructional material, but it is particularly evident in most algebra textbooks.

By examining the kinds of problems we wish students to be able to understand and solve, we can now discover sets of productions that are effective in solving these sorts of problems, then construct sets of worked out examples for the students to use in acquiring their own production systems (both legitimate actions and conditions for their application), and additional problems to test the correctness of what they have learned. Notice that the method does not assume or imply that the students will learn verbal rules equivalent to the productions; just that they will store procedures equivalent to these productions in memory and so will be capable of executing them when they are evoked in appropriate situations (i.e., in situations where the conditions of the productions are satisfied).

Adaptive production systems are now widely used as models of processes for learning procedures. Curriculum design methods utilizing learning from examples techniques based on adaptive production systems have been employed in the People's Republic of China, without any use of computers, to construct a complete 3-year curriculum in middle school algebra and geometry. The curriculum has been used with great success (good posttest results at the end of the course and a year later, and significant time savings) since the middle 1980s, for the instruction of students in various parts of China, now about 20,000 students annually. The classroom materials are paper and pencil workbooks. The teachers do almost no lecturing, devoting almost all their time to tutoring students who are having problems. Classes typically have 40 to 50 students. The entire curriculum was created by six people, including experienced teachers and an educational psychology researcher at the Psychology Institute of the Chinese Academy of Sciences.

John Anderson and his colleagues tell a similar success story about their computer tutor programs, which are now being used extensively in American schools (Anderson et al., 1995). The basic approach to task analysis and curriculum construction is essentially the same as the one I have just described, but the final products are tutorial courses in which the students interact directly with a computer.

Clearly, these methods are not restricted in application to mathematics, although they are probably applied most easily in the sciences, where there is already a tradition of conducting a large part of the learning through problem-solving exercises. Nor as the successful program in China shows, need they always be carried to the stage of computer implementation. This volume provides several other examples of such formal task analyses that approach the precision of computational models; Lovett's application to college level statistics (chap. 11), Kalchman, Moss, and Case's to the teaching of number sense (chap. 1), and Carver's to the design and administration of an entire preschool program (chap. 12).

Extending such task analysis to subjects like history and English literature requires much initial thought about defining the skills that the learner is to attain and the kinds of examples that can be developed to help students learn those skills.

Just the exercise of going through this planning step to define the learning goals and experiences that could be useful in reaching them, would be of substantial benefit to learning in these subjects, over and above its contribution to the design of effective curricular materials. Notice that the procedure I have been describing is significantly different from the notion of "learning by doing" or "learning from problem solving," for the worked-out examples provide a trail of crumbs through the forest, eliminating a great deal of the tiresome and excessively difficult search students are subjected to if they are thrown into problems without an appropriate level of guidance. The detail in the sequence of exemplary steps can be regulated to adjust the difficulty of the learning task as students' skills advance.

CONCLUSION:
THE TOOLS OF MODERN THEORY

The first of the three examples I have discussed (EPAM) shows how cognitive modeling has provided us with a broad and deep understanding of the cognitive bases for human expertise, in particular, the roles of perception and memory-based pattern recognition in expert performance. The second example (ZBIE), through its capabilities for acquiring both the syntax and semantics of natural languages, instructs us about processes through which these skills can be learned and the structure of curricula for employing these processes. The third example (adaptive production systems) demonstrates an effective set of procedures, learning from examples, that has led to an effective model for building curricula in algebra and geometry.

Of course, this is not the only useful purpose that modeling serves. Computer models are a powerful and natural language of theory for psychology in general, and cognition in particular. Perhaps their most important use is identical with that of theories in every field of science; to give the researchers themselves a language in which to think and communicate, that provides a clear, precise, and powerful representation of the situations and problems with which they are dealing. In psychology, we have not in the past commonly had that kind of clarity and precision. It is now available, and we should not delay in taking utmost advantage of it. Our problems are difficult enough without handicapping ourselves by using ordinary language as our only medium of representation, communication, understanding, and explanation.

The Social Dimension of Learning

In my remarks, I have not given equal time to the four major themes of this volume. I have had a good deal to say about development and learning, both in general and in my discussion of ZBIE as a model of first language learning. I have used both EPAM and adaptive production systems to examine some aspects of teaching strategies. I have discussed the computer as a learning tool, at least in two of its uses (understanding the learning process and designing curricula and specific learning experiences within them). But I have had little to say about the social context of learning except insofar as I described the expert's memory as the product of social experience.

My relative neglect of social context does not reflect my assessment of its importance, especially in relation to issues of motivation, and of training in social skills, broadly construed (i.e., the skills of living immersed in a social world). These matters receive extensive discussion in other chapters, so I limit myself to just a few comments on broad questions that I believe need more attention than they have received elsewhere.

First, I must express my disappointment at the controversial spirit in which the discussion of alternative approaches to instruction is often carried on; disappointed, but not surprised, because it is not just a debate among scientists and scholars, or practitioners, about the facts of the matter, but also a much broader public and political debate about the schools, often leading (in both the scientific and public communities) to expressions of extreme "constructivism" on the one hand, and to extreme advocacy of "a return to the fundamentals" on the other. We must expect such debates to generate heat as well as light, but usually much more of the former than the latter. The discussion in this book has a much more objective tone.

Second, there has been considerable conflation of two quite separate issues; the contribution, on the one hand, of educational settings to the social development of the child, and the contribution, on the other hand, of the social structure and processes of the educational setting to children's learning. The first issue is concerned with how far the school is and should be concerned with the child's skills in interacting with other children and people generally; the second is concerned with whether, and what kinds of, group activities among the children contribute to the substantive learning goals (Okada & Simon, 1997). Should algebra be taught so as to improve children's social skills, or should children's social skills be used to teach algebra through group activities? Or both, or neither?

On both issues, the educational world is in considerable need of more solid facts, and while waiting for them, is full of strong and very divergent opinions. On these topics, I have nothing to add beyond what I have already said, in collaboration with several colleagues, in other places (Anderson, Reder, & Simon, 1996, 1997, 1998; Vera & Simon, 1994).

GENERAL CONCLUSION

There is today a science of learning, however incomplete and imperfect. This science has a great deal to say about how learning environments have to be designed for learning to proceed in effective ways. To make use of this know-how, we have to create strong bonds between the research community and the teaching community that do not exist today. And we have to realize that the research community has as much to learn from the teaching community as the latter from the former.

Closer bonds—as illustrated by Klahr, Chen and Toth (chap. 3)—will give a tremendous impulse to our basic research on learning, and will greatly accelerate our progress toward a deep understanding of the human mind; while, as Carver's chapter shows (chap. 12), fundamental principles from cognition can be used to encourage multiple levels and goals in an ongoing school. Looking directly at the phenomena of the real world is the way that all science begins, and the schools are a principal place where the phenomena of learning are found in a form that is easily observed.

REFERENCES

Anderson, J. R., Corbett, A. T., Koedinger, K. R., & Pelletier, R. (1995). Cognitive tutors: Lessons learned. *Journal of Learning Science, 4*, 167–207.

Anderson, J. R., Reder, L. M., & Simon, H. A. (1996). Situated learning and education. *Educational Researcher, 25* (4), 5–11.

Anderson, J. R., Reder, L. M., & Simon, H. A. (1997). Rejoinder: Situative versus cognitive perspectives: Form versus substance. *Educational Researcher, 26* (1), 18–21.

Anderson, J. R., Reder, L. M., & Simon, H. A. (1998). Radical constructivism and cognitive psychology. In D. Ravitch (Ed.), *Brookings papers on education policy* (pp. 227–278). Washington, DC: Brookings Institution.

Feigenbaum, E. A. (1960). The simulation of verbal learning behavior. In E. A. Feigenbaum & J. Feldman (Eds.), *Computers and thought* (pp. 297–309). New York: McGraw-Hill.

Feigenbaum, E. A., & Feldman, J. (1963). *Computers and thought*. New York: McGraw-Hill.

Feigenbaum, E., & Simon, H. A. (1984). EPAM-like models of recognition and learning. *Cognitive Science, 8,* 305–336.

Gobet, F., Richman, H., Staszewski, J., & Simon, H. A. (1997). Goals, representations and strategies in a concept attainment task: The EPAM model. In D. L. Medin (Ed.), *The psychology of learning and motivation* (Vol. 37, pp. 265–290). San Diego, CA: Academic Press.

Gobet, F., & Simon, H. A. (1998). Expert chess memory: Revisiting the chunking hypothesis. *Memory, 6,* 225–255.

Greeno, J. G. (1976). Indefinite goals in well-structured problems. *Psychological Review, 83,* 479–491.

Langley, P., Simon, H. A., Bradshaw, G. L., & Zytkow, J. M. (1987). *Scientific discovery: Computational explorations of the creative processes*. Cambridge, MA: MIT Press.

Neves, D. M. (1978). A computer program that learns algebraic procedures by examining examples and working problems in a textbook. *Proceedings of the Second Conference of Computational Studies of Intelligence* (pp. 191–195). Toronto: Canadian Society for Computational Studies of Intelligence.

Newell, A. (1990). *Unified theories of cognition*. Cambridge, MA: Harvard University Press.

Newell, A., & Simon, H. A. (1972). *Human problem solving*. Englewood Cliffs, NJ: Prentice-Hall

Newell, A., & Simon, H. A. (1976). Computer science as empirical inquiry: Symbols and search. *Communications of the Association for Computing Machinery, 9* (3), 113–126.

Okada, T., & Simon, H. A. (1997). Collaborative discovery in a scientific domain. *Cognitive Science, 21* (2), 109–146.

Pople, H. E., Jr. (1982). Heuristic methods for imposing structure on ill-structured problems: The structure of medical diagnostics. In P. Szolovits (Ed.), *Artificial intelligence in medicine* (pp. 119–190). Boulder, CO: Westview Press.

Postle, B. R., & D'Esposito, M. (in press). "What"—then—"where" in visual working memory: An event-related fMRI study. *Journal of Cognitive Neuroscience*.

Richman, H. B., Staszewski, J. J., & Simon, H. A. (1995). Simulation of expert memory using EPAM IV. *Psychological Review, 102* (2), 305–330.

Siklóssy, L. (1972). Natural language learning by computer. In H. A. Simon & L. Siklóssy (Eds.), *Representation and meaning* (pp. 288–328). Englewood Cliffs, NJ: Prentice-Hall.

Simon, H. A. (1975). Learning with understanding. *The ERIC Science, Mathematics and Environmental Education Clearinghouse*. Columbus, OH.

Simon, H. A. (1994). Bottleneck of attention: Connecting thought with motivation. In W. D. Spaulding (Ed.), *Integrative views of motivation, cognition, and emotion* (pp. 1–21). Lincoln, NE: University of Nebraska Press.

Simon, H. A. (1996). *The sciences of the artificial* (3rd ed.). Cambridge, MA: MIT Press.

Tabachneck-Schijf, H. J. M., Leonardo, A. M., & Simon, H. A. (1997). CaMeRa: A computational model of multiple representations. *Cognitive Science, 21* (3), 305–350.

Vera, A. H., & Simon, H. A. (1994). Reply to Touretzky and Pomerleau: Reconstructing physical symbol systems. *Cognitive Science, 18* (2), 355–360.

Zhu, X., Lee, Y., Simon, H. A., & Zhu, D. (1996). Cue recognition and cue elaboration in learning from examples. *Proceedings of the National Academy of Sciences, 93,* 1346–1351.

Zhu, X., & Simon, H. A. (1987). Learning mathematics from examples and by doing. *Cognition and Instruction, 4* (3), 137–166.

Part III

Tools for Learning
from Instruction

8

What Role Do Cognitive Architectures Play in Intelligent Tutoring Systems?

John R. Anderson
Kevin A. Gluck
Carnegie Mellon University

In his "A Bridge Too Far" article, Bruer (1998) suggested that cognitive psychology serves as an "island" to link research on the brain with research on instruction. He argued that a bridge going all the way from brain to instruction is impossible without this intermediate point to interpret the results from brain research and determine their implications for instruction. This chapter is concerned with the issue of how one can bridge from basic cognitive psychology to education. A great deal of basic research and theory in cognitive psychology studies behavior in small tasks isolated from one another. Cognitive psychologists study how subjects recognize symbols, memorize lists of items, reason about syllogisms, process syntactic ambiguity, and so forth. Much of recent research in cognitive neuroscience has looked for brain correlates of such simple tasks. If there is going to be a bridge between cognitive psychology and education, it is going to have to provide a bridge between such simple tasks and the much more complex cognition that occurs in the classroom.

Unfortunately, there is a large gap between such laboratory research in cognitive psychology and education. As Newell (1973) lamented over 25 years ago, such research has failed to provide a characterization that integrates human cognition. Such an integration is absolutely essential for educational applications. In learning geometry, for instance, students have to simultaneously deal with recognizing symbols, memorizing new information, processing the syntax of instruction, reasoning about the material, and much more. Although he was not specifically concerned with educational applications, Newell introduced cognitive architectures as a solution to the problem of integration. Cognitive architectures are computational systems that try to characterize how the different aspects of the human system are integrated to achieve coherent thought.

This chapter is concerned with the implications of the *ACT* architecture for education. It begins with a description of the ACT architecture (Anderson, 1983) and how this served as the basis for a generation of intelligent tutoring systems (e.g., Anderson, Corbett, Koedinger, & Pelletier, 1995). It discusses the factors that motivated the development of the ACT-R architecture (Anderson & Lebiere, 1998). *ACT-R* is an architecture that analyzes cognition at the grain size that characterizes much of laboratory research and is also capable of putting these pieces together in a model of complex cognition. Thus, it provides the potential bridge between basic cognitive psychology and education.

We first review the ACT theory and its connection with education through the construction of cognitive tutors. The key assumption of this theory is that complex cognition can be decomposed into simpler units. ACT-R currently analyzes cognition at a much finer grain size than did past versions of the ACT theory and we consider the consequences of this fine grain size for tutoring. We show that it implies that it is important to monitor students at a much more detailed level than has been typical of our past tutors. Using eye movement studies, we show that there are indeed instructional advantages to be obtained by what we call high-density sensing of the student. We end the chapter with an assessment of whether it is possible to build one bridge that goes all the way from the simple tasks of cognitive psychology to instruction, or whether more bridges are needed.

THE ACT THEORY
AND COGNITIVE TUTORS

The basic assumption in all the ACT theories is that human cognition emerges through an interaction between a procedural memory and a declarative memory. Interestingly, this procedural–declarative distinction is finding increasing support from cognitive neuroscience with procedural learning associated with the basal ganglia and declarative learning associated with the hippocampus (e.g., Knowlton, Mangels, & Squire, 1996; Poldrack, Prabakharan, Seger, & Gabrieli, in press). Declarative learning results in the acquisition of various facts such as the fact that 3 + 4 = 7. Procedural learning results in the acquisition of production rules that retrieve this information to solve particular problems. Thus, a student might be in the midst of solving the following multicolumn addition problem:

```
 336
+848
────
   4
```

If the student is in the midst of working on the multicolumn addition problem, the next production to apply might be:

IF   the goal is to add n1 and n2 in a column and n1 + n2 = n3
THEN set as a subgoal to write n3 in that column.

This production would retrieve the sum of 3 and 4 from declarative memory and embellish the goal with the information that 7 is the number that should be written out. Then other productions would apply that might deal with things like processing the carry into the column. The basic premise of the ACT theory is that cognition unfolds as a sequence of such production-rule firings. Furthermore, ACT implies that learning involves the acquisition of such production rules.

In the 1980s and 1990s, we engaged in a process of analyzing the production rules that were necessary to achieve competence in a number of domains of mathematics and computer programming. The following are typical of the production rules that we proposed:

LISP
IF   the goal is to get the nth element of the list
THEN code "car"
      and set as a subgoal to get the $n-1^{st}$ tail of the list.

Geometry
IF   the goal is to prove two triangles congruent
THEN set as subgoals to prove corresponding parts congruent.

Algebra
IF   the goal is to solve an equation in x
THEN set as subgoals to graph the right and left sides of the equation
      and find the intersection point(s).

Given the assumption that learning in these domains involves the acquisition of such production rules, it follows that we should try to diagnose whether students have acquired such production rules and provide instruction to remediate any difficulties they have with specific rules. This led to the design of cognitive tutors that ran production-rule models in parallel with the students and attempted to interpret student behavior in terms of the rules in the models. The tutors use computer interfaces in which students can solve problems—for instance, a structured editor for programming or a graphical proof-planning interface for geometry. A process called model tracing tries to find some sequence of productions that produces the behavior exhibited by the student. This interpretation of the behavior controls the tutorial interactions in three ways:

1. If students ask for help, it is possible to give help appropriate to where they are in the problem-solving process, thereby individualizing instruction.
2. If students appear to be progressing correctly, the student model updates its confidence that they know the rules and therefore promotes them through the curriculum. Thus, there are cognitively based mastery criteria for promotion through the curriculum.
3. If students make what appears to be an identifiable error, it is possible to intervene and provide appropriate instructions.

For purposes of later discussion, there are two features to emphasize about this approach. First, the tutor only has access to a narrow "window" of student behavior; mouse clicks, key presses, and their directions from which to make its inference about the student's thinking processes. Second, the typical time span of these steps is on the order of 10 seconds or more. We later describe in this chaper what happens when we consider other behavioral indicants and cognition at a finer grain size.

Validity of the Approach

There are two ways to assess the validity of this approach and the assumptions on which it is based. The first is by assessing its educational outcomes and the second is by looking in detail at the behavior of students working with the tutor.

Achievement Gains. There are a number of assessments (Anderson, et al., 1995; Koedinger, Anderson, Hadley, & Mark, 1997) that converge on the conclusion that students using these tutors perform about a letter grade (approximately one standard deviation) better than students who do not. The approach also appears to produce more motivated students and considerable teacher acceptance. It is harder to know how to measure motivation and acceptance but one thing we can point to is the fact that the tutors are currently used in about 300 schools around the country and teach about 50,000 students. This practical success in acceptance reflects a lot more than the achievement gains associated with the tutor. An analysis of just what is behind the practical success of the tutors remains to be done.

From the perspective of cognitive psychology, the achievement gain is the most interesting aspect of the evaluation. Figure 8.1 shows the results of a typical evaluation. This was an evaluation of the PAT Algebra 1 tutor that targets teaching problem-solving skills and use of mathematical relationships. As is apparent, it was having large positive effects (compared to the control) on these skills and smaller but still positive effects on traditional measures of algebraic performance that it was not targeting. For the targeted skills, the effect size was on the order of one standard deviation.

For two reasons, it is quite problematical to know how to assess an achievement gain of one standard deviation. First, it is hard to say how big

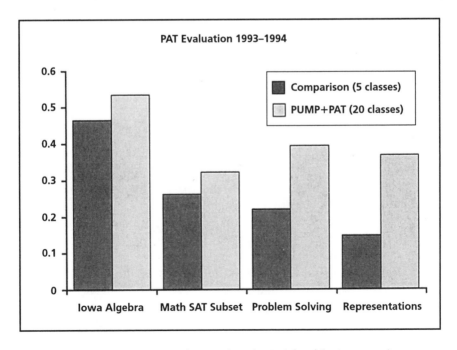

FIG. 8.1. Comparison of control and tutorial subjects on various tests of algebraic problem solving. Percent correct answers.

an effect this is. One standard deviation achievement gain means that the distribution of student performance with the tutor is shifted up about one standard deviation from the distribution of students without the tutor. Because standard deviation is measured with respect to variance in the population, this says as much about the population variability as the effect size. Second, it is hard to know how large an effect could be achieved. Bloom (1984) is famous for claiming an effect size of two standard deviations for human tutoring. However, other assessments have produced smaller effects (Cohen, Kulik, & Kulik, 1982).

Despite the uncertainty about how big an effect is possible, it is generally conceded within our group that our tutors are not having as positive an instructional effect as possible. That is, students should be able to learn more per unit time than they are with the tutors. One sign of this is the low absolute levels of performance in Fig. 8.1. There clearly is a lot of room for improvement. These data come from regular urban mathematics classes and are undoubtedly impacted by difficulties of lack of preparation, nonattendance, and so forth. Still, we know that there are times when students are not getting all they should from their instruction. For instance, there are numerous examples of profitless interaction where the student has a misunderstanding that the tutor cannot address. The fact that, despite these weaknesses, they are doing better than control classrooms might be seen more as an indictment of the control classrooms than as praise for the tutoring manipulation.

Analysis of Tutor Interactions.   The key assumption in these tutors has been that competence in a domain decomposes into a set of components and that the overall learning of the skill is just the learning of the individual components. This is a view of competence that many educators do not share, and the opposite opinion informs many educational programs, such as those produced by radical constructivists in mathematical education (for a discussion see Anderson, Reder, & Simon, 1998). The hard-line constructivist view (Lesh & Lamon, 1992; Shepard, 1991) is that it is not possible to break down a competence into its components, and any attempt to do so will lead to failed education. The success of our tutors clearly contradicts this.

In addition to their overall success, the tutors afford more direct evidence on the issue of the decomposition of knowledge. In tracking knowledge, the cognitive tutors keep track of how well students are doing on various components. Figure 8.2 shows some data making this point from Corbett, Anderson, and O'Brien (1995). The data come from the LISP

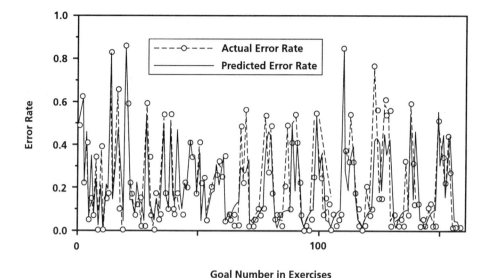

Goal Number in Exercises

FIG. 8.2.   Actual predicted error rates across subjects at each goal
in a set of required tutor exercises. From "Student Modeling in the
ACT Programming Tutor," by A. T. Corbett, J. R. Anderson and A. T.
O'Brien, 1995, in *Cognitively Diagnostic Assessment* (p. 25).
Hillsdale, NJ: Lawrence Erlbaum Associates.

tutor. Students are asked to write a number of LISP functions and the figure shows their error rate at each point in each function across the early
material. Students show a lot of jumps and drops in their error rates at different points. As the figure shows, our model successfully predicts these
jumps and drops. The model assumes that each production rule has its
own learning curve. Figure 8.3 averages together those points where the
same production rule is applying. As Fig. 8.3 illustrates, there is smooth
learning over these points. Thus, the reason for the rises and falls in Fig.
8.2 is the fact that new production rules are being introduced at different
points in the curriculum. The success in accounting for complex behavioral profiles like Fig. 8.2 is for us the most compelling support for the
decomposition of knowledge. However, it needs to be noted that this success depends on a very careful task analysis. The original production rule
set in the LISP tutor did not yield such regular learning data. The final set
resulted from an iterative process of refinement. Indeed, we view the ability to come up with such systematic learning curves as a measure of
whether the right production rules have been identified.

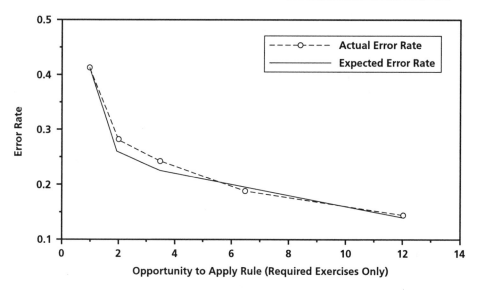

FIG. 8.3.   Mean actual error rate and expected error rate for the ideal
coding rules across successive rule applications.

The Grain Size of Cognition

There is growing evidence that despite their successes, the cognitive tutors
are modeling cognition at too large of a grain size and are consequently
failing to capture some of the regularities in learning. Although results like
Fig. 8.2 are compelling evidence for decomposition, there is reason to
believe that these learning curves actually reflect the aggregate results of
a variety of simpler cognitive steps. Research in the ACT-R laboratory has
supported the decomposition of cognition into subsecond units. In one
study of a simulated air-traffic control task, Lee and Anderson (in press)
found that the overall task decomposed into unit tasks of the multisecond
level typically modeled in the past generation of tutors. However, more
careful analysis indicated that each of these unit tasks decomposed into
simple actions of moving visual attention and issuing individual key-
strokes.

Movement in the direction of a finer temporal resolution is not something that is unique to the ACT research group. Indeed, reflecting an
emerging consensus in cognitive psychology about the grain size of cognition, the architectures for human cognition have all moved to a small

cycle size. In a symposium on production system architectures at the 1995 Cognitive Science meeting (Anderson, et al., 1995), it was noted that the four production systems (ACT, Soar, EPIC, and CAPS) had all converged to a minimum cycle time of only 50 ms. This reflects the efforts of these cognitive architectures to accommodate the detailed data about human cognition.

The strongest regularities in human cognition have come from studies of learning that look at small units of knowledge and studies of performance that look at brief tasks. These tasks are typically on the order of one second in length, and subtracting out encoding and motor time reveals that the cognitive component is often only a few tenths of a second.

Many educators decry the emphasis in the classroom on problems that span only a few minutes. They argue that it leads the child to believe that all problems only require this amount of effort. Still, the contrast is at least three orders of magnitude between the time scale of these classroom tasks and the few hundred milliseconds that cognitive psychology has identified as the place where the real regularities appear in cognition. This contrast has led to an unfortunate disconnect between much of cognitive psychology and much of education.

Many educators do not believe that anything at the subsecond time scale could possibly be relevant to understanding the tasks of significance they study. As we already noted, some hold the belief that task decomposition is just not possible. We think these beliefs are wrong and we have the evidence to show that such task decomposition is indeed possible. Others, however, just believe as a practical matter that it is not possible to do the work to develop such decompositions for the learning phenomena of interest. The cognitive tutoring work involves task decompositions probably two orders of magnitude above the level identified in modern cognitive psychology. It is a legitimate question to ask whether it is a bridge too far to go from the low-level cognitive tasks popular in laboratory psychology to educational applications.

For their part, many cognitive psychologists distrust the research that involves complex tasks spanning time scales of many tens of seconds. They hold the view that such complex tasks are inherently too messy to be given systematic analysis. Again, we think the cognitive tutoring work has proven this view to be false. On the other hand, there is a weaker and more reasonable bias. This is that the one-second laboratory task offers the necessary control and ability to isolate phenomena of interest. A similar concern over experimental control and the isolation of specific phenomena makes researchers in cognitive neuroscience reluctant to image complex tasks because they fear that too many neural areas will be involved and it will be impossible to pull them apart. Although these are legitimate concerns, their consequence is that there has been a failure to make the connection between basic cognitive psychology and education.

Perhaps the correct solution is to introduce another island along the path from neuroscience to education. In this conception, there would be three bridges altogether. The bridge from neuroscience to basic cognitive psychology would be one that aggregates neural detail into units of psychological significance. The bridge from these basic cognitive processes to something like the unit tasks in our cognitive tutors would reflect an aggregation of these units into units of educational significance. The bridge from this unit-task level to education would show how to construct significant intellectual competences.

Although this three-bridge proposal has a lot of plausibility, this chapter is devoted to exploring the idea that the basic subsecond cognitive level can inform the multi-minute level of education. We show that instructional opportunities become available by attending to what is happening at the subsecond level.

THE ACT-R THEORY

We close out this section by describing the ACT-R theory, which is a cognitive architecture that embodies this subsecond level of analysis. Figure 8.4 illustrates the control structure in ACT-R. Cognition is controlled by the current goal, and a production is selected that matches the current goal. This production can cause both actions to be taken in the real world and retrieval requests to be made of declarative memory. The actions in the external world can include shifts of attention, which in effect also retrieve information, but from the external world. This retrieved information results in changes in the goal and the cycle can progress again. This cycle of production firing, retrieval, and goal modification takes on the order of a few hundred milliseconds or less. Thus, it reflects the loop of cognition that has become the focus of analysis in basic cognitive psychology.

The inner loop in Fig. 8.4 reflects a slower learning loop by which knowledge structures can be modified. New chunks are added to declarative memory when goals are achieved. For instance, if a child sets the goal to add $4 + 3$, counts up, and finds 7 as the answer, this goal is popped and stored as a chunk that can be retrieved with the answer.[1] Chunks are also

---

[1]Of course, only after repeated practice will this fact be strong enough to be successfully retrieved.

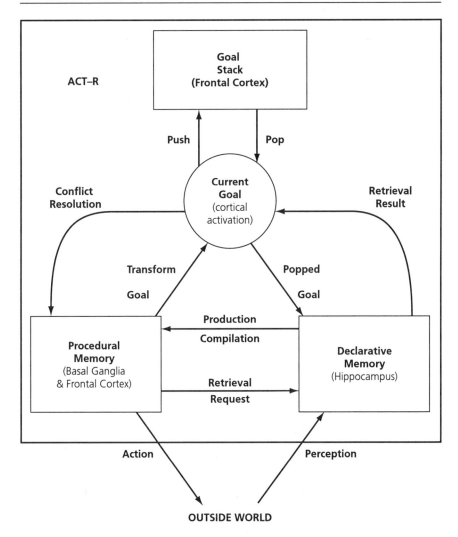

FIG. 8.4.   A representation of the memories in ACT-R and the flow of information among them.

formed by encoding information from the environment. New production rules can be formed by compiling representations of past solutions in declarative memory. Finally, production rules can call for pops and pushes of goals that change the goal state. Pushes store an intention and focus on a more immediate goal. Pops retrieve an old intention and supplant the current goal with it.

The cognitive architecture in Fig. 8.4 reflects an abstraction from underlying neural processes, as indicated by the labels bearing probable brain correlates. The goal state is really the current active cortical state. There is evidence (Wise, Murray, & Gerfen, 1996) that the basal ganglia receive activation from the full cortex and recognize patterns and send these recognized patterns to the frontal cortex, which selects an appropriate action. Thus, production memory is really implemented in basal ganglia and frontal cortex. There is a great deal of evidence pointing to the hippocampus as playing a major role in the creation of declarative memories and the frontal cortex as responsible for the maintenance of intentions, which is abstracted in ACT-R as the goal stack.

When we talk about ACT-R in terms of chunks and productions, we are treating cognition as a symbolic system, which is a useful abstraction. However, productions and chunks vary in their availability, which reflects the underlying, more continuous neural computation. There is a subsymbolic level of ACT-R that models cognition at this level. Much of the important learning in ACT-R is at this subsymbolic level and involves making chunks and productions more available with practice and success. We do not model actual neural learning processes, but rather model their effect by a set of equations that characterize these processes. In this way, ACT-R is an attempt to abstract away from the neural detail to what is relevant to human cognition. These subsymbolic learning processes are very important to learning. Anderson and Schunn (2000) wrote about their implications for educational practice.

When one models cognition at a fine grain size, it becomes important to consider the relationship of cognition to perception and action. Therefore, Byrne (Byrne & Anderson, 1998) created an extension of ACT-R called *ACT-R/PM*, which is represented in Fig. 8.5. All of ACT-R from Fig. 8.4 is embedded in the cognitive layer of Fig. 8.5. In the perceptual layer are a number of independent modules that control hand movement, speech, movement of visual attention, and movement of auditory attention. Each of these peripheral modules is capable of running in parallel with cognition and with each other. However, each of these modules is serial within itself, only doing one thing at a time even as ACT-R can only fire one production at a time. This leads to a complex set of predictions about exactly what can be done within a specified period of time, and these predictions seem largely to be confirmed (Byrne & Anderson, in press).

Initial control of each of these modules in Fig. 8.5 seems to begin in the frontal cortex but each action module and the perceptual module involves

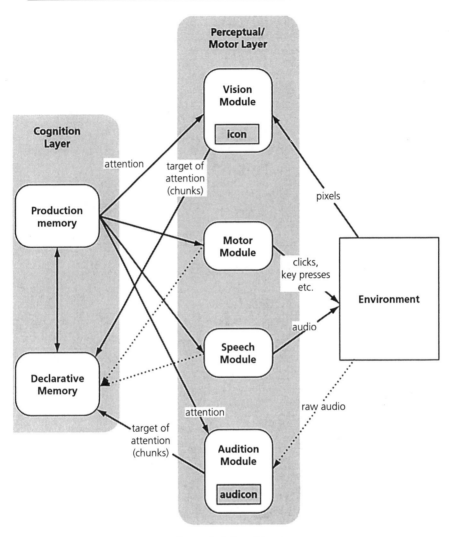

FIG. 8.5. Overview of ACT-R/PM architecture.

a great deal of other neural structures. It is sobering to realize that much more cortex is given over to perception and action than things we would associate with ACT-R or other cognitive architectures. This should make us aware of how important it is to consider human perception and action in a complete account of human cognition.

HIGH-DENSITY SENSING

We argued earlier that significant acts of cognition are happening at the subsecond level and that at least some of them have behavioral indicants. Thus, it is possible to increase one's sensitivity to students by monitoring their behavior at a high temporal density and using this data to make inferences about student cognition. One advantage of human tutors over computer tutors is that humans have such fine grain access to their students' behaviors. This allows for far greater sensitivity and adaptability in a tutorial interaction. A human tutor can see frustration on the pupil's face, hear uncertainty in an utterance, and is aware of how long the student is taking to solve a problem. These are examples of types of input that are typically not used by computer tutors. VanLehn (1988) referred to the amount and quality of the input available to a tutor as an issue of "bandwidth." He identified three bandwidth categories that constitute three different levels of information regarding problem-solving processes. In increasing order of information detail, they are final states, intermediate states, and mental states. A mental states level of bandwidth is necessary to support the model tracing approach used in the ACT tutors, and this can be done with keystroke and mouse click data. However, technological advancements and recent changes in the grain size at which cognition is analyzed in the ACT-R theory have led us to speculate that additional instructional opportunities are afforded by increasing the bandwidth even further.

There are obvious indicants of confusion or understanding such as facial expression and speech. One might think the student could type the same information that they speak but students find it much easier to speak their minds than to type their minds. A frequent occurrence in the tutor classrooms is that students will point to something on the screen and ask somebody "What does this mean?" (Where they could ask the same questions of the tutor with clicks and key presses.)

Of most importance to the main point of this chapter, humans also have an ability to monitor what students are attending to visually. For instance, in a study of human accuracy in gaze estimation, Gale (1998) found that humans could estimate where someone was looking with a root mean square error of about 2 to 4 degrees.

When construction of the cognitive tutors started in the 1980s, it was beyond the realm of possibility to think about using information at the grain size of speech or eye movement. The computers were hard pressed to keep up with an interpretation of students' key presses and mouse clicks in real time. Things have dramatically changed on this score. Speech recognition software now comes as a standard component with many computer systems. Mostow (1998) showed that using speech recognition software, which is only modestly more tuned than the standard commercial software, one can monitor and instruct students' reading. His demonstration is important because it shows how one can use the constraints of the instructional situation to facilitate speech recognition. It is also now possible to attach a camera to a computer, monitor the student's face, recognize expressions and emotions (Cohn, Zlochower, Lien, & Kanade, in press), and track where the eyes are gazing. In our own lab, we demonstrated that it is possible to compute interpretations of the student's eye movements in real time (Salvucci, 1999). Thus, it is now possible to think of the computer tutor as having as rich a perceptual access to the student as does a human tutor.

There are three significant issues that such access raises. The first is more apparent than real but needs to be addressed: privacy and intrusiveness. The second is the core of the instructional issue: what instructional opportunities are created by such high-density access. The third is the cognitive and technical issue: how to place a cognitive interpretation on the information that one gets from such high-density sensing. We address each of these issues in turn.

Privacy and Intrusiveness

Some people set up Web pages where they provide camera access to their private lives. However, most of us (and most students) would find abhorrent the prospect of the world having such access to our lives. On the other hand, virtually no one finds abhorrent the fact that a computer is tracking how they are moving the mouse. This reflects the fact that we want the computer to be sensitive to what we are doing but we do not want it to be a means of broadcasting (or recording for the world) what we are doing.

The situation with respect to the proposed high-density sensing is somewhere in between the two previous examples. Just as current speech recognition software does not keep a permanent record of all the speech (not just out of concern for privacy, but because it would be too much information), any sensing technology would not store a record of the entire sensory signal it was getting from the student. As with speech or mouse movements, it would extract an interpretation of the student from the raw signal. Note that this is equally true of human tutors, who do not remember exactly what they heard and saw. On the other hand, in the tutoring situation, there is a natural desire to maintain a permanent record of that interpretation both for purposes of informing further interactions with the student (this is what individualizes the tutor dialog to the student) and for purposes of later assessment. Despite this, it is probably the case that the actual interpretation of the student will be no different than the interpretations currently stored of the students in our tutors. There will not be more detailed records kept—just more accurate ones. Typically, our tutors only keep summary estimates of how well students are doing on particular cognitive objectives (for future diagnosis) and which problems students have done (for teacher information and to inform future problem selection). Except in experimental situations, we do not even keep a high-level record of the key and mouse interactions. For example, we have never recorded in our tutors mouse trajectories over the screen. Therefore, despite some people's initial reactions to the contrary, the introduction of high-density sensing does not change the recording of the student beyond what one would find in a teacher's grade book. The only difference is the degree to which the record reflects accurate cognitive diagnosis.

Intrusiveness is a somewhat different issue than privacy. Interacting with a high-density tutor would be very much like interacting with a human tutor, where every gesture is interpreted. This humanlike quality might seem a clear benefit, but there is an intrusive nature to such interactions that might not always be desired. Students sometimes like the ability to do their work out of the public eye. A frequent positive comment about our computer tutors from students is that they feel more at ease with them than with human tutors because the computer tutors appear less judgmental. Because of its potential intrusiveness, it is not obvious that high-density sensing would always be a win and one might well want to have the opportunity to turn the high-density sensing off or, indeed, give the student that option. Giving the option to turn the high-density sensing off is really no different than the options that now exist to use or not use the tutor. We would just be providing the student and teacher with another option in their learning interactions.

Instructional Opportunities

Although speech and face recognition offer potentially powerful ways to give computer tutors better access to the student's mental state, our focus in the rest of the chapter is on eye movements as a window into the student's mind. We have done research on the instructional opportunities afforded by eye movement information in the context of the PAT algebra tutor. The ninth-grade algebra tutor, PAT, is the most widely used of the cognitive tutors. (Figure 8.1 shows the results from an earlier version.) Therefore, it seems wise to focus on the opportunities for eye movements to inform instruction with this tutor. The PAT tutor is concerned with teaching students to relate graphical, symbolic, verbal, and tabular representations of mathematical functions. The graphing features are only introduced after a couple of lesson units and for technical reasons, we chose to study the version of the tutor from the early lessons without the graphing interface. To help eye movement resolution, we altered somewhat the exact size and arrangement of material on the screen but otherwise deployed a system that faithfully reproduces the instructional interactions in the actual classroom.

Figure 8.6a shows a screen display as it appears at the beginning of a problem. The student's task is to fill in the column labels and units, enter a variable and an expression written in terms of that variable, and then answer whatever result-unknown and start-unknown questions are present. Figure 8.6b displays the completed problem. The key aspect of the problem is the expression $12 + 45x$, which the student fills in. The real goal of the lesson is to teach the student how to create such expressions and use them to solve problems. There are a total of 18 problems, all similar in form to this one. Two of the problems are used strictly for introducing students to the task, and the other 16 are completed while the student is calibrated on the eye tracker. Each participant completed these problems at a rate of four per day, for 4 days in a row. The participants were students in prealgebra and beginning algebra classes, as are the students who use the PAT tutor in actual classrooms.

The eye tracker used in this study was a head-mounted unit designed by ISCAN, Inc. It was lightweight and rested on the student's head like a visor. Low-level infrared illumination provides a corneal reflection that is used with the pupil center to provide point-of-regard (POR) estimates.

Our research with the system was concerned with collecting descriptive statistics of eye movements and characterizing learning trends. Having access to such visual attention data allows us to infer a great deal about a student's problem-solving processes. In cognitive psychology, there is nothing new about using eye movements to reveal the microstructure of a cognitive process. It is new, however, to investigate ways that we can leverage off this sort of data in a real-time tutoring situation. One of the primary motivations for this project was to explore the kinds of instructional opportunities brought about by increasing the bandwidth of information available to a computer tutor. We also wanted to develop an ACT-R/PM model that was capable of interacting with the tutorial

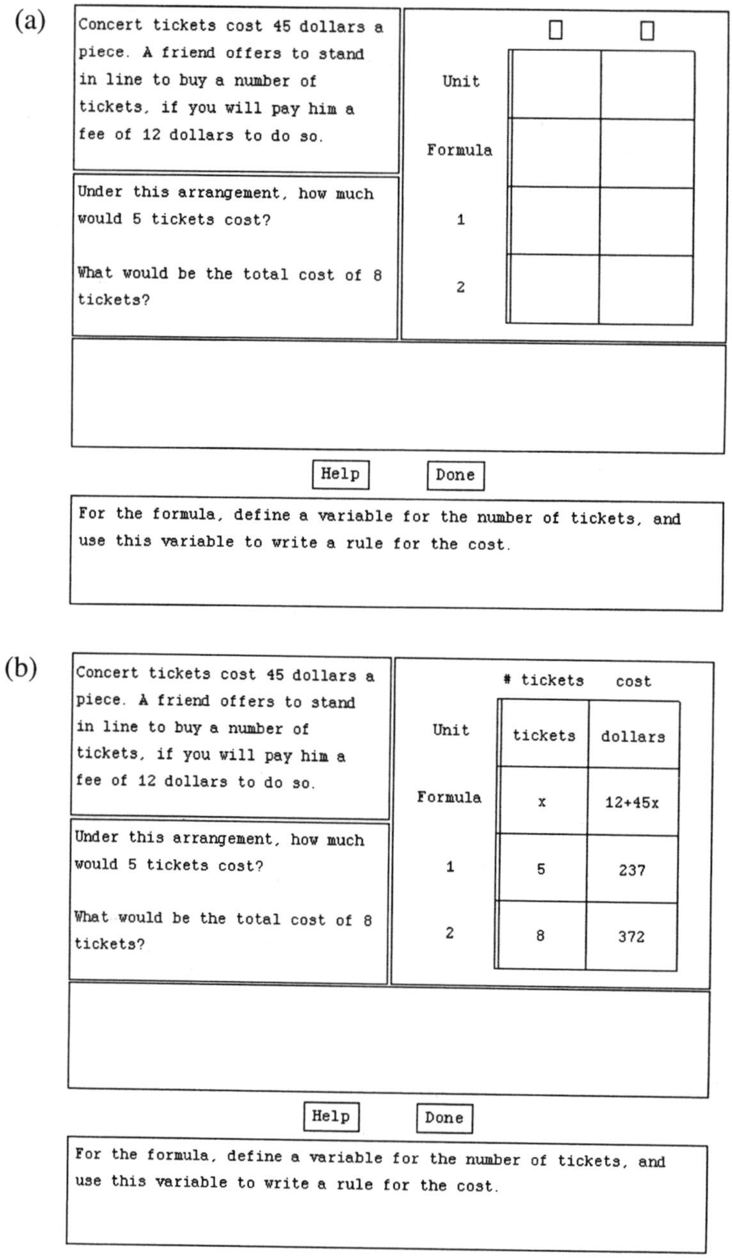

(a)

		☐	☐
Concert tickets cost 45 dollars a piece. A friend offers to stand in line to buy a number of tickets, if you will pay him a fee of 12 dollars to do so.	Unit		
	Formula		
Under this arrangement, how much would 5 tickets cost?	1		
What would be the total cost of 8 tickets?	2		

Help   Done

For the formula, define a variable for the number of tickets, and use this variable to write a rule for the cost.

(b)

		# tickets	cost
Concert tickets cost 45 dollars a piece. A friend offers to stand in line to buy a number of tickets, if you will pay him a fee of 12 dollars to do so.	Unit	tickets	dollars
	Formula	x	12+45x
Under this arrangement, how much would 5 tickets cost?	1	5	237
What would be the total cost of 8 tickets?	2	8	372

Help   Done

For the formula, define a variable for the number of tickets, and use this variable to write a rule for the cost.

FIG. 8.6. The tutor screen at the beginning of the problem (a) and at the end of the problem (b).

interface in the way students are. However, for current purposes, we just report some of the types of instructional opportunities that we found. These opportunities reflect different ways that eye movements enhance our ability to diagnose the student's cognitive state. We consider six examples of such instructional opportunities.

In the sections that follow, we provide examples of typical eye movements that indicate an instructional opportunity. These eye movements are represented as a series of "blobs" on the screen that show where the student's eye was fixated during the episode. These fixation blobs move from light to dark with the passage of time. We also provide statistics to indicate how representative these individual examples are. Each fixation typically occupies a few hundred milliseconds.

1. Student has Shifted Attention to a Different Part of the Problem Without Informing the Tutor.

The tutor problems are typical of many significant mathematical problems in that they have a number of components and it becomes an issue to make sure that the tutor knows what part of the problem the student is currently thinking about. The student can be working on one part of the problem whereas the tutor thinks the student is working on another part of the problem. A classic example of this that occurs in the PAT tutor is that the student selects one of the columns but gives the answer for the other column. For instance, a number of our students clicked the first column in which one enters givens but then went ahead and calculated the result that went into the second column. Not surprisingly, students display very different eye movements when they are entering the given versus calculating the results. Figure 8.7a and 8.7b display a typical contrast. Figure 8.7a shows a successful episode in which the student fixated the *5 hours* in the first question and entered the 5 in the column. The few fixation blobs indicate how brief and direct the eye movements are. In contrast, in Fig. 8.7b, the student chose the cell to enter the given but got ahead of himself and calculated the altitude rather than simply entering the time. Note all the eye fixations over the problem statement—an indication that the student was calculating the result and not entering the given.

The error of putting the solution in the given cell may not seem like a particularly interesting error. That is exactly the problem. From an instructional standpoint, it is not an interesting error. This is not an impasse arising out of some fundamental conceptual error that the student could learn about and overcome by working through the error. There is little, if any, additional learning gain that arises out of a student's having committed

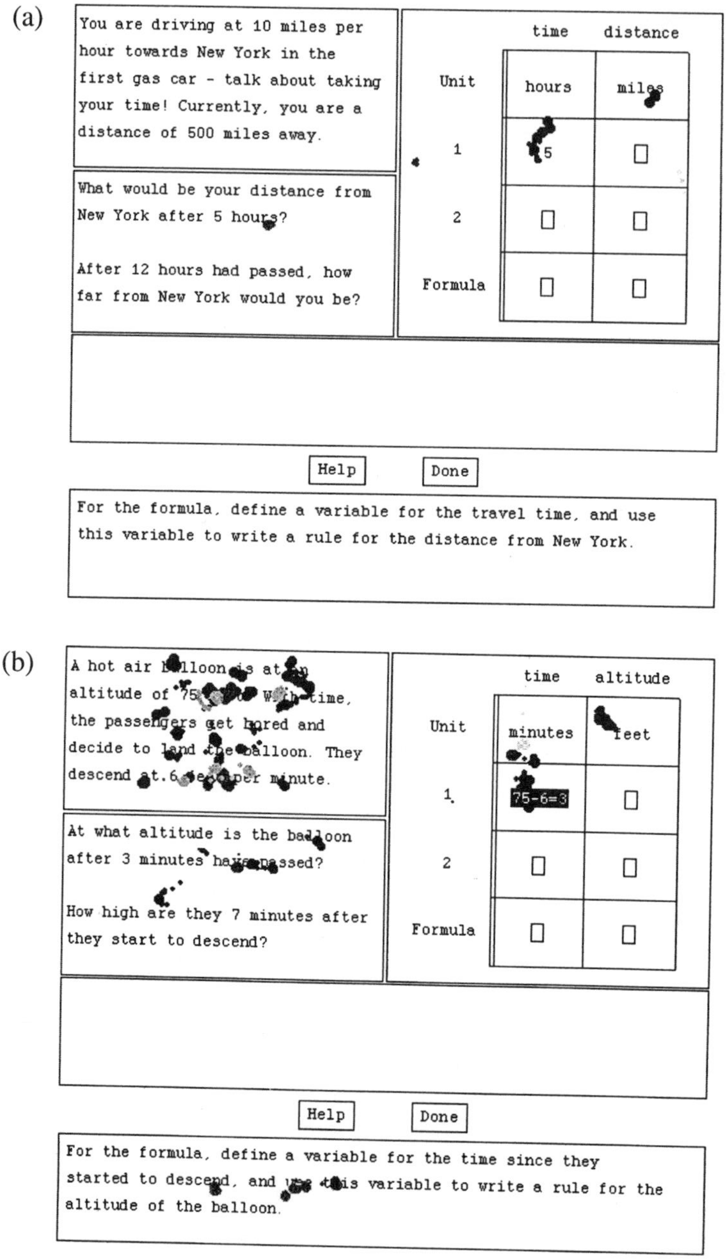

(a)

You are driving at 10 miles per hour towards New York in the first gas car - talk about taking your time! Currently, you are a distance of 500 miles away.

What would be your distance from New York after 5 hours?

After 12 hours had passed, how far from New York would you be?

Unit	time	distance
	hours	miles
1	5	
2		
Formula		

Help   Done

For the formula, define a variable for the travel time, and use this variable to write a rule for the distance from New York.

(b)

A hot air balloon is at an altitude of 75 feet. With time, the passengers get bored and decide to land the balloon. They descend at 6 feet per minute.

At what altitude is the balloon after 3 minutes have passed?

How high are they 7 minutes after they start to descend?

Unit	time	altitude
	minutes	feet
1	75-6=3	
2		
Formula		

Help   Done

For the formula, define a variable for the time since they started to descend, and use this variable to write a rule for the altitude of the balloon.

FIG. 8.7.   Eye movements when a student does not make an attention shift (a) and when a student has (b).

this error. Not only is there little to be gained, but there sometimes is considerable confusion and frustration that arises out of having committed this error. Students do not always see the bug message that appears ("You typed that in the wrong column."), and when they do not see that message, and they are pretty confident they did the computation correctly, it is hard for them to understand why the tutor considers it wrong. Some students even reenter the solution in the wrong cell, to see if the tutor will accept it *this* time. Given the lack of instructional utility and the confusion it sometimes creates, it is an error to be avoided, if possible. One way of avoiding this error is to use the student's eye movements to detect the cognitive attention switch and intervene before the error is committed. Ignoring for now the issue of what the intervention should be, we first explore the possibility of detecting these cognitive attention shifts on the fly.

The eye movement data used in this analysis were those collected during first attempts at cell Q1-Left (the cell on the left side of the row for responses related to question 1). Because the students completed 16 problems on the eye tracker, and there is one first attempt at each cell per problem, this results in 16 part-tasks from each student for this analysis.[2] Eye movement data were extracted from the beginning of each part-task to just before the first character of a response was typed. Examining responses from each student individually (on first attempts in Q1-Left only), it was found that 6 students committed this error three or more times. It is the data from these 6 students that are used to try to predict a cognitive attention shift based on eye movement data.

We started with a shotgun approach to predict when such a shift of attention would occur. The predictor variables were fixation counts and gaze time in every point-of-regard (POR) region, as well as latency from the beginning of the part-task to the first key press. Gaze time in a POR region was computed as the sum of the fixation times for all of the fixations in that region. If we included fixations offscreen, fixations to the keyboard, and fixations to MON ("middle of nowhere"—fixations on the screen that are not in any of the defined regions), there were 23 different POR locations. With two variables (fixation count and gaze) for each region, plus the latency variable from the beginning of the part-task to the first key press, we had a total of 47 predictor variables available.

---

[2]Except for two students who have missing data. One of them had 12 part-tasks total (lost an entire day of data), and the other had 15 part-tasks (lost one problem's worth of data). In both of these cases, the data were lost because the students managed to crash the tutor midtask, before the data were written out.

The two variables with strongest correlation with probability of an attention shift were number of fixations on the problem statement and amount of time fixating the problem statement. After either of these were added to the predictive equation, no other variable had much of a correlation. Figure 8.8 shows the probability of an attention shift as a function of number of fixations of the problem statement. It is apparent that once the number of fixations equals or exceeds 15, it is almost certain that there will be an attentional switch.

One needs to be fairly conservative in predicting an impending attention shift error, and this is exactly what one would want in a real-time tutoring situation. Imagine how frustrating it would be to find out the tutor thinks you are about to make an error, when in fact you are quite aware that you are *not* about to make that error. Ideally, the tutor would only intervene when it was highly confident that the student was headed into a mistake, and it could help the student avoid the additional confusion and lost time.

Given these promising results, we are confident that it is possible to identify cognitive attention shifts of this sort and enable the tutor to be more closely aligned with the student. It is another question of what to do in such a situation. We used the generic term "intervention" several times

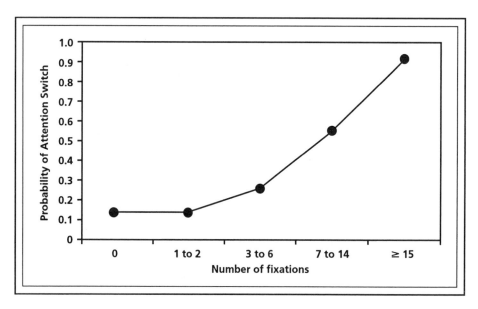

FIG. 8.8.   Probability of attention shift as a function of number of fix-ations on the problem statement.

in the preceding discussion. What might this intervention be? One possibility is to be reactive and simply tell the student after the fact why the answer was an error. With respect to this latter possibility, we should note that, as it currently exists, the tutor will give the student such an error message should they type the value that belongs in a different column. However, eye movements would allow the tutor to be more confident in that diagnosis and identify cases where students try to perform the calculation and make a mental arithmetic error instead. We give an example of such a disambiguation in section 4. Another proposal is to be proactive and warn the student with a (perhaps spoken) message "You should be working on the given." A final possibility, and one that is especially intriguing, is to design the tutor to modify itself to accommodate the assessment that a cognitive attention shift has taken place. For instance, if the model is predicting an attention shift error for the current part-task, the tutor could simply change the cell selection so that the solution cell (Q1-Right) is selected. When the student starts typing, the solution would be entered in the correct cell, thanks to the eye movement data.

2. Disambiguation of Solution Method. Students do not all solve these problems in the same way. With respect to the algebra problems we have been working with, differences in solution paths are apparent by examining how students calculated the solution. An interesting contrast is between students who use the algebra expression to calculate an answer and students who go back to the verbal problem and reason from that. Koedinger and colleagues (Koedinger & Anderson, 1998; Koedinger & Tabachneck, 1995) reported that students sometimes find it easier to reason about word problems than to perform the analogous symbolic manipulations, and Koedinger and MacLaren (1997) developed a model in which there are both algebraic and verbal methods for solving problems. Our eye movement research clearly validates that distinction and allows us to tell which method a particular student used to produce an answer. Figure 8.9a shows a subject using the expression and Fig. 8.9b shows a subject using the problem statement. In the case where the expression is used, the student shows repeated fixations on the expression. In the case where it is not used, the student never fixates the expression but rather fixates the problem statement while reasoning verbally through the problem.

One can wonder whether students are more accurate when they calculate the answer using the expression in the problem statement. To address this question, we looked at fixation frequencies in the problem statement

(a)

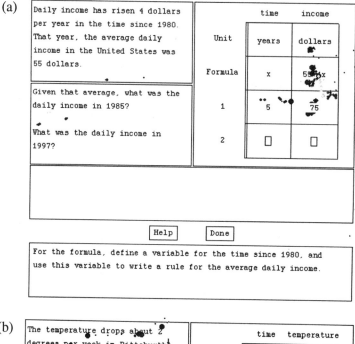

(b)

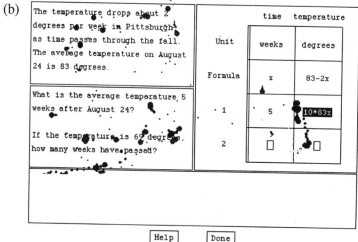

FIG. 8.9. Eye movements when a student calculates the answer using the expression (a) and when a student calculates the answer using the problem statement (b).

and in the expression while participants were working on their first attempt at calculating the answers. Each part-task was labeled as to the presence of fixations in the two regions of interest. If there were one or more fixations in the expression, but not in the problem statement, the part-task was labeled "expression." If there were one or more fixations in the problem statement, but not in the expression, the part-task was labeled "problem statement." Part-tasks were also labeled as "both" or "neither," as appropriate. Table 8.1 shows the results in the form of the percentage of part-tasks that fell into each of these categories and the proportion of correct first attempts within each category.

At the aggregate level, these data indicate that students looked at the expression 54% of the time on their first attempt at solving question 1, suggesting that the traditional model of this process is about half right. The accuracy data show an advantage for using the expression over using the problem statement. There was a main effect of fixation pattern on accuracy, $F(3, 142) = 3.68, p < .02$, and a post hoc Scheffe's test indicated that those who attended to the expression (but not the PS) while solving the result-unknown responded more accurately than those who looked at just the problem statement ($p < .02$). The other differences were not significant. There was also a main effect of fixation pattern on part-task completion time, $F(3, 142) = 19.69, p < .001$, with attending to neither region significantly faster than all of the other fixation patterns and attending only to the expression faster than attending to either just the problem statement or both.

One goal of the curriculum is to help students understand the value of mathematical expressions. With respect to solving result-unknown questions, the expression is useful in that it provides external memory for the computations required to arrive at a solution, and our performance data do indeed show an advantage for those part-tasks in which students looked at

TABLE 8.1
Distribution of fixation patterns during Q1-Right 1st attempts

Fixation Pattern	% of Part-Tasks	Prop. Correct	Time (sec)
Expression (but not PS)	30.1	.88	13.2
PS (but not Expression)	12.6	.50	21.2
Both	23.8	.76	21.1
Neither	33.6	.71	7.7

the expression. These strategies cannot be distinguished on the basis of answer alone, but they *can* be distinguished by a tutor that has access to a student's eye movements. Although the details need to be worked out, the obvious instructional intervention would be to guide the student in the use of the expression.

3. Failure to Read Messages.

One thing that became apparent with our very first pilot subject is that students often fail to read messages that appear on the screen. For instance, often a student will make an error, the tutor will correctly diagnose that error and present a bug message, but the student will not read the message. Figures 8.10a and 8.10b present an interesting example that are two parts of a student's reaction after making the classic error of entering a result in the given (same kind of error as described in section 1). The tutor presented the error message "You typed that in the wrong column." Figure 8.10a illustrates the student's eye movements for the first 18 s where the student failed to read this message and looked through the problem for a possible explanation of his error. Finally, in Fig. 8.10b the student looked at the error message and quickly corrected his error.

The even more extreme case is when a student never reads the bug feedback at all. We saw examples of this during data collection, and became interested in how often this actually happened. To investigate this, we extracted data from only those part-tasks that immediately followed a part-task where an error occurred and led to the display of a bug message. So, in all of the part-tasks used in this analysis, the student had just committed an error and there was a bug message on the screen. We also used only the data from the beginning of each part-task to the first mouse click (a click clears the message window). Figure 8.11 shows the high number of part-tasks in which students did not look at the bug message at all. They failed to fixate the message window in 41% of the part-tasks in which a bug message was present.

The instructional response to such failures to pay attention might seem obvious. Students could receive a spoken prompt to read the message or perhaps we should flash the message to grab attention. There is a possible complication here, however, which is that the tutor messages are not always perceived as useful by the students. For some time now, there have been anecdotal observations of students who, with experience, seem to learn *not* to pay attention to these messages. It turns out there is little evidence for this in the eye tracking data. Table 8.2 lists the proportion of bug

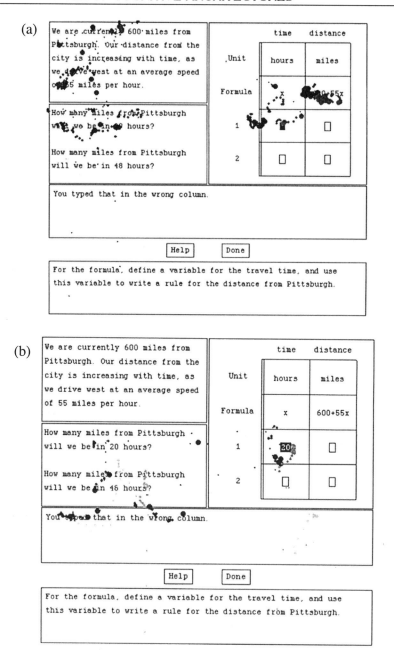

FIG. 8.10. Students eye movements in the first 18 seconds before reading an error message (a) and in the 6 seconds after (b).

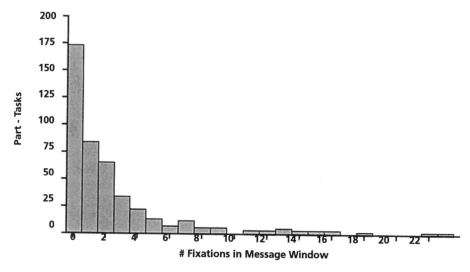

FIG. 8.11. Frequency of fixation in the window that contains the
error message after an error.

TABLE 8.2
Proportion of Bug Messages Ignored Each Day

Day	Proportion Ignored
2	.41
3	.37
4	.40
5	.48

messages that were ignored (i.e., no fixations in the message window) across the 4 days that eye movement data were collected. There is somewhat of an increase on the last day, but this hardly constitutes the sort of clear trend one would want to use as evidence that students are learning to ignore the bug messages.

Another way in which the eye movement data are useful in this context is to help in the evaluation of messages. It is interesting to know whether the help and feedback messages are having their intended effect. One might think that this issue can be investigated in the absence of eye movements. This is true, but in that case, the analysis is done under the assumption that the student is reading the message when it is displayed. As is evident in Fig. 8.11, this often is not the case. Eye movement data allow the researcher to determine with certainty whether a student has read a message. If a student gets some bug feedback and then fails to correct the error, we would not want to blame the message if the subject did not read it. We should note that sometimes a subject makes an error, a message is presented, and the subject corrects the error without ever having read the message. In this case, we would not want to credit the message. Thus, eye movement data make it possible to identify which messages, when read, lead to improved performance.

4. Disambiguation of an Error. There are a number of situations where students make errors that are hard to interpret. One reason for this is that the same error could have multiple causes. Although this is a frequent outcome in our tutors in general, it does not happen in the portion of curriculum that we were studying. The other situation is where the student makes a miscalculation and produces an error that is bizarre. This does happen in our curriculum and eye movements offer an opportunity to disambiguate this class of errors. Figure 8.12 shows an example of this. The student made the same mistake as in Fig. 8.8a, where the result was calculated in the cell where the student should have put the given. However, the student failed to correctly calculate the result, producing an error that would seem totally anomalous to our existing tutor. Note that the eye movements, however, reflect the telltale pattern of calculating a result. If the tutor were designed to do so, it could identify this pattern of fixations and tailor the feedback appropriately—perhaps noting in the message that the student's solution is incorrect (and by the way, the solution is supposed to go in the *other* column!).

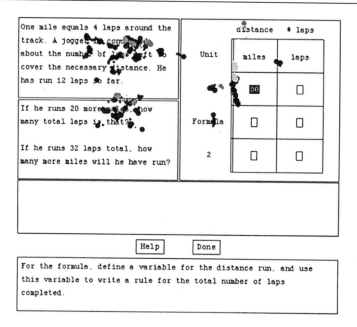

FIG. 8.12. Eye movements when the student has both miscalcu-
lated a result and placed it in the wrong column.

5. Student has Failed to Process Some Critical Information for Answering a Question.

Students are notorious for not reading problems carefully before answering them. A nice example of this appears in Fig. 8.13. The subject entered the data directly from question 1, whereas the formula required the subject to read the earlier problem statement and find the difference between 1985 and 1980. The student's eyes never come close to the 1980 information. Again, the instructional intervention seems obvious and is one that teachers are forever giving their students; "Read the problem statement." An eye-tracking tutor can be more confident that the student has indeed failed to read the problem and can be more certain that such a message is appropriate.

6. Student is Off Task.

There is another class of behavior that we have not seen in our laboratory work with the eye tracker but that we know happens with some frequency in the classroom: Students are just off task and are not looking at the screen. It is not clear that we want to take any actions to correct this behavior but it can inform tutor diagnosis. For

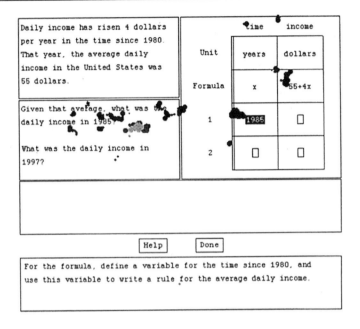

FIG. 8.13. Eye movements when a student has failed to subtract the date, 1980, in the problem statement from the date, 1985, in the question.

instance, it would enable us to use latency of response to infer when a student is having real difficulties. In the current tutors, we do not know during a long-latency response whether the student is looking at the screen and is stuck, or perhaps has turned around and is talking to a neighbor or the teacher. If the student is busy scanning around the screen during this long latency, then we can be fairly confident that they are indeed stuck or confused and can volunteer some help.

Although we do not have instances in our laboratory work of students off task, we certainly have instances of students searching the screen for an answer. Figure 8.14 displays the bandwidth of information that would be available to an eye tracking tutor. The eye movements in the figure reflect the more than 30 s that have passed so far in this part-task, and they reveal that the entire time was spent trying to arrive at a solution for this cell, with multiple saccades among the intercept, the slope, and question 1. This is clear evidence that the student needs help, but the typical computer tutor would be aware only that the cell has been selected.

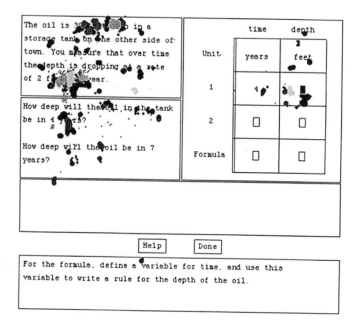

FIG. 8.14.   Eye movements taking place when a student is having difficulty answering the question.

IMPLICATIONS FOR MODEL TRACING

Our goal in presenting these examples is to demonstrate that cognition at the grain size currently monitored in the tutors is supported by cognition at a much finer grain size and that we can gain instructional leverage by monitoring the student at this finer temporal resolution. These examples are also further support for the general thesis that the complex cognition in the classroom can be decomposed into cognitive units of the subsecond level.

Although the decomposition thesis is clearly supported, it does not follow that we have to model cognition at such a fine grain size to achieve our instructional leverage. Recall that our tutor models the problem solving in productions that span many seconds. All the examples that we described so far could be handled by recognizers that looked for a pattern of eye movement that was indicative of that solution method, that bug, or that failure in instruction processing. These recognizers could be attached to existing production rules. We would not really have to produce a process model that actually simulated cognition at such a fine grain size.

There are a lot of reasons to want to keep our instructional models at their current large grain size. Obviously, it is less work to model problem solving at this granularity. Moreover, there are also serious problems of nondeterminacy at the lower level of granularity. For instance, although there are patterns of eye movements that implement using the expression and others that implement using the problem statement, there is not a unique sequence of such eye movements. Although ACT-R is a nondeterministic model that is perfectly capable of accounting for such variation, and much of our research has dealt with distributions of behavior, computationally it can become intractable to trace the subject through a large nondeterministic space of cognitive states.

Salvucci (1999) worked on developing an application of hidden Markov models for interpreting eye movements. Provided there are not huge numbers of states, it achieves efficient recognition of the correct cognitive interpretation of eye movements. It is the sort of algorithm that would work well if we wanted to recognize the general patterns but that would become intolerably slow if we wanted to actually track the system through the exact ACT-R sequence of subsecond cognitive states.

CONCLUSIONS

As a scientific statement, complex cognition can be decomposed into units of cognition of a few hundred milliseconds. We suspect there is no further decomposition of cognition beyond this point that does not involve going to brain models. The cognitive tutoring work has progressed at a much higher level, analyzing cognition into unit tasks of often more than 10 s. As a practical matter, it may be that this is as fine a grain size where one can trace human cognition in an instructional environment. However, the most important properties of an architecture like ACT-R do not show through at this temporal grain size and really only show through at the subsecond level. We showed that, although one might not be able to model trace human cognition at such a fine grain size, behavior occurring at this grain size can inform instruction. It is an open issue just what the magnitude of the instructional leverage is at this grain size, but it is possible that much of the advantage claimed for humans over computers might be due to the fact that they are sensitive to information at this grain size.

To return to the issue of bridges from the brain to instruction, it seems plausible that at least three bridges are required. The first would get from the brain to models of the simple steps of cognition that are primitive steps of cognition in ACT-R. The second would go from these components to performance of unit tasks. The third would compose these unit tasks into educational competences of true significance. ACT-R provides a system in which we can model these bridges. Although ACT-R may inform the construction of the third bridge and facilitate instruction, it does not seem profitable to cast our educational models at the level of detail of ACT-R models.

ACKNOWLEDGMENTS

This research was supported by grant CDA–9720359 from the Natuional Science Foundation and by funding from the Air Force PALACE Knight program to Kevin Gluck.

REFERENCES

Anderson, J. R. (1983). *The architecture of cognition*. Cambridge, MA: Harvard University Press.

Anderson, J. R., Corbett, A. T., Koedinger, K., & Pelletier, R. (1995). Cognitive tutors: Lessons learned. *The Journal of Learning Sciences, 4,* 167–207.

Anderson, J. R., John, B. E., Just, M. A., Carpenter, P. A., Kieras, D. E., & Meyer, D. E. (1995). Production system models of complex cognition. In J. D. Moore & J. F. Lehman (Eds.), *Proceedings of the Seventeenth Annual Conference of the Cognitive Science Society* (pp. 9–12). Hillsdale, NJ: Lawrence Erlbaum Associates.

Anderson, J. R. & Lebiere, C. (Eds.). (1998). *The atomic components of thought*. Mahwah, NJ: Lawrence Erlbaum Associates.

Anderson, J. R., Reder, L. M., & Simon, H. A. (1998). Radical constructism and cognitive psychology. In D. Ravitch (Ed.), *Brookings papers on education policy 1998*. Washington, DC: Brookings Institute Press.

Anderson, J. R., & Schunn, C. D. (2000). Implications of the ACT-R learning theory: No magic bullets. In R. Glaser, (Ed.), *Advances in instructional psychology: Educational design and cognitive science* (Volume 5), pp. 1–34. Mahwah, NJ: Lawrence Erlbaum Associates.

Bloom, B. S. (1984). The 2 sigma problem: The search for methods of group instruction as effective as one-to-one tutoring. *Educational Researcher, 13,* 4–16.

Bruer, J. T. (1998). Education and the brain: A bridge too far. *Educational Researcher, 26,* 4–16.

Byrne, M. D., & Anderson, J. R. (1998). Perception and action. In J. R. Anderson & C. Lebiere (Eds.), *The atomic components of thought*. Mahwah, NJ: Lawrence Erlbaum Associates.

Byrne, M. D., & Anderson, J. R. (in press). *Serial modules in parallel: The psychological refractory period and perfect time-sharing*. Psychological Review.

Cohen, P. A., Kulik, J. A., & Kulik, C. L. C. (1982). Education outcomes of tutoring: A meta-analysis of finds. *American Educational Research Journal, 19,* 237–248.

Cohn, J. F., Zlochower, A., Lien, J., & Kanade, T. (in press). Automated face analysis by feature point tracking has high concurrent validity with manual FACS coding. *Psychophysiology*.

Corbett, A. T., & Anderson, J. R. (1992). The LISP intelligent tutoring system: Research in skill acquisition. In J. Larkin, R. Chabay, & C. Scheftic (Eds.), *Computer assisted instruction and intelligent tutoring systems: Establishing communication and collaboration* (pp. 73–110). Hillsdale, NJ: Lawrence Erlbaum Associates.

Corbett, A. T., Anderson, J. R., & O'Brien, A.T. (1995). Student modeling in the ACT Programming Tutor. In P. Nichols, S. Chipman, & B. Brennan (Eds.), *Cognitively diagnostic assessment.* (pp. 19–41). Hillsdale, NJ: Lawrence Erlbaum Associates.

Gale, C. (1998). Looking around in media spaces: Some quantitative data on gaze awareness. Unpublished manuscript.

Knowlton, B. J., Mangels, J. A., & Squire, L. R. (1996). A neostriatal habit learning system in humans. *Science, 273,* 1399–1402.

Koedinger, K. R., & Anderson, J. R. (1998). Illustrating principled design: The early evolution of a cognitive tutor for algebra symbolization. *Interactive Learning Environments, 5,* 161–179.

Koedinger, K. R., Anderson, J. R., Hadley, W. H., & Mark, M. (1997). Intelligent tutoring goes to school in the big city. *International Journal of Artificial Intelligence in Education, 8,* 30–43.

Koedinger, K. R., & MacLaren, B. A. (1997). Implicit strategies and errors in an improved model of early algebra problem solving. In M. G. Shafto & P. Langley (Eds.), *Proceedings of the Nineteenth Annual Conference of the Cognitive Science Society* (pp. 382–387). Hillsdale, NJ: Lawrence Erlbaum Associates.

Koedinger, K. R., & Tabachneck, H. J. M. (1995, April). Verbal reasoning as a critical component in early algebra. Paper presented at the annual meeting of the *American Educational Research Association,* San Francisco, CA.

Lee, F. J., & Anderson, J. R. (in press) Does learning of a complex task have to be complex? A case study in learning decomposition. *Cognitive Psychology.*

Lesh, R., & Lamon, S. J. (1992). *Assessment of authentic performance in school mathematics.* Washington, DC: AAAS Press.

Mostow, J. (1998). Evaluating tutors that listen. In K. Forbus & P. Feltovich (Eds.), *Invited papers on artificial intelligence in education.* AAAI Press.

Newell, A. (1973). You can't play 20 questions with nature and win: Projective comments on the papers of this symposium. In W. G. Chase (Ed.), *Visual information processing* (pp. 283–310). New York: Academic Press

Poldrack, R. A., Prabakharan, V., Seger, C., & Gabrieli, J. D. E. (in press). Striatal activation during cognitive skill learning. *Neuropsychology.*

Salvucci, D. D. (1999). *Mapping eye movements to cognitive processes.* Doctoral Dissertation, Department of Computer Science, Carnegie Mellon University, Pittsburgh, PA.

Shepard, L. A. (1991). Psychometricians' beliefs about learning. *Educational Researcher, 20,* 2–16.

VanLehn, K. (1988). Student modeling. In M. C. Polson & J. J. Richardson (Eds.), *Foundations of intelligent tutoring systems* (pp. 55–78). Hillsdale, NJ: Lawrence Erlbaum Associates.

Wise, S. P., Murray, E. A., & Gerfen, C. R. (1996). The frontal cortex—Basal ganglia system in primates. *Critical Reviews in Neurobiology, 10,* 317–356.

9

BGuILE: Strategic and Conceptual Scaffolds for Scientific Inquiry in Biology Classrooms

Brian J. Reiser
Northwestern University

Brian K. Smith
MIT Media Laboratory

Iris Tabak
UCLA

Franci Steinmuller
Northwestern University

William A. Sandoval
UCLA

Anthony J. Leone
Northwestern University

AMBITIOUS SCIENCE LEARNING FOR CLASSROOMS

The current focus of much work in science education reform is to bring more ambitious science into classrooms. Education reformers have argued that students need to learn more rigorous scientific content than what is typically taught (AAAS, 1990). In addition, reformers are attempting to bring more of the practices of scientific inquiry into student learning activities (NRC, 1996). This means establishing a learning setting in which students can take ownership of the questions they pursue, can design and implement an investigation to pursue their questions, and can interpret and communicate their results to others (Linn, diSessa, Pea, & Songer, 1994).

These goals have emerged from research documenting the shallow level of understanding engendered in what is argued to be a decontextualized approach to teaching science.

In our view, meeting these science learning goals requires helping students make the connection between inquiry processes and the products that result from inquiry, such as theories, models, and explanations. Although there is often debate that reform science efforts focus too much on process at the cost of students learning scientific content, we argue that this debate is misguided. Developing a deep understanding of science entails understanding the nature of scientific explanations, as well as the practices used to generate and evaluate those explanations. We argue that the most effective way to teach these scientific practices is to ground students' use of them within their learning about the specific theoretical frameworks of particular scientific disciplines. In other words, effective learning of scientific investigation processes requires using the structure of particular scientific frameworks, such as the theory of natural selection or the framework of behavioral ecology, to tailor strategies for investigation, including framing questions, formulating hypotheses, constructing comparisons in data, and evaluating hypotheses. In order to learn scientific processes, students need to understand how the general strategies of science (controlling variables, discriminating hypotheses) are realized within particular scientific domains. A rigorous understanding of science entails recognizing that theoretical frameworks of scientific disciplines may require different investigation methods.

Acquiring this understanding requires engaging in rich investigations. Yet, creating these learning opportunities for students presents two types of challenges; cognitive complexity and classroom culture. First, engaging in sustained investigations requires investigation strategies and an understanding of scientific epistemology that poses challenges for students (Carey, Evans, Honda, Jay, & Unger, 1989; Klahr & Dunbar, 1988; Kuhn, Schauble, & Garcia-Mila, 1992; Schauble, 1990; Schauble, Glaser, Duschl, Schulze, & John, 1995). A second obstacle is the existing culture of the science classroom, which is most typically focused on the transmission of knowledge, where the subject matter is presented as solved problems codified as terminology, theories, and laboratory techniques (Lemke, 1990). The epistemology of science that emerges is one of fixed and unchanging "right answers"(Songer & Linn, 1991). Students' views of science learning lead to strategies appropriate for the acquisition of facts rather than to constructive argumentation and reflective inquiry.

To create inquiry classrooms in which students learn through investigation requires basic changes in the rules of the game for science classrooms—new curricula and tools must be accompanied by new teaching approaches and an explicit attention to shifting students' attitudes toward science and science learning. Engaging students in this type of learning requires different values and expectations. It requires creating a different type of classroom culture (Brown & Campione, 1994; Crawford, Krajcik, & Marx, 1999; Duschl, 1990).

To overcome these obstacles requires two complementary forms of support; support for scientific practice, and creation of a classroom culture of inquiry. Support for scientific practices is needed to help students develop the content knowledge required to raise questions and negotiate novel problems in the domain, plan and pursue systematic analyses of complex datasets, synthesize these findings into well-supported cogent explanations, and reflect on the implications of these findings for understanding key scientific topics. Creating a classroom culture of inquiry consists of communicating and establishing a culture that sets knowledge construction and the evaluation of knowledge claims in light of empirical evidence as the primary goals of classroom work.

One strategy for reform utilizes new technologies to expand the learning opportunities for students (Means, 1994; PCAST, 1997). Technological tools can provide a venue for rich investigations, providing both access to data and powerful analytical tools. Such tools can provide scaffolding to support scientific practice and can be integral in new classroom inquiry practices. To be effective, use of these tools must be embedded in technology-infused curricula, that contain articulated problem contexts, tools, and resources so that students can work through investigations crafted to engage them in the target learning outcomes.

In this chapter, we describe our approach for supporting ambitious science in classrooms. Our work focuses in particular on designing learning environments for students engaged in scientific investigation and explanation of biological phenomena. In this project, called BGuILE, *Biology Guided Inquiry Learning Environments*, we have been developing and studying the use of technological and curricular supports for the teaching and learning of biology. BGuILE technology-infused curricular units center on investigation activities in which students construct empirically supported explanations from a rich base of primary data. These investigations are made possible through software environments that serve as the investigation context that provide access to the primary data, and that provide support tools for analyzing the data and synthesizing explanations.

Activities preceding investigations are designed to help students build the rudimentary knowledge and skills that facilitate a thoughtful and thorough treatment of the problem investigations. In addition, informal and structured discussions are interspersed throughout all the activities in order to provide opportunities for reflection and for sharing and critiquing ideas.

We begin by describing our approach to supporting student inquiry. We then describe the design principles for technology-infused curricula that emerged from this research. We illustrate these principles with particular curricula and tools that we developed for courses on evolution, ecosystems, and behavioral ecology at the high school and middle school levels. Finally, we summarize the evidence that we gathered to date in support of this approach.

A DISCIPLINARY APPROACH FOR SUPPORTING INQUIRY

A Vision of Inquiry for Science Classrooms

In this design effort, a key step is to articulate a vision of scientific inquiry for students. Although there is much interest in involving students in "authentic" scientific reasoning, designing environments for learning requires an articulation of the aspects of scientific practice to establish as goals for students, and consideration of how to integrate those practices within the practices of classrooms. There are several aspects to the argument for involving students in authentic inquiry. The goal is to move classrooms away from "cookbook" or "toy" problems typical of traditional curricula, in which students perform experiments that are given to them. The claim is that instead, students should participate in constructing empirical investigations to address questions they have identified as deserving attention. One strong form of the argument posits that students should work on problems for which a community of researchers is still currently investigating and debating the answers (Means, 1998; Tinker, 1997). Although such problems can offer compelling learning contexts and can allow students to contribute data that can be used by practicing scientists, we suggest that there are other strategies that can be effective. More important, in our view, is establishing what practices of scientific inquiry and argumentation are the core cognitive and social practices we want students to experience, and what practices are most effective in deeply engaging students in reasoning about scientific phenomena.

The construction of scientific knowledge is a complex enterprise, involving both cognitive and social factors. A cognitive analysis aims at characterizing the mechanisms for making sense of scientific phenomena (Clement, 1988; Confrey, 1990; Dunbar, 1995; Tobin & Tippins, 1993), and reasoning about the connection between hypotheses and empirical support (Klahr & Dunbar, 1988; Kuhn, Amsel, & O'Loughlin, 1988). From a social perspective, the choice of experimental procedures and hypotheses are a result of communication, debate, and negotiation with peers (Cetina, 1995; Hawkins & Pea, 1987). Even when scientists are working alone, their actions are driven by considerations of their community, of the audience for the products of their work (Latour, 1988).

Although science is often considered a single, unified enterprise, recent sociological and philosophical studies depict the scientific enterprise as a family of distinct sciences. Scientific disciplines, such as experimental high energy physics or molecular biology, are distinguished on many levels, in their framing of questions and their criteria for knowledge claims (Knorr-Cetina 1996, 1999). Indeed, even within a scientific domain such as biology, individual disciplines differ in significant ways in their approaches. Whereas molecular biologists primarily build theories through experimentation, research in evolutionary biology typically requires observational arguments and model testing rather than controlled experiments.

This examination of authentic scientific practice has several implications for science education. First, students should employ a multiplicity of cognitive, social, and material tools in order to negotiate primary data and construct explanations for novel phenomena. Second, science classrooms need to include social contexts in which learners present and defend their ideas, and negotiate actions and interpretations as a community. Third, the specific practices that distinguish particular scientific disciplines should be a focus of science learning.

Theory Articulation in Problem Scenarios

An important aspect of crafting inquiry experiences for students, which is consistent with this characterization of science, is to expose students to a wide variety of scientific endeavors. These design efforts should focus more on maximizing the breadth of conceptual and material approaches, rather than on maximizing a breadth of content topics, in order to provide students with a fuller perspective of the many facets of scientific inquiry. In the BGuILE project, we directed our design efforts toward supporting a type of investigation that has not received much attention in science education (particularly in the realm of technology-supported inquiry). To articulate this approach, we can characterize investigations according to (1) the investigation method and (2) the relationship between the investigation and theory development.

1.   Observational investigations: Most of the BGuILE investigations employ an observational methodology. The scientific enterprise is most commonly associated with experimentation in which knowledge claims are based on comparing observed outcomes resulting from the control and manipulation of variables. Indeed, educators often speak of "the" scientific method, referring to the process of hypothesis testing through experiments (DeBoer, 1991). In contrast, observational investigations are used in those investigations within scientific disciplines where it is not possible to manipulate variables, such as many investigations in astronomy, earth sciences, ecology, and evolutionary biology. In lieu of manipulating variables, comparisons are constructed across time, location, events, objects, and populations. These comparisons can reveal changes, trends, and differences. Scientists use these patterns of data to test models and construct arguments based on patterns of converging evidence.

2.   Theory articulation: A common image of science is Newton sitting under a tree, observing an apple fall to the ground, and formulating laws to explain and predict these types of phenomena. However, the discovery and formulation of new laws and theories is not the sole orientation that scientists take toward theories. In many cases, scientific activity involves theory articulation—elaborating a theory, and enriching the corpus of evidence in its support by applying an existing theory to explain novel phenomenological instances (Kuhn, 1970). Much of the research on scientific reasoning assumes rule discovery as the paradigm of scientific work and neglects this critical type of reasoning (Ohlsson, 1992).

This approach of theory articulation seems particularly well suited for crafting problems in rich observational domains. In some domains, the goal is to develop simple formal laws. For example, in the physics domains of optics and mechanics, students can experiment in order to conjecture and test simple empirical laws. In contrast, in many domains with probabilistic systems, such as evolutionary biology, animal behavior, and ecosystems, learning involves understanding the application of a general theory to the different types of examples that can elaborate a core concept. For example, the theory of natural selection can be simply stated, but much of the science involves understanding how that theory plays out in different ecological settings with different types of organisms (Mayr, 1988). All living organisms have to obtain food and avoid predators in order to pass on genes, but there are many different forms of the solutions to these problems. Thus, the study of natural selection entails learning the important dimensions on which an organism is adapted to its ecosystem, and the common types of adaptation solutions.

Our goals of observational investigations and theory articulation have led us to adopt a problem-based learning approach (Bransford, Sherwood, Hasselbring, Kinzer, & Williams, 1990; Williams, 1992). The strategy is to craft an investigation around a complex interesting problem that requires the student to apply the target scientific theories and skills. For example, in one BGuILE unit, students investigate a crisis in an ecosystem, and need to explain the death and differential survival of organisms in that ecosystem. Students need to apply the theory of natural selection in order to identify the factors constituting a stress on the population, identify the traits of the organism that are variable and important to the organisms' survival, and link the patterns of survival to patterns in these traits.

Thus far, we have articulated a strategy integral to many science disciplines in which students collect observations to test hypotheses. Their goal is to elaborate theories by applying them to make sense of complex, often nondeterministic phenomena in puzzling problems. We turn next to the question of the types of understandings and skills that are involved in using theories to make sense of problems.

Connecting Investigation Goals, Domain Theories, and Investigation Strategies

Learners need to ground their understanding and practice of inquiry processes in an understanding of the goals and products of inquiry. Students cannot be taught the processes without engaging in reasoning about why these processes are both necessary and effective in testing and arguing for theories.

In our view, the particular inquiry processes students practice are a result of viewing general argumentation goals through the lens of particular scientific disciplines. For example, a general scientific goal, such as articulating causal explanations, leads to a core strategy, such as conducting controlled comparisons in order to isolate causal factors. However, practicing scientists understand more than the general need for articulating hypotheses, conducting systematic comparisons, and supporting claims with evidence. Experts know what types of relationships and arguments prevail in their field, and what type of observations and comparisons can yield relevant data for examining their hypotheses. As a result, science in the different disciplines takes on a somewhat different character. The theoretical frameworks within scientific disciplines suggest the types of causal relations necessary for an argument. This type of knowledge is critical in conducting scientific investigations, and is likely to be an area in which novices lack knowledge and skills.

In our designs, we explore an approach that tries to make the relationship between argumentation goals, domain theories, and investigation strategies explicit for students. There are two types of relationships we need to support for students. The first is the connection between the argumentation goals and investigation strategies. In learning and practicing a strategy, students need to see how that strategy affects the type of inquiry product they produce. The second connection is between the general scientific and the discipline-specific levels. We design tools and artifacts that make the discipline-specific strategies and characteristics of the resulting explanations explicit for students. This approach is illustrated in Table 9.1.

Table 9.1 shows how we go from general scientific to discipline-specific to the design of the associated tools. In the first row are examples

TABLE 9.1
Discipline-Specific Scientific Reasoning Model

Knowledge About Inquiry Goals and Products	Investigation Strategies	Tools and Scaffolding
General Science Explanations should articulate causal mechanisms that can explain data patterns. Causal relationships should be supported by sufficient and relevant data.	Perform controlled manipulations of variables to isolate the role of factors in causal relations. Focus on collecting data that can be used as evidence.	
Discipline-specific Explain how environment can select particular traits of an organism. Explain how selected traits provide reproductive advantage.	Look for factors in the environment that can apply selective pressure. Look for trait variations that enable or impede crucial behaviors.	Students ask to compare across time on environmental factors Students compare survivors and casualties on physical and behavioral characteristics.

of general scientific goals and the associated strategies. In the second row, we see how these goals and strategies are specified within a particular discipline, in this case, natural selection. Opposite the investigation strategies are tools we have built to enable students to perform that strategy. As we will see, the tools are designed to make these strategies observable and explicit in students' interactions with data.

Consider a specific path through the table. We see that a general goal of scientific argumentation is to articulate a causal mechanism that explains patterns of data. The need to generate causal mechanisms suggests the use of controlled comparisons, because they enable us to isolate and identify causal factors. Within the domain of natural selection, the goal is to describe the causal components that show how an environmental pressure selects for a particular trait in a population. This suggests that the controlled comparisons should be applied to observations of the populations' environment (the source of pressures) across time (to identify changes). We provide students with a tool that lets them specify comparisons by selecting a comparison type (e.g., across time) and variable type (e.g., environmental factors such as temperature or rainfall). In this way, we communicate that (a) comparisons to isolate variables are a key component of data analysis and (b) examining environmental factors across time is desirable and effective in this domain.

Making the connection between domain theories and investigation strategies explicit may be particularly productive for achieving a balance between content and process goals in science classrooms, because students are continually grappling with content topics as they plan and execute their investigations. Providing support for the acquisition of content knowledge as well as the development of inquiry skills extends beyond the design of software scaffolds to the design of classroom discussions, activities, and curricular materials in order to shape the full set of mechanisms through which knowledge is constructed in classrooms.

We have discussed how theories, goals, and strategies interrelate, and the implications of these relations for the design of supportive tools. Scientific goals determine the characteristics of the products of inquiry (column 1). The desired characteristics of the inquiry products determine the needed investigation strategies (column 2). Goals and products can be described at the general scientific level (row 1), but must be articulated at the discipline-specific level (row 2) by taking a general science characteristic and specifying it in terms of the properties of particular theoretical frameworks of the discipline. Tools then can be designed (column 3) to enable the needed investigation strategies, and to make clear to students what these strategies are, and how they tie into the type of products they need to create. As we see in part 4, our key design strategy is to establish and reinforce these connections between strategies and products in the software and classroom activities.

A Classroom-Centered Design Paradigm

Our design goals are to provide tools and curricula that help learners engage more deeply with subject matter. A key strategy is to consider not only the cognitive demands of this type of learning, but to focus on the influence of the social context of the classroom. Designing tools and curricula must tackle not only the needs of individual learners, but also those challenges and opportunities provided by the social context of the classroom. We have called this approach *classroom-centered design* (Loh, et al., 1998; Smith & Reiser, 1998). We need to design interventions that can work within and help shift the social context of classrooms in which the software scaffolds will be used.

There are several implications of the classroom-centered design approach. Although our goal may be for software tools to dramatically change the type of work students do in classrooms, it is important to design these tools so that they can be integrated within the existing work practices of classrooms. If technology is going to become an integral part of classrooms, its use must also be seamless. Another consideration of classroom environments is that the teacher will have to play a key role cultivating a classroom culture that emphasizes the values that are inherent in inquiry. Therefore, tools should be designed in a way that allows for teacher–student interactions around the tools, rather than created as self-contained activities. In addition, the use of these software environments should be woven within a web of discussions and activities using both traditional and computational media.

BGUILE TECHNOLOGY-INFUSED SCIENCE CURRICULA

In this section, we present a brief overview of *Struggle for Survival*, a BGuILE technology-infused curriculum, to provide a context in which to describe our design principles. The Struggle for Survival is a unit for middle school, in which students learn about ecosystems and natural selection through their investigations of a crisis in a Galapagos island ecosystem. Students investigate the various interacting components of a complex ecosystem in order to find out what is killing many of the animals on this island, and whether there is a pattern that explains how some of the animals have managed to survive the crisis. The problem becomes an opportunity for students to apply and extend their knowledge about species interactions, structure and function relationships, and natural selection.

The Struggle for Survival unit is summarized in Table 9.2. This 6 to 7 week unit is built around an investigation using the BGuILE software

TABLE 9.2
The Struggle for Survival Middle School Curriculum

Phase A: General Staging Activities (10 Classes)	Staging activities provide background knowledge and motivation for the investigation. Brainstorming activities reveal what students believe and understand about island ecosystems. Activities include a geography game using characteristics of tropical islands as clues, student research on how animals are adapted to the local ecosystem of an island, a background video, and readings on Darwin and the Galapagos.
Phase B: Background for Investigation (5 classes)	Activities focus directly on the Galapagos ecosystem and understanding how to investigate ecosystem data. Activities include a video introduction to the Galapagos and the methods scientists use to study the ecosystem, brainstorming about hypotheses, and a mini paper-based investigation in which students work with a small dataset from the software and make a graph that backs up a claim about the data.
Phase C: Software Investigation (10 classes)	Students investigate data using The Galapagos Finches software environment, documenting their developing explanations as the progress. At the midpoint, student teams pair up and critique each other's explanations.
Phase D: Presenting and Discussing Finding (6 classes)	Student teams prepare their reports. Each team presents their findings, and the class analyzes key points of agreement and dissension.

environment *The Galapagos Finches* (Tabak, 1999; Tabak & Reiser, 1997a; Tabak et al., 1995; Tabak, Smith, Sandoval, & Reiser, 1996). The unit has four basic phases. The introductory activities of Phase A are staging activities, which introduce background knowledge about island ecosystems and motivate the study of an island in crisis in the Galapagos. The unit begins with activities that introduce the influences of geography and climate on ecosystems in general, and then focuses on the particularly rich ecosystem of the Galapagos islands. Phase B brings the specifics of the problem to the foreground, and connects what students are learning generally about island ecosystems to the specific problem in the investigation, a Galapagos island in crisis.

The computer investigation, Phase C, is the core of the unit. Students work in teams using The Galapagos Finches software to study a rich dataset from the island habitat Daphne Major in the Galapagos (Grant, 1986). Through this dataset, they can explore relevant environmental characteristics of the island and background information about other species of plants and animals. The core of the dataset tracks the physical and behavioral characteristics of the finch population under threat. Students can read through field notes and can examine quantitative data about morphological features of both populations and individual finches. Students can compare subgroups of the population and can look for changes across time to identify trends and relationships that can help explain the effects of the crisis. (We describe some of the specific software tools students use to access and manage data in Part 4.) In Phase D, the unit concludes with student presentations and a discussion to highlight the important positions and evaluate points of consensus and dissension.

This example demonstrates how we use problem-based learning scenarios to provide opportunities for theory articulation. Although students need some basic understanding of the theory of natural selection to make progress in the investigation, they need to extend their understanding to make sense of the problem. For example, students acquire a simple understanding of environmental stress and survival value, but the problem context allows the students to consider different environmental factors as candidate stresses, and requires them to work though the implications of an environmental stress for a population.

To date, we have developed four investigation environments now in use in middle and high school classrooms, summarized in Table 9.3. These environments are used to illustrate our principles of scaffolding in the next section.

TABLE 9.3

BGuILE Interactive Learning Environments

Environment	Technology-Infused Units	Description
The Galapagos Finches	Struggle for Survival, Evolution (high school)	Students learn about natural selection by investigating how a drought affects the animal and plant populations on a Galapagos island. Students can examine background information about the island, read through field notes, and examine quantitative data about the characteristics of the island's species at various time points to look for changes in the populations.
TB Lab	Evolution (high school)	Students perform simulated experiments on strains of *M. Tuberculosis* to investigate how antibiotics affect bacteria and how bacteria can become resistant to antibiotics. Facilities allow growth and sensitivity experiments, biochemical assays to examine how antibiotics affect the bacteria's metabolism, and sequencing experiments that allow students to look for genetic differences between strains of bacteria.
Animal Landlord	Behavior Matters (middle school), Behavioral Ecology (high school)	Students investigate variation and similarity in examples of animal behavior, studying topics such as predation, competition, and social groups. Students use video analysis tools to extract frames, comparing and annotating them with their observations and interpretations.
The Florida Panther	Conservation Biology	Students learn about speciation and the use of scientific research for policy decisions. Students evaluate recovery plans to save the endangered Florida Panther. Students can examine background information about the panthers and their habitat, read through field notes, and examine quantitative data about genetics and phenotypic characteristics of the panther population.
Explanation Constructor	Used in conjunction with Galapagos Finches, TB Lab, and Florida Panther	A computer-based journal in which students construct their explanations incrementally while in the midst of an investigation. Students organize explanations around questions and subquestions, and insert evidence from the investigation environment to back up claims.

275

PRINCIPLES OF SUPPORT
IN CURRICULUM AND TECHNOLOGY

Our design represents the union between the general design principles of cognitive apprenticeship (Collins, Brown, & Newman, 1989) and our particular approach to scaffolding inquiry (described in part 2.3) of making the relationship between general inquiry goals, disciplinary theories, and investigation strategies explicit. Earlier we argued that the theoretical frameworks of particular scientific disciplines lead to a tailoring of investigation and argumentation strategies. Our designs attempt to help students understand and practice these investigation and argumentation strategies by making them explicit in both the tools students use and the work products or artifacts they create:

• Strategic Tools: We design the tools students use to access, analyze, and manipulate data to make the implicit strategies of the discipline visible to students. For example, when students construct data queries, they articulate their query in terms of the key distinctions in the types of comparisons used to build theory in the domain, rather than solely in terms of surface data parameters.
• Strategic Artifacts: We design the work products that students create to represent the important conceptual properties of explanations and models in the discipline. For example, we have students construct hypermedia documents that make explicit the rhetorical structure of their arguments.

In this section, we describe our design principles for supporting student inquiry, and illustrate the principles with examples from curriculum and software. These principles are summarized in Table 9.4.

Explanation-Driven Inquiry

Explaining how and why things occur as they do is one of the central aims of science. The goal of explanation is emphasized throughout BGuILE investigations and is apparent in the design of tools, artifacts, and discussion activities.

We focus on two broad criteria that carry particular epistemological weight: (1) Explanations should articulate causal mechanisms; and (2) Explanations should account for observed data. Thus, in our learning activities, students are asked to construct explanations that provide a causal account for why something happens in the way it does.

TABLE 9.4
BGuILE Strategic Design Principles

Structure inquiry around explanatory goals.
• Students generate strategic artifacts representing conceptual and epistemic properties (section 4.1).
Embed the structure of theories and strategies in the tools students use and the artifacts they create.
• Tools structure students' explanation within discipline-specific theoretical frameworks (section 4.2.1)
• Tools for access and analysis of data are structured according to explicit, discipline-specific investigation strategies (section 4.2.2)
• Tools and artifacts explicitly represent the students' epistemological commitments (section 4.2.3)
• Investigations are focused on providing inquiry products that represent causal explanations and models (section 4.2.4).
Integrate classroom and technology-supported learning activities
• Existing learning activities are integrated to introduce skills and concepts needed for the investigation (section 4.3.1)
• Staging activities enable students to practice requisite strategies in miniinvestigations prior to the core investigation (section 4.3.2).
Support ongoing reflection within the structure of the learning activities
• Reflective tools are integrated into the environment students use to investigate data (section 4.4.1).
• Small-group and whole-class discussion activities are integrated within investigations to analyze strategies and build consensus and shared understanding from findings (section 4.4.2).

Furthermore, these explanations should articulate how key theoretical principles in the discipline are applied to particular situations or phenomena. For example, while working on the Galapagos Finches investigation in our evolution unit, students must explain in causal terms how natural selection operates on a particular population in a particular environmental context. Thus, it is not enough to determine what factor is the cause of a crisis on an island or to determine that a particular generalization has empirical support. The goal is to go further to construct a causal explanatory account of the empirical findings.

In BGuILE units, the teacher performs the initial framing of inquiry as explanation. Prior to students' first investigation in a unit, the teacher directs a class discussion in which students' ideas are solicited about what counts as a good explanation and what counts as evidence. This discussion is directed toward the two criteria previously mentioned. When a particular investigation is introduced, teachers reaffirm these criteria and continually help students to apply them. For instance, in the Galapagos Finches scenario, the driving investigative focus is to explain why some finches survive when others do not. In the TB Lab problem, the focus is to explain how tuberculosis bacteria can develop antibiotic resistance. The lion hunt investigation asks students to explain the factors that combine to cause a hunt to succeed or fail.

Once framed, software scaffolds integrate explanatory and investigative supports to maintain the explanatory focus of students' inquiry. Each investigation environment includes a software component to guide students' construction of an explanatory representation of their understanding of the problem. These scaffolds are described in the following sections. In addition, the explanatory thread is maintained throughout inquiry by interleaving self- and peer evaluation activities with investigation. Using rubrics designed with collaborating teachers, these evaluations are focused on the adequacy of students' current explanations and their evidentiary support. Thus, students' inquiry goals are focused on general epistemic concerns grounded in specific disciplinary frameworks and their investigation strategies, as described in Table 9.1. The culminating activity for the investigations consists of some form of public communication and critique of students' explanations, either in the form of group presentations or in the form of constructing a class consensus explanation. This type of culminating task situates the learning within a community, which provides an audience for the work and a context in which students are contributing knowledge to the group (Brown & Campione, 1994; Crawford et al., 1999; Scardamalia & Bereiter, 1994).

Explicit Representation of Theories and Strategies

A key aspect of scaffolding is to represent knowledge explicitly that is usually tacit (Collins et al., 1989), and to do so in a way that helps bridge the way novices think about the problem with more skilled reasoning practices (Merrill, Reiser, Beekelaar, & Hamid, 1992). BGuILE's software tools explicitly represent discipline-specific theories and strategies in ways that guide students' inquiry processes and emphasize general, epistemological goals for their inquiry products. The focus on integrating this discipline-specific level of support complements but differs from the scaffolding strategy of providing tools to support general scientific processes, such as the process support of Symphony (Quintana, Eng, Carra, Wu, & Soloway, 1999) and modeling support tools (Jackson, Stratford, Krajcik, & Soloway, 1994; Stratford, Krajcik, & Soloway, 1998).

The next four sections outline our design approaches for embedding the structure of theories and strategies in the tools students use and the artifacts they create.

Representing Theoretical Frameworks in Tools and Artifacts. Scientific theories are generative explanatory frameworks that provide a way to make sense of particular phenomena. One BGuILE software tool, the ExplanationConstructor, represents relevant explanatory frameworks within the structure of the students' computer-based journal (Sandoval, 1998; Sandoval & Reiser, 1997). As students explore the data in one of the BGuILE investigation environments, such as the Galapagos Finches or TB Lab, they incrementally articulate an explanation using ExplanationConstructor. This tool is essentially an outline and word processing system tailored for scientific argumentation. Students articulate their research questions and attach one or more candidate explanations to each question. As they write the text of their explanation, they can refer to the *explanation guides* that represent the key causal components of the explanatory framework. For example, the explanation guide invoked with the Galapagos Finches includes the major causal components of a natural selection explanation. These include the identification of an environmental change that can exert a selective pressure; the individuals affected by that change; the trait variation that provides a survival advantage; and the mechanism of advantage. In addition to indicating the content of a particular explanation within a given framework, guides can focus students' investigative activities on generating data that can further their explanation. Components of the theory, as represented in the explanation guides, suggest specific kinds of data to look for in the problem.

These explanation guides provide prompts for students to join the components of their explanation together, rhetorically and conceptually. These prompts are given in discipline-specific terms, but they function in a more general way to emphasize that there are separate components to explanations that have to hang together in a coherent manner. In this sense, explanation guides are an instantiation of Collins and Ferguson's (1993) notion of *epistemic forms*, particular forms of knowledge representation that afford particular *epistemic games*, reasoning strategies and manipulations of the representation that allow particular forms of knowledge construction. Thus, these explanation guides link the general epistemological criterion for causal coherence to discipline-specific conceptual scaffolds, as in column one of Table 9.1.

Figure 9.1 shows an explanation constructed by a student working on the TB lab problem, using biochemical assays to explore how antibiotics disrupt cellular processes in TB bacteria, and investigating how TB have become resistant to those attacks.

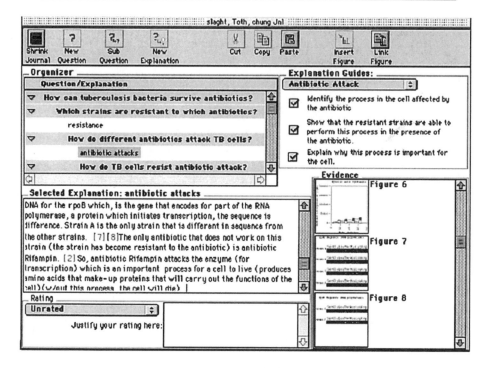

FIG. 9.1. The ExplanationConstructor used to articulate questions, explanations, and the backing support. Shown is a high school student's explanation for the TB Lab problem. The outline of questions, subquestions, and explanations is shown in the upper left Organizer panel. Explanation guides are shown in the upper right. The selected explanation (antibiotic attacks) is shown in the explanation window, and miniature versions of the embedded evidence are displayed in the lower right panel.

The following example demonstrates how the explanation guides can help structure students' analysis of their findings. In this example, the students' attempt to satisfy the explanation guides provokes debate on one of the key ideas in the domain, the nature of traits. In considering whether their finding fits the goal of identifying traits, the group disagrees about whether food choice qualifies as a trait. In the course of this debate, the group brings in key ideas about physical traits and the relation between structure and function. In essence, having to structure their analysis of their findings in terms of the theoretical framework embedded in the tools helps students structure their understanding of the specifics of the case in terms of principles of the domain.

Evan: *(reading prompt)* "Environment causes ..."
Janie: No!
Evan: Yeah, "to be selected for ..."
Janie: Yeah, but that means like ...
Evan: // what food they eat //
Janie: ... organism with these trait
Evan: // the trait being the food
Franny: Yeah, that's right.
Janie: No, because like, if my trait is to eat steak, and there's no steak, I'm immediately gonna go to something else.
Evan: If you're only a vegetarian and you only eat ... you don't eat meat, you're not gonna eat meat. Well, that depends ...//
Janie: Are you insane!?
Franny: Ok, Ok. Don't think of people. Think of these guys (the finches). If they only eat one type of seed with their beaks and that seed is gone then they can't live anymore.

ExplanationConstructor also represents and emphasizes several general aspects of scientific explanations. The ExplanationConstructor representation makes salient the rhetorical structure of arguments. The structure of the journal asks students to articulate questions, and to associate explanations with questions. It is clear from the interface that multiple explanations can be associated with a single question, reminding students that they should be pursuing competing hypotheses.

Finally, and perhaps most important, is that ExplanationConstructor makes the evidentiary basis for the argument explicit. The hallmark of scientific arguments is that claims have to be defended with evidence. Clarity of argument is essential so that the community can evaluate the evidence presented in support of an argument. As can be seen in Fig. 9.1, students embed references to supporting evidence directly within the prose of their argument. Students paste in evidence directly from the investigation environment, and can link it to assertions in their explanation.

In making the argumentative structure an explicit part of the tools students use, ExplanationConstructor is similar to other software tools for hypermedia argumentation, such as CSILE (Scardamalia & Bereiter, 1994), the Collaboratory Notebook (Edelson, Pea, & Gomez, 1996), and SenseMaker (Bell & Linn, 2000). It differs in the incorporation of discipline-specific structures to guide the argumentation, and in the tight coupling of the explanation environment with the associated investigation environments.

This conceptual and strategic organization of ExplanationConstructor is an example of both strategic tools and strategic artifacts. The functionality of the tool is designed to encourage students to consider the appropriate discipline-specific components of an explanation, to tie claims to evidence, and to organize their explanations around explicit questions. In addition, the explanation product that results is a strategic artifact that represents the rhetorical structure of scientific argumentation in the particular discipline. Students can clearly evaluate their product in terms of both its conceptual and epistemic adequacy.

Representing Investigation Strategies. As with the explanation support, our supports for investigation strategies embody general scientific goals within discipline-specific frameworks. This support in the strategic tools for accessing and displaying data helps focus students' reasoning on the core strategies of the discipline, and on aspects of the phenomena that students often find problematic.

The first type of advantage is in making important strategies apparent in the tools. In understanding natural selection in the wild, it is important to examine the survival value of traits that vary within a population. Investigating natural selection entails examining variation in physical and behavioral traits, and looking for patterns of survival that are influenced by those trait differences. Consideration of a trait requires demonstrating a link between structure and its function, to argue for the survival value of the trait. This framework poses conceptual challenges for students, who tend not to see the importance of individual variation in the process of selection (Bishop & Anderson, 1990; Greene, 1990; Settlage, 1994).

To collect data within this framework of evolutionary explanations, scientists do cross-sectional comparisons, comparing different segments of a population, to understand how they differ, and longitudinal comparisons, to compare a population across time. These two types of comparisons are made explicit to the student in the conceptually based interface in The Galapagos Finches. In deciding what data to access and display in a graph, students have to articulate the type of comparison that fits their investigation goals and current hypothesis. Figures 9.2(a) and 9.2(b) demonstrate a query constructed in the population query interface and the resulting data display. The first column shows the two types of comparisons, longitudinal, called "seasons," and cross-sectional, called "subgroups." The next part of the query specifies the type of analysis within that general comparison type. Thus, students are guided to think strategically about not only what variable they want to view (selected in the menu entitled "physical traits"), but also must articulate the type of analysis they wish to perform. Their options are; (1) individual differences—examine individual

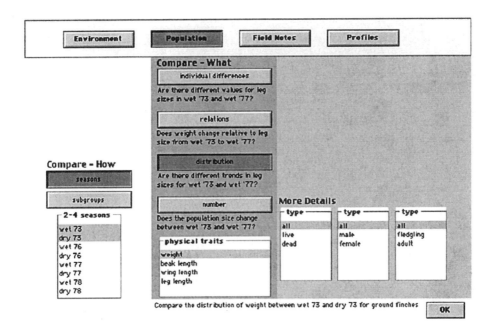

FIG. 9.2.(a) The query screen from The Galapagos Finches. The student has selected a comparison between seasons (first panel), and has selected "distribution" as the comparison type (second panel). Examples of each comparison type are shown beneath each menu item. The particular constructed query is assembled at the bottom of the screen as the students make their menu selections. A seasons comparison distribution graph is shown in (b).

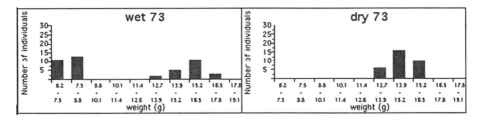

FIG. 9.2.(b) The resulting comparison graph.

283

values of population members on a target trait; (2) relationship—plot the relationship between two variables; (3) distribution—display the distribution of values on the trait within the population; and (4) number—display categorical data about the numbers of segments of the population, such as fledgling/adults, male/female. Using this strategic tool moves students' access of data from a focus on which variables and parameters to select to a conversation about what they are trying to accomplish, and what strategy they are using to test an idea against the data. In this way, investigation strategies become connected to discipline-specific knowledge goals (row 2, Table 9.1).

Representing Epistemological Commitments.   Our representations of explanatory frameworks and investigative strategies not only guide students' inquiry, but also communicate general, epistemological criteria for both their inquiry methods (i.e., strategies) and their products (i.e., explanations). These and other scaffolds reflect epistemological commitments, or "ways of knowing," that we want students to appropriate through inquiry.

As we have already mentioned, students often hold a view of science that fails to distinguish between theories and the experiments and data that support them (Carey et al., 1989). This failure to hold theory and evidence as distinct often interferes with students' abilities to reason about data and hypotheses (Kuhn, 1993; Kuhn, et al., 1988). One of our design goals was to make this distinction salient in both tools and artifacts, to highlight the epistemological distinction between theory and data, and to encourage students to actively evaluate their emergent explanations in terms of available data. In ExplanationConstructor, students actively select data from their investigation environments to link as evidence to causal claims, and these data are represented as distinct from the text of students' explanations. In the Animal Landlord, students study examples of animal behavior to isolate and model the key components of complex animal behavior (Smith & Reiser, 1997, 1998). In a unit on predation, students deconstruct lion hunts into what they see as the important causal events, and for each event, students record their observation of the event and their inference of the importance of that event. Thus, the representations that students construct of their emergent understanding of a problem allow them to maintain a distinction between theory (or interpretation of data) and evidence, saliently depicted as the distinction between "observation" and "interpretation" in the interface (see Fig. 9.3). This explicit distinction facilitates discussions geared at understanding the relationship between the two.

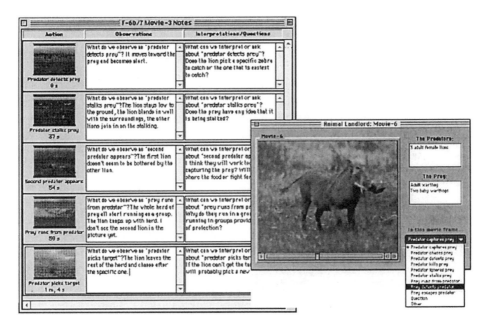

FIG. 9.3. Observation and interpretation are explicit objects of the task, which are made visually distinct in the Animal Landlord interface

For example, in the following classroom dialogue, the teacher questions a pair of students writing their observations and interpretations on an event in one of the lion video segments. Some simple questions provoke a debate between the two students about whether they can assert that the animal is "being sneaky" from the evidence in the video, or whether that is a speculative interpretation of the evidence. The goal of representing strategies and epistemological commitments in tools and artifacts is to focus students on these distinctions and thereby provoke productive debates of this sort.

Ms. C.:	What is the lion doing? *(points to screen)*
Anna:	It's being sneaky.
Ms. C:	"Sneaky?" I'm not sure what you mean.
Anna:	Sneaky. You know, it sneaks around. It's being clever.
Beth:	Yeah, but that seems different from the other things. Shouldn't it be stalking?
Anna:	Whatever. It's still being sneaky
Ms. C:	How do you measure sneaky?
Anna:	What do you mean?

Ms. C: How do you describe it?
Beth: You mean how can you tell it's being sneaky?
Ms. C: Yes.
Anna: It's creeping along in the grass. It's trying not to be seen. It's
          being sneaky.
Beth: Yeah, but that's stalking. Sneaky is more like an interpretation ...
          Sneaky doesn't say how the lion acts.
Anna: It's acting sneaky!
Beth: But what is it *doing*? It's crouching and going slow in the grass.
          So it's stalking.

Focus on Inquiry Products.   Earlier design research on scientific inquiry stressed the importance of having students create concrete products or artifacts that represent their understanding (Blumenfeld et al., 1991; Crawford et al., 1999). Our focus on reflecting the discipline-specific nature of arguments has led us to create strategic artifacts that represent students' knowledge-building contributions. The goal of the inquiry should be a documentation (in text or diagrams) of students' explanation or model. For example, the students' ExplanationConstructor journal represents a clearly structured recounting of the questions, explanations, and supporting and disconfirming evidence that they have assembled. The journal artifact represents the students' explanation. In investigations using the Animal Landlord, the goal is an explanatory model of animal behavior, which abstracts from the specifics of the data.

Working with the Animal Landlord, students use video as data to construct models of animal behavior (e.g., the interactions between predators and their prey). They begin by annotating the video clips, labeling important actions in the films that contribute to final outcomes (e.g., capturing prey). This results in a collection of "plot structures" that can be compared to look for behavioral variations and similarities across a number of films. For instance, stalking behaviors may look different when the prey animal being hunted is a zebra rather than a buffalo. A software comparison tool helps students compare actions across their annotated video corpus, allowing them to see differences in actions and the ways that various behaviors unfold.

In a sense, the students are using video to perform a common scientific exercise—moving from raw data (the video clips), assigning structure to the data, making comparisons between the relevant features, and finally, creating explanatory models. In this case, the modeling activity involves the creation of decision trees, probabilistic models representing the causal paths leading to outcomes (Fig. 9.4). After using the computer tools to

FIG. 9.4.   A student explaining behavioral paths in a decision tree from the behavioral ecology unit.

find variations in behaviors, students create these decision trees on poster-sized pieces of paper and display them around the classroom. Classroom discussions occur around the trees as students and teachers pose questions for the groups' proposed models, asking why certain nodes and branches appear, and the nature of the supporting evidence. Teachers may ask why a predator would ignore its prey if that node appears in the tree, helping students think about energy benefits (and costs) to a creature.

The decision trees also serve as predictive models. In some of our classrooms, teachers played additional hunting videos after using Animal Landlord. Because the decision trees were still displayed on the walls, students could use them to predict the behaviors of these new creatures. When they discovered that sharks display different types of behaviors than the lions studied in Animal Landlord, they revised their decision trees to reflect this new information. In this way, the exercise of model revision and prediction continued to be a part of classroom activity.

Integrating Classroom and
Technology-Supported Learning Activities

Helping students take up the intellectual practices and value system of a discipline is the goal underlying the principles of cognitive apprenticeship (Collins et al., 1989). Learning the "ways of doing" and the "ways of knowing" in a discipline involves developing knowledge of underlying domain principles and skills for data analysis. Instruction involves gradually building students' expertise in orchestrating this knowledge and these skills while engaging in compelling inquiry. Constructing a technology-infused curriculum requires designing both classroom-based activities that prepare students for complex software investigations, and off-computer activities interspersed with students; work on the software, that set the students' interactions with the technology in a broader set of social interactions (Edelson, Gordin, & Pea, 1999; Tabak & Reiser, 1997a). Our designs include two components that address this issue. One component involves integrating and adapting activities from curricula typically used in schools, and the other involves designing constrained investigations that conform to our approach for inquiry support.

ntegrating Existing Learning Activities Within a Project-Based Unit.   The goal of the activities that precede BGuILE investigations are to prepare students' conceptual understanding and skill base needed to plan and manage their investigations. We design this sequence by articulating both the disciplinary understanding and skills needed and the cognitive obstacles posed by typical student prior conceptions. This leads to a set of content and process targets for our activities. Once these targets are identified, we draw on existing, commonly used curricula and construct a sequence of activities leading up to investigation activities. For example, analyses of the study of natural selection point to the primacy of variation and structure–function relationships, as well as to the significance of reasoning about changing distributions in a population (Bishop & Anderson, 1990; Demastes, Good, & Peebles, 1995; Jensen & Finley, 1996). This led us to incorporate two activities, one on variation and one on structure–function relationships, from existing curricula into our technology-infused high school unit on evolution. In one activity, students measure the femur length of all the students in the class and construct a histogram of these measurements in order to appreciate that variation preexists in populations, and to develop proficiency in ways of representing and reasoning about distributions of traits in a population. In the second activity, students try to perform everyday functions, such as using scissors and opening a door, without the benefit of their thumb (their thumb is taped and immobilized), in order to appreciate how a physical characteristic can enable particular functions.

We contextualize these activities by foreshadowing the driving question of the investigation and noting the relationship between these activities in class discussions. For example, the introductory discussion of the variation activity notes that the students will need to examine the variation of finches on a Galapagos island in order to investigate the crisis in the upcoming investigation. In follow-up discussions to the structure–function activity, the class considers how differences in a trait in a population could affect the type of behaviors that the individuals in the population perform.

Drawing on existing curricula is an important part of integrating these new curricula within existing practice. We are building on the infrastructure that already exists for supporting science learning, and on teachers' experience. Rather than introducing the software investigations as self-contained activities, the ideas are strongly linked to concrete experiences that precede the software investigation.

Staging Activities to Prepare Students for Investigations. Although we provide some semblance of the full task by framing the introductory and follow-up activities in terms of the upcoming investigations, this does not provide the same type of experience and opportunity to learn as drawing on the core concepts and strategies within the context of an investigation. Engaging in investigations is key to learning how to orchestrate the necessary knowledge and skills. However, trying to coordinate such practices for the first time in the context of an extended investigation of a rich dataset poses many serious challenges. The investigation requires learning complex scientific content, learning to link mathematical expressions to a characterization of phenomena (Lehrer & Romberg, 1996), as well as investigation of management skills (Krajcik et al., 1998; Loh et al., in press). In order to address these issues, we include staging activities in our unit to incrementally prepare students for the more open-ended nature of an investigation.

Staging activities capture the essential features of conducting an investigation—students have a driving question, and they must negotiate primary data in order to construct an explanation. However, they involve a simpler data set and familiar media, such as paper-based materials, and typically involve more guidance in the materials and from the teacher.

For example, we designed a staging activity as part of the middle school Struggle for Survival unit (described in section 3). In this miniinvestigation, students are given individual data records of 12 finches, and asked to study the records and attempt to discern any patterns. At this point in the curriculum, they know they are going to be investigating a crisis on a Galapagos Island, and they have seen a video showing how the scientists collect data (banding birds, weighing and measuring them, etc.). They are told that prior to getting the full dataset on the computer, they will have some practice drawing inferences from data.

After studying the raw data, and making a table of the trends they notice, they then construct a graph that "tells the story" that they see in the data. For example, in recent classroom trials, students have noticed trends such as the finding that the weight of the birds seems to be lower in the dry season than the wet season, and that the male birds are slightly larger in wingspan and weight than the female birds. Students are not told what kind of graph to make and need to consider how to convey the trend they detect.

This staging activity serves to familiarize students with the data in a more familiar medium (printed tables of data) before they use the computer interface to access the data. Second, it provides students practice in asking questions of data in the context of constructing an explanation, but with a simplified dataset. Rather than a graph providing an answer to a question posed by the teacher, in this activity, students have to interpret the data and construct a graph that shows the pattern they want to communicate. In this way, it introduces the idea that one can focus on different patterns and tell different stories from the same data.

The staging activity we designed for the high school unit on evolution took on a somewhat different form. In this activity, The Marine Iguana, students are presented with a "problematic" natural phenomenon that they are asked to explain, similar to the Galapagos Finches investigation. In this problem, students are asked to explain why subgroups in a population of Galapagos marine iguanas forage at two different sites. Students receive a packet of paper materials that includes the same type of information that is available in the Galapagos Finches investigation, such as graphs showing morphological population data (e.g., snout length), profiles of individual iguanas, and field notes with behavioral descriptions (e.g., descriptions of iguanas foraging). Moreover, the data is structured in the same way as it is structured in the Galapagos Finches, according to our articulation of the intersection of theoretical principles and investigation strategies in this domain.

This activity starts as a teacher-directed activity, and students gain control and direct the activity midway through the investigation. The teacher initially leads the investigation, helping students formulate subquestions and hypotheses, decide on relevant observations, as well as analyze and interpret the data. The activity continues with students completing the investigation in small groups. This structure provides an opportunity for the teacher to model how to execute particular strategies, as well as to voice the rationale for performing these strategies at particular junctures in the investigation. This form of teacher modeling prior to student-directed practice with the strategies is important in helping students learn to direct their own learning (Brown & Campione, 1994; Brown & Palincsar, 1989; Loh et al., in press; Palincsar & Brown, 1984).

Designing different staging activities around investigations provides a mechanism for tailoring investigation-based units that utilize the same software environments to different audiences. For example, the middle school activity addressed the needs of the middle school students who were less proficient with graphs than the high school students. The Iguana activity catered well to the more stringent requirements for the high school students to achieve content learning goals by providing additional experience in applying principles that were drawn from the theory of natural selection to explain an episode in nature.

Ongoing Reflection

A key need in conducting complex investigations is to engage in ongoing reflection as the work proceeds (Collins & Brown, 1988; Loh et al., in press). Students need to continually reevaluate their investigation plans, evaluate the status of their hypotheses, synthesize findings so far, reconsider previous understandings, and redirect their investigation as needed. We have two complementary strategies for supporting these reflection processes. First, we provide tools that encourage and structure reflection while students are conducting their investigations within the software environment. Second, we provide support for reflection by interleaving discussion sessions with investigation sessions.

Integrating Reflection Within Software Investigations.
A key problem in an investigation is managing the information collected, documents created, and generally keeping track of what has been understood and established so far. Students often fail to revisit previous interpretations in light of new and possibly conflicting data (Kuhn et al., 1992;

Schauble, 1990). Creating tools that support the process of reflection has been a focus of our design.

One strategy we discussed earlier is the integration of artifact creation within the process of investigation. The structure of the Explanation-Constructor is tailored to the particular theoretical frameworks being explored, and it is used in an ongoing fashion as students are conducting their investigation. Students need to consider, as they review the data they have collected so far in a session, what data they should insert into their journal. Teachers stress the incremental elaboration of explanations in students' journals as they progress through the investigation.

We have also incorporated tools specifically designed to help students manage their collected data and their interpretations. In the TB Lab, Galapagos Finches, and Florida Panther environments, all data displays constructed by students are automatically stored in a data log (see Fig. 9.5). The data log records the time of the data collection, the nature of the comparison (saved as the title), and the data display itself. In addition, any background data that students retrieve can also be saved in the data log. A typical investigation results in 30 to 40 items in the data log over a period of 1 to 2 weeks. The data log allows students to easily retrieve important data they viewed earlier. In addition, students are encouraged to record their interpretations directly on the record in the data log in an annotation field. Students document what important pattern they noticed in the data display, its significance for the investigation, questions that it raised, and so on. These annotations can help students locate particular data they felt was important when they are writing their explanations in the ExplanationConstructor.

Another important tool in the data log for managing the collected data is the ability to classify the significance of data with respect to the investigation goals. Again, we structure this process from the discipline-specific theoretical frameworks driving the investigation. The data log implemented within the Florida Panthers and Galapagos Finches is tailored with a particular set of categories. For example, the available categories in the data log for the Galapagos Finches are baseline, changes, differential survival, explaining fitness, and variations. Students can classify any data record as belonging in one of these categories, and can later sort the records according to these categories (see Fig. 9.6). In this way, the important components of an argument suggested by the discipline-specific theoretical frameworks drive students' access of the data in the query interface, their management of the data in the data log, and their synthesis and articulation of their interpretations in the ExplanationConstructor.

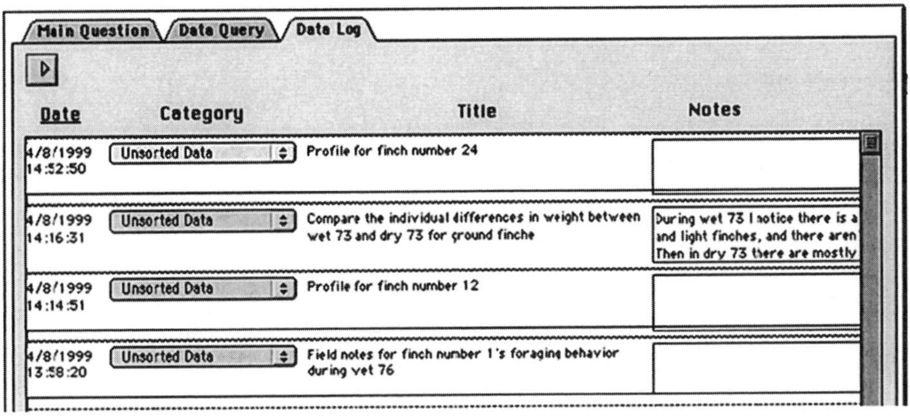

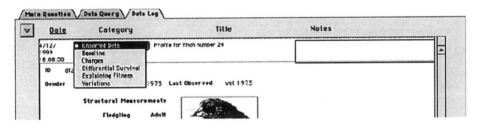

FIG. 9.5.   Collecting data in the data log.

FIG. 9.6.   Managing data through conceptual categories in the Data Log. The group has selected an individual finch data record stored in the data log, and is encoding this data record according to the relevance of the data to their argument.

Integrating Discussion Activities Within Investigations.
A second component of the support for reflection is to structure discussion activities that take place throughout the investigation. Midinvestigation critiques provide students with opportunities to assess their progress while they can still revise and extend their work. Postinvestigation assessments provide opportunities for students to compare their explanations, and to develop consensus explanations.

The evaluation criteria for critiques are established during the initial framing discussion in which students and teachers develop criteria for evaluating explanations. As discussed earlier, these discussions are directed to focus students on assessing the causal coherence of their own and their peers' explanations, and to take an active stance in evaluating the relevance and sufficiency of evidence for particular causal claims. The goal is that students be able to reason about which explanations might be better than others and why. These framing discussions result in a written rubric that is available for subsequent critiques.

The creation of software-based artifacts can play a key role in classroom-based discussion activities. As we have described, in most investigations, students create strategic artifacts that represent their interpretations within the theoretical framework of the discipline, and help make clear the strategies used in the investigation and argument. These artifacts can be used in classroom activities in which students reflect on these artifacts as objects of their cognition (Kuhn, 1993). These discussions may focus on the progress of investigations, comparisons of strategies and results, and so on.

For example, we orchestrate midinvestigation critiques at least once during the course of an investigation. These are supported by specific software scaffolds. We have structured these critique sessions both as evaluative and collaborative exercises. Within ExplanationConstructor, each explanation can be evaluated with a rating and a justification for the rating. These reviews become part of students' work product, and students are encouraged to justify their ratings in terms of the rubric. Using this feature, we have had groups review each other's work during investigation.

In the predator–prey investigation, reflection is woven into the investigation itself. Students collaborate during the annotation and comparison of video clips, labeling important features and identifying variations between various hunting episodes. The software highlights similarities and differences between the students' coding of the hunts, but the students must do the real work of interpreting the data and constructing models to explain what they see. During the unit, groups collaborate to consider how and why variations arise and question their representations of the hunting process.

After investigations, we take a number of approaches to facilitate reflection. These include groups' self-assessment of their final explanations, using the rubric developed earlier, as well as group presentations to the class in which students need to communicate and defend their findings. Also, consensus-building class discussions are used to generate a shared explanation for the problem at hand, and to push students to generalize from the particulars of an investigation to the broader domain theory. For example, in the high school evolution unit, following the second investigation, students are asked to consider whether or not the seemingly very different finch and TB problems are the same type of problem and what relation they have to one another.

STUDIES OF BGUILE IN THE CLASSROOM

In this part, we briefly summarize some of the findings from our empirical studies of students and teachers using BGuILE technology-infused curricula in classrooms. Our empirical studies are presented in more detail elsewhere (Sandoval, 1998; Sandoval, 2000; Sandoval & Reiser, 1997; Smith & Reiser, 1998; Tabak, 1999; Tabak & Reiser, 1997a 1997b).

Analyses of Work Products

At a global level, our analyses of the products students produce in their classroom work suggest that they are generally successful at engaging in inquiry in these rich problems. Most groups of students are able to arrive at reasonably well-justified explanations and models and can recount the evidence on which their explanations are based. For example, in the predation unit, students arrive at qualitative decision trees of predation behavior that mirror the quantitative analyses developed by behavioral ecologists. There is a diversity of models across student groups, but the groups typically succeed in being able to justify their model from their analyses of video data in presentations and classroom discussions. In fact, they notice subtle properties of the behavior in their analyses that take them to advanced topics in animal behavior not usually included in high school textbooks (Smith & Reiser, 1998).

In both the middle and high school units on evolution based on the Galapagos Finches, we see students able to articulate explanations in terms of the theory of natural selection (Sandoval, 2000; Tabak, 1999). As with the predation unit, there are different explanations developed by different groups of students that all find backing in the data. In one study, the vast majority of student groups articulated explanations that contained all the causal components of a natural selection explanation; identifying the environmental pressure (e.g., a drought); how it affected individuals (e.g., it led to competition for reduced food); identifying a physical trait that differentiated surviving finches from those that died (e.g., larger beaks); and explaining how that trait provided an advantage (e.g., larger beaks allowed finches to crack open the remaining hard-shelled seeds). This stands in contrast to the difficulty most students experience in articulating the importance of variation in natural selection (Bishop & Anderson, 1990).

We have also considered the inferential validity (Kuhn et al., 1992) of the explanations students produced. That is, are students' causal claims based on valid inferences from data that they have examined? Perhaps not surprisingly, the validity of inferences decreased in the more demanding parts of the explanation (Sandoval, 2000). For example, more students were able to correctly cite an empirical trend in the data that identified a trait that differentiated survivors, but fewer were able to articulate a survival advantage that was based on observable data. Students had largely identified the needed components of an explanation and typically filled those parts of the explanation with plausible and relevant claims, but had some difficulty navigating the complex dataset to find the best explanations.

Sandoval (2000) developed a measure to assess the causal coherence of students' explanations independently of their accuracy (i.e., inferential validity). This argument coherence measure is roughly based on analyses of text structure (Trabasso, Secco, & Broek, 1984), and measures whether cause and effect chains are explicitly articulated and connected to the central causal chain of the explanation. In the study just mentioned, students' explanations were largely coherent, even when they included unsupported claims, suggesting that students understood what it means to write a clearly articulated causal explanation.

Overall, the results suggest that the discipline-specific strategic scaffolds are promising. Although not all students can construct equally well-grounded explanations, students generally are able to navigate very complex datasets and construct a causally coherent explanation that exemplifies the target discipline theory.

Studies of Conceptual and Strategic Understanding

Our initial studies of improvements in students' performance are encouraging. For example, the intensive type of engagement in explaining lion hunting behavior in the Animal Landlord predation unit results in better performance on transfer essay questions from pretest to posttest. The essays on the posttest contain more causal arguments and a greater proportion of justified points drawn from the behavioral ecology theoretical framework, rather than from common sense claims (Smith & Reiser, 1997).

Similarly, there is some initial evidence that high school students working with the Galapagos Finches-based evolution unit become better at writing evolutionary explanations, as judged by their performance on pretests and posttests (Sandoval, 1998). Students improve on near-transfer problems that ask them to explain a natural selection event using a small dataset. In particular, after the unit, students make fewer unwarranted inferences on these problems, suggesting that they learn a generalizable notion of the need for causally coherent explanations (Sandoval, 1998).

Studies of the Investigation Process

Perhaps the most revealing analyses are the case studies in which we examine the work of individual student groups and the studies of whole classroom discourse. These studies are where we can see the most direct impact of our tools and curricula. In these case studies, we have recorded students' conversations within their group and with their teacher, and their interactions with the software throughout the investigation. Our analyses focus on their incremental understanding of the problem (as manifested in their conversations and their writing in their data log and journals), their strategic decisions, and the construction of their explanations. When we examine the work of individual student groups, we see the guiding effects of the strategic tools, such as the strategic query interface and the ExplanationConstructor. For example, students' investigations are consistently driven by explanatory goals. Students appear to be looking at data to generate ideas for an explanation to their current question, or they are looking for evidence to support a just-recorded partial explanation, or an explanation guide prompt (Sandoval, 1998). The strategic query interface seems to focus students on the types of comparisons they need for their investigation, and becomes a vehicle for teachers to have strategic conversations with students about what they are trying to achieve and what they will learn from particular queries of the data (Tabak & Reiser, 1997a, 1997b).

The strategic tools also seem to play a role in the groups' self-monitoring. Our case studies suggest that groups' monitoring of their progress is very focused on their explanatory goals. They evaluate their progress in terms of their current explanation, its completeness, the evidence they have to support it, and their remaining questions (Sandoval, 1998).

In classrooms using BGuILE materials, we see moves toward a discourse of science. We see teachers systematically and continually pushing students to defend their ideas and back up their claims with evidence (Smith & Reiser, 1998; Tabak, 1999; Tabak & Reiser, 1997a). Teachers helped students elaborate their reports to be more explicit about cause and effect, and to connect their findings to the theoretical framework of natural selection (Tabak, 1999; Tabak & Reiser, 1997a). For example, consider the following dialogue from an urban high school classroom, taken from the midinvestigation strategy discussion.

Ms. Patrick:	A., how do you know that the young ones died off? ... (*turning attention to whole class*) I want to hear how she came up with that because she didn't give me any evidence to support that.
Amalia:	Because we went into graphs. We asked them to show us all the dead birds and the graph was mostly all young.
Ms. Patrick:	Ok, so you did look at a graph of all dead ones. Did you look at a comparison of dead ones versus live ones?
Amalia:	Yes.
Ms. Patrick:	So you know when you looked at the comparison it was the low weight birds that were dead?
Amalia:	Yes.
Ms. Patrick:	And were you sure they were all fledglings or could they have been low weight adults?
Amalia:	No, we checked that.
Ms. Patrick:	How did you check that?
Amalia:	We looked at the profiles.

(*Several minutes later.*)

Ms. Patrick:	What's doing the selecting?
Kevin:	Maybe the owls, since all the small ones are dying maybe the big ones are able to fight off the owls.
Ms. Patrick:	Fight the owls? Do you know, and this is truly a question that I don't know the answer to, do you know if the owls and the finches might be in competition for food at all?
Student:	Yeah, each other.
Kevin:	Oooh (*yells back to classmate*) Didn't you say the owls were eating the finches! (*gets confirmation*) The owls ate all the small finches and all the ones that could fight back survived.
Ms. Patrick:	Oh, so that's an interesting idea, so you think the bigger ones can survive the attacks by owls. What else might be going on? Why are the finches surviving then?
Lisa:	Maybe the finches are adults, and maybe they are more fully developed.
Ms. Patrick:	What does fully developed mean, what's your idea Allan?
Allan:	Maybe some of them are smarter than the owls.
Ms. Patrick:	Maybe some of them are smarter than the owls? Could be, could be. What do you think is the selective pressure here,

	in other words, what's doing the selecting between those who lived and those who died?
Allan:	Yeah, their prey ... no, no its the finches if its the ones that is big, no I mean that is little, that can't do nothing, obviously they are going to die.
Kevin:	It could be the finches because if, um, you say the rainy season is mostly when they mate and it didn't hardly rain in '77 so they might not have mated.
Allan:	ooh, ooh!
Ms. Patrick:	You know you guys have got a lot of stuff to juggle here. I forgot about the mating, so they are not mating in the wet season either!

In this example, we see students able to defend their findings and point to specific evidence that warranted their claims. We see the teacher continually challenging students to back up their claims, and sometimes suggesting alternatives for them to rule out. At one point, the teacher asks a question for which she says she does not know the answer. In one case, we see a student turn to another for information rather than the teacher (about owls eating finches). Clearly, students are still in the process of connecting their understanding to natural selection (some are confused in attempting to articulate the selection pressure). Yet, the picture that emerges is one in which students are taking ownership over what they are producing rather than turning to the teacher as the sole authority in the classroom, and in which the teacher helps to establish a set of norms about claims and evidence that characterize scientific discourse.

Teaching Practice

Another focus of our efforts is to examine the teaching practice that is effective in creating and sustaining a climate of inquiry. As is clear in the previous example, the role of the teacher is key in structuring science discourse and guiding student investigations. Tabak has characterized two collections of strategies teachers use to support inquiry in their classrooms (Tabak, 1999; Tabak & Reiser, 1997a). First, teachers reinforce software scaffolds, by making the conceptual distinctions represented in the software tools a focus of their interactions with students, pushing students to evaluate their claims in light of data, articulate explanations more fully, and so on. Teachers also augment what is supported in the software, prompting students to assess their own progress, helping them evaluate inquiry plans, and establishing norms for discourse that encourage hypothesizing and defending claims with data.

Of course, there are many challenges in moving this type of technology-infused curricula from the "early adopters" who worked directly with our research group to a broader audience of teachers who may be less prepared for these pedagogical approaches. In other work, we are exploring the challenges teachers perceive in incorporating inquiry and technology in their teaching, and the ways their practice changes when they experiment with technology-infused curricula (Reiser et al., 2000).

CONCLUSIONS

In this chapter, we argued that the approach of providing instruction and support at the level of general scientific process needs to be augmented with a focus on designing discipline-specific instruction and supports. We articulated a set of design principles that implement this level of support in the tools students use to investigate and manage data, and in the artifacts they create.

This attention to explanatory frameworks provides a resolution to the false dichotomy plaguing education reform in both the "math wars" and the science reform debates. Education reformers often point to the proceduralized and decontextualized way that many students learn mathematics and science—without connection to their lives, without deep understanding, and focused on vocabulary and algorithms. They are accused by "traditionalists," including some leading scientists and mathematicians, of trivializing the disciplines in favor of being enamored of process. In our view, to teach scientific process is to teach deep engagement with content. To teach students to do inquiry is to teach them to grapple with data by extensively mapping a theoretical framework to rigorously analyze a dataset. To teach scientific process well means not only to teach the process, but to have students engage with the content much more deeply than teaching the content didactically apart from its use in investigations.

It is important to consider the design trade-offs inherent in this discipline-specific strategy for support. An important goal in designing computer supports in general, and supports for learners in particular, is generality. Naturally, a tool that could be used across a range of domains, such as a spreadsheet, has enormous appeal. Why create separate tools for business, science, and mathematics applications? Indeed, a push toward generality has motivated much tool design in the educational technology field. For example, collaborative tools for argument and knowledge building can be applied across a wide range of educational applications

(Edelson et al., 1996; Scardamalia & Bereiter, 1994; Suthers, Weiner, Connelly, & Paolucci, 1995). General modeling tools can be used to capture and explore the behavior of a wide range of phenomena (Jackson et al., 1994; Resnick, 1996; Stratford, et al., 1998). General process supports can be built to support the common practices of scientific disciplines (Quintana et al., 1999).

In contrast, a focus on discipline-specific supports entails tailoring the scaffolds to particular scientific disciplines, at a cost in generality. However, it also enables a degree of integration of tools and potential utility that complements and goes beyond what the general tools can offer. Students using the Galapagos Finches and ExplanationConstructor use two very complex collections of software tools, and yet, manage to move seamlessly between them, exploring data in the investigation environment and periodically returning to the explanation journal to review outstanding questions, insert data, or add to the written explanation. These tools can embody a level of direction in strategic prompts not possible with more general tools. The issue of what will transfer to new science settings is an open question. However, given the situated nature of learning, and the difficulty in demonstrating transfer very removed from the original conceptual domain, it seems overconfident to attempt to solve the transfer problem by teaching skills and providing supports at a very general level.

Just as with the specious process versus content debate, we do not suggest we should propose discipline-specific tools rather than general tools, or vice versa. Instead, we suggest that the field needs to explore the design strategies for crafting each type of support, ways to document what each can achieve, and then compare the design trade-offs.

ACKNOWLEDGMENTS

This research was funded by the James S. McDonnell Foundation, Cognitive Studies for Educational Practice. Additional support for curriculum development and studies of enactment has been provided by the National Science Foundation to the Center for Learning Technologies in Urban Schools (NSF grant #REC-9720383). Opinions expressed are those of the authors and not necessarily those of these foundations.

We are grateful for discussions with our collaborator, James P. Spillane. Richard Leider programmed TB Lab and provided graphics design assistance on the Galapagos Finches. We are also indebted to Susan Margulis and Hans Landel for guidance on the scientific content of our Animal

Landlord and Florida Panthers environments, to Renee Judd for content guidance on TB Lab, to Angie Agganis, Pamela Lentine, and Eric Fusilero for assistance with software and curriculum design, and to Tammy Porter Massey for assistance with background research. BGuILE would not be possible without the valuable assistance of the teachers who have helped us develop curriculum and provided input into our technology development, in particular Linda Patton, David Goodspeed, Carlos Rodriguez, and Eva Laczina. To request further information about BGuILE software or curricula, see the BGuILE web site: http://www.ls.sesp.nwu.edu /bguile/ and the LeTUS website: http://www.letus.org/.

REFERENCES

AAAS. (1990). *Science for all Americans: Project 2061*. New York: Oxford University Press.

Bell, P., & Linn, M. C. (2000). Scientific arguments as learning artifacts: designing for learning from the web with KIE. *International Journal of Science Education, 22*, 797-817.

Bishop, B. A., & Anderson, C. W. (1990). Student conceptions of natural selection and its role in evolution. *Journal of Research in Science Teaching, 27*, 415–427.

Blumenfeld, P. C., Soloway, E., Marx, R. W., Krajcik, J. S., Guzdial, M., & Palincsar, A. (1991). Motivating project-based learning: Sustaining the doing, supporting the learning. *Educational Psychologist, 26*, 369–398.

Bransford, J. D., Sherwood, R. D., Hasselbring, T. S., Kinzer, C. K., & Williams, S. M. (1990). Anchored instruction: Why we need it and how technology can help. In D. Nix & R. Spiro (Eds.), *Cognition, education, and multimedia: Exploring ideas in high technology* (pp. 115–141). Hillsdale, NJ: Lawrence Erlbaum Associates.

Brown, A. L., & Campione, J. C. (1994). Guided discovery in a community of learners. In K. McGilly (Ed.), *Classroom lessons: Integrating cognitive theory and classroom practice* (pp. 229–270). Cambridge, MA: MIT Press.

Brown, A. L., & Palincsar, A. S. (1989). Guided, cooperative learning and individual knowledge acquisition. In L. B. Resnick (Ed.), *Knowing, learning, and instruction: Essays in honor of Robert Glaser* (pp. 393–451). Hillsdale, NJ: Lawrence Erlbaum Associates.

Carey, S., Evans, R., Honda, M., Jay, E., & Unger, C. (1989). "An experiment is when you try it and see if it works": A study of grade 7 students' understanding of scientific knowledge. *International Journal of Science Education, 11*, 514–529.

Clement, J. (1988). Observed methods for generating analogies in scientific problem solving. *Cognitive Science, 12*, 563–586.

Collins, A., & Brown, J. S. (1988). The computer as a tool for learning through reflection. In H. Mandl & A. Lesgold (Eds.), *Learning issues for intelligent tutoring systems* (pp. 1–18). New York: Springer-Verlag.

Collins, A., Brown, J. S., & Newman, S. E. (1989). Cognitive apprenticeship: Teaching the crafts of reading, writing, and mathematics. In L. B. Resnick (Ed.), *Knowing, learning, and instruction: Essays in honor of Robert Glaser* (pp. 453–494). Hillsdale, NJ: Lawrence Erlbaum Associates.

Collins, A. M., & Ferguson, W. (1993). Epistemic forms and epistemic games: Structures and strategies to guide inquiry. *Educational Psychologist, 28*, 25–42.

Confrey, J. (1990). A review of the research on student conceptions in mathematics, science, and programming. In C. B. Cazden (Ed.), *Review of research in education* (pp. 3–56). Washington, DC: American Educational Research Association.

Crawford, B. A., Krajcik, J. S., & Marx, R. W. (1999). Elements of a community of learners in a middle school science classroom. *Science Education, 83*, 701–723.

DeBoer, G. E. (1991). *A history of ideas in science education: Implications for practice.* New York: Teachers College Press.

Demastes, S. S., Good, R. G., & Peebles, P. (1995). Students' conceptual ecologies and the process of conceptual change in evolution. *Science Education, 79* (6), 637-666.

Dunbar, K. (1995). How scientists really reason: Scientific reasoning in real-world laboratories. In R. J. Sternberg & J. E. Davidson (Eds.), *The nature of insight* (pp. 365–395). Cambridge, MA: MIT Press.

Duschl, R. A. (1990). *Restructuring science education: the importance of theories and their development.* New York: Teachers College Press.

Edelson, D. C., Gordin, D. N., & Pea, R. D. (1999). Addressing the challenges of inquiry-based learning through technology and curriculum design. *The Journal of the Learning Sciences, 8*, 391–450.

Edelson, D. C., Pea, R. D., & Gomez, L. M. (1996). The collaboratory notebook: Support for collaborative inquiry. *Communications of the ACM, 39*, 32–33.

Grant, P. R. (1986). *Ecology and evolution of Darwin's finches.* Princeton, NJ: Princeton University Press.

Greene, E. D. (1990). The logic of university students' misunderstanding of natural selection. *Journal of Research in Science Teaching, 27*, 875–885.

Hawkins, J., & Pea, R. D. (1987). Tools for bridging the cultures of everyday and scientific thinking. *Journal of Research in Science Teaching, 24*, 291–307.

Jackson, S. L., Stratford, S. J., Krajcik, J., & Soloway, E. (1994). Making dynamic modeling accessible to precollege science students. *Interactive Learning Environments, 4*, 233–257.

Jensen, M. S., & Finley, F. N. (1996). Changes in students' understanding of evolution resulting from different curricular and instructional strategies. *Journal of Research in Science Teaching, 33*, 879–900.

Klahr, D., & Dunbar, K. (1988). Dual space search during scientific reasoning. *Cognitive Science, 12*, 1–48.

Knorr-Cetina, K. (1995). Laboratory studies: The cultural approach to the study of science. In S. Jasanoff, G. E. Markle, J. C. Petersen, & T. Pinch (Eds.), *Handbook of science and technology studies.* (pp. 140–166) London, UK: Sage.

Knorr-Cetina, K. (1996). The care of the self and blind variation: An ethnography of the empirical in two sciences. In P. Galison & D. J. Stump (Eds.), *The disunity of science: Boundaries, contexts, and power.* (pp. 287–310). Stanford, CA: Stanford University Press.

Knorr-Cetina, K. (1999). *Epistemic cultures: How the sciences make knowledge.* Cambridge, MA: Harvard University Press.

Krajcik, J., Blumenfeld, P. C., Marx, R. W., Bass, K. M., Fredericks, J., & Soloway, E. (1998). Inquiry in project-based science classrooms: Initial attempts by middle school students. *Journal of the Learning Sciences, 7*, 313–350.

Kuhn, D. (1993). Connecting scientific and informal reasoning. *Merrill-Palmer Quarterly, 39*, 74–103.

Kuhn, D., Amsel, E., & O'Loughlin, M. (1988). *The development of scientific thinking skills.* San Diego, CA: Academic Press.

Kuhn, D., Schauble, L., & Garcia-Mila, M. (1992). Cross-domain development of scientific reasoning. *Cognition and Instruction, 9*, 285–327.

Kuhn, T. S. (1970). *The structure of scientific revolutions* (2nd ed.). Chicago, IL: University of Chicago Press.

Latour, B. (1988). Drawing things together. In M. Lynch & S. Woolgar (Eds.), *Representation in scientific practice* (pp. 19–68). Cambridge, MA: MIT Press.

Lehrer, R., & Romberg, T. (1996). Exploring children's data modeling. *Cognition and Instruction, 14*, 69–108.

Lemke, J. L. (1990). *Talking science: language, learning, and values.* Norwood, NJ: Ablex.

Linn, M. C., diSessa, A., Pea, R. D., & Songer, N. B. (1994). Can research on science learning and instruction inform standards for science education? *Journal of Science Education and Technology, 3*, 7–15.

Loh, B., Radinsky, J., Russell, E., Gomez, L. M., Reiser, B. J., & Edelson, D. C. (1998). C.-M. Karat, A. Lund, J. Coutaz, & J. Karat (Eds.), The Progress Portfolio: Designing reflective tools for a classroom context. In *Proceedings of CHI 98* (pp. 627–634). Reading, MA: Addison-Wesley.

Loh, B., Reiser, B. J., Radinsky, J., Edelson, D. C., Gomez, L. M., & Marshall, S. (in press). Developing reflective inquiry practices: A case study of software, the teacher, and students. In K. Crowley, C. Schunn, & T. Okada (Eds.), *Designing for science: Implications from everyday, classroom, and professional settings.* Mahwah, NJ: Lawrence Erlbaum Associates.

Mayr, E. (1988). *Toward a new philosophy of biology: Observations of an evolutionist.* Cambridge, MA: Harvard University Press.

Means, B. (Ed.). (1994). *Technology and education reform.* San Francisco, CA: Jossey-Bass.

Means, B. (1998). Melding authentic science, technology, and inquiry-based teaching: Experiences of the GLOBE program. *Journal of Science Education and Technology, 7*, 97–105.

Merrill, D. C., Reiser, B. J., Beekelaar, R., & Hamid, A. (1992). Making processes visible: Scaffolding learning with reasoning-congruent representations. In C. Frasson, G. Gauthier, & G. I. McCalla (Eds.), *Intelligent Tutoring Systems: Second International Conference, ITS '92* (pp. 103–110). New York: Springer-Verlag.

NRC. (1996). *National science education standards.* Washington, DC: Author.

Ohlsson, S. (1992). The cognitive skill of theory articulation: A neglected aspect of science education? *Science & Education, 1*, 181–192.

Palincsar, A. S., & Brown, A. L. (1984). Reciprocal teaching of comprehension-fostering and comprehension-monitoring activities. *Cognition and Instruction, 1*, 117–175.

PCAST. (1997). *Report to the President on the use of technology to strengthen K–12 education in the United States.* Washington DC.: panel on Educational Technology.

Quintana, C., Eng, J., Carra, A., Wu, H.-K., & Soloway, E. (1999). Symphony: A case study in extending learner-centered design through process space analysis. In M.Altom & M. Williams (Eds.), *Proceedings of CHI 99 Conference on Human Factors in Computing Systems* (pp. 473–480). Reading, MA: Addison-Wesley.

Reiser, B. J., Spillane, J. P., Steinmuller, F., Sorsa, D., Carney, K., & Kyza, E. (2000). Investigating the mutual adaptation process in teachers' design of technology-infused curricula. In B.J. Fishman & S.F. O'Connor–Divelbiss (Eds.), *Proceedings of the International Conference of the Learning Sciences.* (pp. 342–349). Mahwah, NJ: Lawrence Erlbaum Associates.

Resnick, M. (1996). Beyond the centralized mindset. *The Journal of the Learning Sciences, 5*, 1–22.

Sandoval, W. A. (1998). *Inquire to explain: Structuring inquiry around explanation construction in a technology-supported biology curriculum.* Unpublished doctoral dissertation, Northwestern University.

Sandoval, W. A. 2000. *Students' understanding of causal explanation and natural selection in a technology-supported inquiry curriculum.* Manuscript submitted for publication.

Sandoval, W. A., & Reiser, B. J. (1997, March). *Evolving explanations in high school biology.* Paper presented at the Annual Meeting of the American Educational Research Association, Chicago, IL.

Scardamalia, M., & Bereiter, C. (1994). Computer support for knowledge-building communities. *The Journal of the Learning Sciences, 3*, 265–283.

Schauble, L. (1990). Belief revision in children: The role of prior knowledge and strategies for generating evidence. *Journal of Experimental Child Psychology, 49*, 31–57.

Schauble, L., Glaser, R., Duschl, R. A., Schulze, S., & John, J. (1995). Students' understanding of the objectives and procedures of experimentation in the science classroom. *The Journal of the Learning Sciences, 4*, 131–166.

Settlage, J. (1994). Conceptions of natural selection: A snapshot of the sense-making process. *Journal of Research in Science Teaching, 31*, 449–457.

Smith, B. K., & Reiser, B. J. (1997). What should a wildebeest say? Interactive nature films for high school classrooms. In J.D. Hollan & J.D. Foley (Eds.) *ACM Multimedia* (pp. 193–201). New York: ACM Press.

Smith, B. K., & Reiser, B. J. (1998). National Geographic unplugged: Designing interactive nature films for classrooms. In *Proceedings of CHI 98* (pp. 424–431). New York: ACM Press.

Songer, N. B., & Linn, M. C. (1991). How do students' views of science influence knowledge integration? *Journal of Research in Science Teaching, 28,* 761–784.

Stratford, S., Krajcik, J., & Soloway, E. (1998). Secondary students' dynamic modeling processes: Analyzing, reasoning about, synthesizing, and testing models of stream ecosystems. *Journal of Science Education and Technology, 7,* 215–234.

Suthers, D., Weiner, A., Connelly, J., & Paolucci, M. (1995). Belvedere: Engaging students in critical discussion of science and public policy issues. In J. Greer (Ed.), *Proceedings of AI-ED 95: World Conference on Artificial Intelligence in Education* (pp. 266–273). Washington, DC: AACE.

Tabak, I. (1999). *Unraveling the development of scientific literacy: Domain-specific inquiry support in a system of cognitive and social interactions.* Unpublished doctoral dissertation, Northwestern University.

Tabak, I., & Reiser, B. J. (1997a). Complementary roles of software-based scaffolding and teacher–student interactions in inquiry learning. In R. Hall, N. Miyake, & N. Enyedy (Eds.), *Proceedings of Computer Support for Collaborative Learning '97,* (pp. 289–298). Mahwah, NJ: Lawrence Erlbaum Associates.

Tabak, I., & Reiser, B. J. (1997b). Domain-specific inquiry support: Permeating discussions with scientific conceptions. In *Proceedings of From Misconceptions to Constructed Understanding.* Ithaca, NY.

Tabak, I., Sandoval, W. A., Smith, B. K., Agganis, A., Baumgartner, E., & Reiser, B. J. (1995). Supporting collaborative guided inquiry in a learning environment for biology. In J. L. Schnase & E. L. Cunnius (Eds.), *Proceeedings of CSCL '95: The First International Conference on Computer Support for Collaborative Learning* (pp. 362–366). Mahwah, NJ: Lawrence Erlbaum Associates.

Tabak, I., Smith, B. K., Sandoval, W. A., & Reiser, B. J. (1996). Combining general and domain-specific strategic support for biological inquiry. In C. Frasson, G. Gauthier, & A. Lesgold (Eds.), *Intelligent Tutoring Systems: Third International Conference, ITS '96* (pp. 288–296). Montreal, Canada: Springer-Verlag.

Tinker, R. F. (1997). Student scientist partnerships: Shrewd maneuvers. *Journal of Science Education and Technology, 6,* 111–117.

Tobin, K., & Tippins, D. (1993). Constructivism as a referent for teaching and learning. In K. Tobin (Ed.), *The practice of constructivism in science education* (pp. 3–21). Hillsdale, NJ: Lawrence Erlbaum Associates.

Trabasso, T., Secco, T., & Broek, P. V. D. (1984). Causal cohesion and story coherence. In H. Mandl, N. L. Stein, & T. Trabasso (Eds.), *Learning and comprehension of text* (pp. 83–111). Hillsdale, NJ: Lawrence Erlbaum Associates.

Williams, S. M. (1992). Putting case-based instruction into context: Examples from legal and medical education. *The Journal of the Learning Sciences, 2,* 367–427.

10

Tools to Assist Learning by Doing: Achieving and Assessing Efficient Technology for Learning

Alan Lesgold
Martin Nahemow
University of Pittsburgh

Within the past few decades, many important foundations for a cognitive science of learning have been established. Much remains to be done, of course, and many of the contributors to this volume continue to advance the science. In addition to cognitive scientists, there are those, like us, who view themselves as cognitive engineers. Our goal is to use the accumulated understanding and principles from the cognitive science of instruction to address major design problems for the worlds of schooling and training. Like any engineer in a university faculty, we do research, but of a different form. Engineering research is generally driven by real world problems of complex scale. Experiments are conducted and design principles are tested. Often though, the scale of human enterprises prevents the same kind of reductionist single-factor validation that is possible in the laboratory. Rather, efforts are made to demonstrate the efficacy of particular design approaches and to understand the range of contexts in which those approaches can be effectively, efficiently, and safely used.

Consider, for example, the engineering of bridges. Clearly, this is an enterprise that must be informed by materials science and mechanics.

However, there will never be a universal answer to such questions as "which is better, a suspension bridge or double-lenticular truss bridge." Rather, the conditions under which each is safe and effective are established approximately, and trade-off studies are conducted to determine the range of situations in which one design is favored over the other. For a substantial body of cases, there is no research-based answer to the question, leaving the choice as one to be driven more by aesthetics than by science.

We believe that the same state of affairs exists in education. Multiple methods of learning have been engineered, including learning by doing, didactic presentation, peer collaboration and argumentation, drill, and so forth. Each of these methods has costs and benefits that determine whether it is reasonable to use it in specific circumstances. For example, many simple arithmetic skills, like single-digit addition, probably benefit from a bit of drill, although drill is probably not the way to understand electricity and magnetism. Similarly, whereas a few work situations can best be addressed through brief didactic presentations, many others are better addressed through learning by doing. The job of the cognitive instructional research engineer is to design new instructional approaches and to establish something of their effectiveness, efficiency, and safety. In this chapter, we discuss some of the effectiveness and efficiency concerns that arise in developing and applying learning by doing as a training strategy. Safety is gained largely by using simulated rather than real work environments.

THE ECONOMICS
OF TRAINING SYSTEM DEVELOPMENT

Throughout this chapter, we present discussions of specific training situations, including those arising in a joint project with a major high technology manufacturer, Intel. We have worked with several companies over the past decade and also with governmental and quasi-governmental agencies. We have learned from this work that the cost constraints on training system development are a significant barrier to the successful implementation of better training systems. Although one level of this cost concern is inevitable and sensible, there is a second level that also plays a major role. The first level is straight cost–benefit decision making. No company will invest in training that does not return more than it costs to produce—in improved plant and employee efficiency. This itself presents a problem to the education and training world, which historically has not directly compared costs and benefits.

A second financial factor is also important, though. This is the organizational structure and traditional training operations of businesses. Most businesses have relatively low training investments for any specific job and—at least in some cases—correspondingly low outcomes. Intelligent-coached apprenticeship environments, the primary approach described in this chapter, have been extremely costly to develop. The earliest systems cost about $2,000,000 each to develop, and costs have been decreasing so that they are now in the range of a few hundred thousand dollars. This is still an order of magnitude higher than the average training course produced in industry today for the kinds of jobs we have addressed. As a result, a decision to implement an intelligent-coached apprenticeship environment is a courageous one for any training manager—it will likely be the biggest project he or she undertakes. Even if the return on this investment is very good—and our experience has indicated that it is—deciding to develop such a system is a big risk for the decision maker. Throughout this chapter, we address issues of cost and efficiency precisely because of this reality. To be used in training on a large scale, intelligent-coached apprenticeships not only must be a good business investment, they must also not be too much more expensive than other training approaches, regardless of rate of return, or adoption will proceed very slowly.

LEARNING BY DOING

Learning by doing is a central way in which people acquire substantial expertise. It offers a number of advantages over other learning approaches. Most important, it avoids many aspects of the inert knowledge problem. The term *inert knowledge* was introduced by Alfred North Whitehead (1929). He used the term mainly in the context of not having sufficient connections between ideas or sufficient depth to ideas, but we use it more to denote specifically the situation in which the referential meaning of a term has not been fully acquired. We believe that we are addressing the same concern as Whitehead, although he might well have argued that a community school, in which teachers and students share a body of common experiences, can reasonably include considerable didactic presentations grounded in those experiences. Conceivably, it is the pluralism of experience and background that makes learning by doing more important than it might have been in the past.

When principles are acquired through experience, the terms used to state those principles have clear referential meaning, at least within the scope of that experience. Learning by doing also affords opportunities for learning how to manage the full complexity of a real domain, at least when the learning tasks are of the same difficulty and complexity as the harder tasks posed in real life. In this chapter, we explore some of the tools and approaches that allow learning by doing to be a powerful scheme for education and training. First, though, we need to say a little about why learning by doing schemes remain hard to develop.

Three Levels of Facility

Learning by doing facilitates development of all three levels of knowledge that Rasmussen (Rasmussen, Petjersen, & Goodstein, 1994) proposed. Rasmussen, reflecting on the different ways that technicians solve problems in their work, suggested that three levels of knowledge can be involved in expert performances, as listed in Table 10.1. First, there are highly overlearned skills, generally direct connections between recognition of a situation and an action sequence keyed to that situation. Second, there is an intermediate level of performance driven by cognitive rules. That is, action is not reflexive and immediate but is guaranteed as a set of productions (if–then rules). Finally, at the fringes of expertise, performance is driven by conceptual knowledge from which an expert can often infer a course of action using "weak" methods.

It is important to note that there is not really an extended body of laboratory research confirming that the three levels identified by Rasmussen involve different cognitive or brain processes, although there are hints here and there of multiple learning and performance mechanisms. The claim we make is that attention to these three different aspects of competence is essential for any kind of training or education that aims at high levels of performance and adaptive flexibility. It is quite possible to construct a cognitive theory that has only a single formalism for representing knowledge, including both conceptual and procedural knowledge (cf. Anderson & Gluck, chap. 8; Hunt & Lansman, 1986). But, such a unified model would still need some tools to help instructional designers determine what knowledge needs to be captured for a given training task, and whether that knowledge is usefully considered to have multiple levels or forms.

This multilevel character for technical expertise presents several major problems for those who build learning-by-doing systems. Cognitive task

TABLE 10.1
Rasmussen's Three Types of Knowledge

Knowledge Type	Description	Trigger	Example
Skills	Direct connections between perceptual recognitions and specific cognitive or behavioral actions	Perceptual features	Recognizing an unsafe condition in a plant and taking the standard action to restore safety
Rule-Based Knowledge	Specific productions for expert routine	Skills failure	Diagnosing and repairing a piece of equipment when the failure is one for which one has been trained
Conceptual Knowledge	Conceptual understanding of the domain plus mappings of this knowledge to models of domain problem situations	Rules failure plus connections between problem manifestations and relevant understanding	Diagnosing and repairing a piece of equipment when the failure is beyond the specifics of one's training

analysis methods tend to involve a mixture of demonstration by an expert of problem-solving activity and commentary by that expert on such performances. For any given problem that is solved, a given expert will use some combination of knowledge at Rasmussen's three levels. That combination may not—indeed probably will not—be the same as we would see in a trainee. For example, an expert might know a number of explicit rules that permit a rapid solution of a problem and may even recognize exactly what do to (equivalently, have a compiled rule that is directly triggered by recognition and does a major piece of the complete task). It is more likely that a trainee will not know exactly what to do and will therefore need support at the conceptual level and possibly even guidance in making inferences from conceptual understanding of the problem situation. In other cases, an expert may provide commentary that is conceptual even though neither experts nor novices actually use the conceptual knowledge in their performances.

One alternative is to focus completely on the middle, rule-based level of knowledge. This, in essence, is how the model-tracing approach of Anderson (Anderson & Corbett, 1993) works, and it does an excellent job of teaching rule-based knowledge. The problem is that often the real goals of training are not only to teach explicit algorithms for specific problems but also to expand conceptual understanding and to provide practice in the conceptually driven level of problem solving, that is, to teach for transfer. This, in turn, requires that the cognitive task analysis that drives a training system must focus heavily on the conceptual level.

One peril of such an analytic approach is that there is no limit to the potentially relevant conceptual knowledge an expert will cite when asked to state what one needs to know to understand how to work in a domain. The history of both schooling and training is replete with examples of excessive theory being taught in the absence of relevant tasks requiring the theory and also of drill on procedures not anchored to theory, as Whitehead (1929) observed. This happens because experts generally do not know explicitly how their conceptual understanding is linked to their practical (rule-based) knowledge (Chi, Glaser, & Farr, 1988). In order to make some progress in overcoming this problem, we need to have a sense of

- what the learning goals for a training course should be,
- how to extract the needed knowledge to support those goals from subject-matter experts, and
- how to use that extracted knowledge to build a strong training system.

Knowing a Fixed Algorithm
Versus Knowing a Generative Algorithm

Boshuizen and van de Wiel (1999) are among those who have explored the relationship between the knowledge acquired directly concerning routine problem situations and the more conceptual level of knowledge required to deal with the unexpected and with situations that stretch beyond one's explicit training. They have suggested an approach that, while controversial in its detailed assumptions, captures well the role of problem-based learning in building the mix of knowledge levels needed to deal with the unexpected. Writing about medical education, they noted that in trying to diagnose specific patients,

> ... links between concepts that are applied together in the diagnosis, expla-
> nation, or treatment of a patient are strengthened, leading to clusters of con-
> cepts that are closely linked; the encapsulating concepts that summarize the
> knowledge in these clusters are, in fact, no more and no less than concepts

that have acquired a central status in such a cluster, since they are directly and strongly linked to sets of clinical features, other encapsulating concepts, and causes of disease.... routine cases activate a path of encapsulating concepts between signs and symptoms and diagnosis. In more difficult cases, such a path cannot be set up instantaneously, hence spreading activation activates the underlying more detailed concepts leading to a reasoning process in which biomedical concepts play a role.

Implicit in the Boshuizen and van de Wiel formulation is the notion that simply teaching fixed algorithms and practicing cases for which the algorithms work is insufficient for producing flexible, extensible expertise, the kind needed in many modern jobs. This is an issue of practical importance. For example, hospitals employ phlebotomists who do nothing but draw blood for lab tests. Most of what they do is routine, but they must be prepared for bad reactions by patients, damaged and difficult-to-tap blood vessels and other situations that differ in part from any prior case they have experienced. We suggest that only experience combining rules with conceptually based activity can prepare a person for this kind of work.

Having rejected the idea of teaching fixed rule sets of fixed algorithms,[1] we must consider what we do want to teach. One way of thinking about this is to imagine a generative algorithm that involves a combination of specific rule-based activity with reasoning from conceptual knowledge and problem-specific data. As we see it, such a generative algorithm must include schemes for representing a problem, conceptual knowledge sufficient to drive the inference of problem solution steps from the specific details of the problem, and collections of rules for carrying out parts of the problem solution for which fixed algorithms have already been acquired. Our purpose then can be recast as learning how to teach generative algorithms for large classes of problems to trainees, including the knowledge needed to produce such training as well as the methods to be used.

---

[1]Although this rejection extends to the basic model-tracing approach of Anderson and his colleagues (Anderson & Corbett, 1993), it is important to note that the relevant transfer studies to support such a rejection have not been performed. It is quite possible that acquisition of certain rule systems results in a more general ability to transfer to tasks those systems cannot quite handle by themselves. We do have at least "proof of concept" data that the approach we describe in this chapter will yield such transfer (Gott & Lesgold, in press).

PROBLEMS
OF MULTIPLE REPRESENTATION LEVELS

There are a few problems in specifying the multiple knowledge levels needed for expert performance. First, there is no guarantee that the terms used and the forms of encoding for a given object will be the same in each level. Often, the engineering knowledge behind a particular system is a mixture of many different forms. For example, in work we are doing training people who repair ion beam implant devices, we see signs of competence that can be related to various snippets of knowledge from quantum physics, magnetics, optics, and physical chemistry, and it is not clear that the technicians really think about the systems in exactly the terms of any of those domains of knowledge, although their knowledge bears family resemblance to aspects of each.

Further, most technicians have gaps in any one form of knowledge that could support expert performance. They do well precisely because their knowledge, although fragmentary from any one viewpoint, is redundant with respect to the demands made on it. This makes knowledge engineering extremely difficult. Even if every technician in a particular job had the same fragmentary knowledge, the same gaps, and the same redundancies, it is never as easy to teach partly incoherent knowledge as it is to use it once it happens to be acquired. Somehow, a means must be found for building sufficient but flexible competence in technical jobs without forcing the prior acquisition of all the relevant areas of conceptual understanding as a prerequisite to having a particular job.[2]

An additional problem is the lack of certainty that the constructs of one body of knowledge will translate easily into those of another. Consider medicine, for example. Diseases arise and are defined by their symptoms. Over time, the medical world learns associations between particular symptoms and particular diseases. While all this is happening clinically, medical scientists are also trying to understand the mechanisms of a particular disease. Sometimes, it can occur that a diagnostic rule or a treatment rule can develop completely independent of any substantial underlying conceptual understanding. An example of this might be seen in the development of aspirin. At first, certain natural substances like wintergreen were associated with pain relief. Then, the chemistry of salicy-

---

[2]We fully value deep understanding and the teaching of core concepts in ways that achieve completeness and coherence of understanding. However, it may not be practical to insist on this conceptual completeness as a minimal requirement for a job.

lates was understood well enough to begin refining acetylsalicylic acid. Then, molecular manipulations were performed in hopes of producing compounds that might be more effective, still without complete knowledge of how aspirin-type drugs worked. Only very late in the process has the mechanism of aspirin become understood. In turn, this has provided a more coherent understanding of why some chemicals work better than others. However, that knowledge is generally in a language that many health care workers refer to minimally if at all, even though they dispense a lot of aspirin.

Consider, then, how one might tutor a nurse-practitioner today on issues relating to aspirin. For the most part, the practical knowledge of when to administer aspirin remains about what it was before the drug's effects were well understood. A few new uses that have become clear with the improved chemical and pharmaceutical knowledge—like using aspirin in first responses to apparent heart attacks—can be taught as rules just as earlier rules were taught. However, it must surely be the case that aspects of an understanding of how aspirin works could be useful in dealing with difficult cases. Perhaps only physicians need this additional knowledge, but there surely is need for reliable expertise with drugs like aspirin that has access to all the relevant pharmacology and can apply it when rule-based decision making is insufficient. Ideally, this conceptual knowledge would be linked to specific characteristics of situations that can benefit from its use.

A Hypothesis

As noted earlier, Boshuizen and van de Wiel (1999) argued based on earlier work by Boshuizen and Schmidt (1992), that experience with a specific problem (in their work, a medical case) provides an opportunity for linking the various bits of knowledge that are related to the solution of that problem. This would include both specific rules and various fragments of conceptual knowledge that might come up during problem solution, including comments from tutors, ideas considered and abandoned, and so forth. Further, experience with difficult problems itself provides interconnections among the different levels of practical knowledge. As Boshuizen and Schmidt (1992) noted:

> A critical body of knowledge needed for effective performance of complex tasks—and hence for coaching of that performance—is the collection of connections between rule-based and conceptually-driven representations of the task domain.... [R]epeated applications of biomedical knowledge in

clinical reasoning at the earlier stages of development toward medical
expertise result[s] in the subsumption of lower level, detailed [biomedical]
propositions under higher level, sometimes clinical propositions.

The Encapsulation
(Schematization) Process

A general plan for encapsulating or schematizing knowledge from cases
seems to have evolved in the cognitive apprenticeship literature (cf.
Boshuizen & Schmidt, 1992; Brown, Collins, & Duguid, 1991; Collins,
Brown, & Newman, 1989). The plan has three basic parts:

- Develop an articulate conceptual framework
- Reflect on situated rule-driven performances in real task situations
- Elaborate connections between situated (and rule-driven) knowl-
  edge and the global framework

There are natural roles for tutoring in this kind of scheme. First, the
tutor can present at least a rough skeleton of a conceptual framework that
the trainee can use to organize new knowledge and experience. Then, it
can support a process of reflection on the experiences of solving a particular problem or otherwise dealing with a particular situation. Finally, the
tutor can help the trainee discover some of the powerful connections
between successful performance in the situation and the conceptual
knowledge base(s) that can facilitate that performance. There are a number of different ways that such tutors can work.

Designing Learning Systems
to Support Encapsulation

The overall goal of a tutor, within this viewpoint, is to find ways to connect conceptual knowledge to "clinical" or rule-driven knowledge. There
are several ways this might be done, varying mostly in the grain size of
the effort to connect rule-based and conceptual knowledge. Generally,
those systems that focus on teaching a body of conceptual knowledge
using problems as a means of shaping concepts work with coarse-grained
connections between specific problem situations, specific concepts, and
concept networks. So, for example, VanLehn's ANDES system (Gertner,
Conati, & VanLehn, 1998) attempts to determine what knowledge is present and what is absent in a student's understanding of mechanics, based

on the student's problem-solving performance. What is unique to the ANDES approach, though, is multiple levels of focus. One addition to ANDES deals exclusively with self-explanation and coaches the student to carefully work through each example problem solved by the expert system, explaining why each expert step was taken (Conati & VanLehn, 1999). Another variant provides a small minilesson covering, in a coherent way, a set of concepts that seem relevant to the kinds of mistakes the student has been making (Albacete, 1999).

An alternative approach, which we discuss in more detail later, is to provide very explicit links between particular features of problem situations and particular bits of conceptual knowledge. The advantage of this approach is that it focuses very directly on the specific problem of linking conceptual and other knowledge forms around specific problems. The possible disadvantage is that there may be little connection built up between the various conceptual fragments triggered by different problem situations. Compared to the macrolevel approach of VanLehn and his colleagues, this microapproach promotes connections among knowledge bases explicitly and assumes that linkages within a knowledge base will be handled by the trainee or will have been previously acquired. The VanLehn approach makes less complete explicit connections between problem situational specifics and conceptual knowledge, leaving some of that work to the student, but its variants seem to foster learning of more intraknowledge base connections by addressing them more explicitly. However, neither approach was designed to test this distinction; further research is needed to identify how explicit these different kinds of connections must be in the course of coaching complex problem solving.

FORMS OF KNOWLEDGE NEEDED
TO SUPPORT LEARNING BY DOING

Learning by doing systems require several forms of data in order to be fully effective. In this section, we describe these data varieties. To be more concrete, we speak of the needs for a specific class of learning by doing systems, namely systems that teach diagnosis of complex equipment failures. Later, we discuss how these requirements generalize to other areas of learning. The following knowledge bases are needed for building such systems; (1) a simulation of the technicians' work environment; (2) specifications for a set of problems that reasonably cover the range of difficult-to-diagnose failures that we would like technicians to be able to handle; (3) a set of rules that capture sufficient expertise to permit the training system to solve every problem used for training; and (4) to support coaching, a set of conceptual principles that connect specific troubleshooting rules to core principles that lie behind the thinking experts bring to difficult problems.

It is important to bear in mind the three forms of expertise identified by Rasmussen when considering what knowledge is needed. Rasmussen suggested that technicians often operate at a level of practiced routine, in which they simply recognize what to do based on automated, overlearned perceptual knowledge. When that fails, Rasmussen suggested, they elevate their cognitive processing to a richer representation of the task situation, to which they apply domain-specific operating rules. When that also fails, they elevate further and apply weak methods (general problem-solving strategies) to their conceptual representation of the problem.

When we look at the goals of the training systems we have built, we see that we are preparing technicians for the nonroutine parts of their work, the really hard stuff. We did not focus on the practiced routine—that seems to be handled well by cheaper approaches. We also did not focus on the more common components of rule-based expertise, because again that seems to get acquired via experience and "war stories." Rather, we focused on a mixture of the conceptually based "weak methods" reasoning and the most sophisticated of the rule-based processing, the parts most dependent on a powerful representation of the work domain in systemic terms. Connecting specific troubleshooting rules with deeper conceptual content is a critical part of building the knowledge base for that kind of learning by doing system. Further, because expertise does leverage the rule-based and skills levels of knowledge when appropriate, we need to be sure that the most important aspects of those levels are captured as well. We now consider these various knowledge requirements.

No matter which knowledge forms are most critical to achieving particular learning or training goals, it is likely that a number of different forms will be needed to support one aspect or another of an effective coached learning environment. First, the work environment itself must be represented so that it can be simulated. In addition, expert rule-based problem-solving knowledge must be represented, because it is helpful for the system to be able to demonstrate how a problem can be solved or to take over in the midst of problem solution if the student is completely stymied. As we have already discussed, the conceptual knowledge that supports expert procedures must be defined and its connections to rule-based knowledge explicitly represented. Finally, a rationale must be developed for selecting learning tasks (problems for the student to solve).

The Work Environment

The relevant knowledge base about the environment for which students are being trained includes all of the attributes and methods needed to produce the level of simulation relevant to training. At one time, we had hoped that knowledge related to the work environment could be imported automatically from design databases used in building the work place (e.g., the computer-assisted design databases used in developing new machinery). Although part of the needed knowledge can indeed come from that source, additional knowledge must come from experts who use or maintain the work environment. Specifically, we need to be concerned with three aspects of knowledge structure here, the *contents of the individual objects* that comprise the device simulation, the *classification hierarchies* that interrelate those concepts, and the *information paths* that comprise the work environment.

Function. The content of individual objects in the work environment can indeed be extracted from documentation of the environment's design, for example, vendor manuals. In addition, though, it is important to know how experts organize the work environment into functional subsystems. This expert knowledge should be used to organize how the work environment is represented. The interface for access to the simulation should have a hierarchical display and menu scheme that recapitulates the expert decomposition of the work environment.[3] This allows every interaction with the interface to reinforce in the trainee a decomposition of the system that experts would apply. The purposes of components and subsystems need to be recorded as part of the knowledge base as well.

Classification and Flows. In addition, the various components of the work environment need to be organized categorically, into an inheritance hierarchy. This is important in developing the object definitions that turn the knowledge base into a learning environment. Another kind of knowledge needs to come from experts, too. This is knowledge about the flows of material, energy, and information between components. Consider, for example, the path that antifreeze takes in the engine of your

---

[3]Note that we speak of the interface to a training system, not a work interface. Making the interface look like the work environment would make it quicker to use, but then the interface would not teach the trainee anything. By organizing it to reflect expert thinking, it becomes an instructional tool. This will work so long as the interface remains understandable and navigable by the trainee.

car (see Fig. 10.1). The engine receives coolant from the radiator and transmits it to the heater core. If the water pump fails, then the engine will receive no coolant. So, we can define the water pump in part as passing on input water at a particular flow rate when it is running and otherwise, as simply blocking the line. Further, if we could verify that the radiator has a good water flow through it, we could infer that the water pump is at least partly operative. This sort of information, on what can be inferred about other system components from any given observation of some particular component, is needed to drive simulations of the work environment. Each component must know which other components to "tell" when its inputs or outputs change. And the input–output relationships within a component also must be represented. Much of this connection information can be inferred from the design documents for a machine, but some may need to be extracted from a technical expert. Also, design documents may contain a great deal of information that is not relevant to a particular problem domain. The expert often sees this as noise to be filtered out, and in complex domains, failure to filter out this "noise" produces cognitive overload and thus limited performance.

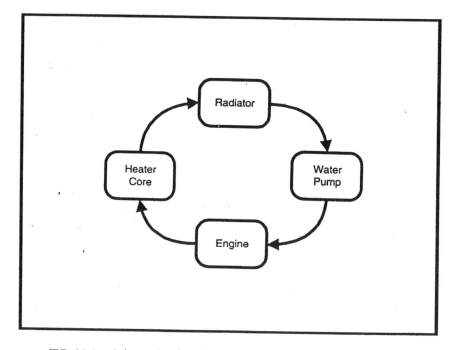

FIG. 10.1.   Schematic of cooling system.

The Data That Signal a Problem. In order to present learning by doing simulations that are contextualized, it is necessary to acquire information about how problems manifest themselves. For example, if we were building a water pump tutor, we would need to know that water pump problems can manifest themselves via the signal for an overheated engine, through certain kinds of noises associated with a breakdown of the bearings or the rotating parts, and perhaps occasionally through large puddles of water under the car. Experts use this kind of symptom or context information to shape a representation of the problem and a plan for its solution.

Often, various kinds of instrument and console displays are part of the work environment. In such cases, part of the staging of a problem will include aspects of these displays. Figure 10.2 shows an example of this from a training system built by a joint team of Intel and University of Pittsburgh colleagues. In this case, a special kind of display illustrating the surface of a wafer (from a computer chip processing machine) is

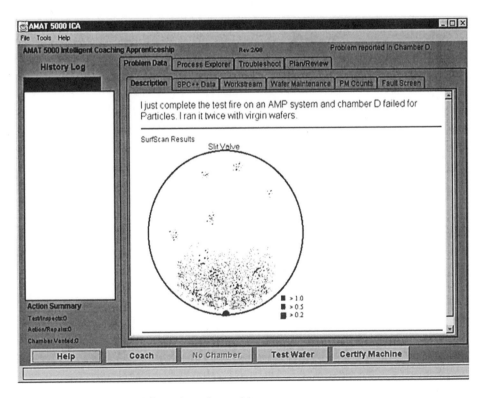

FIG. 10.2.   Initial staging of a problem.

included in the specification of the problem, and other tabs in the display frame (e.g., "SPC++ Data") provide access to additional displays from various consoles that might be relevant to the problem. Overall, a number of forms of data that fix the context for a problem may be needed, including some that need not be dynamically represented during the process of problem solving. For example, the log of past actions on a machine can be represented statically—the past will not change while a trainee is working on a problem. On the other hand, a statistical process control (SPC) chart may well need to be incremented as the technician cycles the system through activities that would ordinarily produce chart entries.

Expert Diagnostic Knowledge

Rules.   In any domain of expertise, much of routine activity is, as previously noted, rule driven. Consequently, it is important to identify the rules that characterize the process the expert uses to represent and solve a problem. These can be inferred from protocols of experts solving target problems out loud or, even better, by having experts go through a trace of their actual diagnostic activity while solving a problem, giving a justification for each action taken and an indication of what was learned from taking that action. As Gott has suggested (Gott, 1987; Gott, Bennett, & Gillet, 1986; Hall, Gott, & Pokorny, 1995; Means & Gott, 1988), much of this information can be gathered using a "stimulated recall" approach,[4] which is discussed later. As is discussed later, various tools are available that allow an analyst both to identify statements in thinking-aloud protocols from which rules should be inferred and to generate rules efficiently from those statements.

Expectations About Actions.   In addition to explicit cognitive rules, experts often have expectations about the results of an action. This permits a relatively automated level of self-monitoring in which the violation of an expectation becomes a signal that the expert's model of the

---

[4]We have not been able to find the source of the term *stimulated recall*, although it seems to have become a widely used method (e.g., Ericcson & Simon, 1993; Nunan, 1992; Wixon & Ramey, 1996). Basically, it refers to a scheme in which a think-aloud protocol is recorded, usually on video but not always, and then the person who did the thinking aloud is stepped back through the protocol and asked focused questions about each step of the problem solution process. Gott and her colleagues used a variation in which the protocol was taken down in notes by a knowledge analyst who then cycled through each recorded step asking several specific questions about each.

current task situation needs repairs. It is quite reasonable to represent many expert rules in the form

IF <condition> THEN do <action> and EXPECT <outcome>

Other rules presumably are learned that have the satisfaction or nonsatisfaction of an expectation as their conditions. A specific kind of violation of expectations can itself signal an appropriate next step in the problem solution process. In some areas of expertise, the relatively automated ability of experts to check their decision making by generating expectations and monitoring whether they are met is especially important. For example, the tendency of physicians to converge on a diagnostic schema quickly is counterbalanced by their ability to do quick checks on whether the triggered schema matches the current situation (cf. Lesgold, 1984).

A further role for expectations is to stimulate the conceptual knowledge-driven level of cognitive activity. Rasmussen et al. (1994) suggested that failure of lower levels of knowledge to drive problem solution triggers higher levels of knowledge. Whereas some such failures will arise from other kinds of impasses—"I don't know what to do here"— very often it will be the violation of an expectation that triggers conceptually driven processing. If an intelligent learning by doing system for training is to address the multiple levels of expertise, then it needs to include information about expectations for actions, especially actions driven by perceptual motor or rule-based knowledge.

Expert Conceptual Knowledge

Expert conceptual knowledge is most useful for intelligent learning by doing systems when it is interconnected with the manifestations that can occur in training problems. This allows the conceptual knowledge to be made available at times when it can be connected to situations in which it might be needed, thus avoiding Whitehead's "inert knowledge" problem. However, it has always proven difficult to organize conceptual understanding in this way. In school, this happens in a somewhat degenerate form when a class is presented a collection of problems in a specific form directly tied to the day's lesson, after which that form may never appear in class again. For example, physics classes offer inclined plane problems, and algebra classes have their unit on mixture problems. This level of attachment of conceptual knowledge is too coarse grained. In real life, we do not encounter pure mixture problems all on a single day or pure

inclined plane problems for one week and then no longer. We need to connect conceptual knowledge to something more like a symptom or manifestation of a problem. This may produce multiple candidate fragments of
potentially relevant conceptual knowledge, but at least it will bring the
right candidates to mind at the right time.

Martin Nahemow developed this idea in a particular instructional
device he calls a *process explorer*. Basically, the idea is to organize conceptual knowledge according to kinds of functions served by various
aspects of the work environment. For example, in machines that put layers onto silicon wafers as part of the process of making computer chips,
plasma processes are involved. This means that some of the basic functions in such machines include the delivery of various gasses into the
chamber in which a plasma reaction will take place, provision of energy
to the chamber in the form of heat and electrical power with certain properties (voltage and frequency), and robotic processes that move the wafer
to the right place, and so forth.

But this is not enough. These causal aspects must be mapped onto the
outcomes that can occur in the work environment (in the present example,
that environment is a wafer layering machine). This mapping can be formalized as a matrix that maps the connections between problem specification data and a prioritized set of functional models. This requires that
we distinguish two different mappings of models and other practical and
conceptual knowledge. In designing a system (i.e., a work environment),
one implicitly is developing a process matrix P_{ij} that maps functional
models, here represented by a vector F_j of parts of the system (often seen
by the expert explicitly as subsystems) into states or parameters of the system's outputs, here represented by a vector N_i;

$$N_i = P_{ij} \times \{F_j\}$$

One difficulty is that much of instruction has traditionally consisted of
explication of this set of relationships that drive a system's design.
However, when problems occur in a system, a different set of relationships
must be known, namely the relationships between subsystem models and
deviations of the system's outputs from accepted levels. This deviation can
be is represented by a vector Δ_i and the critical mappings for training problem solving then are represented by a matrix M_{ij} such that $F_j = M_{ij} \times \{\Delta_i\}$

Thinking more broadly, P_{ij} could be thought of as the engineer's
worldview and M_{ij} as the technician's worldview. One of the most chal-

lenging tasks for knowledge engineering results from the fact that M_{ij} and P_{ij} are often rather orthogonal. Generally, there is no way to map one into the other directly or to observe them both at the same time. For coaching purposes in a learning by doing system, we must capture the essence of the troubleshooting experts' worldview and knowledge. This must be consistent with the engineering model but may not be easily related to it. And, it is seldom articulated as completely or available as readily as the engineer's worldview. Yet, we think that directly teaching the relationships in the technicians' worldview, M_{ij}, is a critical part of effective intelligent coached apprenticeship.

We have developed a practical form—which we call the *process explorer*—that is suitable for making conceptual knowledge available to trainees for examination during problem solving. It consists of a matrix corresponding to M_{ij} for which each cell is a hyperlink to an explanation of the relationship between a problem state defined by Δ_i and a functional model F_j. The icon for each hyperlink is drawn to represent the type of relationship between the problem manifested by Δ_i and the functional subsystem represented by F_j. For example, if a manifestation like grit on the wafer were more likely when the heat system was not delivering sufficient heat, then the cell in M_{ij} representing the connection between heat and grit might contain a $\downarrow$ to show that when heat drops, grit increases. Such icons themselves might give the trainee enough of a hint to help him or her limit the set of subsystems that could cause the set of fault indicators, and the hyperlinks could connect to additional graphics and text that further enhance the understanding of relationships and allow for finer tuning of the development of an action plan.

In addition to being part of the mapping between conceptual knowledge and problem manifestations, the breakdown of conceptual knowledge according to functional subsystems of the work environment also supports a scheme for reifying expert functional understanding in the interface to the simulated work environment. We have used schematic diagrams as parts of the menu systems that trainees use to access specific components of the simulated work environment. Each functional subsystem in the simulation is represented by a schematic diagram that shows all the system components that can be acted on within that subsystem.

One important task is to decide on the submatrix of the complete mapping M_{ij} that should be on the screen for a given problem. Ordinarily, one specific cell of the matrix will contain the symptom–concept mapping that is directly relevant to the solution of the problem being posed. However, in order to support search of the problem space and in order not to give away the solution to the problem, it is important to display more of the mapping than that single cell. On the other hand, the matrix is quite large and likely to be confusing if presented in its entirety. So, it is necessary to decide on an appropriate submatrix for each problem that contains cells that might be the basis for sensible query but does not contain irrelevant rows or columns. This can be done by working from the matrix cell that represents the problem in two directions. First, the matrix should include, as rows, all conceptual categories with strong associations to the particular experience the problem manifests (e.g., if the problem is excess stress, then show all conceptual categories associated with a deviation in stress). Second, the experiential categories associated with the most likely conceptual categories should be represented as columns of the process explorer matrix. An example of an actual submatrix for a problem in one of our systems is shown in Fig. 10.3. The basic idea is that the technician

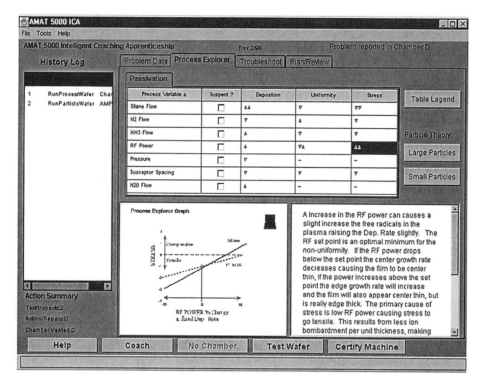

FIG. 10.3.   Example of process explorer.

will tend to notice some category of malfunction in the system he is being trained to fix, such as excessive stress on the surfaces of wafers coming out of the machine (i.e., the surface layers are excessively pulling the outside of the wafer toward the center, which can produce curling). He can then look in the column labeled stress to see which subsystems or system parameters are associated with this kind of problem. In Fig. 10.3, this can be seen in the matrix cell that has been darkened because the trainee clicked on it. That cell showed a strong positive relationship between the output of the RF power unit and the amount of excessive stress. Clicking on the relationship (indicated by the symbol ↑↑) produces a display of both the functional relationship between RF power levels and stress (lower left) and a textual explanation of the cause of this relationship (lower right).

The Problem Set

The final form of knowledge that must be gathered to support learning by doing is a class of troubleshooting problems that span the range of situation types that an expert can expect to face. Presumably, the first concern in developing a problem set is to "cover" the conceptual hierarchy. That is, each kind of system breakdown should be represented in one or more problems. If enough resources exist, one scheme would be to look at the set of surface manifestations for each conceptual category that bears a strong relationship to it and write a problem for each such pairing. For example, if there are a set of conceptual categories of problem areas F_j and a set of experiential categories of failures Δ_i, then the set of problems is given by the set of ij pairs for which $p(\Delta_i/F_j) \geq \Theta$, where Θ is the lowest level of event probability for which we want to provide training. That set will likely be too large. Although no pruning process is guaranteed to work, those selection schemes that give some exposure to each of the functional subsystems seem most sensible.

One reasonable scheme is to define the problem set after a preliminary round of task analysis aimed at defining P_{ij} and M_{ij}. Having these defined permits a rational approach to specifying a sufficient set of problems, namely to attempt to cover as many of the cells of M_{ij} as possible, or, as suggested earlier, at least as many of the rows and columns as possible. Once the problem set is defined, it may be appropriate to revisit the specification of the simulation, the process explorer content, and the expert rule set to be sure that all and only the knowledge needed for training using the defined problem set is specified. Put another way, any iteration in the process of task analysis and system development will pivot on the problem set. The other knowledge is needed to specify roughly a sensible problem set, and the final problem set is the appropriate base for testing the adequacy of the rest of the knowledge base for the training system.

TOOLS
FOR BUILDING LEARNING SYSTEMS

Initial Domain Constraints

The following schemes aim at representing expertise in solving troubleshooting problems. Although a perfect sense of the boundaries of relevant knowledge may not be attainable until one has done some of the task analysis tasks described later, we have still found it useful to do a quick front-end analysis that aims at producing a preliminary set of problems for which detailed task analysis can then be performed. We are doing further work on the specifics of this preliminary or front-end work, but we do know already that front-end analysis can help to constrain the overall task analysis job and therefore to make it more valuable.

The Knowledge Gathering Process

The basic knowledge engineering method is to record an expert solving a problem while thinking aloud, to infer a set of rules from the recorded verbal protocol, to apply those rules to solutions of related problems, to get expert critique of the rule-based solutions, and then to edit the rules to take account of the critique. The last three steps (solve using rules, get critique, edit rules) are iterated as necessary until the rules seem to work adequately. This approach is sufficient when the goal is simply to establish the rule system that an intelligent tutoring system is to train. However, it is insufficient when the broader goals of learning by doing are present.

Several approaches have been developed to facilitate gathering the richer data needed for systems that support deeper learning. One, mentioned earlier, was the PARI (Precursor–Action–Result–Interpretation) method (Gott, 1987; Gott et al., 1986; Hall, et al., 1995; Means & Gott, 1988). In this approach, several additional steps are added to the stimulated recall approach previously discussed. Experts solve real-world problems that are presented verbally, with the tester providing a verbal response to each proposed action. For example, if the domain were flashlight repair and the problem was to figure out why a flashlight is not working, the expert might suggest testing the voltage drop across each of the flashlight's batteries. The tester would then tell the expert what voltage levels to assume, the expert would then propose a next action, the tester would indicate the result, and so on until the expert stated a proposed repair. The tester would then tell the expert whether the repair was successful. After this process was completed, the tester would walk the expert through each of the actions he took, asking, in turn, four questions about each:

- Precursor: What did you know at this point, prior to taking this next action?
- Action: What actions were potentially reasonable, and why did you pick the one you picked?
- Result: What were the possible results of your action?
- Interpretation: What did you learn given the results that actually were reported to you?

From the combination of the actual problem-solving steps and the subsequent responses to the probe questions, it is possible to develop a list of the subsystems and components that need to be understood in order for problems of the type used to be solved expertly. From the response to the various queries, it is possible to develop the specifications of the expert conceptual and diagnostic knowledge that are embodied in the solution offered by the expert. So, the PARI approach is extremely useful for getting from problem solution protocols to a knowledge specification. However, more work is needed in order to get all the knowledge described in the previous section.

One additional requirement is the clear specification of the knowledge that might be available and relevant to initial specification of the problem. It is necessary to ask experts about this specifically. Further probing is needed to establish all the knowledge relevant to the device simulation and to experts' structuring of their own representations of the device. This process can begin with a list of system components mentioned during the solutions to various problems that are generated as part of the PARI process just described. Then, it can be useful to get from experts a sense of how these components should be classified. This can be done through card-sorting processes or through the use of tools for specifying inheritance hierarchies (the card sort and laddering tools from Shadbolt's PC PACK suite, described later, are useful for this purpose).

The precursor information can be used to develop rules that will become part of the expert diagnostic knowledge component of the knowledge base. Suppose that prior to taking action α_i, the expert noted precursor states π_1, π_2, π_3, π_4, and π_5. This might prompt a task analyst to propose a candidate rule of

IF π_1, π_2, π_3, π_4, and π_5 THEN α_i

This rule could be edited further by discussing it directly with the expert, and it would certainly need to be tested as part of the overall rule base.

Similarly, the expected-results information can be used to generate additional candidate rules, especially if the expert is probed for the implications of the possible outcomes to any action he takes. For example, when diagnosing a flashlight, if one measures the voltage levels of the batteries, there are two basic outcomes. Either the voltage level is close to nominal for a functioning battery (1.5v for lead-zinc batteries), or it is close to zero. If the batteries are weak, then the solution is to replace them. On the other hand, if they are adequate, then an expert might move on to examine the bulb. This simple choice can itself be expressed as a couple of rules:

IF battery-voltage-level « 1.2v, THEN replace battery

IF battery-voltage-level ≈ 1.5v, THEN assume-battery-good AND assess-lightbulb

Rule editors (discussed below) can be helpful in formulating rules from the problem-solving protocols and the probe questions. Any such formulation, however, is an induction from a single instance and must be validated. This validation, moreover, cannot be completed until the entire set of problems for a training system has been defined, because the ultimate test of any rule is that it contributes to (or at least does not interfere with) an efficient solution for each problem in the domain. For this reason, expert diagnostic knowledge must be tested repeatedly and not accepted until it is proven to work successfully with any problem that falls within the scope of the domain for which the training system is being built.

It is sometimes possible to infer certain kinds of rules from declarative knowledge. Consider, for example, Table 10.2, which one might build based on the knowledge needed to simulate working and broken flashlights.

This table could be used to infer a set of rules that would probably be an adequate set for this very simple domain. What is not present in the

TABLE 10.2
Device Information From Which Rule Might Be Inferred

Item	State	Manifestation
Batteries	Adequate	Voltage ≈ 1.5v
	Inadequate	Voltage << 1.5v
Bulb	Working	Filament appears intact
	Not Working	Filament appears broken
Switch	Working	Continuous path (low resistance) through switch on; high resistance when off
	Not Working	Resistance constant whether on or off
Caps	Working	Screwed fully into position
	Not Working	Not screwed down completely or lopsided

information of the table, however, is any information about the optimal sequence for carrying out the possible actions. Still, it can be useful to have inference engines to build rule sets from this kind of data, because often it is easier for experts to provide data in tabular form.

Deciding on Conceptual Knowledge and Connecting It to Problem Contexts

Determining the necessary conceptual knowledge to include in a coached learning environment and the connections that knowledge should have to particular problem situations involves several steps. The relevant knowledge must be identified, and it must be linked to problem contexts for which it is relevant. A crude way to do this is simply to note any conceptual content that is provided by subject matter experts during the precursor and interpretation phases of the PARI method previously discussed. From the specifics of expert replies to the PARI probes, it is generally possible to determine whether the expert relied on conceptual knowledge to take a step or simply added such knowledge as an elaboration of the account of problem-solving activity.

For example, if the action taken by an expert technician and the PARI responses he or she provided suggest a specific diagnostic rule and the subject matter (engineering or design) expert confirms that this is a good rule, then there was probably not much reliance on conceptual knowledge to take the action. On the other hand, if no rule seems both to fit the technician expert's actions and to gain acceptance by the subject matter expert, then it is likely that the technician expert had to appeal to conceptual knowledge to arrive at the action taken. In this case, the relevant conceptual knowledge is likely to be in the precursor and interpretation replies, although follow-up confirmation is desirable if time and resources permit.

As the body of conceptual tidbits (the rows of the matrix that maps conceptual knowledge to problem situation features) and the contexts to which they are tied (the cells of the mapping matrix) accumulate, it becomes necessary to place some further organization on both. The organization of a set of conceptual knowledge fragments will be determined by the disciplinary character of those pieces. For example, if there are a number of pieces of conceptual knowledge that all deal with the gas laws of temperature and pressure, then it may be sensible to collapse these into a single explanation of those laws that connects a number of more specific instantiations of that basic account. In one system for which we designed training, problems tended to involve abnormal aspects of gas delivery, of energy supplied to certain reactions, and of robotic transport, so those could have become the organizing categories for conceptual knowledge for that domain. The instantiations become part of the content for the cells in the process explorer matrix that connect the gas laws with particular problem contexts (an example is given by the lower right section of Fig. 10.3).

The contexts that are represented by the columns of the mapping matrix can themselves be organized in a number of ways, depending on which situational features are important in the domain's expertise and how fault states are defined. For example, in one training system for repair of a certain computer chip-making machine, we had broad context features like grit on the wafers, improper wafer thickness, and surface stress outside of quality limits. We might have chosen other categories if they seemed more salient to technicians, such as valve problems, robotic problems, electrical problems, and so forth.

The choices of categorization schemes for both rows and columns of the mapping matrix are important. It is rare for complete linkage and conceptual information to come out of a single round of task analysis with PARI probing. Rather, it is generally necessary iteratively to

- add to the mapping matrix based on responses to postsolution probing (e.g., PARI),
- organize the rows and columns categorically, checking for missing rows and columns (kinds of knowledge or situations that experts feel were left out),
- develop more problems to cover the matrix (as discussed earlier), and then
- gather additional data from experts who solve those problems and then respond to probe questions.

Some Available Tools

Tools to support cognitive task analysis are extremely important to efficient development of training systems. The high cost and inadequate results of many instructional and training technology efforts have been due partly to a lack of schemata for assuring the completeness and depth of the analyses performed and also to a gap between the discursive style of many analyses and the knowledge structures needed to support rich learning by doing approaches. Even in our own work, we initially found that we needed to add additional knowledge acquisition sessions at the last minute, because content was incomplete or insufficiently understood. In the industrial environments in which we work, a single extra knowledge acquisition trip may generate $5,000 to 20,000 in added costs for travel, replacement on the factory floor of experts being interviewed, transcription, and so forth. Given that we aim for a technology that can produce a learning by doing system for under $100,000 (we're not quite there yet), we cannot afford unpredicted costs in this range. So, tools and approaches that assure completeness are essential to our work, especially those that cut the interval between initial interviews and final data structure specification.

Because tools for cognitive task analysis have coevolved with analytic approaches, one way to better understand some of the methods for getting knowledge from experts is to look at some of the tools that have been built. We focus in this section on tools built by Nigel Shadbolt and his colleagues and now sold as a product called PC PACK.[5] This is a tightly

---

[5]See http://www.epistemics.co.uk/ for information on PC PACK, which is a trade name of Epistemics, Ltd. The authors have no connection with Epistemics, Ltd. We simply chose to use it as an example because the particular tools it contains match well with our overall approach. Our own work has used self-built tools (largely developed by Dan Peters at LRDC, now at Intel, and Scott Smith at Intel) because we needed a few capabilities not included in PC PACK and because we did not have time to train our colleagues to use the PC PACK system given the deadlines set for the project.

integrated set that has a number of useful components. While we have not found it perfect for our needs, it has been useful, and we have been stimulated by it to develop some of our own, more tailored tools.

One reason for picking this particular tool kit as an example is that it is object based. That is, any component that is explicitly or implicitly identified through the use of any of the tools is represented in an object database that is active whenever any of the tools are being used. Further, because a given kind of object can be identified many different ways, it is important that the tools be integrated. So, for example, a concept that is identified through marking a word or a phrase with a protocol mark-up tool will also be available to tools like the card-sorting tool and the tool for developing inheritance hierarchies.

Protocol Editor.   As we consider each kind of knowledge needed for a learning by doing system, we can see that each would benefit from some specific tools. In addition, certain more general tools are broadly useful. One such general tool is a protocol editor. This is a tool that takes the transcript of an interview with an expert and allows it to be marked up to indicate the categories with which each statement should be associated. The most important categories for learning by doing include concepts, attributes, values, relations, and rules. Figure 10.4 provides an example of a piece of protocol document that is marked with one color in two places to indicate text implying a rule and another color in one place to indicate text implying a process. The ability to systematically catalog all prose segments that imply the need for various knowledge structures is extremely important in making the protocol analysis process efficient and complete.

Card Sort Tool.   Another tool in the Epistemics PC PACK is the card sort tool. From the earliest cognitive task analyses designed to support the building of learning by doing systems (cf. Gitomer, 1988), one way to get attributes and values assigned to objects is via card-sorting tasks. The expert is given cards on which the names of objects are placed and asked to sort them into groups that share properties. Once this scheme has gone far enough for those properties to be identified and labeled, then additional concepts can be sorted into those categories.

PC PACK supports this via a virtual card-sorting scheme. Attributes and values are assembled into hierarchical lists, and then concepts can be dragged on the screen into the appropriate "pile." For example, in one

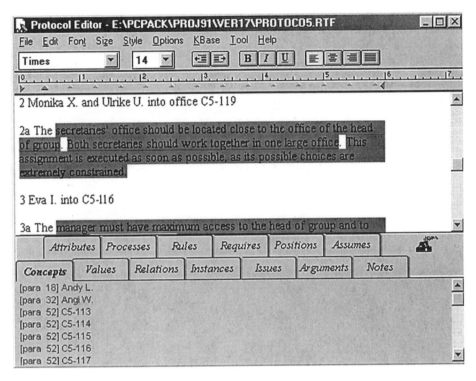

FIG. 10.4.   Example of PC PACK protocol editor.

recent task analysis to support development of an intelligent coached apprenticeship environment, it turned out that experts roughly classified components of a complex system as energy related, gas related, or mechanical–robotic (the system used energy and gasses to create plasma fields into which other objects had to be transported very precisely). Once this distinction is mentioned in an interview, it is possible either to record enough interview content to permit later concept sorting by the task analyst or even to let the expert use a card-sorting tool to classify system components him or herself. Figure 10.5 shows an example of a few "cards" naming components of a mythical system sorted into the three "piles" indicated above. These cards would likely have been generated automatically after a knowledge analyst marked phrases in an interview transcript or the documentation for the system involved, perhaps using the protocol editor described earlier.

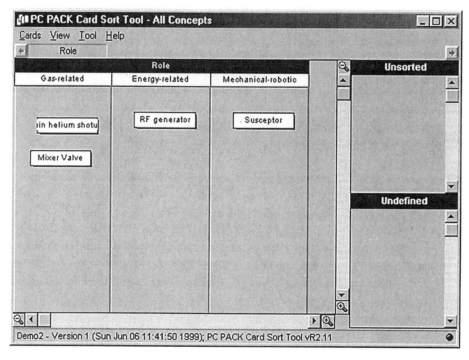

FIG. 10.5.   Card Sort Tool.

Laddering Tool.   The laddering tool supports the accumulation of
attribute and category information through a different approach, namely
hierarchy specification. This can also be an effective way to conduct part
of the task analysis needed to support training system development.
Consider, for example, the concepts sorted in Fig. 10.6. If one were to
begin developing an inheritance hierarchy for these concepts (i.e., a hierarchy that showed the level of abstraction at which different properties are
defined for various classes of objects), it might look something like that
shown in Fig. 10.6. The laddering tool in PC PACK permits cognitive analysts to build such hierarchies directly. New concepts can be added to a
list, and individual concept boxes dragged to appropriate places in the
hierarchy. As with everything else in PC PACK, information represented
with the laddering tool is automatically included in relevant object definitions that are stored in the object database. Figure 10.7 shows one example of a simple object definition that was created by the placement of the
"mixing valve" box in the laddering display. From the laddering display,
the system has noted that mixing valve is an instance of "gas-related
device." If any properties were defined for all gas-related devices, they
would automatically be "inherited" by the mixing valve.

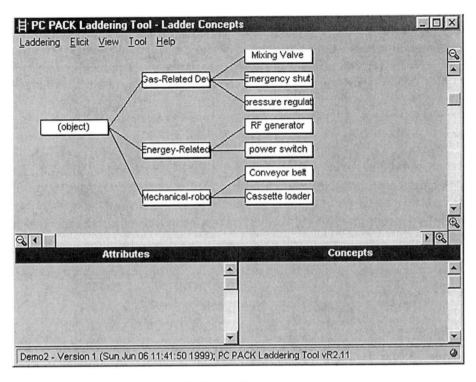

FIG. 10.6. Example of Laddering Tool.

This ability to convert the manipulations of a knowledge-gathering interface into formalized objects is a central part of the tool requirement for efficient cognitive task analysis. Software designers can elaborate computational objects so that they include not only attributes and values but also "methods." For example, one use we made of an object architecture was to generate displays of schematic information intelligently. Each object to be displayed knew how to draw itself, and an object at a given level knew how to allocate its overall space in a drawing to the objects of which it was composed. Finally, there was an attribute for each system object that indicated whether, in the current context of a problem solution, an expert would be thinking about that object. Objects being thought about were given more space and made more salient by the self-drawing method. This meant that the final diagram drawn on the screen when a part of the system was asked by the program to draw itself was dynamically altered to draw attention to the part(s) an expert might be focusing on in the instant context.[6]

---

[6]Edward Hughes developed this approach while at LRDC.

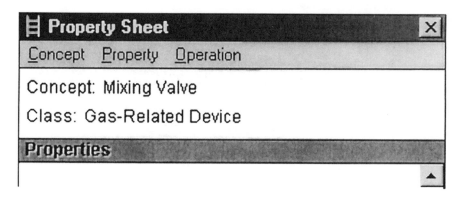

FIG. 10.7.   Example of one object defined by laddering tool.

Rule Inference and Rule-Editing Tools.   The other major formalized knowledge form is the rule. Actually, we have pretty good schemata for writing down rules, because most cognitive analysts have had some exposure to the formalism of production systems. However, it can be much more efficient to have automatic cross-referencing of the objects named in rules to the contents of the declarative knowledge base. This is especially important in light of the need for connections between conceptual and procedural knowledge discussed earlier. This kind of cross-referencing can permit at least an approximation to the final process explorer matrix, and such an approximation can focus and contain the total time that must be invested in developing this matrix of connections among levels of knowledge.

PC PACK contains several mechanisms for developing rules. First, they can be defined directly, one at a time. Second, they can be inferred from "dependency tables" such as the one shown in Table 10.2. For example, the table implies rules such as "IF the battery voltage is much less than 1.5V, THEN replace the battery."

ASSESSMENT IN THE CONTEXT
OF LEARNING BY DOING SYSTEMS

As noted earlier, an engineering research approach would not address the generic question of whether learning by doing works. Rather, it would focus on establishing some of the boundary conditions under which it is effective and would also attempt to develop measures that might support trade-off studies comparing learning by doing to other approaches as solutions to specific training or education problems. We have begun to do this kind of work in some of our joint activities with industry. To do this, we have had to choose—and to some extent develop—appropriate measures for assessing the yield of learning by doing systems.

Across our various projects that produced training systems, we have relied on three different kinds of evaluation. First, and most important, we have assessed the ability of trainees to solve hard problems from the target domain and even from transfer domains that bear some similarity to the target domain. Because we needed to develop training problems of this type as well, it was easy to stretch the process and develop additional problems for pre and post testing. Second, we have developed various schemes for assessing technicians' ability to explain actions that they or others take in trying to solve a difficult problem. Finally, we have attempted to train neural networks to recognize more versus less expert patterns of problem-solving activity by technicians.

Scoring Performances
Using Policy-Capturing Methodology

The most straightforward test of competence in a domain is to place a person in that domain and give them a very hard problem[7] to solve. Then, it is necessary to evaluate the person's problem-solving performance, to determine its value. In many cases, the goals of training represent a mixture of assimilation of expert processes and learning to optimize the value of one's performance within a local economy of practice. To get the needed information on the value of performances and to achieve the appropriate mixture of criteria, Gott and colleagues (Gott, Pokorny, Kane, Alley, & Dibble, 1997) used a policy-capturing approach (Hobson & Gibson, 1983) to establish the features of valued performance in the evaluation of the Sherlock intelligent coached apprenticeship system (Lesgold, Eggan, Katz, & Rao, 1992; Lesgold, Lajoie, Bunzo, & Eggan, 1992).

The approach consisted of having technicians solve difficult real-world troubleshooting problems that were presented verbally, with follow-up structured interviews. The interviews used the same probe questions

---

[7]Actually, this is already a value decision. Our training goals have always been to produce people who could stretch their knowledge to handle extremely difficult and often novel problems in their work. One could readily imagine a variety of training demands that would focus on routine work instead. For such training, different assessment measures would likely be more appropriate.

employed in Gott's task analysis methodology, the PARI method (Gott, 1987; Gott et al., 1986; Hall et al., 1995; Means & Gott, 1988). These questions probe for understanding of the current problem solution context, understanding of available options, and having accurate expectations of the likely results of contemplated next actions and the meaning of such results.

The anonymous solution traces were then given to job experts, who were asked to order the performance traces according to how well they represented desirable performance within the particular work context these technicians occupied.[8] Details of the approach are described later.

Such a scoring scheme can also be used for criticism of trainees' performances in the simulated work environment, provided that all of the features can be operationally defined in terms of patterns of activity a trainee might exhibit while solving a troubleshooting problem. Further, if the presence of each feature is inferable from some aspects of the trainee's performance, then each element of a critique can be "explained" by reconstructing the inference path that led to its being listed for a given problem-solving performance.

To summarize, both the evaluation of trainee performance and the criticism of that performance can be based on features of performances that are derived via policy capturing, provided that for each such feature, there is a way to reliably infer the presence or absence of that feature from the activity of the trainee.

Policy-Capturing Approach. The basic policy-capturing scheme is very straightforward. Records of various people's performances on a set of problems are given to a panel of experts to score. Their first step is to rank the performances from best to worst. Then, they are prompted to account for the ordering by pointing out features that are present in some performances but not in others. These features constitute a set of variables that are candidate features for scoring. Via regression or other less formal schemes, points are assigned to the various features, so that the rankings can be recovered from the features present or absent in the various performances. These point values then constitute a scoring rubric for scoring future performances by others. It is essential in this

---

[8]Some worked in the Central Command, where they had adequate parts inventories and a strong mandate to repair equipment as fast as possible. Others worked at reserve bases or other sites where minimizing the use of new parts was the primary requirement, even if this meant longer diagnostic sessions to absolutely confirm the need for any part before it was ordered.

process to work with the expert panel to assure that all the features are defined objectively, so that nonexperts can do future scoring if necessary.

Our Sherlock experience (Lesgold, Eggan, et al., 1992; Lesgold, Lajoie, et al., 1992) taught us that there are two basic ways to do the policy-capturing and competence assessments. One is to administer the problems completely verbally. That is, an assessment technician states the problem to the person being tested, and the person then tells what his first action will be. The results that would occur in the real world if that action were taken, given the predesignated system fault, are then stated verbally by an expert who works with the assessment technician. After the problem is solved, structured probe questions are used to get additional information about the testee's goals and understanding at different points in the solution process.

The other way to administer problems is to present them via the simulation capabilities of the learning by doing system itself. It would be possible to prompt for additional information in a manner similar to the probe questioning, using either text windows or audio recording to capture the responses. This has the advantage that it does not require a domain expert to be present during all the testing. It has the disadvantage that trainees who have been using the system may be more able to work easily on criterion problems and thus, may have an advantage over a control group even if the training taught them nothing specific. This disadvantage seems minimal with a group of technicians who are used to using computers, and it can be further ameliorated by allowing testees to take as long as they need to do the problems and using audio recording to capture the responses to probe questions.

Mapping Competence to Value.   It is important when doing policy-capturing work to be sure to distinguish an evaluation of performance focused on understanding of the system and its possible failures from an evaluation based on cost–benefit optimization. The policy-capturing scheme just described is very important for training development and refinement, because it can reveal specific areas of competence that are addressed either well or poorly by the evolving system. However, in order to determine the economic value of a training approach, it is helpful to have a second kind of evaluation that focuses directly on the cost and value of trainee actions in simulated troubleshooting tasks. This second approach also starts with performance on problems presented either verbally by a training technician or else via the learning by doing simulation.

In this case, though, each action the trainee takes is assigned a cost that is determined by the amount of the trainee's time the action would take in real life, the cost of any materials that would be used, and the cost in terms of the duration that other employees and/or machinery would be unable to function. It is possible in our learning by doing systems to place such cost assignments on a scale that is anchored by the cost that would result from the fault if it were immediately addressed by the training system's expert model and by the expected cost for a fault of that type in a work environment with a recently acquired and consequently minimally trained workforce (something that would have to be estimated by an expert).

This kind of cost-based scoring can be done substantially by nondomain experts, but experts will occasionally need to be consulted to clarify time estimates for different actions and to delineate the full range of cost sources. Also, cost scoring can, to a large extent, be linked to the policy-capturing scheme, so that approximate cost values are assigned to each feature used in scoring.

Questions Focused on Explanation and Understanding

Another form of assessment focuses on understanding. In this approach, the assessment "items" begin with accounts of some aspect of troubleshooting and then ask the trainee to explain an action that might be taken or to explain some aspect of the situation that has been described. This approach has the advantage that it can be administered and scored by nonexperts, once the items are developed, at least if "objective" forms like multiple choice are used. Further, this approach has been shown to produce results that bear a reasonable relationship to the results of performance tests like those described earlier (Gott, 1987; Gott & Lesgold, in press). The primary danger in relying exclusively on such items is that over time, training may evolve to focus only on conceptual understanding and not on the decision making that goes into complex problem solving. Explaining someone else's decisions is quite different from making them oneself (those who describe championship chess tournaments are not always able to win one!).

Scoring With Neural Networks

We have conducted one last kind of analysis of the protocol data from our direct performance testing. This is a test of whether the difference in overall pattern of performance between pretest and posttest subjects on a given problem was sufficient to be discernible in every individual case. The way we tested this was to ask if a simple (three hidden units in a single layer) neural network could identify pretest versus posttest protocols. There are a variety of tools available in the traditional statistician's arsenal to do this kind of analysis, including discriminant analysis. However, those tools make a variety of assumptions that may not be met or may not be validated very easily. The reader can think of neural network approaches such as the one described next as a sort of nonparametric approach to discriminant analysis. Given the clarity of our results, we believe that the approach has been reasonably used. More generally, we expect that future training systems will likely make use of neural network schemata, at least for assessment decisions.

We built neural networks in which each possible action (test, adjustment, or part replacement) that could be performed was assigned a separate input unit. Two output units were established, representing the choice between pretest and posttest. The individual protocols were then used as training cases to train the network to recognize whether a given case was a pretest performance or a posttest performance. This was done separately for each of the four problems. The networks were standard three-layer networks, and backpropagation was the network training method.

Table 10.3 reports the results of a neural network analysis for an evaluation of one of the training systems we built jointly with Intel Corporation. We used four troubleshooting problems from a library of problems—other problems in the library were selected for use in the training system itself. These problems were problems 3, 7, 8, and 12 of this library and hence are referenced below by those numbers. In this analysis, 0 was the arbitrary value assigned to the classification value for pretest performances and 1 was the value for posttest performances. Hence, the

TABLE 10.3
Neural Network Classifications

Problem	Mean Output Score for Pretest Cases	Mean Output Score for Posttest Cases
3	.026	.704
7	.102	.863
8	.016	.907
12	.063	.845
Average	.052	.830

neural network would have classified perfectly if it had learned to generate a 0 for every pretest case and a 1 for every posttest case. In fact, the network converged on a strong solution for problems 3, 7, and 8, and it produced almost as good a result for problem 12. Again, it was easier to distinguish pre and postperformances on problems 7 and 8, just as they also gave stronger differences on the action counts, but all four problems showed clear differences between the patterns of pretest and posttest performance. Although it is not easy to provide a concise statement about the exact pattern differences between pretest and posttest, the data are consistent with the claim that technicians were learning from the ICA system to avoid time-wasting strategies in their diagnostic work that were either unnecessary or not very informative.

Overall, the multiple evaluation methods described are helpful in determining the effects of learning by doing environments, especially if the goal is to produce expertise sufficient for addressing rare and difficult problems that are especially expensive sources of difficulty for complex work systems.

CONCLUSIONS

We have described the knowledge requirements for learning by doing systems, especially those focused on complex problem solving. In doing so, we have argued that an important form of knowledge that is seldom addressed sufficiently are the connections between rule-based knowledge as it is applied in various problem situations and conceptual knowledge that provides the basis for stretching rules to fit new situations. We have presented a justification for focusing on such knowledge, derived from the work of Rasmussen and more recent work on knowledge encapsulation by Schmidt, Boshuizen, and van de Wiel.

We have suggested specific methods for gathering the full range of data that learning by doing systems require and have discussed some of the relationships among different parts of that data. Out of this has come an initial proposal for selection of problem situations to be presented by a learning by doing system, namely to select problems to cover the space defined by the mappings between conceptual knowledge fragments and problem situations. Although we have not yet performed specific tests of this selection approach—because it is hard to define an appropriate comparison group—it does at least have a reasonable rationale, and systems built on this scheme have proven effective.

Existing tools are a useful beginning, but none have the needed mixture of tight anchoring in an engineering theory of learning by doing system design plus sufficient usability and generality to be readily deployed for new training system development by instructional design experts or subject matter experts who may lack software backgrounds. The biggest gap is in systems for directly and completely conducting the iterative process that is needed to develop the mapping matrix relating conceptual to situational and rule-based knowledge. We hope eventually to design such tools if they do not appear from other sources.

Finally, we have reviewed several evaluation schemata that seem appropriate to assessment of learning by doing systems. The schemata have been used in our own work, and they have considerable face validity. What is still needed though is a richer evaluation model. After all, the history of instructional innovation has been that every intervention works in some "hothouse" environment and that almost all fail in some of the environments in which they are eventually applied. This strongly suggests that the ultimate goal of evaluation must be to establish the range of training requirements that can be addressed by a given approach, not simply to show that it worked somewhere.

REFERENCES

Albacete, P. (1999). *An intelligent tutoring system for teaching fundamental physics concepts.* Unpublished doctoral dissertation, University of Pittsburgh, Pittsburgh.

Anderson, J. R., & Corbett, A. T. (1993). Tutoring of cognitive skill. In J. R. Anderson (Ed.), *Rules of the mind* (pp. 235–255). Hillsdale, NJ: Lawrence Erlbaum Associates.

Brown, J. S., Collins, A., & Duguid, P. (1991). Situated cognition and the culture of learning. In M. Yazdani & R. W. Lawler (Eds.), *Artificial intelligence and education* (Vol. 2, pp. 245–268). Norwood, NJ: Ablex.

Boshuizen, H. P. A., & Schmidt, H. G. (1992). On the role of biomedical knowledge in clinical reasoning by experts, intermediates and novices. *Cognitive Science, 16,* 153–184.

Boshuizen, H. P. A., & van de Wiel, M. W. J. (1999). Using multiple representations in medicine: How students struggle with them. In M. W. van Someren, P. Reimann, H. P. A. Boshuizen, & T. de Jong (Eds.), *Learning with multiple representations.* Amsterdam: Pergamon.

Chi, M., Glaser, R., & Farr, M. (Eds.) (1988). *The nature of expertise.* Hillsdale, NJ: Lawrence Erlbaum Associates.

Collins, A., Brown, J. S., & Newman, S. E. (1989). Cognitive apprenticeship: Teaching the crafts of reading, writing, and mathematics. In L. B. Resnick (Ed.), *Knowing, learning, and instruction: Essays in honor of Robert Glaser* (pp. 453–494). Hillsdale, NJ: Lawrence Erlbaum Associates.

Conati C., & VanLehn, K. (1999). Teaching meta-cognitive skills: Implementation and evaluation of a tutoring system to guide self-explanation while learning from examples. *Proceedings of AIED '99, 9th World Conference of Artificial Intelligence and Education,* Le Mans, France.

Ericcson, K. A., & Simon, H. A. (1993). *Protocol analysis: Verbal reports as data.* Cambridge, MA: MIT Press.

Gertner, A. S., Conati, C., & VanLehn, K. (1998). Procedural help in Andes: Generating hints using a Bayesian network student model. *Proceedings of the Fifteenth National Conference on Artificial Intelligence AAAI-98.* (pp. 106–111) Cambridge, MA: MIT Press.

Gitomer, D. H. (1988). Individual differences in technical troubleshooting. *Human Performance, 1,* 111–131.

Gott, S. P. (1987). Assessing technical expertise in today's work environments. *Proceedings of the 1987 ETS Invitational Conference* (pp. 89–101). Princeton, NJ: Educational Testing Service.

Gott, S. P., Bennett, W., & Gillet, A. (1986). Models of technical competence for intelligent tutoring systems. *Journal of Computer-Based Instruction, 13,* 43–46.

Gott, S. P., & Lesgold, A. M. (in press). Competence in the workplace: How cognitive performance models and situated instruction can accelerate skill acquisition. In R. Glaser (Ed.), *Advances in instructional psychology.* Hillsdale, NJ: Lawrence Erlbaum Associates.

Gott, S. P., Pokorny, R. A., Kane, R. S., Alley, W. E., & Dibble, E. (1997). *Understanding the acquisition and flexibility of technical expertise: The development and evaluation of an intelligent tutoring system: Sherlock 2* (AL/HR Tech. Rep. No. 1997-0014). Brooks AFB, TX: Armstrong Laboratory, Human Resources Directorate.

Hall, E. P., Gott, S. P., & Pokorny, R. A. (1995). *A procedural guide to cognitive task analysis: The PARI methodology* (Tech. Rep. No. 1995-0108). Brooks AFB, TX: Armstrong Laboratory, Human Resources Directorate.

Hobson, C. J., & Gibson, F. W. (1983). Policy capturing as an approach to understanding and improving performance appraisal: A review of the literature. *Academy of Management Review, 8,* 640–649.

Hunt, E., & Lansman, M. (1986). Unified model of attention and problem solving. *Psychological Review, 93,* 446–461.

Lesgold, A.M. (1984). Acquiring expertise. In J. R. Anderson & S. M. Kosslyn (Eds.), *Tutorials in learning and memory: Essays in honor of Gordon Bower* (pp. 31–60). San Francisco: Freeman.

Lesgold, A., Eggan, G., Katz, S., & Rao, G. (1992). Possibilities for assessment using computer-based apprenticeship environments. In W. Regian & V. Shute (Eds.), *Cognitive approaches to automated instruction* (pp. 49–80). Hillsdale, NJ: Lawrence Erlbaum Associates.

Lesgold, A. M., Lajoie, S. P., Bunzo, M., & Eggan, G. (1992). SHERLOCK: A coached practice environment for an electronics troubleshooting job. In J. Larkin & R. Chabay (Eds.), *Computer assisted instruction and intelligent tutoring systems: Shared issues and complementary approaches* (pp. 201–238). Hillsdale, NJ: Lawrence Erlbaum Associates.

Means, B., & Gott, S. P. (1988). Cognitive task analysis as a basis for tutor development: Articulating abstract knowledge representations. In J. Psotka, D. Massey, & S. Mutter (Eds.), *Intelligent tutoring systems: Lessons learned* (pp. 35–59). Hillsdale, NJ: Lawrence Erlbaum Associates.

Nunan, D. (1992). *Research methods in language learning.* Cambridge, England: Cambridge University Press.

Rasmussen, J., Petjersen, A., & Goodstein, L. (1994). *Cognitive systems engineering.* New York: Wiley.

Whitehead, A. N. (1929). *The aims of education and other essays.* New York: The Free Press. [Available as of August 1999 from http://dept.english.upenn.edu/~rlucid/A_Whitehead.html]

Wixon, D., & Ramey, J. (1996). Field oriented design techniques: Case studies and organizing dimensions. *SIGCHI Bulletin 28* (3), 21–26.

Part IV

Social Contexts of Instruction and Learning

11

A Collaborative Convergence on Studying Reasoning Processes: A Case Study in Statistics

Marsha Lovett

Carnegie Mellon University

This chapter begins with a memory experiment, and you, the readers, are the participants! Please read the brief story below and try to memorize it. There will be recall questions asked later. [You may recognize the story, as it is quoted verbatim from an already published work (Gick & Holyoak, 1983.)]

The General

A small country was ruled from a strong fortress by a dictator. The fortress was situated in the middle of the country, surrounded by farms and villages. Many roads led to the fortress through the countryside. A rebel general vowed to capture the fortress. The general knew that an attack by his entire army would capture the fortress. He gathered his army at the head of one of the roads, ready to launch a full-scale direct attack. However, the general then learned that the dictator had planted mines on each of the roads. The mines were set so that small bodies of men could pass over them safely, since the dictator needed to move his troops and workers to and from the fortress. However, any large force would detonate the mines. Not only would this blow up the road, but it would also destroy many neighboring villages. It therefore seemed impossible to capture the fortress.

However, the general devised a simple plan. He divided his army into small groups and dispatched each group to the head of a different road. When all was ready he gave the signal and each group marched down a different road. Each group continued down its road to the fortress so that the entire army arrived together at the fortress at the same time. In this way, the general captured the fortress and overthrew the dictator. (pp. 35–36)

INTRODUCTION

This chapter focuses on the problem of improving young adults' statistical reasoning skills, with a particular emphasis on transfer outside the original learning context. Effective transfer is critical here because statistical reasoning is applicable across a wide variety of domains and in daily life; statistical reasoning skill is of little value if it can only be applied in the statistics classroom. And yet, students have great difficulty learning statistical reasoning skills in a transferable way (e.g., Garfield & delMas, 1991; Pollatsek, Konold, Well, & Lima, 1984). These instruction-oriented studies document that many current approaches to teaching statistics—even modern reform-based pedagogy—leave significant room for improvement, but they provide relatively little guidance about how to proceed.

Learning the appropriate representations for knowledge (not overly specific, not overly general) is key for effective transfer. Understanding how knowledge representations are formed and changed during learning is one of the foci of cognitive theory. This suggests that a successful route to improving students' transfer of statistical reasoning skill may rely heavily on integrating instructional and cognitive theory, while maintaining a link to the realities of the classroom. Unfortunately, the fundamental tension between theoretical and applied methods over the last 30 years has led to the emergence of three distinct approaches, each primarily emphasizing a single perspective:

1. Develop cognitive theories to describe knowledge representations that explain observed performance on simplified statistical reasoning problems;
2. Conduct empirical work to study students solving simplified statistical reasoning problems in real-world contexts.
3. Work in the classroom, with all the complexity that doing so implies, to develop new instructional techniques based on instructors' expertise, but without much guidance for or contribution to theory.

Which of these approaches should cognitive scientists and educational researchers take to best address the problem of improving students' statistical reasoning abilities? (Hint: Think back to the story about the general!) The response advocated here is analogous to the general's solution: Do not use one or another solution approach by itself, but rather employ a *convergence* of multiple approaches. This chapter begins with the story about the general not as part of a memory experiment (are you surprised?) but rather as a "source" problem to be applied by analogy to help solve the problem of improving statistics instruction (see Gick & Holyoak, 1983, for more details on their analogical problem-solving experiment).

Although it is difficult to take a multidisciplinary approach to any research problem, the work of Ann Brown shows that it is possible and indeed can lead to striking benefits. In Brown's 1992 "Design Experiments" paper, she emphasized the importance of bringing multiple perspectives to bear for the success of her work. Brown's training in experimental psychology spurred her initial theoretical ideas, based on memory and learning research, regarding how to improve instruction. These ideas led to instructional interventions (e.g., Palincsar & Brown, 1986) that she and her colleagues tested in the laboratory and then in the classroom, where they have become fairly widely used. More recently, she extended her applied side even further by playing the role of "learning community" builder in order to address issues of acceptance and impact so that her instructional innovations could produce larger educational changes. This integration of pure and applied work is a model for the success of the convergent approach to be discussed in the context of statistics education.

The next part defines the term "statistical reasoning." Then, a brief historical review of cognitive science research on statistical reasoning is presented, highlighting how the three approaches previously mentioned map onto the development of the field over the past 30 years.

- 1970s   Cognitive science theories were developed to explain fallacies in people's statistical reasoning.
- 1980s   New empirical work was conducted to study students' statistical reasoning.
- 1990s   Students' difficulties in statistical reasoning (and associated instructional innovations) were studied in the context of classroom practice.

These examples of single-perspective research are then followed by a description of some of my own research in which the aim is to bring these different solution approaches together to improve students' ability to transfer their statistical reasoning skills.

WHAT IS STATISTICAL REASONING?

Statistical reasoning is the use of statistical tools and concepts (e.g., hypothesis testing, variation, correlation) to summarize, make predictions about, and draw conclusions from data. Two examples illustrate this definition in a more probabilistic and a more statistical problem, respectively.

Example #1:

A certain town is served by two hospitals. In the larger hospital, about 45 babies are born each day, and in the smaller hospital, about 15 babies are born each day. As you know, about 50% of all babies are boys. However, the exact percentage varies from day to day. Sometimes it may be higher than 50%, sometimes lower.

For a period of one year, each hospital recorded the days on which more/less than 60% of the babies born were boys. Which hospital do you think recorded more such days? The larger hospital; the smaller hospital; or about the same (i.e., the two hospitals are within 5% of each other; (Kahneman & Tversky, 1972, p. 443).

Solution to Example #1:

The smaller hospital likely recorded more days with more than 60% boys because when sample sizes are smaller, the observed distributions are more likely to diverge from that of the population at large.

Solving this problem requires reasoning about the impact of sample sizes on variability and involves making a prediction based on this relationship. Thus, this example fits the definition of statistical reasoning because (a) it employs the use of statistical concepts (e.g., sample size and variability), and (b) it involves making a prediction based on the given data (two separate samples with sample sizes equal to 15 and 45).

Example #2:

A weather modification experiment was conducted in Florida to investigate whether "seeding" clouds with silver nitrate would increase the amount of rainfall. Clouds were randomly assigned to be seeded or not to be seeded, and data were collected on the total rain volume falling from each cloud. A variable named *group* contains data on whether each cloud was seeded or not, and a variable named *rain* contains data on each cloud's rain volume. Does cloud seeding increase rainfall? To answer this question, perform any appropriate statistical analyses of the given data set and interpret the results accordingly.

(Partial) Solution to Example #2:

Solving example #2 requires performing exploratory and confirmatory data analyses. It thus fits the definition of statistical reasoning because (a) it employs the use of several statistical tools and concepts (e.g., boxplots, confidence intervals, hypothesis testing), and (b) it involves drawing conclusions based on these analyses. It is important to note that the complete solution to this problem would involve more than the displays and statistics presented in Fig. 11.1. For example, the skewness of the data suggests reanalyzing the rain volume data after performing a transformation, an analysis not presented in Fig. 11.1. More importantly, a complete solution would include a more thorough interpretation of the various results in terms of the question at hand, "Does cloud seeding increase rainfall?" (Note that this is a test problem used in the statistics course that provides a classroom context for much of my work described later.)

HISTORICAL REVIEW

The question motivating this volume (and the Carnegie Symposium that it documents) asks how far we have come in applying cognitive research to instruction in the past 25 years. In this spirit, it is worth considering the development of past research relevant to statistical reasoning as a benchmark for current work in this area. Moreover, by looking at the past work on statistical reasoning—theoretical in the 1970s, empirical in the 1980s, and classroom based in the 1990s—one can see how these different research approaches perform at their best in isolation, thereby gaining insights into how they might be profitably integrated.

A Template for Comparison

Four questions serve to structure this historical review of cognitive science research on statistical reasoning. The corresponding answers highlight how the social context of the research in each era influenced the nature of the research. A discussion of each of these questions follows.

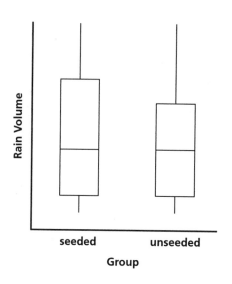

	N	MEAN	MEDIAN	SD
Seeded	45	61.33	40	45.31
Unseeded	45	44.67	40	35.07

The exploratory analysis (i.e., boxplots and descriptive statistics) suggest that there is great overlap in the distributions of rainfall among the "seeded" and "unseeded" clouds. [Ideally, student would also notice skewness of rainfall data and hence would perform inferential statistics on transformed data.

$$95\% \text{ Confidence interval for } \mu_{seeded} - \mu_{not}: (0.02, 0.583)$$

$t\text{-test for } H0: \mu_{seeded} = \mu_{not}$ $\qquad H_A: \mu_{seeded} \neq \mu_{not}$

$$t = 2.11 \; p = 0.038 \; df = 85$$

These inferential statistics suggest that, with an alpha level of 0.05, these data show significant evidence to reject the null hypothesis of no difference between seeded and unseeded clouds' rainfall volumes. This is consistent with the 95% confidence interval that falls completely above 0.0, suggesting that the seeded clouds' rainfall volume is greater than the unseeded clouds'.

FIG. 11.1. Components of a solution to the cloud-seeding problem.

Who are the Researchers? The answer to this question may be cognitive scientists, education researchers, teachers, domain experts, or some combination. It is an important question to consider because the background and experience of the researchers involved can greatly influence the direction of the research, both in terms of the questions being asked and the methods used to address them. In terms of identifying research that takes a "convergence" approach to studying statistical reasoning, the main distinction to be made regarding this question is whether or not the research integrates expertise from multiple disciplines (regardless of whether that multidisciplinary expertise comes from one or more than one person).

What is the Goal of the Research? The various answers to this question are of course quite involved, but they may be categorized into different types of goals, such as developing or extending a body of theory, adding to an empirical database, testing an educational intervention, or assessing educational outcomes (at a classroom or institutional level). Although the goal of a particular project may not fall completely into one of these categories, it is likely that one emerges as most representative of the emphases in that project.

What is the Context of the Research? This question can be answered at many levels, as there are many ways of interpreting the term "context." For simplicity, a basic interpretation answers the question in terms of the *physical context* in which the research is pursued. Even at this basic level, there are vastly different possibilities, including the cognitive psychologist's laboratory, the school classroom, or everyday life situations. Each of these different physical contexts tends to have a unique social and cultural context that can, in turn, influence the nature of the research.

How is the Research Being Applied? The most salient application area is education and, more specifically, the improvement of instructional practice. This application may be a direct part of the work or a potential future outlet for the work. Alternatively, the research may not be directed toward any explicit application, or its application may be mostly self-directed, that is to extend or test a current theory. This question, then, does not address the nature of the work itself as much as the implications of the research, for example, what impact will it have on science or society and what audience will be concerned with its results?

With these framing questions outlined, the next three subparts briefly sketch research on statistical reasoning produced in three different periods; the 1970s, the 1980s, and the 1990s. The purpose of this review is not to provide complete coverage but to convey the general tenor of the work produced in each of the different periods. For each period, these questions will be answered based both on "typical" work and on specific papers from that era.

Theoretical Focus of the 1970s

Cognitive science in the 1970s savored the somewhat new concept that mental representations can offer important insights into human behavior. Applying this concept to the domain of statistical reasoning—specifically, to the question of how people make judgments under uncertainty—led to a body of work that is best represented by Kahneman, Slovic, and Tversky's (1982) book, entitled *Judgment Under Uncertainty: Heuristics and Biases*. In this book, the editors, along with many other cognitive psychologists and social scientists working at that time, documented their research from the preceding decade. They presented a variety of behaviors that people exhibit when reasoning about probabilistic and statistical situations, and they posited specific mental processes as leading to these behaviors. In most cases, the behaviors demonstrate people's *errors* in reasoning. For example, the hospital babies problem presented earlier (example #1) is taken from a study performed by Kahneman and Tversky (1972) in which more than half of the participants answered that the two hospitals would have the same number of days with more than 60% baby boys (despite the fact that one hospital delivers three times as many babies per day as the other). This answer fails to take into account the relationship between sample size and variability (i.e., the probability of extreme measurements), so it highlights the fact that people do not always employ correct statistical reasoning.

Other statistical reasoning fallacies (e.g., the gambler's fallacy, the conjunction fallacy, overconfidence, and insensitivity to base rates) were documented by these researchers. However, the main goal of the work was to develop and test a theory that explains why people make these reasoning errors. Relying on the importance of mental representations and processes in understanding behavior, this theory proposed that people reason about uncertain situations by applying particular heuristics and biases that generally work well (i.e., produce "good" reasoning) but that fail under particular circumstances. Thus, it should be emphasized that this era evinces a positivist perspective, comparing human performance against logical ideals without much attention to the general value of using heuristics and biases (e.g., they are easy to apply, not overly computation or memory intensive, and make accurate predictions in many situations).

An example of one of these heuristics, proposed by Kahneman and Tversky, is the *representativeness heuristic*, which states that people make relative probability judgments about events A and B according to how representative A is of B. In the hospital problem, this heuristic applies when people consider the bigger and smaller hospital to be equally representative of the population of baby-delivering hospitals and therefore judge them both to have the same probability of delivering more than 60% baby boys on a given day. The representativeness heuristic explains several other errors in statistical reasoning as well. For example, Kahneman and Tversky (1973) showed that, in particular circumstances, individuals are insensitive to the prior probabilities of two events and that this insensitivity can be explained by application of the representativeness heuristic. When given brief personality descriptions of several individuals taken from a pool of 70% engineers and 30% lawyers, participants rated the following individual as equally likely to be from either profession:

> Dick is a 30-year-old man. He is married with no children. A man of high ability and high motivation, he promises to be quite successful in his field. He is well liked by his colleagues. (p. 242, Kahneman & Tversky, 1973)

Because this description was designed to convey no information particular to Dick's profession, the prior probabilities of the two professions would suggest that Dick was more likely an engineer than a lawyer. However, participants on average judged this probability to be 0.5. Kahneman and Tversky argued that this response stems from the representativeness heuristic because Dick's description is equally representative of a lawyer and of an engineer, so the probability judgment is reasoned to be that he is equally likely to be one or the other.

Table 11.1 encapsulates the 1970s research on statistical reasoning by answering the four framing questions of this historical review. In summary, the research of this era mainly followed a theory-based approach to try to understand how people solve (or fail to solve) statistical reasoning problems. Little attention was paid to the realities of everyday problem solving, let alone classroom learning, and yet several new ideas and constructs were developed (e.g., reasoning heuristics) that could later be applied in more practical settings.

TABLE 11.1

Contrasting Historical Periods of Research on Adult Statistical Reasoning

Question	1970s Answer	1980s Answer	1990s Answer
Who are the researchers?	Cognitive psychologists and social scientists	Cognitive psychologist	Psychologists, educators, and instructors
What is the goal of the research?	Developing and testing a theory positing that people use certain heuristics and biases	Primarily testing theory but also documenting abilities of statistics students	Documenting students' difficulties in statistical reasoning
What is the context of the research?	The psychologist's laboratory, with sanitized versions of real-world problems	Studying students outside the context of statistics class, with pseudoreal-world problems	Studying students in the classroom
How is the research being applied?	To develop and test theory	To test theory; could also be applied to instructional design.	To provide information to instructors of similar courses

Empirical Focus of the 1980s

Toward the end of the 1970s, researchers interested in science and math education were starting to get excited about the ways in which cognitive science theories and results (similar to those described earlier) could be applied to improve instruction (cf. Klahr, 1976). However, this potential influence between cognition and instruction did not immediately impact the domain of statistical reasoning. It was not until the 1980s that several researchers interested in statistical reasoning started working on the question of how students, who have been trained in a probability and statistics course, fare on similar tests of statistical reasoning (e.g., Fong, Krantz, & Nisbett, 1986; Konold, Pollatsek, Well, & Lohmeier, 1993; Pollatsek et al., 1984; Pollatsek, Well, Konold, & Hardiman, 1987). These researchers tested students on problems that resembled those from Kahneman and Tversky's work. Presumably, a reasonable prediction at the time was that these students, thanks to their coursework in probability and statistics, would demonstrate better statistical reasoning than that exhibited in the earlier studies where the participants had no special training. However, this prediction did not generally hold true. For example, Fong et al. (1986) found that students had significant difficulty answering such questions outside the classroom context. Indeed, this experiment warrants special attention not only for its results on students' statistical reasoning but for its serious attention to the issue of transfer of relevant knowledge and skills outside the statistics classroom.

In Experiment 4, Fong et al. (1986) selected students at random from a college-level introductory statistics course; half of the students were tested during the first week of the semester, and the other half were tested during the last week of the semester. The "test," however, did not consist of a typical set of questions given in connection with the students' statistics course. Instead, students were contacted by phone (completely outside the context of any course) and asked if they would have time to answer some questions for a campus survey on students' opinions about sports. Following two questions that actually did ask students about their opinions regarding sports issues, four statistical questions—couched in terms of sports cover stories—were asked. An example of such a question that was designed to tap students' understanding of the concept of "regression to the mean" is as follows:

> In general, the major league baseball player who wins Rookie of the Year does not perform as well in his second year. This is clear in major league baseball in the past 10 years. In the American League, eight Rookies of the Year have done worse in their second year; only two have done better. In the National League, the Rookie of the Year has done worse the second year 9 times out of 10. Why do you suppose the Rookie of the Year tends not to do as well his second year? (Fong et al., 1986, p. 279)

Other statistical questions included in the survey involved the statistical concepts of sample size (cf. example #1 presented earlier) and confounding variables.

Students' responses to the four statistical questions were rated for evidence of statistical thinking and for the quality of the statistical response. For two of the questions, there was no significant difference between the two test periods (before and after students had taken a relevant course) in their use of statistical thinking. For the other two questions, there was a significant difference in the use of statistical thinking between the two testing times. However, in each of these latter two cases, the effect reflected only an additional 20% of students giving statistically related responses (with little concern of ceiling effects limiting the possible improvement). For example, for the question given earlier, only 37% of students tested at the end of the term used statistical reasoning in their answers, compared to 16% of students tested at the beginning.

Regarding the *quality* of statistical reasoning, only one out of the four questions showed a significant increase between students' responses collected at the two testing times. While these results do suggest that a statistics course can, for particular questions, produce transfer effects in students' statistical reasoning, an interpretation of the practical significance of these results (and similar results in Experiment 3 of the same paper) seems more akin to a glass half empty.

Placing this work in its historical context, it is important to note that the motivation behind these experiments was not to understand students' statistical reasoning in their college courses but rather to test the hypothesis that people in general tend to use abstract rules in their application of statistical concepts, such as the law of large numbers. This theoretical basis for studying students' statistical reasoning is also true of other work in this period. For example, a series of studies by Konold, Pollatsek, Well, and their colleagues was aimed at better understanding why students might demonstrate the various fallacies documented in the 1970s (Konold et al., 1993; Pollatsek et al., 1984, 1987). One such study tested two alternative hypotheses for why students reason incorrectly about random sampling: Is it because they hold a passive, descriptive view of sampling that merely does not include the notion of independence of trials or is it because they hold an active-balancing model in which earlier trials influence later trials, thus countermanding the notion of independence (Pollatsek et al., 1984)? By varying the original paradigm used by Tversky and Kahneman, these researchers were able to distinguish that students' judgments were not consistent with an active-balancing model, thereby suggesting a descriptive view of sampling. These results helped to distinguish different underlying statistical conceptions that students might have, thereby expanding the 1970s theoretical work on reasoning fallacies; they were not, however, directly applied to the improvement of classroom instruction.

In summary, the research conducted during the 1980s, like that of the 1970s, was mainly theoretical in nature. However, there was a new trend toward studying statistical reasoning in more realistic situations. Moreover, the research participants were often college students who had taken a course in probability and/or statistics. In this way, the results were more relevant to an applied audience including university instructors and instructional designers. Again, Table 11.1 summarizes the answers to the four framing questions for this era.

Classroom Focus of the 1990s

By the 1990s, the reform movement in math and science education had taken a foothold in statistics instruction. Many new textbooks focusing on the practice of statistics were being used in courses whose curricula now emphasized reasoning about data rather than memorizing formulas. Along with this change in content, there was a change in the techniques of instruction: Students were getting more hands-on practice (typically in computer laboratories where they used statistical software packages to analyze data); they were solving more real-world problems; and they were getting access to computer simulations of various statistical phenomena (e.g., the central limit theorem).

With all these changes in statistics instruction, many researchers were asking the question: What do our students know and what problems can they solve coming out of these new courses? The motivation seems not to have been to compare previous, traditional instruction with the new, nor to directly explore the application of previous research to college instruction, but rather to document students' strengths and weaknesses under the reformed courses and, in some cases, to evaluate the potential of specific instructional innovations. For example, Garfield and delMas (1991) tested students' conceptions of probability at the start and end of an introductory course by asking questions such as the following: Which of several coin flip sequences is most likely? least likely? How should one interpret a medicine label warning that there is a 15% chance of developing a rash? Each question had a set of multiple-choice answers. Comparing students' results from before and after the course showed that students did show an overall increase in correct responses. Nevertheless, particular misconceptions were maintained after instruction, leaving the absolute performance levels at posttest well below perfect performance. In a similar vein, Melvin and Huff (1992) listed and described several difficulties that their students demonstrated regarding various statistical concepts required for analyzing data and interpreting statistical results. In both of these studies, the results highlighted that students have difficulty applying particular statistical concepts even in the same context where these concepts were learned (i.e., not a case of real transfer).

Other work during this period shares the focus on assessing students' strengths and weaknesses but does so in the context of evaluating a particular new teaching intervention. For example, Cohen and his colleagues conducted several studies in which the students were tested before and after taking a statistics course that either did or did not employ a new instructional software package (Cohen & Chechile 1997; Cohen, Smith, Chechile, Burns, & Tsai 1996; Cohen, Tsai, & Chechile 1995). The questions were designed to test students' ability to apply the statistical concepts taught by the software package. Although the "experimental" students exhibited greater learning gains (posttest–pretest) than did "control" students, Cohen and Chechile (1997) remarked that "even those students with adequate basic mathematical skills [who had used the hands-on instructional software] still scored only an average of 57% [correct] on the [post] test of conceptual understanding" (p. 110). Although this result demonstrates an improvement relative to that group's average pretest score of 42% correct, it shows that students' ability to reason statistically could still be greatly improved.

To summarize the research conducted during the 1990s, the main focus was on studying students' statistical reasoning (and difficulties thereof) in the classroom. (See Table 11.1 for the 1990s answers to the framing questions.) Although there was little attempt to draw on previous theoretical work that might have helped to explain why these difficulties arose, there was a solid contribution in practical knowledge for teachers regarding where students' difficulties lie. Perhaps even more importantly, research in this era provided public documentation that there is still ample room for improving statistics instruction. It is this last point that may have provided an impetus for researchers to look to multiple perspectives in trying to make headway against the challenging problem of improving students' statistical reasoning.

Islands of Integrative Research in the Mid-1990s and Beyond

As described earlier, most of the work on statistical reasoning during the 1970s, 1980s, and 1990s employed a single research approach (i.e., theoretical, empirical, or classroom based). This past research also emphasized the products of learning and reasoning rather than the processes. There have been some recent studies, however, in which the focus is more process oriented and multiple approaches have been integrated. These bridging examples generally use the results of one approach to motivate or justify new research using a second approach. For example, Garfield

(1995) provided a review of past results on probabilistic reasoning fallacies (highlighting some of the same 1970s research previously described). She described results, which were generated to test a more general psychological theory, but she did so in a way that draws on her own applied perspective and that reaches a classroom-oriented audience (e.g., high school and college statistics instructors).

Another article by Garfield (1994) described a fairly traditional assessment of students' statistical reasoning ability but added to this applied topic a more theoretical perspective on learning. In particular, the assessment asked students not only for their answer to each question, but also which of several different modes of reasoning led them to their chosen answer. This approach enabled the teacher/assessor to identify not only when and how often a student answers correctly/incorrectly but what mental processes and concepts led them to their answers. These additional data led Garfield to look for patterns of responding across related questions to make better inferences about what mental models of statistics each student might have. More generally, it suggests to instructors and assessors to consider, in the abstract, what knowledge is required for statistical reasoning and how students' knowledge differs.

This approach is closely related to Hunt and Minstrell's DIAGNOSER research (e.g., Hunt & Minstrell, 1994) in which students were asked to complete assessments that required them to select among options that reflected both their solutions and their reasoning (i.e., both the products and processes of their problem solving). In this way, the assessment made it possible to diagnose which *facets* of knowledge and understanding students have. Thus, like the theoretically focused work of the 1970s, this research made inferences about students' internal mental states. In Minstrell and Hunt's work, however, the DIAGNOSER went beyond inference to intervention in students' learning by providing feedback tailored to students' particular choices and by asking additional questions tailored to the inferred facets of knowledge. This research integrates a theoretical and applied approach because it includes both the development of new theoretical constructs (i.e., facets of knowledge that represent certain profiles of understanding) and the development of an empirical database describing real students' various levels of understanding. Although Hunt and Minstrell's earlier work focused on students' understanding of physics, their approach was more recently applied to the domain of probability (Schaffner, 1997).

A CONVERGENT ASSAULT
ON STATISTICAL REASONING

The remainder of the chapter describes some of my recent work on examining Carnegie Mellon students' learning of statistical reasoning. This work is part of a project aimed at both understanding students' learning processes and improving their statistical reasoning abilities by creating new instructional environments. Exploratory and inferential data analysis (like that exemplified in the cloud-seeding example presented earlier) are the focus of our work. Our approach involves using cognitive theory to help achieve instructional goals, instructional results to help inform theory, and technology to help both. We integrate all three approaches mentioned earlier; theoretical, empirical, and classroom based. In contrast with the work of the 1970s, 1980s, and 1990s, we are able to integrate these approaches in large part because of the multidisciplinary team working on this project. In our work, the researchers consist of cognitive psychologists, statistics instructors, educational researchers, and instructional technologists.

Our convergent approach is also made possible by the varied contexts in which we are conducting the research. These diverse contexts reflect a mixture of the psychology laboratory and the statistics classroom. In particular, the classroom context for our work is an introductory statistics class taken by more than 250 first-year undergraduates each semester. These students come from a variety of majors in the humanities, social sciences, and architecture.

Because of this strong link between our research program and the course mentioned earlier, it is important to briefly describe the content and format of the course. The instructors' goals in designing this course were to help students learn to (1) apply the techniques of exploratory data analysis, (2) understand the concept of sampling variability, (3) critically evaluate the effectiveness of different study designs, and (4) use and interpret inferential statistical procedures. (As previously mentioned, exploratory and inferential analyses—goals 1 and 4—are the focus of our work.) The course deemphasizes the memorization of statistical formulas in favor of students practicing statistics in authentic situations. Specifically, the students analyze real data sets in order to address current scientific and policy-oriented questions (e.g., Does seeding clouds with silver nitrate increase rainfall? Which of two new drugs is most effective in reducing the recurrence of depression? Do female professors earn less than their male counterparts?).

The format of the course includes two hour-long lectures and one hour-long computer laboratory session per week. In each laboratory session, students work in pairs at a computer, using a commercially available statistics package (Minitab, 1999) to complete assigned exercises. These exercises are presented in the form of a lab handout that describes a data set, provides detailed instructions to guide students through the analysis, and asks them to interpret the results of their analysis. Similar exercises are assigned as homework, where students apply the same skills without the supervision of laboratory instructors.

As it stands, this course uses several innovative instructional design techniques (e.g., collaborative learning, hands-on practice). However, given the 1990s research on similar reform-based courses, it seemed quite possible that students could be exiting the course without the desired statistical reasoning skills and transfer abilities. To address these potential areas of poor learning and transfer, we could have jumped in with a variety of new, "better" ideas to test in the class. Unfortunately, however, the existing research on students' difficulties in learning statistical reasoning does not offer much explanation of what causes these difficulties nor does it provide much guidance in devising specific solutions for overcoming them.

Thus, instead of relying on our intuition to guide us where past research could not, we take a systematic approach toward describing and understanding students' learning processes before we begin any instructional interventions. Our approach involves developing a model of how students learn statistical reasoning, testing that model empirically, and using that model to inform instructional innovations. The products of our approach include: (1) a cognitive model of statistical reasoning that is detailed enough to solve the same problems that students are asked to solve in an instructional setting, (2) well-tested instructional innovations, and (3) a computerized learning environment, based on (1) and (2), for students to use in the statistical reasoning class.

The remainder of this part documents four studies we conducted that exemplify (1) and (2). Then, the following part describes how the results of these studies were instrumental in our ongoing development of (3), a new computerized learning environment for statistical reasoning.

Task Analysis

Analyzing the knowledge and skills required for reasoning statistically is an important first step both for understanding how this skill is learned and for designing a learning environment to help teach it. Cognitive theory provides a mechanism for representing knowledge and can make detailed predictions about how that knowledge is learned and used. Within the ACT-R cognitive theory (Anderson & Lebiere, 1998), knowledge is represented in one of two ways; as declarative facts arranged in a semantic network or as procedural skills embodied in a set of production rules, each of which specifies an action to be taken under particular circumstances. These pieces of knowledge can be inferred from traces that document the steps a solver takes at each point in a problem. Once the set of production rules and semantic network are specified, the corresponding problem-solving performance can be generated by simulation using the ACT-R computational engine. Putting these knowledge pieces into a cognitive model makes it possible to compare the theory's predictions with observed behaviors and to evaluate or refine the model.

We began this process of knowledge decomposition by focusing on the first and last of the four course goals that were specified by the instructor (as listed earlier). These goals refer to students' ability to apply the techniques of exploratory data analysis and inferential statistics. By collecting talk-aloud protocols (Ericsson & Simon, 1993) from the statistics instructors and analyzing what they considered to be "ideal" student solutions to typical data analysis problems, we generated a sequence of steps that reflect their problem-solving process (see Fig. 11.2). Note that this sequence of steps can be applied to solve the cloud-seeding example presented earlier. To refine this analysis and obtain a further specification of each step, we generated an initial set of production rules and corresponding declarative facts that enabled the ACT-R simulation program to perform each of the steps (correctly and at the appropriate points in problem solving). Testing the model on sample problems assigned in the course, comparing the model's performance to that of actual students', and identifying parts of problems where the model lacked appropriate knowledge, we iteratively refined our cognitive model. The model thus represented (to a reasonable level of completeness) the facts and skills that students would need in order to solve each part of a typical problem.

Given our focus on improving students' ability to transfer their statistical reasoning ability, we were interested in how much of this knowledge would be general (i.e., applicable in multiple contexts for multiple problems) and how much of it would be case specific (i.e., only applicable under specific circumstances). The model was helpful in making this distinction because it highlighted the fact that there were particular production rules that were used regardless of the specifics of the problem. For

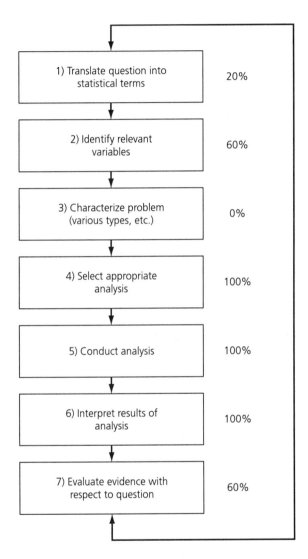

FIG. 11.2. Task analysis of major steps in solving exploratory data analysis problems. Note that this is a cyclical process in which initial analyses may suggest further questions for analysis. Percentages to the right of each step represent the percentage of students in a protocol study who showed explicit evidence of engaging in that step.

example, Table 11.2 shows several of these production rules, translated into pseudocode for easier reading. The first production rule represents the knowledge for executing a particular step, namely, choosing an appropriate graph. Notice, however, that even this particular graph choice step is represented with sufficient generality that it applies to problems with different types of variables. The second and third production rules in the table represent a small part of the common goal structure that guides the application of particular problem-solving steps throughout the solution. This goal structure is depicted at a high level in Fig. 11.2 and, like that figure, applies to almost any exploratory data analysis problem.

For the purpose of understanding students' learning processes, this production representation raised the question: At what level of generality do students learn these rules? For example, students could learn lots of specific rules to apply in different situations instead of the more general rules in our model, or they could learn overly general rules that do not adequately account for the specific conditions under which particular steps are appropriate. For the purpose of improving students' learning via our new learning environment, this question led to the further consideration of how we could design the learning environment to emphasize the common goal structure so that students' internal knowledge representations would be at an appropriate level of generality, like the model's (see the next major part for more details on this issue).

TABLE 11.2
General Production Rules in Cognitive Model of Statistical Reasoning

IF the goal is to address question q with data set d & the relevant variables are x and y & the type of x is x-type & x is the explanatory variable & the type of y is y-type & y is the response variable & a graphical tool for y-type versus x-type data is graph g THEN produce a graph g of y versus x
IF the goal is to address question q with data set d & relevant variables have not yet been selected & variables x and y are in data set d and relevant to question q THEN select x and y as the variables to be analyzed
IF the goal is to address question q with dataset d & the relevant variables are x and y & the type of variable x (quantitative/categorical) has not yet been identified THEN set a subgoal to inspect variable x as to type

This analysis and model development were also quite helpful in establishing a common language among the statistics instructors and cognitive psychologists that facilitated the collaboration in our group. As we developed the model and discussed its possible refinements, the instructors had opportunities to indicate precisely which aspects of the problem-solving process they found important, and the cognitive psychologists had concrete, domain-specific examples to use in discussing how knowledge comes in different forms (e.g., procedural vs. declarative) and the implications of different levels of generality.

Large-Scale Assessments

Having generated a model describing what students need to know to reason statistically on data analysis problems, we next wanted an idea of students' knowledge, both before and after taking the course. This information would be especially helpful for our applied goal of improving instruction because it would indicate students' strengths and weaknesses, that is, where we needed to work most to improve their statistical reasoning abilities. In addition, because of our focus on transfer, we wanted some assessment of how students would perform outside the original learning context. To obtain this information, we created an assessment instrument designed to tap students' statistical reasoning abilities. In particular, we used the results of our task analysis to generate separate questions for each separate concept (a part of the model's semantic network) or skill (a subset of the model's production rule set). In this way, we tried to achieve a close correspondence between items on the instrument and particular pieces of knowledge identified in our task analysis as critical for statistical reasoning.

For ease of administration, scoring, and analysis with large groups of students, we designed the questions in multiple-choice format. Although this conveys more information about the products of problem solving (which is different from most of our other work that emphasizes process), the fact that the questions focus on small subparts of each problem gives some intermediate information about students' problem-solving process. As examples of the content and format of the assessment, Fig. 11.3 shows two questions that were designed to test students' knowledge of how to choose an appropriate graph.

We administered the complete assessment according to a pretest/ posttest design with two groups of students participating—those who did and those who did not take the course between the pretest and posttest

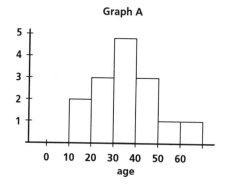

Graph A

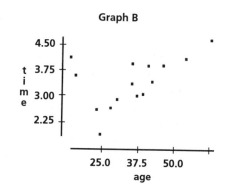

Graph B

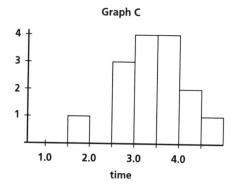

Graph C

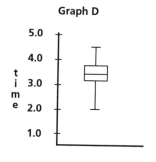

Graph D

12. Suppose you wanted to show a group of new members how much joining this team improves people's running times. Which of the four graphs above would you use? [Answer choices: A, B, C, D, or none of the above]

13. Suppose you were interested in how running times tend to change as people get older. Which graph would you use to get an idea of what this trend looks like? [Answer choices: A, B, C, D, or none of the above]

FIG. 11.3. Two sample assessment questions on choosing appropriate statistical display.

phases. The latter group served as a control so that we could determine what statistical reasoning abilities students in the course were gaining above and beyond those attributable to maturation or exposure to the general college environment. Both groups of students took the pretest in an extracurricular testing session given at the beginning of the school year. Then, at the beginning of the second semester of that same year, students took the posttest in the context of a separate statistics course.

This posttest context represented our attempt at establishing a near-transfer situation; "near" because the testing environment was another statistics course (as opposed to, say, an economics course) but still "transfer" because that course was different from students' original learning environment. Given poor results in the studies reviewed earlier, it seemed prudent to test for near transfer before expanding to more distant transfer tests. Note that the context of this posttest also had important ecological validity that was of interest to the statistics instructors; we were testing students' ability to retain and apply what they learned in one course to a related course downstream in their program of study.

Here, we summarize the results of this assessment and describe how they were helpful to the different members of our group. (Lovett, Greenhouse, & Johnson, 1999, provides a more thorough report of our analyses of the data.) Panel A of Fig. 11.4 presents total percentage correct for each group of students at pretest and posttest. These results were encouraging in that they showed that students who took the statistics course improved their total scores more than did the students who had not taken the statistics course. Such aggregate results, however, do not provide any diagnosis of students' potential areas of strength and weakness. We therefore conducted item-based analyses of students' responses and found three distinct categories of items; (1) items for which the statistics class students increased the accuracy of their responses but for which the other group of students did not, (2) items for which both groups of students showed no increase in accuracy but could have, and (3) items for which both groups of students showed no increase in accuracy due to a ceiling effect at the pretest. Panels B, C, and D of Fig. 11.4 show the average proportion correct for group of students for each of these categories of items, respectively. Only the pattern of results in Panel B demonstrates learning of statistical reasoning skills that can be attributed to the course.

By identifying which items on our test fall into these three categories, we were able to glean important information both about students' areas of strength and weakness (i.e., in what components of statistical reasoning skill are inherently difficult?) and/or how the course might be improved

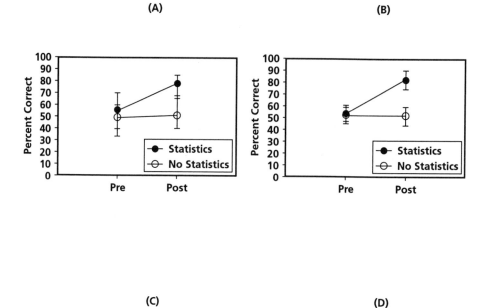

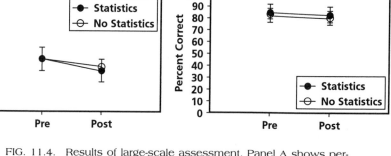

FIG. 11.4.   Results of large-scale assessment. Panel A shows percentage correct over all items. Panel B shows percentage correct for items on which students who took the course improved from pre to posttest. Panel C shows percentage correct for items on which both groups of students showed no improvement, even though they could have. Panel D shows percentage correct for items on which both groups of students showed no improvement, presumably due to a ceiling effect at pretest.

(i.e., in what part of the course is the instruction insufficient?). For example, the first category of items included skills such as interpreting descriptive and inferential statistics and defining statistical terms (e.g., correlation). These skills appear to be well learned from the course, and there is not much need for improvement. The second category of items included skills such as choosing appropriate statistical displays (including the example questions from Fig. 11.3) and drawing conclusions from statistical analyses. The corresponding pattern of performance in Fig. 11.4c suggests that students have particular difficulty with these skills—both before and after the course—and that our efforts at improving the course should be directed at these areas. Finally, the third category of items included interpreting boxplots and scatterplots. That students had an especially easy time with these subskills was somewhat surprising to the instructors. This result implies that the course need not emphasize these subskills as much as it does, something that we could also take into account in our plan for a new learning environment.

Assessing students' abilities skill by skill with this instrument gave the instructors more precise information about the areas of strength and weakness than they could previously obtain. Final exam questions given by instructors often require synthesis of a variety of skills (an important ability to test) but do not offer the same diagnostic capability, nor do they offer a controlled comparison to students' abilities before the course or without having taken the course. In summary, these assessment results provided important information to the instructors about their students' strengths and weaknesses, and they provided initial pointers for the project team as a whole in terms of where we should concentrate our further study of why students have difficulty reasoning statistically.

Detailed Study of Individual Students

As a result of the large-scale assessments, we knew that students exited the course without having fully learned particular subskills important to statistical reasoning (e.g., choosing appropriate analyses, drawing conclusions, etc.), but we did not know the source of these problems. Moreover, we wanted to know how students were able to combine these and their better learned skills in the context of solving authentic problems. To address these questions, we conducted a very different type of study, focusing on individual students' ability to apply statistical reasoning in solving open-ended problems. We asked individual students who had taken the statistics course under study to come into the psychology laboratory and provide talk-aloud protocols while they solved a few data analysis problems analogous to the ones they had encountered in class. They were allowed to use whatever statistics package they preferred (usually the one they had used in the statistics class). The main difference between these experimental sessions and students' computer laboratory sessions in the course was that our problems were stated with only three basic pieces of information; the background needed to understand the problem, the research question being asked, and a description of the data to be analyzed. In contrast, in most of the computer laboratories in the statistics course, students received this information plus an entire lab handout guiding them explicitly as to how they should proceed in their problem solving. Instead of constraining students to a single solution path, we wanted to investigate how they would approach these problems in a much more open format, such as what ideas and strategies for data analysis they would generate on their own. Moreover, this served as a different kind of transfer test to see how well students could solve problems without the typical aid of a lab handout to guide them.

We collected students' talk-aloud protocols and synchronized these with the computer traces of their interactions with the statistics package. Together, these two streams of data offered a rich description of the mental and physical steps students were taking as they solved the problems. Here is a sample problem from our study:

> In men's golf, professional players compete in either the regular tour (if they're under 51 years old) or in the senior tour (if they are 51 or older). Your friend wants to know if there is a difference in the amount of prize money won by the players in the 2 tours. This friend has recorded the prize money of the top 30 players in each tour. The variable *money* contains the money won by each of the players last year. The variable *tour* indicates which tour the player competed in, 1 = regular, 2 = senior. The variable *rank* indicates player rank, 1 = top in the tour.

We analyzed students' verbal and computer protocols in several ways to get a full description of their problem-solving behavior. First, we coded the combined protocols according to the main steps of problem solving (see Fig. 11.2): If a given protocol segment or computer interaction offered evidence that the student had considered one of these steps, we would code the step as attempted. Figure 11.5 shows a protocol excerpt and our coding of each segment. The percentage of students who showed evidence of engaging in each step is presented in Fig. 11.2 next to the box corresponding to that step. It is clear that students were often not engaging (at least

1) Oh, okay. So we need to, he wants to know whether there is a difference in the amount of prize money, the amount of money won by players in the two tours.

2) So, I think this is the prize money, uh, money contains the prize money won by each of these players. Tour indicates which tour the player competes in. Well, you don't really need rank, in order to solve this, right? Cause like, well, I don't know.

4) Um ... I'm gonna do a boxplot ...

5) [Subject uses statistics package to make a boxplot] oh, cool (laugh)— I did it.

6) All right, uh, so just looking at the average. It looks like the people in the senior tour get less money. Um, and there's a lot less variation in the amount of money that, like all the prizes. A couple little outliers in each which means like, I don't know, like some people won, like a lot of money at a time.

FIG. 11.5. Sample protocol with each step coded according to the major steps of statistical reasoning (see Fig. 11.2). Notice that there is no evidence for steps 3 and 7. Also notice that the interpretation is somewhat inaccurate in that boxplots display the median, not the mean as a measure of central tendency.

explicitly) in the first three steps and the last step of our problem-solving sequence. Although it is possible that experts could skip the first three steps and initiate their problem solving at Step 4 (selecting the appropriate analysis), this sample of students did not demonstrate such expertise. Although 100% of protocol subjects showed evidence of attempting to select the appropriate analysis, their accuracy in doing so was only 50%. Thus, it seems likely that inaccuracy in Step 4 was in part caused by skipping Steps 1 through 3. Separate analyses supported this idea by demonstrating that the probability of a correct Step 4 was much higher in cases when the preceding steps were not skipped compared to when they were skipped. Also, note that although 100% of subjects gave some interpretation of their results, only 80% provided accurate interpretations.

Given students' difficulty with Step 4, choosing the appropriate analysis, our next step was to review the protocols to explore the nature of students' inappropriate choices. More specifically, what (if anything) were students doing instead of applying the preceding three steps that could lead them to an appropriate analysis? An "interpretation approach" (Chi, 1997) was used where the protocols were examined to facilitate interpretation of the computer data. In many of the verbal protocols, we found evidence that students were relying on the statistics package as a crutch to get a reasonable analysis on screen. Two such examples are presented. In the first, the student does not systematically derive the appropriate analysis given the problem information but rather uses the statistics package's menu list as an idea generator:

> Oh, okay. Um, I'm not really sure if—do I need to uh we can just, like, graph it, right? Uh line plot, I guess. ... oh, uh histograms, barcharts maybe a boxplot? Uh, no .... Uh, uh histogram, um data table, um ....

In this case, there is no clear constraint on the student's selection process, nor is it guided by a conceptual understanding of the task.

In the second protocol example, a different student uses two separate heuristics for selecting the appropriate analysis, neither of which is related to the specifics of the problem or an understanding of the task. The first heuristic involves relying on what is typically a correct choice in this task (i.e., following the base rates of success on past problems). The second heuristic involves using the statistics package's warning message as feedback that the chosen analysis is not appropriate:

> Oh well, maybe, hmm ... if I highlight all of them [the variables in the data set], and then, maybe make a boxplot cause, in statistics class that always worked when you got stuck, just make a boxplot, and see what happened. So uh, I'll boxplot them, um, *y* by *x*. [quack] Uh oh, it says the variable rank has 30 categories, shall I continue? Usually that was bad, so I cancel that, because it shouldn't come out like that.

These protocol examples offer a preliminary hypothesis for why students were (1) skipping the first three planning steps of the problem-solving process, and (2) relatively inaccurate in selecting an appropriate analysis. Namely, by using the statistics package interface cues, they were able to apply a basic guess-and-test strategy in order to generate analysis.

Our third analysis of the students' problem-solving traces looked for quantitative evidence supporting this hypothesis. In particular, we analyzed various features of the analyses students performed on each problem. We found that, on average, students performed approximately 11 separate analyses per problem, even though only 3 analyses at most could be deemed truly appropriate. Also, of the analyses students generated in their problem solving, approximately 3 per problem were exact repeats of a previously generated (usually inappropriate) analysis. These two results suggest that students were not using an efficient search strategy because they were generating so many extra (generally useless and often redundant) analyses. Moreover, the sequence of analyses generated by the students did not follow what the course had taught. On average, the most informative statistical analysis (i.e., the one that the course instructor would have performed first and the one that was most consistent with the teaching in the course) was the *6th* analysis attempted by these students.

There are at least two possible explanations for this pattern of results. One is that students have not yet learned a systematic procedure for selecting appropriate displays that works for all sorts of data analysis problems. Thus, they do not see the common structure across problems and do not know how to proceed in a systematic fashion. Another possible explanation is that students have arrived at a suboptimal strategy that enables them to "get by" with arbitrary selections but without understanding of the reasoning behind their steps. Both of these suggest that our computerized learning environment should emphasize the common goals and procedures across problems and monitor students' choices to assess the effectiveness of their selection strategies.

Experimental Study of Learning

The previous results helped us uncover an important area of difficulty in students' statistical reasoning—the ability to systematically plan an analysis based on the problem information and on an understanding of statistical displays. Tackling this difficulty area thus became one of our new goals. In particular, we wanted to design our computerized learning environment to facilitate students' planning processes so they could more easily learn to choose appropriate statistical displays and acquire the corresponding skills at an appropriate level of generality. We generated various ideas, based on past research, that would *scaffold* students in this planning process. Before implementing any of our ideas in the context of a full-scale learning environment, however, we compared two potential design variants in a controlled experiment. Our motivation for doing so was twofold. First, as a basic research goal, we wanted to gather more, fine-grained data on how students' learn these planning skills. Note that the studies presented earlier involved either students who had already taken the statistics course (i.e., were not in an initial learning phase) or a data collection procedure that produced very coarse-grained information (i.e., provided data only on students' answers, not their processes). In the following description, we describe data collected at a fine grain from students who had not taken a previous statistics course. Our second motivation was an applied research goal. We wanted to gather some preliminary data on whether our ideas for scaffolding students' planning skills would actually aid learning. In particular, we wanted to compare two versions of a computer interface that manipulated the degree of scaffolding students would receive as they learned how to choose appropriate statistical displays.

The procedure of this experiment involved assigning students to one of two conditions (i.e., end only and immediate feedback) and then asking them to complete four experimental phases (i.e., pretest, instruction, problem solving, and posttest). The first phase involved a set of pretests to assess students' preexperimental understanding of statistical displays and planning. These tests included problems where students had to consider the entire problem-solving situation, not just the step of choosing appropriate displays. The second phase involved an instructional phase in which students read various materials (on the computer) that described different statistical displays, how they are produced, and under what conditions they are appropriate. These materials were made available to students throughout the course of the experiment, whenever students chose to access them. The third phase, the only phase to differ between the two groups, involved a series of 16 problems that students were asked to solve on the computer. Depending on their assigned condition, students received more or less specific feedback as they worked through each problem. Figure 11.6 shows the problem-solving interface. Students in the end-only scaffolding condition were asked to make all five selections shown, in any order, and then to submit their answer. On doing so, they were shown the corresponding statistical display (regardless of whether their selections were correct) and binary feedback (correct/incorrect) regarding their entire response. Note that incorrect feedback for the end-only group did not disambiguate which of the five choices was incorrect. In contrast, students in the intermediate-feedback condition received correct/incorrect feedback after making the first four choices (choosing the response/ explanatory variables and their quantitative/qualitative type). If incorrect, they were forced to try again until these choices were correct. The procedure thus implies that this group of students would only be selecting a type of display (i.e., making the fifth choice) after they had correctly classified the problem situation. Further, it implies that their end-of-problem feedback (same as in the other group) unambiguously referred to the cor-

A dog breeder breeds Great Danes. She has measured the
height and weight of various Great Danes at her kennel.
The variable **height** measures each dog's height in inches.
The variable **weight** measures each dog's weight in
pounds. This breeder is interested in how the dogs' heights
influence their weights. If there is a relationship, she
would like to be able to guess a dog's weight by looking at it's
height.

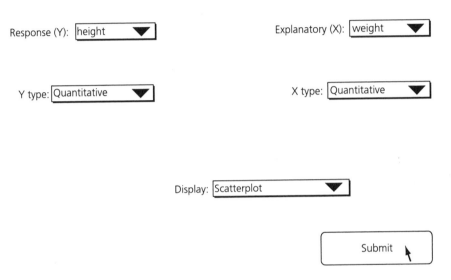

FIG. 11.6. Interface displayed to subjects in learning experiment.

rectness of the fifth (display type) choice. The fourth phase of the experiment involved the same tests used in the first phase.

The data gathered in this experiment consisted of students' answers to
the pre and postexperimental tests (Phases 1 and 4) and complete traces of
their interactions with the computer during Phases 2 and 3. Figure 11.7A
shows that, based on their pre and posttest scores, students improved
a great deal in their ability to select appropriate data displays,
$F(1, 50) = 69.6$, $MSE = 2.83$, $p < .01$. As a point of comparison, it is
interesting to note that students in this experiment, who had taken no previous statistics class and who spent approximately 45 minutes working
with these instructional materials and problems, showed posttest scores
that were comparable to those of students who had taken the full semester course and then participated in the same experiment. This comparison

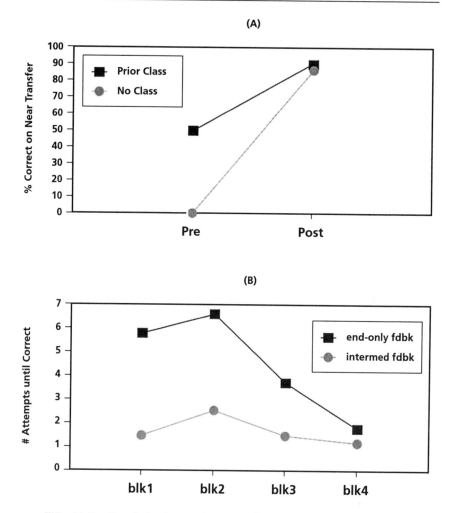

FIG. 11.7. Panel A shows the overall improvement in pre and posttest scores for the two groups of student—those with and without previous statistics courses. Panel B shows the improvement throughout the course of the experiment for the two different conditions (end-only vs. intermediate feedback), including only those students who had no prior statistics classes.

does not suggest that students can learn an entire statistics course in 45 minutes, but rather that the set of subskills involved in selecting appropriate analyses can be reasonably well learned in a short, focused lesson that forces students to practice making these selections on their own. It is often the case in the context of an actual statistics class that students do not actually have many opportunities to make such choices on their own; these choices are either made for them explicitly (in homework or lab assignments that indicate which analysis is appropriate and ask for students' interpretation of the results) or implicitly (in cases where there is only one new analysis being taught in a given week and that analysis is the correct one for the problems assigned that week).

Perhaps more interesting than the pre and posttest data are the data collected while students were learning. On average, the number of attempts made on each problem decreased with problem number for both conditions in the experiment, $F(3, 54) = 2.9$, $MSE = 13.6$, $p <. 05$ (see Fig. 11.7B). In other words, students were getting better at solving the problems over the course of the experiment. Moreover, the number of attempts across blocks of the experimental phase was lower for the intermediate-feedback group, suggesting that this version of the interface made the learning process go more smoothly and quickly, $F(1, 18) = 3.9$, $MSE = 37.3$, $p < .06$ (see Fig. 11.7B). The advantage of the intermediate-feedback group was also revealed when analyzing a particular set of "difficult" problems where it was predicted that students would tend to make errors. On these problems, the intermediate-feedback group chose the correct analysis first 82% of the time, whereas the end-only feedback group chose the correct analysis first 40% of the time.

These results support two general points about how students learn to choose appropriate statistical displays. First, students can acquire mastery of this skill by practicing it in isolation with adequate feedback. This supports the notion that decomposing the task of statistical reasoning into the required knowledge and skills for good performance can lead to targeted, effective instructional interventions. Of course, this knowledge-decomposition idea also acknowledges the value of giving students practice at the "synthesis" skills that are required for handling whole-problem solutions. Second, the fact that intermediate feedback helps students learn this skill more efficiently suggests that students can benefit from more than a standard statistical software package when learning. In particular, the feedback offered by a statistical software package is limited in that (1) it relies on the student's ability to interpret a dubious display as such, (2) it does not indicate what aspect of the student's selection is incorrect, and (3) it does not provide any information to help the student to correct the error. In contrast, the intermediate-feedback condition of this experiment provided enough information to avoid all three of these problems. In our learning environment, we are incorporating feedback features that avoid these problems as well as offering students information on why their selections were wrong.

A CONVERGENT ASSAULT:
PUTTING IT ALL TOGETHER

As these studies show, understanding how students learn statistical reasoning can be studied effectively from many different perspectives. Moreover, greater gains can be achieved when these perspectives are brought together to influence each other. In each of the four studies described, multiple perspectives were integrated (e.g., theoretical and empirical, empirical and classroom-based, etc.) to study a particular aspect of students' statistical reasoning. These four studies also serve to provide important results that are informing the design of our computerized learning environment for statistical reasoning. In this way, all three perspectives converge to impact the way students learn statistical reasoning in the classroom.

The design considerations offered by the above studies' results are as follows. First, the task analysis highlighted the general skills that correspond to the goal structure present in many data analysis problems. Ideally, then, our learning environment should help students to learn these skills in a general way so that they can transfer what they learn to a variety of problem contexts. Second, the large-scale assessment indicated that, although students improved overall on statistical reasoning questions after taking a course, there are particular areas (e.g., selecting appropriate displays, and evaluating the strength of evidence) with ample room for improvement. Our learning environment should give special attention to these aspects of statistical reasoning, such as scaffolding students' intermediate steps. Third, the detailed, process-based study showed that students' difficulties in planning stemmed from the application of nonoptimal strategies for selecting appropriate analyses (e.g., guessing through menu items in the statistics package). Our learning environment thus should discourage students from using these strategies and instead should teach them to apply a systematic strategy based on an understanding of data types and experimental designs. Fourth, the laboratory study showed that practice on planning steps improves students' ability to select appropriate analyses and that intermediate feedback increases students' efficiency of learning.

Applying all these considerations jointly leads to the design of a learning environment that has the following features. First, to highlight the general scheme for solving data analysis problems, the learning environment should make the goal structure explicit. Other researchers achieved this by labeling important goals and subgoals in problem solutions (Catrambone 1995, 1996) and by emphasizing the commonalties across problems

(Cummins, 1992). Figure 11.8 presents a snapshot of a prototype for the interface to our learning environment. Notice that the outlinelike format presents major goals and subgoals with expand/compress buttons for focusing on particular parts of the problem. The labels for these goals and subgoals are the same for all data analysis problems, regardless of the particulars of the data set or questions. Second, our learning environment scaffolds students in their planning processes. The goal structure highlighted in the interface includes steps for considering the relevant variables and their types that students must complete before selecting a particular analysis for the given problem. Here, the aim is to reduce students' "dive in" tendency and to encourage them to explicitly plan their analysis. This interface also makes the invisible skills of planning visible (cf. Koedinger & Anderson, 1993) by giving external actions for steps that ordinarily would only take place "in the students' head." These external actions then enable the third design consideration, offering feedback to students at critical points in problem solving. When students can communicate their intermediate planning steps to the problem-solving interface in Fig. 11.8, the problem-solving engine behind this interface can offer feedback on these steps individually. For example, if a student identifies

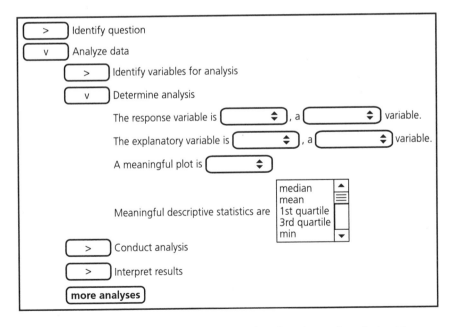

FIG. 11.8. A snapshot of a prototype interface to our learning environment.

the response variable incorrectly, that mistake can be indicated and explained before the student goes on to conduct and interpret analyses that have no relevance to the question at hand. Note that the problem-solving engine here is based on the cognitive model of statistical reasoning developed in the task analysis study; it makes our learning environment an example of an intelligent tutoring system because it can track students' problem solving and offer hints and feedback accordingly.

As we develop and refine this learning environment, we will not abandon the convergent approach that motivated its development; our evaluation protocol for our own system will be based on empirical studies conducted both in the laboratory and the classroom, and we will use these results in combination with theoretical considerations and the guidance of our domain experts to improve the effectiveness of the system. Part of this further development will include going beyond exploratory and inferential data analysis to emphasize the other two goals of the course, namely, sampling variability and experimental design.

Making the General's Strategy Work

Although it was not discussed in the opening story about the General, an important prerequisite for the success of his convergent strategy is effective communication. Coordinated timing was the key to the strategy; if communication among the various troop units was not strong, the whole plan could have been dashed. Similarly, in the collaboration discussed in this chapter, effective communication among the different team members has been critical. Such communication, however, takes time to establish in a multidisciplinary situation. Early in the project, team members with different areas of expertise spoke somewhat different languages. It took collaboration on specific problems of mutual interest, where everyone was willing to consider alternative perspectives, to establish a common language. As this common language has been refined through our work on the project, the synergy of our multiple perspectives has increased.

ACKNOWLEDGMENTS

The author would like to thank Joel Greenhouse, Brian Junker, Rob Kass, and Ken Koedinger who have been and continue to be key collaborators in this project. This work is partially funded by the National Science Foundation, grant number 97–20354.

REFERENCES

Anderson, J. R., & Lebiere, C. (1998). *Atomic components of thought.* Mahwah, NJ: Lawrence Erlbaum Associates.

Brown, A. L. (1992). Design experiments: Theoretical and methodological challenges in creating complex interventions in classroom settings. *Journal of the Learning Sciences, 2,* 141–178.

Catrambone, R. (1995). Aiding subgoal learning: Effects on transfer. *Journal of Educational Psychology,* 87 (1), 5–17.

Catrambone, R. (1996). Generalizing solution procedures learned from examples. *Journal of Experimental Psychology: Learning, Memory, and Cognition,* Vol. 22, no.4, 1020–1031.

Chi, M. T. H. (1997). Quantifying qualitative analyses of verbal data: A practical guide. *The Journal of the Learning Sciences, 5,* (3), 271–315.

Cohen, S., & Chechile, R. A. (1997). Overview of ConStats and the ConStats Assessment. In J. B. Garfield and Burrill (Eds.), *Research on the role of technology in teaching and learning statistics* (pp. 101–110). Voorburg, The Netherlands: International Statistical Institute.

Cohen, S., Smith, G., Chechile, R. A., Burns, G., & Tsai, F. (1996). Identifying impediments to learning probability and statistics from an assessment of instructional software. *Journal of Educational and Behavioral Statistics, 21,* 35–54.

Cohen, S., Tsai, F., & Chechile, R. (1995). A model for assessing student interaction with educational software. *Behavior Research Methods, Instruments, and Computers, 27,* 251–256.

Cummins, D. D. (1992). Role of analogical reasoning in induction of problem categories. *Journal of Experimental Psychology: Learning, Memory, and Cognition, 18,* 1103–1138.

Ericsson, K. A., & Simon, H. A. (1993). *Protocol analysis: Verbal reports as data* (Rev. ed). Cambridge, MA: MIT Press.

Fong, G. T., Krantz, D. H., & Nisbett, R. E. (1986). The effects of statistical training on thinking about everyday problems. *Cognitive Psychology, 18,* 253–292.

Garfield, J. (199f). Beyond testing and grading: Using assessmentto improve students' learning. [35 paragraphs]. *Journal of Statistics Education* [On-line serial]. Available E-mail: archive@jse .stat.ncsu.edu Message: Send jse/v2n1/garfield.

Garfield, J. (1995). How students learn statistics. *International Statistical Review, 63,* 25–34.

Garfield, J., & delMas, R. (1991), Students' conceptions of probability, In D. Vere-Jones (Ed.), *Proceedings of the Third International Conference on Teaching Statistics* (Vol. 1, pp. 340–349). Voorburg, The Netherlands: International Statistical Institute.

Gick, M., & Holyoak, K. J. (1983). Schema induction and analogical transfer. *Cognitive Psychology, 15,* 1–38.

Hunt, E., & Minstrell, J. (1994). A cognitive approach to the teaching of physics. In K. McGilly (Ed.), *Classroom lessons: Integrating cognitive theory and classroom practice* (pp. 51–74). Cambridge, MA: MIT Press.

Kahneman, D., & Tversky, A. (1972). Subjective probability: A judgment of representativeness. *Cognitive Psychology, 3,* 430–454.

Kahneman, D., & Tversky, A. (1973). On the psychology of prediction. *Psychological Review, 80,* 237–251.

Kahneman, D., Slovic, P., & Tversky, A. (1982). *Judgment under uncertainty: Heuristics and biases.* New York: Cambridge University Press.

Klahr, D. (1976). *Cognition and instruction.* Hillsdale, NJ: Lawrence Erlbaum Associates.

Koedinger, K. R., & Anderson, J. R. (1993). Reifying implicit planning in geometry: Guidelines for model-based intelligent tutoring system design. In S. P. Lajoie & S. J. Derry (Eds.), *Computers as cognitive tools* (pp. 15–45). Hillsdale, NJ: Lawrence Erlbaum Associates.

Konold, C., Pollatsek, A., Well, A., & Lohmeier, J. (1993). Inconsistencies in students' reasoning about probability. *Journal for Research in Mathematics Education, 24,* 392–414.

Lovett, M. C., Greenhouse, J. B., & Johnson, M. (1999). *Assessing an introductory statistics course.* Manuscript in preparation.

Melvin, K. B., & Huff, K. R. (1992). Standard errors of statistics students. *Teaching of Psychology, 19* (3), 177–178.

Minitab (Student Version 9) (1999). [Computer Software]. Reading, MA: Addison-Wesley.

Palincsar, A. S., & Brown, A. L. (1986). Interactive teaching to promote independent learning from text. *Reading Teacher, 39,* 771–777.

Pollatsek, A., Konold, C. E., Well, A. D., & Lima, S. D. (1984). Beliefs underlying random sampling. *Memory & Cognition, 12,* 395–401.

Pollatsek, A., Well, A. D., Konold, C., & Hardiman, P. (1987). Understanding conditional probabilities. *Organizational Behavior and Human Decision Processes, 40,* 255–269.

Schaffner, A. A. (1997). Tools for the advancement of undergraduate statistics education [Doctoral dissertation, University of Washington, 1997]. *Dissertation Abstracts International, 58* (08A), 3056.

12

Cognition and Instruction: Enriching the Laboratory School Experience of Children, Teachers, Parents, and Undergraduates

Sharon M. Carver
Carnegie Mellon University

The primary focus of this symposium volume is advances in the understanding of teaching and learning that have developed because of the increasingly reciprocal relationships between psychology and education, between research and practice, and between laboratory and classroom learning contexts. The beneficial synergy between theory, research, and practice has been exemplified in each chapter by fruitful researchers who have contributed significantly to our understanding of cognition and instruction.

The purpose of this chapter is to describe the ways that such research can impact an entire school when the Director of the school, trained as a cognitive psychologist, assumes the responsibility for fostering the development of every child in the school, in every domain, every day of the school year, across, in this case, a 3-year period of preschool and kindergarten. With that as a foundation, I also highlight the ways that the same cognitively based approach has been applied across all aspects of the school's mission,[1] including the professional development of teachers, the interactions with parents of the children in the school, and the undergraduate academic opportunities. Despite the daunting size and incredible complexity of this task, I consistently conclude that the educational experience of each constituent is enriched by the contributions of this field. By sharing these laboratory school experiences, I hope to encourage the continued progress of cognition and instruction research, such as that represented by the other chapters in this volume, and to suggest areas for future expansion of the field in theory, research, and practical impact.

THE CENTRAL PROCESS:
EXPLICIT GOALS DRIVING INSTRUCTION
AND ASSESSMENT DESIGN

My thinking about the link between cognition and instruction was heavily influenced by one point that Jim Greeno (1976) raised at the original Cognition and Instruction symposium in 1974; that is, his notion of using cognitive objectives as opposed to the traditional behavioral ones. He suggested that

> ... the explicit statement of instructional objectives based on psychological theory should have beneficial effects both in design of instruction and assessment of student achievement. The reason in simple: we can generally do a better job of accomplishing something and determining how well we've accomplished it when we have a better understanding of what it is we are trying to accomplish. (p. 123)

For the past 17 years, I have used the three-fold process suggested by this quote to direct my own research, as well as my consulting on others' educational and research designs (see Table 12.1). I begin with a formal domain analysis specifying the declarative, procedural, and metacognitive knowledge that a learner at a given developmental level and with a typical

---

[1]The Children's School is the laboratory school for Carnegie Mellon's Psychology Department. Its goals and responsibilities include (1) development and management of laboratories for research in developmental psychology, (2) training of undergraduate and graduate students in child development theory and research, (3) implementation of a model half-day preschool and full-day kindergarten program for children ages 3–6, (4) provision of resources to parents, (5) provision of resources to the community of early childhood educators, and (6) training of students earning teaching certificates (in collaboration with other local colleges and universities).

TABLE 12.1
GOALS → PROGRAM → ASSESSMENT Approach

Goals:	Detailed Task Analysis Considering Developmental Level Considering Knowledge Base Considering Available Time
Program:	Explicit Focus on Target Consistent with Cognitive Principles
Assessment:	Cognitive Assessments of Process Covering the Full Target

knowledge base could reasonably be expected to acquire in the designated period of time. I then design instructional interventions to explicitly target the identified goals in ways that are consistent with well-established cognitive principles and develop cognitive assessments of learning that cover the full range of the targeted skills. The arrows in the title of Table 12.1 connote the essential alignment of the goals, program, and assessment rather than indicating a rigid sequence of design. In practice, the consideration of possible assessments helps sharpen the goal specifications and narrow the program options, and program constraints impact both goals and assessment.

My first attempt to apply this approach began with a limited but tractable set of debugging skills (Carver & Klahr, 1986; Klahr & Carver, 1988), one of the powerful ideas that many educators believed elementary school children would discover via experience with well-designed programming languages. First, I specified a model of basic LOGO debugging skills, including key knowledge and strategies necessary for identifying the likely type and location of a bug before beginning to search the program code. I found that students with extensive but unstructured LOGO experience did not build a useful knowledge base of bug types or discover these effective debugging skills. I then developed a 30-minute lesson to teach the search narrowing skills explicitly and found that elementary students were able to utilize the strategies with minimal teacher support. In several studies, I then demonstrated that students applied the target debugging skills on program debugging tasks, transferred them to noncomputer debugging tasks (specifically, finding the mistake in a written set of directions), and maintained their new level of performance after a semester's delay (Carver, 1988). In other words, short-term explicit instruction can promote significant learning, transfer, and retention, at least for this well-defined domain in a small class context, with me as the teacher, using assessments that are carefully designed to have goal structures isomorphic to the instruction.

In an attempt to work more closely with teachers on a topic of broader educational significance in a more realistic school setting, I studied the "research and communication skills" necessary for urban students doing typical middle school reports. In a 4-year series of studies that involved major redesign of middle school curriculum,[2] my students and I found that by identifying the goal structure and key strategies involved in the process, we were able to design explicit instruction that was successful in promoting middle school students' use of the targeted process (Carver, 1995, in press). For example, in one study that I did with Myunghee Kang (Carver, in press; Carver & Kang, 1999), we focused on the process of organizing notes into a coherent structure that could be represented in HyperCard. Kang developed instruction that focused the students on intentionally completing each step in the organization process and evaluating their own and other students' stacks for their organizational quality. Using a split-class design, she showed that the half of each class that got the focused instruction based on her model improved more from pretest to posttest than did the other half of the students on three different assessments, an interview conducted during their own process of organizing material for a class project, an analysis of the organizational quality of the stack they produced, and a written test with questions about how they conduct research projects. Once again, the key finding was that an explicit link between goals, program design, and assessment provides a powerful means of enhancing learning. However, we found that it was much more difficult and complicated to use this approach in a real school context, for an extended period of time, while targeting a broader set of skills. Also, although the collaborative approach between researchers and teachers proved useful in many ways, the project was plagued with high teacher mobility rates and an inconsistent commitment of the public school system. This situation caused frequent frustrations, ones that are commonly experienced by many of the researchers who contributed to this volume.

Thus, when presented with the opportunity to gain more control of the administrative aspects of my school site by becoming a Director, I decided to shift career tracks to head a psychology department laboratory school. The challenge is, of course, that now I am responsible for the education of

---

[2]This research was supported by grants from the James S. McDonnell Foundation's Cognitive Studies in Educational Practice Program, by Apple Computer, Inc.'s Crossroads Program, and by a subcontract from the Center for Technology in Education.

children, teachers, parents, and undergraduates, not to mention the public relations, facilities, and other school issues that are beyond the scope of this chapter. The relevant question for this volume is: To what extent can I use principles derived from cognitive theories and research, together with experience from educational practice, to set appropriate goals for development, to design an instructional program that will encourage growth, and to assess each individual's progress? Table 12.2 shows how I summarize the approach in teacher and/or administrator training contexts.

Integrating cognition and instruction across an entire school required me to simplify the approach that I had used in my earlier research. I needed to find a practically useful level of application for the cognitive principles and research strategies that shaped my work on debugging and on research and communication. Jim Minstrell's description of continually switching hats from teacher to researcher while adapting his goals, instructional approaches, and even assessments "online" (chap. 4) parallels my situation. As with most new problem-solving contexts, I initially applied "weak methods," general heuristics based on well-established cognitive principles, and then developed stronger, more context-specific methods via experience and refinement cycles. We have been the most thorough and made the most progress in using clear goals to design the children's program and assessments, so I present that first. Then, I briefly discuss the ways that the same approach applies to the teachers, parents, and undergraduates, even though we have spent less formal development time on those aspects.

TABLE 12.2
The G → P → A Approach as Presented in Training

Children's School
Goals → Program → Assessment (GPA) Approach

• Specify developmentally appropriate learning objectives (GOALS) re: the Whole Child and the specific population served.

• Use the goals as a systematic framework for focusing PROGRAM and ASSESSMENT design.

   Structure the Early Childhood Program to Foster Development
   • Teaching Strategies
   • Classroom Routines & Transitions
   • Curriculum Content with Developmentally Appropriate Activities
   • Learning Environment

   Focus Assessment on the Goals
   • Teacher Observations
   • Teacher Documentation
   • Parent Conferences

GOAL-DRIVEN DESIGNS
FOR YOUNG CHILDREN

Specifying Goals

Given the wide range of social, cognitive, and physical development goals for young children, doing a full task analysis of each subgoal was not practical. We used the strategy of starting with a global level analysis and then made continual refinements to get more specific, particularly for areas that required more program input for their development. My teachers and I started with specifying and prioritizing the general areas of development for which we would set goals (see Table 12.3). At an early childhood level, fostering "Self-Esteem and Independence" and "Interaction and Cooperation" should get top priority because students entering elementary school without those skills have the greatest difficulty succeeding. The more traditionally cognitive domains of development were also strongly emphasized. We used the terms "Communication" and "Discovery and Exploration" to focus explicitly on the cognitive foundations for academics rather than on subject areas, like language arts, science, and math. "Physical Capabilities" was included but with a low priority because both small and large motor development progresses without much intervention, assuming that the child has ample opportunity for productive movement. Finally, "Creativity" was added because we wanted

TABLE 12.3
Learning Goals Underlying Program and Assessment

Children's School
Basic Learning Goals
1. **Self-Esteem & Independence**—encouraging each child's pride in individual characteristics, families, experiences, and accomplishments and each child's responsibility for personal care, actions, and words.
2. **Interaction & Cooperation**—promoting children's social skills for diverse adult and peer relations, including listening, turn taking, following directions, rules and routines, group participation, care for shared materials, and conflict resolution.
3. **Communication**—facilitating comprehension and expression skills beginning with oral and progressing to written language.
4. **Discovery & Exploration**—fostering a positive attitude toward learning through questioning, observing, and experimenting with varied materials related to diverse themes.
5. **Physical Capabilities**—giving children opportunities to use their growing bodies to develop small and large motor skills and coordination.
6. **Creativity**—cultivating each child's ability to express ideas and emotions through art, music, movement, and drama.

to promote children's ability to express themselves and their ideas in a variety of ways.

Specifying categories such as these is important for establishing a consistent framework for the school (including the education of teachers, parents, and undergraduates), but this level of description is not otherwise useful for instruction and assessment design. Our staff works from goal specifications that we developed at one level deeper than those in Table 12.3 and that indicate the anticipated progression from age 3 to 5. We developed these more detailed specifications by collecting educational goal statements for preschoolers from around the country and then using the teachers' experience and my knowledge of developmental research to refine them. Typically, the developmental literature led to added breadth and depth in the cognitive areas, and it also helped ensure that we were following natural developmental sequences, like those that Kalchman, Moss, and Case described for mathematics (chap. 1).

To exemplify the level of task analysis we used, Appendix A includes the full outline and parts of our specification for the domains of Communication and of Discovery and Exploration.[3] For the Communication domain, we focus on speaking, literature/reading, and writing, each of which is divided into subcategories. For the Discovery and Exploration domain, we focus on foundations for scientific and mathematical thinking. Each domain includes goals for generalizable attitudes, concepts, and skills. Bob Siegler raised the question of how to inculcate the "habit of mind" to pursue meaning (chap. 6). At the Children's School, we make "approaches to learning" an explicit goal for young children and then design program routines, teaching strategies, and curriculum activities to foster such development. At this level of education, we are not particularly concerned with children developing a specific, well-defined body of conceptual knowledge from social studies or science, but we do vary our units to expose children to a range of topics for study. For each thematic unit, we identify the basic concepts related to the topic, introduce them in a variety of ways, and reinforce them via diverse activities. Because the units vary from year to year and the conceptual content for each is extensive, only key concepts that are relevant in many units are listed as general goals. For example, the goals for Discovery and Exploration include basic number, space, and measurement concepts (see the outline in Appendix A). Our goal specification does, however, include an extensive

---

[3]The full specification for all six domains listed in Table 12.3 is available by contacting Dr. Sharon M. Carver at the Children's School, Carnegie Mellon University, Pittsburgh, PA 15213.

list of skills because most of the skills that we emphasize in all six domains are applicable across topics of study. Taken together, the general approaches to learning, basic concepts, and widely applicable skills that we have specified represent our understanding of the early childhood development that our program is designed to support and foster.

Designing a Model Program

Having clear goals for the children's development guides our program design and refinement efforts, but where does cognitive theory and research fit? A Piagetian might stress the importance of creating an environment in which preoperational children can engage in active learning, continually assimilating new experiences and accommodating schemata until they eventually reorganize their cognitive structures to reach a new level of concrete reasoning (Miller, 1993). A Vygotskian would place more emphasis on the social interactions involved in the learning process by focusing on ways an adult or more skilled peer could provide scaffolding so that the child is able to practice and eventually master tasks at the higher end of her zone of proximal development (Miller, 1993). Teachers are, in fact, drawn to these approaches because they are highly general "rules of thumb" that can be used to label, describe, or justify many of the strategies that excellent teachers use naturally.

Applying the more detailed principles from the field of Cognition and Instruction offers a clearer vocabulary for discussing the predicted effects of particular program features, a level of description one level deeper than the approaches I just mentioned (e.g., Klahr, Chen, & Toth distinguish between domain-general and domain-specific knowledge, chap. 3), and a more systematic focus on the process of change. Together, these benefits enable us to move beyond the artificial constraints imposed by stage boundaries to consider the specific conditions under which particular children progress toward each goal most effectively. They also specify a wide variety of scaffolding strategies so teachers can purposefully choose among them in different contexts. As Palincsar and Magnusson suggested in chapter 5, researchers need to focus on a smaller grain size in their analyses of teaching and learning to specify why certain approaches, like their use of the scientist's notebook to model scientific inquiry processes, have particular effects.

Lists of such "key principles" are widely available, typically in texts with titles such as *Cognitive Psychology for Teachers* (Glover, Ronning, & Bruning, 1990) or *Cognitive Classroom Learning* (Phye & Andre,

1986), and each researcher in the field, at least implicitly, has a favorite set. In this chapter, I describe the top five metaprinciples that we use to shape our early childhood program. Each of these is typically part of expert teachers' repertoire of strategies, but I have found that making them explicit during design discussions increases the likelihood that they are consistently and effectively taught and applied.

Metaprinciple 1: Build on Prior Knowledge. An extensive body of literature from cognitive and developmental psychology indicates the importance of activating prior knowledge in order to get effective storage and, ultimately, retrieval of new knowledge (Anderson, 1983), as well as the impact of a learner's correct and incorrect models of a domain (Siegler, 1998). In addition, learners typically demonstrate the most advanced processing in familiar contexts and show the greatest attention span and memory in situations for which they have developed a high level of automaticity of their procedures (Chi, 1981).

At the Children's School, we begin our instructional design process with an understanding of the foundations with which individuals enter our learning context. Based on both the developmental research literature and practical teaching experience, we expect a typical range of information-processing capacity, knowledge, strategies, and metacognitive skill in social, cognitive, and physical development based on the children's ages and background. With this in mind, we formulate what we believe to be developmentally appropriate daily schedules, classroom routines, and physical arrangements of the learning environment for each group of students. To offer a simple example, the size and spacing of the furniture in the classrooms changes in accordance with the children's physical stature and with the increasing control of their bodies. Similarly, the classroom routines become more elaborate and rely more heavily on the children taking responsibility as their level of independence for self-care and cognitive capacity for following multistep procedures improves.

The Children's School curriculum is designed to build on children's prior knowledge and to foster growth toward mastery of the goals we have specified. We develop thematic units that invite children to explore specific topics in depth while challenging them in each of the six domains. Our teachers explicitly take prior knowledge into account in planning the units by specifying the topic-related concepts that they anticipate the group already possesses (including possible "preconceptions," as Minstrell calls them in chap. 4) and then identifying key concepts that they intend to help the children develop. When designing a unit, the teachers use their knowledge of the unit's timing within the year and sequence relative to other units to specify which aspects of each goal domain should be emphasized. They list theme-related activities designed to foster development within each domain. Appendix B includes excerpts from the study of "Ponds" that was in progress at the Children's School during the symposium.

Evidence for the centrality of this prior knowledge principle exists within this very volume, in the frequency with which it drove the researchers' task analyses and intervention designs. The application of Metaprinciple #1 was clearly evident in the developmental sequence of layers in the conceptual structure for number, the explicit links between instruction and the students' existing knowledge of percents, and the "walk-a-thon" problems (Kalchman, Moss, & Case, chap. 1). Palincsar and Magnusson's explicit links between second-hand investigations and the students' own experiments (chap. 5), rather than the commonly used reverse order, exemplifies instructional design based on maximizing prior knowledge effects. Minstrell's specification of knowledge "facets" and choice of instructional prompts based on a diagnosis of a student's current set of facets (chap. 4) is also a direct application of Metaprinciple #1. Similarly, Lehrer, Schauble, Strom and Pligge's instruction built carefully on students' "intuitive theories," and new concepts were "anchored" in concepts built during the prior year's instruction (chap. 2). At a more philosophical level, their whole project stemmed from a claim about the importance of prior knowledge, that is, that mathematizing ideas creates a firm foundation for understanding science.

Metaprinciple 2: Make Thinking Explicit.   Research in cognitive psychology has documented the value of explicit communication for explaining properties of the task (Carver & Klahr, 1986), directing learners' attention to key features, which in turn aids encoding, clarifying declarative, procedural, and, especially, metacognitive components of the learning task (Siegler, 1998), highlighting distinctions between similar concepts and procedures (Anderson, 1983), and providing effective feedback (Anderson, Corbett, Koedinger, & Pelletier, 1995). Developing specific prompts for the key steps in a cognitive activity, whether they are verbally given by a teacher, embedded in a visual model (Carver, 1995), or supported by an intelligent tutor (Anderson et al., 1995), both strengthen and fine tune the thinking process.

Klahr, Chen, and Toth's primary manipulation (chap. 3) directly tested this explicitness principle and showed that combining clear probes with training yielded the best performance. Other researchers' work demonstrated the important point that explicitness does not necessarily imply direct "telling." Lehrer, Schauble, Strom, and Pligge used "inscriptions" to make thinking explicit (chap. 2); Palincsar amd Magnusson invented the "scientist's notebook" (chap. 5); and Minstrell fashioned a set of queries posed by the "Diagnoser" in response to student answers that reveal "preconceptions" (chap. 4).

At the Children's School, having thematic units developed with specific focus on the key concepts and developmental goals is an important first step in making thinking explicit (Appendix B). The teachers, themselves, are clearer about what they are trying to teach and they are more likely to stress key concepts and balance their emphasis on all six domains of development. In addition, the teachers use many verbal and gestural strategies to direct the children's attention to the central elements of a concept or task. In one recent book reading session on the solar system, a preschool teacher used (a) increased volume and enunciation, (b) verbal repetition, (c) representational gesture with one finger, and even (d) full-body enactment to highlight the difference between rotation of the earth and revolution around the sun. As the children ask questions and offer examples during discussions, the teachers explicitly shape their understanding via direct instruction, posing questions, and encouraging comparison and contrast.

One striking example that integrates both of the first two metaprinciples is our approach to fostering conflict resolution in young children. Initially, the teacher intervenes in the process to explicitly model strategies for identifying the problem from both children's point of view, proposing solutions, agreeing on one, and then implementing it. As the children become familiar with the process, the teacher becomes a coach who prompts them for each step of the process as necessary, until the children become comfortable doing it independently. Recently, in the context of working with our youngest and least skilled children on conflict resolution, we began to discuss the cognitive capacity constraints on the process. We found that the demands of formulating sentences in an emotionally charged context were too high for the youngest children, so we began offering sentence templates and using gestures instead. Similar approaches have been utilized effectively at the Child Development Center at U.C. Davis (Linda Acredolo, personal communication, 11/5/98), and the potential for gestural evidence of cognitive states preceding verbal evidence has been documented in the laboratory (Alibali & Goldin-Meadow, 1993).

Analyzing two individual cases in which children had extreme difficulty with conflict resolution revealed contrasting starting points for intervention and differential focus for explicitness. In one case, the child entered the program viewing verbal and physical aggression as a game of control, so the teachers supplemented the modeling described earlier with explicit prompting to consider other children's perspectives and to notice the positive outcomes of nonaggressive interactions. Another child with similar aggressive tendencies had proprioceptive difficulties monitoring and controlling his own body, which then required us to focus our explicit discussion and modeling on the physical aspects of conflict resolution, such as increasing the amount of space between the children in conflict and the amount of physical support the teacher used.

Metaprinciple 3: Emphasize Links.   In Siegler's discussion of the first five chapters in this volume (chap. 6), he extracted this metaprinciple as a common thread, phrased as "the meaning is in the links." Minstrell's example of comparing and contrasting the forces acting on varied supports for a book (chap. 4), Kalchman, Moss, and Case's development of manipulatives to embody mathematics concepts (chap. 1), and Lehrer, Schauble, Strom, and Pligge's multiple representations for ratios (chap. 2) all exemplify instructional designs based on extensive research documenting the advantages of cognitive organization and elaborative processing (Siegler, 1998). Using advanced organizers, providing multiple representations of concepts, generating examples and explanations, and otherwise elaboratively processing information contribute to the development of better integrated and more complex knowledge structures (Glover, Ronning, & Bruning, 1990). These connections, in turn, improve retrieval, help fill gaps in recall, and generally improve one's comprehension.

During individual lessons within a unit, our teachers use a variety of strategies for encouraging the development of a well-integrated knowledge base. They routinely combine visual and verbal representations, invite students to share their experiences related to a given lesson, and intentionally ask children to recall aspects of prior related lessons. To represent specific connections, they often draw concept webs for a given topic during their discussions with the children in their group. Typically, the web is started as a means of activating prior knowledge during the introduction of a topic, and then ideas are added during subsequent sessions in which nonfiction books are read, artifacts are explored, experiments conducted, and so forth. Even for nonreaders, this webbing strategy explicitly emphasizes the relationship between concepts and encourages the children to begin intentionally connecting ideas.

Emphasizing one theme for an extended time period, such as the 2 to 3 weeks of our units, allows the children to explore multiple aspects of a concept. For example, we began the "Ponds" unit by studying the water, progressed to exploring the plant life in and around the water, and then continued with the animal life. The children made repeated trips to the pond near campus, each time reinforcing and extending their concepts, making connections between what they discussed at school and what they experienced at the pond.

Although our teachers continually refine their use of strategies such as webbing and extended thematic units, studying their specific impact on children's developing concepts is an untapped research area in early childhood development. As we explore the effectiveness of modifications such as adding graphic images to webs, we are also planning to develop research procedures that can be used within our program while maintaining experimental control.

Metaprinciple 4: Provide Practice Opportunities. The necessity of repetition in varied contexts for the development of proficient and efficient skills has been well documented (Anderson, 1983). Basic findings of frequency and distributed practice effects are easily applied in educational contexts. We discuss the importance of practicing routines to develop strong scripts, and repetition of existing skills to develop the automaticity that frees capacity for more advanced tasks or combination of skills. We balance that with the importance of providing a wide variety of contexts for knowledge and skill application to heighten the distinctiveness of both concepts and strategies, as well as improve the generality of their application (Glover, Ronning, & Bruning, 1990). In addition to the standard cognitive literature, specific recommendations for sequencing practice opportunities are discussed in the cognitive apprenticeship literature (Collins, Brown, & Newman, 1989; Collins, Hawkins, & Carver, 1991).

The consistent repetition of the Children's School daily and weekly routines, as well as the consistent expectations for behavior, increases the strength of their memory and ease of retrievability, which, in turn, sets the stage for the children's comfort with and independence in our learning environment. Offering opportunities for repeated practice of foundational skills encourages children to work toward mastery, which also increases self-esteem. Kalchman, Moss, and Case's high ratio of problems per representation (chap. 1) focuses on the repetition aspect of the practice principle and also emphasizes the ways that cognitive gains underlie social and motivational improvements.

Within a thematic unit, children have varied opportunities to acquire, strengthen, and refine their concepts via experimentation, stories, dramatic play, art, games, computer activities, and so forth. We also attempt to develop a conceptual progression across units that reinforces and extends children's concepts. For example, we recently planned a sequence for the fall that involves studying ourselves and our families, where we live (country and city, buildings, transportation, and community helpers), what we eat (food, farms, grocery stores, and restaurants), and what we wear (clothing, shoes, hats, work clothes, dress clothes). In the winter, we will then study China, comparing and contrasting all of the same aspects. In addition to supporting conceptual development, our thematic units actually serve as varied contexts for growth in each of the six domains. Within each unit, we purposely provide activities that foster increasingly diverse and complex uses of the skills in each of our six developmental domains. This distributed practice in varied and increasingly challenging contexts promotes skill acquisition that is impressively generalizable. Similar applications of Metaprinciple #4 are clearly evident in Palincsar and Magnusson's "cycles of inquiry" (chap. 5), Minstrell's combination of work with the Diagnoser, labs, and class discussions (chap. 4), and Reiser, Tabak, Sandoval, Smith, Steinmuller, and Leone's integrated design for technology-infused curricula (chap. 9).

Metaprinciple 5: Expect Individual Variability. Often times, cognitive and developmental psychologists focus on establishing characteristics of cognitive processing, developmental progressions, and the effects of experience at a group level. As I have already discussed, these findings are clearly useful for establishing reasonable developmental goals and metaprinciples of design for educational contexts. At the same time, researchers who analyze their data at an individual level, such as Klahr, Chen, and Toth's analysis of different learning patterns for individual students (chap. 3), often discover dramatic contrasts in the learning process. Similarly, at the classroom level, the impact of individual variability is often a significant factor, and our success in responding to the full range typically determines our overall effectiveness.

In our preschool, we divide our preschool children into groups with only a 6-month range of ages, which limits the developmental range more than most schools and allows our teachers to focus their lessons on a narrower range. Nonetheless, we find a wide variability in developmental levels that is exaggerated by divergent background experiences, even for our young 3-year-olds, and by individual differences such as those Gardner (1993) might characterize as intelligence profiles, or others might describe as "learning styles" (Tobias, 1994). In addition, individual variability in home situations and the presence of developmental disabilities, however subtle, need to be included in the instructional planning process. For that reason, we also incorporate periods of time when children interact across groups, both indoors and outdoors. In these contexts, children are more able to interact with children of similar interests and abilities, independent of age grouping.

This principle highlights one limitation of applying the theories, methods, and findings of research in the field of cognition and instruction, and often makes me wish I had degrees in medicine, counseling, and special education. The key is that we need to focus on the integration of social, cognitive, and physical domains within one child and realize that what happens during the 18 to 20 hours per day the child spends outside of school impacts what happens in school. We need to evaluate the individual combination of developmental, experiential, and potential ability and disability factors that impact a child's progress so that we can plan individualized strategies for fostering development.

For example, many kindergartners start the year with poorly developed fine motor skills, partly because of developmental constraints and partly because of the types of experience available in the previous years both in and out of school. Typically, such skill limitations cause no problem because physical maturation in the 5th and 6th years and the fine motor activities in our kindergarten program together yield impressive progress for almost all children. One child, however, did not progress like the others, despite strong cognitive skills. The fact that he could not dress himself, open his lunchbox, and ride a tricycle started impacting his self-confidence and his social interactions. Increasing frustrations in both social and physical domains yielded further isolation and emotional breakdowns, which eventually started impacting the cognitive progress as well. Obviously, inadequacies in any of these domains have mutual influence in a negative direction here. Thus, we began to explore factors beyond maturation and experience as the primary cause of the problem. To make a long story short, we relied on counseling skills in working with the parents to encourage developmental screening and neurological diagnostics, then consulted with medical personnel to eventually reach a diagnosis of dyspraxia (poor motor planning), and finally integrated some basic special education strategies to identify ways to use the child's cognitive strengths to explicitly coach himself in motor planning.

Discovering and dealing with such individual variability essentially means that we must utilize a case study approach to determine the key goals for emphasis and effective instructional strategies relative to each child's specific foundations. That requires an acceptance of nonstandard instruction. Although designing the instructional program in advance is important, as described earlier, our success with whole, individual children depends largely on the teacher's ability to adapt her program to each individual student based on her concurrent assessment of the child's understanding, progress, attitude, and so forth. In addition, unlike a research project that targets one specific set of skills per instructional program, in a real classroom, multiple goals are simultaneously being targeted. In many cases, a teacher will use one activity to strengthen different skills in individual children. For example, a teacher might play the familiar game of Chutes & Ladders with three preschoolers, emphasizing the number patterns with Nina, who already taught herself to read in both English and Russian, focusing on politely taking turns and encouraging each other with Mary, who was diagnosed with autism, and physically directing Justin's hand to move appropriately from square to square to help refine his proprioceptive control of motor direction and force.

Assessing Progress

The online adaptation that characterizes our instructional approach is, in a sense, our primary method of assessment. As such, it involves the same cognitive principles of (1) identifying a child's prior knowledge, (2) following her thought processes as she communicates them via actions and words, (3) noting the connections she makes between ideas, (4) tracking her applications and improvements in various contexts of practice, and (5) consciously recording individual factors of maturation, environment, and abilities or disabilities.

We use our six domains of development to structure our assessment process. The product is a conference form that summarizes a child's progress in each area via a brief checklist and a paragraph of explanation (see Appendix C for examples related to Communication and Discovery & Exploration). The teacher talks with the child's parents about each aspect of development to provide additional explanation, detail, and often strategies for improvement. Having consistent categories and types of items within them helped us to get diverse teachers to talk about the same aspects of development with parents across the 3 years of our program.

The teachers develop these summaries based on longitudinal observation of the child in the natural school context. They record anecdotes about the child's interaction with others, response to activities, and so forth. They save products of the children's exploration where possible or take photos of others, such as block structures built. Our collection of varied evidence within the classroom context is similar to Minstrell's use of discussion comments, test performance, lab activities, and other written work as the basis for assessing his students (chap. 4).

For domains where classroom observation is impractical because of the number of children or the complexity of the target skills, we have developed some structured, individual assessments that are conducted by a research assistant who then communicates the results to the child's teacher in writing. The sessions are also videotaped so that the teacher can watch them if necessary. For example, we developed an assessment this semester that tapped a variety of communication skills within a single session (see Appendix D).

Although the level of detail possible with such structured assessments could be very useful, it is not practical to assess every detail of every subgoal for all six domains. For that reason, we reserve the most detailed analysis and documentation for cases of developmental difficulty or significant delay, such as those previously described as struggling with aggression or dyspraxia. Challenging situations in both instruction and assessment arenas are also the ones where we analyze our own applications of the cognitive metaprinciples most closely, because that is where we stand to benefit most from the time and effort required to do the analysis. As the next part indicates, such analyses are central to the alignment of goals, program, and assessment for the adult learners in the laboratory school.

GOAL-DRIVEN DESIGNS
FOR ADULT LEARNERS

Although we have not described our approach with teachers, parents, or undergraduates in as much detail as we have for the children, the essential process of basing program design and assessment on clear specifications of developmental goals and on strong cognitive principles is the same. From the start, we have a simpler case because we can typically assume the fully developed adult cognitive system at the outset. Also, our responsibility is primarily for fostering growth in the cognitive domain, although each individual's interaction skills, relational context, health status, and so forth, often have a major impact on the outcomes.

At a global level, my goal for all of the adults in the laboratory school context is to understand and to be able to utilize information from theory,

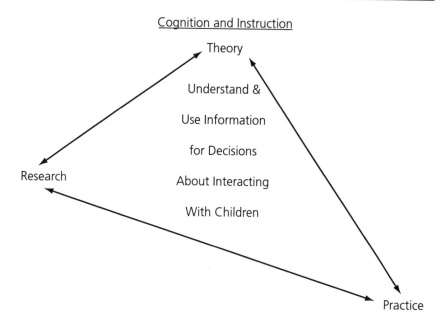

FIG. 12.1.   Contributions from theory, research, and practice.

research, and practice to make sound decisions about the ways that they interact with young children. The differences in approach for adult learners in the laboratory school stems primarily from the differing amounts of background they have with each part of the theory, research, and practice triangle (Fig. 12.1).

Staff Development

Teachers at the laboratory school start with a strong foundation in the practice part of the triangle—excellent interaction styles, prior knowledge of which activities work and which do not, and lots of experience adapting their approaches to a wide variety of children. All have some coursework in child development and most are active readers of early childhood journals, which occasionally mention psychology theories or research findings while describing effective educational methods. Despite teaching in CMU's laboratory school, none of the teachers on the staff when I arrived had formal knowledge of information-processing theories, even those that were developed via research in their own school, and I have never been able to hire a teacher who has already had such training.

Given that my goal is to strengthen and better integrate each part of the triangle, what "program" can I provide for teachers and how can I assess their progress? As a director, I work with the teachers through the formal professional development opportunities that I offer, the informal consulting on program, students, and so forth that I provide, and the collaborative work I do with teachers when we become the teachers of teachers, parents, and undergraduates. Progress is most directly evident in the teachers' dialogue with me and each other and in their written work, but it can also be inferred by observing them in the classroom. Most of my assessment involves ongoing and informal evaluations that impact my staff development program; although I do have a more formal, annual evaluation meeting with each staff person to discuss their progress and the next steps in each of seven categories.[4]

Because practical knowledge was the clearest strength of my staff, I began 6 years ago by using professional development time to explicitly discuss the teachers' goals for their students, to agree on a consistent vocabulary for goal categories, and to establish an appropriate progression of expectations for the 3 years of our program, based on the foundations with which children typically enter our program and the common developmental changes they may experience. We then altered our assessment process and conference forms to align with the six goal categories, so that teachers would discuss the same aspects of development in each of their reports each year. Once we were clear about our goals and the aspects of each that we would be assessing, the next step was to plan our program to foster each aspect of development. What we learned was that having the goals framework helped us to determine whether our program was providing a well-balanced set of learning experiences, to choose among the many possible activities, and to intentionally focus activities on the areas in which a particular student or group of students was weak. This process has made our thinking about early childhood education explicit, and the goal framework has helped organize the links we form as we read new articles, visit other programs, and integrate new methods and materials into our program.

---

[4]Teacher assessment categories include Interactions with Children, Program Planning & Implementation, Knowledge/Expertise, Professional Approach to Work, Problem Solving, Team Approach to Staff Interactions, and Other Professional Interactions. This set is broader than the staff development goal discussed in this chapter.

As with any learner, practice dramatically affects the depth of acquisition and utility of application in new contexts. Each staff member is responsible for coordinating one or two of the thematic units for the year, so each individual has an opportunity to independently practice identifying the conceptual foundations and goals for a topic and to specify ways in which each of the six domains can be advanced by our program. During that process, I am available for consultation and can provide a level of guidance and instruction that is appropriate for each individual. The teachers get a similar opportunity to work independently or consult with me when they teach other teachers, either the student teachers that they supervise, colleagues at a professional conference, or teachers that attend the professional development sessions that the Children's School offers. For example, several teachers collaborated on a presentation about the ways that we integrate cooking activities into our thematic units and discussed the specific aspects of each developmental domain that can be intentionally fostered via cooking. Talking about the six domains with parents during conferences and with undergraduate interns provides additional opportunity for them to strengthen their own understanding.

My staff development examples thus far have focused on formal professional development that involved essentially the whole staff, with basic modifications or extra work with people who had weaker foundations. My informal, more individual, interactions with teachers typically focus on discussing why some part of the program did not work or how to help a particular child who is experiencing a developmental difficulty or delay in one or more areas. In such cases, like the example of fostering conflict resolution, I typically use the same cognitive principles to guide the discussion. Did we assume some prior knowledge, skill, or interest that the children did not have? Did we make the process, expectations, and so forth explicit enough for them to use as a guide? Did we intentionally connect with the children's existing knowledge or in other ways help them elaborate on the experience? Did we give them enough opportunities to learn and practice the desired skill to gain mastery? Did the program work better with some children than with others (older? more verbal? etc.)? In this way, I hope to reinforce the teachers' use of these metaprinciples so that they will eventually integrate them automatically into their instructional and assessment designs.

These examples demonstrate how I can strengthen the theory–practice link through both formal and informal coaching. Emphasizing the research link can enhance the whole system. My emphasis is heaviest on learning about research. We read and discuss research articles or reviews that are relevant to issues that we are facing; staff members who attend conferences present abstracts of research sessions that they found helpful; and all of the researchers who conduct studies at the Children's School give brief presentations to our staff. In all of these contexts, I serve somewhat as a translator, or perhaps more of a "connector," trying to activate the prior knowledge that I know exists, to explicitly label and define concepts that may be presented in cryptic form, to elaborate points with examples from our shared experience, and to reiterate key concepts during a discussion. Although any one article or presentation is unlikely to dramatically affect our "system," it has been interesting to watch the depth of discussion develop over the course of repeated exposures to different studies within a research program or a particular subfield. For example, our staff discussions of the role of gesture in development and education have grown deeper with each presentation that one of our faculty gives (Alibali & Goldin-Meadow, 1993).

Involving the teachers more directly in research has benefits for them and the researchers. We have researchers talk with teachers prior to the beginning of a given study so that the teachers can offer suggestions about the design. Not surprisingly, they often comment about the interaction of a specific task with the children's prior knowledge (e.g., the potential impact of one year's "letter of the week" project on a study of children's ability to identify the initial letter of words presented orally, a study that was slated to happen just after "J" week). They suggest ways to make the child's task clear (both through explicit instructions and by using "games" that have a common script) and to make it interesting enough to get them through the often large number of trials necessary in experimental designs.

In my own lab, I choose to explore the aspects of development that most trouble, puzzle, or otherwise interest my teachers, and my research assistant involves the teachers in both the design of the task and of the report format, so that the teachers will be able to use the information gained to help them understand their children. The communication assessment in Appendix D is an example of this type of involvement with research. Because my lab is such an integral part of the school, the teachers both give and receive feedback in shorter cycles than is typical in research contexts. In this case, they suggested the topic, helped revise the assessment, and got data on almost all of their children within one semester. With the help of undergraduate students, we have developed similar assessments on a wide variety of topics, including comparison–contrast skills, leadership, decision making, cooperation, and so forth.

Overall, the benefit of this emphasis on the research links in the theory–research–practice triangle is that teachers' theoretical concepts deepen and become better integrated with their understanding of both research and practice. In addition, they have become more "experimental" in their classrooms, purposely trying different strategies with individual children or groups, in a more reflective, although not controlled, way than I had previously witnessed.

Parent Education

The case of parent education is both simpler and more difficult because of the limited interaction and responsibility that we have with parents. For most parents, with the notable exception of psychologists from the university and professional communities, prior knowledge about cognitive and social development is limited to practical experience with their own children and their children's friends, and access to theory or research is limited to what they hear in the popular media, which typically distracts them. We begin our parent education when prospective parents first visit our school by introducing them to the six domains of development in Table 12.1 and our rationale for the priority order. We discuss our educational program, and, in lay terms, the cognitive foundations for its design. We especially emphasize the goal-driven nature of our instruction and assessment approaches. Once parents have children attending our school, we begin more detailed descriptions of the ways that our program is designed to foster skills in particular domains, or the ways that certain activities, like cooking or dramatic play, can be used to foster development in all six domains. Appendix E includes sample parent newsletter articles, including one that focused explicitly on the metaprinciples underlying our use of thematic units, such as the "Ponds" study (Appendix B). Conference discussions with teachers provide yet another context for parents to develop an understanding of developmental theory in relation to their child.

We also begin our parent education about developmental research at the prospective parent stage. One requirement for entry into our program is that parents sign a blanket permission form for the child to participate in any research projects conducted at the Children's School. Helping them become comfortable with that requirement involves explicitly describing the low-risk types of research conducted and the high-quality procedures that we have developed to ensure that the children's experience meets all of the ethical standards and is consistent and well integrated with their school experience. For some parents, it also involves countering misconceptions and fears about research that relate to their prior experience with medical research or highly publicized cases of ethical breeches. Once the family becomes part of our school, they can read abstracts of studies being conducted and summaries of completed studies in our monthly newsletter.

The most in-depth application of metaprinciples from cognition and instruction is with parents whose children are experiencing a developmental delay or difficulty. In these cases, the parents' models of development and of their child have a dramatic effect on their ability to understand the presenting problem, its underlying causes, and the steps that can be taken to improve the child's functioning, if not eliminate the causes altogether. One interesting example relates to the two children whose difficulties with conflict resolution were described earlier. Both children were in the same preschool class and their consistent and dramatic aggressive behavior was impacting the whole class negatively. Through careful observation of the contexts, triggers, patterns, and resolution strategies related to these aggressive episodes, as well as conversations with the parents about the nature of similar episodes at home, we diagnosed one child's difficulty as resulting from a lack of clear structure in the home and anger at the family situation. In contrast, we felt strongly that the other child's behavior was the result of physiological issues with proprioception and motor control. Our ability to work with the parents of both children was hampered considerably by the fact that neither set of parents shared our model of the child's behavior. The prior personal and cultural experience of the first family led them to describe their child as cute, funny, assertive, a negotiator, and rambunctious, so they were slow to respond to the needs the child was expressing through his aggression. The second family viewed their child as in control of his behavior and purposefully being oppositional, so they responded with increased strictness, punishment, and so forth. Our eventual success with both sets of parents, and ultimately with their children, depended heavily on our identification of the prior conceptions with which they entered the process, explicit discussion of alternate models and ways to distinguish between them, emphasis on connecting the scenarios experienced at home and at school with the models that best explain them, repeatedly over the period of an entire year, with sensitivity to the individual characteristics and needs of each parent.

It is clear that we integrate the cognitive metaprinciples into both our general parent communication and our work with parents whose children are struggling. Our goal for the general parent population is merely exposure, so we have no formal assessment of our success, although it would be an interesting study to conduct. For the parents whose children are struggling, we have a clearer goal for them to make good choices about diagnostics and interventions, as well as to have the relevant knowledge to advocate effectively for their children. As with assessment of the children themselves, assessment of our success with parents in these situations is essentially a longitudinal case study. Although the impact of cognition and instruction is evident in our approach as I have described it, it is insufficient for dealing with the socioemotional aspects of the situation, where counseling skills are essential.

Undergraduate Learning Experiences

Undergraduates are an interesting contrasting case to teachers and parents. They come to us with more current theoretical background—having taken child development recently, plus most courses here emphasize an information-processing approach and highlight research methods and findings. Also, they may have taken other research methods courses before taking the developmental course. On the other hand, most have limited practical experience with children, perhaps some babysitting or interactions with younger siblings.

For undergraduates, we have two learning options, one with goals for building practical skills for working with children and the other for building developmental research skills. Many of our students participate in both aspects of our program, but we have to design programs that can be taken in either order.

The practicum option involves a guided field experience designed to help students deepen their understanding of developmental psychology by assisting in a preschool or kindergarten classroom and discussing the ways that their experiences relate to the theories and research they have previously studied, as well as to new readings. The classroom observation, interaction with the children and teachers, and experimentation with strategies for promoting children's development yields the fodder for the course discussions. As the course instructor, I intentionally work with the students during our formal seminar time and our informal interactions at the school to explicitly label the episodes they describe with theoretical terms, to make connections between theories by comparing and contrasting their perspectives on interesting episodes, and to link episodes with the research presented in our course readings. By using these strategies each week with respect to a new reading topic, I offer the students opportunities to practice making the links and communicating explicitly about them. As the semester progresses, the students begin to identify the theoretical perspectives that are most useful for helping them understand their experiences in the classroom.

Individual students in the practice track also have the opportunity to work independently toward the goal of integrating theory, research, and practice by writing weekly entries in their course journal that explicitly discuss the connections and by developing a case study of one child. The case study is structured by the Children's School's six domains of development, and students gather information by naturalistic and structured observation, interviews with the teacher, and occasionally, interaction with the parents. Here again, the emphasis is on theoretical explanation for the child's development and prediction of what strategies might foster development, as well as links to research findings that support the student's claims. These two written projects, plus an oral presentation of the case study, serve as the assessment of each student's progress toward the goal of integrating their theory and research knowledge with educational practice.

The research option involves a research methods course with a laboratory component at the Children's School. The goal of the course is to help students acquire an understanding of the concepts and issues in developmental research and to provide hands-on experience in conducting developmental research. Because instructors other than myself actually teach the seminar portion of the course, my participation is limited to working with the students on the laboratory component. Nonetheless, the goal of integrating theoretical, research, and practical knowledge and the application of the cognitive metaprinciples are still a major part of the process. Because we are aware that the weakest aspect of the students' prior knowledge is typically the practical side of conducting research with young children, we have designed explicit procedures and support students' use of them by working closely with them during their initial lab setup and initial contact with the children. In our group introduction to the research procedures and in our involvement with each research group, we explicitly highlight the rationale behind our procedures (the theoretical principles, the research ethics, and the practical aspects of work with young children). As they progress from one lab to the next, we repeatedly emphasize the decision-making process underlying the design of the projects. Eventually, they develop a final project of their own design and then receive feedback from both me and their course instructor. During the inevitable revision process, we emphasize the design decision process explicitly and encourage links to research examples with which the students are already familiar. Although the course is only long enough to permit students to conduct one study of their own design, interested students have numerous opportunities to conduct research projects in the context of upper level courses, independent research with faculty members, and senior honors theses. Although I have no formal role in evaluating the students' progress in research, I continue to review their requests to use the Children's School laboratory and monitor the conduct of their research there. In that context, I have observed that the students make better research design decisions, understand my suggested revisions and the rationale for them more easily, and develop better interaction strategies in research contexts with young children as they gain more experience.

COGNITION AND INSTRUCTION
IN THE LABORATORY SCHOOL
AND BEYOND

Applying the cognitive technique of task analysis at an educationally practical level has significant benefits for designing effective instruction and assessments. We demonstrated this point most effectively with respect to the children in our laboratory school, but we are also witnessing the positive impact of the approach in our work with teachers, parents, and undergraduates. In a similar way, we have found the cognitive metaprinciples that I described to be broadly useful in focusing design discussions on effective strategies for both instruction and assessment. Constraints imposed by the enormous scope of applying both the task analysis and the metaprinciples across the curriculum for all learners require a streamlined approach for most aspects, with more detailed applications in only the most important or difficult cases. Nonetheless, we continue to improve our own applications and to spend a significant portion of our teacher training and consulting efforts encouraging others to use this $G\rightarrow P\rightarrow A$ approach.

In fact, beginning in 1998, we founded an Early Childhood Professional Development Center[5] to develop ways of using our approach to help educators to improve their own programs. (See Appendix F for the center philosophy and a sample seminar schedule.) By familiarizing ourselves with trainees' programs in advance of training and by conducting

---

[5]Our Early Childhood Professional Development Center is supported by the Alcoa Foundation.

introductory activities at the seminars, we estimate the trainees' prior knowledge and existing practice. Our seminar activities and handouts explicitly detail our approach and provide visual examples. By encouraging sharing of ideas among trainers and trainees, we build links between seminar principles, existing practice, and future directions. Our 2 day and week-long seminars include opportunities for practicing the G→P→A alignment as it relates to diverse aspects of an early childhood program. We also explicitly emphasize our goal of teaching a design strategy that is individually applicable to diverse programs, rather than suggesting that participants mimic our specific program. Feedback during and immediately after each seminar reveals that trainees both understand the basic G→P→A Approach (Table 12.2) and anticipate being able to apply it to their program improvement efforts. More importantly, our subsequent interactions with both teachers and directors reveal that significant progress is occurring. Such reports indicate that the strategies of using task analysis and metaprinciples are applicable beyond the laboratory school and in diverse programs that are unlikely to have a cognitive psychologist on staff;[6] but, once again, formal study of the specific ways professional development impacts program improvement is needed.

In addition to the impact of dissemination efforts, such as those of our Professional Development Center, laboratory school practice such as ours can impact the field of cognition and instruction during the next 25 years in several ways. At some level, our efforts exemplify the ultimate goal of the field: to understand the processes of teaching and learning well enough to provide ideal learning environments for varied individuals at all levels of the system. As such, we serve as a cautionary reminder of the "big picture" and encourage others to broaden their research to include an integration of social, cognitive, and physical development in a realistic context.

Because that task may seem daunting, I suggest several more manageable, but highly valuable contributions that researchers could make toward the ultimate goal.

1. Develop practical techniques for streamlined task analysis.
2. Specify the set of metaprinciples that serves as the foundation for your instructional designs and write about them more fully than is typically allowed in our field's journals.

---

[6]In addition to our early childhood professional development work with educators in our community, I have applied the same G→P→A approach (Table 12.2) to the redesign of an elementary school curriculum, reviews of several college programs, and a training program for postcollege campus ministers. Theoretically, the approach can be applied to learners of any age and across many domains.

3. Experiment with assessments that are short and straightforward enough to be used for large numbers of children in school contexts.

4. Develop scoring systems and analysis techniques that can be used validly and reliably, even in nonstandardized contexts with a wide range of learners.

Then, take these new approaches and use them to set new goals for teacher training, to design effective instruction for teachers, and to assess their progress. For example, Minstrell cited the significant changes he has witnessed because of helping teachers learn to use research to address their own educational problems (chap. 4). This step is essential because there will never be enough well-trained researchers to fully apply even what we know now about cognition and instruction. Broad impact will be possible only when the skills are broadly distributed.

Finally, take collaboration to the next level, from the level of a whole course to a whole domain, to a full program, to an entire school. Psychologists in positions like mine do not have time to fully implement all of our ideas, let alone study the impact of the designs we develop, even for one set of learners in one domain. Enrich the field by collaborating with us during the next 25 years of Cognition and Instruction research.

ACKNOWLEDGMENTS

The progress described in this chapter is the result of close collaboration between the author and the staff at the Children's School. Thanks to each staff member for seeking continual improvement both individually and as a team. Special thanks to Donna Perovich, Jean Simpson, and Jolene Watson for capably designing documents, orchestrating programs, and keeping the many facets of our work organized.

Correspondence concerning this chapter should be addressed to Sharon M. Carver, Children's School, Carnegie Mellon University, Pittsburgh, PA 15213.

REFERENCES

Alibali, M. W., & Goldin-Meadow, S. (1993). Gesture–speech mismatch and mechanisms of learning: What the hands reveal about a child's state of mind. *Cognitive Psychology, 25*, 468–523.

Anderson, J. R. (1983). *The architecture of cognition.* Cambridge, MA: Harvard University Press.

Anderson, J. R., Corbett, A. T., Koedinger, K., & Pelletier, R. (1995). Cognitive tutors: Lessons learned. *The Journal of the Learning Sciences, 4* (2), 167–207.

Carver, S. M. (1988). Learning and transfer of debugging skills: Applying task analysis to curriculum design and assessment. In R. E. Mayer (Ed.), *Teaching and learning computer programming: Multiple research perspectives* (pp. 259–297). Hillsdale, NJ: Lawrence Erlbaum Associates.

Carver, S. M. (1995). Cognitive apprenticeships: Putting theory into practice on a large scale. In C. N. Hedley (Ed.), *Thinking and literacy: The mind at work* (pp. 203–228). Hillsdale, NJ: Lawrence Erlbaum Associates.

Carver, S. M. (in press). The Discover Rochester design experiment: Collaborative change through five designs. In J. Hawkins & A. Collins (Eds.), *Design experiments: Integrating technology into schools.* New York: Center for Technology and Education.

Carver, S. M., & Klahr, D. (1986). Assessing children's LOGO debugging skills with a formal model. *Journal of Educational Computing Research, 2* (4), 487–525.

Carver, S. M., & Kang, M. (1999). *Modeling, teaching, and assessing knowledge organization skills.* Manuscript in preparation.

Chi, M. T. H. (1981). Knowledge development and memory performance. In J. P. Das & N. O'Connor (Eds.), *Intelligence and learning.* New York: Plenum Press.

Collins, A., Brown, J. S., & Newman, S. E. (1989). Cognitive apprenticeship: Teaching the crafts of reading, writing, and mathematics. In L. B. Resnick (Ed.), *Knowing, learning, and instruction. Essays in honor of Robert Glaser* (pp. 453–494). Hillsdale, NJ: Lawrence Erlbaum Associates.

Collins, A., Hawkins, J., & Carver, S. M. (1991). A cognitive apprenticeship for disadvantaged students. In B. Means, C. Chelemer, & M. S. Knapp (Eds.), *Teaching advanced skills to at-risk students: Views from research and practice* (pp. 173–194). San Francisco: Jossey-Bass.

Gardner, H. (1993). *Frames of mind: The theory of multiple intelligences* (10th anniversary edition). New York: Basic Books.

Glover, J. A., Ronning, R. R., and Bruning, R. H. (1990). *Cognitive psychology for teachers.* New York: Macmillan.

Greeno, J. G. (1976). Cognitive objectives of instruction: Theory of knowledge for solving problems and answering questions. In D. Klahr (Ed.), *Cognition and instruction* (pp. 123–160). Hillsdale, NJ: Lawrence Erlbaum Associates.

Klahr, D., & Carver, S. M. (1988). Cognitive objectives in a LOGO debugging curriculum: Instruction, learning, and transfer. *Cognitive Psychology, 20*, 362–404.

Miller, P. H. (1993). *Theories of developmental psychology.* New York: Freeman.

Phye, G. D., & Andre, T., (Eds.). (1986). *Cognitive classroom learning: Understanding, thinking, and problem solving.* San Diego, CA: Academic Press.

Siegler, R. S. (1998). *Children's thinking* (3rd ed.). Upper Saddle River, NJ: Prentice-Hall.

Tobias, C. U. (1994). *The way they learn.* Colorado Springs, CO: Focus on the Family.

APPENDIX A

Samples From the Children's School Goal Specifications

3. COMMUNICATION—facilitating comprehension and expression skills beginning with oral and progressing to written language.

A. SPEAKING
Phonetics, Vocabulary, Grammar, Oral Expression

B. LITERATURE/READING
Story Listening

3→	4→	5→
enjoy books with pictures enjoy silly stories	listen attentively to story identify characters ask questions	predict next events
listen to story on tape		listen when peers read
recall main idea relate story to own exp.	recall plot in order (literal events) recall small details	listen for meaning and answer comprehension questions draw conclusions
fill in missing words identify missing object from set of four or class identify missing part of picture	fill in missing actions (not saying thanks)	use more abstraction in what's missing

Story Telling

3→	4→	5→
retell two or more facts from story read two times	retell story in own words identify beginning, middle, end	retells in order with details borrowed stories (new twist on an old favorite)
make up stories	use expressive language and sounds	tell original story use descriptive words illustrate/write own books
	simple story grammar (beginning, middle, end)	use standard story frame (once upon a time)

Story Analysis, Pretend Reading, Sounds & Symbols, Print Formats

C. WRITING
Letter Recognition/Formation, Writing Format, Writing to Communicate

4. DISCOVERY & EXPLORATION—fostering a positive attitude toward learning through questioning, observing, and experimenting with varied materials related to diverse themes.

A. APPROACH TO LEARNING

3→	4→	5→
positive attitude self-motivation / initiative accepting of mistakes as learning resourceful	complete task with persistence	plan for task (e.g., gather materials) seek more than one solution

B. COLLECTING AND OBSERVING

3→	4→	5→
aware of senses describe basic features	describe characteristics and behaviors of present and imagined objects	more complex description
collect and sort objects compare and contrast basic dimensions	classify and order added variation and # of dimensions	
count objects	estimate number measure with units create balance	use standard measure weigh objects
magnify objects associate objects (e.g., bird with nest)	record observations with drawing or photo	use standard symbols use graphs
recognize map	identify land and water relate personal experience to map	use simple map and globe

C. QUESTIONING & PREDICTING
D. EXPLAINING & REPORTING
E. NUMBER
   Comparing, Sorting, Ordering, Number, Operations
F. SPACE (both two- and three-dimensional understanding)
   Lines (components of shapes), Shapes, Position, Patterns
G. MEASUREMENT
   Length, Weight & Volume, Temperature, Speed, Time, Money, Graphing

APPENDIX B

Outline and Excerpts From the Summer 1999 Pond Unit

Carnegie Mellon University Children's School
Ponds Unit
Summer 1999

Plan to Subdivide the Four Weeks of the Ponds Unit:
Water (Week 1)
Plants (Week 2)
Animals
    Fish, Frogs, and Turtles (Week 3)
    Insects & Spiders (Week 4)

Likely existing concepts (depending on individual experience)
Everything needs a place to live.
  A pond is a small body of water.
  Can describe water—typically wet, clear, cool, etc.
    May know different forms of water.
    Can describe ways people use water.
  Can list and describe some plants and animals that live in
        or near ponds—typically ducks, frogs, turtles, fish, bugs.
May identify basic parts of plants and what they need to live.
May identify basic parts of animals and what they need to live.

What they're unlikely to understand is the concept of *habitat* and
        the *interdependence* of the living and nonliving things in a
        habitat. They're unlikely to link the features of plants and
        animals to the ways that they are *adaptations* to the particu-
        lar habitat. These are the key points to emphasize in the
        unit. The concepts listed below expand on these basic
        points.

Concept of "A Pond as a Habitat"

Habitat Basics
    Living vs. nonliving things.
        Living things need food, water, and air to stay alive.
        Most living things grow and change.
    Variety of living things (plants and animals).
    Many different places to live.
        Every living thing needs a place to live—a home.
        Each living thing lives in a
        HABITAT = A PLACE WHERE SOMETHING LIVES
        Every habitat has living and nonliving parts.
        A habitat provides food, water, air, temperature, safe spaces
            that a plant or animal needs.
        Different habitats meet different needs.
        A living thing also gives something back to a habitat.
            Each living thing has a job to do.
    In habitats, all the parts fit together.
    Common needs, Diversity of approaches to meeting them in
        diverse habitats, interdependence
    Importance of taking care of habitats

Water habitats
    Earth has more water than land.
    Two types of water habitats; freshwater and saltwater
    Freshwater habitat (*ponds*, bogs, swamps, lakes, rivers)
        Climate varies
            Water can be cold or warm
            Water can be still or flow fast
        Plant & animal life depends on type of water
    A *pond* is an enclosed body of fresh water that is smaller than
        a lake (i.e., still water but could be cold or warm)

Unit continues with concepts about each week of the unit
    Water (Week 1)
    Plants (Week 2)
    Animals—Fish, frogs and turtles (Week 3)
    Animals—Insects & spiders (Week 4)

Developmental Objectives for Focus in the Ponds Unit

Objectives for all six domains are listed in the unit. Key excerpts for two domains are included here.

3. Communication—facilitating comprehension and expression skills beginning with oral and progressing to written language.

Speaking
- Learn new vocabulary—habitats, pond, vapor, cattails, water lily, shelter, fins, gills, minnow, catfish, bass, amphibian, tadpole, reptile, antenna, metamorphosis ...
- Use body language, act out certain animals/pond life, role play
- Identify and name pond/pond life objects
- Convey ideas regarding pond, discuss cycles and activities that go on at a pond

Literature/Reading
- Read books about the pond and pond life
- Predict what happens next in stories and/or life cycles of pond life
- Retell stories and/or life cycles in correct order
- Tell original stories involving pond habitat or pond life
- Recognize words related to pond and identify the word when it is next to a picture

Writing
- Dictate pond stories and write some words from story
- Make books, sign, pictures related to pond
- Label categories for sorting pond items

4. Discovery & Exploration—fostering a positive attitude toward learning through questioning, observing, and experimenting with varied materials related to diverse themes.

- Collect and sort items from pond according to various categories such as plant vs. animal, living vs. nonliving, land vs. water, insect vs. reptile, fish vs. mammal
- Ask questions about pond/pond life
- Observe the various types of pond life at the pond
- Describe characteristics and attributes of pond items collected
- Count items relating to pond
- Identify the different parts of an insect or plant
- Magnify, measure, and weigh pond items
- Compare and contrast the length and weight of items
- Record observations of pond/ pond life with drawings & charts

- Make a simple map of the pond
- Understand and follow sequences in relation to pond life cycles and water cycle
- Add and subtract using pond related objects
- Match pictures with pond objects collected

Pond Resources found at the Children's School:

Puzzles / Games:
    Pond Life
    Duck Pond
    Fishing Game
    and so on
Manipulatives:
    Insect Collection
    See and Do Nature Series
    and so on
Computer CDs:
    Sammy's Science House—Seasons at the Pond
    Amphibians and Reptiles
    and so on

Pond Books found in the Children's School Library

Habitats / Pond:
    Birds and Their Environment, Frances Todd Stewart
    All About Water, Melvin Berger
    and so on
Plants:
    The Story of the Root-Children, Sibylle von Olfers
    The Giving Tree, Shel Silverstein
    and so on
Frogs, Fish, and Turtles:
    The Magic Fish, Freya Littledale
    The Tortoise and the Hare, Aesop Fable
    and so on
Insects and Spiders:
    Feely Bugs, David Carter
    The Very Busy Spider, Eric Carle
    and so on

Activities Bibliography

Exploring Water and The Ocean, Gayle Bittinger (Green)
The Kids' Nature Book, Susan Milord (Salmon)
and so on

APPENDIX C

Samples From the Children's School's
Kindergarten Conference Form

Communication

Speaking:
- ✓ uses 100% intelligible speech
- ✓ has age-appropriate vocabulary
- ✓ speaks in complete sentences
- ✓ participates in conversation
- ✓ participates in group discussion
- ✓ presents information to the group

Beginning Reading:
- ✓ listens attentively for meaning
- ✓ answers comprehension questions
- ✓ follows left to right progression
- ✓ follows top to bottom progression
- ✓ identifies rhyming words
- ✓ recognizes upper case letters A through Z
- ✓ has been exposed to lower case letters a through z
- ✓ finds name on list and writes a check mark

Beginning Writing:
- ✓ forms upper case letters A through Z
- ✓ prints full name
- ✓ asks for spellings of words

Name ... (teacher writes a paragraph of evidence, explanation, and suggestions)

Discovery & Exploration

- ✓ exhibits a positive approach to learning
- ✓ completes an age-appropriate task with persistence
- ✓ asks Who? What? Why? Where? When? How? questions
- ✓ seeks answers through exploration

Beginning Math:

- ✓ can count from 1–30 by rote
- ✓ counts to 20 with 1 to 1 correspondence
- ✓ forms numerals from 1–20
- ✓ recognizes numerals 1–20
- ✓ recognizes and names complex shapes
- ✓ recognizes and forms simple patterns
- ✓ classifies and orders objects independently
- ✓ compares and contrasts length, weight, volume
- ✓ recognizes time cycles
- ✓ tells time by hours
- ✓ understands use of money for buying
- ✓ reads and forms bar graphs

Name ... (teacher writes a paragraph of evidence, explanation, and suggestions)

APPENDIX D

Sample Report From a Structured Assessment of Communication

Child's Name *NB*   Date Observed *4/29/99*
Observer's Name *Jolene*

The ABC Game—A Communication Task

NB was asked to *find her name* on a list of all 23 kindergartners. She was able to do this right away. She was also able to make an X by her name.

Next, she was asked to *name rubber letters* of the alphabet and correctly named all 26 upper and 25 lower case letters (she didn't know the q, but it's an odd q, with a short straight tail).

When *listening* to a brief (approx. 6 minute) story tape, NB was 100% engaged with the book, and 100% engaged with the tape, during the first 4 minutes. She seemed to enjoy the story, but was somewhat distracted by the tapeplayer. Her answers to several *comprehension* questions indicated that she paid attention and understood the story. NB showed a strong *interest in words*. Answering one question, she said the giant was big, hairy, scary, mary, gary. Also, she was very interested in oversized words in the text.

When asked to *follow on a page* read aloud with her finger, NB was able to follow from top to bottom and from left to right.

NB appropriately *named the story* "The Giant." She knew how to spell THE, and carefully *sounded out* GYNT. NB was able to *write* her first and last name.

APPENDIX E

Sample Parent Education Articles
From the Children's School Monthly Newsletter

Director's Corner (for November '98 Newsletter)

The development of *Communication Skills* is an important aspect of the preschool years because these skills enable increasingly effective social interaction and increasingly complex learning. Young children's listening, speaking, reading readiness, and writing readiness skills contribute to their foundation for success in elementary school.

Communication is a part of the Children's School day from the moment the teacher and child greet each other at the car through dismissal. By repeating standard phrases, songs, and fingerplays, together with relevant visual cues, we encourage children's listening comprehension and fluent speech. As the teachers introduce and reinforce concepts related to our themes, the children learn and begin to use new vocabulary. While exploring these topics, we encourage children to ask questions, describe their observations and experiences, and formulate explanations for events. Frequent story reading and re-reading helps children practice their comprehension skills, as well as promoting interest in books. Teachers also provide a wide variety of opportunities for sharing personal stories and knowledge informally. We encourage formal sharing via "Sharing Days" in the preschool and "Discovery Table" presentations in the kindergarten.

In addition to promoting oral communication, we encourage children's interest in written communication by providing frequent exposure to reading and writing in inviting contexts. Children have many opportunities for quiet "reading" times to explore books individually. We talk about letters, the way they look, the way they sound, and the places we see them in our environment. In the preschool, names have special significance, as do words like "open" and "closed." Similarly, our writing centers are places for children to experiment with drawing and writing. Teachers follow the children's interest with help in letter formation and spelling. Children in the preschool are also invited to dictate stories that can then be reread in the classroom and at home. In the kindergarten, the opportunities for exploring reading and writing are expanded to include the "Morning News," the "Wall of Words," journal writing, group stories, and many other activities. In all cases, the teachers tailor the program to the needs of each year's class and modify activities to challenge individual children ranging from prereaders to fluent readers.

A short walk through the school while the program is in session will provide a vibrant demonstration of the many ways our teachers work to promote strong comprehension and expression so that our children become effective communicators. Feel free to join us one day soon!

Director's Corner (for March '00 Newsletter)

Thanks, again, to the many parents who helped make our Heritage Celebration a wonderful event! I enjoyed interacting with all of the families and hearing about how much the children have learned from the China and Canada units. As you probably know, such in-depth units are rarely attempted in other early childhood programs and some educators claim that it is impossible for young children to learn about topics beyond their immediate environments (e.g., China, dinosaurs, and outer space) in developmentally appropriate ways. At the Children's School, we utilize key principles from cognitive psychology to help us create ways for our students to experience concepts directly and to build a strong knowledge base about a variety of topics that interest them.

Build on Prior Knowledge
Before each unit begins, the teacher who has volunteered to be the Theme Leader collects factual information about the topic and identifies concepts that the children are likely to know already as well as those that are within their reach. They prepare a booklet for the whole staff that includes these concepts, as well as more in-depth background information that we might need for answering children's questions as they arise. Each unit begins with circle time discussion of what the children already know about a topic. The 4's and kindergarten teachers often record this information on chart paper as a list or web that can be consulted and expanded throughout the unit.

Make Thinking Explicit

The Theme Leader also collects a wide variety of materials from the Children's School shelves and local libraries that will help the teachers and children use their senses to observe important properties related to the topic. We utilize a wide range of fiction and nonfiction books, particularly ones with clear photographs and we attempt to have authentic artifacts for the children to handle. For example, you might have visited the Beaver Museum in Canada during the Heritage Festival to see the beaver artifacts that we borrowed from the Carnegie Museum and the beaver dam that the kindergartners designed.

Emphasize Links

Studying one topic for an extended period of time allows the children to explore multiple aspects of a concept. For example, the Forest unit involved a comparative study of the plants and animals in Deciduous and Coniferous Forests. Throughout the unit, teachers routinely combine verbal and visual representations, provide a variety of exploration activities related to the topic, and intentionally ask children to recall aspects of prior related lessons. We also sequence our units to maximize the useful connections between them. In the preschool, our China unit was purposely designed to link with our Where We Live, What We Wear, and What We Eat units in the fall.

Provide Practice Opportunities

Both proficiency and efficiency of knowledge application are dependent on repeated practice in a variety of contexts. Within a thematic unit, children have varied opportunities to acquire, strengthen, and refine their concepts via experimentation, stories, dramatic play, art, games, computer activities, etc.

Expect Individual Variability

The diverse opportunities that children have for exploring a theme throughout our daily schedule allow for individual choice related to the special interests and talents of each child. At the same time, the availability of activities that are not related to the theme allows children to explore other interests and the teachers to work on skill development in all areas, regardless of particular thematic relation. The broad range of themes that we study in a given year are purposely designed so that there will be a few that spark particular excitement from each child.

Feel free to visit the school to see the key principles in action. Reading books and talking with your child about our unit topics will give you a chance to observe his or her developing concepts. For topics of special interest to you, consider talking to your child's teacher about how you can help extend the theme at school or at home.

APPENDIX F

Professional Development Center Philosophy and Sample Seminar Schedule

Early Childhood Professional Development Center
Sponsored by the Children's School
at Carnegie Mellon University
Supported by the Alcoa Foundation

- The purpose of the Professional Development Center is to improve the reflective practice of early childhood educators by
    1) training educators to use clear objectives for children's development as the basis for developmentally appropriate program and assessment, and
    2) consulting with administrators and their staff members during the process of implementing new approaches.

- Our Professional Development Center programs are based on the philosophy that trainers are most effective when they are master teachers themselves, have advance knowledge of the contexts in which trainees work, and can have long-term contact with trainees for both initial training and follow-up consulting. Similarly, trainees learn best in small groups that are conducive to discussion, when they have detailed documentation of seminar principles and clear practical examples to follow, and with strong support from their administrators and active consulting on implementation after the initial training.

- We design unique programs that equip individual educators or staffs to apply the seminar principles to their centers based on their students, staff, clients, and facilities.

Developmentally Appropriate
Goals, Program, & Assessment
The Children's School, Carnegie Mellon University

Goals for Day 1

- Using developmentally appropriate goals to structure program and assessment design
- Developing practical classroom strategies for fostering the development of preschool and kindergarten children
- Using thematic units that meet your program's specific goals

9:00am	Introductions / Overview
9:30am	The Goals → Program → Assessment Approach
10:00am	Identifying Goals for a Child's Development
10:30am	BREAK
10:45am	Designing the Program to Meet Goals
12:00pm	LUNCH
12:30pm	Studying Themes to Meet Goals
1:00pm	Exploring Unit Samples
2:30pm	BREAK
2:45pm	Assessing Progress → Goals
3:45pm	Closure / Q & A / Evaluation

Goals for Day 2

- Exploring ways to use Phys Ed, Computers, Science, and Visual Arts to provide a variety of unique learning experiences that meet your goals and provide evidence of children's growth

9:00am	Introductions
	Review of the Goals → Program → Assessment Approach (GPA)
9:30am	Visual Arts Exploration (Red Room)
10:45am	Computer (Kindergarten)
12:15pm	LUNCH
12:45pm	Science (Green Room)
2:00pm	Physical Education (Outside, we hope!)
3:30pm	Closure / Q & A / Evaluation

13

Themes in Cognitive Science and Education

Earl Hunt
University of Washington

The chapters in this part of the volume range over a wide variety of processes and topics. Processes range from Carver's focus on the interaction between social, cognitive, and motor maturation in young children (chap. 12) to Anderson and Gluck's analysis of young adult problem-solving skills based on traces of their eye fixations as they scan the displays from an intelligent tutor (chap. 8). Topics range from Lovett's discussion of university-level statistics (chap. 11) to Reiser, Tabak, Sandoval, Smith, Steinmuller, and Leone's instruction in high school biology (chap. 9). In spite of this variety, and probably because the symposium was limited to less than 3 years duration, no attempt was made to include chapters that cover the full curriculum at all grades and for all topics.

For all of this diversity, I believe that there are some common ideas in this set of chapters. I am not sure whether they should be called themes within the chapters or dimensions along which the chapters can be compared. The first theme (or dimension) deals with the balance between engineering and science in instructional applications of cognitive science, and the second deals with the role of the teacher in such applications. I also comment on the issue of classroom culture and group work. This topic—too often ignored in the application of cognitive science to education—was introduced at the symposium by Ellis and Gregoire but, unfortunately, it could not be included in this book.

COGNITIVE ENGINEERING
AND THE ROLE OF THEORY

Lesgold and Nahemow call the design of educational techniques "cognitive engineering" (chap. 10). The same idea appears in the chapters by Lovett (chap. 11) and by Carver (chap. 12). As Lewis Carroll said, in *The Hunting of the Snark,* what I tell you three times is true. Every one of the applications of cognitive science described in this book is really cognitive engineering.

Engineering certainly uses science but it does not necessarily wait for science. In keeping with the very latest ideas about the use of far analogies to develop understanding, I offer a very far one indeed. I hope it will make the point.

In the late 15th century, the English man-of-war *Mary Rose* sank suddenly, in an accident that was no reflection on Tudor naval engineers.[1] Underwater archeologists raised the ship in the 1980s. They were struck by the *Mary Rose's* systems of pulleys, levers, and winches. More than a hundred years before Newton was born, the ideas of Archimedes, amplified by hundreds of now forgotten Roman and medieval engineers, let Henry VIII's shipyard redirect and amplify forces. It seems to me that the chapters in this volume show that—with respect to the relation between our science and our engineering—cognitively-based education is about where Henry's naval architects were.

Modern cognitive psychology is making a great deal of progress toward establishing a science of memory and learning at the level of brain mechanisms. The scientific effort is exciting, newsworthy, and fundable. However the knowledge is far too microscopic to be of any use to a classroom teacher in the near future, and quite possibly not in the far future either. The relation between neurosciences and cognition may be analogous to the relationship between quantum mechanics and automobile mechanics. But this does not mean that cognitive science is irrelevant to education. Cognitive psychologists have had some good ideas, but certainly not complete scientific theories, about how learning takes place. These ideas lead us to emphasize the use of certain techniques for developing and redirecting ideas, just as Henry's shipbuilders used certain techniques for redirecting forces in order to raise anchors and hoist sails,

---

[1]The *Mary Rose* had opened all its gun ports, preparing to enter a battle with an attacking French fleet. A sudden gust of wind caused the ship to heel over. Water entered through the lower ports, capsizing and sinking the ship.

without being able to say, with modern mathematical precision, how levers and winches work.

This can be seen in the Anderson and Gluck chapter (chap. 8). The computer-program tutors that they describe are organized around the well-known production principle; recognize a pattern and do an action. Hundreds, if not thousands, of papers published since 1950 have shown that extremely complex problem solving can be built from simple productions. In the abstract, though, none of these papers were needed to establish that production systems could do these things. Unrestricted production systems are equivalent to unrestricted Turing machines, so they can compute anything that is computable.

Anderson and Gluck's project clearly indicates that today we know how to write such programs, which is a step beyond knowing that the programs can be written. In doing so, Anderson and Gluck develop the first working principle of (educational) cognitive engineering. The pattern part of a pattern-action sequence is important. Learning when to apply actions is as important as learning how to apply them. This rule clearly applies in geometry, algebra, and computer programming, where Anderson and his colleagues gathered a good deal of data. The same point appears in Lovett's discussion of the statistical reasoning of college students (chap. 11). The students do well in interpreting graphic presentations, where the pattern is presented to them explicitly. They do poorly when they have to map concrete situations onto abstract ones, in order to recognize that a particular analytic method is appropriate.

Both Anderson and Gluck and Lovett stress the importance of pattern recognition in order to activate learned procedures, but no use is made of any models of how pattern recognition takes place. In fact, Anderson himself, in numerous other papers, proposed models of the process of production activation. In the educational application the mechanisms of production activation are taken for granted. And that is how it should be, because going to a finer level of detail would be of little use to the classroom teacher.

The projects described by Reiser, Tabak, Sandoval, Smith, Steinmuller, and Leone (chap. 9) and by Carver (chap. 12) are clearly inspired by principles of cognitive psychology. However, even more than the Anderson and Gluck, Lesgold and Nahemow, and Lovett chapters, the Reiser, Tabak, Sandoval, Smith, Steinmuller, and Leone and Carver chapters use these principles to emphasize certain aspects of instruction, rather than showing that science dictates them. Carver enunciates five principles of cognitive instruction. These are stated very broadly, for example, "Build on prior knowledge." One can justify this principle by talking about schema, semantic networks, and the like, but to do so is pointless, for no serious use will be made of the justification. Besides, virtually any intelligent educator would agree with the principle, once it is stated. Nevertheless, Carver's principles are not vacuous, for they direct attention to certain aspects of teaching. This is an engineering principle, analogous to the old Roman rule of thumb: Build the bridge so that it will withstand loads substantially greater than those you think will go over it.

David Klahr (personal communication, June 11–13, 1999) has, on several occasions, commented on the role of theory in education. Whereas in most areas of science the function of a theory is to account for a body of data, in education, it seems, a theory is not intended to account for any particular body of data, but rather, to serve as a framework for a set of plausible ideas, often with a strong value component. Klahr's assessment can be applied to all five chapters here. They are good ideas about education, suggested by people's knowledge of modern day cognitive psychology. The ideas are not formally dictated by cognitive theory, nor need they be. The present evidence, and other evidence that is being accumulated, are that the ideas put forward in these chapters are indeed good ones. There is nothing wrong with this. Engineering and education can both use good ideas.

THE ROLE OF THE TEACHER

Although the five chapters share an emphasis on cognitive engineering, they differ on a very important point, the role of the teacher. Two extreme positions are taken. Anderson and Gluck (chap. 8) and Lesgold and Nahemow (chap. 10) barely discuss the role of the teacher at all. Anderson and Gluck are concerned with the design of a computer-tutor that is presented as if it operated independently of the teacher. (In practice, I suspect that this is not the case, but we must take the chapter for what it says.) Lesgold and Nahemow are concerned with ways of extracting information from experts, presumably teachers, in order to design an autonomous tutor. They are certainly not alone. I suspect that many advocates of distance education would like to see something like the Anderson and Gluck, Lesgold and Nahemow approach developed in university education. It saves salaries.

At the other end of the spectrum, Carver (chap. 12) goes to great lengths to involve teachers both in a philosophy of teaching and in research on teaching in their own classes. In between, Lovett's analysis of statistical problem solving implies the existence of a teacher (chap. 11), and Reiser, Tabak, Sandoval, Smith, Steinmuller, and Leone (chap. 9) provide a role for a teacher, as a coach while the students play a game of science in a computerized world.

One way to understand this continuum is to look at it as an outcome of historical trends. Lovett points out that history of the interaction between cognitive psychology and education reflects a trend going from theory testing (1970s) to the design and testing of theory-driven methods in the classroom (1980s) to studies centered on classroom dynamics (1990s) and intended to improve student performance. Furthermore, it is historically accurate to say that Anderson and Lesgold's work is very much in the 1970 to 1980s tradition (and started there), whereas Carver's is newer. However, time itself is not a causal variable. There has to be another explanation.

It might be that the differences in the way that these various chapters view the teacher has to do with the level of student. Anderson and Gluck, Lesgold and Nahemow, and Lovett were dealing with young adults. Carver was dealing with young children, Reiser, Tabak, Sandoval, Smith, Steinmuller, and Leone were concerned with middle school students. It could be argued that the younger the students are, the more general the goals of education. Therefore, when we deal with young children we need to rely on a sensitive teacher who can recognize rather vaguely defined situations. At the high school and college levels, specific skills and knowledge are being taught, so progress toward educational goals can be defined more precisely. A computer can be programmed to recognize the misapplication of an algebraic transformation. It takes a human to recognize that a child is frightened and defensive in class because of tensions in the home. To the extent that these factors are operating, the teacher should be paramount in K through 4 education, important in middle school, not negligible in high school (but a computer can help), and replaceable by a computer in the university. It follows that the University of Phoenix should replace Harvard in a very few years.

I do not think this will happen, but my example is not entirely facetious. One prominent opponent of the use of computers in the schools, Clifford Stoll (1999), leveled his most cogent criticisms at the use of computers to educate grade school children. I believe that he has a point when he argued that young children, who have to learn about the world of nature and social interactions, should learn about it directly rather than through the World Wide Web. In Stoll's spirit, I defy someone to run a first-grade class over the Internet. Analogs to the computer chat room can supplement university level instruction. I have used them personally, to good effect. The same thing can be said of distance learning in which middle and high school classes communicate with other classes in different schools. However, even at the university level, there are limits on what you can do without a teacher.

Stoll argued that the give and take of ideas that characterizes a good university seminar cannot be replicated by impersonal exchanges of information using electronic media. Research on cooperative work in industry seems to back him up. Electronic media can be used to facilitate cooperation between people at distant sites, providing that they know each other and have periodic meetings. On the other hand, my own university has a 700-person "classroom," so students in the back row are already enrolled in a distance learning course. Why not use technology?

Very much the same thing can be said of exchanges of information between students and computers. There is certainly a role for computer-oriented gaming, as in Reiser, Tabak, Sandoval, Smith, Steinmuller, and Leone and, in some ways, Lovett's statistical problems, interaction with tutors (Anderson and Gluck, Lesgold and Nahemow), and the use of computer simulations and analytic packages. These can virtually substitute for teachers in very large courses, with mature and motivated students. They are, I think, of only marginal use in the early elementary grades.

The problem is how to define the role of the teacher and the computer in intermediate size, intermediate level courses of 20 to 30 people. This includes most high school science and mathematics courses, and a very large number of university courses in between the freshman and graduate levels. At least in their chapter in this volume, Anderson and Gluck leave the impression that the computer tutor is to be primary, while the teacher is somewhere in the background (chap. 8). Quite the opposite view is taken by Minstrell (chap. 4), who goes to great effort to enroll teachers into the spirit and practice of facet-based learning, and then offers a computer program as a device for assisting and supplementing the teacher's instruction. Reiser, Tabak, Sandoval, Smith, Steinmuller, and Leone (chap. 9) are not too clear on the point. I imagine that in practice, teachers have a great deal of flexibility in the way they use BGuILE.

I think there has been too little discussion of this topic. Part of the reason is because of audience interest. When Minstrell and I present our work on facet-based instruction and the DIAGNOSER, there is a sharp bifurcation of audience interest. Practicing teachers want to know about what the instructor does; cognitive science researchers want to know the program works. At one level, this is hardly surprising. Each member of the audience wants to learn something that they can take away and use in their own work, relatively soon.

At another level, the problem is serious. The fact that different audiences have different interests indicates that teachers and cognitive scientists will find it quite easy not to talk to each other. What is worse, it is possible to give the illusion of talking by having real discussions with a few individuals but having very little impact on the target audience as a whole. Cognitive scientists can easily find dedicated, competent master teachers who will work with them, as fellow researchers or subject matter experts, in the design of programs. Except in Lake Wobegone, most teachers are not outstanding, dedicated people. They are ordinary folks working in a highly time-constrained setting. Because of the situational demands on them, they look for practical information that they can use in the next class period, with minimum preparation time. In order to make effective use of technology-oriented applications of cognitive science into education, there have to be guidelines for the interaction between technology and teaching methods.

The guidelines are not going to be easy to establish. They will depend on the interaction between subject matter, social setting of the class, and capabilities of the teacher and program. Therefore, we need to have a better taxonomy of the cognitive demands of different academic topics, and we have to study how the average teacher can use them, in a way that that teacher regards as cost effective.

This effort is important for two reasons. The first is that if teachers do not regard using the programs as a cost-effective way of using teaching (and preparation) time, then the programs will not be used. There is a simple marketing principle here; reduce the up-front and maintenance costs to the consumer.

The second reason for stressing the teacher's role in technologically oriented education is that there are some very unrealistic ideas about the magnitude of the problem. As Stoll (1999) pointed out, enthusiasts for educational technology have seriously maintained that teachers do not need training to use computers because the students will teach the teachers. Although students can, on many occasions, help teachers, the idea that the schools should rely on students to do this is naïve beyond belief. Yet, it seems to be reflected in the huge disparity between school budgets for computer equipment and for computer support and training. The extreme enthusiasts have even claimed that by building good science and mathematics into computer programs, we can obviate the problem of inadequate teacher training in a content field. No way!!

THE CLASSROOM CULTURE

A third way of ordering these chapters is to compare them on the extent to which they are concerned with the social setting of the classroom. Anderson and Gluck are concerned with a duet between a student and a computer (chap. 8). Lesgold and Nahemow are interested in facilitating learning by doing, in the context of industrial settings, such as maintaining aircraft (chap. 10). Thus Anderson and Gluck leave it up to some mysterious agency (the teacher, maybe?) to explain to the student why he or she should be doing algebra at all. Lesgold and Nahemow's clients know perfectly well why they are doing what they are doing. The purpose of the tutor is to provide knowledge on demand. Predictably, Carver is at the other end of the dimension, for several of her examples are concerned with student social interactions rather than the teaching of well-defined knowledge and skills (chap. 12). In between, Reiser, Tabak, Sandoval, Smith, Steinmuller, and Leone (chap. 9) and Lovett (chap. 11) are clearly advocates of increasing learning and motivation by group work. The conventional knowledge is that this is a good thing. Well, is it?

Most modern theories of education advocate group work almost as fervently as religious organizations advocate group worship. (But recall my earlier cautionary note about the role of theory in education.) Business and industrial leaders also smile on group work, for they complain that the schools do not teach students to work in teams. Expanding on the theme developed by Ellis and Gregoire, I take a skeptic's view of the conventional wisdom.

There are three arguments for group problem solving. They are (a) that it actually improves learning, because group members share and criticize each other's ideas, (b) that group interactions maintain motivation, and (c) that training students to work in groups is valuable in itself.

The goal of point (c), training people to work in teams, can hardly be denied. Outside of school, most serious work is accomplished with some form of cooperation. The efficacy of group problem solving, as it is practiced in the schools, as a way of teaching teamwork, can be questioned. There are major differences between groups of students working on a problem and teams of engineers, scientists, building contractors, and lawyers.

School problem-solving groups are made up of individuals with basically the same skills, they are (in American educational philosophy) aggressively nonauthoritarian, and the problem is attacked to show that the students can do it, rather than because its solution contributes to a group goal. Outside the school, problem-solving teams are usually composed of specialists who are supposed to complement each other's contributions, they almost always have clearly defined leadership structures backed with very real authority, and the problem arises in the course of pursuit of a larger goal.

Of course, there are real-world groups that do partly mimic school group work. Academic committees, juries, and political councils spring to mind. These are part of the world, but they are not all of it. I do not maintain that group work is an ineffective training device for later teamwork. I am making the much weaker, more defensible, point that the assertion that group work does teach important social skills *that would not be learned otherwise, outside the classroom,* seems to be an assertion rather than a conclusion supported by evidence.

The issue of whether or not group learning improves individual learning is a complex one. As a simple statistical issue, if k people are presented with a problem, and there is a probability p that any one of them will solve it, then assuming no interactions between members, the probability is $1 - (1-p)^k$ that at least one member of the group will solve it. This means that if a problem is hard enough so that only 50% of students will solve it on their own, the probability that a group of four students will solve it is .9375. So if the group shares the insights of its members, education should triumph.

In practice, groups seldom work out this well, but the probability of a group solution is higher than the probability of an individual solution. There are also other models, for problems that have to be solved in stages, that suggest even larger advantages for groups. However, these are all no-interaction models. Most educators would regard them as faulty, because the interactions between members are seen as being valuable in themselves. In particular, group work is often said to be more motivating than individual work. Because group problem solving is enjoyable, individual students become more involved and learn more.

Ellis and Gregoire questioned this bit of conventional wisdom. They pointed out that American middle school and high school students are extremely conscious of social status. When it is time for group work, marginal students are denigrated. This is particularly the case when the problem to be solved is ostensibly an intellectual one, such as the problems

posed by BGuILE (chap. 9). Most American adolescent and subadoles-
cent societies contain powerful social pressures against "being a brain."
(Being a jock is ok.) It is even worse, though, to be thought stupid.
Therefore, in many situations, students, especially adolescents, will share
ideas only when they know that it is safe to share them. It is never safe for
the unpopular student. On listening to the Ellis and Gregoire presentation
(and watching their videotapes of faces of unpopular students when group
work was announced), I was reminded of a line in one of Ring Lardner's
stories; "Shut up!" he explained. Not all students are motivated by the
prospect of group work.

This point is extremely important for any educational method that, like
Reiser, Tabak, Sandoval, Smith, Steinmuller, and Leone's (chap. 9) and
Lovett's (chap. 11), relies partly on discussion and group problem solving
as a technique of teaching. Teachers who use Minstrell's facet-based
instruction method, and Minstrell himself, go to some lengths to ensure
that the classroom culture distinguishes between questioning an idea and
attacking the person who proposes the idea (chap. 4). The distinction has
to be made by both the attacker and the attackee. The way you defend your
ideas should be different from the way you defend an attack on your personal competence and integrity. No one, including scientists, attains this
level of sainthood all the time, but some of us do better than others.

Carver (chap. 12), and many other progressive educators who deal with
young children, can rightly claim that they try to teach children respect for
others, sharing, and so forth. However a high school or university instructor cannot rely on having students who have passed through such programs. Also, there are elements in both the peer and adult culture that
actively encourage an "assert or withdraw" strategy for participating in
groups. They even encourage the strategy of regarding any attack as an
attack on the person. There are very few TV shows where an attractive person puts forward a poor idea, to be corrected by an unattractive one. When
a new educational method is introduced into a class, the classroom culture
must be considered. And remember, the classroom culture is only part of
a larger culture, over which the teacher may have very little control.

My remarks should not be taken as a universal attack on group problem
solving. In general, it is a good thing. So is the encouragement of the isolated problem solver. Creative solutions are not facilitated by a requirement that a group come to a consensus. The educator's problem is to
decide when to encourage which method of teaching. The cognitive scientist acting as a consultant should not ignore the issue. When I reviewed
the five chapters here in the light of the Ellis and Gregoire presentation, I

realized that we need a lot more research on when and how to use group problem solving.

CONCLUSION

Cognitive science in general, and cognitive psychology in particular, has provided important principles of educational practice. These are engineering principles rather than scientific facts. That is not bad. However, we would like to have a better scientific base for designing both our teaching methods and teaching technology. This can only be done by moving from the grain size of pattern recognition and working memory phenomena to the grain size of idea grasping, analogical reasoning, and schema building. The necessary research is feasible. It requires the study of large scale phenomena directly. The move toward narrowing the grain size from elementary behavioral to neural events (i.e., moving from cognitive psychology to cognitive neuroscience), although good in itself, is unlikely to provide very much help for education.

As part of this effort, we are going to have to broaden our idea of what cognition is. My remarks about the interaction between technology and the teacher mix social and cognitive psychology. Certainly my remarks about group problem solving are more social than cognitive. In the field, one discipline merges into the other. The social–cognitive distinction may be a useful way to organize academic disciplines, but it is not a useful way to organize teaching and thinking.

ACKNOWLEDGMENTS

My own research in this area has been supported by the James S. McDonnell Foundation and the National Science Foundation. I am also happy to acknowledge the many conversations I have had with my colleague Jim Minstrell on topics related to education.

REFERENCES

Carroll, L. (1891). *The Hunting of the Snark*. Page 46, MacMillan & Co.

Lardner, R. (1934). *First and Last*, The Young Immigrants, C. Scribner's Sons.

Stoll, C. (1999). *High tech heretic: Why computers don't belong in the schools*. New York: Doubleday

Part V

Cognition and Instruction:
The Next 25 Years

14

A Third Metaphor for Learning: Toward a Deweyan Form of Transactional Inquiry

Timothy Koschmann
Southern Illinois University

...[F]or one may explain (or predict) behavior by observing what are the "obvious" things to do to attain the goal (even though they may be insufficient), and therefore what are the things that the problem solver, being a bear of little brain, will do.
—Newell & Simon (1972, p. 79)

The attempt to clarify the concept of situated learning led to critical concerns about the theory and to further revisions that resulted in the move to our present view that learning is an integral and inseparable aspect of social practice.
—Lave & Wenger (1991, p. 31)

These steps were all definitely in the line of the transactional approach: the seeing together, when research requires it, of what before had been seen in separations and held severally apart. They provide what is necessary at times and places to break down the old rigidities: what is necessary when the time has come for new systems.
—Dewey & Bentley (1949/1991, pp. 106–107)

This volume marks the anniversary of an earlier Carnegie Symposium on the topic of cognition and instruction that took place 25 years ago. David Klahr (1976), in the preface to an edited collection of papers from that symposium, quoted Forehand (1974) who observed, "In what seems remarkably few years, information-processing psychology has come to dominate the experimental study of complex human behavior" (p. 159). Forehand went on to predict that the potential of information-processing theory "for illuminating recalcitrant problems in education seems evident" (p. 159). Klahr observed that the chapters comprising the volume from the first cognition and instruction symposium served as evidence that this potential had already begun to be realized.

Looking at the papers presented at the more recent symposium, it is clear that our community no longer possesses such a unified theoretical foundation. The cognition and instruction research community has grown since the first symposium, and with this growth has come plurality with respect to our foundational theories of learning and problem solving. The emergence of new theories has been attended with extensive (and sometimes rancorous) debate (cf. Anderson, Reder, & Simon, 1996, 1997; Cobb & Bowers, 1999; Greeno, 1997; Norman, 1993). Information-processing theory itself has been subjected to critical reappraisal from both within (Greeno & MMAP, 1998; Scardamalia, Bereiter, & Lamon, 1996) and outside (Bredo, 1994, 1997; Dreyfus & Dreyfus, 1986; Lave, 1988) this community.

As Sfard (1998) pointed out, advocates of different sides in this debate have appealed to different metaphors of what constitutes learning and, as a consequence, have developed incommensurable vocabularies, making productive dialog difficult. Although the debate about how to appropriately frame research into human learning and problem solving is multifaceted, it is useful for the purposes of this discussion to characterize the controversy, as Sfard did, as a conflict between two specific metaphors— an *acquisition metaphor* by which learning is treated as "gaining possession over some commodity" (p. 6) and a *participation metaphor* by which learning is "conceived of as a process of becoming a member of a certain community" (p. 6). This division can be seen in microcosm in the chapters of this book—a few standing defiantly on one side of the divide or the other, others being more ambivalent with respect to the metaphor underlying the work.

To ultimately overcome this division will require finding a new metaphor for learning. I argue that some useful clues for how this might be accomplished can be found in the writings of the American philosopher, John Dewey. Dewey was a tireless crusader against all forms of dualism. He endeavored in his writing to demonstrate that many of the intractable problems of Western philosophy were an outcome of the way in which the questions were initially framed. Dewey's methods may prove useful, therefore, in overcoming the acquisition–participation dualism currently dividing the educational research community. In fact, it is my hope that he can provide us with a new vocabulary for discussing human problem solving that will enable us to bridge this division. Before turning to Dewey's writings, however, I begin by summarizing the basic tenets of two currently prominent theories of learning, one that entails a metaphor of learning as acquisition and another that employs a metaphor of learning as participation.

LEARNING AS ACQUISITION

Sfard (1998) observed that the view of learning as achieving "ownership over some kind of self-sustained entity" (p. 5) is so deeply engrained in our thought and language that it is difficult to consider it any other way. Information-processing theory, mentioned earlier by virtue of its historical importance to research in cognition and instruction, is one example of a theory constructed on this metaphor. Information-processing theory is by no means the first or the only theory of learning to embrace the metaphor of learning as acquisition—it is just one in a long tradition that stretches back to the work of Thorndike and other early learning theorists (Koschmann, 2000).

Newell and Simon (1972) summarized the underlying principles of information-processing theory in the form of four interlocking claims:

1. A few, and only a few, gross characteristics of the human IPS [Information-processing System] are invariant over task and problem solver.
2. These characteristics are sufficient to determine that a task environment is represented (in the IPS) as a problem space, and that problem solving takes place in a problem space.
3. The structure of the task environment determines the possible structures of the problem space (i.e., the class of admissible problem spaces).
4. The structure of the problem space determines the possible programs that can be used for problem solving. (p. 788–789)

Three concepts fundamental to these postulates are the *IPS* as a problem-solving "processor," the *problem space* within which the problem solver operates, and the *methods* by which the problem solver produces a solution.

In information-processing theory, the computer serves as both a metaphor and a medium for modeling human problem-solving capabilities. As Newell and Simon (1972) put it: The "programmed computer and human problem solver are both species belonging to the genus IPS" differing only in "memory organization, elementary processes, and program organization" (p. 870). They described an IPS as "a serial system consisting of an active processor, input (sensory) and output (motor) systems, an internal LTM and STM and an EM" (p. 808). In the human problem solver, LTM (long-term memory) is described as being of indefinite capacity and organized associatively. STM (short-term memory), on the other hand, has extremely limited capacity (on the order of five to seven symbols) but is immediately accessible to the processor. Representation in the LTM and STM of the human problem solver are assumed to be "homogenous," that is "sensory patterns in all sensory modalities, processes, and data patterns are symbolized and handled identically" (p. 808). EM (external memory) is defined as "the immediately available visual field" (p. 809).

As stipulated in the second postulate, problem solving is said to occur by searching a *problem space*. A problem space can be defined formally as:

1. *A set of elements*, U, each representing a "state of knowledge."
2. *A set of operations*, Q, each of which allows transformations from one knowledge state to another.

A problem on a space so defined is specified by an initial state, u_0, and a set of one or more possible goal states. A problem space is a representation of a particular task environment, but any given task environment can be represented in a variety of ways, although the authors conceded that problem solving can be effective "only if significant information about the objective environment is encoded in the problem space" (p. 790). Information-processing theory, therefore, seeks to understand problem-solving performance through detailed study of the problem itself and the processes by which the problem might be solved, that is through a careful cognitive task analysis.

Finally, Newell and Simon introduced the notion of methods that are "organizations for behavior that bear a rational relation to solving a problem," in which "rational" is taken to mean, "if the premises of the method are granted, then it is possible for the method to produce a solution" (p. 835). Methods are implemented as a program. The program envisioned by Newell and Simon by which the IPS performs the search for the goal state(s) is implemented as a production system comprised of a set of stimulus–response couplings known as *productions*. Appropriate productions are triggered by the appearance of a particular symbol or symbols in the STM augmented by the foveal EM.

Newell and Simon (1972) acknowledged that any useful account of human problem solving must include a description of the process or processes by which the capacity for problem solving develops ontogenetically, or stated in their own terms, "the processes by which the contents of the LTM of the human adult are *acquired*" (p. 866, italics added). Newell and Simon were silent on what these processes might be, but extensive work has been carried out in cognitive psychology to provide an information-processing account of development (cf. Case, 1985; Klahr & Wallace, 1976; Siegler, 1989).

That information-processing theory has not been abandoned as an inspiration for current research in cognition and instruction is demonstrated most clearly by Anderson and Gluck (chap. 8). They begin by noting the substantial difference in scale between the types of tasks studied by cognitive psychologists (e.g., memorizing a list of nonsense syllables, recognizing a symbol) and the more complex types of activities studied by educational researchers (e.g., proving a theorem, writing a computer program, solving an algebra word problem), and they propose *cognitive architectures* as an conceptual framework for decomposing the more complex activities into components that can be studied in the laboratory. They define cognitive architectures as computational models of complex problem solving and describe one such model based on Anderson's ACT theory. ACT theory is an elaboration of information-processing theory that conceptualizes cognition as "a sequence of ... production-rule firings" (p. 223). The findings they describe include eye-tracking data for students engaged in a solving problems posed by a computer-based algebra tutor. In Newell and Simon's terms, the students can be construed as IPSs employing portions of the computer screen as a "foveal EM" in their problem solving. Studies employing "high-density sensing" data, such as this, could provide a basis for making conjectures about the problem-solving methods used by the students, the problem-solving spaces they might construct, and the specific productions used in solving the problem.

The acquisition metaphor appears in different guises in other chapters, as well. Klahr, Chen, and Toth (chap. 3) describe work done in both the laboratory and the classroom to facilitate children's acquisition of a strategy for designing experiments. Carver's description (chap. 12) of doing task analyses of the instructional activities of an experimental preschool, although less bound to classic information-processing theory than the

Anderson and Gluck chapter, still embraces a view of learning as acquisition. Lesgold and Nahemov (chap. 10) begin their chapter with the proposition: "Learning by doing is a central way in which people *acquire* substantial expertise" (p. 303, italics added). Their model of the knowledge underlying expert performance, although more complex than the one proposed by Newell and Simon (1972), appeals, nonetheless, to the traditional metaphor.

Chapters by Kalchman, Moss, and Case (chap. 1), Minstrell (chap. 4), Reiser, Tabak, Sandoval, Smith, Steinmuller, and Leone (chap. 9), and Lehrer, Schauble, Strom, and Pligge (chap. 2) all emphasize the importance of learners' active engagement in the learning process, stressing themes consistent with constructivist theories of learning (e.g. Steffe & Gale, 1995). Constructivist theories represent a departure from more traditional theories of learning that treat the learner as a passive object written on (the *tabula rasa* of British empiricism) by experience. When construction becomes an alternative means to acquisition, however, the underlying metaphor is, nevertheless, preserved.

LEARNING AS CHANGE
IN PARTICIPATION

Lave began *Cognition in Practice* (1988) with the declaration:

> There is reason to suspect that what we call cognition is in fact a complex social phenomenon. The point is not so much that arrangements of knowledge in the head correspond in a complicated way to the social world outside the head, but that they are socially organized in such a fashion as to be indivisible. (p. 1)

This radical reconstrual of cognition as a fundamentally social process necessitated a corresponding rethinking of what it means to learn and a number of authors (e.g. Bruffee, 1993; Gee, 1992; Lave & Wenger, 1991; Nunes, Schliemann, & Carraher, 1993; Smith, 1988) have made moves in this direction. Ellis and Gregoire[1] discussed some of the implications of reconceptualizing learning in this way.

---

[1]Shari Ellis and Michele Gregoire, University of Florida, made a presentation entitled, "Sociocultural and cognitive aspects of teaching and learning in mathematics and science classrooms" at the June 1999 Carnegie Symposium. It does not appear in this volume.

Lave and Wenger's social practice theory is one of the most influential and better elaborated formulations based on a view of learning as modal changes in participation in a socially organized activity. There are three key concepts associated with this theory; *communities of practice, legitimate peripheral participation*, and *participants' developing identities*. They defined a community of practice as "a set of relations among persons, activity, and world, over time and in relation with other tangential and overlapping communities of practice" (p. 98). They stressed that this definition does not necessarily imply "co-presence, a well-defined, identifiable group, or socially visible boundaries," but does require "participation in an activity system about which participants share understandings concerning what they are doing and what that means in their lives and for their communities" (p. 98). Although they conceded that their definition leaves community of practice "largely as an intuitive notion" (p. 42), they strengthened the intuition by providing many practical examples (e.g., midwife and tailor apprentices, participants in an AAA "12-step" programs) from the world around us.

Lave and Wenger described legitimate peripheral participation as opportunities extended to newcomers to a community of practice to learn, that is "of both absorbing and being absorbed in—the 'culture of practice'" (p. 95). Herein lies their solution to the problem of how to describe learning in strictly social terms; they stipulated "learning occurs through centripetal participation in the learning curriculum of the community" (p. 100). This is a crucial point, with respect to a participation view of learning—learning is not simply construed as joining or entering a community of practice (that is, as a one-time event), but rather represents continuous changes in the nature of participation over time. Greeno (Greeno & MMAP, 1998) highlighted this point by defining a participant's identity as, "regularities of an individual's activities, in a trajectory that spans participation at different times in a community and participation in different communities" (p. 6), a definition he credited to Wenger (1999).

The Palincsar and Magnusson chapter exemplifies some aspects of this view of learning as changing participation (chap. 5). They describe a series of studies involving what they term "second-hand investigations" (p. 152) in the context of guided inquiry instruction. In these studies, they employed a particular set of teaching materials; a text designed to resemble a scientist's notebook. Palincsar and Magnusson make explicit their view of the classroom as a "community of inquiry" (p. 158). Inquiry in such a classroom is a form of social practice in which students, in the process of becoming active participants in a community of practice, take up a new set of discursive practices, (we hope) eventually mastering the more precise language and argumentation methods of bench scientists involved in scientific investigations. Legitimate peripheral participation is reflected in the distinction made in the chapter between firsthand and secondhand investigations that might be construed as different modes of participation within a community of inquiry. The pre- and post-test data reported in the chapter are actually more consistent with a view of learning as acquisition, but I interpret this more as a bridge-building move on the part of the authors that does not fundamentally detract from a more generally expressed treatment of learning as a participatory trajectory.

Minstrell's chapter also addresses learning as a change in participation (chap. 4). Although his description of student learning vacillates between a focus on outcome measures (acquisition) and a concern with the learner's changing ability to articulate their physics understanding (participation), his description of his own professional trajectory as a teacher and researcher is more consistently in keeping with a view of learning as a restructuring of relationships within particular communities of practice.

Other chapters also contain hints and suggestions of a participatory view. The Klahr, Chen, and Toth chapter (chap. 3) and the chapter by Reiser, Tabak, Sandoval, Smith, Steinmuller, and Leone (chap. 9), for example, describe efforts to construct and sustain scientific communities of practice within classrooms. Similarly, the chapter by Lehrer, Schauble, Strom, and Pligge (chap. 2) describes students' changing identities as model builders, a practice clearly relevant to becoming a science practitioner. Kalchman, Moss, and Case (chap. 1) also addressed learner identity issues in their discussion of children's acquisition of numeracy. In each case, learning is presented as occurring within a particular social and material setting.

DEWEY ON INFORMATION-PROCESSING AND SOCIAL PRACTICE

Dewey's Notion of Inquiry

I would contend that Dewey could be read selectively to provide support for either information-processing theory or social practice theory. This is because, as I argue, Dewey espoused a broader view of learning and human problem solving that subsumes both of these theories. To see this, let us turn first to Dewey's account of reflective inquiry.

In *How We Think*, a text written for schoolteachers, Dewey (1933/1989) described what he termed "the five phases of reflective thought":

> ... as states of thinking, are (1) *suggestions*, in which the mind leaps forward to a possible solution; (2) an intellectualization of the difficulty or perplexity that has been *felt* (directly experienced) in a *problem* to be solved, a question for which the answer must be sought; (3) the use of one suggestion after another as a leading idea, or *hypothesis*, to initiate and guide observation and other operations in collection of factual material; (4) the mental elaboration of the idea or supposition as an idea or supposition (*reasoning*, in the sense in which reasoning is a part, not the whole, of inference); and (5) testing the hypothesis by overt or imaginative action. (p. 200)

Although sometimes understood by readers as a linear process, Dewey made clear that these are phases, not steps. The order in which the phases occur (and reoccur) is indeterminate and the overall process is more recursive than sequential.

Dewey's description, written for a lay audience and stated in everyday terms, highlights a number of issues that concerned Dewey throughout his career. In *How We Think*, he argued that learning is a process of developing new adaptive "habits," habits that enable us to conduct our lives more easily and more comfortably. Reflective thought is only one of several available means by which new habits can be developed, but it is also a habit itself, one that can, therefore, be developed and fostered through educational activities (Dewey, 1916/1985). This, in fact, was the central function of schools for Dewey—to help students develop robust habits for reflective thinking.

Dewey (1929/1988) developed these ideas further when he wrote: "Thinking is objectively discoverable as that mode of serial responsive behavior to a problematic situation in which transition to the relatively settled and clear is effected" (p. 181). Dewey later introduced a more general term, inquiry, to describe the process of human problem solving, which he (1938/1991) defined as *"the controlled or directed transformation of an indeterminate situation into one that is so determinate in its constituent distinctions and relations as to convert the elements of the original situation into a unified whole"* (p. 108).

It should be noted that Dewey's definition of inquiry, at least by a casual reading, is not inconsistent with the descriptions of problem solving offered by Newell and Simon (1972). This can be seen most strikingly in his discussion of symbolic reasoning. Dewey (1929/1988) wrote:

Organic biological activities end in overt actions, whose consequences are irretrievable. When an activity and its consequences can be rehearsed by representation in symbolic terms, there is no such final commitment. If the representation of the final consequence is of unwelcome quality, overt activity may be foregone, or the way of acting be replanned in such a way as to avoid the undesired outcome. (p. 63)

There are some important differences, however, between Dewey's account of inquiry and the approach to studying problem solving advocated within information-processing theory.

Newell and Simon (1972) wrote, "Restricting the discussion to symbolic entities and processes does not severely limit our analysis or problem solving, except at physiological boundaries (e.g., the physiological aspects of sensory and motor skills, especially those requiring real-time action and coordination)" (p. 72), a position that Dewey would contest. He (1929/1988) emphasized that knowledge could not be separated from its contexts of use and wrote: "Knowing is, for philosophical theory, a case of specially directed activity instead of something isolated from practice" (p. 163). Dewey later (1938/1991) stipulated "the position here taken is that inquiry effects *existential* transformation and reconstruction of the material with which it deals" (p. 161). He acknowledged the possibility and importance of what might be termed the cognitive phases of inquiry, but also stressed that inquiry entails additional phases of observation, testing, and implementation, what Hickman (1998, p. 184) referred to as the "excursus" and "recursus" of inquiry, and can only be understood as a cohesive unit.

Situating Meaning in Conjoint Activity

Dewey (1938/1991) further elaborated his views on the nature of symbol grounding when he wrote:

... [T]he meaning which a conventional symbol has is not itself conventional. For the meaning is established by agreements of different persons in existential activities having reference to existential consequences.... For agreement and disagreement are determined by the consequences of conjoint activity. (p. 53)

He went on to observe, "Meanings hang together not in virtue of their examined relationships, but because they are current in the same set of group habits and expectations" (pp. 55–56) and, as a consequence, "[a] word means one thing in relation to a religious institution, still another thing in a business, a third thing in law, and so on" (p. 56). Dewey concluded, "Genuine community of language or symbols can be achieved only through efforts that bring about community of activities under existing conditions" (p. 56).

These ideas resonate with certain themes developed in conjunction with social practice theory. Greeno and MMAP (1998), for instance, argued "Conventions of interpreting meanings of symbols, icons, and indexes are a crucial part of social practices, and attunements to those constraints and affordances of interpretation are a crucial part of individuals' participation in those practices" (p. 10). Wenger (1999) developed this further by observing that the ability to participate in meaning negotiation itself controls the possibility for learning within a community of practice. He contended:

> A split between production and adoption of meaning ... compromises learning because it presents it as a choice between experience and competence: You must choose between your own experience as a resource for the production of meaning and your membership in a community where your competence is determined by your adoption of other's proposals for meaning. In other words, learning depends on our ability to contribute to the collective productions of meaning because it is by this process that experience and competence pull each other. (p. 203)

By the tenets of social practice theory, learning is conceptualized as a trajectory of changing participation within a community. Producing and adopting new meanings and interpretations is one aspect of practice. It would be consistent with such a theory to study meaning negotiation within a community of practice as a basis for understanding how learning is accomplished.

The point was made earlier that one could not (at least by Dewey's lights) understand inquiry by focusing exclusively on the cognitive aspects of the process. A similar point can be made with respect to studying learning exclusively as a process of social interaction. Dewey would argue that it is not sufficient to understand inquiry purely as an interactional achievement[2]—a full understanding must include both "the *opus operatum* and the *modus operandi*" (Bourdieu, 1990, p. 52) of inquiry.

---

[2]I use the term *interactional* here in the sense in which it is employed in ordinary parlance and not in the special sense in which Dewey (as we will see in the next part) used it in his later works. To make the distinction clear, I use the hyphenated form (i.e., *inter-action*) when using the term in the technical sense proposed by Dewey.

TRANSACTION:
A THIRD METAPHOR FOR LEARNING

Toward the very end of his career, Dewey jointly published a volume with Arthur Bentley, entitled *Knowing and the Known*. It was written, among other purposes, to provide a more disciplined terminology for doing behavioral inquiry. In this work, Dewey used the notion of inquiry not only as a description of how human problem solving is accomplished, but also reflexively as the means by which all valid understandings are to be developed, including our understanding of inquiry itself.

Dewey and Bentley (1949/1991) elaborated that inquiry can be conducted at three levels or stages of development, namely:

Self-action: where things are viewed as acting under their own powers.

Inter-action: where thing is balanced against thing in casual interconnection.

Trans-action: where systems of description and naming are employed to deal with aspects and phases of action, without final attribution to "elements" or other presumptively detachable or independent "entities," "essences," or "realities," and without isolation of presumptively detachable "relations" from such detachable "elements." (pp. 101–102)

Self-actional inquiry results in types of prescientific explanations employed by primitive cultures as accounts of natural phenomena, although Dewey and Bentley cited examples of self-actional accounts in contemporary writings. Much influenced by contemporary developments in the physical sciences, they viewed classical Newtonian mechanics as exemplifying inter-actional inquiry, whereas they considered the just emerging theories of quantum mechanics to represent a shift toward a trans-actional perspective.

Dewey and Bentley stipulated that transactional inquiry must proceed without preestablished conceptualizations and specifications, that interacting components cannot be studied in isolation except in and for the purposes of forming preliminary and partial descriptions, and that phenomena under study must be researched in full extension, both in space and time. They wrote:

Transaction is the procedure which observes men talking and writing, with their word-behaviors and other representational activities connected with their thing-perceivings and manipulations, and which permits a full treatment, descriptive and functional, of the whole process, inclusive of all its "contents," whether called "inners" or "outers," in whatever way the advancing techniques of inquiry require. (p. 114)

With respect to the need to subject human behavior to a more transactional form of analysis, Dewey and Bentley wrote:

> In ordinary everyday behavior, in what sense can we examine a talking unless we bring a hearing along with it into account? Or a writing without a reading? Or a buying without a selling? Or a supply without a demand? How can we have a principal without an agent or an agent without a principal? We can, of course, detach any portion of a transaction that we wish, and secure provisional descriptions and partial reports. But all this must be subject to the wider observation of the full process. (p. 127)

Dewey introduced the idea of transactionalism in earlier writing. For example, in *Experience and Education* (1938/1988) he wrote, "An experience is always what it is because of a *transaction* taking place between an individual and what, at the time, constitutes his environment" (p. 25, italics added). In *Knowing and the Known* (1949/1991), Dewey and Bentley attempted to make this notion more concrete through appeal to the example of a simple sales transaction:

> Th[e] transaction determines one participant to be a buyer and the other a seller. No one exists as buyer and seller save *in and because* of a transaction in which each is engaged. Nor is that all; specific things *become* goods or commodities because they are engaged in the transaction. There is no commercial transaction without things which only are goods, utilities, commodities, in and because of a transaction. Moreover, because of the exchange, or transfer, both *parties* (the idiomatic name for *participants*) undergo change; and the goods undergo at the very least a change of *locus* by which they gain and lose certain connective relations or "capacities" previously possessed. (p. 242)

This description might be seen as an alternative metaphor for the learning process; one that illustrates that learning is a process that not only transforms the learner, but also the environment within which the learning occurs. Observations, facts, and suggestions become knowledge by virtue of the unfolding transaction between the learner and the learner's environment. The acquisition metaphor, which focuses exclusively on the changes presumed to be taking place within the learner, is like describing a sales transaction as a simple entry on a balance sheet. By the same token, a participatory account of such a transaction would only reveal the sociointeractional aspects of the event. A Deweyan transactional analysis, on the other hand, would subsume both forms of description into a single account.

TOWARD A FORM OF TRANSACTIONAL INQUIRY INTO INQUIRY

Invoking Dewey is a familiar move in educational writing and I am not the first to suggest that his ideas might be helpful in resolving the divisions within our research community (cf. Altman & Rogoff, 1987; Bredo, 1994; Clancey, 1993, 1997; Greeno & Moore, 1993; Greeno & MMAP Group, 1997). Bredo (1994) came closest to the position being argued here; namely that there is a need for a more pluralistic approach that honors and incorporates both perspectives. That Dewey would endorse such a move can be inferred from his comment in the preface to *Knowing and the Known* (1949/1991):

> In advancing fields of research, inquirers proceed by doing all they can to make clear to themselves and to others the points of view and the hypotheses by means of which their work is carried on. When those who disagree with one another in their conclusions join in a common demand for such clarification, their difficulties turn out to increase command of the subject. (p. 3)

Boisvert (1998) recounted how the metaphor of philosopher as mapmaker is a recurrent one in Dewey's writing. In the cursory survey presented here, I have attempted to show how certain contributions from Dewey's work might be used as a basis for charting a new direction in research on cognition and instruction. Like a roadmap, Dewey's ideas provide guidance, but unfortunately lack detail with respect to how such a research agenda might actually be implemented. Instead, Dewey proposed standards for what would constitute a methodologically adequate account of learning and problem solving, leaving the implementation to others. Information-processing theory and social practice theory both address important aspects of Deweyan inquiry although neither alone meets his standards for a transactional account. Developing a more comprehensive framework, therefore, remains an open challenge for the next generation of researchers as we enter our second 25 years of research in cognition and instruction.

ACKNOWLEDGMENTS

I would like to thank Eric Bredo, Paul Feltovich, David Klahr, and Gerry Stahl for their useful comments on an earlier draft of this chapter.

REFERENCES

Altman, I., & Rogoff, B. (1987). World views in psychology: Trait, interactional, organismic, and transactional perspectives. In D. Stokols & I. Altman (Eds.), *Handbook of environmental psychology* (pp. 7–40). New York: John Wiley & Sons.

Anderson, J., Reder, L., & Simon, H. (1996). Situated learning and education. *Educational Researcher, 25* (4), 5–11.

Anderson, J., Reder, L., & Simon, H. (1997). Situative versus cognitive perspectives: Form versus substance. *Educational Researcher, 26* (1), 18–21.

Boisvert, R. (1998). Dewey's metaphysics: Ground-map of the prototypically real. In L. Hickman (Ed.), *Reading Dewey: Interpretations for a postmodern generation* (pp. 149–166). Bloomington, IN: Indiana University Press.

Bourdieu, P. (1990). *The logic of practice* (R. Nice, Trans.). Stanford, CA: Stanford University Press.

Bredo, E. (1994). Reconstructing educational psychology: Situated cognition and Deweyean pragmatism. *Educational Psychologist, 29,* 23–35.

Bredo, E. (1997). The social construction of learning. In G. Phye (Ed.), *Handbook of academic learning: The construction of knowledge* (pp. 3–43). New York: Academic Press.

Bruffee, K. (1993). *Collaborative learning.* Baltimore, MD: Johns Hopkins University Press.

Case, R. (1985). *Intellectual development: Birth to adulthood.* Orlando, FL: Academic Press.

Clancey, W. (1993). Situated action: A neuropsychological interpretation response to Vera and Simon. *Cognitive Science, 17,* 87–116.

Clancey, W. (1997). *Situated cognition: On human knowledge and computer representation.* NY: Cambridge University Press.

Cobb, P., & Bowers, J. (1999). Cognitive and situated learning: Perspectives in theory and practice. *Educational Researcher, 28* (2), 4–15.

Dewey, J. (1985). Democracy and education. In J. A. Boydston (Ed.), *John Dewey; The middle works, 1899–1924* (Vol. 9, pp. 1–370). Carbondale, IL: SIU Press. (Original work published 1916)

Dewey, J. (1988). The quest for certainty. In J. A. Boydston (Ed.), *John Dewey: The later works, 1925–1953* (Vol. 4, pp. 1–250). Carbondale, IL: SIU Press. (Original work published 1929)

Dewey, J. (1988). Experience and education. In J. A. Boydston (Ed.), *John Dewey: The later works, 1925–1953* (Vol. 13, pp. 1–62) Carbondale, IL: SIU Press. (Original work published 1929)

Dewey, J. (1989). How we think. In J. A. Boydston (Ed.), *John Dewey: The later works, 1925–1953* (Vol. 8, pp. 105–352). Carbondale, IL: SIU Press. (Original work published 1933)

Dewey, J. (1991). Logic: The theory of inquiry. In J. A. Boydston (Ed.), *John Dewey: The later works, 1925–1953* (Vol. 12, pp. 1–506). Carbondale, IL: SIU Press. (Original work published 1938)

Dewey, J. & Bentley, A. (1991). Knowing and the known. In J. A. Boydston (Ed.), *John Dewey: The later works, 1949–1952* (Vol. 16, pp. 1–294). Carbondale, IL: SIU Press. (Original work published 1949)

Dreyfus, H. L., & Dreyfus, S. (1986). *Mind over machine: The power of human intuition and expertise in the era of the computer.* Oxford, England: Basil Blackwell.

Forehand, G. (1974). Knowledge and the educational process. In L. W. Gregg (Ed.), *Knowledge and cognition* (pp. 159–166). Hillsdale, NJ: Lawrence Erlbaum Associates.

Gee, J. (1992). *The social mind, language, ideology, and social practice.* New York: Bergin & Garvey.

Greeno, J. (1997). On claims that answer the wrong questions. *Educational Researcher, 26* (1), 5–17.

Greeno, J., & MMAP Group. (1997). Theories and practices of thinking and learning to think. *American Journal of Education, 106,* 85–126.

Greeno, J., & MMAP Group. (1998). The situativity of knowing, learning, and research. *American Psychologist, 53,* 5–26.

Greeno, J., & Moore, J. (1993). Situativity and symbols: Response to Vera and Simon. *Cognitive Science, 17,* 49–60.

Hickman, L. (1998). Dewey's theory of inquiry. In L. Hickman (Ed.), *Reading Dewey: Interpretations for a postmodern generation* (pp. 166–186). Bloomington, IN: Indiana University Press.

Klahr, D. (Ed.). (1976). *Cognition and instruction.* Hillsdale, NJ: Lawrence Erlbaum Associates.

Klahr, D., & Wallace, J. G. (1976). *Cognitive development: An information-processing view.* Hillsdale, NJ: Lawrence Erlbaum Associates.

Koschmann, T. (2000). The physiological and the social in the psychologies of Dewey and Thorndike: The matter of habit. In B. Fishman & S. O'Connor-Divelbiss (Eds.), *Fourth International Conference of the Learning Sciences* (pp. 314–319). Mahwah, NJ: Lawrence Erlbaum Associates. Retrieved August 4, 2000 from the World Wide Web: http://www.umich.edu/~icls/proceedings/pdf/Koschmann.pdf

Lave, J. (1988). *Cognition in practice.* New York: Cambridge University Press.

Lave, J., & Wenger, E. (1991). *Situated learning: Legitimate peripheral participation.* New York: Cambridge University Press.

Newell, A., & Simon, H. (1972). *Human problem solving.* Englewood Cliffs, NJ: Prentice-Hall.

Norman, D. (Ed.). (1993). Special issue on situated action. *Cognitive Science, 17* (1), 1–133.

Nunes, T., Schliemann, A., & Carraher, D. (1993). *Street mathematics and school mathematics.* New York: Cambridge University Press.

Scardamalia, M., Bereiter, C., & Lamon, M. (1996). The CSILE project: Trying to bring the classroom into World 3. In K. McGilly (Ed.), *Classroom lessons: Cognitive theory and classroom practice* (pp. 201–228). Cambridge, MA: MIT Press.

Sfard, A. (1998). On two metaphors for learning and the dangers of choosing just one. *Educational Researcher, 27* (2), 4–13.

Siegler, R. S. (1989). Mechanisms of cognitive growth. *Annual Review of Psychology, 40,* 353–379.

Smith, F. (1988). *Joining the literacy club.* Portsmouth, NH: Heinemann.

Steffe, L. P., & Gale, J. (Eds.). (1995). *Constructivism in education.* Hillsdale, NJ: Lawrence Erlbaum Associates.

Wenger, E. (1999). *Communities of practice.* New York: Cambridge University Press.

15

Supporting the Improvement of Learning and Teaching in Social and Institutional Context

Paul Cobb
Vanderbilt University

The charge the editors gave me for this chapter was to "push the envelope" by raising methodological issues and by indicating phenomena that might be included within the scope of future cognitive science research. In seeking to fulfil this charge in what I hope will prove to be a constructive manner, I consider two points of methodology in the first part of the chapter. The first of these concerns the relation between the development of cognitive or learning theory on the one hand and the improvement of instructional practice on the other. The second methodological point brings to the fore the need for interpretive frameworks that enable us to analyze students' learning as it occurs in the social context of the classroom. This discussion then provides a backdrop for the second part of the chapter in which I focus on two general phenomena that typically fall beyond the purview of cognitive research but that are significant in the current era of educational reform. These phenomena concern the institutional context of the school and the cultural diversity of the students whose learning we seek to support.

COGNITIVE THEORY
AND INSTRUCTIONAL PRACTICE

It is helpful if I clarify at the outset that I am neither a psychologist nor a cognitive scientist. Instead, my professional identity is that of a mathematics educator. As a consequence, my colleagues and I spend a considerable amount of our time in classrooms attempting to understand and improve the process of learning and teaching mathematics in specific content domains. As the work of several contributors to this volume indicates, this focus on classroom instructional processes and students' learning as they participate in them also motivates an important strand of cognitive science research (e.g., Griffin & Case, 1997; Lehrer & Romberg, 1996; Lehrer, Schauble, Carpenter, & Penner, in press; Moss & Case, 1999). In our own work, the basic methodology that we have sought to refine over the past 13 years is that of the classroom teaching or design experiment (Brown, 1992; Cobb, in press; Confrey & Lachance, in press; Simon, in press). Our goal in these experiments, which can last up to a year, is both to develop sequences of instructional activities and associated tools, and to conduct analyses of the process of the students' learning and the means by which that learning is supported and organized. Research of this type falls under the general heading of design research in that it involves both instructional design and classroom-based research.

Gravemeijer (1994) wrote extensively about the first aspect of the design research cycle shown in Fig. 15.1, instructional design, and clarifies that the research team conducts an anticipatory thought experiment when preparing for the design experiment. In doing so, the team formulates a hypothetical learning trajectory that involves conjectures about both a possible learning route or trajectory that aims at significant mathematical ideas, and the specific means that might be used to support and organize learning along the envisioned trajectory. It is important to emphasize that these two aspects of a hypothetical trajectory are interrelated in that the realization of the conjectured learning route is seen to depend on the use of the proposed means of support. Thus, the proposed learning route might well depart quite radically from accounts of cognitive development in the domain of interest that are based on either naturalistic observations or on analyses of the learning of students who have received traditional forms of instruction. The envisioned trajectory is therefore hypothetical in the sense that it embodies hypotheses about what might be possible for students' mathematical learning in a particular domain.

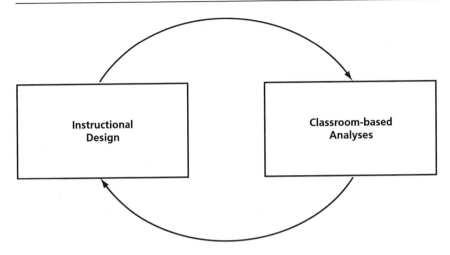

FIG. 15.1. The Design Research Cycle.

The speculative nature of this trajectory does not of course imply that it is fabricated in an unrestrained ad hoc manner. Instead, its formulation is subject to two types of constraints. The first type stems from the designers' general theoretical perspective on learning in instructional situations. Carver (chap. 12) illustrates constraints of this type when she discusses what she terms metaprinciples of domain-independent cognitive theory, such as building on prior knowledge. In the case of myself and my colleagues, the background theory that orients our design work is a version of social constructivism.[1] The second type of constraint on the design process derives from the syntheses that we develop of prior research on learning in the mathematical domain of interest. Significantly, we have found that exclusively cognitive studies that merely report misconceptions or sequences of levels in students' reasoning have been, at best, of limited value to us. In contrast, studies that attempt to document the process of students' learning in innovative instructional situations have proven to be of great value. Unfortunately, the number of studies of the first type heavily outweighs the number of studies of the second type in most mathematical domains.

---

[1]A discussion of our general theoretical orientation can be found in Cobb, Stephan, McClain, and Gravemeijer (in press). It is important to stress that this background theory has itself evolved as we have worked in classrooms in that we initially took a relatively individualistic psychological constructivist perspective.

Turning now to consider the proposed means of support inherent in a hypothetical learning trajectory, it is important to clarify that they are construed broadly and include:

- Resources typically considered by materials developers (e.g., instructional activities together with the notational schemata and the physical and computer-based tools that students might use).
- Classroom social context (e.g., the general classroom participation structure and the nature of specifically mathematical discourse).
- The teacher's proactive role in supporting the emergence of increasingly sophisticated ways of reasoning.

Although instructional planning at this level of detail is unusual in the United States, there are several notable exceptions (e.g., Confrey & Smith, 1995; Lehrer et al., in press; Simon, 1995). In addition, an encompassing approach of this type is the norm in Japan where members of professional teaching communities often spend several years teaching and revising the hypothesized learning trajectories that underpin a sequence of mathematics lessons (Stigler & Hiebert, 1999).

It is important to stress that the conjectures inherent in a hypothetical learning trajectory are just that—they are tentative, provisional, eminently revisable conjectures that are tested and revised on a daily basis once the experiment begins. Our goal when experimenting in a classroom is therefore not to try to demonstrate that the instructional design formulated at the outset works. Instead, it is to improve the design by testing and modifying conjectures as informed by ongoing analyses of both students' reasoning and the classroom learning environment. As a consequence, although we formulate a hypothetical learning trajectory in advance and also outline possible types of instructional activities, we develop the specific instructional activities used in the classroom only a day or 2 before they are needed. I mention this to clarify that the methodology is relatively labor-intensive. It is essential, for example, that the senior researchers be present in the classroom each day and that they lead debriefing meetings of the research team after every classroom session. Formal design experiments should therefore not be confused with informal explorations in which research assistants are delegated to work in a classroom in a less principled way.

My immediate purpose in outlining the methodology that my colleagues and I use is to highlight what I take to be a defining characteristic of design research, the tightly integrated cycles of design and analysis. Gravemeijer (1998) differentiated what he refers to as daily minicycles from macrocycles that span an entire teaching experiment. This latter, longer term cycle involves a retrospective analysis that is conducted once the design experiment is completed and that can feed forward to guide the formulation of a revised learning trajectory for follow-up teaching experiments.

My larger purpose in discussing design experiments is to describe a methodological approach in which instructional design serves as a primary setting for the development of theory. This characteristic of design experiments becomes apparent once I clarify that the questions and concerns that arise while an experiment is in progress are typically pragmatic and relate directly to the goal of supporting the participating students' learning. In contrast, the intent when conducting a retrospective analysis of an experiment is to contribute to the development of a domain-specific instructional theory (see Fig. 15.2). This theory emerges over the course of several macrocycles and consists of a demonstrated learning route that culminates with the emergence of significant mathematical ideas, and substantiated means of supporting and organizing learning along that trajectory. As Steffe and Thompson (in press) clarified, it is this theory that makes the results of a series of design experiments potentially generalizable, even though they are empirically grounded in analyses of only a small number of classrooms. In their terms, this is generalization by

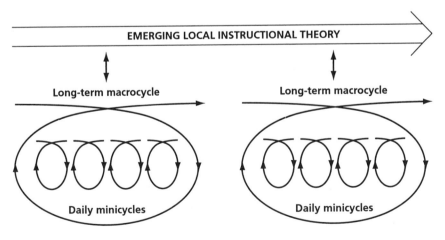

FIG. 15.2. Design minicycles and macrocycles (adapted from K. Gravemeijer, 1998).

means of an explanatory framework rather than by means of a representative sample in that the insights and understandings developed and tested during a series of experiments can inform the interpretation of events and thus pedagogical planning and decision making in other classrooms.

Design experiments in which the development of theory and the improvement of an instructional design coemerge can be contrasted with an alternative approach to design that involves a sequence of steps:

1. The development of cognitive theory.
2. The derivation of principles for design from the cognitive theory.
3. The translation of the principles into concrete designs.
4. The assessment of the designs to test whether they work as anticipated.

It is, of course, debatable whether this putative sequence is ever strictly adhered to in practice. However, research reports are often written so as to imply that the development of the design involved a one-way chain of reasoning from cognitive theory to instructional practice. The general approach is therefore alive in research discourse, where it is frequently treated as the ideal. It is this ideal that I want to scrutinize from my perspective as a mathematics educator.

As an initial observation, I should clarify that assessments conducted as part of this design approach can involve the generation of qualitative and process data as well as quantitative outcome measures. Thus, my primary concern is not with the nature of the assessment data, but with the intent that underlies their generation. The key point to emphasize is that, in this orientation to design, the anticipated or targeted ways of reasoning (often those of experts) are typically used as normative standards against which students' reasoning is compared. As a consequence, the purpose of the assessment is usually to evaluate rather than to understand students' reasoning in that the analysis focuses on the extent to which their reasoning deviates from the standard rather than on understanding how they are actually reasoning and on explaining why they came to reason in these ways. As someone who sees considerable merit in Toulmin's (1963) argument that explanation and understanding constitute the driving forces of scientific inquiry, I find the priority given to evaluation troubling. In addition, I am also concerned about the relatively weak feedback loop from the final assessment phase to the design principles and cognitive theory. It is not clear, for example, that these principles and the underlying theory are open to the results of an unfavorable assessment of a specific design. This is disconcerting if one takes the view that educational reform should be an ongoing, continual process of iterative improvement characterized by what Lampert (1990) termed a "zigzag between conjectures and refutations."

Beyond these general observations, I also wonder about the practical feasibility of this idealized approach to design in specific mathematical domains. For example, my colleagues and I have recently completed a sequence of two classroom design experiments that focused on statistical data analysis at the middle school level. In preparing for these experiments, we conducted a reasonably extensive review of the literature but found only a small number of studies that could guide our formulation of a hypothetical learning trajectory.[2] There did not even appear to be a consensus on the overarching statistical ideas that should constitute the potential endpoint of a learning trajectory. However, rather than waiting for development of cognitive theory, we drew on the available literature to formulate initial conjectures about major shifts in students' statistical reasoning and the means by which these shifts might be supported. Not surprisingly, a number of these conjectures proved to be unviable when we began experimenting in the classroom. We therefore began the process of revising conjectures online and eventually formulated a new learning trajectory that was empirically grounded in our work in the two classrooms. We contend that what we learned about the learning and teaching of statistical data analysis by proceeding in this way can contribute to an emerging instructional theory that aims at a significant statistical idea, that of distribution.

It is important to note that the lack of an adequate research base is not unique to statistical data analysis. The same observation applies to areas such as algebra and geometry that are also undergoing relatively profound disciplinary changes (Cobb, 1997; Kaput, 1994; Lehrer, Jacobson, Kemney, & Strom, 1999). In domains such as these, the idealized top-down approach to instructional design in which cognitive theory trickles down to instructional practice appears to be untenable. Instead, the

---

[2]McGatha (2000) described the year-long process of preparing for the first of these experiments in considerable detail. As she documented, it involved reviewing the research literature, the available research-based curriculum materials, and the available data analysis tools. In addition, we analyzed videorecordings of individual student interviews and whole class performance assessments that we conducted as part of our pilot work.

bootstrapping approach integral to design research in which theory and instructional designs evolve together appears to be more feasible. The contributions to this volume by Case and colleagues and by Lehrer and Schauble serve to substantiate this claim. Some years ago, the Dutch mathematician and mathematics educator Hans Freudenthal (1973) argued that psychology should follow instructional design rather than the reverse. Although this might be too strong, it does seem reasonable to think in terms of a symbiotic relationship between cognitive theory and instructional practice, and between the discipline of cognitive science and so-called applied fields such as mathematics education.

In concluding this discussion, it is worth clarifying that the arguments I have advanced about the relative merits of design research have not been cast in absolute terms. Instead, they reflect the view that methodologies are conceptual tools that are more appropriate for some purposes than for others. It would, therefore, be naive to reject treatment-control experiments of the type frequently conducted by cognitive scientists out of hand. I would, however, contend that such experiments are relatively blunt instruments that are not well-suited to the demands of instructional design. A fundamental difficulty is that these experiments do not produce the detailed kinds of data that are needed to guide the often subtle refinements made when improving an instructional design. In contrast, treatment-control experiments are highly appropriate for another purpose for which design research is less well-suited, that of generating the types of data that we need in order to participate in public policy debates about education. Relevant assessment studies of this type include those that compare matched groups of students in experimental and traditional classrooms on a range of measures such as basic computational skills, mathematical understanding, motivations for engaging in mathematical activity, and beliefs about the general nature of mathematics in school (e.g., Cobb et al., 1991; Wood & Sellers, 1996). We have found the results of studies of this type to be invaluable in persuading school district administrators and other policymakers of the potential value of the instructional sequences developed during design experiments. In addition to conducting further studies of this type as part of our ongoing work in statistics, we also plan to compare the capabilities of middle school students in experimental classrooms with university undergraduate and graduate students. These studies should enable us to both triangulate the findings of a series of design experiments and to frame our claims in the linguistic currency of public policy discourse, that of inferential statistics.

LEARNING AND TEACHING
IN SOCIAL CONTEXT

The second methodological issue I raise builds on the first by focusing on the need, within design research, for interpretive frameworks that enable us to analyze students' learning as it occurs in the social context of the classroom. As we know all too well, classrooms are messy, complex, and sometimes confusing places. One of the concerns that my colleagues and I have struggled with as we have worked in classrooms is that of developing an analytic framework that enables us to come to terms with this complexity so that we can begin to see some pattern and order in what appear at first glance to be ill-structured events.

I would argue that an interpretive framework that is appropriate for the purposes of instructional design should satisfy the following criteria:

1. It should result in analyses that feed back to inform the improvement of instructional designs.
2. It should enable us to document the developing mathematical reasoning of individual students as they participate in the practices of the classroom community.
3. It should enable us to document the collective mathematical learning of the classroom community over the extended periods of time spanned by design experiments.

The rationale for the first criterion follows directly from the tightly integrated cycles of design and analysis that I discussed at both the micro and macrolevel (see Figs. 15.1 and 15.2). The second criterion, which emphasizes the importance of focusing on the nature and quality of individual students' reasoning, probably needs little justification for most cognitive scientists. Nonetheless, I give a brief rationale to clarify the pragmatic origins of this criterion. Briefly, the classroom sessions that we conduct during a design experiment are frequently organized so that students initially work either individually or in small groups before convening for a whole-class discussion of their interpretations and solutions. A pedagogical strategy that we have found productive involves the teacher and one or more members of the project staff circulating around the classroom during individual or small group work to gain a sense of the diverse ways in which students are interpreting and solving instructional activities. Toward the end of this phase of the lesson, the teacher and project staff members confer to prepare for the whole-class discussion. In doing so, they routinely focus on the qualitative differences in students' reasoning in order to develop conjectures about mathematically significant issues that might, with the teacher's proactive guidance, emerge as topics of conversation. Their intent in doing so is to capitalize on the diversity in the students' reasoning by identifying interpretations and solutions that, when compared and contrasted, might lead to substantive mathematical discussions that advance their current pedagogical agenda. It is because of this crucial role that a focus on individual students' reasoning plays in our instructional decision making that we require an analytic approach that takes account of the diverse ways in which students participate in communal classroom practices.

The third criterion, which introduces a focus on the mathematical learning of the classroom community, is probably more controversial. Its rationale stems from the observation that the conjectures the designer develops when preparing for an experiment cannot be about the trajectory of each and every student's learning for the straightforward reason that there are significant qualitative differences in their reasoning at any point in time. In my view, descriptions of instructional approaches written so as to imply that all students will reorganize their thinking in particular ways at particular points in an instructional sequence involve, at best, questionable idealizations. An issue that arises is therefore that of clarifying the focus of the envisioned learning trajectories that are central to our (and others') work. The resolution that we propose involves viewing a hypothetical learning trajectory as consisting of conjectures about the collective mathematical learning of the classroom community. This proposal in turn indicates the need for an interpretive framework that enables us to analyze collective mathematical learning as well as the learning of the individual students as they participate in this communal process.

The interpretive framework that we currently use to organize our analyses of classroom data is shown in Fig. 15.3. As can be seen, it addresses the last two criteria by coordinating a psychological perspective on individual students' reasoning with a social perspective on communal classroom processes (cf. Cobb & Yackel, 1996). The three entries in the column headed "Social Perspective" indicate three aspects of the classroom microculture that we have found it useful to differentiate. The first of these, classroom social norms, provides a way of documenting what both Erickson (1986) and Lampert (1990) termed the "classroom participation structure." Examples of social norms for whole class discussions include that students are obliged to explain and justify solutions, to attempt to make sense of explanations given by others, to indicate under-

Social Perspective	Psychological Perspective
Classroom social norms	Beleifs about own role, others' role and the general nature of mathematical activity in school
Sociomathematical norms	Mathematical beliefs and values
Classroom mathematical practices	Mathematical interpretations and reasoning

FIG. 15.3. A framework for analyzing individual and communal mathematical activity.

standing or nonunderstanding, and to ask clarifying questions or challenge alternatives when differences in interpretations have become apparent.

It is readily apparent that these social norms are not specific to mathematics, but instead apply to any subject matter area. For example, one might hope that students would explain their reasoning in science or history classes as well as in mathematics. In contrast, sociomathematical norms focus on regularities in classroom actions and interactions that are specific to mathematics (cf. Simon & Blume, 1996; Voigt, 1995; Yackel & Cobb, 1996). Examples of sociomathematical norms include the criteria that are established in a particular classroom for what counts as a different mathematical solution, a sophisticated mathematical solution, and an efficient mathematical solution, as well as for what counts as an acceptable mathematical explanation.

If sociomathematical norms are specific to mathematics, then classroom mathematical practices are specific to particular mathematical ideas and are thus concerned with the emergence of what is traditionally called mathematical content. A hypothetical learning trajectory can in fact be viewed as consisting of an envisioned sequence of mathematical practices together with the means of supporting and organizing the emergence of each practice from prior practices. To give one brief example that is taken from a second-grade design experiment, the students typically solved arithmetical tasks by counting by ones at the beginning of the school year. However, some of the students also developed solutions that involved conceptualizing numbers as composed of units of 10s and 1s. When they did so, they were obliged to explain their numerical reasoning. This contrasted with observations we made at the midpoint of the school year in that students who conceptualized numbers in this way were no longer obliged to give justifications. Instead, it appeared to be taken for granted, at least in public classroom discourse, that numbers were composed of units of 10s and 1s. This way of construing numbers was now treated as a self-evident mathematical fact. It was at this juncture that we inferred that this way of talking and reasoning had been established as a classroom mathematical practice.

It is important to clarify that an assertion that a mathematical practice has been established does not enable us to make claims about the reasoning of any particular student. As a consequence, we find it essential to complement an analysis of the mathematical development of the classroom community with analyses of individual students' mathematical activity. These psychological analyses invariably reveal that there are qualitative differences in students' reasoning even as they participate in the same practice. In general, a practice can be thought of as constituting the immediate social context in which students' learning occurs. We take the relationship between practices and the reasoning of the participating students to be reflexive (cf. Cobb et al., in press). Although relationships of this type are nondeterministic, they are nonetheless relatively strong and imply that individual students' reasoning does not exist apart from communal practices and vice versa. On the one hand, we view the practices being continually regenerated by the teacher and students as they mutually adapt to each other's actions in the classroom. On the other hand, we view individual students' reasoning as acts of participation in communal practices and contend that the types of reasoning we observe would not have emerged but for the students' history of participation in specific classroom mathematical practices. This does not, of course, imply that students can only reason in particular ways if they are actually engaging in collaborative activity with others in the classroom. The eventual goal is that students will be able to participate in communal practices on their own outside the classroom.[3] The processes involved in this development are discussed in some detail by Beach (1999).

---

[3]Stated in this way, it might appear that we frame our overall instructional goals in purely functional terms. However, in preparing for a design experiment, we attempt to explicate the overall goals in terms of Greeno's (1991) metaphor of knowing in a particular domain as acting in and reasoning with the resources of a particular environment. One of the attractive features of this metaphor is that it enables us to transcend the dichotomy between subject and object by simultaneously specifying both the taken-as-shared mathematical environment in which we hope that students will come to act and the taken-as-shared ways of reasoning and communicating mathematically that we hope will emerge in the course of a design experiment.

It is apparent from this brief overview that analyses developed by following the general approach of coordinating social and psychological perspectives result in situated accounts of learning. I can further clarify this point by drawing on an analogy that Herbert Simon introduced in his presentation at the symposium that led to this book. He proposed that the relation between mind and the environment is analogous to that between jello and the mold. In developing the entailments of the analogy, he argued that just as we should study the mold if we want to understand the shape of the jello, so we should analyze the environment if we want to understand the mind. Extending this analogy to the analytic approach I have presented, individual students' reasoning corresponds to the jello, and communal practices correspond to the mold. The analogy helps to make explicit a contrast with the cognitive paradigm discussed by Simon in that the mold (i.e., communal practices) is not viewed as pregiven with respect to the mind. Instead, the mold is viewed as a collective accomplishment of the community of which the students are members. Further, the reflexive relation between the psychological and social perspectives implies that students actively contribute to the continual regeneration of the mold that enables and constrains the development of their reasoning.

Thus far, in outlining the interpretive framework that my colleagues and I currently use, I have said little about the first of the three criteria that I stated earlier, namely that analyses should feed back to inform the ongoing instructional design effort. In this regard, I contend that the situated nature of our analyses is a good thing given the concerns and interests that motivate our work in classrooms. It is a strength rather than a weakness in that it results in accounts of students' learning that are tied to analyses of the actual environment in which that learning occurs (i.e., the classroom microculture). As a consequence, we can disentangle aspects of this environment that served to support and organize the development of the students' reasoning. This, in turn, makes it possible for us to develop testable conjectures about ways in which we might be able to improve those means of support and thus our instructional design.

It is important to note that this argument in support of a situated approach is not ideological, at least in the pejorative sense of the term. I have not, for example, presented a barrage of citations to claim that cognition is situated and that anyone who thinks otherwise has got the mind wrong. Instead, the gist of my argument is that it is useful for the purposes of design research to view students' reasoning as situated with respect to communal classroom processes. The argument is, therefore, pragmatic and reflects the view that the interpretive framework, as an aspect of our methodology, is a conceptual tool that is appropriate for certain purposes but not others.

BROADENING THE CONTEXT

Thus far, in raising methodological issues, I have limited my focus to the social context of the classroom. I now discuss two broader phenomena that are pragmatically significant in the current era of reform, the institutional context of the school, and the cultural diversity of the students whose learning we attempt to support. Although my intent is to bring to the fore two complex sets of issues that are not usually considered in cognitive science research, I should acknowledge that my own research has also failed to take explicit account of these phenomena to this point. Consequently, in proposing issues that might be included in future cognitive science research, I also indicate directions in which I believe my own and my colleagues' work should move. As our attempts to develop an initial theoretical orientation are still ongoing, my primary concern is to justify why cognitive scientists might want to give the two phenomena serious attention.

The Institutional Context of the School

To frame issues relating to school context, I return briefly to the design experiment methodology. An important aspect of our work concerns the negotiations that occur as we seek entry into a school. In these negotiations, we request that we be given responsibility for a group of students' mathematics instruction for an agreed-upon period of time. Further, as part of the negotiation process, we seek to insulate the design experiment classroom from many of the institutional constraints of the school (e.g., use of adopted textbooks, content coverage prescriptions, norms for the structure of lessons and students' engagement in them). Negotiations of this type are, of course, not unique to design research but are instead undertaken routinely in a range of school-based research endeavors. Typically, there are good reasons for attempting to insulate the school-based research site in this way. In the case of design research, for example, I would argue that this insulation is justifiable when the purpose is to develop a local instructional theory by investigating what might be possible in students' mathematics education. However, it can become problematic in this and other types of research if the researchers overlook the effort they expend to create and maintain temporary lacunae within the institutional structure of the school. Documenting these efforts is particularly important if the eventual goal is to use the products and findings of the research as a basis for the development of a professional teaching community to be established in collaboration with a group of teachers.

A primary difficulty that arises concerns the potential tensions and conflicts between the forms of instruction institutionalized in the school (or school district) and those that emerge both within the capsule of the research site and within the professional teaching community. Frequently, these two forms of instruction are organized by contrasting overall intentions or motives. The motive of school instruction might, for example, be competent performance on a relatively limited range of tasks as assessed by teachermade, textbook, and state-mandated tests of skills. However, the overall motive of the forms of instruction nurtured in the professional teaching community might be mathematical understanding as assessed by the teachers' observation and documentation of their students' reasoning.

The need to make this potential conflict a focus of inquiry becomes particularly pressing if one is concerned about the sustainability of the instructional approaches the teachers create in the course of the collaboration. In this regard, Cole (1996) noted that although it might be possible to nurture novel forms of instruction in almost any institutional setting by supplying the material and human resources necessary to create appropriate conditions, it is often not possible to sustain those conditions once the resources have been withdrawn. This observation obviously indicates the importance of involving administrators, parents, and other stakeholders in the activities of the professional teaching community (cf. Lehrer & Shumow, 1997; Price & Ball, 1997). The intent in doing so is to bring the instructional goals of the professional teaching community and of the school into closer alignment, for the teachers' emerging instructional approaches must come to fit with institutional goals if they are eventually to be sustained by local resources.

This discussion of sustainability illustrates the complexity of teacher professional development in that the goal is to support both the professionalization of teaching and the emergence of institutional conditions that enable teachers to act as professionals. The realization that professionalization is distributed in turn gives rise to a theoretical challenge, that of coming to understand the relations between teachers' participation in multiple communities. The design experiment methodology provides a point of reference in that the focus is on students' learning as they participate in the practices of a single community, that of the classroom. In contrast, analyses of teachers' learning that are adequate for our purposes necessitate the development of interpretive frameworks that make it possible for us to understand how teachers' participation in two distinct communities, the professional teaching community and the school community, influence their pedagogical activity in the classroom. To be sure, an appropriate framework should enable us to analyze individual teachers' planning and decision making. However, in addition to enabling us to locate that reasoning in the immediate social context of their interactions with students, it should also enable us to see their reasoning as situated within the broader institutional context of their schools.

The extent of this theoretical challenge is indicated by a dichotomy that is apparent in the literature on teacher change (cf. Engestrom, 1998). One body of scholarship focuses on the role of professional development in supporting teachers' views of their instruction and themselves as learners. A second body of scholarship is concerned with the structural or organizational features of schools and with how changes in these conditions can lead to changes in classroom instruction. The task, as I see it, is to transcend the dichotomy between these two largely independent lines of work, one oriented toward teachers' learning as they participate in professional teaching communities and the other toward broader policy considerations. Although this challenge is central to our own and others' current work (e.g., Cobb & McClain, 1999; Spillane, 1999; Stein, Silver, & Smith, 1998). I contend that it is also of critical importance to cognitive scientists who want to leverage their research by collaborating with teachers and administrators to influence public school instruction.

Cultural Diversity

As was the case with the social context of the school, the design experiment methodology provides a useful starting point from which to approach issues of cultural diversity. I have already noted that the design experiment classroom is insulated from the institutional constraints of the school to a considerable degree. A second kind of insulation is inherent in the analytic approach that my colleagues and I follow in that we characterize students' reasoning solely in terms of their participation in the practices of the classroom community. In adopting this analytic stance, we fail to take account of students' participation in the practices of either their local home communities or of the cultural groups within the wider society of which they are members. This second form of insulation is, I believe, less justifiable than the first, particularly as our espoused goal is to support all students' development of what current reform documents label as mathematical power (NCTM, 1989).

The consequences of this limitation become apparent when we consider the various ways in which students' participation in out-of-school practices can influence their activity in the classroom. There is evidence, for example, that students make a range of suppositions and assumptions when interpreting mathematical problems set in real-world scenarios that reflect the practices of their communities. As an illustration, Ladson-Billings (1995) presented the following task to suburban students and to their inner city counterparts:

> It costs $1.50 to travel each way on the city bus. A transit system fast pass costs $65.00 a month. Which is the more economical way to get to work, the daily fare or the fast pass? (p.123)

Ladson-Billings reported that the suburban students assumed that the scenario was about a person who commuted to work in the city. They therefore calculated the cost of the daily fare as $3.00 per day for 5 days each week. In contrast, the inner city students asked a number of questions: How many jobs are we talking about? Are these part-time or full-time jobs? As Ladson-Billings noted, these differing responses reflect differences in the economic practices of the two groups of students' home communities. Although there has been some acknowledgment in the cognitive science literature that the process of interpreting story problems involves implicit suppositions and assumptions of this type (e.g., De Corte, Verschaffel, & De Win, 1984), they are typically characterized in purely individualistic psychological terms. In exploring links with the practices of students' home communities, Ladson-Billings oriented us toward an explanation that, in my view, makes such issues more tractable for teachers.

In addition to influencing how students interpret instructional activities in the classroom, students' home communities can involve differing norms of participation, language, and communication, some of which might actually be in conflict with those that the teacher seeks to establish in the classroom (Cazden, 1988; Delpit, 1988; Fine, 1987; Philips, 1972). For example, Cazden (1988) identified two distinct types of narrative style, topic-centered and episodic, that differ in thematic structure and organization when she analyzed a group of first-grade students' activity during sharing time at school. As she clarified, topic-centered narratives focus on one topic whereas episodic narratives focus on a number of events with shifting scenes. Cazden reported that most of the students who gave topic-centered narratives were White whereas most who gave episodic narratives were African American. This finding takes on added significance in light of a follow-up study in which Cazden investigated adults' reactions to videorecordings of children giving topic-centered and episodic narratives. She discovered that the White adults found the episodic narratives hard to follow and typically judged the child to be of low ability. In contrast, the African American adults were more likely to value both narrative styles even though they were aware of differences between them. These results are important given that schools, in general, and mathematics classrooms, in particular, privilege topic-centered narratives. In particular, the results illustrate how differences in the discourse patterns of students' home communities may influence how they are perceived in the classroom and how their contributions are treated by teachers and other students. These reactions can, in turn, influence whether students perceive themselves as supported or as marginalized and silenced in the classroom, thus leading to inequities in both opportunities and motivations to learn.

It should be clear from this discussion of Cazden's work that the implications of potential conflicts between home and school norms are not limited to the establishment of general classroom social norms and the classroom participation structure but also relate specifically to the teaching and learning of mathematics. For example, the notion of mathematical proof is central to any coherent instructional program. Within the discipline, proof serves both as a means of inquiry for individual mathematicians and as a means by which they convince others of the validity of their reasoning (Hanna, 1989; Schoenfeld, 1983). It is part of the linguistic currency of mathematics and can be seen to originate in discussions conducted in the early grades in which students are expected to justify their reasoning by developing and refining arguments. In this case of proof, potential conflicts between the forms of discourse targeted in the mathematics classroom and the norms of communication in students' home communities therefore penetrate to the core of teachers' instructional agendas. This observation is not, however, unique to proof but also holds for other central aspects of mathematical activity such as modeling, symbolizing, inference, and indeed the very process of mathematizing (cf. O'Conner, 1998).

From the point of view of instructional design, the issues I have raised emphasize the importance of attending explicitly to the diversity in the practices of students' home communities when formulating the starting points of a hypothetical learning trajectory. In addition, they indicate the need to be cognizant of these out-of-school practices when analyzing the ways in which individual students participate in the practices of the classroom community. This broadening of the analytical approach is crucial given that analyses of classroom events inform pedagogical judgments and thus impact the quality of students' mathematics education. At a minimum, a broader perspective would enable cognitive scientists to guard against the danger of attributing inherent cognitive deficiencies to students from home communities whose practices conflict with those that are privileged both in school and in psychological research. In addition, it would enable cognitive scientists interested in influencing school instruction to view the cultural diversity of students' discourse and reasoning as an instructional resource to be capitalized on rather than as an obstacle to be overcome. In science education, design experiments conducted by Warren and Rosebery (1995) that focused on scientific argumentation indicate the viability of such an approach.

In stepping back still further to consider the practices of cultural groups within wider society, I draw primarily on the work of my colleague Lynn Hodge (1999). She developed an initial orientation by introducing the notions of dominant cultures and cultural capital (Bourdieu, 1977). As she clarified, cultural capital refers to the ways of speaking, writing, dressing, and so forth that are, in a sense, possessed by members of identifiable cultural groups and that are passed from one generation to the next (see also Zevenbergen, 1996). The idea of dominant cultures indicates that although all cultural groups within society possess cultural capital, these diverse forms of capital are treated differently by a range of societal institutions, including schools. As a consequence, schools can be seen to play a central role in maintaining the dominance of certain cultural groups. Students who talk and act in ways consistent with a dominant culture are, for example, usually at an advantage in gaining access to educational, economic, and professional opportunities.

For mathematics educators and, I suggest, cognitive scientists, the notions of dominant cultures and cultural capital indicate the importance of scrutinizing the instructional goals that constitute the endpoints of learning trajectories. The purpose in doing so is to examine whether the goals can be justified in terms of participation in a democratic society or whether they are tied to taken-for-granted policies and practices that serve to perpetuate the regeneration of inequities. In the two design experiments I referred to earlier that focused on statistical data analysis in the middle grades, we did in fact conduct such an examination by clarifying for ourselves why statistics should be taught in school. Although we identified several rationales in the literature, the argument that we found most compelling took account of the increasing premium being placed on statistical reasoning as a consequence of the increasing use of computers, not just in the discipline but in society more generally (cf. Cobb, 1997). We noted, for example, that there is much talk of preparing students for "the information age," but without fully appreciating that much of this information is statistical in nature. This shift has significant implications for the discourse of public policy and thus for democratic participation and power. It is already apparent that debates about public policy issues tend to involve reasoning with statistical data and that this discourse is increasingly becoming the language of power in the public policy arena. These observations led us to conjecture that the inability to participate in this discourse results in de facto disenfranchisement that can spawn alienation from and cynicism about the political process. From this, we concluded that statistical literacy that involves reasoning with data in relatively sophisticated ways relates directly to both equity and participatory democracy.

Given this image of students, as increasingly substantial participants in public policy discourse, the competencies that we considered critical were those of developing and critiquing data-based arguments. As we have noted elsewhere (Cobb, 1999), in supporting students' development of these competencies in the design experiments, we were simultaneously supporting their eventual participation in the practices of dominant groups. As a consequence, the approach we took to statistics is compatible with Delpit's (1988) admonition that instruction should aim to support students' appropriation of what she called the culture of power. I would argue that learning trajectories that involve the type of analysis I have illustrated, therefore, have the potential to contribute to the reconstruction of schools as institutions that redress rather than regenerate inequities. In my view, such an approach is worthy of consideration by cognitive scientists, given that their work has sometimes been criticized for unquestioningly accepting traditional instructional goals and thus, for tending to support the status quo.

As a further observation, it should also be clear from the illustrations I have presented that issues of diversity, like those relating to the institutional context of the school, give rise to the theoretical challenge of accounting for participation in multiple communities. Hodge's (1999) analysis is again helpful in that she proposed that cultural diversity can be treated productively as a relational notion. The approach she developed grounds students' activity in the practices of the three types of communities I have discussed; the classroom community, the local home community, and the identifiable cultural groups within wider society. She argued that issues that fall under the general rubric of diversity can then be seen to emerge from students' participation in the practices of these different communities. Further, in this scheme, the mathematics classroom is viewed as the immediate arena in which issues of diversity play out at the microlevel of face-to-face interaction. As a consequence, diversity is not equated with students' culturally situated ways of reasoning and talking per se, but is instead framed in terms of relations between those ways of acting and the norms and practices established in the classroom (Crawford, 1996; Moll, 1997; Warren, Rosebery, & Conant, 1994). The arguments I have presented to support a focus on diversity when formulating the starting points and ending points of learning trajectories can, in fact, be viewed as illustrations of the relational view. Although both the specific remarks I have made and the more general relational view are preliminary, I nonetheless hope that they might in some way sustain the emergence of diversity as a shared interest of cognitive scientists and of subject matter specialists such as mathematics educators. The immediate challenge, then, is to develop analytical approaches that treat students' reasoning as situated with respect to their history of participation in the practices of particular communities.

CONCLUSION

In the first part of this chapter, I raised two methodological issues and, in doing so, developed a pragmatic justification for analyzing students' reasoning in situated terms. In the second part of the chapter, I critiqued the situated perspective inherent in the design research methodology as not going far enough. My concern was not whether this situated perspective remained faithful to the basic tenets of what might be termed a strong situated cognition paradigm. Instead, my concerns were again pragmatic and stemmed from the need to integrate a focus on both the institutional context of the school and the student's cultural diversity into our work. This led me to argue that it is insufficient to see teachers' and students' activity as situated merely with respect to the norms and practices of the classroom community. The overriding theoretical issue that then emerged involves coming to understand how teachers' and students' participation in multiple communities plays out in the arena of the classroom. It is this issue that I propose as a prime candidate for inclusion in future cognitive science research.

ACKNOWLEDGMENTS

The analysis reported in this chapter was supported by the National Science Foundation under Grant No. REC9814898 and by the Office of Educational Research and Improvement under Grant No. R305A60007. The opinions expressed do not necessarily reflect the views of the Foundation or of OERI. I am grateful to Sharon Carver for her constructive comments on a previous draft of this chapter.

REFERENCES

Beach, K. (1999). Consequential transitions: A sociocultural expedition beyond transfer in education. In A. Iran-Nejad & P. D. Pearson (Eds.), *Review of Educational Research,* (Vol. 24). Washington, DC: American Educational Research Associaton.

Bourdieu, P. (1977). *Outline of a theory of practice.* Cambridge, MA: Cambridge University Press.

Brown, A. L. (1992). Design experiments: Theoretical and methodological challenges in creating complex interventions in classrooms. *Journal of the Learning Sciences, 2,* 141–178.

Cazden, C. (1988). *Classroom discourse: The language of teaching and learning.* London: Heineman.

Cobb, G. W. (1997). More literacy is not enough. In L. A. Steen (Ed.), *Why numbers count: Qualitative literacy for tomorrow's America* (pp. 75–90). New York: College Entrance Examination Board.

Cobb, P. (1999). Individual and collective mathematical learning: The case of statistical data analysis. *Mathematical Thinking and Learning, 1,* 5–44.

Cobb, P. (in press). Conducting classroom teaching experiments in collaboration with teachers. In R. Lesh & E. Kelly (Eds.), *New methodologies in mathematics and science education.* Mahwah, NJ: Lawrence Erlbaum Associates.

Cobb, P., & McClain, K. (1999, May). *Supporting teachers' learning in social and institutional context.* Paper presented at the 1999 International Conference on Mathematics Teacher Education, Taipei, Taiwan.

Cobb, P., Stephan, M., McClain, K., & Gravemeijer, K. (in press). Participating in classroom mathematical practices. *Journal of the Learning Sciences.*

Cobb, P., Wood, T., Yackel, E., Nicholls, J., Wheatley, G., Trigatti, B., & Perlwitz, M. (1991). Assessment of a problem-centered second grade mathematics project. *Journal for Research in Mathematics Education, 22,* 3–29.

Cobb, P., & Yackel, E. (1996). Constructivist, emergent, and sociocultural perspectives in the context of developmental research. *Educational Psychologist, 31,* 175–190.

Cole, M. (1996). *Cultural psychology.* Cambridge, MA: Belkamp Press.

Confrey, J., & Lachance, A. (in press). A research design model for conjecture-driven teaching experiments. In R. Lesh & E. Kelly (Eds.), *New methodologies in mathematics and science education.* Dordrecht, Netherlands: Kluwer.

Confrey, J., & Smith, E. (1995.) Splitting, covariation, and their role in the development of exponential functions. *Journal for Research in Mathematics Education, 26,* 66–86.

Crawford, K. (1996). Vygotskian approaches in human development in the information era. *Educational Studies in Mathematics, 31,* 43–62.

De Corte, E., Verschaffel, L., & De Win, L. (1984, April). *The influence of rewording verbal problems on children's problem representations and solutions.* Paper presented at the annual meeting of the American Educational Research Association, New Orleans.

Delpit, L. (1988). The silenced dialogue: Power and pedagogy in educating other people's children. *Harvard Educational Review, 58,* 280–298.

Engestrom, Y. (1998). Reorganizing the motivational sphere of classroom culture: An activity-theoretical analysis of planning in a teacher team. In F. Seeger, J. Voigt, & U. Waschescio (Eds.), *The culture of the mathematics classroom* (pp. 76–103). New York: Cambridge University Press.

Erickson, F. (1986). Qualitative methods in research on teaching. In M. C. Wittrock (Ed.), *The handbook of research on teaching* (3rd ed., pp. 119–161). New York: Macmillan.

Fine, M. (1987). Silencing in public schools. *Language Arts, 64,* 157–175.

Freudental, H. (1973). *Mathematics as an educational task.* Dordrecht, The Netherlands: Reidel.

Griffin, S., & Case, R. (1997). Re-thinking the primary school mathematics curriculum: An approach based on cognitive science. *Issues in Education, 3,* 1–49.

Gravemeijer, K. E. P. (1994). *Developing realistic mathematics education.* Ultrecht, Netherlands: CD-β Press.

Gravemeijer, K. (1998, April). *Developmental research: Fostering a dialectic relation between theory and practice.* Paper presented at the research presession of the annual meeting of the National Council of Teachers of Mathematics, Washington, DC.

Hanna, G. (1989). More than formal proof. *For the Learning of Mathematics, 9,* 20–23.

Hodge, L. L. (1999). *Issues in diversity and equity: A synthesis of literature relevant to mathematics classrooms which emphasize understanding.* Unpublished manuscript, Vanderbilt University, Department of Teaching and Learning.

Kaput, J. J. (1994). The representational roles of technology in connecting mathematics with authentic experience. In R. Biehler, R. W. Scholz, R. Strasser, & B. Winkelmann (Eds.), *Dialectics of mathematics as a scientific discipline* (pp. 379–397). Dordrecht, Netherlands: Kluwer.

Ladson-Billings, G. (1995). Making mathematics meaningful in multicultural contexts. In W. G. Secada, E. Fennema, & L. B. Adajion (Eds.), *New directions for equity in mathematics education* (pp. 329–348). New York: Cambridge University Press.

Lampert, M. (1990). When the problem is not the question and the solution is not the answer: Mathematical knowing and teaching. *American Educational Research Journal, 27,* 29–63.

Lehrer, R., Jacobson, C., Kemney, V., & Strom, D. A. (1999). Building upon children's intuitions to develop mathematical understanding of space. In E. Fennema & T. R. Romberg (Eds.), *Mathematics classrooms that promote understanding* (pp. 63–87). Mahwah, NJ: Lawrence Erlbaum Associates.

Lehrer, R., & Romberg, T. (1996). Exploring children's data modeling. *Cognition and Instruction, 14,* 69–108.

Lehrer, R., Schauble, L., Carpenter, S., & Penner, D. (in press). The inter-related development of inscriptions and conceptual understanding. In P. Cobb, E. Yackel, & K. McClain (Eds.), *Symbolizing, mathematizing, and communicating: Perspectives on discourse, tools, and instructional design.* Mahwah, NJ: Lawrence Erlbaum Associates.

Lehrer, R., & Shumow, L. (1997). Aligning construction zones of parents and teachers for mathematics reform. *Cognition and Instruction, 15,* 41–83.

McGatha, M. (2000). *Instructional design in the context of developmental research: Documenting the learning of a research team.* Unpublished doctoral dissertation, Vanderbilt University, Department of Teaching and Learning.

Moll, L. (1997). The creation of mediating settings. *Mind, Culture, and Activity, 4,* 191–199.

Moss, J., & Case, R. (1999). Developing children's understanding of rational numbers: A new model and an experimental curriculum. *Journal for Research in Mathematics Education, 30,* 122–147.

National Council of Teachers of Mathematics (NCTM). (1989). *Curriculum and evaluation standards for school mathematics.* Reston, VA: Author.

O'Conner, M. C. (1998). Language socialization in the mathematics classroom: Discourse practices and mathematical thinking. In M. Lampert & M. L. Blunk (Eds.), *Talking mathematics in school* (pp. 17–55). New York: Cambridge University Press.

Philips, S. (1972). Participant structures and communicative competence: Warm Springs children in community and classroom. In C. Cazden, D. Hymes, & V. John (Eds.), *Functions of language in the classroom* (pp. 370–394). New York: Teachers College Press.

Price, J. N., & Ball, D. L. (1997). "There's always another agenda": Marshalling resources for mathematics reform. *Journal of Curriculum Studies, 29,* 637–666.

Schoenfeld, A. H. (1983). Beyond the purely cognitive: Belief systems, social cognitions, and metacognitions as driving forces in intellectual performance. *Cognitive Science, 7,* 329–363.

Simon, M. A. (1995.) Reconstructing mathematics pedagogy from a constructivist perspective. *Journal for Research in Mathematics Education, 26,* 114–145.

Simon, M. A. (in press). Research in mathematics teacher development: The teacher development experiment. In R. Lesh & E. Kelly (Eds.), *New methodologies in mathematics and science education.* Dordrecht, Netherlands: Kluwer.

Simon, M. A., & Blume, G. W. (1996). Justification in the mathematics classroom: A study of prospective elementary teachers. *Journal of Mathematical Behavior, 15,* 3–31.

Spillane, J. P. (1999). External reform initiatives and teachers' efforts to reconstruct their practice: The mediating role of teachers' zones of enactment. *Journal of Curriculum Studies, 31,* 143–175.

Stein, M. K., Silver, E. A., & Smith, M. S. (1998). Mathematics reform and teacher development: A community of practice perspective. In J. G. Greeno & S. V. Goldman (Eds.), *Thinking practices in mathematics and science learning* (pp. 17–52). Mahwah, NJ: Lawrence Erlbaum Associates.

Steffe, L. P., & Thompson, P. W. (in press). Teaching experiment methodology: Underlying principles and essential elements. In R. Lesh & E. Kelly (Eds.), *New methodologies in mathematics and science education.* Mahwah, NJ: Lawrence Erlbaum Associates.

Stigler, J. W., & Hiebert, J. (1999). *The teaching gap.* New York: Free Press.

Toulmin, S. (1963). *Forsight and understanding.* New York: Harper Torchbooks.

Voigt, J. (1995). Thematic patterns of interaction and sociomathematical norms. In P. Cobb & H. Bauersfeld (Eds.), *Emergence of mathematical meaning: Interaction in classroom cultures* (pp. 163–201). Hillsdale, NJ: Lawrence Erlbaum Associates.

Warren, B., & Rosebery, A. S. (1995). Equity in the future tense: Redefining relationships among teachers, students, and science in linguistic minority classrooms. In W. Secada, E. Fennema, & L. Byrd (Eds.), *New directions in equity for mathematics education* (pp. 298–328). New York: Cambridge University Press.

Warren, B., Rosebery, A., & Conant, F. (1994). Discourse and social practice: Learning science in language minority classrooms. In D. Spener (Ed.), *Adult biliteracy in the United States* (pp. 191–210). Washington, DC: CAL and Delta Systems, Inc.

Wood, T., & Sellers, P. (1996.) Assessment of a problem-centered mathematics program: Third grade. *Journal for Research in Mathematics Education, 27,* 337–353.

Yackel, E., & Cobb, P. (1996). Sociomathematical norms, argumentation, and autonomy in mathematics. *Journal for Research in Mathematics Education, 27,* 458–477.

Zevenbergen, R. (1996). Constructivism as liberal bourgeois discourse. *Educational Studies in Mathematics, 31,* 95–113.

16

Affect and Effect
in Cognitive Approaches
to Instruction

Sam Wineburg
University of Washington

Pam Grossman
Stanford University

The chapters in this volume represent the bold strides that cognitive science has made in the past 20 years. Since the appearance of the last Carnegie Symposium on cognition and instruction (Klahr, 1976), researchers have become more nuanced in conceptualizing the educational process. In particular, three developments represented in this volume come to mind.

DEVELOPMENTS IN CONCEPTUALIZING
THE EDUCATIONAL PROCESS

The Reciprocity of Contexts

Until recently, it was common for researchers to talk about developing a training technique in a laboratory setting and "applying" it in the classroom. The vertical relationship between laboratory and applied setting was taken for granted (cf. Brown, 1992). Against this backdrop, the chapters in this volume represent a sea change. We have come to understand how educational problems, located in the context of the laboratory, turn

479

into different problems once transported into a classroom of 35 children, nested in a particular school, district, and state context. The point is not simply that the real-world conditions of the classroom add complexity to models of intellectual growth. Rather, educational settings themselves restructure intellectual problems, changing their cognitive and social dimensions and giving rise to new problems and variations on the problems originally set (cf. Cole & Means, 1981; Cole & Traupman, 1981). It is now generally recognized that the vertical relationship between laboratory and classroom is more beneficially conceptualized as a reciprocal loop in which both contexts—the lab, which permits us to "freeze the frame" of cognition in ways we can never do in the classroom; and the classroom, which reconstitutes cognition by restoring its intrinsically human and social dimensions—mutually inform and correct one another. These points are hardly new (Cole & Means, 1981; Scribner, 1997), but the chapters in this volume suggest that attention to context is no longer a radical idea.

From Statistically Significant to Educationally Significant Change

Some years ago, Elliot Eisner (1984) chastised psychologists when he reported that the average amount of time spent on educational interventions in the typical research report was less than 50 minutes. Eisner bemoaned the practice among psychologists to pursue statistically significant results that, given their brevity, left nary a trace on the lives of children and teachers. In contrast to such studies, those represented here take seriously the time it takes to effect lasting educational change. In their various dimensions and stages, these investigations respect the complexity of educational change by situating themselves in schools for the long haul.

Domain Specificity of Knowledge

For the most part, these chapters call attention to the fact that different domains in the school curriculum present different cognitive demands. No longer are the disciplines perceived as shells that encase domain-general processes—shells to be discarded once their inner psychological core was reached. Rather, there is an awareness that mathematics, biology, history, physics, and the other subjects of the school curriculum are distinctive ways of thinking and talking (McCloskey, 1985; Nelson, Megill, & McCloskey, 1988; Schwab, 1978). Understanding domains as cultural and linguistic practices, each with rules of argument and means of persuasion, expands the horizon of the psychologist interested in cognition and instruction. Compared to first generation cognitive studies, that pressed knowledge into declarative and procedural straightjackets and sought to strip away context, the investigations here place issues of epistemology and rhetoric at the center of cognitive inquiry. The result is a richer and more textured cognitive science.

COGNITION AND COMMUNITY

These developments, and the considerable achievements of 30 years of cognitive science in education (cf. Bransford, Brown, & Cocking, 1999), led us to initiate a research project in which we sought to create a teacher community informed by the principles of cognitive science. In January 1995, with a grant from the James S. McDonnell Foundation program "Cognitive Studies in Educational Practice," we located ourselves in the midst of an urban high school. We brought together teachers from two different departments to create curricular materials that would focus students on the epistemological and discursive principles of history and literature. We planned to build our teacher community around the reading of texts, seeking to import the social form of the book club from the comfort of the living room to the confines of the urban high school. Grant monies, along with enthusiastic support from the local school district, allowed us to do what few projects have ever been done: We were able to buy teachers' time on a biweekly basis, permitting them to leave the classroom for an entire day (while the grant provided substitutes) to come together to read history and fiction, to discuss disciplinary principles, and to deliberate over curriculum design. After-school meetings were held in the intervening weeks between our all-day project meetings (see Grossman, Wineburg, & Woolworth, 2000; Thomas, Wineburg, Grossman, Myhre, & Woolworth, 1998; Wineburg & Grossman, 1998; 2000a; 2000b). The design of our project explicitly attended to the three developments in the cognitive sciences noted earlier: (1) The context of our innovation was the multifaceted context of its application—the urban high school; (2) we recognized that the kind of change we sought required a major time commitment and figured this into our design; and (3) we took seriously the domain specificity of the high school curriculum by tailoring our program to the entailments and cultures of the humanities, specifically those of history and literature.

Our plans were grand. We would compare our own readings of texts to the think alouds of high school students as they formulated interpretations of literature and history; we would enable teachers to observe in each other's classrooms, where they would engage students in clinical interviews about disciplinary knowledge; we would videotape teachers as they tested parts of the curriculum, and then show the tapes during our group meetings where, as a community, we could engage in the process of design, revision, and reformulation of instruction. Informed by the writings of Ann Brown (1992), Allan Collins (1992), Barbara Rogoff (1994; Rogoff, Baker-Sennett, Lacasa, & Goldsmith, 1995) and others, we argued that instead of locating our work on a bucolic college campus (the typical site of professional development in the humanities), we should create this community amidst the meandering hallways, aluminum-sided trailers, and classrooms without telephones of the urban high school. In summary, we had time, we had resources, we had district and building buy-in, and we had willing teachers who saw the project as a gift. We were ready to hit the ground running.

After one of our early all-day meetings, Dave, an experienced English teacher, called to tell us that he was dropping out. He had spent the morning in a small-group activity working with colleagues and complained that he didn't "have the stomach" to read texts with people who did not share his deep knowledge of literature or his commitment to intellectual inquiry. One of the most dedicated teachers in the school, Dave had trouble making the connection between the 17-year-old students about whom he cared so deeply and the new teachers in their mid-20s and early 30s who recently joined his faculty. More than a personal choice or an act of individual pique, Dave's reaction should be viewed in the context of a profession known for a "culture of privacy" (Little, 1990; Lortie, 1975), with no significant tradition or appreciation of adult-to-adult mentoring. Dave's response to his colleagues reflected longstanding norms of profession—to retreat to the bastion of the classroom, to close the door, and to focus attention on students.

By the fifth group meeting, we began to notice that Heather, an articulate English teacher relatively new to teaching, had grown quiet. In contrast to our early meetings, when Heather was a lively contributor, she now said little. In a one-on-one interview at the end of the first year, Heather explained that she became aware of the costs of talking about books and "making mistakes" in front of her department chair, the person who would decide her fate by assigning her to teach freshmen or seniors, regular or honors students. Heather's contributions to discussions now passed through a filter in which she weighed risks and benefits in a complex personal, vocational, and social calculus.

By the end of the first year, Lee, a history teacher, and Barb, an English teacher, had settled into a predictable routine of tête-à-tête disputes on issues of interpretation (cf. Hamel, 2000; Wineburg & Grossman, 2000b). At issue were questions at the intersection of history and fiction: What is the role of the reader vis-à-vis the text? How stable is the text and what is the "truth" of an interpretation? How do we judge competing interpretations and arrive at criteria for assaying intellectual claims? In these discussions, we heard echoes of the heady epistemological issues that have characterized discussions in the humanities since the linguistic turn. Yet, the teachers in our project seemed to hear something different. To them, these exchanges were emblematic of personality conflicts played out in public view. For many of the teachers, aspects of epistemology were eclipsed by issues of gender, identity, and forms of power exacted through discourse.

Among our 22 participants, Grace immediately stood out. Unlike her liberal colleagues, who espoused progressive educational and social ideals, Grace was conservative in her beliefs and, at least in the early phases of the project, willing to share them. But as the project progressed, Grace began to sense an hostile atmosphere when she expressed ideas that ran afoul of the prevailing ideological current. All diversity is tolerated in this group, she once remarked, on the condition that it is the "right diversity." The books we read and the issues we broached, from the topic of gang rape in Nathan McCall's (1994) *Makes Me Wanna Holler* to notions of Eleanor Roosevelt's alleged homosexuality in Doris Kearns Goodwin's (1994) *No Ordinary Time*; to issues of silencing the other in Stephan Ambrose's (1996) *Undaunted Courage* to questions of "justified murder" in Bharati Mukherjee's (1989) *Jasmine*, touched on questions at the heart of the humanities: What does it mean to be human, in all of its darkest and most sublime dimensions? But on more than one occasion, when Grace spoke her truth, eyes rolled and muttering began. As the year progressed, our group meetings became a place for Grace to mask her real self—not reveal it.

Were the teachers in our project bad people? Were they less generous and more callous than the rest of us, unrepresentative of other adults who might gather at other schools? We believe the opposite is true. If other projects did not experience similar obstacles on the way to creating community, we bet that they either began with self-selected volunteers or met only for a limited time.

Indeed, many teacher development projects are configured to prevent issues of self and professional identity from entering into the workplace and thus end up tinkering at the margins of teacher change (Miller & Lord, 1993). The typical profile of the teacher who seeks professional development in the humanities (the "National Endowment for the Humanities [NEH] Institute junkie") is often the person who needs it least, a self-starter already motivated to learn, to read, and to stretch beyond his or her present understanding. But what about teachers who would never choose to travel to a college campus in the summer to attend an NEH institute? Because our project offered compensation for participation, and because of the convenience of locating ourselves in the workplace, we attracted teachers who would not otherwise have participated in such a project. Furthermore, because we intervened at the department level rather than at the individual level, our allies were the two department chairs, strategic lynchpins typically overlooked in discussions of high school reform (Grossman, 1996). In several instances, department chairs "strongly recommended" that individual members participate in this project, creating a subgroup we referred to as *impressed volunteers* (Grossman, Wineburg, & Woolworth, in press), teachers who technically volunteered but only because their department chairs strongly pressed them to do so. Our final group of 22 teachers, drawn from English and history, with representatives from ESL and special education, was a mix of eager and reluctant learners, fence-sitters, and those who came under gentle duress. In this sense, our group better reflected the overall make-up of teachers in the school than would the participants at a special summer program or brief workshop.

The work of community building was transacted on a public stage, and our community members were "worse than perfect strangers." Strangers may not have a strong basis on which to build community but at least they are not burdened by history. In some cases, teachers in our project had been working side by side for decades, but had never before seen each other teach. Instead, they brought to the table years of hearsay from legions of 14- and 15-year-old informants. These impressions created a charged atmosphere that highlighted the disjuncture between participants' *performed identities* and their *perceived identity* by the group (cf. Goffman, 1959). The social framework that our 22 participants enacted as they and we came together constrained and enabled, setting our parameters and changing them as we went along. Collectively, we resembled the proverbial Gertzian spider caught in webs of interaction that we had woven and that we ourselves would have to undo if we were to create community.

Affect was the common thread in the issues that marked our project in the first $1^1/_2$ years; feelings of tension, anger, fear, exposure, denial, face saving, positioning, ego protecting, and embarrassment. Although we hoped to create a "cognitively based model for teaching," we quickly realized that we were in a social mine field—think alouds and task analyses would have to wait. Our most pressing concerns as project facilitators, researchers, and members of the group had to do with creating and sustaining a safe place for adult learning in the day-to-day grind of the urban school. The challenges of creating such a space constituted a daunting and draining intellectual task. We put down our cognitive psychology books and turned to other literatures not because cognitive psychology was wrong, but because it had little to say about attending to the affective side of cognitive change.

As researchers, we were not as naive as the earlier description suggests. We sensed from the outset that the social issues of adults coming together to read texts in the workplace might present new challenges. But in our theoretical models, as well as in the primary literatures in which we located our work, these issues occupied the shadowy margins, constituting the background or precursor to the important cognitive work to be achieved. Indeed, in the sociocultural context in which we competed for grant monies, it is unlikely that we would have received funding had we showcased the social aspects of our work and downplayed the cognitive ones. To be sure, there was a recognition that teachers had to be motivated to do this work, and had to find a way to work together, but these issues were often viewed as items to be checked off before the real work could proceed.

All affect is not negative. Emotions in our project spanned the range from despair to elation. Positive affect, in fact, was the glue that held the project together, that ultimately made the struggle worthwhile. The joy of learning in a group, the élan that develops among people who work hard together, is also a missing element from the literature on cognition. Current formulations of distributed cognition ignore issues of desire, fondness, affection, and respect—feelings that ultimately determine our willingness to learn from and with others. The emotional context underlying social forms of learning must be addressed as we move from highly individualistic models of cognition to models of cognition as a social enterprise. Groups can possess tremendous social and intellectual capital, but if the individuals in them are not ready to relinquish prior grudges and start over, the rich cognitive resources of the group will go untapped.

Although we provided examples of charged and tense manifestations of affect, our project could not have progressed had we not also experienced moments of goodwill and esprit de corps. And so, Dave, who left the project, returned out of respect for a colleague's report that good things were in the making. With his deep background in literature, Dave had little to learn about subject matter. But the group offered Dave a chance to craft a professional identity that took seriously his own responsibility for the learning of new department members. Grace also left the project for a while. She, too, rejoined at her colleagues' urging, ultimately forging close relationships with people whose political views she strongly opposed.

If the last 5 years have taught us anything, it is that we cannot treat issues of social context, workplace and vocational norms, interpersonal histories and issues of identity as someone else's theoretical problem. These issues are not prerequisites before we turn to the "real" work of school change. If we want to create a cognitive science that has relevance outside of the laboratory, we must, in a Lewinian spirit, make the social world our lab. In the social world—in schools, universities, hospitals, prisons, accounting firms, or anywhere where people work together on a daily basis—individuals bring to the table histories of beliefs, grudges, fears, insecurities, and the need for approval. Working through these issues— indeed, creating the structures for group cognition that deal with these issues systematically—must be at the forefront of our collective research agenda. Otherwise, we will continue to experience success in changing isolated parts of the school day—one section of the science or math curriculum—but we will not, in any fundamental way, alter the cognitive, social, or moral landscape of the workplace.

REVISITING ASSUMPTIONS

As we reviewed the other chapters in this volume, several themes echoed between the lines. In the spirit of bringing underlying assumptions to the surface for scrutiny and examination, we note four themes that weave themselves through some of these chapters.

Kids are Smart but Teachers are Dumb

One of the major achievements of cognitive science has been to show the varied and nuanced dimensions of children's thought. School children, it turns out, can reason in sophisticated ways about various species of finches, unconfound thorny scientific variables, model the slopes of lines, and engage in all kinds of intellectual processes that overzealous misinterpretors of Piaget claimed they could not. But something happens as these bright and gifted children grow up, enter adulthood, and choose to become teachers. It would seem from some of these chapters that a stumbling block to creating exciting educational settings is the limited capacity of the adults at the helm. How can it be, we wondered, that children are so capable of sophisticated thought but, as adults, they seem incapable of continued growth and change?

The Domain-Specificity of School Learning Only Goes So Far

Many of these chapters reflect a deep sensitivity to the problems of disciplinary knowledge, and as such, represent a marked advance over the first generation of "knowledge-lean" problems on which early models of learning were based (cf. Glaser, 1984). But, as psychologists, we, too, are conditioned by history and tradition. Our search for the nomothetic finds its way into our language when we move from a discussion of, say, the teaching of high school chemistry or physics to a discussion of what "the teacher" needs to know. A deep abyss separates the teaching of physics from the teaching of English literature, and one should not serve as the model for the other. Although our research has become more attuned to the particularities of content, our generalizations all too often remain deaf to issues of grade level and subject matter. Despite our attention to disciplinary context, we still seem fidgety and uneasy with its attendant constraints.

A similar process is evident in the appeal to task analysis as a primary tool—indeed the prerequisite—to understanding the cognitive processes of school learning. As originally conceptualized by Gagné (1965) and others, task analysis is a useful analytic strategy that can be productively exploited. But, like any generic technique, task analysis has limitations, especially when it isolates tasks from the larger disciplinary calculus that gives them meaning. For example, concentrating on the processes needed to decode the words and interconnections of historical documents in an interpretive task, apart from how the disciplinary community convinces itself and others of the truth of its claims, misses the point (cf. Fish, 1980; Hexter, 1971; Scholes, 1989; Wineburg, 1998; 1999). In this sense, the ultimate meaning of a task inheres not in its concrete material dimensions (the specific documents used or even the psychological processes needed to understand them), but in the norms, practices, conventions, and ways of arguing that characterize communities of practice.

The School Day in North America is Composed of Two Subjects; Science and Mathematics

Judging by the contributions to this volume, an uninformed reader might conclude that children go to school to learn two subjects; math and science. But the truth is that school children learn much more—by the fourth or fifth grade, they encounter literature, history, geography, and in many places art, music, and drama. In this sense, the image of cognition and instruction presented in this volume is more an artifact of funding patterns among cognitive researchers (as well as researchers' proclivity to study scientific and mathematical topics) than a representative portrait of the cognitive challenges faced by children and teachers during the school day.

Educational Improvement Will Come About by Working on Each Part of the Curriculum as a Separate Entity and Then by Adding the Parts Together

The complexity of the school day and the multiple subjects in it means that, as a research community, we must engage in a division of labor, with some of us studying math, others history, others science, and so on. Although rarely articulated in our journals and conferences, the presumption behind this division of labor is that all of the separate pieces will come together so that the teaching and learning of all subjects will be enhanced. But rarely, if ever, do we engage in any formal analysis of how these subjects do and do not interrelate.

Our interventions are typically focused on one part of the school day, and we often have little sense of the effect of our new science or math curriculum on the teaching and learning of social studies or English. So, for example, consider the situation fifth graders face as they move from science to history during portions of the same school day. In both subjects, students hear words like "evidence, "cause," and "argument." Beneath this linguistic similarity rests profound conceptual and epistemological differences. At the same time, it is fair to say that there is a closer relationship between "evidence" in science and history than between science and literature (cf. Haskell, 1998; Ozick, 1999; Wood, 1982).

What, then, are the points of departure and what are the points of overlap? Such questions are rarely marked for students; rarely are they topics of classroom debate. Work on interdisciplinary curriculum in K through 12 settings tends to be interdisciplinary in name alone, more often appealing to common sense notions than pulling together powerful techniques and ways of thinking from the disciplines (Gardner & Boix-Mansilla, 1994; Wineburg & Grossman, 2000a). In most cases, students are left on their own to make connections from one subject to the next. What ends up happening is that those least able to bring conceptual order to the school day—young children—end up shouldering the burden of having to do so (Wineburg, Stevens, Herrenkohl, & Bell, 1999).

At present, our various research specialties—science researchers, math researchers, literacy researchers, and so forth—reflect the structure of the academy rather than the structure of the school day. Classroom teachers who recognize the problem of fragmentation must either strive to connect subjects on their own or let the pieces fall where they may. As a field, we lack an understanding of the intellectual connections among school subjects. Pursuing this understanding would elect a different path from the one that led psychologists to claim that there was no basis for the different school subjects, except as "divisions of time devoted to these subjects during a school day" (Gagné, 1976, p. 30). Instead, this new path would seek to articulate the connections and differences among the intellectual traditions known as disciplines. Such a comparative psychology of school subjects would come to see the different parts of the school day not as historical accidents but as valuable resources that, properly understood, could lead to the enhanced learning of all subjects (Wineburg et al., 1999).

CONCLUSION

Cognitive researchers will need to tackle these limitations if the field is to continue to progress. As our discussion of affect indicates, cognitive researchers will need to navigate beyond the mind and into the emotional worlds of individuals and groups. Knowing that individual children are capable of mastering complex mathematical or literary ideas is one step; understanding classrooms, as social units composed of leaders and slackers, the motivated and the disaffected, must be the next.

Cognitive researchers will need to learn to see teachers as resources, not solely as obstacles, for children's learning. If the next decade can provide models of teacher learning that are as nuanced and respectful as the portraits drawn of children's learning, we will have made enormous progress. Such models must account for the differences, as well as the similarities, between adults' and children's learning, and must address the deep issues of professional identity that are evoked in teacher development. What would it mean to proclaim, as we do now for children, that all teachers can learn? What would need to change in the landscapes of teacher education, schools, and professional development to provide meaningful opportunities for teachers' ongoing growth? What does it really mean to learn from and in practice and how could we design environments that support such learning (cf. Ball & Cohen, 1999)?

Finally, cognitive researchers will need to find ways to study the curricular mélange experienced by students. The current respect for the domain specificity of knowledge is a virtue, but any virtue carried to excess can become a blind spot. In our efforts to unravel the weave of the curriculum into distinct topics that can be studied in depth, we may have lost sight of the tapestry that children encounter. The next generation of researchers will need to look at cognitive resonance across the curriculum. Do children see the study of Emperor Penguins as different from the study of empires? How do the habits of mind and argument developed during math class resonate in arguments over historical or literary interpretation? Such questions also pose serious challenges to the preparation of elementary teachers. How can teachers develop the deep, disciplined understanding of subject matters that would enable them to nurture children's cognitive growth across the full curriculum?

The agenda we have outlined would require that cognitive researchers stretch beyond the current boundaries and definitions of the field. It would also require that they work in more interdisciplinary partnerships with colleagues in social psychology, sociology, and the disciplines themselves. But if cognitive research is to effect deep educational change—change that will endure beyond the limited scope of our interventions—we see no other way.

REFERENCES

Ambrose, S. E. (1996). *Undaunted courage: Meriwether Lewis, Thomas Jefferson, and the opening of the American West.* New York: Simon & Schuster.

Ball, D. L., & Cohen, D. K. (1999). Developing practice, developing practitioners: Toward a practice-based theory of professional education. In L. Darling-Hammond & G. Sykes (Eds.), *Teaching as the learning profession: Handbook of policy and practice* (pp. 3–33). San Francisco, CA: Jossey-Bass.

Bransford, J., Brown, A., & Cocking, R. (1999). *How people learn.* Washington, DC: National Research Council Press.

Brown, A. L. (1992). Design experiments: Theoretical and methodological challenges in creating complex interventions in classroom settings. *The Journal of the Learning Sciences, 2*, 141–178.

Cole, M., & Means, B. (1981). *Comparative studies of how people think.* Cambridge, MA: Harvard University Press.

Cole, M., & Traupmann, K. (1981). Comparative cognitive research: Learning from a learning disabled child. In W. A. Collins (Ed.), *Aspects of the development of competence: The Minnesota Symposium on child psychology* (Vol. 14, pp. 125–153). Hillsdale, NJ: Lawrence Erlbaum Associates.

Collins, A. (1992). Toward a design science of education. In E. Scanlon & T. O'Shea (Eds.), *New directions in educational technology* (pp. 15–22). New York: Springer-Verlag.

Eisner, E. W. (1984). Can educational research inform educational practice? *Phi Delta Kappan, 66*, pp. 447–452.

Fish, S. (1980). *Is there a text in this class?* Cambridge, MA: Harvard University Press.

Gagné, R. M. (1965). *The conditions of learning.* New York: Holt, Rinehart & Winston.

Gagné, R. M. (1976). The learning basis of teaching methods. In N. L. Gage (Ed.), *The psychology of teaching methods: Seventy-fifth yearbook of the National Society for the Study of Education* (pp. 21–43) Chicago: University of Chicago Press.

Gardner, H., & Boix-Mansilla, V. (1994). Teaching for understanding in the disciplines and beyond. *Teachers College Record, 96*, 198–218.

Glaser, R. (1984). Education and thinking: The role of knowledge. *American Psychologist, 39*, 93–104.

Goffman, E. (1959). *The presentation of self in everyday life.* New York: Anchor.

Goodwin, D. K. (1994). *No ordinary time.* New York: Touchstone.

Grossman, P. L. (1996). Of regularities and reform: Navigating the subject-specific territory of high schools. In M. W. McLaughlin & I. Oberman, (Eds.), *Teacher learning: New policies, new practices* (pp. 39–47). New York: Teachers College Press.

Grossman, P., Wineburg, S., & Woolworth, S. (in press). In pursuit of teacher community. *Teachers College Record.*

Hamel, F. (2000). Disciplinary landscapes, interdisciplinary collaboration. In S. Wineburg & P. Grossman (Eds.), *Interdisciplinary curriculum: Challenges to implementation* (pp. 74–92). New York: Teachers College Press.

Haskell, T. L. (1998). *Objectivity is not neutrality.* Baltimore: Johns Hopkins University Press.

Hexter, J. H. (1971). *The history primer.* New York: Basic Books.

Klahr, D. (1976). *Cognition and instruction.* Hillsdale, NJ: Lawrence Erlbaum Associates.

Little, J. W. (1990). The persistence of privacy: Autonomy and initiative in teacher professional relations. *Teachers College Record, 91*, 509–536.

Lortie, D. (1975). *Schoolteacher: A sociological study.* Chicago: University of Chicago.

McCall, N. (1994). *Makes me wanna holler: A young black man in America.* New York: Random House.

McCloskey, D. N. (1985). The problem of audience in historical economics: Rhetorical thoughts on a text by Robert Fogel. *History and Theory, 24*, 1–22.

Miller, B., & Lord, B. (1993). *Staff development in four districts.* Newton, MA: Educational Development Center.

Mukherjee, B. (1989). *Jasmine.* New York: Fawcett Crest

Nelson, J. S., Megill, A., & McCloskey, D. N. (1987). *The rhetoric of the human sciences.* Madison, WI: University of Wisconsin Press.

Ozick, C. (1999). The rights of history and the rights of imagination. *Commentary, 46*, 22–27.

Rogoff, B. (1994). Developing understanding of the idea of communities. *Mind Culture and Society, 1*, 209–229.

Rogoff, B., Baker-Sennett, J., Lacasa, P., & Goldsmith, D. (1995). Development through participation in sociocultural activity. In J. Goodnow, P. Miller, & F. Kessel (Eds.), *Cultural practices as contexts for development* (pp. 45–65). San Francisco: Jossey-Bass.

Scholes, R. (1989). *Protocols of reading.* New Haven, CT: Yale University Press.

Schwab, J. J. (1978). Education and the structure of the disciplines. In I. Westbury & N. J. Wklkof (Eds.), *Science, curriculum, and liberal education* (pp. 229–272). Chicago: University of Chicago Press.

Scribner, S. (1997). Mind in action: A functional approach to thinking. In M. Cole, Y. Engstrom, & O. Vasquez (Eds.), *Mind, culture and activity* (pp. 354–368). Cambridge, England: Cambridge University Press.

Thomas, G., Wineburg, S., Grossman, P., Myhre, O., Woolworth, S. (1998). In the company of teachers: An interim report on the development of a community of teacher learners. *Teaching and Teacher Education, 14,* 180–195.

Wineburg, S. (1998). Reading Abraham Lincoln: An expert/expert study in the interpretation of historical texts. *Cognitive Science, 22,* 319–346.

Wineburg, S. (1999). Historical thinking and other unnatural acts. *Phi Delta Kappan, 80,* 488–499.

Wineburg, S., & Grossman, P. (1998). Creating a community of learners among high school teachers. *Phi Delta Kappan, 79,* 350–353.

Wineburg, S., & Grossman, P. (Eds.). (2000a). *Interdisciplinary curriculum: Challenges to implementation.* New York: Teachers College Press.

Wineburg, S., & Grossman, P. (2000b). Scenes from a courtship: Some theoretical and practical implications of interdisciplinary humanities curricula in the comprehensive high school. In S. Wineburg & P. Grossman (Eds.), *Interdisciplinary curriculum: Challenges to implementation* (pp. 57–73). New York: Teachers College Press.

Wineburg, S., Stevens, R., Herrenkohl, L., & Bell, P. (1999). *A comparative psychology of school subjects: Promoting epistemological sophistication in elementary science through the study of history.* Proposal funded by the National Science Foundation. (http://www.nsf.gov/cgi-bin/showaward?award=9980536)

Wood, G. (1982, December 16). Writing history: An exchange. *New York Review of Books,* p. 59.

17

Progress Then and Now

Robert Glaser
University of Pittsburgh

To place this volume in historical perspective, I revisited two early compilations on the subject of learning and instruction: *Training Research and Education* (Glaser, 1962/1965), as well as David Klahr's original *Cognition and Instruction* (Klahr, 1976). My book resulted from a conference sponsored by the Office of Naval Research (ONR) involving experimental psychologists interested in problems of training and the underlying phenomena of learning. Before this time, many psychologists had conducted research on training, and the goal of this conference was to examine what the work could bring to education more generally.

TRAINING, RESEARCH AND EDUCATION–1962

The chapters of almost 40 years ago are of interest in their contemporary flavor. Nearly all of them emphasized the importance of procedures for task analysis and specification of instructional objectives for training (e.g., Miller, 1965). There were chapters on tests of individual differences and the assessment of change. Contrasts were made between testing and training. In testing, practical books were many and theoretical books were few. In learning, theoretical books were common and practical books on the psychology of training and education were few, if one disregarded texts on classroom methods.

Chapters that reflected a theoretical orientation toward research on training and learning included Fleischmann (1965) and Fitts (1965). Fleischmann's (1965) factor analytic study showed the differential involvement of various abilities as training proceeded; general abilities being helpful initially, and more specialized performance accounting for skill later in learning. This well-cited study was concerned with motor skill tasks, such as tracking and rotary pursuit. Fitts (1965), on the other hand, focused on more complex skilled performance, and proposed three phases in the progression of proficiency; (1) a cognitive phase—where skill learning involves early stages of "intellectualization" and is of relatively short duration in comparison to the next phase; (2) a fixation phase—where patterns of behavior are established by continued practice that may last for weeks or months, and where most laboratory experiments are terminated too early; and (3) an autonomous phase—where advanced proficiency is characterized by increasing speed, increasing accuracy of performance, and increasing resistance to stress and interference from outside activity. Fitts also talked about the learning of subroutines and absence of plateaus and asymptotes during practice under certain circumstances. He also mentioned the significance of over-practice, component subroutines, and possible artificial limits to performance (e.g., code transmission rates, and lack of feedback).

The nature of proficiency was also discussed in another chapter, in relation to achievement tests. The necessity for specifying detailed objectives of instruction was raised once again, followed by a discussion of types of evaluation measures and the value of performance tests (Frederiksen, 1965). The more general issue of the relationship of psychological research to educational practice was raised by Travers (1965). He pointed out that over 100 years ago, the German philosopher Herbart proposed that educational procedures should be guided by scientific research, and that some studies of this kind were carried out in German laboratories.

The 1962 ONR conference arose out of an interest in the adaptability of military training research to education and the cast of authors came from that background. It is interesting to note that prior to their engagement in training research, many appeared to agree that there was no unified science of learning to be applied. In general, the conception was that basic and applied research were antithetical, and that the kind of learning or the task selected as an object of investigation somehow determined whether the research was basic or applied.

At the time, one notion about the relationship between basic and applied studies was described by Estes (1960), who pointed out that as the psychology of learning begins to show signs of maturing, the relationship to education would be more like that of physiology to medicine, than that of medicine to the patient. Direct transfer from theory or laboratory findings was argued to be a false expectation and a source of disappointment. The only realistic expectations from the science of learning were a deeper understanding of school learning and guidance in conducting appropriate research.

Estes also reacted to the fact that applications of learning theory to educational psychology often took the form of tests of purportedly opposing theories. When Thorndike and Guthrie wrote textbooks on educational psychology, they made recommendations about educational practices. This advice was taken as deduction from theory, so that a comparison of teaching methods emphasizing drill and practice versus methods emphasizing understanding mistakenly gave the impression of a test of behavorists versus field theories of learning. Estes (1960) wrote

> tests of this sort are logically on a par with one that would appraise the relative contributions of chemical and electrical theories to the automotive industry by conducting a race between a stock model Chevrolet [gasoline-driven] and a Sturges Electric [powered by electricity]. (p. 752)

However, what was known about learning in the early 1960s continued to be obtained, for the most part, in artificial settings remote from ordinary experience. Standard reference laboratory tasks were the order of the day. Scientists did express some hope of an eventual rapprochement between the laboratory and the classroom in the study of human learning. After all, a fertile field had been found in applications to military training, and attention could be directed toward education in our classrooms. In this atmosphere, the Learning Research and Development Center (LRDC) emphasizing research on learning and instruction was launched in 1963 (Glaser & Gow, 1964).

At this time, Bruner (1964) contrasted the nature of a theory of instruction with a theory of learning. He pointed out that a theory of learning is descriptive, whereas a theory of instruction is prescriptive, in the sense that it sets forth rules concerning or specifying the most effective way of achieving knowledge or mastering skills. A theory of learning describes, after the fact, the conditions under which some behavior was acquired. A theory of instruction is a normative theory in that it sets up a criterion and then states the conditions for meeting it. The first two reviews of Instructional Psychology appeared in the *Annual Review of Psychology.* In the late 1960s and early 1970s, Gagné and Rohwer (1969) wrote:

Remoteness of applicability to instruction, we note with some regret, characterizes many studies of human learning, retention, and transfer, appearing in the most prestigious of psychological journals ... the conditions under
which the learning is investigated, and the tasks set for the learner are often
unrepresentative of conditions under which most human learning occurs ...
this is not to imply that such studies do not further an understanding of the
learning process. However, it would seem that extensive theory development centering upon learning tasks and learning conditions will be required
before one will be able to apply such knowledge to the design of instruction. (p. 381)

A few years later, Glaser and Resnick (1972) pointed out that an
increasing number of experimental psychologists were turning their enterprise to analyses and investigations of instructional processes.

COGNITION AND INSTRUCTION–1974

In 1974, David Klahr organized the symposium that resulted in the 1976
volume of *Cognition and Instruction*. Klahr foresaw an emerging new
field; the rapid success of cognitive psychology in the laboratory and in
theory now needed to be examined in the context of its applications. Klahr
organized a seminal symposium and labeled a field. (Like the 1962 conference, it was supported by ONR's continuing interest in science and
practice.) The resulting book was representative of efforts that made a
start in attempting to relate work in cognitive psychology to the solution
of problems in instructional design.

In writing my general comments for that volume, I used a framework
that assisted me in thinking about components of instructional design
(Glaser, 1976).

1. *Description and analysis of competent performance*—The state of
knowledge and skill to be achieved. This component required the development of procedures for analyzing tasks and specifying the content and
context of learning.

2. *Description and analysis of the initial state with which an individual begins the course of learning*—This entails assessing prior knowledge
and the use of this knowledge, as well as the long-term predictive utility
of aptitudes.

3. *Conditions that foster learning and the acquisition of competence*—
The point was made that this knowledge needs to be cast into the mold of

a design science, thereby calling for new forms of experimentation where the tactic is to test existing models by using them for maximizing learning effects.

4. *Assessment and evaluation was concerned with the effects of instructional implementation in the short and long run*—The short run involves supplying classroom feedback and information during the course of learning. In the longer run, the emphasis is on transfer, generalized patterns of behavior, and ability for further learning.

In terms of these four components, Klahr's volume rated high on the explication of performance theory and the analysis of states of competence. The new topic was cognitive task analysis and the problem solving and thinking processes to be taught in contrast to earlier forms of behavioral objectives. The chapters in the volume had less to say about the diagnosis of initial state; several themes were mentioned, however, such as a psychometrics of process for initial state assessment, consideration of developmental growth changes, and the notion of schema discrepancies between initial performance and later competence. The third component, which specifies processes of learning from initial state and prior knowledge to competent performance, was addressed only somewhat in most chapters. But reference was made to the various properties of performance that are involved when one proceeds from novice to expert. Attention was called to the importance of time when attaining competence. There was the employment of an optimization procedure involving learning functions for very simple kinds of behavior. And there were models of understanding in math word problems and reading text that suggested modes of instruction.

The fourth component involving the measurement of achievement, that is, the effects of the conditions provided for instruction, was considered tangentially in the chapters. However, it has taken on a special crusade in my current interests—the main theme involving the insularity of the psychometrics of testing and assessment from modern knowledge of human cognition. Some effort must now be devoted to an integrative field of cognition, performance measurement, and psychometric practices.

Learning Theory

The ongoing paradigm change in the study of learning and instruction was examined in the chapter by Carroll (1976) on the teaching of language skills. He pointed out that, despite a good deal of publicity and experimentation, behavior theory had not become particularly popular with most language teachers. However, behavior theory has been the precipitating factor in research attempting to teach language systems to chimpanzees. Behavior theory also stimulated interesting work in the development of programmed instruction for the teaching of foreign languages and of English, and was a basis for the behavior modification techniques employed for influencing language behavior in slow young learners and emotionally disturbed children. These successes have served to sort out critical elements in learning theory and have revealed some of the weaknesses of the behavioristic approach.

In offering some general prescriptions for instruction, Carroll, in the tradition of behavioral technologists, recommended careful analysis of what is to be learned. However, this analysis, with respect to language learning, was to be made in terms of information structures that correspond to meanings and communicative intentions that are manifested in overt behavior. In the preparation of instructional materials, account must be taken of what new information is presented to the learner in relation to the prior information presumed to be available. "There must be great concern with exactly what new information is presented from moment to moment in the instruction, with reference to what processing of that information is likely to be performed by the learner" (Carroll, 1976, p. 21). Rather than speaking of reinforcement, the role of certain types of information in directing the cognitive processes of the learner should be emphasized.

Task Analysis

Several other chapters (Greeno, 1976; Hayes, 1976; Norman, Gentner, & Stevens, 1976; Resnick, 1976; Simon & Hayes, 1976) again emphasized the importance of task analysis. However, rather than specifying behavioral objectives, the recommendation was that "cognitive objectives" be developed by analyzing the psychological processes and structures in memory that are sufficient to produce the target behaviors.

The research described in *Cognition and Instruction* (Klahr, 1976) makes it apparent that cognitive psychologists were preparing to study the problems of the acquisition and utilization of the intellectual skills of everyday life. For the scientists involved, an adequate theory of learning would embrace inferred covert events such as the processing of complex information, and memory storage and retrieval. These cognitive actions would include the organization of knowledge structures in memory, and shifts and differences in modes of cognitive functioning that occur as children grow up and that result from the particular cultural environment to which they are exposed. At that time, however, work focused largely on understanding how acquired complex cognitive tasks were performed, to much less of an extent than on how these activities were learned. For significant influence on educational practice, the problem of learning and the acquisition of performance—the *how* of learning and teaching—must now also be considered.

COGNITION AND INSTRUCTION–1999

Twenty-five years later, the work reported at this symposium appears to encompass the components of instructional design as an integrated task. In comparison to the past, the present-day chapters reflect less of a one-way movement from research to practice, but more of a supportive, productive interaction between modern knowledge of learning and development, and instructional theory. Ann Brown's work has been a prototype (Brown, 1992). Her general approach described a methodology adopted by mature sciences at various periods in their advancement where investigation contributes to both theoretical development and practical application. The design of the transistor alongside the emergence of solid state theory illustrates this mode, as does space engineering, which involves the rejuvenation of optical theory and advances in laser communication. In a recent book, *Pasteur's Quadrant: Basic Science and Technological Innovation* (Stokes, 1997), the interrelationship between fundamental science and application was exemplified by Pasteur who sought to understand microbiological processes, as well as to control their effects on various products such as the pasteurization of milk. In contrast, the physicist Neils Bohr's work on a model of atomic structure was pure theoretical description. The work of Edison and his coworkers pursued application without attention to theoretical knowledge. Pasteur's work, however, was practically useful for deriving alcohol from beet juice and for pasteurization but also sought to extend the frontiers of understanding microorganisms. Research efforts were embedded in theoretical description, targeted invention, and immediately applied goals. Much of the work reported at this symposium shows a realization of the significance of this form of mutually catalytic effort for the development of cognitive science and instruction.

It is interesting to speculate about the relationship between research and applied design in the work reported, and to ask how close the instructional effort is to theoretical description, and in what way theory and research are mutually supportive. Furthermore, the terms reasoning, understanding, explanation, interrogation, and participation are pervasive in the chapters and we wonder how future learning theory and instruction will be influenced.

Cognitive Development and Learning

A developmental theme is evident in the chapters by Lehrer, Schauble, Strom, and Pligge (chap. 2); Kalchman, Moss, and Case (chap. 1); and Palincsar and Magnusson (chap. 5). These authors describe working relationships with teachers to plan, design, and redesign instruction so that students' thinking is engaged. The work is distinguished by inventive generative topics—like model-based reasoning, number concept tasks, and text integration. Of theoretical interest and instructional utility are frameworks describing developmental progressions of cognitive processing. For example, in Lehrer, Schauble, Strom, and Pligge's work, there is attention to the development of models and reasoning with them, moving from physical models to symbolic conceptual models, and the use of mental models, analogies, and mathematical description as tools for understanding (chap. 2). Predisposing a student to cognitive activities like modeling drives the development of procedures and concepts, and assists the advancement to richer knowledge structures for complex thinking.

Curricula of this kind—based on a developmental paradigm of learning combined with continuing analysis of children's growing competence, and innovative practice environments—raise questions for research on educational design. Three general points for study are (a) the disciplinary concepts used in a curriculum and their generative power, (b) the developmental progression postulated, and (c) the adaptive feedback characteristics of instruction to the learner's performance. A developmental psychology of learning seems a more apt term than just learning theory.

Interaction Between Theory and the Design of Instruction

In other chapters, there is attention to the various components of design that I have described. The mode of proceeding seems to be more seamlessly accomplished; each of the components required is subsumed in the next activity as instructional design proceeds. The work by Palincsar and Magnusson is a good example of an interactive design task in that there is adjustment to maximize instructional attainment and to gain understanding of learning (chap. 5). The objective of inquiry is different from typical hands-on science activity because of the opportunity for the kind of text interrogation encouraged. The research described shows how text, without its "formidable authoritarian presence," can become an interactive aspect of student–teacher and classroom community activity that can advance inquiry skills and conceptual understanding (see also Beck, McKeown, Hamilton, & Kucan, 1997). The design problem is how to construct and use text to support cognitive activity. The way in which the teacher mediates the student's reading and understanding of the text is a fascinating event for study. Rather than a declarative text, the student is given a description of individuals' adventures in the course of their work; what they did, how they thought, how they conjectured. In this sense, an active life and mind is presented where questions can be engaged, in contrast to situations that encourage more passive reading.

Minstrell applies another "engineering" approach that involves this adjustment of instruction to address student performance and to influence their understanding of the processes of science (chap. 4). Dynamic instructional adjustment is displayed in the design of relevant experiences for the student. The instructional exercise involves an analysis of the components of knowledge that build a level of understanding, questions designed to diagnose students' thinking, and instruction based on the diagnosis that enables the effective choice of experiences to engage students' thinking and to foster interpretation and explanation of events. The active encounter with the progress of student knowledge is ordered by a computer program, making us aware that the online decision making of an effective teacher may require assistance in some form that can be part of future instructional situations. Both the teacher and the instructional designers can profit from this information.

Reiser, Tabak, Sandoval, Smith, Steinmuller, and Leone have designed an active environment for facilitating understanding that involves the construction of explanations (chap. 9). The instructional setting begins with an investigation through a series of questions about a phenomena, and students attempt to construct explanations based on the information obtained. As students construct explanations, they are prompted and scaffolded by a computer-based "explanation template." Students write questions and explanations, and the software supports their construction to meet general criteria for scientific explanations. A research issue is how using an "explanation constructor" that represents students' constructions (explanations) as a network of relations can assist an analysis of the causal coherence of explanations. Reiser, Tabak, Sandoval, Smith, Steinmuller, and Leone's efforts at design are interwoven with research questions, such as students' handling of evidence and the ability of students to assess themselves according to criteria for their performance (i.e., sufficiency of data support, the relevance of their data, its clarity, and possible alternative explanations). Further relevant research could include how explanations serve as products for reflection and evaluation, and contribute to the growth of students' knowledge and its competent use.

Moving From Laboratory Study to Classroom Design

The chapter by Klahr, Chen, and Toth is categorized separately because it has a different take on the idea of continuous instructional adjustment that is informative for the researcher and the teacher (chap. 3). Mutual stimulation between basic and applied research is activated in the course of the transition from laboratory study to classroom design as decisions are made for classroom instruction. The hope is to learn from change and to find out what instructional questions need to be studied in order to make this transition. A goal of this approach is to inform teachers of the research techniques underlying the development of instructional procedures and new content, so that teachers can translate cognitive research and adapt it to their practice for developing interesting methods of instruction. Perhaps conducting experiments in the classroom makes teachers more convinced of the value of attempting new methods and of the difficulty of translating research to the practical situation; researchers can learn about factors that are influencing the application of their research.

Questions have come forward in moving from the lab to the classroom, such as: How do fourth graders learn to transfer in the classroom? What new issues and difficulties occur in the classroom setting? How do students learn to evaluate experiments conducted by others when in a classroom group? Do they acquire domain knowledge from experimentation? These issues are a combination of experimental outcomes and design questions. It is especially interesting to note that the complexity of the classroom forces experimenters to engage students in formative assessment to keep track of their own performances.

Computer-Assisted Instruction and Task Analysis

The Anderson and Gluck chapter (chap. 8) reminded me of the Isaac Asimov story entitled *The Fun They Had* (1963). As I remember it, this short story tells of two children, who, after completing their work in the lesson room of their house, went up to the attic to play. They rummaged around and found a book; the little girl said "What is that?" and her big brother replied "It's a book." She asked, "What's a book?" He said, "A book was something they used in school a long time ago, the teacher helped children learn things from the book." The little girl asked, "What's a teacher?" The boy said it was a person. The little girl was appalled, saying that no person was smart enough to be a real teacher, and nothing that looked like this book could really help children learn. The eye-tracking study in the Anderson and Gluck chapter also made me feel that, in the course of learning in the future, there will be few places to hide.

Nevertheless, in computer-assisted tutorial instruction, grain size in the analysis of performance is a fascinating issue. It arises from the forms of analysis used in experimental work that indicate significant learning indicators such as shifts in attention, disambiguation of strategies, the nature of error, and information about whether the student is on an unproductive track that will interfere with an experiment. Manipulating grain size for studies of instructional design is an important endeavor; perhaps we can determine the level of analysis that can be imposed for initial effort and then gradually change the level to see how learning is influenced. Manipulations might be made in the size of a presented unit and the size of the required response in order to see how various amounts of information can be processed as learning occurs. Increasing the organization of information as instruction proceeds may help assess patterns of competence that are developing. It might be possible to assess the automaticity of various levels of performance so that they can be managed in a way that differs from other aspects of performance. It would be interesting to analyze the level of a good teacher's grain size when interacting with students and compare that with the grain size of a possible computer tutor.

Lesgold and Nahemow have persistently investigated the nature and development of expertise (chap. 10). In the course of their research, they have taken on complex technical tasks, such troubleshooting test equipment for aircraft systems and systems for the design of intricate computer chips. What is always impressive is the detailed task analysis that is necessary and the methods they have developed for analyzing complex performances. These procedures should be considered and further techniques worked out for the analysis of advanced school learning. More than most instructional developers, Lesgold has been a victim or benefactor of the operational details of the performance for which he has designed training systems. The training he undertakes involves expensive errors, and requires elaborate guiding structures for scaffolding learning and practice capabilities for principled performance leading to the ability to transfer to new systems. Minimizing the length of training time for technical personnel while maximizing their ability to transfer have been competing objectives.

While being an active theorist in connection with task analysis and learning principles, Lesgold's work shows his capability to transform himself into a skilled educational engineer—more than most of us, who are inhibited by our academic training. Investigation of Alan's ability to shift from a theorist to engineer, and the differences between his personas and tactics in this regard would be a significant study in instructional design.

Situated Cognition
and Instructional Design

As they turn their interest to education and the design of settings for learning, Cobb (chap. 15), Ellis and Gregoire[1] embraced the practical implications of situated cognition, if not the explanatory theory. This framework connects what students learn with the environments in which they learn to offer a unit of analysis for the design of instruction. Participation and engagement with others and with objects, and the affordances they offer in this sociopsychological setting is a major mechanism for learning. Regardless of the debate surrounding the notion of situativity, the unit of learning appears to be a useful framework to these researchers for the engineering of learning situations. Cobb reports that a shift has taken place in his theoretical orientation as a result of his work in classrooms over the past 10 years (chap. 15), and Ellis and Gregoire documented the change in classroom context for them. This shift has been away from a definition of learning and mathematical proficiency in terms of individu-

---

[1]Shari Ellis and Michele Gregoire, University of Florida, made a presentation entitled, "Sociocultural and cognitive aspects of teaching and learning in mathematics and science classrooms" at the June 1999 Carnegie Symposium. It does not appear in this volume.

alistic characterizations of students, to a view of performance being characteristic of an individual's way of participating in a community. For the purposes of instructional design, this framework involves "classroom mathematical practices" and the evolution of such practices that can document the learning trajectory of the classroom community. The grain size of analysis for the instructional designer is a so-called "reflective relation" between the psychological activities of the individual and the social contributions of the students in the classroom activities. Cobb indicates that learning occurs and is assessed through the coordination of social and psychological perspectives that are used to analyze the development of students' mathematical reasoning in the situations in which they participate.

From the point of view of instructional design, and the facilitation of learning, the social participation of the group can be constantly renegotiated in terms of such activities as the obligation of students to explain and justify their reasoning, to listen and attempt to understand other's explanations, or to attempt to indicate their lack of understanding in some form of displayed community activity. There can be continued adjustment between student reasoning and the environmental resources or tools involved in the situation; instructional design is informed by this interplay.

The Community of the Classroom and Learning Concepts

Carver's point of view about cognition in the community environment of the classroom represents an important perspective (chap. 12). A significant problem is enriching the experience not only of children and teachers in terms of concepts of cognition and learning, but also to get this viewpoint considered by parents and undergraduates in the course of their education. Carver's notion of metaprinciples is also interesting from a design and implementation point of view. These principles include building on prior knowledge, making thinking explicit, emphasizing links, providing opportunities for practice, and acknowledging the presence of individual variability. She indicates that these are inevitably a part of teachers' repertoires of strategies, and points out that making these topics explicit during instructional design increases their effective application, and the consistency and adaptability with which they become part of the instructional environment. Too often these principles become shallow slogans without the deeper structure of knowledge and practice which is necessary.

CONCLUDING COMMENTS

In writing a history of instructional psychology and the influence of modern knowledge in cognitive science on instruction, it appears that Carver and Klahr's symposium and this book will end the 20th century with significant attention to instructional design for the purposes of theory building and educational innovation. A strong focus will also involve improving the cognitive capabilities of individuals as they learn the disciplines and subject matters of education. We can look forward to a teaching profession empowered by modern knowledge of mature cognition and child development, and the related design of curriculum content and teaching methods. We will see that most of our students not only have information, but are also using their knowledge for problem solving, invention, conceptual exploration, and reasoned judgment.

In accomplishing these objectives, the fundamental task requires a design or engineering stance through which we can build cognitively enriched learning environments while at the same time developing relevant science. This task will be constrained by variation in the structure of the different disciplines to be learned and in the cognitive skills involved; different subject matter environments may not look alike as they are learned. Additional attention will also be paid to the nesting of participation in school environments and in the larger society of communities and cultures.

At the present time, scientists interested in instructional design are working with teachers and school administrators. This grouping of talent will need to change its character as concepts of learning and cognition become explicit enough to enable teachers and educators to introduce a profession of educational designers focusing on significant educational goals. It is difficult to judge how soon the designer-practitioner will become a recognized intermediary in the teaching profession. For now, however, the practitioner, scientist, instructional developer, and active policy manager team seems an important way to proceed for future progress.

REFERENCES

Asimov, I. (1963). The Fun They Had. In I. Asimov & G. Conklin (Eds.) Fifty Short Science Fiction Tales (pp. 25–28), New York: Collier. (original work published in 1951).

Beck, I. L., McKeown, M. G., Hamilton, R. L., & Kucan, L. (1997). *Questioning the author: An approach for enhancing student engagement with text.* Newark, DE: International Reading Association.

Brown, A. L. (1992). Design experiments: Theoretical and methodological challenges in creating complex interventions in classroom settings. *The Journal of the Learning Sciences, 2* (2), 141–178.

Bruner, J. (1964). Some theorems on instruction illustrated with reference to mathematics. In E. R. Hilgard (Ed.), *Theories of learning and instruction: The 63rd yearbook of the NSSE*, (*Part I,* pp. 306–335). Chicago, IL: NSSE.

Carroll, J. B. (1976). Promoting language skills: The role of instruction. In D. Klahr (Ed.), *Cognition and instruction* (pp. 3–22). Hillsdale, NJ: Lawrence Erlbaum Associates.

Estes, W. K. (1960). Learning. In C.H. Harris (Ed.) *Encyclopedia of educational research* (3rd ed., pp. 752–767). New York: Macmillan.

Fitts, P. M. (1965). Factors in complex skilled training. In R. Glaser (Ed.), *Training research and education* (pp. 177–197). New York: Wiley.

Fleishman, E. A. (1965). The description and prediction of perceptual-motor skill learning. In R. Glaser (Ed.), *Training research and education* (pp. 137–175). New York: Wiley.

Frederiksen, N. (1965). Proficiency tests for training evaluation. In R. Glaser (Ed.), *Training research and education* (pp. 323–346). New York: Wiley.

Gagné, R. M., & Rohwer, W. D., Jr. (1969). Instructional psychology. *Annual Review of Psychology, 20,* 381–418.

Glaser, R. (Ed.). (1965). *Training research and education.* New York: Wiley. (Original work published in 1962)

Glaser, R. (1976). Cognitive psychology and instructional design. In D. Klahr (Ed.), *Cognition and instruction* (pp. 303–315). Hillsdale, NJ: Lawrence Erlbaum Associates.

Glaser, R., & Gow, G. S., Jr. (1964). The Learning Research and Development Center at the University of Pittsburgh. *American Psychologist, 19,* 854–858.

Glaser, R., & Resnick, L. B. (1972). Instructional psychology. *Annual Review of Psychology , 23,* 207–276.

Greeno, J. G. (1976). Cognitive objectives of instruction: Theory of knowledge for solving problems and answering questions. In D. Klahr (Ed.), *Cognition and instruction* (pp. 123–159). Hillsdale, NJ: Lawrence Erlbaum Associates.

Hayes, J. R. (1976). It's the thought that counts: New approaches to educational theory. In D. Klahr (Ed.), *Cognition and instruction* (pp. 177–196). Hillsdale, NJ: Lawrence Erlbaum Associates.

Klahr, D. (Ed). (1976). *Cognition and instruction.* Hillsdale, NJ: Lawrence Erlbaum Associates.

Miller, R. B. (1965). Analysis and specification of behavior for training. In R. Glaser (Ed.), *Training research and education* (pp. 31–62). New York: Wiley.

Norman, D. A., Gentner, D. R., & Stevens, A. L. (1976). Comments on learning schemata and memory representation. In D. Klahr (Ed.), *Cognition and instruction* (pp. 177–196). Hillsdale, NJ: Lawrence Erlbaum Associates.

Resnick, L. B. (1976). Task analysis in instructional design: Some cases from mathematics. In D. Klahr (Ed.), *Cognition and instruction* (pp. 51–80). Hillsdale, NJ: Lawrence Erlbaum Associates.

Simon, H. A., & Hayes, J. R. (1976). Understanding complex task instructions. In D. Klahr (Ed.), *Cognition and instruction* (pp. 269–285). Hillsdale, NJ: Lawrence Erlbaum Associates.

Stokes, D. E. (1997). *Pasteur's quadrant: Basic science and technological innovation.* Washington, DC: Brookings Institution Press.

Travers, R. M. W. (1965). A study of the relationship of psychological research to educational practice. In R. Glaser (Ed.), *Training research and education* (pp. 525–558). New York: Wiley.

Author Index

Subject Index

F

Facets of thinking, 127–148, 361
    diagnosis of, 139–143
    facet-based learning environments, 128–147
Feedback, 140–142, 252–255, 376–381
    end only vs. immediate, 376–381
Fluid properties, 128–131, 133, 135–138,
    143–144
Fractions, 6–8, 13–15, 18–19, 22–23

G

GIsML (Guided Inquiry supporting Multiple
    Literacies), 157–174, 178
Goals framework, 386–392, 401–404, 410–411
G→P→A (Goals→Program→Assessment)
    approach, 389, 410–411
Gravity, 128–129, 144–145
Group work, 434–437
    individual learning and, 435
    motivation and, 435–436
    school vs. workplace, 434–435

H

Heuristics, 354–356
High-density sensing, 228, 240–242
    and intrusiveness, 242
    and privacy, 241–242
High-level skills, 197–198
High school, 123, 220, 242, 266, 274, 290–291,
    295, 431–432, 481–484
Humanities education, 481–486
Hypotheses, 78–81, 112, 147, 179, 264, 267,
    269–270, 281, 284, 291, 350–351, 447

I

Individual differences, 398–400
Information processing theory, xx, 402,
    439–444, 446–448, 452
Inquiry, 112–113, 152–154, 156, 158–159,
    173–175, 179, 183–185, 263–301,
    445–446, 450–452, 501
    community of, 158, 445–446
    goals of, 269–272, 276, 278

guided, 153, 156, 159, 173–175, 183–185,
    265–301, 445
products of, 264, 269–272, 286–287,
    295–296
reflective, 446–448
transactional, 450–452
Instruction, xviii, 82, 84–87, 95–97, 102, 104,
    109, 113–114, 196–200, 387–400, 406,
    408–410, 459–463, 495–496, 499, 505
    direct, 82, 84–87, 95–97, 102, 104, 109,
        113–114
    explicit, 387–388, 394–396
    strategies for, xviii, 389–400, 406, 408–410,
        463, 505
    theories of, 84, 459–462, 495–496, 499
Instructional design, xv, 11–12, 36, 213,
    386–387, 456–462, 472–475, 499–501,
    504–506. see also Design principles
Instructional interventions, 82, 96, 123,
    359–360, 363, 469–470, 488–490
    interdisciplinary integration of, 488–490
    sustainability of, 469–470
Instructional technology, xix, 25, 29–30,
    208–209, 224, 265, 270–272, 274–276,
    278, 286, 288–292, 299–301, 307, 345,
    360–363, 375–382, 431–434, 501,
    503–504. see also Tutors, computer
    integration of, 288–292
    training for, 433–434
Investigations, 152–157, 159–174, 180–185,
    264–301, 445–446
    first-hand, 159–160, 171–173, 180–185
    preparation for, 289–291
    second-hand, 152–157, 159–174, 180–185,
        445–446
    strategic artifacts of, 276, 281–282, 294
    strategic tools for, 276, 281–282,
        297–299
    strategies for, 264, 269–272, 276–278,
        282–284, 297–299

K

Knowledge, 2, 24, 53–54, 89–90, 93, 96, 98,
    102, 105, 108, 110–113, 125–132, 147,
    172, 175, 177–179, 199–200, 232–236,
    258, 265, 271, 309–318, 322–333,
    344–345, 364–367, 379, 393–394,
    396–397, 448, 496–498

P

PARI (Precursor-Action-Result-Interpretation)
method, 328–329, 331–333
PAT algebra tutor, 231, 242–258
Pattern recognition, 429
PC PACK, 333–338
  card sort, 334–335
  laddering, 336–337
  protocol editor, 334
  rules, 338
Percents, 6, 13–19, 22–23
  estimating, 15
Perception, 216–217, 238–239
Physics education, 123–148
Piaget, Jean, 206, 392, 486
Practice, 213, 218, 397–398, 404, 494
Preschool education, 222, 385–412, 431
  cognitive goals, 390–392
  physical goals, 390, 399
  social goals, 390
  thematic units in, 391, 393–398
Problem solving, 223, 231, 240, 243, 258–259,
  310–312, 317–331, 339–344, 355, 361,
  367, 372–374, 429, 434–437, 439–443,
  446–448, 450–452, 497
Process explorer, 324–328
Production systems, 218, 220–224, 229–230,
  235–239, 364–366, 429, 442–443
Public policy, 462, 474

Q

Qualitative reasoning, 41–43, 143–144
Quantitative reasoning, 41–43, 50, 53

R

Rational numbers, 1, 6–8, 13–23
Ratios, 43–44, 48–53, 61
Reflection, 104, 179, 264, 277, 291–295,
  446–448
Representation, xvii, 2–8, 11–12, 18–20,
  23–35, 48–52, 58–62, 66–69, 96–98,
  114–115, 174, 180–181, 184, 201,
  278–286, 288, 290, 314–317, 325–327,
  332–333, 348, 354, 364–366, 396–397
  algebraic, 24–27, 48, 60–62
  concept webs, 396–397

of epistemological commitments, 284–286
graphs, 8, 24–35, 48–52, 58–62, 66–69,
  282–283, 290
integrative, 6–8, 11–12
of knowledge, 348, 364–366
matrix, 325–327, 332–333
multiple levels of, 314–317
of strategies, 282–284
tables, 24–26, 96–98
of theories, 279–282

S

Scaffolding, 184, 265, 270–271, 274, 276, 278,
  299, 375–381, 392, 501
Schemata, 2–3, 6, 8–11, 13
Science education, 39–72, 77–80, 95–114, 116,
  151–185, 197, 201–202, 263–301, 488.
  see also Biology education, Physics
  education
Scientific argumentation, 71–72, 183–184,
  197–198, 266–267, 269–271, 276,
  279–282, 297–299, 446
Scientific claims, 161–175, 182–184, 200
Scientific disciplines, 264, 267–271, 276,
  301
Scientific literacy, 153, 159
Scientific reasoning, 77–81, 83, 152, 174,
  176–177, 183–185, 266–268
Situated cognition, xx, 467–468, 475, 504–505
Social context, xix-xx, 207–209, 224–225, 272,
  278, 351–354, 358, 455, 458, 463–475,
  482–486, 489
  classroom, 358, 458, 463–475, 489
  of learning, xix-xx, 207–209, 224–225
  of professional development, 482–486
  of research, 351–354, 358
Social process theory, 444–446, 449, 452
Sociocultural theory, 152, 157
Software, see Instructional technology
Statistical reasoning, 350–352, 354–382
  choice of analyses, 373–375, 376–382
  errors in, 354–356, 359
  goal structure of, 380–381
  planning in, 374–375, 381
  steps in, 372–374
Statistics education, 146, 222, 347–382,
  461–462, 473–474
Strategies, xvii, 16, 20–23, 35, 45–47, 252,
  372–375, 380, 387–388. see also